TDBoK™ Guide

Talent Development Body of Knowledge

2nd Edition

First edition published as
Talent Development Body of Knowledge™

Association for Talent Development
Alexandria, VA

© 2024 ASTD DBA the Association for Talent Development (ATD)
All rights reserved. Printed in the United States of America.

27 26 25 24   1 2 3 4

No part of this publication may be reproduced, distributed, or transmitted in any form or by any means, including photocopying, recording, or other electronic or mechanical methods, without the prior written permission of the publisher, except in the case of brief quotations embodied in critical reviews and certain other noncommercial uses permitted by copyright law. For permission requests, please go to www.copyright.com, or contact Copyright Clearance Center (CCC), 222 Rosewood Drive, Danvers, MA 01923 (telephone: 978.750.8400; fax: 978.646.8600).

ATD is the world's largest association dedicated to those who develop the knowledge and skills of employees in organizations. ATD Press is an internationally renowned source of insightful and practical information on talent development, training, and professional development.

Association for Talent Development
1640 King Street
Alexandria, VA 22314 USA

For information about purchasing and licensing options for the *TDBoK™ Guide*, visit td.org/tdbok.

Library of Congress Control Number: 2023943977

ISBN 10: 1-957157-31-3
ISBN 13: 978-1-957157-31-3
e-ISBN: 978-1-957157-32-0

ATD *TDBoK™ Guide* Editorial Staff
Director, ATD Press: Sarah Halgas
Vice President, Learning: Courtney Vital
Project Manager, Education Product Development: Mindi Smith
Manager, ATD Press: Melissa Jones
Developmental Editor, ATD Press: Jack Harlow
Production Editor, ATD Press: Katy Wiley Stewts
Text Designers: Rosemary Aguilar Mingo and Shirley E.M. Raybuck
Cover Designer: Rose Richey

Printed by BR Printers, San Jose, CA

TABLE OF CONTENTS

Foreword xvii

Introduction xix

Editors and Contributors xxv

1.1 Communication 1
    1.1.1   Skill in Expressing Thoughts, Feelings, and Ideas in a Clear, Concise, and Compelling Manner 1
            I. Effective Communication for TD Professionals 1
    1.1.2   Skill in Applying Principles of Active Listening 5
            I. Effective Communication Skills and Strategies 5
    1.1.3   Skill in Using Communication Strategies That Inform and Influence Audiences 8
            I. Communicating to Inform and Influence 8
    1.1.4   Skill in Applying Persuasion and Influencing Techniques to Gain Agreement, Commitment, or Buy-In From Stakeholders 10
            I. Using Communication to Persuade and Influence 10
    1.1.5   Skill in Conceiving, Developing, and Delivering Information in Various Formats and Media 11
            I. Developing Materials for Results 11
    1.1.6   Skill in Applying Verbal, Written, or Nonverbal Communication Techniques 14
            I. Communicating to Be Heard and Understood 14
    1.1.7   Skill in Facilitating Dialogue With Individuals or Groups to Help Them Identify, Articulate, or Clarify Their Thoughts and Feelings 16
            I. Dialogue for Clarity 16
    1.1.8   Skill in Articulating and Conveying Value Propositions to Gain Agreement, Support, or Buy-In From Stakeholders 17
            I. Using Value Propositions 17
    References 19
    Recommended Reading 20

1.2 Emotional Intelligence & Decision Making 21
    Emotional Intelligence 21
    1.2.1   Knowledge of Theories of Emotional Intelligence 21
            I. Emotional Intelligence Models and Theories 21
    1.2.2   Skill in Assessing and Managing One's Own Emotional State 24
            I. Managing Personal Emotions 24

Table of Contents

1.2.3	Skill in Identifying Personal Biases That Influence One's Own Cognition and Behavior	25
	I. Understanding the Relationship of Bias to EI	25
1.2.4	Skill in Observing and Interpreting the Verbal and Nonverbal Behavior of Individuals or Groups	27
	I. Interpreting Verbal and Nonverbal Behavior	27
1.2.5	Skill in Adjusting One's Own Behavior in Response to or Anticipation of Changes in Other Peoples' Behavior, Attitudes, or Thoughts	29
	I. Developing Emotional Intelligence	29
1.2.6	Knowledge of Techniques and Approaches to Learn or Demonstrate Resilience	30
	I. Developing Resilience	30

Decision Making 31

1.2.7	Knowledge of Decision-Making Models	31
	I. Making Decisions	31
1.2.8	Skill in Using Logic and Reasoning to Identify the Strengths and Weaknesses of Alternative Solutions, Conclusions, or Approaches to Problems	34
	I. Exploring Critical Thinking	34

References 38

Recommended Reading 39

1.3 Collaboration & Leadership 41

Collaborating With Others 41

1.3.1	Knowledge of Theories, Methods, and Techniques to Build and Manage Professional Relationships	41
	I. Build and Manage Professional Relationships	41
1.3.2	Knowledge of Methods and Criteria for Establishing and Managing Collaboration Among Various Units	43
	I. Methods and Techniques to Build a Collaborative Environment	43
1.3.3	Skill in Building and Managing Teams and Work Groups	44
	I. Build and Manage High-Performance Teams	44
1.3.4	Skill in Integrating and Synthesizing Others' Viewpoints to Build Alignment of Diverse Perspectives	48
	I. Building Alignment and Synergy From Diversity	48
1.3.5	Knowledge of Conflict Management Techniques	49
	I. Models and Techniques for Conflict Resolution	49
1.3.6	Skill in Managing Conflict	51
	I. Managing Conflict	51

Managing and Leading Others 52

1.3.7	Knowledge of Methods and Techniques for Managing and Supervising Others	52
	I. Managing and Supervising Methods	52
1.3.8	Skill in Matching, Assigning, and Delegating Work to Others	55
	I. Delegation	55
1.3.9	Knowledge of Principles and Techniques for Providing Feedback	57
	I. Importance of Feedback	57
1.3.10	Knowledge of Theories of Leadership	59
	I. Key Leadership Theories	59

References 61

Recommended Reading 62

1.4 Cultural Awareness & Inclusion 63
Cultural Awareness 63
- 1.4.1 Knowledge of Cultural Differences in the Workplace 63
  - I. Cultural Differences in the Workplace 63
  - II. Cultural Dynamics 64
- 1.4.2 Knowledge of Social and Cultural Norms That Influence Decision Making and Behavior 71
  - I. Social and Cultural Norms 71
- 1.4.3 Knowledge of Methods and Techniques to Foster Cultural Awareness, Encourage Cultural Sensitivity, and Broaden Viewpoints 76
  - I. Develop Intercultural Awareness and Competence 76

Diversity, Equity, and Inclusion 77
- 1.4.4 Skill in Adapting and Adjusting Attitude, Perspective, and Behavior to Function Effectively in Diverse Environments or Situations 77
  - I. Maximizing Workplace Diversity 77
- 1.4.5 Knowledge of Approaches to Encourage and Promote Workplace Diversity, Equity, and Inclusion 82
  - I. Promoting Workplace Diversity, Equity, and Inclusion 82
- 1.4.6 Skill in Integrating DEI Principles in TD Strategies and Initiatives 85
  - I. Workplace Diversity, Equity, and Inclusion Planning 85

References 92
Recommended Reading 94

1.5 Project Management 95
- 1.5.1 Knowledge of Project Management Principles and Processes 95
  - I. Project Management Principles 95
  - II. The Project Management Process 97
- 1.5.2 Skill in Coordinating the Logistical Tasks Associated With Planning Meetings 101
  - I. The Roles of a Project Sponsor and Project Manager 101
- 1.5.3 Skill in Evaluating and Prioritizing Implications, Risks, Feasibility, and Consequences of Potential Activities 103
  - I. Defining the Project Purpose 103
- 1.5.4 Skill in Developing Project Plans and Schedules That Integrate Resources, Tasks, and Timelines 104
  - I. Project Management Planning 104
- 1.5.5 Skill in Adjusting Work Processes and Outputs in Response to or Anticipation of Changes in Goals, Standards, Resources, or Time 105
  - I. Project Management Implementation 105
- 1.5.6 Skill in Establishing, Monitoring, and Communicating Progress Toward the Achievement of Goals, Objectives, and Milestones 106
  - I. Assessing Project Management Progress 106

References 109
Recommended Reading 109

1.6 Compliance & Ethical Behavior 111
- 1.6.1 Skill in Acting With Integrity 111
  - I. Principles of the Ethical TD Professional 111

	1.6.2	Skill in Establishing, Maintaining, and Enforcing Standards for Integrity and Ethical Behavior in Self and Others 113
		I. Creating a Culture of Ethics, Integrity, and Compliance 113
	1.6.3	Knowledge of Laws, Regulations, and Ethical Issues Related to the Access and Use of Information 115
		I. Laws, Regulations, and Ethical Issues Related to Data and Information.............................115
	1.6.4	Knowledge of Laws, Regulations, and Ethical Issues Related to the Development of Instructional Content 117
		I. Legal, Regulatory, and Ethical Requirements Related to Instructional Content................ 117
	1.6.5	Knowledge of Laws, Regulations, and Ethical Issues Related to Human Resources and Talent Development 119
		I. Laws, Regulations, and Ethical Issues in Talent Development... 119
	1.6.6	Knowledge of Laws, Regulations, and Ethical Issues Related to the Employment of Permanent, Contingent, or Dispersed Workforces 121
		I. Laws, Regulations, and Ethical Issues Related to Employment 121
	1.6.7	Knowledge of Regional and Market-Specific Education and Labor Public Policies...........123
		I. Global Laws and Regulations Affecting Talent Development 123
	References 125
	Recommended Reading 126

1.7 Lifelong Learning 127

	1.7.1	Knowledge of How a Desire to Learn Can Lead to the Expansion and Development of Knowledge and Skills Over Time..127
		I. Lifelong Learning...127
	1.7.2	Knowledge of Resources for Career Exploration and Lifelong Learning for Self and Others.............. 130
		I. Fundamentals of Career Exploration 130
	1.7.3	Skill in Acquiring New Knowledge Through Professional Development Activities for One's Self..133
		I. Professional Learning Activities 133
	1.7.4	Skill in Developing, Maintaining, and Leveraging Networks Across a Range of People and Groups Inside and Outside the Organization 134
		I. Networking Principles 134
	References 139
	Recommended Reading 140

2.1 Learning Sciences 143

	2.1.1	Knowledge of the Foundational Learning Theories of Behaviorism, Cognitivism, and Constructivism.. 143
		I. Foundational Learning Theories... 143
	2.1.2	Knowledge of the Principles and Applications of Cognitive Science for Learning 145
		I. Principles of Cognitive Science for Learning... 145
	2.1.3	Knowledge of Theories and Models of Adult Learning 148
		I. Theories and Models of How Adults Learn 148
		II. Theories and Models of Design That Ensure Learning 152
	2.1.4	Knowledge of Communication Theories and Models and How They Relate to Learning.....................156
		I. Conceptual Models of Communication 156

  2.1.5 Skill in Applying Principles of Cognitive Science and Adult Learning to Design Solutions That Maximize Learning or Behavioral Outcomes 159
    I. Applications of Cognitive Science in Adult Learning 159
    II. Maximizing Learning and Behavioral Outcomes 160
 References 165
 Recommended Reading 168

2.2 Instructional Design 169
Foundational Principles of Design 169
  2.2.1 Knowledge of Instructional Design Models and Processes 169
    I. Learning Design Basics 169
    II. Instructional Systems Design (ISD) Models and Processes 171
    III. The ADDIE Model 173
  2.2.2 Knowledge of Needs Assessment Approaches and Techniques 177
    I. Needs Assessment for Instructional Design 177

Objectives 183
  2.2.3 Knowledge of Methods and Techniques for Defining Learning and Behavioral Outcome Statements 183
    I. Designing to Meet Organizational Requirements 183
  2.2.4 Skill in Developing Learning and Behavioral Outcome Statements 184
    I. Writing Objectives 184
  2.2.5 Knowledge of the Criteria Used to Assess the Quality and Relevance of Instructional Content in Relation to a Desired Learning or Behavioral Outcome 186
    I. Clarifying Desired Outcomes 186

Design 187
  2.2.6 Skill in Designing Blueprints, Schematics, and Other Visual Representations of Learning and Development Solutions 187
    I. The Design Process 187
  2.2.7 Knowledge of Instructional Modalities 189
    I. Instructional Modality Options 189

Development 191
  2.2.8 Knowledge of Methods and Techniques for Planning, Designing, and Developing Instructional Content 191
    I. Methods and Techniques to Develop Content 191
  2.2.9 Skill in Eliciting and Using Knowledge and Information From Subject Matter Experts to Support or Enhance Learning 193
    I. Using SMEs in Instructional Design 193
  2.2.10 Knowledge of Types and Applications of Instructional Methods and Techniques 195
    I. Planning for Instructional Delivery 195
  2.2.11 Skill in Selecting and Aligning Delivery Options and Media for Training or Learning Events to the Desired Learning or Behavioral Outcomes 196
    I. Aligning Delivery Options to Objectives 196
  2.2.12 Skill in Designing and Developing Learning Assets 198
    I. Creating Materials 198

Additional Design Approaches 201

    2.2.13 Knowledge of How Design Thinking and Rapid Prototyping Can Be Applied to the
Development of Learning and Talent Development Solutions 201

        I. Using Design Thinking for Instructional Design..201

    2.2.14 Knowledge of How Formal and Informal Learning Experiences Influence and
Support Individual and Group Development 203

        I. Awareness of How Learning Influences Development...203

  References 204

  Recommended Reading 206

2.3 Training Delivery & Facilitation 207

    2.3.1 Skill in Coordinating the Logistical Tasks Associated With Planning
Meetings or Learning Events 207

        I. Planning and Coordinating Learning Events 207

        II. Facilitator Preparation..210

        III. Prepare Participants and Their Managers 211

        IV. Planning and Coordinating Meetings..212

    2.3.2 Skill in Facilitating Meetings or Learning Events in Face-to-Face and Virtual Environments 213

        I. Facilitating Groups 213

        II. Managing Effective Meetings...215

    2.3.3 Knowledge of Facilitation Methods and Techniques 216

        I. Understanding the Role of Facilitation 216

        II. Engagement Methods and Techniques..221

    2.3.4 Skill in Creating Positive Learning Climates and Environments 222

        I. Creating Climates Conducive to Learning... 222

    2.3.5 Skill in Selecting and Aligning Delivery Options and Media for Training or Learning
Events to the Desired Learning or Behavioral Outcomes 224

        I. Ensuring Delivery Options Align With How Employees Learn.. 224

        II. Learning Preferences 225

        III. Presentation and Training Tools..228

    2.3.6 Skill in Delivering Training Using Multiple Delivery Options and Media.....................................229

        I. Delivering Formal Learning...229

        II. Applying Learning Science 230

        III. Exploring Informal Learning...231

        IV. Self-Directed Learning Approaches 233

    2.3.7 Skill in Designing or Developing Learning Assets That Align to a Desired Learning
or Behavioral Outcome..235

        I. Creating Course Materials... 235

  References 238

  Recommended Reading 240

2.4 Technology Application 241

Administering a Learning Technology Ecosystem 241

    2.4.1 Skill in Selecting, Integrating, Managing, or Maintaining Learning Platforms 241

        I. Selecting, Integrating, Managing, and Maintaining Learning Platforms 241

Assessing, Selecting, and Implementing Learning Technology 245

- 2.4.2 Skill in Identifying, Defining, and Articulating Technology System Requirements to Support Learning and TD Solutions 245
  - I. Identifying, Defining, and Articulating Technology System Requirements 245
- 2.4.3 Knowledge of Criteria and Techniques for Evaluating and Selecting E-Learning Software and Tools 248
  - I. Evaluating and Selecting E-Learning Software 248
- 2.4.4 Skill in Identifying, Selecting, and Implementing Learning Technologies 250
  - I. Identifying, Selecting, and Implementing Learning Technologies 250
- 2.4.5 Knowledge of Methods and Techniques for Testing the Usability and Functionality of Learning Technologies and Support Systems 251
  - I. Methods and Techniques for Testing Usability 251

Building a Workplace Technology Ecosystem 254

- 2.4.6 Knowledge of Existing Learning Technologies and Support Systems 254
  - I. Existing Learning Technologies 254
- 2.4.7 Knowledge of Human Resources Systems and Technology Platforms and How They Integrate With Other Organizational and Business Systems and Processes 256
  - I. Integrating Human Resources Systems and Technology Platforms With Other Systems 256
- 2.4.8 Knowledge of Communication Technologies and Their Applications 257
  - I. Communication Technologies and Their Applications 257

Building Learning Technology Tools 259

- 2.4.9 Knowledge of Principles of User Interface Design 259
  - I. User Interface Design Principles 259
- 2.4.10 Skill in Developing Artificial Intelligence, Machine Learning Algorithms, Augmented Reality, Virtual Reality, and Mixed Reality Tools That Are Ethical and Free of Bias 261
  - I. Developing AI, Machine Learning Algorithms, AR, VR, and Other Mixed Reality Tools 261

Applying Learning Technology 265

- 2.4.11 Skill in Using E-Learning Software and Tools 265
  - I. Using E-Learning Software and Tools 265
- 2.4.12 Knowledge of Functions, Features, Limitations, and Practical Applications of the Technologies Available to Support Learning and Talent Development Solutions 268
  - I. Functions, Features, Limitations, and Application of Available Technology 268
- 2.4.13 Skill in Using Human Resource Technology Systems to Store, Retrieve, and Process Talent and Talent Development–Related Information 269
  - I. Using Technology to Store, Retrieve, and Process Talent Information 269
- 2.4.14 Knowledge of Techniques and Approaches to Leverage Social Media Platforms and Tools to Support Knowledge Sharing, Idea Exchange, and Learning 270
  - I. Techniques and Approaches That Leverage Social Media Platforms 270

Advancing the Learning Technology Ecosystem 273

- 2.4.15 Knowledge of Artificial Intelligence, Machine Learning Algorithms, Augmented Reality, Virtual Reality, and Mixed Reality Trends That Are Ethical and Free of Bias 273
  - I. Knowledge of AI, Machine Learning Algorithms, AR, VR, and Mixed Reality Trends 273

References 276

Recommended Reading 276

2.5 Knowledge Management 279

Knowledge Management 279

- 2.5.1 Knowledge of Principles of Knowledge Management 279
  - I. Principles of Knowledge Management 279
- 2.5.2 Knowledge of Methods and Techniques for Capturing and Codifying Knowledge 284
  - I. Knowledge Mapping 284
- 2.5.3 Skill in Designing and Implementing Knowledge Management Strategy 287
  - I. Designing and Implementing a KM Strategy 287
- 2.5.4 Knowledge of Methods, Techniques, and Structures for Disseminating and Sharing Knowledge Across Individuals, Groups, and Organizations 290
  - I. Techniques to Establish Knowledge Sharing 290

Curation 293

- 2.5.5 Skill in Identifying the Quality, Authenticity, Accuracy, Impartiality, and Relevance of Information From Various Sources 293
  - I. Establish Governance for Content Curation 293
- 2.5.6 Skill in Organizing and Synthesizing Information From Multiple Sources 294
  - I. Map Information From Knowledge Sources to Application 294
- 2.5.7 Skill in Curating Instructional Content, Tools, and Resources 295
  - I. Curating Content, Tools, and Resources for Knowledge Management 295

Applying KM in Talent Development 296

- 2.5.8 Skill in Identifying the Type and Amount of Information Needed to Support TD Activities 296
  - I. Identifying Information for Talent Development 296
- 2.5.9 Skill in Developing, Managing, Facilitating, and Supporting Knowledge Networks and Communities of Practice 297
  - I. Develop and Manage KM Networks and Communities of Practice 297

References 300
Recommended Reading 301

2.6 Career & Leadership Development 303

Career Development 303

- 2.6.1 Knowledge of Career Models and Paths 303
  - I. Career Models and Paths 303
- 2.6.2 Skill in Facilitating the Career Development Planning Process 305
  - I. Supporting Individual Lifelong Learning and Career Development 305
- 2.6.3 Skill in Developing, Administering, and Debriefing Results of Assessments of Intelligence, Aptitude, Potential, Skill, Ability, or Interests 308
  - I. Using Assessments for Career Development 308
- 2.6.4 Knowledge of Career Development Methods and Techniques 309
  - I. Development Approaches for Key Roles and Jobs 309
- 2.6.5 Skill in Conducting Individual and Group Career Planning Sessions to Provide Guidance Across Career Phases 309
  - I. Supporting Employees' Career Cycle 309
- 2.6.6 Knowledge of How to Develop and Implement Qualification Programs 311
  - I. Develop and Implement Qualification Programs 311

Leadership Development 314
    2.6.7   Knowledge of Leadership Development Practices and Techniques 314
            I. Understanding Leadership Development 314
    2.6.8   Skill in Sourcing, Designing, Building, and Evaluating Leadership Development Experiences 316
            I. Designing a Leadership Development Initiative 316
            II. Build a Leadership Development Plan 318
    References 323
    Recommended Reading 325

2.7 Coaching 327
    2.7.1   Knowledge of Organizational Coaching Models 327
            I. Coaching Basics 327
    2.7.2   Skill in Helping Individuals or Teams Identify Goals, Develop Realistic Action Plans,
            Seek Development Opportunities, and Monitor Progress and Accountability 330
            I. The Coaching Process 330
            II. Following a Coaching Process 333
    2.7.3   Skill in Coaching Supervisors and Managers on Methods and Approaches for
            Supporting Employee Development 334
            I. Coaching Managers to Support Improved Performance and Employee Development 334
    2.7.4   Skill in Creating Effective Coaching Agreements 337
            I. Establishing a Coaching Engagement 337
    2.7.5   Knowledge of Methods and Techniques to Evaluate the Effectiveness of Coaching 339
            I. Evaluating a Coaching Engagement 339
    2.7.6   Skill in Establishing an Environment That Fosters Mutual Respect and Trust With
            Coaching Clients 341
            I. Creating an Environment That Supports Coaching 341
    2.7.7   Skill in Recruiting, Training, and Pairing Coaches and Mentors With Employees 344
            I. Fostering an Active and Enduring Coaching Initiative 344
    2.7.8   Knowledge of Professional Standards and Ethical Guidelines for Coaching 345
            I. Professional Standards and Ethical Guidelines for Coaching 345
    References 348
    Recommended Reading 349

2.8 Evaluating Impact 351
    2.8.1   Knowledge of Models and Methods to Evaluate the Impact of Learning and Talent
            Development Solutions 351
            I. Assessing and Evaluating the Impact of TD Solutions 351
            II. Evaluation Methodologies 354
    2.8.2   Knowledge of Qualitative and Quantitative Data Collection Methods, Techniques, and Tools 358
            I. Qualitative and Quantitative Data Collection Methods 358
    2.8.3   Skill in Identifying and Defining Individual and Organizational Outcome Metrics
            Based on Evaluation Strategy or the Business Objectives of a Solution 361
            I. Identifying Outcome Metrics 361
    2.8.4   Skill in Creating Data Collection Tools 366
            I. Steps for Creating Evaluation Instruments 366

2.8.5	Knowledge of Research Design Methodologies and Types	369
	I. Research Methods and Design	369
2.8.6	Skill in Selecting or Designing Organizational Research	370
	I. Designing Organizational Research	370
2.8.7	Skill in Analyzing and Interpreting Results of Data Analyses to Identify Patterns, Trends, and Relationships Among Variables	375
	I. Analyzing and Interpreting Results	375
References		379
Recommended Reading		380

3.1 Business Insight 383

3.1.1	Knowledge of Business and Organizational Processes, Operations, and Outputs	383
	I. Organizational Insight	383
3.1.2	Knowledge of Business Strategies and Factors That Influence an Organization's Competitive Position in the Industry	385
	I. Understand What Makes an Organization Successful	385
3.1.3	Knowledge of How Organizations Provide Customer Service	387
	I. Customer Service Fundamentals	387
3.1.4	Knowledge of How Talent Development Contributes to an Organization's Competitive Advantage	389
	I. Understanding Talent Development's Contribution to Organizational Outcomes	389
3.1.5	Knowledge of Financial Management Principles	391
	I. Business Acumen: Critical Concepts for TD Professionals	391
3.1.6	Skill in Managing Budgets and Resources	392
	I. Budgeting, Accounting, and Financial Management	392
3.1.7	Skill in Creating Business Cases for Talent Development Initiatives Using Economic, Financial, and Organizational Data	394
	I. Business Cases for TD Initiatives	394
3.1.8	Skill in Communicating Business and Financial Information to Different Audiences Using Appropriate Terminology and Relevant Examples	395
	I. Communicating Business and Financial Information	395
References		397
Recommended Reading		398

3.2 Consulting & Business Partnering 399

3.2.1	Skill in Establishing and Managing Organizational and Business Partnerships and Relationships	399
	I. Talent Development's Role As a Trusted Advisor	399
3.2.2	Skill in Partnering With Other Organizational Units to Provide Guidance on Departmental or Organizational Talent Requirements	405
	I. Partnering Across the Organization	405
3.2.3	Skill in Managing Stakeholders on an Ongoing Basis to Sustain Organizational or Business Relationships	407
	I. Building and Managing Stakeholder Relationships	407
3.2.4	Knowledge of Needs Assessment Approaches and Techniques	409
	I. Designing Organizational Needs Assessments	409

	3.2.5	Skill in Synthesizing Information to Formulate Recommendations or a Course of Action to Gain Agreement, Support, and Buy-In From Stakeholders 412
		I. Gain Agreement, Support, and Buy-In From Stakeholders: Synthesizing Information 412
	3.2.6	Skill in Conveying Recommendations or a Course of Action to Gain Agreement, Support, and Buy-In From Stakeholders 414
		I. Gaining Agreement, Support, and Buy-In From Stakeholders: Communicating Recommendations 414
	3.2.7	Knowledge of Methods and Criteria for Sourcing, Establishing, and Managing Partnerships 416
		I. Establishing External Partnerships 416
	3.2.8	Skill in Identifying, Minimizing, and Overcoming Organizational Barriers to Implementing Talent Development Solutions or Strategies 417
		I. Overcoming Barriers and Resistance to TD Solutions 417
References 419
Recommended Reading 420

3.3 Organization Development & Culture 421

Organization Development 421

	3.3.1	Knowledge of Organization Development Concepts 421
		I. Organization Development Basics 421
	3.3.2	Skill in Designing and Implementing an Organization Development Strategy 424
		I. Designing and Implementing an OD Strategy 424
	3.3.3	Knowledge of Theories and Frameworks Related to the Design, Interaction, and Operation of Social, Organizational, and Informational Systems 425
		I. General Theories Supporting Organization Development 425
	3.3.4	Skill in Identifying Formal and Informal Relationships, Hierarchies, and Power Dynamics in an Organization 427
		I. Understanding Organizational Relationships, Hierarchies, and Power Dynamics 427
	3.3.5	Knowledge of the Principles of Organizational Management 428
		I. Principles of Organizational Management 428
	3.3.6	Knowledge of Work Roles, Relationships, and Reporting Structures Within an Organization 430
		I. Organizational Reporting Structures 430

Culture 431

	3.3.7	Knowledge of Strategies and Techniques for Building, Supporting, or Promoting an Organizational Culture That Values Talent and Learning as Drivers of Competitive Advantage 431
		I. Fostering a Learning Organization 431
	3.3.8	Skill in Creating a Culture That Encourages or Creates Opportunities for Dialogue and Feedback Between Individuals and Groups 438
		I. Learning Cultures Encourage Dialogue, Feedback, and Collaboration 438
	3.3.9	Skill in Articulating and Codifying Talent and Leadership Principles, Values, and Competencies That Guide the Organization's Culture and Define Behavioral Expectations 439
		I. Defining and Articulating an Organization's Culture 439

Engagement 441

	3.3.10	Knowledge of How Employee Engagement and Retention Influence Organizational Outcomes 441
		I. Employee Engagement and Retention 441
	3.3.11	Skill in Assessing and Evaluating Employee Engagement 444
		I. Assessing and Evaluating Employee Engagement 444

3.3.12 Skill in Designing and Implementing Employee Engagement Strategies 445
    I. Designing Employee Engagement Strategies 445
3.3.13 Knowledge of the Principles, Policies, and Practices Associated With Programs and Initiatives Designed for Organizational Well-Being 447
    I. Well-Being for Organizational Success 447
References 449
Recommended Reading 452

3.4 Talent Strategy & Management 453
3.4.1 Knowledge of Talent Management Functions 453
    I. Integrated Talent Management Functions 453
3.4.2 Skill in Creating and Aligning Talent Development Vision and Strategy With Organizational and Business Vision and Strategy 457
    I. Aligning Talent Strategy to Organizational Strategy 457
3.4.3 Skill in Developing a Talent Strategy That Aligns to Organizational Strategies to Positively Influence Organizational Outcomes 461
    I. Talent Development's Role in Influencing Positive Organizational Outcomes 461
3.4.4 Skill in Designing and Implementing Strategic Plans for Talent Development Projects, Programs, and Functions 464
    I. Planning for Talent Development Work 464
3.4.5 Skill in Identifying Anticipated Constraints or Problems Affecting Talent Development Initiatives........... 466
    I. Identifying and Overcoming Constraints and Problems With TD Initiatives 466
3.4.6 Skill in Establishing and Executing a Marketing Strategy to Promote Talent Development Activities 467
    I. Creating a TD Marketing Strategy 467
3.4.7 Skill in Designing and Implementing a Communication Strategy to Drive Talent Management Objectives 471
    I. Creating a TD Communication Strategy 471
3.4.8 Skill in Communicating How Talent Development Strategies and Solutions Support the Achievement of Targeted Business and Organizational Results 472
    I. Communicating the Value of Talent Development 472
3.4.9 Skill in Communicating the Value of Learning and Professional Development 474
    I. Communicating the Value of Continuous Learning and Development 474
3.4.10 Skill in Developing Workforce Plans That Articulate Current and Future Talent and Skill Requirements...476
    I. Strategic Workforce Planning 476
3.4.11 Knowledge of Succession Planning and Talent Review Processes 478
    I. Succession Planning and Talent Reviews 478
3.4.12 Knowledge of Approaches for Identifying and Developing High-Potential Talent 480
    I. Developing High-Potential Talent 480
3.4.13 Knowledge of Methods to Identify Critical Requirements of Tasks, Jobs, and Roles 483
    I. Identifying Tasks, Jobs, and Role Requirements 483
3.4.14 Knowledge of Talent Acquisition Strategies and Concepts 486
    I. Talent Acquisition Strategy and Concepts 486
3.4.15 Skill in Comparing and Evaluating Advantages and Disadvantages of Talent Development Strategies... 488
    I. Sources of Talent: Build, Buy, Borrow, Bound, Bounce, or Bind 488

    3.4.16 Skill in Designing and Implementing a Performance Management Strategy 491

                I. Performance Management 491

    References 494

    Recommended Reading 495

3.5 Performance Improvement 497

    3.5.1   Knowledge of Theories, Models, and Principles of Human Performance Improvement 497

                I. Principles of Performance Improvement 497

    3.5.2   Knowledge of Performance Analysis Methods and Techniques 502

                I. Business, Performance, and Gap Analysis 502

    3.5.3   Knowledge of How Human Interactions With Work Environments, Tools, Equipment, and Technology Affect Individual and Organizational Performance 505

                I. Influences on Individual and Organizational Performance 505

    3.5.4   Skill in Conducting a Performance Analysis to Identify Goals, Gaps, or Opportunities 506

                I. Conducting a Performance Analysis 506

    3.5.5   Skill in Designing and Developing Performance Improvement Solutions to Address Performance Gaps 507

                I. Selecting HPI Solutions to Address Gaps 507

    3.5.6   Skill in Designing and Implementing Performance Support Systems and Tools 512

                I. Designing and Implementing Performance Support 512

    3.5.7   Skill in Conducting Analysis of Systems to Improve Human Performance 514

                I. Analysis of Systems to Improve Performance 514

    References 519

    Recommended Reading 520

3.6 Change Management 521

    3.6.1   Knowledge of Change Management Models, Theories, and Tools 521

                I. Change Management Models, Theories, and Tools 521

    3.6.2   Knowledge of How Change Affects People and Organizations 526

                I. The Impact of Change on People and Organizations 526

    3.6.3   Skill in Assessing Risk, Resistance, and Consequences to Define a Change Management Approach 533

                I. Assessing Change Risk, Resistance, and Consequences 533

    3.6.4   Skill in Designing and Implementing an Organizational Change Strategy 537

                I. Designing and Implementing an Organizational Change Strategy 537

    References 548

    Recommended Reading 549

3.7 Data & Analytics 551

    3.7.1   Knowledge of Principles and Applications of Analytics 551

                I. The Importance of People Analytics 551

    3.7.2   Skill in Gathering and Organizing Data From Internal or External Sources in Logical and Practical Ways to Support Retrieval and Manipulation 555

                I. Selecting a Project for an Analytics Initiative 555

Table of Contents

- 3.7.3 Skill in Identifying Stakeholders' Needs, Goals, Requirements, Questions, and Objectives to Develop a Framework or Plan for Data Analysis 557
  - I. Developing a People Analytics Plan 557
- 3.7.4 Skill in Analyzing and Interpreting Results of Data Analyses to Identify Patterns, Trends, and Relationships Among Variables 558
  - I. Analyzing Data and Interpreting Results 558
- 3.7.5 Knowledge of Data Visualization, Including Principles, Methods, Types, and Applications 561
  - I. Data Visualization Principles 561
- 3.7.6 Skill in Selecting or Using Data Visualization Techniques 563
  - I. Selecting Data Visualization Techniques 563
- 3.7.7 Knowledge of Statistical Theory and Methods Including the Computation, Interpretation, and Reporting of Statistics 564
  - I. Principles, Definitions, and Applications of Statistical Theory 564
- References 567
- Recommended Reading 569

3.8 Future Readiness 571

- 3.8.1 Knowledge of Internal and External Factors That Influence Talent Development 571
  - I. Influences on the Workplace of the Future 571
- 3.8.2 Skill in Conducting Environmental Scanning to Identify Current and Emerging Trends in the Economy, Legislation, Competition, and Technology 577
  - I. Environmental Scanning 577
- 3.8.3 Knowledge of Techniques to Promote, Support, or Generate Innovation and Creativity 580
  - I. Fostering Innovation and Creativity 580
- 3.8.4 Knowledge of Emerging Learning Technologies and Support Systems 583
  - I. Evaluating Emerging Learning Technologies 583
- 3.8.5 Knowledge of Information-Seeking Strategies and Techniques 587
  - I. Identifying Information Sources 587
- 3.8.6 Skill in Applying Previous Learning to Future Experiences 589
  - I. Learning Agility 589
- References 594
- Recommended Reading 595

Glossary 597

Acronyms 645

FOREWORD

For 80 years, ATD has served the development needs of learning professionals as the talent development field has evolved to meet the knowledge and skill requirements of organizations, industries, and a dynamic business environment. Throughout our organization's history, what has remained constant is our purpose of empowering TD professionals like you to lead the important work of developing people. We have always worked to help people grow their knowledge, skills, and capabilities so they can help unleash human potential in the workforce and, in so doing, contribute to achieving the strategic goals and success of their organizations. Never has this been more essential than in today's environment as leaders and organizations wrestle with economic, technological, and workplace disruption.

These changes require members of this field to adapt and constantly upskill and reskill our workforce. A recent ATD research report, *The Future of Work: Technology, Predictions, and Preparing the Workforce*, revealed that a majority of organizations (76 percent) are concerned that their workforces may not be properly skilled for the future of work. In the postpandemic era with evolving employee expectations around employment, talent concerns may be the most critical challenge facing businesses today.

Opportunities to harness innovative approaches to planning, managing, and developing talent in organizations are endless. C-level executives can—and must—use their talent development functions strategically. Doing so positions their organizations for growth, creates high-performance workplaces, increases employee engagement and retention, and generates greater profitability. Forward-thinking organizations are forming working groups to plan for the future of work and help leaders think about the organizational changes that need to be made in the coming years. This requires talent decisions to be made based on future needs, and for talent development professionals to be prepared to handle the increasing strategic demands that will be expected of them.

For many decades, ATD has published competency and capability models to help professionals in the field understand what they need to know and do to be successful in their work. ATD introduced the Talent Development Capability Model several years ago to better reflect the current state of the profession—and where it's headed. This modernized model has filled a critical need for the field—a significant shift in focus from competence to capability, which speaks to the expansion of the role and skill requirements necessary to lead talent in today's environment. ATD has structured the Talent Development Capability Model and the supporting Body of Knowledge (TDBoK™) with a broad-based perspective and future-focus because we see the talent development field's growing importance, influence, and impact.

Foreword

Since its original publication in 2020, the definitive TDBoK has been an invaluable resource for the field, providing global talent development professionals a comprehensive collection of concepts, definitions, methodologies, and examples that help readers understand how to apply the concepts and theories. Inside you will find the knowledge and skill statements for each of the 23 capabilities in the three domains of practice identified in the Talent Development Capability Model.

This second edition of the *TDBoK Guide* represents an exciting new phase for this resource. As our field continuously evolves, so too must the insights and information that equip the profession. We've scanned the environment, curated perspectives from industry leaders, and surveyed those of you who perform the noble work of talent development every day to synthesize the most relevant and up-to-date information on what you need to know and do to guide the workforces you support in these complex times.

The development of human capability, knowledge, and skills is critically important to our society. This is about more than training—it is about fostering cultures of lifelong learning that drive performance, innovation, engagement, and opportunity. As Peter Drucker wrote, "We now accept the fact that learning is a lifelong process of keeping abreast of change. And the most pressing task is to teach people how to learn."

ATD's Talent Development Capability Model and this new edition of the *TDBoK Guide* are a blueprint for your own learning at this crucial time. Please continue to use these resources to help create a world that works better.

Tony Bingham
President and CEO, Association for Talent Development

INTRODUCTION

About the Association for Talent Development (ATD)

The Association for Talent Development, formerly the American Society for Training & Development, is the world's largest association dedicated to those who develop talent in organizations. Founded in 1943, ATD's mission is to support those who help others achieve their full potential by improving their knowledge, skills, and capabilities. ATD's members come from more than 120 countries and work in organizations of all sizes and in all industry sectors. This global community of practitioners looks to ATD's publications, digital content, career resources, events, education courses, and professional certification programs to elevate their skills and advance their careers.

ATD also leads the profession by setting standards and assessing competence against those standards. Since 1978, ATD has published nine competency models that have tracked the profession's evolution from training to the broader, more strategic function of talent development. These models have each answered the question: What do professionals in the field need to know and do to be successful? Based on ATD's competency model research and vetted by experts, these models provide a blueprint for individuals to determine their current knowledge of professional concepts and the areas in which they need further development.

ATD offers more than 100 training courses that enable professionals to expand their knowledge and build new skills across the competencies within the talent development industry. The ATD Certification Institute (ATD CI) offers two professional certifications and five assessment-based certificate programs to assess and recognize a practitioner's mastery of the knowledge and skills that make up talent development best practices. ATD's competency models form the foundation of our education and credentialing programs, giving TD professionals the ability to build a structured and progressive pathway for professional development and career advancement.

The Talent Development Capability Model

In 2019, ATD conducted its latest competency research, culminating with the launch of the Talent Development Capability Model. With the intent to establish a new standard for the TD professional, the model is a framework to communicate what practitioners need to know and do to develop themselves, others, and their organizations. The book *Capabilities for Talent Development: Shaping the Future of the Profession* details the trends affecting our profession today, the knowledge and skill areas addressed in the model, and the research behind it.

In 2021, ATD conducted a pulse survey to identify how the perceived importance of the capabilities in the Capability Model has evolved over time, specifically due to the COVID-19 pandemic. The study aimed to

Introduction

articulate and synthesize the disruptions to how we work and how we develop talent. The results of the study provided insights that were used to inform the modifications and enhancements in this second edition. The core structure of the Capability Model itself remains untouched; however, additional information has been incorporated to reflect the present-day climate of talent development.

The Talent Development Capability Model features three domains of practice:

- Building Personal Capability
- Developing Professional Capability
- Impacting Organizational Capability

Within the three domains are 23 capabilities spanning a broad spectrum of disciplines that, when integrated and leveraged holistically, enable professionals to effectively develop employees in the workplace. Each capability is further broken down into knowledge and skills statements, with the 186 total across the entire model.

Domain 1. Building Personal Capability

1.1 Communication
1.2 Emotional Intelligence & Decision Making
1.3 Collaboration & Leadership
1.4 Cultural Awareness & Inclusion
1.5 Project Management
1.6 Compliance & Ethical Behavior
1.7 Lifelong Learning

Domain 2. Developing Professional Capability

2.1 Learning Sciences
2.2 Instructional Design
2.3 Training Delivery & Facilitation
2.4 Technology Application
2.5 Knowledge Management
2.6 Career & Leadership Development
2.7 Coaching
2.8 Evaluating Impact

Domain 3. Impacting Organizational Capability

3.1 Business Insight
3.2 Consulting & Business Partnering
3.3 Organization Development & Culture
3.4 Talent Strategy & Management
3.5 Performance Improvement
3.6 Change Management
3.7 Data & Analytics
3.8 Future Readiness

The Talent Development Body of Knowledge (TDBoK)

Information about talent development practices has never been more readily available. In addition to the publications, events, and education products offered by ATD, TD professionals can easily access the latest ideas, opinions, and research from thought leaders and industry experts through websites and social media platforms. As the field continues to transform to match business and organizational strategic priorities, it is important to have a codified set of standards that define talent development.

To support the Talent Development Capability Model and all TD professionals, ATD embarked on researching, documenting, and evaluating the concepts, topics, theories, models, and activities that define the profession. The Talent Development Body of Knowledge (TDBoK) was released in 2020 and is the comprehensive resource for information that guides the work of those who develop talent in the workplace. After two years of extensive use in the profession, the TDBoK has been revised. ATD leveraged more than 100 subject matter expert contributors and curated perspectives from thousands of publications to produce an updated resource for the field.

Although the Capability Model's core structure was exempt from editing during this standard revision, the entire TDBoK content was reviewed and edited for consistency in terminology, to correct unclear or incorrect content, and to address input received directly from TDBoK users. In addition, six capabilities were targeted for an in-depth review and revised to incorporate updates and changes based on ATD's 2021 pulse survey and trends in the profession. The six capabilities that received a detailed review were:

- 1.4 Cultural Awareness & Inclusion
- 2.4 Technology Application
- 3.4 Talent Strategy & Management
- 3.6 Change Management
- 3.7 Data & Analytics
- 3.8 Future Readiness

Consistency of terminology throughout this second edition is a priority. For example, we use "talent development" to refer to the profession, "talent development professional" to refer to the associated career, and "facilitator" to refer to an individual who is guiding learning. We recognize that you may use other terms such as "trainer" to define what you do. Our purpose is to achieve consistency and clarity and to avoid confusion; it is not our intent to eliminate specific terms. The glossary, which has also been updated, provides additional definitions and clarity. Please use it freely.

ATD's goal is to ensure that the *TDBoK Guide* will:
- **Serve as a definitive, ongoing, centralized source and reference guide** for TD best practices and the knowledge and skills required for success in the profession.
- **Enable easy access to theories, models, insights, and answers** through a structured, searchable publication.
- **Provide an overview of the broad array of disciplines in talent development** (23 unique capabilities) so TD professionals can get exposure to new proficiency areas, identify what more they need to learn, and tailor their future development plan.
- **Give TD professionals a shared set of terminology and definitions** to create a common language.
- **Ensure alignment of professional resources** that TD professionals use to expand and develop their career—from credentials to courses and conferences to publications and online content.

The *TDBoK Guide* also addresses the current needs of diverse audiences. It will:
- Give **individuals who are new to talent development**, or who are looking to formalize their expertise, an understanding of the breadth of knowledge covered within the field.
- Offer **talent development managers** a resource for creating shared understanding and language with their teams.
- Guide **individual and team development planning** by identifying the knowledge and skills required for success.
- Serve as **a source for creating business cases** with leadership to validate appropriate approaches and the benefits of talent development.
- Enable **educators and curriculum developers** to align their offerings to a research-based, vetted framework that defines excellence in talent development.

The Talent Development Capability Model is the foundation for ATD CI's certification programs, the Associate Professional in Talent Development (APTD) and the Certified Professional in Talent Development (CPTD). The *TDBoK Guide* can serve as an important resource for exam preparation.

How to Use the *TDBoK Guide*

This book is structured to mirror the Talent Development Capability Model. It comprises three sections, one for each domain in the model, and the 23 capabilities are spread across those three sections. A descriptive paragraph accompanies each capability to establish what TD professionals need to know and be able to do to achieve the standard of performance defined by the Capability Model. Within each capability, TD professionals will find knowledge and skills statements describing the concepts, terminology, and models associated with the topic.

A numbering system allows for quick referencing of the domain, capability, and knowledge and skills statements. For example, 1.1.1 refers to "skill in expressing thoughts, feelings, and ideas in a clear, concise, and compelling manner"—the first knowledge and skill statement in the communication capability, which is the first capability in the first domain (Building Personal Capability).

The *TDBoK Guide* also includes these content elements:
- **Cross-references** indicate where you can find additional information about a topic within another section; for example, [See 5.1.2].
- **References** provide the direct sources cited in the publication.
- **Recommended reading** outlines supplemental resources for further background and knowledge.
- **The glossary** defines key terms.

Feedback and Future Updates

ATD's Talent Development Capability Model and the resources aligned to it are regularly revisited and updated to keep up with with evolutions in society, the workplace, and our profession. The TDBoK's content is periodically reviewed and modified to align with these changes. ATD keeps its members and subscribers informed of updates to its products and invites feedback to ensure we are delivering high-quality offerings. For more information, please visit td.org/tdbok, or contact ATD Customer Care at 1.800.628.2783 or customercare@td.org.

EDITORS AND CONTRIBUTORS

This publication is possible because of the collaboration, expertise, and dedication of a team of volunteer contributors and ATD staff. ATD is especially grateful to Elaine Biech for the thousands of hours she devoted to the development of this book and its subsequent second edition.

Principal Designer and Curator
Elaine Biech, CPTD Fellow

Elaine Biech is a consultant, facilitator, and author of the *Washington Post* number 1 bestseller *The Art and Science of Training*. With four decades of experience and more than 80 published books, she has been called "one of the titans of the training industry." She is a dedicated lifelong learner who believes that excellence isn't optional and is the recipient of numerous professional awards, including ISA's 2022 Thought Leader, ATD's 2020 Distinguished Contribution to Talent Development Award, Bliss Award, Torch Award, and Staff Partnership Award. She served on ATD's board of directors, CCL's board of governors and executive board, and ISA's board of directors, and she is the inaugural CPTD Fellow Honoree from ATD's Certification Institute. Elaine is a consummate TD professional who has been instrumental in guiding the talent development profession throughout her career.

Lead *TDBoK Guide* Advisor
Courtney Vital, CPTD, Vice President, Learning, ATD

Chapter Authors and Significant Contributors
- **Holly Burkett,** Evaluation Works
- **John Coné,** i4cp and The 11th Hour Group
- **JD Dillon,** Axonify and LearnGeek
- **Barbara Goretsky,** Barbara Goretsky Consultancy
- **Jonathan Halls,** Trainer Mojo and George Washington University
- **Mason Holloway,** Deltek
- **Cindy Huggett,** CPTD, Independent Consultant
- **Lou Russell,** Moser Consulting

Editors and Contributors

TDBoK Guide, Second Edition, Advisory Board
- **Elaine Biech,** Advisory Board Chair
- **Rita Bailey,** Up to Something, LLC
- **Holly Burkett,** PhD, SPHR, hb Consulting | Evaluation Works
- **John Coné,** i4cp and The 11th Hour Group
- **Jonathan Halls,** Jonathan Halls LLC
- **Karl Kapp,** EdD, Bloomsburg University
- **Dana Alan Koch,** MA, Accenture Institute for Applied Learning Sciences
- **Patti Phillips,** PhD, CPTD, ROI Institute, Inc.
- **Eivind Slaaten,** Hilti Corporation

TDBoK Guide, Second Edition, Development Team
- **Melissa Jones,** Manager, ATD Press, ATD
- **Mindi Smith,** Project Manager, Education Product Development, ATD
- **Katy Wiley Stewts,** Production Editor, ATD Press
- **Jeanna Sullivan,** Manager, Education Product Development, ATD
- **Jeff Surprenant,** CPTD, Associate Director, Education Product Development, ATD
- **Courtney Vital,** CPTD, Vice President, Learning, ATD

TDBoK Guide, Second Edition, Subject Matter Experts
- **Michelle Braden,** MBA, WEX
- **Wendy Gates Corbett,** MS, CPTD, Signature Presentations, LLC
- **Wagner Denuzzo,** LCSW, Prudential Financial
- **Joel DiGirolamo,** BSEE, MBA, MS I/O Psychology, International Coaching Federation
- **Joe Folkman,** President, Zenger | Folkman
- **Bahaa Hussein,** CPTD, SIMDUSTRY
- **Graham Johnston,** Deloitte Services LP
- **Amy P. Kelly,** GPHR, SPHR, SHRM-SCP, The Amy P. Kelly Companies
- **Debra McKinney,** SPHRi, Independent Consultant
- **Margie Meacham,** Chief Freedom Officer, Learningtogo
- **Kristopher J. Newbauer,** EdM, MHRM, SPHR, SHRM-SCP, CPTD, CPT, Rotary International
- **Almira "Myra" Roldan,** MS Ed, MBA, AWS
- **Tom Stone,** Senior Research Analyst, i4cp
- **Eddie Turner,** Eddie Turner, LLC
- **Dana Vogelmeier,** CPTD, Vogelmeier Consulting, LLC
- **Travis Waugh,** MS, TD SYNNEX
- **Joe Wilmore,** Willmore Consulting Group
- **Tonya J. Wilson,** MAIOP, CPM, AFC Consulting Group
- **Kathryn Zukof,** PhD, MBA

Talent Development Body of Knowledge Subject Matter Experts
- **Rita Bailey,** Up to Something
- **Mimi Banta,** Banta Training Services
- **Robert Brinkerhoff,** Brinkerhoff Evaluation Institute and Western Michigan University
- **Diane Elkins,** Artisan E-Learning
- **Barbara Goretsky,** Barbara Goretsky Consultancy
- **Tracy Harris-Bennett,** Bennett Global Group
- **Bahaa Hussein,** CPTD, Abudawood Group
- **Jenn Labin,** MentorcliQ
- **Lynn Lewis,** CPTD, Learning Solutions
- **Seema Nagrath Menon,** CPTD, Independent Consultant
- **Renie McClay,** Inspired Learning
- **Sarah Mercier,** Learning Ninjas
- **Julie O'Mara,** The Centre for Global Inclusion
- **Maureen Orey,** CPTD, Workplace Performance Group
- **Julie Patrick,** JP Learning Associates
- **Chris Ross,** CPTD, The Engagement Effect
- **Eddie Turner,** Eddie Turner, LLC
- **Dana Vogelmeier,** CPTD, Vogelmeier Consulting

Talent Development Capability Model Advisory Panel
- **Britt Andreatta,** Andreatta Consulting
- **Elaine Biech,** ebb associates inc
- **Nicole Carter,** Signature Health
- **John Coné,** i4cp and The 11th Hour Group
- **David Forman,** Sage Learning Systems and Pepperdine University
- **Wendy Gates Corbett,** CPTD, Refresher Training
- **Jonathan Halls,** Trainer Mojo and George Washington University
- **Karl Kapp,** Bloomsburg University and 2K Learning
- **Dana Alan Koch,** Accenture
- **Jennifer Martineau,** Center for Creative Leadership
- **Patricia McLagan,** McLagan International
- **Kara Miller,** Comcast
- **William Rothwell,** Rothwell & Associates and Pennsylvania State University

Talent Development Capability Model Task Force
- **Grace Amos,** Cisco Meraki
- **Jennifer Brink,** Comcast University
- **Brian Davis,** CPTD, Washington Suburban Sanitary Commission

- **Jessica Gil,** European Wax Center
- **Jennifer Halsall,** TD Bank
- **Stephanie Hubka,** CPTD, Protos Learning
- **Bahaa Hussein,** CPTD, Abudawood Group
- **John Kostek,** Hitachi Vantara
- **Lance Legree,** Hilti
- **Jay Maxwell,** CPTD, Call Center Optimization Group
- **Kent Nuttall,** CPTD, Torch Solutions Group
- **Joseph Reamer,** HSBC
- **Wei Wang,** CPTD, ATD Global

ATD Staff Contributors

- **Eliza Auckerman,** Senior Project Manager, Education Product Development
- **Holly Batts,** Associate Director, Credentialing
- **Amber Bronder,** Senior Marketing Manager
- **Justin Brusino,** Director, Content
- **Alexandria Clapp,** Content Manager, Learning Technologies and Sciences
- **Christopher Collins,** Instructional Design Specialist
- **Carrie Cross,** Project Manager
- **Elizabeth Decker,** Senior Manager, Education Product Development
- **Kristen Fyfe-Mills,** Director, Marketing and Strategic Communications
- **Patty Gaul,** Writer/Editor
- **Sarah Halgas,** Director, Production, Editorial, and Creative
- **MJ Hall,** Content Manager, ATD Forum
- **Jack Harlow,** Developmental Editor, ATD Press
- **Amy Harrison,** Technical Project Manager
- **Kay Hechler,** Senior Manager, Publications and Content Marketing
- **Morgean Hirt,** Director, Credentialing
- **Maria Ho,** Associate Director, Research
- **Jennifer Homer,** Vice President, Content and Communications
- **Sue Kaiden,** APTD, Senior Project Manager, Credentialing
- **Paula Ketter,** Senior Manager, Content Strategy and Communications
- **Allison Rafti,** Director, Marketing
- **Rose Richey,** Creative Director
- **Kathy Stack,** Director, Enterprise and Education Marketing

Domain 1
Building Personal Capability

1.1 COMMUNICATION

Communication is about connecting with others. Effectively communicating requires a knowledge of communication principles and techniques that allows a person to articulate the appropriate message for a particular audience. It requires active listening, facilitating dialogue, and the ability to express thoughts, feelings, and ideas clearly, concisely, and compellingly.

1.1.1 Skill in Expressing Thoughts, Feelings, and Ideas in a Clear, Concise, and Compelling Manner

> **I. Effective Communication for TD Professionals**
> As the employee development representative, effective communication is at the base of everything that TD professionals do.

1.1.1.1 Value of Good TD Communication

Good communication is essential to creating a productive and efficient workplace. Effective communication helps build the working team, boost employee engagement, increase customer satisfaction, improve productivity, and grow the bottom line. The cost of poor communication is measureable. The Society for Human Resource Management (SHRM) surveyed 400 companies with more than 100,000 employees and found an average loss per company of $62.4 million per year due to inadequate communication. The *2018 State of Employee Communication and Engagement* report conducted by an independent market research company surveyed 1,072 US employers and found that 56 percent struggled to keep employees engaged and informed (Dynamic Signal 2018).

The value TD professionals can contribute to improving communication in their organizations should be a priority.

1.1.1.2 The Communication Process

The communication process is the transmission of a message from a sender to a receiver. The sender uses a medium to send the message, which then goes through the sender's and receiver's filters before the receiver decodes the message. The receiver's interpretation of the message then becomes part of the feedback to the sender.

1.1 Communication

TD professionals should understand the concepts that describe the communication process:
- **Environment.** The conditions or circumstances within which the communication process operates; it may enhance or block communication
- **Message.** The information that is communicated
- **Sender.** The person communicating the message
- **Filter.** A mindset, bias, or opinion that hinders the flow of information between the sender and receiver, usually based on past experiences
- **Medium.** The method used to convey the message, such as voice, reports, or email
- **Receiver.** A person or device that receives the message and decodes or processes it
- **Encoding.** The process of translating the message by the sender
- **Decoding.** The process of translating the message to thoughts and understanding
- **Feedback.** Communication that gives individuals information about the effect of their communication

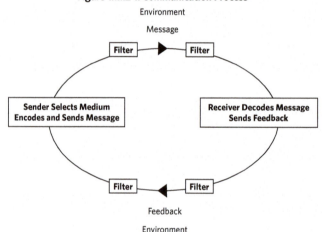

Figure 1.1.1.2-1. Communication Process

Source: Adapted from a drawing by Elaine Biech.

1.1.1.3 Effective Communication

As the voice of employee development, TD professionals must be able to interpret the needs of the organization, employees, and other stakeholders and communicate with each. Effective communication can be defined by the six Cs of communication; TD professionals should deliver messages that are clear, correct, complete, concise, coherent, and courteous:
- **Clear.** Choose audience-appropriate words that are precise and descriptive.
- **Correct.** Select accurate words and use correct grammar; avoid using the wrong words.
- **Complete.** Articulate comprehensive messages that are transparent and include all the details.
- **Concise.** Use short, specific sentences and phrases; avoid rambling.
- **Coherent.** Maintain consistency, select simple sentence structures, and present in an easy-to-follow order.
- **Courteous.** Form respectful and authentic messages with words that are friendly, positive, gender neutral, and sensitive; avoid accusing or blaming.

1.1.1.4 Create a Compelling Message
A compelling message incorporates four elements. It must:
- Include a benefit to listeners and why they should invest their time.
- Be unique, inspiring, or exciting and answer the question, "What's different about this message?"
- Be complete with data, examples, or a story that relates the message to what the listener wants to hear or answers the question, "How do I know?"
- Include a call to action or what the listener should do. This could include anything on a continuum from responding to the message to completing a task; it answers the question, "So what?"

1.1.1.5 Selecting Appropriate Communication Media
Communication media—or the method used to convey a message—includes but is not limited to voice, reports, or email. Media can be divided several ways depending on whether the message is meant to be one-way or two-way, with immediate or delayed feedback, or to one person or more. The TD professional should not become overly reliant on one medium. Immediate feedback can be provided using one-to-one, large, or small meetings; video conferences; phone calls; or word of mouth. The delayed feedback media could include intranet, newsletters, corporate communication, social media, infographics, fact sheets, reports, emails, text messages, or mail.

Guidelines to determine the choice of communication medium include:
- What kind of message is it? Is it routine and open to anyone, or is it confidential?
- How long is the message?
- How urgent is the timeline to deliver the message?
- What's the cost and does the result justify the expenditure?
- Does the message require a record of distribution?
- Is the size and the distribution of the group receiving the message important?
- Who is the audience, and what's the relationship of the sender and receiver?
- What technology is available to send the message? [See 2.3.5.12]

1.1.1.6 Barries to Effective Communication
Due to the high cost of poor communication, TD professionals should ensure that they review communication barriers and do what they can to eliminate their personal barriers. In addition, they need to be aware of other's barriers. Barriers include, but are not limited to:
- **Physical barriers**—environment, location, medium selected, technology, distance between communicators, and disruptive or uncomfortable settings
- **Perceptual barriers**—preconceived ideas, expressed disinterest, behavior patterns, misinformation, uncomfortable previous experiences, conflicting nonverbal and verbal communication, and distractions caused by other's dress or grooming
- **Emotional barriers**—lack of self-confidence, transparency, trust, or flexibility; information overload; and feelings of defensiveness, superiority, or inferiority [See 1.2]
- **Interpersonal barriers**—inability to connect with others, misunderstood body language, lack of social skills or flexibility, avoidance of others, reluctance, and misunderstanding of importance
- **Inability to listen**—distracting eye contact, thinking of what to say next, impaired hearing, distraction from a more pressing concern, poor timing, and preoccupation with internal dialogue

- **Language**—different languages, differing meanings of words to individuals, generational differences, industry-specific jargon, accent, and distraction from negative or positive trigger words
- **Cultural, gender, or other differences**—lack of knowledge, understanding, or respect

Even with the best intentions, messages can become distorted and confused (Booher 2015). [See 1.1.1.5]

1.1.1.7 Importance of Overcoming Communication Barriers

Effective communication with colleagues, stakeholders, customers, and others is one of the most valuable skills a TD professional can possess. At times they must overcome communication barriers to influence, articulate decisions, motivate team members, solve problems, and complete other tasks to ensure a more productive exchange.

Many things can prevent message reception and interpretation. Miscommunications, censored feedback, and poor listening can diminish a conversation or communication. People may not understand what others mean even if they hear the words being spoken. Communication between two people goes through each person's filters, and the meaning of the message may change as it passes through those filters (mindset, biases, and opinions) of the sender and receiver.

It is important to identify and prevent or eliminate communication barriers, because they can increase accidents, cause unnecessary expenses, limit a company's ability to optimize performance, reduce profits, and lead to the loss of customers. Inadequate communication or misunderstood messages can create a culture of distrust, reduced employee engagement, uncertainty, ineffective customer interaction, increased errors, lack of teamwork, increased conflict, low morale, and dozens of other effects that can reduce job satisfaction.

TD professionals should be prepared to address current barriers and prevent others in the future. For example, if physical barriers make it difficult to concentrate and understand a message, TD professionals may identify a different location. If language, jargon, or clarity is a problem, TD professionals can opt for using an interpreter to help explain what's necessary. If emotions are causing the misunderstanding, TD professionals may have to identify another time that is convenient for everyone involved.

TD professionals should use a process like this one to overcome communication barriers:
1. Identify the barrier and ensure everyone understands and agrees.
2. Enlist those involved to determine the reason it is (or has become) a barrier.
3. Identify resources required to clarify the cause of the barrier (other people, data, or perhaps a survey).
4. Schedule dedicated time and open a discussion or dialogue. Practice the six Cs of communication to create a plan to overcome the barriers. [See 1.1.1.3 and 1.1.7]

Understanding communication barriers and overcoming them will save time, money, and relationships. Excellent communication can heighten TD professionals' productivity, reputation, trustworthiness, and admiration. They will enhance their professionalism and be viewed as respected leaders.

1.1.2 Skill in Applying Principles of Active Listening

> **I. Effective Communication Skills and Strategies**
>
> TD professionals should engage in active listening techniques, strive to understand the speaker's perspective, and clarify information to better understand the message; active listening is the key to exceptional workplace relationships. Active listening is based on work by Carl Rogers, who called it reflective listening. Rogers and Richard Farson (2015) coined the term *active listening* and wrote, "Despite the popular notion that listening is a possible approach, clinical and research evidence clearly shows that sensitive listening is the most effective." TD professionals should use active listening skills in classrooms with learners, in the C-suite with leaders, and externally with vendors and consultants. Honing active listening skills will help them build relationships, understand requirements, make better decisions, gain knowledge, and reach mutual agreements (Hoppe 2014). [See 2.1.3.2]

1.1.2.1 Levels of Listening

Communication is a complex process that involves different degrees of listening. TD professionals should be aware that there are different levels and when to use each. The levels should not be understood as better or worse than the others, but rather appropriate at different times. Listening may include, although is not limited to, these levels:

- **Passive listening**—demonstrating nonverbal behaviors, such as affirmative head nodding, making eye contact, note taking, smiling, or presenting a thinking pose at appropriate moments
- **Listening for knowledge**—listening first for facts and logic, and then mentally listing things in a sequence or pattern to form conclusions
- **Active listening**—demonstrating a high level of interaction with the speaker; for example asking questions to increase understanding of the message, observing the speaker's body language for underlying messages, or showing concern
- **Listening for clarification**—paraphrasing in different words to help increase understanding of previous comments and dialogue
- **Empathetic listening**—identifying feelings by confirming with the speaker if an intuition about their feelings is correct

1.1.2.2 Developing Listening Skills

"Listening, really listening, is tough and grinding work, often humbling, sometimes distasteful," says author Robert H. Waterman Jr. (1987). When TD professionals are on the receiving end of a message, they may come up against barriers to understanding; awareness of them is the first step to avoiding mistakes.

Nichols and Stevens (1957) were the first to establish that the fundamental problem with learning to listen is that most people can process messages much faster than those who are sending them. Although scientists differ in exact speeds, they all agree that listeners can understand at least 275 words per minute, while a typical speaker talks anywhere from 120 to 180 words per minute. If the speaker simply talks faster, however, the words sound rushed or anxious (Wingfield 1996).

Several skills contribute to a TD professional's ability to listen well. They fall into three skill clusters: attending and focusing, following, and reflecting.

1.1.2.2.1 Attending and Focusing Skills

Attending and focusing skills indicate that TD professionals are giving their physical attention to others. They are nonverbal messages that show the TD professional cares and is listening:

- A posture of involvement means inclining the body toward the speaker, facing them squarely, maintaining an open position (arms uncrossed, for example), and positioning themselves at an appropriate distance.
- Appropriate body motion means using receptive body gestures (such as nodding their heads) and not using disruptive body motions (like fidgeting nervously or drumming their fingers).
- Eye contact indicates a desire to listen. It should be consistent but not intense.
- A nondistracting environment requires finding a place away from potential interruptions.

1.1.2.2.2 Following Skills

Following skills are those that help TD professionals stay focused on the speaker. Listeners who ask many questions, interrupt with their own viewpoints, or talk too much miss out on others' perspectives.

- Door openers are gentle invitations to talk and are used when listeners sense someone may want to say more.
- Minimal encouragers are words and phrases that encourage others to continue, such as, "Tell me more" or "And then?"
- It usually makes sense to ask some questions, but they should be infrequent. The idea is to understand speakers, not divert them.
- Listeners should avoid leading questions, which are asked in a way that make others believe they are looking for a specific answer. For example, "You didn't let that upset you, did you?" is a leading question that may influence the person to say they were not upset, even if they were.
- Attentive silence means offering a quiet space to the speaker.

1.1.2.2.3 Reflecting Skills

Reflecting skills are the essential range of skills used when TD professionals are actively listening:

- Paraphrasing is restating the message in the listener's own words.
- Reflecting feelings are statements in the listener's words about the emotional content that is being communicated.
- Reflecting meaning is a response that joins the feelings and the facts the listener believes are being communicated.
- Summative reflections are brief statements about the main themes and feelings that were expressed during the conversation. They are useful to move the conversation along or bring it to a close.

All the skills described contribute to a TD professional's ability to be a skilled listener.

1.1.2.3 Observing and Sending Nonverbal Messages

If nonverbal messages conflict with verbal messages, receivers tend to place more trust in the nonverbal messages. Communication experts believe that more than half of all communication may be nonverbal. Albert Mehrabian (1971), who may have been the first person to study the topic, stated that 55 percent of any message is conveyed through nonverbal elements. Others claim that up to 90 percent of a message depends on nonverbal behavior. Although there is disagreement on the exact ratio, it is more important to remember that most communication is nonverbal, and nonverbal elements are crucial aspects of any message (Pease and Pease 2006). Vocal clues communicate much of this nonverbal meaning; however, a great deal of meaning is also transmitted physically, including behaviors like patterns of movement, facial expression, and eye contact. TD professionals must be attuned to the nonverbal messages they send and the nonverbal messages others display.

There are three different types of nonverbal messages:
- **Patterns of movement** include gestures, physical posture, and head movement. The appropriate use of gestures can motivate and excite others. Inappropriate gestures can be distracting. Physical posture affects interaction whether it is relaxed or intense, open or closed.
- **Facial expression** can be welcoming or distracted, express feelings, or demonstrate a TD professional's desire to communicate. It can encourage someone to share more or not, to increase trust or not, or to be helpful or not.
- **Eye contact** can send a welcoming or unwelcoming message. Direct eye contact can be intimidating or encouraging. When done well, it demonstrates interest and focus.

When TD professionals communicate, they should consider how their nonverbal message aligns with their verbal message and how it will affect their listeners. Additionally, they should learn to read the nonverbal messages others are sending (Zenger and Folkman 2016).

1.1.2.4 Choosing Responses Carefully

Almost nothing can influence how a message is received by others more than the chosen language. Although this section is about how a TD professional would respond in an active listening scenario, the suggestions here work for any communication situation:
- **Be concise.** Avoid language that is complex or cluttered; use common words and phrases.
- **Be objective.** To keep the language objective, avoid overuse of superlatives and flowery words. Use precise words whenever possible.
- **Be positive.** Whenever possible, express the message in positive rather than negative terms.
- **Use inclusive neutral language.** Use gender neutral and other inclusive words that do not set people apart.
- **Express clear ideas.** To be understood, avoid language that is inappropriate or outdated. If unsure, ask.
- **Use personal pronouns.** Personal pronouns have a special effect on people. Especially when communicating positive information or good news, use pronouns that focus on the listeners (like *you*, *your*, and *yours*).
- **Pay attention to word choice and pronunciation.** Using words incorrectly or pronouncing them incorrectly can significantly limit the effectiveness of a message. When in doubt of a word's meaning, leave it out.

TD professionals who select the right words ensure that those listening will be receptive to hearing and understanding their messages.

1.1.3 Skill in Using Communication Strategies That Inform and Influence Audiences

> **I. Communicating to Inform and Influence**
>
> TD professionals should be skilled at both informing and influencing because they have many opportunities to communicate with others and use the principles of influence.

1.1.3.1 Talent Development's Role in Informing and Influencing

TD professionals are increasingly expected to deliver solutions better, faster, and cheaper. They are expected to interact with executives and articulate how they can help the organization accomplish its goals and objectives. If TD professionals are expected to influence the organization's vision and initiatives, they must be able to customize the message, read and react to a learner's body language, facilitate question-and-answer sessions, handle tough questions, and deliver memorable messages that learners will use.

The first step in effective communication is deciding what to communicate. Begin by making a list of items to address, and then formulate more detailed ideas based on those items. Ensuring that there are logical segues between conversation points helps communication flow in an orderly way. Unmanaged communication becomes diffused and unspecific, and it can be interpreted arbitrarily. Problems occur when people say one thing, but their behavior suggests the opposite. TD professionals must be authentic when communicating to transmit messages that are trusted.

TD professionals will likely find themselves presenting the value of developing talent; supporting management as a consultant, advisor, coach, or advocate; facilitating team meetings [See 2.3.2]; and communicating as a facilitator. Before presenting in any of these instances, they must always be prepared, anticipate questions that will be asked, and think of ways to enhance the presentation through visual aids. These skills will help TD professionals regardless of the communication situation.

1.1.3.2 Principles That Inform and Influence

TD professionals will have many opportunities to inform and influence people at all levels in their organizations. For example, they may ask leaders and managers to use their services, supervisors to coach their employees, or participants to use new skills back on the job. These principles not only ensure that TD professionals influence or inform effectively, but that they also build relationships as a side benefit:

- **Communicate authentically.** TD professionals should say what they mean and mean what they say. It is impossible to be someone they aren't. Influencing others is easier when built on authentic trust.
- **Build long-term relationships.** Those who aggressively go about meeting their own needs without regard for how their actions affect others are short-term strategists and may get what they want this time—but that success probably won't continue in the long term.
- **Clarify the outcomes.** TD professionals need to be clear about the purpose of the communication. Know the goals in advance. They also need to have a positive mindset about the outcomes—attitude affects communication.
- **Speak the right language.** Influencing others depends on speaking their language. Whether speaking to people in the C-suite or on the factory floor, use words that resonate with the audience.

- **Start with the bottom line.** TD professionals who know the outcome they want and present it up front will gain trust and have a better chance of influencing others.
- **Identify and communicate personal value.** Bill Treasurer (2019) says that the most important four words in building relationships and personal value ask the question, "What do you want?" Certainly, TD professionals want and need communication, but when they learn what another person wants first, their chances of influencing them increase.
- **Use data to communicate a relevant story.** Data is important and when used to tell a relevant story, it can be powerfully influential.
- **Reciprocate self-disclosure.** Self-disclosure means sharing information with others. It can be personal or not—but it needs to be related to the communication situation. Sharing something personal sends an invitation to others to do the same. Self-disclosure is an effective strategy for building productive business relationships.
- **Remember the power of language.** Use people's names when speaking with or writing to them. Tuning into the sensory language or pet phrases of others builds instant rapport. Remember, it's not only what speakers say, but how they say it.
- **Gain agreement.** TD professionals communicate so that both parties are on the same side of the fence. When there are issues to work through, decisions to be made, or problems to solve, TD professionals will be more effective if they structure communication so that both people are working on the issue together.
- **Communicate understanding, acceptance, and respect.** The best communicators use an approach that demonstrates that others are accepted, respected, and understood.
- **Remain neutral and objective.** No matter how difficult the situation, TD professionals will be more successful by remaining neutral than by challenging the other person.

TD professionals should use these principles to inform and influence. They will see that a valuable byproduct is positive business relationships and the trust good communication builds (Scharlatt and Smith 2011). This makes influencing easier every time.

1.1.3.3 Depersonalizing and Defusing Anger

TD professionals are in an awkward position when they are the target of someone's anger. Unfortunately, they will likely be on the receiving end of a conversation with a person who is upset. Whatever the complaint or criticism, TD professionals can be prepared with an effective strategy for dealing with angry people.

Defuse anger using these tactics:
- Acknowledge the person's anger by listening to identify the cause.
- Avoid personalizing the complaint.
- Focus on the facts of the complaint.
- Show empathy and avoid defensiveness.
- Assure them that you want to understand their anger.
- Ask relevant questions to clarify the facts.
- When logic doesn't work, agree about the facts or the person's right to be angry.
- Explain what *can* be done, indicating a specific time and date.

- Reach an agreement and confirm the agreement.
- When necessary, defer the conversation.

When people are angry, they don't listen very well. Summarize the agreement and reflect it back to the other person to ensure that both parties heard the same problem-solving information. Both people should be clear about what each must do to resolve the problem.

1.1.4 Skill in Applying Persuasion and Influencing Techniques to Gain Agreement, Commitment, or Buy-In From Stakeholders

> **I. Using Communication to Persuade and Influence**
>
> TD professionals should comprehend persuasion and influencing skills because they will have many opportunities to persuade stakeholders and leaders in their organizations. In addition, these skills help them be more observant of others' attempts to persuade them.

1.1.4.1 Understanding Persuasion Principles

Influence is one aspect of persuasion and can be used to affect another's beliefs, intentions, or behaviors (Gass and Seiter 2010). The Greek philosopher Aristotle identified three essential elements of persuasive communication:

- **Reason** (*logos*)—the ability to articulate points clearly
- **Credibility** (*ethos*)—the ability to convey integrity and goodwill
- **Emotion** (*pathos*)—the ability to create or control emotion in the listeners

A skilled communicator requires these same three qualities to be successful at persuasion. TD professionals can use these methods:

- **Appeal to reason**—logical arguments, data, consequences, or scientific proof
- **Appeal to credibility**—authority, expertise, communication skills, sales techniques, or body language
- **Appeal to emotion**—tradition, mental images, relationships, or stories

Many persuasion theories exist and most are influenced by research that psychologist Robert Cialdini (2006) presented in his book, *Influence: The Psychology of Persuasion*. Cialdini's principles are:

- **Reciprocity**—give first without any expectation of return.
- **Consistency**—commit to behave in the same way as in the past.
- **Social proof**—do something because others are doing the same.
- **Authority**—defer to experts or others with credentials.
- **Liking**—find commonalities.
- **Scarcity**—demonstrate a shortage of items or time to act.

In their book *The Art of Woo*, G. Richard Shell and Mario Moussa (2008) present an approach to strategic persuasion. They explain that persuasion means to win others over, not defeat them. Therefore, TD professionals must see the situation from different angles to anticipate the reactions of other people. The authors recommend confronting five obstacles that pose the greatest risks to a successful influence encounter: relationships, credibility, communication mismatches, belief systems, and needs.

TD professionals should be prepared to persuade others in many situations, including, but not limited to:
- Briefing as a TD representative to senior leadership
- Getting commitment on a proposed TD budget
- Gaining agreement, commitment, and buy-in for a TD initiative
- Presenting compelling rationales for projects or requirements [See 2.1.4.4]

1.1.4.2 Using Communication Styles to Influence

Understanding basic communication styles is helpful in persuasion—especially as it relates to emotions. Communication style has a direct effect on how employees view every situation. While several instruments exist to determine social styles, the two most well-known are the DiSC Personality Profile and the Myers-Briggs Type Indicator (MBTI) assessment. According to David W. Merrill and Roger H. Reid (1992), communicators exhibit four styles. They are are listed here with their corresponding DiSC types in parenthesis and demonstrate how communication styles can be used to increase one's ability to influence an individual: [See 2.3.5.4 and 2.3.5.5]

- **Analytical** (conscientiousness) people tend toward perfectionism and deal in logic and details. They keep feelings to themselves. When influencing them, it's helpful to prepare the case in advance and be accurate and realistic. Provide tangible evidence to support major points.
- **Amiable** (steadiness) people put a high value on people and friendships. They go out of their way not to offend. Despite having opinions, they are not inclined to say what's on their mind. To influence them, draw out their opinions by asking "how" questions and showing how everyone will benefit.
- **Drivers** (dominance) can make high demands on themselves and others, and they tend to be emotionally reserved. They are decisive and results oriented, and they like to give guidance to everyone. When influencing drivers, be brief, specific, candid, and pertinent.
- **Expressive** (influence) people are social. They are enthusiastic, creative, and intuitive but have little tolerance for those unlike themselves. Easily bored, they tend to go on tangents. When influencing this type of person, stick with the big picture, avoid details, and create excitement.

Similar examples could also be matched to the MBTI assessment's 16 personality types.

Although pure communication styles don't exist, most people have a tendency toward one or two. TD professionals who are skilled in recognizing all four communication and social styles know how to best appeal to each persuasively. Moving into another person's comfort zone requires flexibility, which is a learned skill. TD professionals should have a working knowledge of communication styles and how they can be used to influence. They should also use a tool to determine their own styles.

1.1.5 Skill in Conceiving, Developing, and Delivering Information in Various Formats and Media

> **I. Developing Materials for Results**
>
> TD professionals must be able to communicate using the six Cs of communication to produce reports, presentations, executive briefings, business cases, and other documents. [See 1.1.1.3]

1.1.5.1 Instances When Conceiving, Developing, and Writing Materials Is Critical for Talent Development

TD professionals have many opportunities to develop content that is critical to their functions and their jobs. They will create longer content such as talent development's business or strategic plans, reports that summarize the success of an initiative, agreements with consultants, requests for proposals, project management plans, and other opportunities for talent development to complete its work.

TD professionals also develop content that is shorter, including business cases, value propositions, job descriptions, work objectives and goals, blog posts, articles, and performance appraisals.

In addition, they may create training materials used to develop employees such as participant manuals, facilitator guides, role plays, case studies, and critical incidents. [See 2.2.12 and 2.3.7]

In some cases, TD professionals need to include information that may not be text based. For example, training materials may require pictures, diagrams, and graphs. PowerPoint presentations require visuals. Infographics and job aids often need both text and visual content. At other times, a video may deliver the message best.

1.1.5.2 Developing Written Materials

Being able to craft clear and concise written materials is an essential business skill. TD professionals must be able to communicate the details of initiatives in a way that states objectives, identifies intended outcomes, and shares all details required for understanding the document.

Guidelines should be followed regardless of the length of the document or report. All written materials should:
- **Have a single purpose.** Every sentence and paragraph should align with that purpose.
- **Be tailored to the reader.** The language must be completely understandable and readable. Do not include jargon, complicated language, or ambiguous, distorted, or conflicting messages.
- **Ensure economy.** Longer documents do not automatically mean better messages. Every word must count. Every point must be necessary in assisting the reader to understand and act. Documents must be complete, yet concise.
- **Be accurate.** All aspects of the content, data, dates, references, and other details should be verified.
- **Be organized.** Materials should be presented in an easily understood and readable way. The language should display the writer's style, authority, and credibility.
- **Be visually appealing.** Use a consistent typeface, layout, and organizational structure. The document should be easy for the eye to follow, with short paragraphs, white space, headings, bullets, numbers, insets, and so forth.

The astute TD professional will share written documents with someone else to read for comment. They will also conduct a self-edit looking for clarity, accuracy, effective sentence structure, punctuation, grammar, capitalization, titles, correct use of possessives and pronouns, subject-verb agreement, frequently misused words, and typographical errors (Booher 2008).

1.1.5.3 Communicating With Others Through Writing

When crafting written communication, TD professionals must first establish a clear objective: What should the readers take away from the communication? They should streamline written communication so it states objectives and expectations clearly. Readers must know what their responsibilities are after reading the communication.

Written communication should follow a format that is easy to comprehend: The opening states the facts, the middle provides supportive details, and the closing makes a call for action. Written communication falls into three categories: routine (which is initiated by the writer or in response to another's communication), delivery of good news, or delivery of bad news (Appleman 2018; O'Quinn 2017).

- **Routine correspondence** will cause limited emotional reaction for the reader. There are two kinds of routine correspondence:
  - Routine correspondence initiated by the sender should have three parts. It should open with an introduction, if necessary, and state the inquiry or request concisely, specifically, and courteously. The middle should explain the purpose of the inquiry and provide additional information or details. The closing thanks the reader in advance.
  - Routine correspondence that responds to another's correspondence should also have three parts. It should open by concisely referencing the request and adding a thank you. The middle should answer any questions asked, provide sufficient details about the steps to be taken, and provide additional information that would be helpful. The closing expresses appreciation for the contact, hope that the information is helpful, and a willingness to provide additional information or assistance.
- **Correspondence that delivers good news** follows three steps. The opening paragraph should state the good news and what the reader is receiving that is viewed as good news (such as a discount, acknowledgment of being correct, information, a change, or a job offer). The middle provides supportive details such as reassurance, an explanation of past or future steps, or a description of how the actions will be implemented. The closing should repeat the good news and add a goodwill closing, such as congratulations or another positive statement.
- **Correspondence that delivers bad news** uses a format for softening the message. This format does not delay or avoid giving the bad news, but it presents the news in a way that can be understood. Include reasons why and alternatives. The writer should avoid using words and phrases like *unfortunately* and *because you did not* as they may send the message earlier and stronger than intended. Accordingly, this type of correspondence follows three steps. The opening paragraph refers to the situation by stating the request, advising about any action, and making a neutral statement about the situation. The middle places the bad news between details and alternatives. It begins with the details or reasons (for example, "one of the criteria"), states the bad news as clearly as possible, and adds potential alternatives. The closing incorporates a neutral or positive statement, offers additional information, and expresses appreciation for the recipient's interest.

1.1.5.4 Effective Use of Email

Written communication has degrees of formality, with email being one of the most informal. However, the convenience and ease of email can make it risky. People may be careless with email communications and send messages that can be misinterpreted. Because the reader must interpret the sender's tone, problems can occur when the receiver's interpretation of tone does not match the sender's intention (Booher 2019).

1.1.6 Skill in Applying Verbal, Written, or Nonverbal Communication Techniques

> **I. Communicating to Be Heard and Understood**
> Whether communicating verbally or in writing, TD professionals must be skilled in many techniques.

1.1.6.1 Developing and Demonstrating a Professional Presence

TD professionals are only as successful as their ability to communicate ideas, knowledge, and information. Communication skills are essential for developing others' skills as well as for creating collaborative relationships, working in teams, or working across department lines. TD professionals should explain decisions and reasoning and invite questions. They lead meetings, set agendas, and influence others. They communicate to be heard and understood. [See 1.2, 1.3, and 2.3]

All these responsibilities require positive communication that begins with credibility and personal presence. In her book *Creating Personal Presence,* Dianna Booher (2011) writes, "Your presence involves your physical, mental, and emotional essence, as well as character. It encompasses what others think or feel about you, based on their interactions with you over time. When that feeling turns out to be favorable, you earn trust and credibility."

To build professional presence and credibility, a TD professional should begin by knowing how to formulate a strategic message, which entails:

- Stating the conclusion first and then building the case to support it
- Sorting the significant from the trivial
- Delivering the strategic context and specific details
- Using appropriate positive language
- Asking thought-provoking questions
- Taking a point of view
- Making all points memorable (Booher 2014)

Beyond formulating strategic messages, a TD professional demonstrates credibility nonverbally by maintaining a confident posture, following acceptable appearance norms, and practicing deference and respect. The goal is to build rapport with everyone.

1.1.6.2 Giving and Receiving Feedback

Giving and receiving feedback are imperative skills for TD professionals because feedback is a tool for continued learning. In general, when giving feedback, it is important to focus on:

- The issues or behaviors, not the person
- The facts, not opinions
- Sharing ideas and information, not giving advice [See 1.3.9]

Receiving feedback is equally valuable for TD professionals, who will reap more benefits from the feedback if they:
- Respect the person who's offering it, knowing that it isn't easy.
- Listen actively, holding questions until all the feedback is given.
- Define the specific behavior that led to the feedback.
- Identify what could be improved (CCL 2019).

Providing and receiving feedback implies an interest in and concern for the other party, which allows both parties to collect more data about the situation and understand the other party's way of thinking, as well as what can be improved. Feedback is a requirement for continuous open and honest communication.

1.1.6.3 Practicing Questioning Skills

TD professionals use a variety of questioning techniques to stimulate discussion, check for understanding and consensus, and encourage free thinking and brainstorming. Some types of questions that facilitators use are closed-ended, open-ended, and Socratic:

- **Closed-ended questions** require nothing more than a yes or no answer. They may be tacked on to a statement and are often conversation closers. They are most frequently used to get specific information or to reach agreement. [See 2.3.3.10.1]
- **Open-ended questions** are asked when a person needs more than a simple yes or no answer. They are conversation openers and used to understand problems, determine needs, or check for comprehension.
- **The Socratic questioning method** is named for the Greek philosopher and teacher Socrates (470–399 BC). This approach is a form of disciplined questioning when the questioner pretends to be uninformed about a topic to encourage responses. Also known as the dialectical approach, this questioning process can probe for more information, identify assumptions and perspectives, or clarify complex topics. This method generally begins with a statement, claim, or definition that the questioner does not accept as fact or truth. It is followed by additional questions that participants can answer with a yes or no response, combined with supporting data or concepts that uncover contradictions. In the final step, the participants reach the conclusion that what they thought they knew wasn't accurate.

TD professionals can use the Socratic questioning method to help others more clearly state their views and prove the concepts behind their argument. In addition to being a good instructional tool, it helps participants learn to think critically. The goal is to reach deeper understanding because the participants are required to come to their own conclusions.

TD professionals ask questions in many situations, such as obtaining additional information, clarifying a statement, probing for deeper meaning, focusing on the specifics, understanding perceptions, testing for content agreement, planning for implementation, reaching closure, and evaluating a plan or solution. Questioning skills are essential for the TD professional to effectively communicate.

1.1.7 Skill in Facilitating Dialogue With Individuals or Groups to Help Them Identify, Articulate, or Clarify Their Thoughts and Feelings

> **I. Dialogue for Clarity**
>
> TD professionals should understand how to successfully facilitate dialogue. Engaging individuals and groups in discussion is an important aspect of the learning and development process. The rest of their organization is likely to look to them for definition, clarity, and facilitation.

1.1.7.1 Defining and Using Dialogue for Clarity

Dialogue is a discussion between two or more people marked by openness, honesty, and genuine listening. The word comes from the Greek *diá* and *lógo*, which can be interpreted as the "flow of words" or "meaning" from more than one person to clarify all concepts.

1.1.7.2 Principles of Dialogue

Peter Senge (2006) makes a powerful distinction between discussion and dialogue. In *discussion*, opposing views are presented and defended as a team searches for a way to make a decision. People want their ideas to be accepted with an emphasis on winning. In contrast, *dialogue* is "the free and creative exploration of complex and subtle issues, a deep 'listening' to one another and suspending of one's views."

Because people are open to new ideas in dialogue, they can more readily access information. This provides participants with access to knowledge from everyone, allowing them to enlarge ideas, not diminish them. The result explores all options and reaches agreement on what is right.

Senge's ideas about dialogue draw on the work of David Bohm, a contemporary quantum physicist. In introducing dialogue, Senge (2006) discusses Bohm's treatment of the subject: "Dialogue, as it turns out, is a very old idea revered by the ancient Greeks and practiced by many . . . societies such as the American Indians." Besides Bohm, Senge also taps into the work of Chris Argyris and Donald Schon to explain that dialogue requires individuals to be more aware of input and what they do with it, writing that, "All of us have had some taste of dialogue—in special conversations that begin to have a 'life of their own,' taking us in directions we could never have imagined nor planned in advance."

1.1.7.3 Guidelines to Facilitate Dialogue With Individuals

An astute TD professional should be able to facilitate dialogue with individuals. Senge (2006) and Bohm agree on these guidelines. To facilitate effective dialogue, both participants must:
- "Suspend" their assumptions (and actually hold them "as if suspended before us").
- Regard one another as colleagues.
- Communicate in a private and comfortable location.
- Eliminate all distractions and allow enough time.

1.1.7.4 Additional Strategies to Facilitate Dialogue in Groups

TD professionals have a responsibility to help groups identify, articulate, and clarify their thoughts. Senge (2006) believes that "reflection and inquiry skills provide a foundation for dialogue." He defines reflection skills as "slowing down our own thinking processes so that we can become more aware of how we form our mental models and the ways they influence our actions." Inquiry is the process that starts by asking questions prior to reflecting and interpreting the answers. Senge believes "dialogue that is grounded in reflection and inquiry skills is likely to be more reliable and less dependent on particulars of circumstance, such as the chemistry among team members."

The same guidelines for dialogue between individuals are required for groups. Additionally, Senge (2006) and Bohm agree that there must be a facilitator who "holds the context of dialogue" for the group.

Other strategies TD professionals can use in facilitating group dialogue include:
- Recognizing that dialogue in groups with more than 30 members is difficult
- Using a space where all participants can have direct eye contact with one another
- Ensuring that everyone can hear each other easily
- Making sure there are no hierarchical differences in the seating
- Remaining neutral throughout
- Formulating questions that open the exchange of comments
- Accepting that they need strong listening, reframing, and summarizing skills
- Understanding group development as a dynamic process (Ropers 2017)

Dialogue can be a powerful tool for enhancing team learning, building teams, and creating a learning organization. When TD professionals facilitate effective dialogue sessions regularly, team members are better able to develop a relationship of deep trust and a richer understanding of each person's point of view. They know that a larger understanding will often emerge if all members participate. Dialogue leads to learning. [See 2.3.2 and 3.3.8]

1.1.8 Skill in Articulating and Conveying Value Propositions to Gain Agreement, Support, or Buy-In From Stakeholders

> **I. Using Value Propositions**
> TD professionals should use value propositions to gain stakeholder agreement and secure leadership support.

1.1.8.1 Defining Value Propositions
The term *value proposition* comes from the marketing field. Companies promise to deliver value to customers who buy their products. For TD professionals, a value proposition represents a promise of value that they will deliver to their leadership, stakeholders, or clients. The value proposition states the results they can expect from a prospective program, TD solution, or even the TD function itself. [See 3.1.2]

1.1.8.2 When to Use Value Propositions
A value proposition is most useful when introducing a new program or effort. It will explain the benefits the program will provide, for whom, and how. It is typically offered during the initial discussions and proposed solution. It may also be a part of a proposal written internally by the TD function or externally by a consultant.

1.1.8.3 Start With the Bottom Line

A value statement starts with the bottom line—the end benefit that is offered. It should address three things:
- **Relevancy** explains how the product or service solves the stakeholders' problems or improves their situation.
- **Benefit** outlines the quantified value of the proposition (for example, will reduce errors by 50 percent).
- **Differentiation** is what sets this solution apart.

1.1.8.4 Address the Point Quickly

Once the bottom line is presented, the value statement needs to define the supporting points. This could be two to three bullet points that list the supporting benefits or features that make the proposition different from what the organization currently does.

1.1.8.5 Techniques to Present Data and Information

TD professionals have many options for presenting data and information. None are more important than understanding the audience and what they will expect. Generally, it is best to start with the bottom line, and then follow with more information. A TD professional needs to:
- Acquire as much knowledge as possible about the culture of the audience before presenting the information.
- Select media that the audience expects, such as slides, possibly accompanied by identical paper handouts or an infographic.
- Anticipate reactions and questions and be prepared to respond.
- Use line and pie charts, column and bar charts, scatter charts, bubble charts, time series charts, year-over-year comparisons, or any others that clearly make the point. [See 3.7 and 2.8.7]
- If using slides, follow professional guidelines for color, word choice, number of words, images, and other design elements.

1.1.8.6 Tailoring the Messaging to the Audience

The value proposition needs to be written for the stakeholder. It should not use talent development jargon (such as "Level 4 evaluation" or "action learning") if the audience is a C-suite executive. Speak the language the stakeholder speaks—the value proposition should join the conversation that is already taking place in the stakeholder's office and in their mind. To ensure the audience consumes the data, the presenter must:
- Consider the timing of the message; it must give the right people the right information at the right time.
- Focus on what's in it for the stakeholder or listener.
- Start with the end and what the stakeholder needs to hear, and then backfill with the support.
- Use appropriate terminology.
- Create relevant examples.
- Select the best environment and communication medium to reach the intended audiences.

Finally, when delivering a data-rich presentation, don't forget to consider the human impact of an initiative. Presentations will be more effective if the data is matched with real people. "Research shows that people are persuaded to take action or change their minds when you speak to both their heads, and their hearts" (Evergreen 2017). This could be accomplished by simply displaying a photo next to a graph. Good presenters speak to their audience's heads and hearts.

REFERENCES

Appleman, J. 2018. *10 Steps to Successful Business Writing*. Alexandria, VA: ATD Press.

Arnold, K. 2014. "Behind the Mirror: Reflective Listening and its Tain in the Work of Carl Rogers." *The Humanistic Psychologist* 42(4): 354–369.

Booher, D. 2008. *Booher's Rules of Business Grammar: 101 Fast and Easy Ways to Correct the Most Common Errors*. New York: McGraw-Hill.

Booher, D. 2011. *Creating Personal Presence: Look, Talk, Think, and Act Like a Leader*. San Francisco: Berrett-Koehler.

Booher, D. 2014. "Securing Executive Support." Chapter 38 in *ASTD Handbook: The Definitive Reference for Training and Development*, 2nd ed., edited by E. Biech. Alexandria, VA: ASTD Press.

Booher, D. 2015. *What MORE Can I Say? Why Communication Fails and What to Do About It*. New York: Prentice Hall Press.

Booher, D. 2019. *Faster, Fewer, Better Emails: Manage the Volume, Reduce the Stress, Love the Results*. San Francisco: Berrett-Koehler.

CCL. 2019. *Feedback That Works: How to Build and Deliver Your Message*, 2nd ed. Greensboro, NC: Center for Creative Leadership.

Cialdini, R. 2006. *The Psychology of Persuasion*, 2nd ed. New York: Harper Business.

Dynamic Signal. 2018. "The Crumbling State of Employee Communication." In *2018 State of Employee Communication and Engagement*. San Bruno, CA: Dynamic Signal.

Evergreen, S. 2017. *Presenting Data Effectively: Communicating Your Finding for Maximum Impact*. Thousand Oaks, CA: SAGE Publications.

Gass, R.H., and J. Seiter. 2010. *Persuasion, Social Influence, and Compliance Gaining*, 4th ed. Boston: Allyn & Bacon.

Hoppe, M. 2014. *Active Listening: Improve Your Ability to Listen and Lead*. Greensboro, NC: Center for Creative Leadership.

Mehrabian, A. 1971. *Silent Messages: Implicit Communication of Emotions and Attitudes*. Belmont, CA: Wadsworth Publishing Company.

Merrill, D., and R. Reid. 1981. *Personal Styles and Effective Performance*. Boca Raton, FL: CRC Press.

Nichols, R.G., and L. Stevens. 1957. "Listening to People." *Harvard Business Review*, September.

O'Quinn, K. 2017. "Business Writing for Managers." *TD at Work*. Alexandria, VA: ATD Press.

Patterson, K., J. Grenny, R. McMillan, and A. Switzler. 2005. *Crucial Confrontations*. New York: McGraw-Hill.

Pease, B., and A. Pease. 2006. *The Definitive Book of Body Language: The Hidden Meaning Behind People's Gestures and Expressions*. New York: Bantam.

Rogers, C., and R. Farson. 2015. *Active Listening*. Mansfield Centre, CT: Martino Publishing.

Ropers, N. 2017. *Basics of Dialogue Facilitation*. Berlin: Berghof Foundation Operations.

Scharlatt, H., and R. Smith. 2011. *Influence: Gaining Commitment, Getting Results*, 2nd ed. Greensboro, NC: Center for Creative Leadership.

Senge, P.M. 2006. *The Fifth Discipline: The Art and Practice of the Learning Organization*, rev. ed. New York: Currency/Doubleday.

Shell, G., and M. Moussa. 2008. *The Art of Woo: Using Strategic Persuasion to Sell Your Ideas*. New York: Penguin Group.

Treasurer, B. 2019. *Courage Goes to Work: How to Build Backbones, Boost Performance, and Get Results*, 2nd ed. San Francisco: Berrett-Koehler.

Waterman, R. 1987. *The Renewal Factor: How the Best Get and Keep the Competitive Edge*. New York: Bantam.

Wingfield, A. 1996. "Cognitive Factors in Auditory Performance: Context, Speed of Processing, and Constraints of Memory." *Journal of Audiology* 7(3): 175–182.

Zenger, J., and J. Folkman. 2016. "What Great Listeners Actually Do." *Harvard Business Review*, July 14.

Recommended Reading

Blade, V. 2021. *Influence in Talent Development*. Alexandria, VA: ATD Press.

Booher, D. 2017. *Communicate Like a Leader: Connecting Strategically to Coach, Inspire, and Get Things Done*. San Francisco: Berrett-Koehler.

Cialdini, R. 2006. *The Psychology of Persuasion*, 2nd ed. New York: Harper Business.

Scharlatt, H., and R. Smith. 2011. *Influence: Gaining Commitment, Getting Results*, 2nd ed. Greensboro, NC: Center for Creative Leadership.

1.2 EMOTIONAL INTELLIGENCE & DECISION MAKING

Emotional intelligence and the skill to make good decisions are paramount to professional success. *Emotional intelligence* is the ability to understand, assess, and regulate your own emotions, correctly interpret the verbal and nonverbal behaviors of others, and adjust your behavior in relation to others. Emotional intelligence is a key strength in building rapport. *Decision making* requires one to determine the need for and importance of making a decision, identify choices, gather information about those choices, and take action on the appropriate choice.

Emotional Intelligence

1.2.1 Knowledge of Theories of Emotional Intelligence

> **I. Emotional Intelligence Models and Theories**
> TD professionals should understand and implement emotional intelligence as a starting point for most of their professional and personal interactions.

1.2.1.1 History

In the beginning of the 20th century, a formal means of measuring intelligence was developed—the IQ (intelligence quotient) test. IQ is measured using a standardized score based on a ratio of age and performance. In recent years, other theories have used IQ as a springboard to focus on people's emotional intelligence.

Although many believe the misconception that EQ (emotional quotient) and IQ are opposed, they are actually just different. Whereas IQ measures how people learn, understand, and apply information, EQ measures how individuals learn, understand, and apply emotional knowledge. For example, EQ scores reflect how well individuals understand their own and other's emotions, distinguish between them, and use that knowledge to guide their actions and behaviors.

The term *emotional intelligence* (EI) has been around for more than a half century, and it has been presented in various publications over the years. In 1964 Michael Beldoch used the term in a paper. In 1983 Howard Gardner introduced his multiple intelligence theory, which included interpersonal and intrapersonal intelligence to show that IQ failed to explain complete cognitive ability. Peter Salovey and John Mayer published the first

EI model in 1990. Marc Brackett, founding director of the Yale Center for Emotional Intelligence and lead developer of RULER, has produced more than 125 articles related to EI. RULER (recognizing, understanding, labeling, expressing, and regulating emotions) is an evidence-based approach to emotional learning (Brackett 2019). [See 2.2.1 and 2.3.5]

Even with many people researching and writing about EI, it wasn't until Daniel Goleman's book *Emotional Intelligence* was published in 1995 that the term became widely known. In his book, Goleman presented the argument that noncognitive skills can matter as much as IQ for workplace success and leadership effectiveness.

1.2.1.2 Definitions

Emotional intelligence is the potential to monitor and accurately identify, express, and understand one's own and others' emotions and reactions. It also includes the potential to control personal emotions, use them to make good decisions, and act effectively (Mayer, Salovey, and Caruso 1998). Individuals are born with the potential to develop their EI capabilities and are influenced through their life experiences—most notably what they learned emotionally from their parents, teachers, and acquaintances during their formative years.

Emotional quotient (EQ) implies a measure, but EI instruments don't measure emotional intelligence. Emotional intelligence, by definition, emphasizes an individual's ability to *apply* knowledge of emotions to manage their own behavior or to influence others. Even the best EQ test only measures knowledge of emotions and how they work; it can't evaluate the ability to put that knowledge into action. EI assessments are valuable because they provide insight into the knowledge or a starting place. While EQ can be used as shorthand to refer to an individual's knowledge of emotions, recognize that EQ and EI are not interchangeable. Emotional intelligence is a practical ability. And while a person may comprehend the principles of how emotions work, it is the application of that knowledge that truly defines EI.

1.2.1.3 Research on EI

Many studies demonstrate the value of EI, and nearly every facet of work is influenced positively or negatively by emotional awareness and regulation. An individual's emotional state can positively affect memory and learning, boost confidence to make better decisions, improve connections and effective working relationships with others, cause physiological reactions that affect health and well-being, and enhance creativity (Brackett 2019). It even affects something as practical as earnings, which have been shown to be an average of $29,000 more per year for those who have a high EI (Bradberry and Greaves 2009).

1.2.1.3.1 Benefits of EI

A study by John D. Mayer (2008) found that higher emotional intelligence is positively correlated with several worthy results, including:
- Better self-perception of social ability, more successful interpersonal relationships, and less interpersonal aggression and problems
- Being perceived by others as more empathetic, socially skilled, and pleasant to be around
- Better relationships with family and colleagues
- Increased social dynamics at work as well as better negotiating ability
- Higher life satisfaction and self-esteem and lower levels of insecurity or depression (the study also found a negative correlation with poor health choices and behavior)

1.2.1.3.2 Criticism of the Models and Theory

There has been some confusion and controversy concerning EI. To be fully informed, TD professionals should know that there are concerns that the model confuses skills with morals and that EI does not have predictive outcomes academically or in business (Landy 2005). Measurement of the model is also a concern because it is based on self-assessment (Salazar 2017). However, even with these concerns, EI is a critical skill for success in both one's personal and professional endeavors.

1.2.1.3.3 The Future of EI

Bradberry is positive about the future of EI, stating that although some research has shown a drop in the average EI measures around the globe, practice is the key to bringing scores up (Bradberry and Greaves 2009).

1.2.1.4 Three Models

There are three main models of emotional intelligence—the ability model, the mixed model, and the trait model—and each requires different instruments for measurement. Although some of the measures overlap, most researchers agree that they tap different constructs.

1.2.1.4.1 Ability Model

Salovey and Mayer (1990), the creators of the ability model, define emotional intelligence as "the capacity to reason about emotions, and of emotions, to enhance thinking." The model requires evaluting people in four related abilities to determine their EI:

- **Perceiving emotions** involves understanding verbal and nonverbal signals.
- **Reasoning with emotions** means using emotions to solve problems or review situations.
- **Using and understanding emotions** means to use the two previous abilities to analyze emotions and chose an action.
- **Managing emotions** involves regulating emotions to respond appropriately and correctly to other's emotions (Salazar 2017).

1.2.1.4.2 Mixed Model

The mixed model, which is built on five competencies, mixes emotional intelligence qualities with other personality traits unrelated to either emotion or intelligence. The five categories are self-awareness, self-regulation, motivation, empathy, and social skills. The competencies are learned capabilities that must be worked on and can be developed. [See 1.2.2]

1.2.1.4.3 Trait Model

The trait model, developed by Petrides and colleagues (2007), is the most recent model. It is different because it is not an ability-based construct. Instead, the trait model establishes that people have "emotional traits or emotional self-perceptions" as a part of their personality. EI is viewed as individuals' "self-perceptions of their emotional abilities including behavioral abilities" (Salazar 2017). Measures are based on self-reporting.

1.2.2 Skill in Assessing and Managing One's Own Emotional State

> **I. Managing Personal Emotions**
> TD professionals should be skilled in monitoring, identifying, and controlling their emotions and reactions.

1.2.2.1 Goleman's Five Competencies

Goleman's mixed model presents five main areas that define emotional intelligence, which can be divided into two groups: personal and social. Personal includes self-awareness, self-regulation, and motivation; social includes empathy and social skills. In addition, the five competencies encompass 25 emotional intelligence characteristics.

- **Personal competencies:**
    - **Self-awareness** entails knowing one's own internal states, preferences, resources, and intuitions. People who have strong self-awareness can monitor their emotional state and realize what they are feeling and why.
    - **Self-regulation** refers to a person's capacity to manage their internal states, impulses, and resources. People who have strong self-regulation (also called self-management) can control or redirect their impulses and moods in the moment. This involves the ability to suspend judgment and think before responding, even in difficult situations.
    - **Motivation** involves the ability to understand emotional tendencies that facilitate reaching goals. People who have strong motivation demonstrate an internal passion to achieve and pursue goals with energy and commitment (Sallie-Dosunmu 2016).
- **Social competencies:**
    - **Empathy** is the ability to view and understand other's feelings, needs, and concerns. Recognizing emotional needs in others and effectively supporting them in the way that they require are vital to interpersonal relationships.
    - **Social skills** involve managing relationships and building networks in a way that results in being looked on favorably by others. People who excel in social skills can find common ground with others to build rapport and connection.

1.2.2.2 Brackett's RULER Model

Marc Brackett (2019) of the Yale Center for Emotional Intelligence is the lead designer of the RULER model. This evidence-based approach focuses on understanding the importance of emotions and enhancing the skills of EI to build and maintain a positive culture. There are five skills in the RULER model:

- **Recognizing emotions** in the self and in others is the first step to being able to understand anyone's emotional state.
- **Understanding emotions** means understanding what causes them and the consequences that result. (Brackett believes this is the most challenging skill to learn.)
- **Labeling emotions** by using precise words increases the ability to meet other's needs, thus ensuring true empathy.
- **Expressing emotions** is the point when individuals take action and do something about the emotions they are feeling.
- **Regulating emotions** is the final level when individuals implement helpful strategies to choose what emotions they will have and when.

1.2.2.3 Developing Skills to Improve EI

EI is flexible and can be improved through concerted and conscious efforts at self-improvement (Bradberry and Greaves 2009). TD professionals who want to develop their emotional intelligence need to put an improvement plan together. The plan should include these steps:

1. **Understand the concepts.**
2. **Identify a current baseline.**
   o Complete a self-assessment.
   o Gather feedback from others (such as from a multi-rater).
   o Examine personal reactions to stressful situations.
   o Review how current actions affect others.
   o Take responsibility for the actions.
3. **Create a development plan.**
   o Assess motives for change.
   o Identify goals.
   o Determine how to manage negative emotions.
   o Be mindful of vocabulary.
   o Identify stressors.
4. **Practice the skills and behaviors.**
5. **Learn resiliency skills.**
6. **Acquire insight from a mentor or coach.**

1.2.3 Skill in Identifying Personal Biases That Influence One's Own Cognition and Behavior

> **I. Understanding the Relationship of Bias to EI**
>
> TD professionals who understand EI and the roots of bias are better equipped to change their behavior and increase their EI.

1.2.3.1 Roots of Bias, Prejudice, and Discrimination

Bias, prejudice, and discrimination are kinds of emotional learning that begin in childhood. According to Goleman (2006), it's almost impossible to eliminate the emotions of prejudice because they are formed early in life. They are then strengthened later in life because stereotypes have already been formed, and supporting the stereotype is easier than to deny it. [See 1.4.2.1 and 1.4.5.3]

Many people's experiences generally involve being with people who are similar to themselves. This means that their viewpoints often go unchallenged, thus, reinforcing that their views are correct, even if they are not. Eventually, people's brains consistently see patterns and look for what is similar (Rabotin 2011). As a result, stereotypes become stronger.

1.2.3.2 Methods for Uncovering Personal Biases

Uncovering bias is the first step in removing it from the workplace. Bias can be identified by:

- Admitting to having biases
- Reviewing internal conversations
- Attending professional affinity groups to better understand bias, prejudice, and discrimination
- Seeking out regular feedback about personal behaviors and actions
- Evaluating personal actions daily
- Being proactive about recognizing people's different capabilities
- Taking steps to actively support anyone who might feel like an outsider (Wilkie 2014)

1.2.3.3 Effects of Bias

TD professionals should recognize how destructive bias and prejudice can be. Biases can not only cost companies financially in lawsuits, but they also influence a company's reputation by preventing it from hiring the best employees, affecting performance and engagement, resulting in pay discrimination, and negatively affecting recruitment and retention.

1.2.3.4 Personal Bias and Prejudice

Research of hidden bias shows that the human brain is wired to make quick decisions. These decisions are based on assumptions and experiences and sometimes even injudicious generalizations that cause people to unconsciously make incorrect judgements and decisions (Wilkie 2014).

Most people have biases of some sort, and this is not a sign that they're an inadequate or bad person. EI can help people speak up against these biases.

TD professionals can address personal bias in the workplace using the following strategies:
- **Encourage the discussion of biases.** Self-awareness is the first step, with everyone owning up to having biases before they can be addressed.
- **Be aware of the impact that biases may have on decision making** within the organization and discuss how biases can potentially impede progress toward organizational goals.
- **Survey employees about their experiences with unconscious biases,** as well as hidden barriers that may exist within the organization. Tailor TD solutions according to the results.
- **Implement policies and practices that ensure unconscious biases are not impeding efforts toward developing an inclusive and diverse workplace.** For example, review all hiring and interviewing policies. [See 1.4]

1.2.3.5 Personal Empathy for TD Professionals

According to Goleman (2019), when people exhibit empathy (one of the five EI competencies) they exhibit three distinct kinds. Each one is important for effectiveness:
- **Cognitive empathy** is the ability to understand another person's perspective. It enables TD professionals to explain themselves in meaningful ways.
- **Emotional empathy** is the ability to feel what someone else feels. TD professionals need to possess emotional empathy to develop and coach others, interact with stakeholders, and read group dynamics.
- **Empathic concern** is the ability to sense what one person needs from another. Empathic concern enables a TD professional to sense not just how people feel, but what they need. This is important for TD professionals who are in a support function intended to provide support for the organization and its employees.

1.2.4 Skill in Observing and Interpreting the Verbal and Nonverbal Behavior of Individuals or Groups

I. Interpreting Verbal and Nonverbal Behavior
TD professionals should excel at interpreting verbal and nonverbal behavior of individuals and groups.

1.2.4.1 Practical Skills to Improve Effectiveness
Whether TD professionals are aware or not, they are constantly communicating—giving and receiving messages. TD professionals can improve and strengthen their messages and how they send them by following these guidelines:

- Send consistent messages—with matching verbal and nonverbal messages. (For example, it would be difficult to understand a message if an individual said yes while shaking their head no.)
- Strengthen a message by repeating it.
- Ensure that facial expression conveys what is intended. (For example, a frown may indicate concentration or disapproval.) Some facial expressions are universal and can indicate happiness, sadness, fear, anger, uncertainty, surprise, or disgust.
- Ensure eye contact sends the right message; use direct eye contact to show interest, but do not be so direct that it is intimidating.
- Confirm that posture and movement send a message of interest and focus.
- Communicate through positive touch, such as a handshake, pat on the back, or controlling grip.
- Pay attention to how you speak, including timing and pace, volume, inflection, and tone; avoid fillers such as "um" or "like."

It's also important for the TD professional to read others' nonverbal behavior so they comprehend the entire message. TD professionals need to focus on nonverbal behavior in several ways: [See 1.1.2.3]

- Read the combined nonverbal signals and avoid reading too much into a single gesture.
- Pay attention to inconsistencies.
- Listen to and trust your instincts if things don't seem right or if there are mixed messages.
- Look for eye contact, facial expression, posture, tone of voice, intensity, physical contact, or nonverbal sounds that indicate concern or interest.
- Check for confused looks when speaking to others, ask if they understand a reference, and assure them that it is acceptable to ask questions.

1.2.4.2 Observing Behavior in Groups
The challenge in a group is that the TD professional must be able to read anywhere from 10 to 20 to 40 people in one setting. A skilled TD professional can overcome the challenge by connecting with everyone—scanning the entire group while at the same time making eye contact with individuals. They balance their focus on every part of the room, recognizing the location that they focus on the least (usually the side of the room on their nondominant side). They communicate by learning to silently signal to people when they want them to save a question for the end. They watch for people in the group who have tuned out, talk excessively, or are disagreeable, and they have techniques to address each. They use break time to touch base with those people who may need encouragement, advice, support, or feedback.

1.2.4.3 Observing and Interpreting Behavior in Virtual Groups

Virtual groups typically meet online because they are working from different physical locations. When forming a virtual group, TD professionals must establish rules of engagement before beginning the work, project, or course. When a follow-up meeting is held, TD professionals must ensure that all members of the virtual group have received and digested the same communications and have completed any between-session tasks.

TD professionals need to communicate with the group between official meetings to prevent problems, show respect, and be supportive. They should observe behaviors between sessions, such as limited written communication, slow responses, or late or incomplete tasks. They should also start each group meeting with a check-in. TD professionals should ensure that everyone is contributing and ask direct questions if anyone isn't. These observations could signal whether there is a problem. Astute TD professionals will wait to interpret behavior until they have all the facts.

1.2.4.4 Connecting EI to Talent Development

TD professionals should find ways to practice and model EI skills. They could, for example, create an EI development plan that includes some of these items (Bradberry and Greaves 2009; Nadler 2011):

- **Self-awareness tactics:**
    - Keep a journal about their emotions.
    - Seek feedback.
    - Observe the ripple effect from their emotions.
- **Self-management tactics:**
    - Learn to sleep on it or to count to 10 before responding.
    - Interview a skilled self-manager.
    - Control their self-talk.
- **Social awareness tactics:**
    - Plan ahead for social gatherings.
    - Greet people by name.
    - Practice observing and addressing body language.
- **Relationship management tactics:**
    - Tackle a difficult conversation.
    - Acknowledge other peoples' feelings.
    - Build trust.

TD professionals should also be prepared to develop and coach others to enhance their EI skills. They may want to suggest that the individual begins with an assessment. They can then coach them to design a developmental plan that includes some of the same tactics. [See 2.7]

1.2.5 Skill in Adjusting One's Own Behavior in Response to or Anticipation of Changes in Other Peoples' Behavior, Attitudes, or Thoughts

I. Developing Emotional Intelligence
TD professionals should be able to monitor and identify other peoples' behavior and attitudes, and appropriately adjust their own behavior.

1.2.5.1 Situations When Changing One's Behavior Is Required
Many situations exist when TD professionals need to adjust their behavior or understand the situation from another person's point of view. They will then decide what skills they need and practice so that they're prepared for things such as:
- Anticipating individual behavior, attitudes, or thoughts
- Observing verbal and nonverbal messages in groups
- Making a difficult decision
- Addressing challenging situations

1.2.5.2 Using Goleman's Five Competencies
TD professionals should understand that knowledge of EI is a start, but *ultimately* they need to implement EI skills, such as: [See 1.2.2]
- **Self-awareness:**
  - Create a list of strengths and talents that build confidence.
  - Seek development in areas that are not strengths.
- **Self-regulation:**
  - Demonstrate a willingness to try new things.
  - Read a book or attend a class on resiliency.
- **Motivation:**
  - Establish a set of personal goals that align with the department and the organization.
  - Volunteer for the next cross-functional team.
- **Empathy:**
  - Seek out an individual who may not always appear to fit in, and build a relationship with that person.
  - Anticipate a customer's needs and create a plan to address them.
- **Social skills:**
  - Practice active listening, and obtain feedback from a colleague.
  - Collaborate with other people to help them meet their needs.

1.2.5.3 Develop and Adjust Behavior to Improve EI
TD professionals should be aware of situations and be able to adjust their behavior to improve a situation's outcome. The ability to stay calm in difficult situations is valuable—especially in professional situations. TD professionals can develop this ability by reflecting on their own emotions. They can also ask other people for

their perspectives of past situations and explore why they reacted a certain way, what triggered the reaction, and what they could have done differently.

1.2.5.4 EI in the Workplace

Current workplaces require everyone to have EI. Leaders who demonstrate high levels of EI set an example and encourage employee engagement, lower levels of turnover, and increased levels of productivity. Individual contributors must also demonstrate EI for improved communication and collaboration. Workplace characteristics that hasten the need for EI include:
- Need to improve engagement
- Requirements for diversity and inclusion
- Increased globalization
- Increased use of technology
- Increased need for acquiring and retaining employees
- Collaboration and managing priorities
- Need for ensuring a competitive advantage

1.2.6 Knowledge of Techniques and Approaches to Learn or Demonstrate Resilience

I. Developing Resilience

Setbacks are part of life. TD professionals need to examine how they respond to adversity and then practice resiliency.

1.2.6.1 Definition and Characteristics of Resilience

Resilience (or resiliency) is the capacity to adapt and recover quickly when something does not go as planned. There are four characteristics that everyone can develop to build resilience (Hanson 2018):
- Recognize that a challenge is not a paralyzing event. Failures and mistakes are lessons to be learned from and opportunities for growth.
- Find the confidence and commitment to continue working toward personal and professional goals, no matter the setback.
- Regulate thoughts, feelings, and actions to remain positive and learn from daily events. Also, treat people with compassion and empathy.
- Relate skillfully to other people and the wider world.

1.2.6.2 Value of Resilience

Resilient employees are physically and mentally healthier, which saves organizations money. In addition, a resilient workforce exhibits higher productivity and tends to be more willing to learn new skills or take on new roles. Resilient employees perform better under pressure, maintaining their composure when things around them are uncertain—which is beneficial during times of constant change.

Resilience has become a growing focus for many employers, and resilience training programs are becoming increasingly prevalent (Kohill 2017).

1.2.6.3 Techniques to Learn and Practice Resilience

TD professionals develop and maintain resilience in several ways, starting with the basics of exercising regularly, getting enough sleep, and maintaining a healthy diet. Resilience also requires thinking positively and learning from mistakes. There are various skills that can develop this ability, including:

- Build strong relationships with colleagues and friends.
- Try a technique such as meditation or mindfulness.
- Practice thought awareness and prevent negative thoughts from derailing efforts.
- Practice cognitive restructuring to change the perception of negative situations.
- Set measurable personal goals that align with personal values.
- Learn from mistakes and failures.
- Choose positive responses in words and actions.
- Maintain perspective of events.
- Find purpose in life.

1.2.6.4 Helping Other People Improve Resilience

Teaching resilience is one thing that TD professionals can do to help other people improve their resilience, but they should also ensure that measures are in place to foster resilience in the workplace, such as:

- Coach leaders to lead by example and build resilience at the leadership level.
- Foster a sense of purpose by encouraging employees to find meaning in their work.
- Ensure the organization has a culture and plan that supports change.
- Encourage employee teaming and connections on the job and socially.
- Encourage healthy habits.
- Create a positive, flexible, and pleasant atmosphere.

Decision Making

1.2.7 Knowledge of Decision-Making Models

> **I. Making Decisions**
>
> TD professionals should use a methodical decision-making process that enables everyone who needs to be involved to contribute ideas and play an appropriate role in making the decision.

1.2.7.1 Problem-Solving Processes

Problems may be solved more effectively when an organized procedure is followed. Using a process for making decisions helps people remember each step required to reach the best decision. Many processes exist, but most follow these six steps:

1. Define the problem.
2. Research and analyze the problem.
3. Establish a checklist of criteria for evaluating possible solutions.
4. List all possible alternatives.
5. Select the best alternative, and discuss how to implement it.
6. Monitor implementation, and modify it if required.

Most people begin at the fourth step, skipping three important steps—effective decision making depends on defining the problem. A problem is a discrepancy between what is and what should be. It should be stated in the form of a question; for example, asking, "How can we reduce the number of errors on the production line?" is better than saying, "Develop a plan to improve quality."

TD professionals can use these guidelines for developing questions that lead to better decisions (Quinlivan-Hall and Renner 1990):
- *How* questions suggest a process.
- *Where* questions indicate locations.
- *Who* questions identify the people involved.
- *When* questions point to time.
- *What* questions sort process and content.

The more specific the question, the more successful the decision-making process will be.

1.2.7.2 Decision-Making Models

TD professionals should be aware of several well-known decision-making models:
- **The Kepner-Tregoe Decision-Making Methodology** is one of the oldest formal methods used in organizations. This structured process for gathering, prioritizing, and evaluating information was developed by Charles H. Kepner and Benjamin B. Tregoe in the 1960s and is respected in business management circles. An important aspect of the Kepner-Tregoe Decision-Making Methodology is the assessment and prioritization of risk. The idea is not to find a perfect solution but the best possible choice. The process—which involves listing must haves, want to haves, and restraints—attempts to limit conscious and unconscious biases that draw attention away from the outcome. The alternatives are rated against these three items and weighted. The step-by-step approach is easy to use, especially when there are many potential options (Kepner and Tregoe 1997).
- **The Vroom-Yetton-Jago Decision Model** asserts that not all decisions are worthy of the same amount of time investment. The TD professional begins by examining three factors to analyze a decision: the importance of the decision quality, the need for subordinate commitment or buy-in, and time constraints. Depending on the results of this examination, one of three leadership styles is assigned to make the decision: autocratic, consultative, or collaborative (MindTools n.d.).
- **The OODA Loop** includes four stages: observe, orient, decide, and act. Although three of the four stages are self-explanatory, *orient* means that the problem solvers need to introduce themselves to the new information and not be swayed by past experiences (Ullman 2007).
- **Paired Comparison Analysis** uses a comparison matrix to pair each option with all other options to decide the preferred one. It is most useful when many competing options are involved (Newton and Bristol n.d.).
- **The Delphi Technique** uses a carefully designed list of questions that is developed and refined in several rounds. Participants' ideas are confronted as the group of experts work toward a consensus through step-by-step feedback on one another's answers. It is often compared to brainstorming, but there is no direct group interaction when using the Delphi Technique (Mulder 2017).

1.2.7.3 Decision-Making Approaches
Decision making can be done by individuals or groups and teams, and there are several available approaches.

Individual decision-making methods include:
- **A decisional balance sheet** lists the advantages and disadvantages (pros and cons) of each option. This process was suggested by Plato and further developed by Benjamin Franklin.
- **A weighted matrix** lists possible solutions on one axis and weighted criteria on the other to determine which solution has the highest score.
- **Satisficing** is reviewing alternatives until an acceptability threshold is met.

Group decision-making methods include:
- **Consensus** tries to avoid winners and losers and requires that the minority agree to support the decision in words and deeds. The minority can demand that the decision be modified to remove objectionable features.
- **A democratic or majority vote** requires support from more than 50 percent of the members of a group.
- **In authority rule,** one person makes the decision, generally with some group input.
- **Expert decision** is used when there is an identifiable expert who is technically qualified to make the decision.
- **Minority control** enables a minority within a group to make the decision and requires everyone to agree to support the decision.

1.2.7.4 Using EI Knowledge for Improved Decision Making
EI can be helpful when making decisions because it helps people recognize emotional decisions and remove emotions that are not a part of the decision. Emotionally intelligent leaders are less likely to make a mistake because they recognize the source of their emotions. Leaders can also help reduce the impact of other people's anxiety by defining the true source of their emotions based on a decision.

EI may also help people better understand their triggers (or causes of their emotional reactions) and manage automatic reactions to a decision-making situation. A TD professional who is emotionally intelligent will be more likely to stop and consider a decision or respond to a new situation rather than react. Better decisions are made by acting on information from feelings, instincts, and intuition, as well as on information coming from a rational intellect. TD professionals have access to memory (short-term, long-term, and working memory) that assigns a weight or preference to different choices. EI provides guidance to control or access emotions for adapting to change, getting along with others, or dealing with stressful decisions. Finally, EI will help TD professionals remain optimistic about decisions once they are made. [See 2.1.2.2]

1.2.8 Skill in Using Logic and Reasoning to Identify the Strengths and Weaknesses of Alternative Solutions, Conclusions, or Approaches to Problems

I. Exploring Critical Thinking

TD professionals must hone their critical thinking skills to be able to attain the most effective decision-making results.

1.2.8.1 Critical Thinking Skills

TD professionals should practice critical thinking, or the analysis of a situation and the related facts, data, and evidence to make better decisions. Ideally, critical thinking focuses solely on factual information and is done objectively, without influence from personal opinions or biases.

The critical thinking process includes:
- **Identifying and organizing.** Identify the situation and the factors that influence it, organizing them in some categories such as strengths and weaknesses or opinions and facts.
- **Researching.** Find the source of the information and conduct an independent verification.
- **Identifying biases.** Identify one's own and others' biases and not let them cloud judgment; analysis is critical.
- **Inferring to draw conclusions.** Summarize and assess information, and use it to extrapolate potential outcomes without jumping to conclusions; interpretation skills are vital.
- **Solving problems.** Organize one's thoughts and apply problem-solving steps.
- **Determining relevance.** Recognize the most important information.
- **Asking questions and being curious.** Ask open-ended questions.

1.2.8.2 Steps Required for Critical Thinking

Critical thinking is an important skill for TD professionals. It can be presented in six steps that coincide with required skills:

1. **Organize information.** There is no shortage of information, but the key is to select the most important information and group it into categories that reveal connections, themes, or hierarchies.
2. **Structure reasoning.** Opinions will be a part of the critical thinking process, but this step requires that the statements are supported and different opinions are considered. Find a way to display reasoning so the relationship between statements or data can be seen.
3. **Consider evidence.** Closely review the evidence to determine where it originated and how reliable it is—for example, is the information from a biased news source or evidence-based research?
4. **Identify assumptions and biases.** Review the logical structure of the argument up to this point to determine its validity. This requires identifying any assumptions and biases that exist.
5. **Evaluate arguments.** Review the arguments to determine not only the pros and cons, but also the strength of the arguments.
6. **Communicate conclusions.** No matter how strong the argument is, if it is not presented well in writing or orally, it may not be successful.

1.2.8.3 Making Team Decisions

Like individuals, teams need to follow an organized decision-making process. They should have an agreed-upon process for making decisions. The problem-solving model for team decisions is the same six-step problem-solving process presented earlier in this section. [See 1.2.7]

There are advantages and disadvantages of group decision making:
- **Advantages:**
    - Cross-fertilization for more ideas
    - Generally increased buy-in and commitment
    - More solutions
    - Increased risk-taking
    - Encourages creative ideas
- **Disadvantages:**
    - Time consuming
    - Potential unequal participation
    - Conflicts caused by personality types
    - Increased competition
    - Groupthink—when all members conform their thinking to the perceived consensus of the group

Of the disadvantages to team decision making, it's important for TD professionals to be particularly aware of groupthink. Psychologist Irving Janis coined the term in 1972 to describe situations when groups make bad or irrational decisions. The main characteristic of groupthink occurs when each member of the group alters their stated opinions to conform to the perceived consensus of the group. Some conditions that can cause groupthink include isolation of the group, high group cohesion, directive leadership, lack of norms related to methodical decision-making procedures, homogeneity of members, and high stress from external threats.

1.2.8.4 Decision-Making Models

Many decision-making tools exist. TD professionals can choose the best approach or model, which will depend on how many people need to be included, how much time is available, and the relative importance of the decision. Tools that may also be helpful for making decisions include multivoting, affinity diagrams, or a countermeasure matrix. TD professionals can weigh the advantages and disadvantages of each model to choose the best one for the situation (Table 1.2.8.4-1).

1.2 Emotional Intelligence & Decision Making

Table 1.2.8.4-1. Decision-Making Models

Technique	Description	Advantages	Disadvantages
Multivoting (Nominal Group Technique)	A group decision-making method to shorten a list of ideas to a manageable number through a series of structured voting steps	• Works well for a team • Minimizes team dynamics issues • Results in a rank-ordered list • Generates more ideas than discussion • Limits the power of people with strong opinions • Reduces pressure to conform • Allows for democratic prioritization • Usually produces a sense of closure	• Requires preparation • Creates a regimented process • Works best for single, clearly defined problems • Minimizes discussion • Doesn't allow for the full development of ideas
Affinity/Interrelationship Digraph	A tool used to organize a large number of ideas into logical groups based on natural relationships among the ideas	• Encourages balanced input, and considers everyone's ideas • Inspires unconventional thinking • Creates a simple, cost-effective, and thorough process • Obtains consensus on categories • Displays all ideas • Increases understanding of how others think • Works well when facts seem to have no structure • Works well for large or complex issues	• Requires about two hours • Necessitates eliminating distractions for those participating • Follows a regimented process • Causes participants to feel strange during the silent portion • Doesn't show systematic causes of effect • Doesn't show causal interdependency
Countermeasure Matrix	A tool that documents causes, solutions, and implementation priorities of a problem and provides input for developing an action plan	• Encourages critical thinking • Identifies causes, solutions, and implementation priorities • Provides input to develop an action plan	• Needs to have the right people involved • Struggles to achieve balanced participation • Appears to be a complex process

Other tools that TD professionals may want to explore include:
- **Strengths and weaknesses sort** identifies the strengths and weaknesses of alternative solutions.
- **Decision matrix** is a tool that lists values in columns and rows to identify and analyze relationships.
- **Weighted criteria** is a decision-making matrix that compares alternatives on one axis to weighted (prioritized by importance) values on the other.
- **T-chart** is an organizing tool that compares two facets of a solution, such as pros and cons.
- **Decision tree** is a branching model that sorts through decisions and their consequences.
- **Cost-benefit analysis** estimates the value of options by evaluating the best approach to achieve the benefit at the best cost.
- **SWOT** is a two-by-two visual that shows the strengths, weaknesses, opportunities, and threats of an idea, problem, or solution.
- **Force field analysis** is a diagnostic tool developed by Kurt Lewin to assess two types of forces (driving and restraining).
- **Pareto chart** is a vertical bar chart that shows values and a line graph that plots the cumulative total.

Virtual teams may need unique tools for collaborative brainstorming and group decision making. TD professionals should review several tools before selecting the one that best meets their specific needs. It's important to ensure that everyone understands how the electronic tool will process the group's activities. Decision making will typically follow the same process as a group would in person: defining the objective, clarifying criteria, generating ideas, organizing possibilities, evaluating solutions, and selecting the decision. Virtual decision-making tools have the advantage of using electronic means to accomplish some of these steps. For example, some of the tools organize possibilities by merging like alternatives and reducing redundancies. Other tools help participants negotiate solutions with others. The process results in a collaborative agreement.

REFERENCES

Beldoch, M. 1964. "Sensitivity to Expression of Emotional Meaning in Three Modes of Communication." In *The Communication of Emotional Meaning*, edited by J.R. Davitz and M.Beldoch. New York: McGraw-Hill.

Brackett, M. 2019. *Permission to Feel: Unlocking the Power of Emotions to Help Our Kids, Ourselves, and Our Society Thrive*. New York: Celadon Books.

Bradberry, T., and J. Greaves. 2009. *Emotional Intelligence 2.0*. San Diego: TalentSmart.

Cherniss, C., and M. Adler. 2000. *Promoting Emotional Intelligence in Organizations*. Alexandria, VA: ASTD Press.

Gardner, H. 1975. *The Shattered Mind*. New York: Knopf.

Goleman, D. 2001. *Primal Leadership*. Boston: Harvard Business School Press.

Goleman, D. 2006. *Emotional Intelligence: Why It Can Matter More Than IQ*, 10th anniversary ed. New York: Bantam Books.

Hanson, R., and F. Hanson. 2018. *Resilient: How to Grow an Unshakable Core of Calm, Strength, and Happiness*. New York: Penguin Random House.

HBR Press. 2019. *Emotional Intelligence Focus*. Boston: HBR Press.

Hunt, J., and M. Fitzgerald. 2013. "The Relationship Between Emotional Intelligence and Transformational Leadership: An Investigation and Review of Competing Claims in the Literature." *American International Journal of Social Science* 2(8): 30–38.

Kepner, C.H., and B.B. Tregoe. 1997. *The New Rational Manager*. Princeton, NJ: Princeton Research Press.

Kohll, A. 2017. "How You Can Build a More Resilient Workforce." *Forbes*, January 5. forbes.com/sites/alankohll/2017/01/05/how-you-can-build-a-more-resilient-workforce/#536ce39e9b50.

Landy, F.J. 2005. "Some Historical and Scientific Issues Related to Research on Emotional Intelligence." *Journal of Organizational Behavior* 26:411–424.

Mayer, J.D. 2008. "Human Abilities: Emotional Intelligence." *Annual Review of Psychology* 59:507–536.

Mayer, J.D., P. Salovey, and D. Caruso. 1998. "Competing Models of Emotional Intelligence." In *Handbook of Human Intelligence*, edited by R.J. Steinberg. New York: Cambridge University Press.

MindTools. n.d. "The Vroom-Yetton Decision Model: Deciding How to Decide." mindtools.com/pages/article/newTED_91.htm.

Mulder, P. 2017. "Delphi Technique." *Tools Hero*. toolshero.com/decision-making/delphi-technique.

Nadler, R. 2011. *Leading With Emotional Intelligence: Hands-On Strategies for Building Confident and Collaborative Star Performers*. New York: McGraw-Hill Companies.

Newton, P., and H. Bristol. n.d. "Paired Comparison Analysis." Chapter 4 in *Top 5 Decision Making Models*. Free Management Books. free-management-ebooks.com/news/paired-comparison-analysis.

Petrides, K.V., R. Pita, and F. Kokkinaki. 2007. "The Location of Trait Emotional Intelligence in Personality Factor Space." *British Journal of Psychology* 98(2): 273–289.

Quinlivan-Hall, D., and P. Renner. 1990. *In Search of Solutions*. Vancouver, BC: PFR Training Associates.

Rabotin, M. 2011. *Culture Savvy: Working and Collaborating Across the Globe*. Alexandria, VA: ASTD Press.

Salazar, A. 2017. "Emotional Intelligence: What Is It, Interpretation Models and Controversies." CogniFit, July 14. blog.cognifit.com/emotional-intelligence.

Sallie-Dosunmu, M. 2016. "Using Emotional Intelligence in the Workplace." *TD at Work*. Alexandria, VA: ATD Press.

Salovey, P., and J. Mayer. 1990. "Emotional Intelligence." *Imagination, Cognition, and Personality* 9(3): 185–211.

Ullman, D.G. 2007. "'OO-OO-OO!' The Sound of a Broken OODA Loop." *Crosstalk*, April.

Wilkie, D. 2014. "Tips for Rooting Out Hidden Bias." *HR Magazine*, December 1.

Recommended Reading

Bradberry, T., and J. Greaves. 2009. *Emotional Intelligence 2.0*. San Diego: TalentSmart.

Goleman, D. 2006. *Emotional Intelligence: Why It Can Matter More Than IQ*, 10th anniversary ed. New York: Bantam Books.

Heath, C., and D. Heath. 2013. *Decisive: How to Make Better Choices in Life and Work*. New York: Crown Business.

Malone, P. 2021. *Emotional Intelligence in Talent Development*. Alexandria, VA: ATD Press.

1.3 COLLABORATION & LEADERSHIP

Leadership is about influence and vision, which also helps facilitate collaboration. Being good at collaboration requires the ability to foster environments that encourage teamwork and respectful relationships, especially cross-functionally. Both collaboration and leadership require the practitioner to communicate effectively, provide feedback, and assess the work of others. Leadership also requires the ability to effectively align people and tasks to support the organization's strategy. Effective leaders inspire trust and engagement with their employees and teams.

Collaborating With Others

1.3.1 Knowledge of Theories, Methods, and Techniques to Build and Manage Professional Relationships

> **I. Build and Manage Professional Relationships**
>
> TD professionals should understand the methods and techniques needed to build and manage professional relationships because collaborating and working on teams is how most work is accomplished in organizations. [See 1.2]

1.3.1.1 Defining Group Dynamics

TD professionals are members of groups and teams. Group dynamics refers to any group, including social communities, that has something in common. Teams are special groups in which the commonality is a shared goal. Having a goal creates a dynamic between team members, making them dependent on one another for success (a sports team wins or loses as a team, for example). Group dynamics processes ensure that all members are effective contributors.

TD professionals need to be aware of the natural stages that teams move through, know how to help teams navigate these stages, and understand how to deal with counterproductive behavior by participants.

A TD professional's role is to work with individuals and account for all the different characteristics, wants, needs, and behavioral styles that make up their dynamics. Dynamics refers to how individuals interact when working or learning together, and includes setting goals, communicating, making decisions, providing leadership, and resolving conflict.

1.3.1.2 Group Dynamics Processes

Group dynamics is the area of social sciences that focuses on the nature of groups. When individuals come together in groups they may worry about personal identity, how well they will relate to others, and how team membership will affect their work responsibilities. In addition, their desire to belong to or identify with other group members may create distinctly different attitudes (recognized or unrecognized) than an individual normally exhibits. It's also possible that the consensus of the group will influence or overwhelm individual preferences and actions. Group dynamics may also cause a person's behavior to change when they appear before a group.

Groups and teams develop in numerous ways. A facilitator can help move teams and groups from forming to performing stages. In this process, the facilitator's goal is to provide proper feedback and correctly timed facilitation tools to alter the group's actions. Facilitators should carefully watch what the group is doing as a unit, as well as any interactions among individual team members.

Listening is the key tool when observing a group. It shows interest in the individual who is speaking and respect for their experience. There are several levels of listening:

- **Passive listening** describes a situation when the listener has no interaction with the speaker, such as listening to the radio or a podcast.
- **Attentive listening** refers to a situation when the listener has some interaction with the speaker, such as listening for content in class or taking notes in a meeting.
- **Active listening** describes a situation when the listener has a high level of interaction with the speaker, listening for content, meaning, and feelings.

TD professionals should listen actively to build and manage professional relationships. Listening skills are critical when TD professionals are:

- Answering participant questions as they facilitate learning
- Addressing concerns when they coach managers
- Responding to requests from senior leaders
- Solving issues as they consult with managers [See 1.1.2]

1.3.1.3 Leveraging Group Dynamics

TD professionals can leverage group dynamics to build high-performance teams by doing things such as:

- Involving everyone in vision creation
- Clarifying decision-making responsibilities
- Identifying and leveraging collaboration opportunities
- Establishing values or guiding principles

1.3.1.4 Fostering Teamwork and Collaboration

TD professionals can take many steps to foster teamwork and collaboration. Team dynamics are the unconscious, psychological forces that influence the direction of a team's behavior and performance, including creating shared experiences and maintaining excellent communication.

1.3.2 Knowledge of Methods and Criteria for Establishing and Managing Collaboration Among Various Units

I. Methods and Techniques to Build a Collaborative Environment

Collaboration provides every team member with equal opportunities to participate, communicate, and be involved in collectively completing projects and goals. TD professionals should collaborate with colleagues by showing them respect, valuing their skills, and acknowledging their feelings, opinions, and ideas. [See 1.2]

1.3.2.1 Identify Existing Collaborative Networks

TD professionals should start with their team and ensure that everyone uses collaborative skills to accomplish goals. Collaboration is sometimes defined as taking teamwork to a higher level. TD professionals should identify other existing collaborative networks, such as internal customers, suppliers, or other alliances that extend collaboration beyond their immediate teams.

1.3.2.2 Establishing New Collaborative Networks

It's important for TD professionals to establish new collaborative networks in situations such as working across department lines to improve a process, solve a problem, or start a new project. A collaborative network has a common goal that is beneficial to everyone. TD professionals can start by presenting a compelling case about what could be achieved, why networking would be advantageous, how leveraging one another's strengths would be beneficial, and getting buy-in to work together. They can use a collaboration portal to share data, solve issues, and stay up to date with information and changes (Zack 2019).

1.3.2.3 Establish a Motivating Atmosphere

Motivation has its origin in Maslow's hierarchy of needs, which states that once an individual's basic physiological (food, sleep) and safety (stability) needs are met, they are interested in satisfying their belongingness and self-esteem needs. A motivating atmosphere builds self-esteem and includes all actions that positively influence employees to perform. TD professionals should establish a motivating atmosphere because it increases productivity, encourages engagement, and fosters an ongoing commitment to the organization. Because motivation is a component of both the workplace atmosphere and the learning environment, TD professionals should determine how they can satisfy these needs and motivate employees and learners. [See 2.1.3.3 and 3.3.10]

Extrinsic and intrinsic motivation are both important. Intrinsically motivated employees are more likely to be engaged in what they are doing. Several ways to create a motivating atmosphere include:
- Thanking employees and others for a job well done
- Ensuring employees have an opportunity to do what they do best every day
- Providing timely and specific feedback
- Making time to meet with and listen to employees and others formally and informally
- Maintaining a workplace that is transparent, trusting, and fun
- Encouraging and rewarding initiative and new ideas
- Sharing information with employees and others
- Involving employees in decisions

- Providing employees with a sense of ownership of their jobs and the organization
- Giving employees a chance to learn new skills
- Using delegation as a motivational tool

1.3.2.4 Encourage Shared Experiences

A shared experience is seeing, hearing, or doing the same thing as others. Although it's a simple concept, shared experiences have a deep impact on human socialization because they enhance each person's individual experience. A Yale University study demonstrated that when two people ate a piece of chocolate *together*, they described it as more flavorful and enjoyable than when eaten alone (Hathaway 2014). Shared experiences are powerful because they bring people together to enhance one another's experience. TD professionals can use shared experiences to build and manage professional relationships.

1.3.2.5 Recognize, Reward, and Celebrate Collaborative Behavior

Cross, Taylor, and Zehner (2018) suggest that leaders should examine how they reward their employees for effective collaboration. They should note whether collaborative efforts in their organizations are evenly distributed. While employees may achieve their goals, they may not work well with colleagues because they lack the time to focus on both their goals and collaborating. Employees should be rewarded similarly to how soccer players are rewarded for both goals and assists. Organizations are most effective when employees meet their goals and assist their colleagues.

1.3.2.6 Recognize Collaborative Overload

According to data collected over the past two decades, the amount of time spent by managers and employees in collaborative activities has increased by 50 percent or more (Cross, Rebele, and Grant 2016). Although this results in improved cross-functional work and increased connectivity, it's also important to remember that collaboration isn't always perfect in organizations. For example, 20–35 percent of value-added collaboration often comes from only 3–5 percent of employees.

The greater worry is that employees can spend as much as 80 percent of their time on collaborative activities, such as attending meetings, making phone calls, and responding to emails. As a result, they take work home, or their performance suffers, as they are buried under mountains of requests for advice, access, input, or meeting attendance.

TD professionals should evaluate their own collaborative overload and help provide guidance to leadership and managers on how to ensure an optimal amount of collaboration.

1.3.3   Skill in Building and Managing Teams and Work Groups

> **I. Build and Manage High-Performance Teams**
>
> Building teams is a natural task for TD professionals because one of their key roles is to develop the requisite teaming skills in others, such as communicating, problem solving, goal setting, resolving conflict, and decision making.

1.3.3.1 Advantages to Teamwork

Teamwork is the harmony created by the combined actions of a group of people with a common goal, defined roles, effective communication, and a willingness to cooperate and support one another.

Teamwork encourages trust and a sense of identity and increases accountability and internal effectiveness. Effective teams almost always outperform individuals who work independently, especially when various skills are required.

1.3.3.2 Defining High-Performance Teams

The concept of high-performance teams within organizations refers to teams, organizations, or virtual groups that are highly focused on their goals and achieve superior results. High-performance teams outperform other similar teams as well as their own expectations.

1.3.3.3 Characteristics of Successful Teams

Successful teams start with a foundation of clear goals, defined roles, open and clear communication, and effective decision-making skills. Once these are in place, a team can add the next three critical building blocks: balanced participation, valued diversity, and managed conflict. Effective high-performance teams always operate in a positive atmosphere through cooperative relationships. Participative leadership ensures that everyone believes they're part of the team (McDermott 2014).

1.3.3.4 Establishing Rules of Engagement

As a team is forming, it should establish the rules of engagement. These include logistics and meeting expectations, communication expectations, how roles will be established, and how decisions will be made. Defining ways of working and communicating is especially critical for teams in a remote or hybrid workplace where physical co-location does not exist and where work may be conducted at different times. This ensures team members understand what is required of the group as it relates to when and how collaboration will occur. [See 1.2.4.3]

1.3.3.5 Team Development Models

TD professionals should be aware of the most common team development models. Each team progresses through the various stages of team development in a unique way. The goal of all models is to move teams through the initial stages when they are forming to reach a state of productivity as efficiently as possible. Some stages can be more painful than others; teams can also get stuck in a stage and fail to advance. Changes in team membership or circumstances can require the team to return to an earlier stage. It's useful for TD professionals to understand which stage a team is in. There are several classification models to choose from.

1.3.3.5.1 Tuckman's Model

The Tuckman model is the most well-known. In 1965, Tuckman presented a team-maturing model with four stages: forming, storming, norming, and performing. In 1997, Tuckman and Jensen added a fifth stage—adjourning. Progress through these stages isn't strictly linear. Various things affect the development of teams, such as the maturity of the team members and whether facilitation is provided.

The following is a description of the five stages (ATD 2018):
- The **forming stage** is characterized by each team member's reliance on past behavior. Members may be uncertain about why they're there, and they'll look to the team leader for guidance to try to avoid controversy and keep things safe. At this stage, members tend to be extremely polite, may be reluctant to participate, and often avoid serious topics and personal feelings. To grow from this stage to the next, team members must be willing to confront threatening topics and risk the possibility of conflict. Team output at this stage of development is low.
- The **storming stage** is renowned for the conflict and competition that surfaces. Some experience hostility or defensiveness. As the team tries to work together, disagreements may arise about its goals and objectives. During this stage, boundaries are tested, power struggles or conflicts may develop, and cliques may form. Some members may remain silent while others attempt to dominate. To grow from this stage to the next, team members must be willing to give up personal preferences in favor of the requirements of the entire group. Output in this stage is still low.
- The **norming stage** describes when the team begins merging into a cohesive group. More cooperation and understanding occur. The group's goals and objectives are decided and owned by members. The team has now negotiated roles, successfully managed differences, developed written and unwritten norms, recognized the need for interdependence, and mastered decision making. It's ready to complete the defined work. This stage is typified by cohesion and acknowledgment of individual members' contributions. Output at this stage is moderate to high.
- During the **performing stage,** the team identity is complete, and morale is high. Members are task and people oriented. This stage is characterized by a high level of trust. Members are encouraged to use their unique talents. They organize themselves in highly flexible ways and experiment with solutions. When teams reach this stage, their capacity, range, and depth of personal interactions make them independent. If a team can avoid groupthink, output at this level is very high.
- The **adjourning stage** happens when the team prepares for termination. Once they achieve the goal, the team recognizes its own accomplishment, may be rewarded by others, and disbands. Teams may disband because their work is completed or because team members are no longer challenged by the task.

1.3.3.5.2 Cog's Ladder

Another team development model is Cog's ladder, which is similar to the Tuckman model. However, progress through Cog's ladder is not strictly linear. Teams may go back and forth between stages 3 and 2 several times before moving on to stages 4 and 5. Cog's ladder identifies the following maturing stages that teams pass through:

1. **Polite stage.** This is the stage when team players try to make a good first impression.
2. **Purpose.** At this stage, it's typical for members to ask, "Why are we here?" and explore what they are supposed to do. Teams determine goals, objectives, and purposes and define what will be accomplished.
3. **Bid for power.** Team and individual power bases are established. Power, influence, and competence emerge.
4. **Performance progress.** Dynamic interaction begins as the team starts to work together. It is constructive and positive.
5. **Synergy.** By working together, the team accomplishes things that members could not achieve individually. There is a sense of esprit and proficiency.

1.3.3.5.3 Other Team Performance Models

The Drexler Sibbit Performance Model uses seven sequential steps to build teams and team-based cultures. The seven steps are orientation, trust building, goal clarification, commitment, implementation, high performance, and renewal. An important part of the model is the resolved and unresolved traits on either side of each step.

The Katzenbach and Smith model, presented in the book *The Wisdom of Teams*, uses a triangular framework with each point representing the key deliverables of most teams: collective work products, performance results, and personal growth. To reach those goals, teams must work through necessary elements that include skills, commitment, and accountability.

The GRPI Model of Team Effectiveness is a simple model developed by Richard Beckhard, which represents the four fundamental dimensions every team requires: goals, roles, processes, and interpersonal relations. It is used as a planning tool for new teams, a maintenance tool for developing teams, and a diagnostic tool when a teambuilding initiative is required.

Patrick Lencioni's book *The Five Dysfunctions of a Team* defines the five behaviors that create a cohesive team: trust, conflict resolution, commitment, accountability, and results. They are presented as the dysfunction of the team by being described as absence of trust, fear of conflict, lack of commitment, avoidance of accountability, and inattention to results.

1.3.3.6 Building Team Trust

Teams and organizations benefit from full participation of all team members. Individuals bring unique perspectives, skills, and ideas that contribute to the team's successful achievement of a performance solution. These guidelines can help the TD professional ensure that all team members are included and able to participate:

- Establish clear communication methods and styles.
- Establish agreement and maintain focus on the team's project objectives, goals, and mission. Each member must believe that their relationship to the overall project plan is clearly defined. In addition, project timelines should be clear.
- Assist team members with relationship building. The team must have opportunities for group introductions, downtime, and celebrations.
- Ensure that team members remain connected to their daily work. They need to be comfortable with their relationships within the organizational structure.
- Become familiar with any cultural differences and address them with individuals and the team. Team members need to know that they can overcome any cultural differences and that alternative approaches to work will be welcomed.
- Establish a code of conduct. This should include communication style, conflict management, the position of the leader and other roles within the group, the consequences of commitment lapses, and anything that team members may consider a threat. Some codes of conduct include norms, such as all team members must take part in group discussions; members must not interrupt when another member is speaking; and all members will be punctual for meetings.

1.3.3.7 The Team-Building Process

Teams occasionally become less effective as time goes on. At this point, the TD professional may identify someone to lead a team-building process. Although the nature of team building varies in terms of scale and what needs to be accomplished, the best results occur if several things are in place:
- The event is held off-site.
- The team building event lasts one to two days.
- Everyone is required to attend.
- A neutral facilitator is used.
- The team clarifies its goal, identifies inhibitors, and creates actions to remove those inhibitors.
- The facilitator customizes an approach for the team.
- The team uses its own data to address required change.

1.3.4 Skill in Integrating and Synthesizing Others' Viewpoints to Build Alignment of Diverse Perspectives

> **I. Building Alignment and Synergy From Diversity**
>
> TD professionals should use many approaches to maximize success, including identifying, assimilating, and blending a wide variety of ideas. Tapping into the best ideas from many sources increases options and the likelihood of finding a unique solution. It also increases the opportunity for team-wide buy-in.

1.3.4.1 The Value of Communication

Diversity of thought brings fresh ideas and a multifaceted view to the work environment. Cross-cultural communication skills are essential to building alignment and synergy. Having clear, effective communication between co-workers, managers, customers, and executives creates an equal opportunity workplace in which a diverse set of individuals are empowered to excel. Inclusion and respect for everyone in the workplace will benefit performance and working conditions. Communication challenges in a diverse workplace are common due to differences in body language, thought processes, and communication norms, which can lead to miscommunication. Communication is important regardless of job functions in the diverse work environment.

1.3.4.2 Encourage All to Contribute to Success and Achieve Buy-In

Diversity of thought can create differences of opinion and direction. TD professionals should encourage everyone to contribute to the goal and build alignment that inspires all group members to buy in to the same plan to reach that goal. Doing so saves time, energy, and money.

1.3.4.3 Use Critical Thinking Skills

Critical thinking is a process that stresses an attitude of suspended judgment, incorporates logical inquiry and problem solving, and leads to an evaluative decision or action. [See 1.2.8]

1.3.4.4 Demonstrate Innovation and Creative Thinking

Diversity in the workplace is vital because it enhances creativity and increases innovation. Internally, it adds creative ideas to problem solving, increases profitability, and supports innovation for the future. Externally, an innovative environment builds a positive reputation for the organization, leading to the ability to attract and hire skilled employees.

1.3.5 Knowledge of Conflict Management Techniques

I. Models and Techniques for Conflict Resolution
Managing conflict is likely to be a daily occurrence for TD professionals, who should know how to manage it to ensure collaboration and teamwork.

1.3.5.1 Kenneth Thomas and Ralph Kilmann Conflict Model
Skilled TD professionals should seek to understand employees' reactions to conflict, which can differ from person to person. Understanding how this behavior fits into different conflict management styles is critical to recognizing its effect on a conflict situation. The most widely used model is Kenneth Thomas and Ralph Kilmann's Conflict Model, which uses levels of cooperation and assertiveness to define five different modes for responding to conflict (Figure 1.3.5.1-1):

- **Competing.** Using a competitive response, the individuals seek to satisfy their own needs without regard to, and often at the expense of, others involved.
- **Accommodating.** Accommodators neglect their own concerns to satisfy those of other people.
- **Avoiding.** When avoiding conflict, individuals do not address it. They do not seek to satisfy their own interests or the interests of others.
- **Collaborating.** Collaborators work with others to find a solution that fully satisfies all interests.
- **Compromising.** Compromisers seek to partially satisfy all participants.

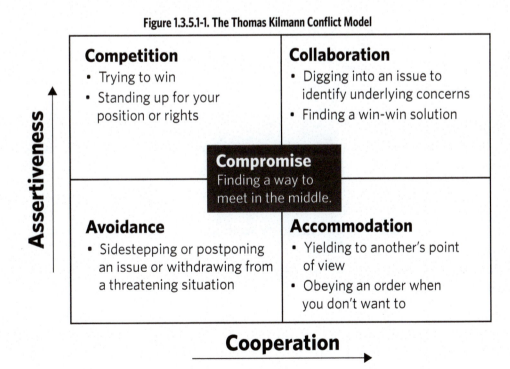

Figure 1.3.5.1-1. The Thomas Kilmann Conflict Model

Source: Batista (2007).

None of the five responses to conflict is inherently superior or inferior. However, one response may be more effective than another depending on the situation. For example, a competitive approach is better than a collaborative approach for handling an emergency. It also may be best to avoid a conflict temporarily to let participants regain composure.

Although individuals may have a preferred response, they can respond to conflicts at home differently than at work. A person's response to conflict is a learned behavior, and it changes as they gain life experience. Understanding one's own preferred response to conflict and its potential positive and negative effects is important for managing conflict. Learning to recognize others' preferences gives TD professionals the tools to communicate better.

Roles are used to establish expectations for how people should act in terms of duties and in relation to others. For example, a leader's role embodies certain expectations about the duties performed and who the leader consults with in the performance of those duties. Conflict within a group can be lessened by developing written expectations for each role.

1.3.5.2 Conflict Resolution Strategies

Knowing how others respond to conflict is important, but it's more important that TD professionals know how they respond to conflict. TD professionals should model and use conflict resolution strategies such as:
- Using "I-messages" rather than "you-messages"
- Addressing conflict directly
- Avoiding the words *always* and *never*, which are exaggerations and rarely true
- Considering what is known about the other person's behaviors and personality
- Thinking about their relationship and history with the individuals, their communication style, and general behavior patterns, which will help them anticipate potential reactions
- Focusing on what they need to talk about and communicating concerns in a clear, specific, and neutral way; for example, identifying the central issue, maintaining focus, and preventing parties from slipping into other matters
- Concentrating on behavior, not personality

1.3.5.3 Managing Team Conflict

All conflict is not one-on-one; sometimes, it occurs between groups within or outside a team. Use these steps to help identify conflict and clarify the situation when a team is in conflict:

1. Identify the root cause of the conflict. [See 3.5.2]
2. Identify what's at stake for the team.
3. Assess how the team is currently managing the situation.
4. Listen to both sides—or more.
5. If necessary, speak with individuals separately.
6. Ask the team to gather the facts.
7. Bring the individuals together.
8. Find a common ground.
9. Be clear about outcome expectations.
10. Create a plan of action as a team.

1.3.5.4 Ways to Diffuse Conflict Situations

At times, it may be necessary to quickly diffuse the situation. A few tactics for doing so are:
- Stay calm.
- Listen to all perspectives.
- Identify points of agreement and disagreement.
- Manage one's own response.
- Set limits and ground rules.
- Handle challenging questions.
- Confront negative feelings.
- Prioritize the main points of conflict.
- Prevent a physical confrontation.

1.3.6 Skill in Managing Conflict

> **I. Managing Conflict**
>
> Conflict can be viewed as good, bad, or neutral. TD professionals should know when it can be addressed and when not to do so.

1.3.6.1 Principles of Conflict Resolution

Every day will not be smooth sailing. There will be conflict. This process works for TD professionals, whether the conflict is with them or between two employees. The guiding principles are be calm, patient, and respectful—and most of all, don't put it off. Tackle it immediately.

A Forward-Focused Resolution Process

These steps will help TD professionals resolve conflict:

1. **Set the stage.** Use specific communication skills to restate, paraphrase, listen actively, and summarize to ensure everyone understands clearly and completely.
2. **Gather information.** Try to understand the motivations and goals and how other actions might affect them in objective terms. Stay focused on work issues. Is something hampering a decision? Disrupting teamwork? Damaging customer service? Listen with empathy, and see the conflict from both sides. Clarify feelings.
3. **Agree on the problem.** This may seem obvious, but if parties can't agree on the specific issue they won't find a solution.
4. **Brainstorm possible solutions.** Everyone must generate some ideas so they feel like part of the solution.
5. **Agree on the solution.** The conflict may have been resolved by this point, but if not, find a solution that satisfies everyone somewhat. This may require negotiation.

Managing and Leading Others

1.3.7 Knowledge of Methods and Techniques for Managing and Supervising Others

I. Managing and Supervising Methods

Successful TD professionals should be strong leaders and managers in many situations. Sometimes they'll manage their own team, but at times they may guide teams they don't directly manage. Leadership means getting people to understand and believe in the vision and to work with the team to achieve the goals. Managing involves administering and ensuring that any day-to-day tasks are happening as they should. Peter Drucker (2001) stated that "Management is doing things right; leadership is doing the right things." Let's begin with the TD professional's role as a manager.

1.3.7.1 Principles of Management

Organizations require a clear management structure. Efficient and well-intentioned management sets the tone for the rest of the staff, which then filters through and influences the entire organization's culture. Thus, it's helpful to have managers establish an excellent example throughout the organization. Henri Fayol (2016), often acknowledged as the founder of modern management, wrote a classic theory on the principles of management, which identifies 14 principles (Northouse 2019):

- Division of work
- Managerial authority
- Discipline
- Unity of command
- Unity of direction
- Subordination of individual interests
- Remuneration
- Centralization
- Scalar chain (chain of command)
- Order
- Equity
- Stability
- Initiative
- Team spirit [See 3.3.5.3]

1.3.7.2 Management Functions

TD professionals require knowledge about finance, accounting, marketing, systems, procedures, structure, and supervision and control of employees. TD managers need to be skilled in these functions so they can apply them in direct supervisory situations, as well as help guide managers to improved performance.

- **Planning.** Good leaders must be forecasters who can set goals and objectives, develop strategies, and establish priorities, and they must be skilled at timing, sequencing, organizing, and budgeting. Planning involves determining objectives and a course or direction for achieving them. TD managers also set product- or service-related goals, such as deciding to migrate three instructor-led courses to blended learning curriculums in the next year. Part of the planning process is breaking down objectives into subobjectives and action plans.

- **Organizing.** A good leader designs a structure that helps accomplish goals and relates human and nonhuman resources to the organization's tasks. This involves dividing work into jobs, assigning those jobs to people, and delegating authority so that employees can effectively perform their jobs. The keys to successful organizing are teamwork and creating an environment of cooperation and understanding.
- **Coordinating.** Coordinating resources is a constant leadership task. It involves using all activities in the organization to give employees the resources and means they need to accomplish goals.
- **Directing.** Leaders at all levels of the organization are responsible for making the right things happen. The purpose and long-range goals help define what is right for a particular organization. The most pertinent responsibility of a leader, at any level, is providing direction.
- **Controlling.** A leader ensures that everything is performed according to plan, which involves evaluating or assessing situations. For example, TD managers compare the actual performance with ideal or expected outcomes and then try to resolve any meaningful differences to keep their operations aligned with the organization's plan. Some means of control that offer valuable feedback include the budget, quality control programs, and the TD manager's observations. Control of information must be timely; if it's not received in time to take corrective action, the control system is inadequate.

1.3.7.3 Solve Problems

Solving problems is a vital part of a TD professional's role as a manager or supervisor because it gives them methods for identifying processes or interactions that are not functioning smoothly, determining why, and creating a plan of action to improve them. This seven-step process works well for making decisions and solving problems:

1. **Identify the decision or issue.** Is it worth investing time?
2. **Gather information and learn others' interests.** What's relevant to know before making the decision?
3. **Analyze the situation.** What alternatives exist?
4. **Develop options or alternatives.** How many options can be generated? Ask, "What if?" questions.
5. **Evaluate the options.** What criteria will be used to evaluate the options?
6. **Select the preferred option.** What risks and problems could this decision create?
7. **Implement the plan.** Do commitment and resources exist for the plan?

1.3.7.4 Improve Processes

Process improvement is the proactive approach of identifying, analyzing, and improving a function's processes. While there are many approaches and methodologies, the TD professional needs to examine the process and identify which steps need attention.

Begin a process improvement initiative by understanding the four basic components of a process:

- **Inputs.** Process inputs are the individual items that are required to perform the process. Traditionally these are called the four Ms and an E: methods, materials, machines, man, and environment.
- **Controls.** Process controls are the information and physical controls that have been developed for the process. Drawings, specifications, procedures, education and training, performer experience, data, competitors, and information are examples of process controls.

- **Outputs.** Process outputs can be either intended or unintended and are defined by determining the process's desired result. *Typically,* this is determined from customer requirements and specifications. The customer can be either internal or external. Completed purchase orders, finished products, facilitator manuals, and paid employees are examples of process outputs.
- **Resources.** Process resources are the equipment, systems, and human resources required to perform the process. Heating, water, and electrical systems; physical plants; equipment and machinery; and personnel are examples of process resources. Resources are not consumed in the process. They remain available for the next run of the process.

To achieve desired process improvement results, more than one process component typically needs to be addressed. Each process can be an input or control for another process. Drawing flowcharts can help show the interrelationships and potential effects of a change on other processes in the system. Expanding the basic model to include two additional components—suppliers at the beginning of the process and customers at the end of the process—may be necessary to identify root causes (for example, defective supplier materials or undocumented customer expectations). [See 3.5.2.5]

TD professionals should learn to use process improvement tools including but not limited to:
- Process maps or flowcharts create a clearer understanding of the process and identify its beginning and end. [See 3.5.2.5]
- The process improvement model is used to provide a repeatable set of steps. One of the more popular models (which was created by Shewhart and popularized by Deming) is the plan, do, check, act (PDCA) continuous improvement model. All processes, whether six or eight steps, follow these same general principles:
    - **Plan.** Determine the problem to be addressed and the improvement opportunity.
    - **Do.** Implement the solutions, action plans, and process changes.
    - **Check.** Track, analyze, and evaluate the result of the change.
    - **Act.** Based on the analysis from the previous step, reflect and act on the lessons learned.
- Affinity diagrams, interrelationship digraphs, multivoting, Pareto Charts, cause-and-effect diagrams, and the five whys technique are all described in other areas. [See 3.5.5 and 3.5.2]

1.3.7.5 Clarify and Articulate Change

Every TD professional will experience an organizational change in their career. It is critical for them to know how to communicate change and to understand why clear communication is important. Change can have a huge impact on employees and organizations. When it is not communicated clearly and completely, change can increase employee anxiety, which may cause them to resist the change. This ultimately affects performance and job satisfaction and can lead to decreased productivity that will be reflected in the bottom line. If the organization and its leaders fail to clearly communicate the change, employees will begin creating their own change story, which is usually worse than the truth.

On the other hand, when change is communicated clearly and employees are kept informed, the likelihood of getting buy-in and support from employees increases. With clearer understanding comes stronger commitment. Employees will be more willing to embrace change and participate in change requirements.

TD professionals can support organizational change efforts by describing what change will occur and why it is necessary. They can act as sounding boards, clarify misunderstandings, ask for suggestions and support, and follow through on any communication needs.

1.3.7.6 Coach Employee Performance

Coaching is an ongoing process that helps employees build competence and overcome obstacles to improving their performance. It is one of the most effective ways TD professionals can develop others—no matter their role. Coaching helps employees develop faster and be more prepared for advancement opportunities. It is good for the organization because improved employee performance leads to better performance and bottom-line results.

TD professionals will have many opportunities to coach employee performance. For example, they could coach a manager to improve communication or coach an employee to learn new skills or change their behavior. There are many models for coaching for improved employee performance, but most follow a similar process. The model presented here is generic and may require slight adjustments depending on who is being coached and their relationship to the TD professional:

1. Describe the performance-related behavior that needs to change.
2. Ask for an employee response.
3. State the expectations.
4. Obtain agreement.
5. Create a collaborative improvement plan.
6. Get commitment and establish a time for the next meeting.

TD professionals will monitor the behavior and then plan and provide feedback and reinforcement.

As they coach employee performance, TD professionals should remember that connecting employees to the organization can be a critical driver of discretionary effort (Scisco, Biech, and Hallenbeck 2017).

1.3.7.7 Develop Employees

TD professionals should connect with employees to coach them to develop skills and help them establish career goals. Be prepared to discuss developmental opportunities, which include but are not limited to coaching, mentoring, stretch assignments, job rotations, and job shadowing. [See 1.2.6.4, 1.4.3, 2.2, 2.3, 2.6, 2.7, and 3.5]

1.3.8 Skill in Matching, Assigning, and Delegating Work to Others

> **I. Delegation**
>
> In their leadership role, TD professionals must delegate. To do so successfully, they need to identify, develop, and tap employee skills and abilities.

1.3.8.1 Delegating Work and Tasks

Delegation is the assignment of tasks or activities accompanied by the authority to complete them; accountability remains with the delegator. Of its many advantages, delegation is motivational, builds trust, is an effective time management technique, creates a positive work environment, forms a strong team, develops others, and enhances solid management practices.

TD professionals should delegate tasks that provide maximum benefit for employees and the function—for example, the parts of a job that offer challenges and opportunities for another to learn and grow are usually the most motivating. In addition, TD professionals can delegate routine tasks that can be performed more than once, research that is clearly defined, statistical analysis that needs focused effort, temporary and ad hoc assignments for a unique experience, or representation at a meeting. Avoid delegating crises or high-pressure assignments, any situation when success will be difficult, tasks that are in a trial period, or representation when a substitute will not be viewed well. Figure 1.3.8.1-1 provides a decision framework to determine appropriate delegation decisions (Biech 2015).

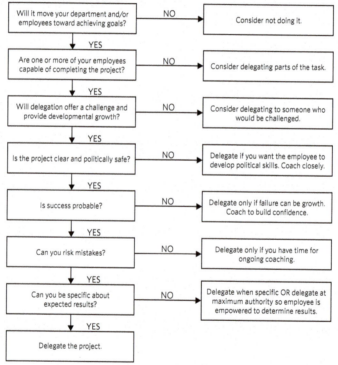

Figure 1.3.8.1-1. Determining Appropriate Delegation Decisions

Source: Biech (2015).

There are four stages in the delegation process: preparation, communication, monitoring, and evaluation.

Preparation Stage

Delegation preparation requires a decision about the desired results, the level of authority that is given, a required timeline, a tracking plan, and the necessary resources. The TD professional will also want to select the right person. Questions they might ask include:
- Who is qualified and available?
- Who can be trained?

- Who will benefit in terms of development?
- Who will be motivated?
- Who will accept the planned authority level?

Communication Stage

When delegating, the TD professional should schedule a meeting time that is convenient for both parties involved. The steps that ensure an effective delegation start are:
- Create a positive climate.
- Gain initial acceptance.
- Deliver the assignment.
- Mutually determine the amount of instruction necessary.
- Work together to prepare an action plan with specific milestones and dates.
- Ensure clear understanding.

Monitoring Stage

Monitoring a delegated project does not mean controlling. It means checking the project at predetermined checkpoints, but not intervening at random. When a TD professional is effectively monitoring, they are providing resources if necessary, answering questions, coaching for improved performance, paving a political path when necessary, and offering support.

Evaluation Stage

A TD professional should evaluate the results of the project and how well the project was delegated. Questions to ask include:
- Were expected results achieved?
- Did the project meet the delegate's developmental goals?
- How skillfully did the manager delegate the project?
- How smooth was the relationship between the manager and the delegate?

Other Considerations

Delegating can be rewarding for everyone involved. Use these tips to build success:
- Delegate the whole project to one person.
- Clearly specify the preferred results.
- Assign the project, not the method.
- Ask employees for their ideas and input.
- Reward results.

1.3.9 Knowledge of Principles and Techniques for Providing Feedback

I. Importance of Feedback

Feedback is the flow of information from one person to another about how useful or successful a process, behavior, or action is. In coaching and all other TD activities, learners need to receive feedback regarding their progress to help with their behavioral change. TD professionals should understand the feedback techniques to help employees and learners see whether they are learning and progressing.

1.3.9.1 Principles of Feedback

Constructive feedback provides useful comments and suggestions that contribute to a positive outcome, a better process, or improved behaviors. It delivers encouragement, support, corrective measures, and direction to the person receiving it.

TD professionals can deliver feedback in a way that employees understand and accept. Feedback must be:

- **Immediate.** Delays will seriously influence the effectiveness of any reward. Thank employees immediately and provide tangible awards as soon as possible.
- **Sincere.** Don't praise employees if it isn't genuine. Insincere praise does more harm than good, both to the employee involved and to others who will discount any praise given in the future.
- **Specific.** Generalizations give employees the idea that the speaker doesn't know what they do. Including the details of their accomplishments lets them know that they are valued and their achievements are known (Weitzel 2007).

1.3.9.2 Using a Process for Feedback

Give constructive feedback and be thoughtful in your approach. There are three steps to the feedback process:

1. Plan.
2. Deliver.
3. Follow up as needed.

1.3.9.3 Guidelines and Techniques for Giving and Receiving Feedback

Feedback supports both professional and personal development. It provides a clear picture of performance and behavior expectations.

Use these guidelines to give feedback that is appreciated:

- Be honest and direct.
- Be specific.
- State observed behaviors.
- Express feelings.
- Time it close to the action.
- Speak for oneself.
- Offer support when appropriate.
- Check for readiness.
- Do not assume intent.
- Check for clarity.
- Specify impact and consequences.
- Offer only what can be acted on.
- Don't exaggerate, use labels, or be judgmental.
- Phrase the issue as a statement.
- Give positive and corrective feedback.

As a manager, supervisor, or TD professional, it is important to give constructive feedback. It is equally important to receive feedback graciously. TD professionals should remember these tips when receiving feedback:

- Have respect for the person offering the feedback.
- Listen actively.
- Ask open-ended questions.
- Continue breathing.
- Ask, "How can I grow from this?"
- Don't become defensive or argumentative.
- Take time to think about the feedback.
- Be willing to change the behavior.

1.3.10 Knowledge of Theories of Leadership

I. Key Leadership Theories

In addition to being an effective manager, a TD professional should be a leader who can inspire a team. They possess or can develop the ability to influence employees and organizational leaders by being a model to others, a developer of employees, and a coach to managers and leaders.

1.3.10.1 Reviewing Common Leadership Theories

Organizations need good leaders to maximize efficiency and achieve their strategic imperatives. Good leaders shape a positive culture and create an engaging workplace that helps attract and retain excellent employees. They know their own strengths and weaknesses and are self-aware and resilient. Good leaders work with others and have excellent interpersonal and communication skills. They also possess employee development skills and can create and actualize a vision.

Leadership theories attempt to explain how and why certain people become leaders. These theories also explain the influence different leadership styles have on organizations. While many theories have emerged, most fall into one of the following categories (Northouse 2019):

- **Great man theories** propose that great leaders are born with the confidence, charisma, and intelligence to be natural-born leaders.
- **Trait theories** suggest that some people have certain qualities that make them better leaders.
- **Behavioral theories** focus on the actions of leaders. In the 1930s, Kurt Lewin argued that there are three types of leaders:
    - *Democratic leaders* allow their team to provide input before they make a decision.
    - *Autocratic leaders* make decisions without consulting their team.
    - *Laissez-faire leaders* allow their team to make decisions without interfering.
- **Contingency theories** suggest that there is no one correct type of leadership and that some leaders focus on particular variables related to the environment.
- **Situational theories** are closely related to contingency theories, when leaders choose the best action based on the situation, the person, and the decision that needs to be made.
- **Participative theories** propose that the ideal style is one that includes other people's input.
- **Management or transactional theories** focus on the role of supervision and group performance. These leadership theories are based on a system of rewards and punishments, and the leader influences others by what they offer in exchange.

- **Relationship or transformational theories** focus on the connections formed between leaders and followers. They inspire and motivate others by helping the team see the higher good of the task. They are also focused on the task but want all team members to fulfill their potential.

1.3.10.2 Contemporary Leadership Theories

"Nobody has really recommended command-and-control leadership for a long time. But no fully formed alternative has emerged either," begins an article in *Harvard Business Review* (Ancona, Backman, and Isaacs 2019). Although it is still too soon for new leadership theories to have emerged in the 21st century, given the changes within organizations relating to structure, the role of technology, and need for agility and innovation, TD professionals should expect to see new leadership approaches and theories soon. The authors of the *HBR* article also highlight that mature companies struggle to balance the need for innovation with the need for discipline.

The article defines three kinds of leaders: entrepreneurial leaders at lower levels, enabling leaders in the middle of an organization, and architecting leaders near the top. Their research—which was done over a 10-year period with a few tenured companies—showed that when companies encouraged employees at all levels to take on leadership roles, they continued to function efficiently and exploited new opportunities quickly (Ancona, Backman, and Isaacs 2019).

Contemporary leadership theories face hurdles and socializing new leadership processes will take time. Many leaders aren't comfortable with what's required. From an organization's perspective, releasing bureaucratic styles increases complexity. However, even with these obstacles, TD professionals should expect to see other leadership types taking shape and gaining traction in this decade. Some examples include:
- **Robert Greenleaf's servant leadership**, which focuses on the development and well-being of people, occurs when leaders share power and put the needs of others ahead of the organization (Blanchard 2010; George 2010).
- **Authentic leadership**, which emphasizes the leader's sincerity and self-awareness, is based on honesty and transparency, values input from employees, and stresses an internal moral perspective (Northouse 2019).
- **Adaptive leadership** focuses on adjusting and thriving in changing environments—it is "purposeful evolution in real time" (Cambridge Leadership Association n.d.).
- **Global leadership** emphasizes the unique requirements of an organization that is based in multiple world-wide regions. It focuses on having profound self-awareness, sensitivity to cultural diversity, professional and personal presence, and the ability to think strategically globally (Rhinesmith 2010; Northouse 2019).

1.3.10.3 Deciding on Leadership for the Situation

TD professionals should spend time determining their own leadership style and whether it is the best for the situation they find themselves in. According to Kouzes and Posner (2017), a leader must model the way, inspire a shared vision, challenge the process, enable others to act, and encourage the heart. Doing so will ensure TD professionals are on their way to building their collaboration and leadership skills.

REFERENCES

Ancona, D., E. Backman, and K. Isaacs. 2019. "Nimble Leadership: Walking the Line Between Creativity and Chaos." *Harvard Business Review*, July-August.

ATD (Association for Talent Development). 2018. *10 Steps to Successful Facilitation*, 2nd ed. Alexandria, VA: ATD Press.

Biech, E. 2015. *New Supervisor Training*. Alexandria, VA: ATD Press.

Blanchard, K. 2010. "Leadership Ethics and Integrity for the 21st Century." Chapter 21 in *The ASTD Leadership Handbook*, edited by E. Biech. Alexandria, VA: ASTD Press.

Cambridge Leadership Association. n.d. "Adaptive Leadership." Cambridge Leadership Associates. cambridge-leadership.com/adaptive-leadership.

Cross, R., R. Rebele, and A. Grant. 2016. "Collaborative Overload." *Harvard Business Review*, January-February.

Cross, R., S. Taylor, and D. Zehner. 2018. "Collaboration Without Burnout." *Harvard Business Review*, July-August.

Drucker, P. 2001. *The Essential Drucker*, 5th ed. New York: HarperCollins.

Fayol, H. 2016. *General and Industrial Management*. Cambridge: Ravenio Books.

George, B. 2010. "The Authentic Leader." Chapter 19 in *The ASTD Leadership Handbook*, edited by E. Biech. Alexandria, VA: ASTD Press.

Hathaway, B. 2014. "Chocolates (and Life?) Sweeter When Shared." *Yale News*, September 9. news.yale.edu/2014/09/09/chocolates-and-life-sweeter-when-shared.

Kouzes, J.M., and B.Z. Posner. 2017. *The Leadership Challenge: How to Make Extraordinary Things Happen in Organizations*, 6th ed. Hoboken, NJ: John Wiley and Sons.

McDermott, L. 2014. "Developing High-Performance Leadership Teams." *TD at Work*. Alexandria, VA: ATD Press.

Northouse, P. 2019. *Leadership Theory and Practice*, 8th ed. Thousand Oaks, CA: SAGE Publishers.

Rhinesmith, S. 2010. "Globally Savvy Leaders." Chapter 25 in *The ASTD Leadership Handbook*, edited by E. Biech. Alexandria, VA: ASTD Press.

Russell, L. 2005. "Leadership Development." *Infoline*. Alexandria, VA: ASTD Press.

Scisco, P., E. Biech, and G. Hallenbeck. 2017. *Compass: Your Guide for Leadership Development and Coaching*. Greensboro, NC: The Center for Creative Leadership.

Weitzel, S. 2007. *Feedback That Works: How to Build and Deliver Your Message*. Hoboken, NJ: John Wiley and Sons.

Zack, D. 2019. *Networking for People Who Hate Networking: A Field Guide for Introverts, the Overwhelmed, and the Underconnected*, 2nd ed. Oakland, CA: Berrett-Koehler.

Recommended Reading

Biech, E., ed. 2010. *The ASTD Leadership Handbook*. Alexandria, VA: ASTD Press.

Johansen, B. 2017. *The New Leadership Literacies: Thriving in a Future of Extreme Disruption and Distributed Everything*. Oakland, CA: Berrett-Koehler.

Zenger, J., and J. Folkman. 2019. *The New Extraordinary Leader: Turning Good Managers Into Great Leaders*. New York: McGraw-Hill.

1.4 CULTURAL AWARENESS & INCLUSION

Cultural awareness and the ability to foster an inclusive work environment are requirements in today's global business climate. Being effective at both means conveying respect for different perspectives, backgrounds, customs, abilities, and behavior norms, and as well as ensuring all employees are respected and involved by leveraging their capabilities, insights, and ideas.

Cultural Awareness

1.4.1 Knowledge of Cultural Differences in the Workplace

> **I. Cultural Differences in the Workplace**
>
> TD professionals should be knowledgeable about the effect cultural differences may have on the workplace. This knowledge increases trust, builds working relationships, improves communication, and increases the likelihood of making more considerate and insightful decisions. TD professionals working in a multinational context should also be aware of past and current national and regional economic, political, and social events that have occurred or are occurring in the areas where they conduct work.

1.4.1.1 Personal Self-Awareness

TD professionals should understand how their unconscious workplace customs, communication styles, and other idiosyncrasies influence their work style and how they may affect others. For example, always opening training sessions with an icebreaker may not relax participants and get them ready to work if their cultural beliefs call for more formal or direct approaches. On the other hand, in countries where people first discuss more personal issues, such as family and one's health, initially focusing on business in a meeting can be viewed negatively.

TD professionals should be aware of how personal differences influence the workplace, as well as the images and feelings they create. Different cultures have different values, attitudes, and beliefs about:
- Communication styles and how to share opinions [See 1.1.4]
- Organizational norms such as roles, rules, and types of interaction
- Business customs including how to show respect and courtesy
- Degree of flexibility
- Personal values and perspectives

- Attire and celebrations
- Family obligations and expectations

1.4.1.2 Building Skills in Cultural Awareness

TD professionals have a dual role in building cultural awareness skills. They should develop and strengthen their own skills as they interact with others; in addition, they should help others develop their skills. They need the capacity to identify ways that individuals differ within and across various cultures. Understanding different people and their respective cultures is critical to reaching a higher level of cultural awareness and building skills for accepting differences. TD professionals should also understand that there are bicultural or multicultural individuals, who may behave differently in different contexts—showing different facets of themselves in a work or public domain than in their personal lives. Achieving cultural awareness requires interacting and communicating with people from other cultures to identify personal obstacles and strengths. The following skills are helpful for TD professionals who seek to accept differences: [See 2.3.2]

- **Knowledge.** Acquire a clear understanding of others by learning about their cultural norms, history, basic language, and religion.
- **Listening.** Take time to listen to the opinions of others; practice active listening and dialogue skills. [See 1.1.2]
- **Empathy.** Ask about, clarify, seek to understand, and relate to the views and perspectives of others toward situations that occur in the workplace. Work toward building understanding and rapport.
- **Self-confidence.** A healthy self-confidence is required to control reactions to personal weaknesses and difficulties. Work to eliminate any difficulties and obstacles to accepting differences.
- **Cultural self-awareness.** Having a clear understanding of what created a current attitude, belief, or value may help people appreciate and accept a different perspective.

1.4.1.3 The Role of Cultural Theories, Models, and Assessments

Cultural theories and models can build greater understanding between people with different cultures in an organization by identifying differences such as in how they view power or competition. Assessments can measure these norms by examining overall organizational culture and exploring individual cultural awareness competency. [See 1.4.1.10]

It may be difficult to fully understand culture from a single theory or model because "researchers have found the influences of national cultures shape strong value systems" (Katz 2005). Therefore, knowing a country's values provides a useful framework for developing global awareness. This framework should be used to describe the general cultural trends of a nation. Organizational consultants Fons Trompenaars and Charles Hampden-Turner (2012) assert, "It is now too simplistic to try to describe the (single) culture of country X without taking into consideration the effects of immigration, the development of multicultural societies, age and generation differences, and where corporate culture is a major variable."

> ## II. Cultural Dynamics
>
> TD professionals understand that cultural dynamics are made up of subtle changes that occur due to the interactions of people, organizations, and their environments. Culture is important to all social groups because it defines each individual and gives them a sense of identity, belonging, and stability in an ever-changing world.

1.4.1.4 Globalization of Culture

Cultural theories describe what distinguishes people from one culture to another. While culture can be understood by comparing beliefs, most approaches are limiting. "Becoming culture savvy," explains author Maureen Rabotin (2011), "means gaining the ability to perceive culture not as a list of differences but as the added value that expands our worldviews and cultural perspectives." By only comparing beliefs, people might mistakenly think they are superior to another group if they become biased by their preset stereotypes based on those limiting comparisons. If given time to interact in a neutral, judgment-free setting, people could better understand their differences and why they are happening. For example, what is commonly accepted etiquette in one culture may be perceived as inappropriate in another.

Edgar Schein (2009) observes that "learning about culture requires effort. You have to enlarge your perception, you have to examine your own thought process, you have to accept that there are other ways to think and do things. But once you have acquired what I would call a 'cultural perception,' what is increasingly labeled as 'cultural intelligence,' you will be amazed at how rewarding it is. Suddenly, the world is much clearer. Anomalies are now explainable, conflicts are more understandable, resistance to change begins to look normal, and most important, your own humility increases. And in that humility, you will find wisdom and increased capacity to work with others whose thoughts and feelings may be very different from yours."

TD professionals often work within the influence of their own culture, other people's cultures, an organization's culture, and possibly other cultures where the organization is located. The differences between these cultures can create conflicts that could impede the organization's ability to execute its global strategic plan. However, if addressed well, this cultural variety can offer new opportunities for collaboration and innovation. TD professionals, particularly those in leadership roles, must appreciate the complexity of culture and the effect that such forces can have on the execution of global strategies and local business practices. Determining how to manage the organization's needs within other cultures can be difficult. In their book *Riding the Waves of Culture*, Trompenaars and Hampden-Turner (2012) discuss "glocalization," saying that "this balance between consistency and adaptation is essential for corporate success."

To be successful within a globalized context, TD professionals should understand the different layers of cultural influence that affect their work. They should ask themselves, "What past and current major economic, political, national, and local events have occurred or are occurring?" Staying informed about global current events and having a basic understanding of national or regional history and geography where an organization conducts business is important.

1.4.1.5 National Culture

Geographic boundaries change over time, and it is not sufficient to try to understand a national culture merely by looking at those boundaries. For that reason, many researchers focus more on societal cultures, which are the larger, yet significant, cultural groupings that exist within a country, such as French- and English-speaking Canadians.

Some researchers even question the degree to which national culture exists in the business world. Data reviewed by Taras, Steel, and Kirkman (2011) shows that while some aspects of different cultures are becoming more alike, others are growing more different. While Western business philosophies may have significantly shaped the international business landscape, the world continues to evolve under new influences. Traditionally, the predominant industrialized countries were the providers and users of highly skilled and educated talent, but that is now shifting to other countries, such as Brazil and India. This shift, according to Towers Watson (2012), has "massive implications, not only for sourcing talent, but also for managing and engaging workforces with multiple generations from an array of different cultures—with many working in nontraditional arrangements." To accommodate these changes—and to start increasing their global mindset—TD professionals will have to learn more about multiple societal cultures and their ways of operating.

1.4.1.6 Subcultures

Members of a subculture have beliefs, values, and behaviors that are distinct from other members of the same society. Everyone belongs to a variety of subcultures—some they are born into and others they join by choice. These groups and the individuals who form them must choose to what degree they want to integrate into or express their differences from the larger society in which they live.

Some subcultures develop from the immigration of new groups into an existing society. "In complex, diverse societies in which people have come from many different parts of the world," people, according to Dennis O'Neil (2013), "often retain much of their original cultural traditions. As a result, they are likely to be part of an identifiable subculture in their new society. Members of each of these subcultures share a common identity, food tradition, dialect or language, and other cultural traits that come from their common ancestral background and experience." For example, India has more than 100 ethnic groups that speak more than 29 major languages, China is made up of many different ethnicities, and Egypt is a blend of many different cultures and religions. "As the cultural differences between members of a subculture and the dominant national culture blur and eventually disappear, the subculture ceases to exist except as a group of people who claim a common ancestry" (O'Neil 2013).

A slight variation on the concept of subculture involves the combination of multiple countries or regions to define a particular shared belief or value. In *Cultural Anthropology*, for example, Ember and Ember (2011) discuss "Western culture (the cultural characteristics of societies in or derived from Europe) or the culture of poverty (the presumed cultural characteristics of poor people the world over)." The influence of these larger, commonly accepted beliefs should also be considered when working in different situations or with diverse groups.

1.4.1.7 Organizational Culture

Organizational culture is the sum of the values, beliefs, practices, and behaviors that contribute to an organization's social and psychological environment. Social psychologist Geert Hofstede believed that while national cultures are based on deeply held values, organizational cultures are more concerned with practices. Organizational cultures are influenced by an organization's industry, its founders' and leaders' personalities, and the types of employees it hires. Organizational cultures define expectations for how people dress (casual or formal), how the organization perceives and values employees (recognition), and how it makes decisions (as a group or by the manager alone; Carpenter and Dunung 2018).

TD professionals should support the evaluation of proposed or existing practices within the overall corporate culture. For example, can the practices be applied uniformly to all areas and all employees in the organization? Have cultural differences been considered? How will these decisions or guidelines be perceived by employees? Although organizations may have characterized their current or desired corporate culture, a written description may or may not exist in the organization. A benefit of documenting organizational culture may be to attract and hire employees. Leading by example is the best way to demonstrate culture, but stating the values that drive the culture helps employees understand why the organization does what it does.

The broadest definition of organizational culture manifests through the day-to-day interactions of employees. Few members of an organization work as individual contributors; most must engage others in a team environment to achieve business results. These teams may be geographically dispersed, and many work virtually. Globalization requires new structures for these teams, such as clearly defining work hours when time zones differ, the preferred communication methods, how roles relate to one another across distances, and new methods for developing trust and creating learning opportunities. Organizations often struggle to balance consistent company values and rules with having the flexibility to adapt to and integrate local influences. [See 3.3.7]

Numerous studies have been conducted to explore the relationship between organizational culture and performance. A study by the Arab Universities for Tourism and Hotels shows that three practices—adaptability, collaboration, and integrity—can establish a strong culture in an organization and create a competitive advantage (Elshaer and Azazz 2016).

1.4.1.8 Environmental Factors

In addition to understanding the company's organizational and national cultures, TD professionals should also explore the influence that logistical factors can have on global business. These factors—for example, political, economic, and legal—affect the organization and its training and development needs. TD professionals who understand these factors and their effects on the organization are better prepared to help their organizations.

An environmental scan is an inventory of the political, economic, sociological, cultural, global, technological, and employment forces that influence the way an organization functions. These factors relate to internal and external influences. The scan involves analyzing the current environment and the trends that may affect it, as well as assessing customer needs and stakeholder expectations. There's no perfect standard for conducting environmental scans, but TD professionals should strive to get as much information as possible on factors that could influence the direction of an organization. Consider these examples:

- **Economic factors** include the effects of employment rates and interest rates on gross domestic product, consumer price index, disposable income, exchange rates, currency devaluation, economic effects on supply chains, and inflation.
- **Political factors** include the level of privatization in governmental services; political trends affecting suppliers, markets, competitors, and customers; and the level of partisanship in governmental bodies.
- **Sociological factors** include worker skills, corporate responsibilities and ethics, population shifts, immigration, migration, age, gender, generational differences, minority groups, and nontraditional labor.
- **Cultural factors** include the effects of national and local cultures on employees and organizations, as well as the effects of corporate cultures on departments, regions, and organizations.
- **Global factors** include the effects of multinational organizations (such as the European Union), that may determine political, social, and economic policies for members. Global influences also include wage comparisons, trade agreements, and other effects of globalization.

1.4 Cultural Awareness & Inclusion

- **Technological factors** include the lack of skills and knowledge or regional complications due to the digital divide.
- **Employment factors** include the effects of recruitment and unions on unemployment, turnover, and relocation, compensation, benefits, and various employee rights. [See 3.8.2]

1.4.1.9 Socioeconomic and Macroeconomic Conditions

Globalization often refers to economic globalization, which is the integration of national economies into the international economy through trade, foreign direct investment, capital flows, migration, and the spread of technology. The changing landscape of competition from other countries often forces organizations to evolve to continue to compete in the market; for example, the global economy and affordable, widely available technology create more competition, forcing organizations to make process improvements, operate with less overhead, and become more efficient.

These factors can significantly affect global businesses. Many organizations will need to develop new knowledge, which means they'll need to conduct extensive research before engaging globally. In addition to doing an environmental scan, organizations must talk with others, engage international consultants, learn about negotiation skills, and develop a plan that includes contingencies.

TD professionals "need to understand regional or country differences regarding the quality and types of skills available, typical turnover rates, employment regulations, costs of labor, healthcare policies and costs, talent mobility policies, cultural norms and values, the strength of the employer brand, and the specific employment value proposition that will attract and retain people" (Gartside and Sloman 2014).

1.4.1.10 Models, Theories, and Assessments Beyond Borders

Beyond global cultural perspectives, several other influential methods and models are used to classify organizational cultures.

1.4.1.10.1 Hofstede's Cultural Dimensions Theory

This theory demonstrates that there are national and regional cultural groups that influence organizational behaviors. Hofstede identifies five dimensions of national culture that determine the values that distinguish countries rather than individuals. These dimensions—power distance, individualism versus collectivism, masculinity versus femininity, uncertainty avoidance, and long-term versus short-term orientation—influence managers who work globally. Hofstede later expanded the original framework to include a sixth dimension—indulgence versus restraint—based on further study and Michael Minkov's research. Hofstede's work is one of the first quantifiable frameworks in the field of cross-cultural communication.

Despite being highly regarded, Hofstede's work is not without criticism. One major critique is that defining a culture using just a few dimensions is oversimplified and does not address the regional differences within a country or cultural lines that have blurred through globalization. In addition, Hofstede's 1973 study does not take into consideration the generation born after 1973 that is influencing culture and society today (UK Essays 2018). Hofstede does not deny that people are affected by regional and other differences, but his and others' research validate the importance of national values to cultural identity.

The six dimensions are best used to compare the cultural attributes of one country or region with another. Here is a more detailed look at each:

- **Power distance.** This dimension expresses the degree to which the less powerful members of a society accept and expect that power is distributed unequally. Countries that score low on this dimension are more likely to prefer more democratic systems of government and challenge inequality.
- **Individualism versus collectivism.** This dimension describes the degree to which people prefer to be integrated within groups. Self-interest is more dominant in individualistic societies, with people focusing more on themselves and their families.
- **Masculinity versus femininity.** Masculine countries are typically more competitive and reflect the more traditionally male values of assertiveness, achievement, and material rewards. Feminine societies prefer cooperation, modesty, caring for others, and a concern for quality of life.
- **Uncertainty avoidance.** This dimension involves a society's level of tolerance for ambiguity when facing new or unknown situations. Countries that avoid uncertainty are more likely to enact numerous rules and regulations to keep unknown situations from occurring.
- **Long-term versus short-term orientation.** Cultures that prefer long-term orientations are more pragmatic and content with waiting on rewards, which is seen in behaviors like saving, adapting, and persisting.
- **Indulgence versus restraint.** This dimension describes countries with indulgent values as those who permit and encourage the gratification of basic needs and desires, whereas restrained countries restrain those needs and desires.

1.4.1.10.2 Trompenaars and Hampden-Turner's Dilemma Theory

Trompenaars and Hampden-Turner (2012) developed the model for dilemma theory in their book *Riding the Waves of Culture*. Their work is based on the concept that humans universally experience problems associated with their relationships to others, time, and the environment. While they argue that these problems are universal, the solutions for dealing with them are not. Their model postulates that cultures approach these universal problems by considering different solutions.

Trompenaars and Hampden-Turner's framework aims to be less dualistic and linear in its approach, which means that having one cultural category does not exclude its opposite. They theorize that the two values influence one another, and if people work together, they can achieve a solution that is better than what one person could achieve independently. The comprehensive model involves much data; however, some critics find the seven dimensions too complicated. A more detailed look at each dimension includes:

- **Universalism versus particularism.** Countries with more universalist preferences view rules, regulations, laws, and obligations as highly important for helping them make decisions. They view rules as more important than the relationships that people have with one another.
- **Individualism versus communitarianism.** Similar to Hofstede's second dimension (individualism versus collectivism), this dimension describes a preference toward individual or group identification. Individualist countries are more oriented around personal responsibility, freedom, and achievement; communitarian countries support group values of safety, support, and loyalty.
- **Specific versus diffuse.** This dimension involves the degree to which people desire separation between their personal and professional lives. In cultures that aspire to a more diffuse outlook, people believe that professional and personal lives should overlap, and that close relationships are important for successful work.

- **Neutral versus emotional.** Neutral cultures prefer to stifle emotions and work from a logical framework in their decision making. Emotional cultures do not avoid expressing emotion and believe it is helpful.
- **Achievement versus ascription.** This dimension describes how people view status. Cultures with an achievement orientation value performance, believing that what a person does defines them and their worth. A value of ascription recognizes power and position for gaining status.
- **Sequential versus synchronous.** This dimension describes the dilemma of how people view and manage time. Sequential cultures value punctuality and planning. Synchronous cultures understand time as more circular and fluid, which results in them being more flexible with planning and follow-through.
- **Internal direction versus outer direction.** An internal direction of control means that people believe they control their environment, and motivation is predominantly internal. People with an external direction of control believe that the environment is more powerful and in control.

1.4.1.10.3 Other Models

Additional researchers have contributed to cultural awareness with other models and assessments:
- **Global Leadership and Organizational Behavior Effectiveness (GLOBE).** Hoppe and Eckert (2012) of the Center for Creative Leadership based GLOBE on the early work of Hofstede and other researchers. Wharton School of Business professor Robert House first envisioned it to answer the question: "How is culture related to societal, organizational, and leader effectiveness?" GLOBE researchers sought to capture how groups actually practiced their beliefs in their current environment. Due to the cultural variations that can exist within countries, the researchers defined their results at the smaller group level of *societies*. GLOBE's nine cultural competencies are assertiveness, future orientation, gender egalitarianism, uncertainty avoidance, power distance, institutional collectivism, in-group collectivism, performance orientation, and humane orientation. Research also found that two characteristics of leaders were valuable in all cultures: charismatic value and team orientation.
- **The Lewis Model of Cross-Cultural Communications** aligns cultural norms to three categories: linear-active, multi-active, and reactive. Like Hofstede, Lewis (2006) states that countries' cultures and behaviors are deeply held and not easily changed. While appreciated for its thoroughness and comprehensibility, some critics state that Lewis's model achieves little beyond communication applications. Critics would prefer that the model address more business contexts.
- **The Organizational Cultural Profile** is a model developed by O'Reilly, Chatman, and Caldwell (1991). It argues that organizational cultures can be distinguished by the values that are reinforced within them. It's a self-reporting tool that distinguishes between eight categories: innovation, support, stability, respect for people, outcome orientation, attention to detail, team orientation, and aggressiveness.
- **Denison's model** asserts that organizational culture can be defined by four dimensions: mission, adaptability, involvement, and consistency (Denison, Haaland, and Goelzer 2004).
- **Deal and Kennedy** (2000) defined organizational culture as "the way things get done around here." They suggest four types of organizational culture: work-hard, play-hard culture; tough-guy macho culture; process culture; and bet-the-company culture.

- **Schein** (1992) states that culture is the most difficult attribute to change and the two key reasons are due to external adaptation and internal integration. He sees culture at three levels: artifacts, espoused values, and basic underlying assumptions.
- **The Organizational Culture Assessment Instrument (OCAI)**, developed by Cameron and Quinn (2011), distinguishes four culture types: clan, adhocracy, market, and hierarchy.
- **Culturally Dynamic Partnership** is based on emerging research by Narayan Gopalkrishnan (2019) that suggests the way society views cultural competence—the awareness, knowledge, skills, and processes for functioning effectively in diverse situations—is not adequate. He argues that current models do not examine the complexity of relationship power nor the dynamic changing nature of cultures. Instead, he offers a collaborative approach, or partnership, to work across cultures in a safe environment for all stakeholders to interact in mutual learning relationships.

1.4.2 Knowledge of Social and Cultural Norms That Influence Decision Making and Behavior

I. Social and Cultural Norms

TD professionals should understand the norms that influence behaviors in organizations.

1.4.2.1 Influence of Social and Cultural Norms on Behaviors

Culture develops and shapes a person's values, assumptions, and behaviors. There are many ways in which people can increase their awareness of cultural norms. TD professionals should start by learning more about themselves before moving on to learning what influences their behaviors.

Self-Awareness

It is important to first acknowledge and understand one's own cultural context and how it influences the perception of others. This step of self-awareness is necessary for all individuals to take, particularly leaders of organizations with a diverse staff who are trying to evaluate policies and practices in a global environment. TD professionals are frequently in critical positions of championing or facilitating cultural self-assessments.

Self-awareness is difficult because most deeply held beliefs and values (of a person or organization) are ingrained and even unconscious. These beliefs can go so deep that they are treated as fact. Without a deliberate approach to increase one's awareness, a person may not realize that they need to question their beliefs or recognize how their beliefs differ from those of others.

Bennett's Developmental Model of Intercultural Sensitivity

Milton Bennett (2004) developed a model—the Developmental Model of Intercultural Sensitivity (DMIS)—to explain why some people improve in their intercultural interactions while others do not. According to Bennett, "as one's experience of cultural difference becomes more complex and sophisticated, one's competence in intercultural relations increases." He identified six stages of increasing cultural sensitivity: denial of difference, defense against difference, minimization of difference, acceptance of difference, adaption to difference, and integration of difference.

Figure 1.4.2.1-1 illustrates Bennett's model. The first three stages are *ethnocentric* (the evaluation of others against one's own set of standards), while the last three stages are *ethnorelative*—the opposite of ethnocentrism—which Bennett explains is "the experience of one's own beliefs and behaviors as just one organization of reality among many viable possibilities."

Figure 1.4.2.1-1. Milton Bennett's DMIS

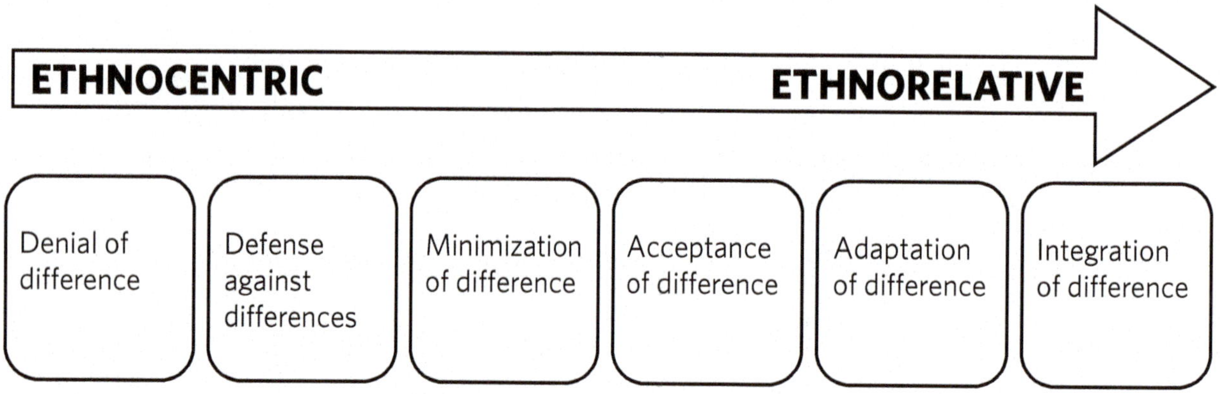

ETHNOCENTRIC → ETHNORELATIVE

| Denial of difference | Defense against differences | Minimization of difference | Acceptance of difference | Adaptation of difference | Integration of difference |

The following is a more detailed look at each stage in Bennett's model:
- **Denial of difference.** People are uninterested in or unaware of cultures other than their own and have little motivation to expand their awareness.
- **Defense against difference.** People might acknowledge cultures outside their own, but they believe that theirs is better, which often results in negative stereotyping and openly expressed disdain of different cultures.
- **Minimization of difference.** At this stage, people acknowledge different outward expressions of culture, such as food and clothing, but do not fully recognize the deeper levels of cultural differences. This increased awareness of differences leads people to be less blatantly stereotypical of other groups. Individuals view themselves as more tolerant and accepting than they actually are.
- **Acceptance of difference.** This is the first stage of sensitivity that comes from an ethnorelative perspective. People recognize that there are multiple cultural views that influence beliefs and behaviors, although they do not always understand them.
- **Adaption to difference.** People are more willing to expand their own worldview through the increased awareness of others' experiences. They can offer empathy and compassion.
- **Integration of difference.** People at this stage can integrate the views of other cultures within their own. They easily move in and out of different cultural perspectives.

1.4.2.2 How Social and Cultural Norms Influence Behaviors and Decisions
Cultural beliefs and behaviors are not innate or genetically inherited; they are learned. Beginning with infancy and continuing throughout adulthood, people learn about how to think and behave by interacting with their environment. *Behaviorism* and *cognitivism* are two explanations of how people acquire and maintain behavior patterns. In addition, *enculturation* is the process by which people gradually acquire the norms and beliefs of their culture. It happens in many ways depending on the context of someone's life, their experiences, and whether they are bicultural or multicultural. TD professionals must not make assumptions about someone based on their ethnicity, language, or other characteristics.

Understanding these processes can help TD professionals be more sensitive to the different contexts in which they work. [See 2.1.1.2]

Values, Beliefs, Preferences, and Attitudes

As young children, people are taught values by parents or other familiar adults. As people age, their experiences grow to include more people they will learn from and different values they may need to choose from. Developing self-awareness of those values can be difficult because they are deeply held and not always articulated. In addition, people do not always act according to what they say that they value—they may go against their stated values in some situations if it appears the reward will be greater for not acting on a stated value, or if another value is more highly prioritized. Values are often realized when someone is challenged to explain or defend why they believe something or act in a certain way, which can be the catalyst that pushes them to stop denying differences and moves them to a more aware stage (as discussed in Bennett's DMIS).

Assumptions and Biases

An *assumption* is something that is accepted as true without proof. Intuition influences how people make assumptions because they use it to attribute meaning to an experience. However, intuition isn't always correct. Because many people only share experiences with others who are similar to them, their viewpoints can go unchallenged. This reinforces their viewpoints as correct, even if they're not. Eventually, their brain will begin to see patterns and look for similarities, which becomes limiting if they engage outside their usual environment (Rabotin 2011).

Bias is prejudice in favor of or against one thing, person, or group compared with another, and it's usually considered to be unfair. People are generally biased in believing that their values are truths that define what is good or bad, right or wrong, fair or unjust. This can be especially true when people are exposed to something that contradicts their beliefs. When assumptions are based on biases, people can feel validated in their actions and deem another culture as wrong. Negative stereotypes may eventually occur as people fit situations into their biased categories. [See 1.2.3]

Behavioral Patterns and Norms

Behaviors are the explicit forms of culture that result from implicit values and assumptions. *Norms* are the "unwritten rules that govern behavior, behavior patterns typical of specific groups, which have distinct identities based on culture, language, ethnicity, race, etc., that separate them from other groups" (Ember and Ember 2011). While individual variations of a behavior may exist, most behaviors fall within culturally accepted limits because cultural consistency is favored within a group. These accepted behaviors play a role in forming cultures.

Semiotics

Semiotics is the study of how meaning is created and communicated to form a culture. A sign is anything that is used for communication—it can be visual and linguistic, and people will give it meaning. For instance, the letters *g-a-t-o* have nothing to do with the furry mammal that purrs—those are simply the letters that were ascribed in the Spanish language to mean that animal. English speakers have ascribed the letters *c-a-t* to the same animal. People do not have to see an actual cat to imagine it or to ascribe characteristics to it.

They learn these signs and internalize meanings so that they can react to them implicitly. The context in which communication happens is as important as the actual language used.

In addition, the same sign can mean different things; for example, in some Western cultures, the action of putting one's thumb up indicates being OK, but if this were to occur while people were diving underwater, it would mean it was time to return to the surface. In some countries the thumbs-up gesture is offensive. The context and the connotation applied by a culture are important parts of meaning.

Gestures and Body Language

The thumbs-up example illustrates the importance of gestures as a form of nonverbal communication. Using specific body movements to express meaning can be as ingrained in a person as their values and beliefs and is easily done without much thought. TD professionals should try not to automatically gesture when in different cultural groups and learn how to recognize through others' expressions if they are offended. For example, pointing at something with a finger—a benign and helpful gesture in some cultures—may be offensive in others. Gestures can illicit strong reactions because they are done automatically and often interpreted immediately, without analysis.

Idiosyncrasies

An *idiosyncrasy* is a behavior that is viewed as peculiar and specific to other people. Such behaviors may be more related to a personality characteristic than cultural influences, but because many cultural behaviors seem peculiar to outsiders, outsiders may label any behavior that they are unaccustomed to as idiosyncratic. Behavior that appears strange can be disconcerting or distracting. TD professionals should be trained to be aware of any idiosyncratic behaviors that they may exhibit, most notably when speaking to groups, such as speaking very loudly or using dramatic hand gestures. Recognizing when one's own culturally accepted behavior may appear strange to those from different cultures can help eliminate problems.

Nuances, Idioms, Expressions, Slang, and Colloquialisms

Language is full of nuance, which can significantly influence meaning. Even in the same language, different cultures may assign special meanings to expressions and terms that cannot be easily understood without significant context. If the language is not one's own, nuances can be even harder to decipher. Because idioms and colloquialisms cannot be translated literally or figuratively, they may appear abstract and nonsensical to the listener. When communicating across cultures, remove culturally specific references, idioms, colloquialisms, slang, and cultural references that may only be understood by a specific group. Whether they're writing or speaking, TD professionals must attempt to remove culturally specific terms when working with groups that are different from their own.

Humor

While every culture has humor, what a culture determines to be funny can vary greatly. Humor can help calm people in new situations; however, if perceived by others as inappropriate, jokes can also be disrespectful. Comedy is often ethnocentric—told from the speaker's perspective. To understand a joke as intended, a listener must understand the context as well. TD professionals should recognize that it is probably better to avoid using humor in a new situation.

Dress Codes

Attire is not merely a covering; it is part of a person's outwardly expressed identity. People are judged by their appearance, and clothes are a major contributor. Clothing can represent culturally bound concepts, such as modesty, conformity, expression, formality, status, or age. Clothing choices may also reflect religious beliefs. In some locations, clothes might also be dictated by weather conditions and the environment. Although less true today, clothing is historically a representation of class standing, serving as a material indication of power differences (Twigg 2009). TD professionals should be aware of the clothing customs and expectations of the countries and organizations in which they work, recognizing that they will be judged by their appearance. Wearing clothes that are more acceptable to different cultures can minimize any distractions brought about by appearance.

Relationship Patterns

Business relationships are often culturally influenced. Cultures that are more collectivist will value different relationships than individualistic cultures. In cultures that deem relationships as significant, people might be expected to engage personally before addressing organizational goals or to maintain relationships beyond a project's or contract's end. TD professionals should not assume what a relationship pattern might look like for a particular culture because their work demands that they form relationships with people from other cultures. They need to understand what business relationships may mean to the people with whom they are working so that they will not be perceived as being too personal or impersonal.

Customs

Customs are established practices of behaviors that have symbolic or emotional meaning. They typically follow a pattern of procedures and are repetitive, often providing guidelines for conduct. Customs can include everyday events, such as greetings or meetings, or special events that occur at regular intervals, such as birthdays, special occasions, or rites of passage like funerals, weddings, or retirements. TD professionals should be aware of the meaning that these activities hold for people and recognize that such meanings cannot simply be forced onto others. Like values, people may not be aware of all that a custom represents until it is challenged or questioned.

Business Norms

Culture can influence business practices in many ways, from how people physically and verbally meet and interact to how an organization approaches selling products or delivering value to customers. These business norms may vary greatly by region or country:

- **Managing employees and projects.** Power distance values may dictate how people are best managed. For projects, collectivist cultures might favor groups, while individualist cultures prefer individual contributions. Cultural understandings of time might result in people doing one project singularly until completion while others might perform multiple projects simultaneously.
- **Propensity for risk taking.** Risk taking can include what information is divulged and to what extent, a willingness to consider new approaches, and the comfort that someone has for tolerating uncertainty. Negotiations between a country that avoids uncertainty and one that prefers group consensus could be more involved than negotiations with countries that are more comfortable with risk.

- **Marketing, sales, and distribution.** Regulations will determine marketing approaches and sales practices in different countries, such as level of comfort with discounts, promotions, product presentation (size, quantity, and packaging), and a willingness to wait for availability.
- **Decision making and negotiating.** Cultural views on negotiating can focus on win-win or win-lose outcomes. Some cultures approach decision making by looking at what's best for individuals but others look at what's best for everyone.
- **Neutral versus emotional.** Neutral cultures prefer to stifle emotions and work from a logical framework when making decisions. Emotional cultures do not avoid expressing emotions and will often do so spontaneously, believing it is acceptable and helpful.

Cross-Cultural Concepts

People observe and evaluate things differently. What is considered acceptable behavior in one culture may be inappropriate in another. Problems arise when people use their meanings to understand other people's reality. With increased self-awareness, people can recognize the influence that their experiences have had on shaping their worldview and can more easily accept this mindset as their own. Becoming self-aware means people must become more:

- Conscious of their own biases and values without favoring them over another's
- Aware of how their own values and biases affect clients from a different cultural group
- Comfortable with these cultural differences
- Aware of any attitudes, beliefs, and behaviors that may be oppressive (Weng 2005)

1.4.3 Knowledge of Methods and Techniques to Foster Cultural Awareness, Encourage Cultural Sensitivity, and Broaden Viewpoints

I. Develop Intercultural Awareness and Competence

TD professionals should have a working knowledge of techniques and best practices to foster cultural awareness in their organizations. Research and practice are in constant evolution, and it is vital to be aware of conceptual changes and emerging trends. TD professionals should focus on their own attitudes and actions, as well as those of others in their organizations.

1.4.3.1 Importance and Relationships

TD professionals should know that promoting cultural awareness is not optional. It helps teams function effectively and make better decisions. Diversity brings fresh ideas and a multicultural perspective to stimulate creativity and broaden messaging to customers. A workplace that values and embraces broad viewpoints can create a corporate identity that attracts and retains a talented workforce.

1.4.3.2 Categories of Cultural Appreciation

TD professionals should foster cultural awareness and encourage individuals to broaden their view at three levels:

- **Personal cultural awareness** relates to self and others.

- **Workplace actions and inclusion** relate to an organization as a whole and the beliefs and values that contribute to the social and psychological environment in which employees interact. Psychological safety is required for open and respectful conversations.
- **A global mindset** is the ability to respectfully observe and learn about traditions and norms from many places throughout the world and determine how to accommodate cultural differences.

1.4.3.3 Promote Cultural Awareness

The workplace has become a blending of culture, which enhances communication and unity in organizations. TD professionals can promote cultural awareness and help others recognize cultural differences. Individuals work better together when they recognize and appreciate these differences. TD professionals can help by:
- Fostering sharing and open discussions about the different cultures in their organization
- Building awareness and knowledge of cultures represented in their organization
- Creating formal learning and assessment opportunities

1.4.3.4 Build Acceptance of Cultural Differences

Once individuals recognize cultural differences, they can build acceptance. Humans share many universal concerns, such as the desire for respect, although the way they handle these concerns may differ. By remembering similarities, individuals can begin to better understand external differences. TD professionals can help by facilitating internal diversity teams and hiring external culture consultants for assistance as they create plans. Building acceptance is a long-term process; it will not be achieved through a short-term promotion. TD professionals support the change by:
- Developing a cultural awareness strategy
- Encouraging cultural sensitivity and empathy to language differences
- Maintaining inclusive activities that are respectful of differences
- Implementing self-awareness tools, dialogues, and education
- Broadening viewpoints through mentorship, partnering, travel, and work in other locations
- Encouraging discovery of cultural differences
- Establishing leadership accountability

Diversity, Equity, and Inclusion

1.4.4 Skill in Adapting and Adjusting Attitude, Perspective, and Behavior to Function Effectively in Diverse Environments or Situations

> **I. Maximizing Workplace Diversity**
>
> TD professionals must be experts at adapting their perspectives and behavior to be effective in diverse situations.

1.4.4.1 Areas of Diversity

TD professionals should focus on how diversity, equity, and inclusion (DEI) can be a natural part of an organization's values and priorities. *Diversity* is a broad term that encompasses race, ethnicity, sexual orientation, faith, age, and other factors that make each person unique. Diversity areas include a focus on gender equality, race awareness, generational differences, personal space, disability awareness, religious accommodations, multiple languages, and diversity of thought. There are multiple factors that TD professionals should recognize that make others different because they come from different circumstances, have a different lifestyle, or are facing unique plights.

Diversity is the presence of differences that may include, but are not limited to, race, gender identity, sexual orientation or attraction, religion, ethnicity, nationality, socioeconomic status, language, physical or mental ability, cognitive processing, and age. Diversity may also include differences in personality, political perspectives, learning requirements, and communications preferences.

Equity promotes justice, impartiality, fairness, and equal access to opportunities, advancement, and participation. It addresses structural inequalities and barriers through fairness in procedures, processes, practices, access, and the distribution of resources.

Equity and equality have two distinct meanings, and TD professionals should understand the difference. Equality implies treating everyone as if their experiences and backgrounds are the same, whereas equity means considering differences in people's experiences and backgrounds when determining what fairness looks like. Equity is the idea of fairness and impartiality, providing opportunities for all employees based on individual needs. Unlike across-the-board equality efforts, equity means acknowledging that different individuals have unique needs and will need support to address those specific needs. Equity usually includes rebalancing existing systems to mitigate disadvantages experienced by marginalized groups.

Inclusion is experienced when environments are created and fostered in which everyone—including members of traditionally underrepresented or marginalized groups—feels respected, welcomed, and that they belong.

Gender Equity

Gender discrimination can exist in the workplace. Specifically, women still experience discrimination in pay and advancement. However, many organizations have become role models of gender equity due to the increasing use of diversity training programs. The importance of gender equality varies by culture, nationality, and country; therefore, TD professionals are well advised to approach such issues on a case-by-case basis.

Gender Identity and Expression

Gender expression, such as pronouns used and gender identity, is an important aspect of diversity in the workplace. Gender identity refers to an individual's own sense of being male, female, both, or anywhere along the spectrum of gender and may be expressed as gender fluid, transgender, or gender neutral (APA 2022). TD professionals should understand the impact of gender identity and expression and ensure talent development activities support both.

Racial Equity

Increasing racial awareness and implementing positive approaches will increase appreciation for diversity, equity, and inclusion. Positive approaches could include establishing mentorship programs for underrepresented groups or an inclusive statement issued by an organization's CEO. Inclusion practices have been shown to lead to better organizational outcomes. Racial awareness is an economically sound choice for organizations because diverse teams lead to better performance organization wide. Diversity also fosters a wider range of employee perspectives, resulting in better decisions, better customer service, innovative product development, and expansion into new markets.

Generational Differences

In today's workplace, TD professionals attract, develop, and engage multiple generations of workers with different work styles and career expectations. Because there are currently multiple generations working side by side, TD professionals need to raise workplace awareness of how different generations perceive and approach work to prevent unnecessary conflicts.

Personal Space

The way people manage personal space varies greatly from culture to culture. People from cultures that use plenty of personal space to reinforce social distance may seem cold and isolating to people from cultures where proximity is the norm. Physical touch can be misinterpreted during intercultural communications, ranging from no touching whatsoever to multiple-kiss greetings and everything in between. *Proxemics* is the relationship of people's positions in space. Researchers state that in a person's brain, the amygdala intercedes to maintain what is believed to be the "right" distance from another human being (Kennedy et al. 2009). TD professionals play a role in increasing awareness of the importance of respecting different ideas of acceptable personal space (for example, in meetings, coaching sessions, and training classes).

Disability Awareness

The Americans With Disabilities Act (ADA) of 1990 and similar legislation in other countries have implications for designing training programs for people with disabilities. In the United States, the ADA prohibits discrimination in employment, public services, transportation, public accommodations, and telecommunications services against people with disabilities. All aspects of employment are covered, including application and selection processes, on-the-job training, wage increases, benefits, and employer-sponsored social activities. Disability awareness has achieved greater accessibility in many domains. It is imperative that TD initiatives align as much as possible to ensure equitable processes and infrastructure.

TD professionals with responsibilities that span multiple countries or regions should stay informed on legal requirements in those places. The United Nations Department of Economic and Social Affairs: Disabilities provides links to legislation in each member country. Also, many multinational organizations, such as the European Union, have guidelines or legal requirements for members or signatories. In many nations, labor unions and public health departments may also have specific binding requirements.

Religious Accommodations

Religion is different from culture. *Religion* is a set of beliefs that go beyond both the self and natural world, defining existence and behavior (Fein 2010). However, religion and culture overlap in some regions. Where religion and government are more clearly separated, it may be easier to view religion as a subculture, but where the two are closely aligned, knowing the religious influences is critical to understanding the lifestyle of a particular community. Some cultures have been changed by religious beliefs, whereas some religions have adapted based on the cultures in which they exist.

1.4 Cultural Awareness & Inclusion

While it's unlikely that TD professionals will directly address religious beliefs in their work, they should be aware of religion's influence in situations when such beliefs can strongly affect organizational culture. Some religious customs or requirements may affect work guidelines, including paid leave for religious rites or celebrations, food choices available in the office, accommodations necessary for religious observance such as time and private space, and even the nature of an organization's holiday celebrations.

Multiple Languages

For face-to-face training and online learning, TD professionals may need to provide instruction and training materials in multiple languages to aid in learning transfer. They may also need to arrange for translators for live instruction and captioning for online learning. Even people who speak the same language may have trouble communicating because of the effort involved in crafting and hearing a message. These communication difficulties are often compounded when the languages are different.

Here are some verbal language factors to consider:

- **Dominant language or lingua franca.** Although an organization may use a single language for business, not every person will feel equally at ease communicating in that language, which may affect an individual's ability to participate fully in an event or have their contributions recognized, ultimately affecting performance appraisals. Offering supplementary language instruction may be necessary.
- **Accent, dialects, and vocabulary.** An *accent* is the way an individual pronounces and articulates words. Whenever possible, TD professionals should provide an instructor who speaks the same language and has a similar accent or dialect as the participants. *Dialect* is the variation from standard language used by members of a specific region or group.
- **Translation.** Translation errors occur frequently and are usually the easiest to detect and correct. The possibility of conflict arises when one party attributes the mistranslation as disrespect for the receiving culture.
- **Nuance errors.** When two parties do not have a similar command of a language, mild distinctions between meanings can lead to misunderstandings. TD professionals must avoid slang, colloquialisms, and, at times, humor.

Neurodiversity Awareness

TD professionals should be prepared to address the needs of neurodiverse populations. *Neurodiversity* is a term that originated in the autism community to explain the normal variations of how individuals' brains learn or think. It describes people who have a broad range of brain functions and behavioral traits such as dyslexia, attention deficit hyperactivity disorder (ADHD), or autism (Lewis 2022). Considerations for a neurodiverse workforce can affect hiring practices, onboarding processes, instructional strategies, and training program delivery. TD professionals' awareness of neurodiversity can influence the organization's approaches in these areas to ensure employees' needs are met.

Diversity of Thought

Diversity of thought refers to employees being hired for their ability to see an issue differently, solve problems differently, or bring a unique thought process to the job. While this may seem like a good idea, the practice has many opponents who think that it should not be viewed at the same level as hiring for demographic diversity because diverse representation will naturally lead to diversity of thought.

The way people think, problem solve, and communicate is shaped by their experiences—the way they learned to think. Therefore, although the concept has both proponents and opponents, TD professionals should consider the specific goal of diversity and have the skills to make space for and respect diverse perspectives that may be based on several dimensions:

- **Personality**—a compilation of character, emotions, temperament, personal values, patterns of thought, strengths and weaknesses, and communication preferences
- **Internal dimensions**—innate characteristics that individuals have no control over, such as neurodiversity and mental ability
- **External dimensions**—aspects of identity individuals have some control over
- **Organizational dimensions**—characteristics related to work or occupational environments
- **Global dimensions**—a broader spectrum of cultural, socioeconomic, and political differences

All these situations are visible diverse areas. However, TD professionals should always be aware of any circumstance that may create a unique situation in which differences prevent compassion, empathy, or understanding.

1.4.4.2 Adaption and Flexibility

The key to functioning effectively in a diverse environment is personal and organizational flexibility. *Personal flexibility* means that an individual can adapt easily to changing circumstances. *Organizational flexibility* means the organization is agile.

Characteristics of a flexible individual include:
- Good listener
- Willing to learn
- Confident
- Resourceful
- Disciplined
- Works collaboratively
- Open to feedback
- Resilient
- Adapts to change easily

Characteristics of a flexible organization include (Biech 2014):
- Employee-friendly workplace and in touch with employee satisfaction
- Flexible benefits, including hours, education benefits, and gradual retirement
- Rapid decision-making and learning cycles
- Next-generation enabling technology
- Culture of creativity, risk taking, and innovation
- Results tailored for clients and customers
- Ability to recover and learn quickly from mistakes
- Willingness to evolve due to external pressures
- Excellent communication
- Focus on improving engagement to benefit employees
- Support for various work environments including in-person, remote, and hybrid

1.4.5 Knowledge of Approaches to Encourage and Promote Workplace Diversity, Equity, and Inclusion

> **I. Promoting Workplace Diversity, Equity, and Inclusion**
>
> TD professionals should be prepared to lead, support, and leverage any organizational strategy that promotes workplace diversity, equity, and inclusion in their organizations.

1.4.5.1 Promote the Value of Diversity, Equity, and Inclusion

A diverse, equitable, and inclusive workforce fosters a more creative and innovative work environment. It attracts talent and avoids employee turnover costs. As organizations adapt to the changing world, diversity helps them increase their competitiveness. TD professionals should promote these advantages to the workforce by implementing specific procedures, including:

- Helping employees acknowledge differences
- Communicating the importance and value of DEI through various communication vehicles
- Creating a business case that examines the cost and the return on investment (ROI), as well as the cost of not promoting the value of DEI
- Asking questions and opening conversations about DEI
- Evaluating recruiting and hiring processes to better attract and retain a diverse workforce
- Assessing practices, policies, and procedures used by the organization to promote equity

1.4.5.2 Create a Shared Sense of Responsibility and Accountability

Effective leaders will achieve buy-in before launching any new strategy. By creating a shared sense of responsibility and clarifying what constitutes accountability for promoting workplace DEI, it becomes everyone's obligation. This is increasingly important as more organizations implement ESG (environmental, social, and governance) and CSR (corporate social responsibility) teams or departments to ensure accountability related to an organization's broader impact. TD professionals have several approaches available to them, including:

- Helping employees identify specific steps they can take toward DEI accountability
- Providing a clear understanding about why DEI is being emphasized
- Ensuring everyone is speaking the same language with clear definitions of all terms
- Encouraging others to get involved to identify targeted solutions

1.4.5.3 Consider the Benefits of DEI Training

DEI training—sometimes called bias, unconscious bias, or sensitivity training—creates value by raising awareness about specific communication or behavioral problems that affect TD and organizational outcomes. Training events may also highlight issues that are overlooked by employees. DEI training can heighten an employee's self-awareness of bias and empathy about others' experiences. To be successful, DEI training programs should be designed specifically for the organization, facilitated by an outside facilitator, and attended by everyone, including senior leaders. Training topics and activities may include:

- Appreciating differences
- Understanding bias
- Using inclusive language and communication

- Any specific barriers or obstacles the organization faces
- Role plays to practice specific skills
- Case studies that highlight acceptable conduct
- Sensitive topics that are difficult to discuss
- Research related to the business case for DEI
- Measuring the ROI of DEI training

Even after learning and participating in training programs on this topic, it is possible that TD professionals or participants may overestimate their knowledge of specific cultures or subcultures, potentially considering themselves competent in the area. TD professionals should recognize the value of cultural humility to understand themselves and others.

1.4.5.4 Provide Mentors, Sponsors, and Allies

Mentoring employees from underrepresented populations ensures their development and success within an organization. The benefit of having the support of someone who knows the organization can be invaluable for the employee and the organization. All mentoring programs require structure—and that is particularly true for a diversity mentoring program. Sponsorship goes a step further than mentorship by fostering trusted relationships between underrepresented populations and an organization's senior leaders, who leverage their power to support their proteges.

TD professionals should develop a plan for mentoring and sponsoring diverse candidates with goals, such as:
- Providing training and support for all involved, including the mentor or sponsor and the employee
- Ensuring funding and staffing
- Establishing goals that align with the organization's DEI strategy
- Rallying committed knowledgeable staff as mentors and sponsors
- Making sure leadership is involved
- Ensuring quality interactions (Labin 2017)

Allyship refers to how an organization leverages its resources, access, voice, and privilege to fight injustice and promote equity in the workplace. Anyone can be an ally by leveraging their voice or resources for another person. Like mentorship and sponsorship, allyship is necessary for the growth, development, and progression of talent within marginalized populations. TD professionals should be allies and role models for others in their organizations.

1.4.5.5 DEI Assessments

TD professionals should use tools that are validated for general assessment or learning-solution purposes. Assessments focus on two targets: the organization and individuals. One commonly accepted tool for organizations is the Global Diversity Equity Inclusion Benchmarks (GDEIB), which provides ample data for developing a comprehensive DEI strategy. The GDEIB is a free resource developed and maintained by a group of DEI experts. Organizational assessments can highlight a company's future educational needs and provide input for strategies.

In addition to conducting an organizational assessment, employees may be encouraged to complete a DEI self-assessment, which is an early step in understanding how personal biases, prejudices, and stereotypes influence perceptions and behaviors. People need to make an intentional effort to examine and expose their deeply held values of what is good, right, and preferred because they're often unknown to others as well as themselves. Regardless of the tool used, an assessment should gather information about knowledge, understanding, acceptance, and behavior.

1.4.5.6 Valuing Diversity

TD professionals should demonstrate how to value diversity, equity, and inclusion, while also coaching others to value diversity and demonstrate inclusion. For example, they can:

- Move team members around to increase development, provide new opportunities, and encourage diversity of work units.
- Celebrate differences to help build awareness of other cultures and groups.
- Emphasize that differences combine to create unique opportunities, and that the whole is worth more than the sum of its parts.
- Promote psychological safety to allow people to make comments about what makes them feel valued.
- Develop diversity mentorship and sponsorship programs.
- Establish transparent leadership and organizational accountability.
- Acknowledge and celebrate the holidays of different cultures.

1.4.5.7 Workplace Inclusion Roles

TD professionals should be prepared to work with various DEI roles and committees. An organization may have a diversity manager or perhaps a chief diversity officer. Both are responsible for fostering, promoting, and monitoring an open and inclusive environment that encourages and supports diversity. Some DEI-focused committees within organizations may be led by organizational leaders while others, such as employee resource groups (ERGs) may be employee-led. Designated DEI leaders in an organization can have responsibilities that span the organization to integrate the DEI strategy.

Responsibilities of diversity managers or chief diversity officers may include, but are not limited to:

- Evaluating the organization's DEI efforts and strategy
- Improving access to development and career opportunities
- Enhancing internal and external relationships
- Increasing the visibility of the organization's diversity strategy
- Providing expertise on issues of diversity, access, and equity
- Increasing the success rate of employees from underrepresented groups
- Recruiting and expanding the number of diverse job applicants and promotions

A workplace inclusion committee can also be helpful when establishing long-term processes and practices. It can help senior leaders understand the nuances associated with diversity and workplace inclusion and nudge them toward doing what's necessary. TD professionals should help the organization see the value of a planned recruitment for committee members. Including skilled employees who are respected and represent a broad organizational perspective will create a more effective team. In addition, the committee must have leadership support, a charter, goals, a budget, specified term lengths, and a plan for communication. Two tasks the committee might undertake are to gather information and to identify cultural influences:

- **Gathering information.** TD professionals use a variety of tools to gather information about culture, equity, inclusion, and diversity, and then analyze the data, which requires objectivity. Data might include information on diverse applicant volume, hiring volume, and salary comparisons. To avoid biased results, use methods and approaches such as trained observers or evaluators with proper instruments. Using multiple data sources as well as multiple observers or evaluators and checklists to aid in observation can also safeguard against observation bias. [See 2.8.6.2]
- **Identifying cultural influences.** Cultural values affect business outcomes, and problems can occur when there is a disparity between the two. TD professionals can use a culture audit or diversity climate survey to analyze an organization's assumptions, norms, philosophy, and values and determine whether they hinder or support its vision and mission.

1.4.6 Skill in Integrating DEI Principles in TD Strategies and Initiatives

I. Workplace Diversity, Equity, and Inclusion Planning
TD professionals should be skilled at integrating DEI into the workplace and business processes.

1.4.6.1 Talent Development's Role in Diversity and Inclusion

TD professionals should acknowledge, accept, and embrace DEI to increase the likelihood that their decisions and their organization's decisions for influencing a DEI culture will be effective. They should make a concerted effort to learn about DEI and then ensure that their organizations have a clear rationale for integrating it into their culture. They should continue by making sure DEI efforts are supported with processes and procedures throughout the organization.

A variety of approaches can maximize workplace diversity. Organizations must understand the various aspects of diversity and put appropriate methods in place to meet strategic initiatives for a diverse population. Diversity strategy should focus on each aspect that makes an individual unique. Changes in an organization's strategic imperative may create implications for reaching out to workers from various backgrounds, generations, and different points of view.

Because more organizations are competing in the global market, TD professionals may need to target global diversity and consider it when creating career planning and talent management programs. This also requires skills in cross-cultural communication and necessitates valuing different cultural models. TD professionals working in multinational contexts should have a clear understanding of DEI policy and law in other locations to integrate these requirements into a single set of company policies. They should also be prepared to assist in identifying appropriate ways to measure their organization's progress in its diversity strategy and its commitment to DEI.

Rationale for Integrating DEI
TD professionals should begin by ensuring that their organizations understand the rationale for integrating DEI into the company culture. Many organizations that lack formal policies about diversity—even if their workforce reflects a racially and culturally diversified population—face potential discrimination lawsuits or complaints from vulnerable populations, which are identified by US federal regulations as more susceptible

to coercion or undue influence such as minors, prisoners, pregnant women, and those who are educationally or economically disadvantaged. Documented policies and procedures are important to support training initiatives and create accountability. At minimum, every organization needs to evaluate its DEI approach and develop a strategy. The best approach is to build a strong case for inclusive practices:

- The organization attracts and retains the best and brightest candidates from a wide variety of experiences, backgrounds, and cultures.
- Due to changing demographics, customer diversity increases market share and creates a loyal, satisfied customer base.
- An organization's customers or members may desire that the companies they do business with demonstrate a commitment to DEI.
- Employees learn to communicate with and truly understand one another, which enables them to be more innovative, responsive, and productive.
- Candidate pools expand, and objective criteria for hiring and promotion increase fairness and opportunity.
- Employee engagement increases, which leads to increased employee retention.
- Diversity fosters a wide range of perspectives, resulting in better organizational decisions. A broader perspective leads to better customer service, innovative product development, and expansion into new markets.
- An inclusive culture develops flexible leaders who think more broadly and are better prepared for a global economy.
- Overall organizational performance improves when people are encouraged to overcome cultural misunderstandings and appreciate differences.
- Employees feel more valued and tend to be more productive.

TD professionals may be involved in helping their organizations identify a rationale for a stronger DEI culture. They should be able to explain how their organization's culture is socially constructed and changed through conversations. *Culture* involves a shared view of the world and value system. It includes how employees talk to one another, their tolerance for uncertainty, their willingness to take risks, and their comfort level in interacting with leaders and peers in an environment sustained by psychological safety. These and other factors have a direct influence on learning and development preferences and how people interact on the job.

Talent Development's Involvement in DEI

TD professionals should be prepared to be involved in many ways as they support their organizations to improve diversity, equity, and inclusion. Once the organization has a clear understanding of its rationale for improving DEI aspects of its culture, TD professionals should review the approaches to encourage and promote workplace DEI and be prepared to assist. [See 1.4.5]

TD professionals may find themselves addressing many aspects of DEI. They must constantly work on enhancing their own cultural awareness, acceptance, and adaptation before trying to determine what others should or might do. Leading by example is vital to prepare for taking on any of these possible roles:

- Developing their organization's DEI strategy [See 1.4.6.2]
- Leading the implementation of their organization's DEI strategy
- Ensuring that the diversity strategy incorporates all locations

- Creating a business case for diversity
- Identifying diversity competencies
- Designing and supporting a diversity recruitment plan
- Designing or leading an equity audit or analysis
- Aligning training and development opportunities to ensure they promote the organization's DEI values, represent different cultures, and are accessible to all
- Providing team building or other exercises to teams and groups to overcome negative stereotypes, develop skills, or improve communication
- Giving DEI support to supervisors and managers who have employees from underrepresented groups
- Establishing a mentorship and sponsorship program for employees from underrepresented groups
- Designing an inclusive succession planning process
- Procuring and administering organizational DEI assessments or self-assessments
- Increasing the rate of success for underrepresented groups throughout the organization
- Proposing suggestions for leveraging employee diversity
- Providing input about how DEI supports the organization's brand and visibility
- Expanding the diversity strategy to customers and suppliers
- Measuring and assessing the effectiveness of the organization's DEI strategies
- Advising leaders whether the DEI strategy has achieved the desired goals
- Helping leaders understand their responsibility to support DEI
- Determining measures of accountability
- Contributing DEI input and perspective for the organization's employer brand and talent acquisition strategy value propositions

Including and Engaging Remote Employees

TD professionals should pay particular attention to identifying ways to champion DEI ideals in a virtual environment, which may seem more challenging when promoting inclusion, but it doesn't have to be difficult. TD professionals can take advantage of a remote setting to build inclusion by adopting some of these approaches:

- Ensure that leaders or facilitators ask about employees' needs, acknowledge them, and address them, when possible, in a virtual setting. For example, include a check-in at the beginning and end of a call or learning session.
- Demonstrate understanding of personal situations due to remote settings, such as limited space or unusual background noise, and ask employees to share any challenges they are facing.
- Help leaders or facilitators adopt a learning stance by admitting to what they don't know or asking questions before stating their own opinions. This is especially critical in a virtual setting when it is more difficult to read body language.
- Model how to be accepting of others, for example by adapting to their communication styles. [See 1.1.4.2]
- Encourage employees to find time to incorporate team building and collaboration by scheduling regular remote sessions that encourage team members to interact with and learn more about each other.
- If working extensively with people from another culture, learn as much as possible about their culture. Understanding the unique differences between the two (or more) groups will help establish successful virtual relationships.

1.4 Cultural Awareness & Inclusion

An organization's culture can enable or hinder DEI success. TD professionals can play a role in the process by aligning the DEI strategy and implementing supporting tactics to build and reinforce the desired culture. They should remember that conversations can change the organization's culture.

1.4.6.2 Developing an Equity Strategy

Equity promotes fairness in the workplace by creating a level playing field for all employees (Biech 2022). An equity strategy could be part of the DEI strategy or a separate initiative. In either case, the focus should include opportunities for career advancement, fair compensation, recognition for work, and an equal voice in decisions that affect employees' work. TD professionals should be prepared to lead their organization's efforts to evaluate equity, address inequities, and integrate equity throughout the organization (Bersin 2021). An equity strategy evaluates practices including hiring, promoting, compensation, and how decisions are made by examining data and current policies.

TD professionals may be responsible for or supporting strategic activities such as:
- Defining what *fair* and *just* practices and policies are in their organizations
- Evaluating practices, policies, and processes for fairness
- Developing impartial processes related to hiring, promotions, and organizational decision-making practices
- Facilitating the creation of new policies and procedures
- Supporting leadership in gaining understanding of the impact of equity
- Defining measures of organizational accountability for equity

1.4.6.3 Implementing an Equity Strategy

Once an equity strategy is in place, TD professionals are likely to be called upon to help their organizations implement it as a part of the overall DEI strategy. In this capacity, a TD professional may be responsible for leading or contributing to any of these tasks:
- Developing an action plan
- Defining measurable goals
- Gathering and analyzing relevant data from multiple sources
- Recruiting employees and leaders to participate in working groups
- Documenting DEI efforts and activities to serve as an employee reference
- Evaluating processes, practices, and policies
- Recommending changes to processes, practices, and policies

1.4.6.4 Developing an Inclusion Strategy

A workplace DEI strategy is a written policy that expresses the belief that DEI must become an essential part of the organization's culture and be integrated into the organizational infrastructure, policies, practices, and procedures. TD professionals are often tapped to lead the development of the entire DEI strategy or, at times, a separate inclusion strategy. The organization's commitment is demonstrated by establishing consistent policies, organizational systems, measurable goals, and a pledge to being held accountable for the strategy's success. There must be buy-in from leadership—a firm, transparent, and demonstrated conviction that DEI is tied to the organization's goals, objectives, and bottom line. A workplace inclusion strategy should include objectives for three areas:

- **Customers**—including goals such as expanding into the global marketplace.
- **Employees**—including goals that will benefit the workforce, such as increasing the retention rates of women or promoting more people from various racial and ethnic backgrounds into leadership positions.
- **Community**—including goals that represent the organization, its community, and diversity all at once, such as donating time and financial resources to worthy causes.

The plan also should include a mission, a vision, and values to help achieve a more inclusive workplace:
- **Vision.** The vision statement sets the desired DEI goal and defines the future. It incites action and generates commitment to achieving the goals. The future of work is strongly connected to technology and the progression of digital transformation, as well as artificial intelligence (AI). It is important to be mindful of potential bias in algorithms and data as goals are established.
- **Mission.** A mission statement must be clear and linked to the organization's identity. It should be motivating and encouraging. Even though it may not seem immediately apparent, all constituents can benefit from a commitment to workplace diversity, equity, and inclusion.
- **Values.** Values reflect the organization's deepest beliefs. They are nonnegotiable and are how the organization identifies and differentiates itself from others. Values should be embodied in specific behaviors that the organization identifies and institutionalizes at all levels. A leader must exemplify the inclusion values of the workplace (Silveira and Walters 2017).

1.4.6.5 Implementing an Inclusion Strategy

TD professionals may be called upon to help the organization implement the inclusion strategy as part of the overall DEI strategy. They may be required to assist, lead, or facilitate others to complete any of these implementation steps:
- Establishing an action plan
- Identifying measures of success and impact
- Assembling, facilitating, or coordinating working groups
- Encouraging involvement
- Setting measurable goals
- Launching mentoring options to support the inclusion strategy
- Identifying best practices that will form an integral part of the organization's policies and procedures
- Evaluating the strategy's success

1.4.6.6 Facilitating Inclusion in the Workplace

TD professionals may need to facilitate the inclusion of new cultural ideas or marginalized or underrepresented groups in the training analysis and planning processes for employee development programs. During this process, the HR function and top management may develop a strategy to interview and hire candidates from different backgrounds to broaden diversity in the organization. In addition to attracting a diverse workforce, facilitating inclusion may involve implementing culture change initiatives and maximizing learning and development:
- **Attracting a diverse workforce.** TD professionals need a corporate structure that is supportive of varying backgrounds and predispositions to attract a diverse workforce. Internal resources with the ability to identify a variety of cultures to attract to the organization are also required. Depending

on the corporate structure, the TD function may work with HR to identify the best sources to find the right people to fill the roles. TD professionals should think ahead to determine whether any additions or changes need to be incorporated in the onboarding process to ensure all new employees feel welcomed and included.

- **Implementing culture change initiatives.** To ensure all employees, especially those from diverse populations, feel invited to fully participate in the organization, TD professionals may be called upon to support culture change efforts. These initiatives may include creating a more psychologically safe work environment and a commitment to ensuring underrepresented groups are involved in decision making.
- **Maximizing learning and development.** TD professionals need to consider all cultural concepts and differences when they design and deliver training programs or interact with the workforce. They should examine the design of all training and development programs, communication efforts, and products and services for a DEI focus, considering accessibility, gender neutral language, appropriate examples, and other aspects of inclusion. Delivery should occur in a psychologically safe atmosphere with jargon-free language and appropriate dress. Attitudes about age, personal space, work, time, and reactions to authority should be respected.

1.4.6.7 Learning Ethical Standards and Legal Issues

TD professionals should follow strict ethical standards regarding the confidentiality of employee information, especially related to counseling and the administration of psychological and personality tests. They should be aware of the credentials required to administer psychological assessments and ensure that they are administered by certified professionals. Understanding the legal ramifications of all aspects of the talent management cycle ensures compliance with applicable laws and regulations.

TD professionals working in multinational contexts will need to be knowledgeable about current standards, regulations, legislation, and guidelines about equal opportunities, disabilities, hiring practices and testing, and selecting learners in each nation in which their organization operates. In addition, countries belonging to groups of nations, such as the European Union and the Association of Southeast Asian Nations (ASEAN), may also have binding agreements with those groups. Therefore, TD professionals must be aware of current legal requirements affecting all regions in which their organization conducts business. TD professionals may rely on their colleagues in other regions for information, but it is their responsibility to ask, update their information, and make sure any decisions or instructions consider all appropriate factors.

Equal Opportunity

In the United States, regulations governing the hiring, promotion, and discharge of employees are administered by the Equal Employment Opportunity Commission (EEOC). These regulations also cover some aspects of training. For example, the EEOC's Uniform Guidelines on Employee Selection Procedures "apply to tests and other selection procedures which are used as a basis for any employment decision" as well as in "hiring, promotion, demotion," and other employment decisions. Additionally, the guidelines say that "other selection decisions, such as selection for training or transfer, may be considered employment decisions if they lead to any of the decisions listed above." TD professionals should know their country's regulations. [See 1.6.5.2]

Disabilities

To be considered a qualified person with a disability in the United States, a job applicant or employee must be able to perform the essential functions of a job. Employers must reasonably accommodate known mental illnesses or physical disabilities unless they can demonstrate undue hardship as regulated by the Americans With Disabilities Act (ADA). However, the ADA does not guarantee an individual with a disability the right to a job they've applied to. An employer is not required to give preference to an applicant with a disability over another applicant but must provide reasonable accommodations to enable them to perform the essential functions of their job. [See 1.6.4.6]

TD professionals should be aware that the ADA requires that effective communication and training not exclude people with disabilities. This may mean providing written materials, sign language interpreters, close-captioned videos, or recorded text or special reading software for people who need them. TD professionals in other countries should check their country's regulations. In some countries, there are even mandates on how much of an organization's workforce must include people with disabilities.

TD professionals may also be called upon to help ensure that neurodiverse employees—and any other employees who require accommodations—receive necessary accommodations to access learning.

Hiring Practices and Testing

Hiring a new employee or promoting an experienced one may cause issues because the stakes are high and no one wants to make the wrong decision. There are many indicators and tests that TD professionals can use to lessen issues during the hiring and career planning processes. They can also use personality or psychological tests for coaching and employee development tools. In fact, many staffing organizations use these tools as a secondary evaluation after conducting a thorough interview. In all situations (and especially in the US), however, be aware of the possible legal or ethical guidelines that dictate the use of tests in hiring. [See 1.6.5.2]

Selecting Learners

The selection of individuals to participate in TD programs is another important legal issue that talent development professionals should know about. They should determine whether their country provides any legal requirements for training prior to job entry, selecting employees to attend training programs, or assigning jobs based on performance in the training program. [See 1.6.5.3]

REFERENCES

American Psychological Association (APA). 2023. "Understanding Transgender People, Gender Identity, and Gender Expression." APA, March 9. apa.org/topics/lgbtq/transgender-people-gender-identity-gender-expression.

Bennett, M.J. 2004. "Becoming Interculturally Competent." In *Toward Multiculturalism: A Reader in Multicultural Education*, 2nd ed., edited by J. Wurzel, 62–77. Newton, MA: Intercultural Resource Corporation.

Bersin, J. 2021. "Elevating Equity and Diversity: The Challenge of the Decade." Josh Bersin blog, February 11. joshbersin.com/2021/02/elevating-equity-and-diversity-the-challenge-of-the-decade.

Biech, E., ed. 2014. *ASTD Handbook: The Definitive Reference for Training and Development*, 2nd ed. Alexandria, VA: ASTD Press.

Biech, E., ed. 2022. *ATD's Handbook for Training and Talent Development*, 3rd ed. Alexandria, VA: ATD Press.

Cameron, K., and R. Quinn. 2011. *Diagnosing and Changing Organizational Culture: Based on the Competing Values Framework*. Hoboken, NJ: John Wiley and Sons.

Carpenter, M., and S.P. Dunung. 2018. *International Business: Opportunities and Challenges in a Flattening World*. Boston: FlatWorld.

Deal, T., and A. Kennedy. 2000. *Corporate Cultures: The Rites and Rituals of Corporate Life, Harmondsworth*. New York: Perseus.

Denison, D., S. Haaland, and P. Goelzer. 2004. "Corporate Culture and Organizational Effectiveness: Is Asia Different From the Rest of the World?" *Organizational Dynamics* 33:98–109.

Ember, C.R., and M.R. Ember. 2011. "Culture and Culture Change." In *Cultural Anthropology*, edited by C.R. Ember and M.R. Ember, 14–39. Upper Saddle River, NJ: Pearson Higher Education.

Elshaer, I.A., and A.S. Azazz. 2016. "An Empirical Study of Hotels and Tour Operators in Egypt." *Journal of Association of Arab Universities for Tourism and Hospitality* 13(2): 65–78. jaauth.journals.ekb.eg/article_49743_e59c120b6087853fc7c85960a8e4f5d0.pdf

Fein, J. 2010. *Module 10: Culture and Religion for a Sustainable Future*. Paris: United Nations Educational, Scientific, and Cultural Organization.

Gartside, D., and C. Sloman. 2014. "Adapting to a Workforce Without Borders." *T+D*, April.

Goldsmith, M., C.L. Greenberg, A. Robertson, and M. Hu-Chan. 2003. *Global Leadership: The Next Generation*. Upper Saddle River, NJ: Pearson Education.

Gopalkrishnan, N. 2019. "Cultural Competence and Beyond: Working Across Cultures in Culturally Dynamic Partnerships." *The International Journal of Community and Social Development* 1(1): 28–41.

Hofstede, G.H. 2001. *Culture's Consequences: Comparing Values, Behaviors, Institutions, and Organizations Across Nations*. Thousand Oaks, CA: Sage Publications.

Hofstede, G., G. Hofstede, and M. Minkov. 2010. *Cultures and Organizations: Software of the Mind*. New York: McGraw-Hill.

Hoppe, M.H., and R. Eckert. 2012. *Leader Effectiveness and Culture: The GLOBE Study*. Greensboro, NC: Center for Creative Leadership.

Katz, L. 2005. "Organizational Versus National Culture." Leadership Crossroads. leadershipcrossroads.com/mat/Organizational%20vs%20National%20Culture.pdf.

Kennedy, D., J. Gläscher, J. Tyszka, and R. Adolphs. 2009. "Personal Space Regulation by the Human Amygdala." *Nature Neuroscience* 12(10): 1226–1227.

Labin, J. 2017. *Mentoring Programs That Work*. Alexandria, VA: ATD Press.

Lewis, J. 2022. "Five Ways Workplaces Can Become More Neuro-Inclusive, According to Neurodiversity Advocates." NeuroLeadership Institute, April 28. neuroleadership.com/your-brain-at-work/five-ways-for-neuro-inclusivity.

Lewis, R.D. 2006. *When Cultures Collide: Leading Across Cultures*, 3rd ed. Boston: Nicholas Brealey Publishing.

Lubin, G. 2013. "The Lewis Model Explains Everything in the World." *Business Insider*, September 6.

Luthans, F., and J. Doh. 2015. *International Management, Culture, Strategy and Behavior*, 9th ed. New York: McGraw-Hill.

Meister, J.C., and K. Willyerd. 2010. *The 2020 Workplace*. New York: Harper Business.

Minkov, M. 2012. *Cross-Cultural Analysis: The Science and Art of Comparing the World's Modern Societies and Their Cultures*. Thousand Oaks, CA: SAGE Publishers.

O'Neil, D. 2013. "Language and Culture: An Introduction to Human Communication." palomar.edu/anthro/language/default.htm.

O'Mara, J., and A. Richter. 2011. *Global Diversity and Inclusion Benchmarks: Standards for Organizations Around the World*. The Diversity Collegium. diversitycollegium.org/GDIB.pdf.

O'Mara, J. and A. Richter. 2017. *Global Diversity, Equity, and Inclusion Benchmarks Assessment*. The Diversity Collegium. centreforglobalinclusion.org/wp-content/uploads/2017/07/GDIB_-AssessmentChecklist_100217.pdf.

O'Reilly, C., J. Chatman, and D. Caldwell. 1991. "People and Organizational Culture: A Profile Comparison Approach to Assessing Person-Organization Fit." *The Academy of Management Journal* 34(3): 487–516.

Rabotin, M. 2011. *Culture Savvy: Working and Collaborating Across the Globe*. Alexandria, VA: ASTD Press.

Schein, E. 1992. *Organizational Culture and Leadership: A Dynamic View*. San Francisco: Jossey-Bass.

Schein, E. 2009. *The Corporate Culture Survival Guide*, rev. ed. San Francisco: Jossey Bass.

Silveira, E., and J. Walters. 2017. "Building Blocks of Workplace Inclusion." *TD at Work*. Alexandria, VA: ATD Press.

Taras, V., P. Steel, and B.L. Kirkman. 2011. "Three Decades of Research on National Culture in the Workplace: Do the Differences Still Make a Difference?" *Organizational Dynamics* 40:189–198.

Thomas, R.R., Jr., 2010. *World Class Diversity Management: A Strategic Approach*. San Francisco: Berrett-Koehler.

Thomas, D.C. 2008. *Cross-Cultural Management: Essential Concepts*, 2nd ed. Thousand Oaks, CA: Sage.

Towers Watson. 2012. "Global Workforce Study Engagement at Risk: Driving Strong Performance in a Volatile Global Environment." Towers Watson. towerswatson.com/assets/pdf/2012-towers-watson-global-workforce-study.pdf.

Trompenaars, F., and C. Hampden-Turner. 2012. *Riding the Waves of Culture: Understanding Diversity in Global Business*, 3rd ed. New York: McGraw-Hill.

Twigg, J. 2009. "Clothing, Identity and the Embodiment of Age." In *Aging and Identity: A Postmodern Dialogue*, edited by J. Powell and T. Gilbert, 1–19. New York: Nova Science Publishers.

UK Essays. 2018. "Is Hofstede's Model Still Relevant Today?" November 2018. UKEssays.com. ukessays.com/essays/business/assessing-the-cultural-model-of-hofstede-business-essay.php?vref=1.

Weng, C. 2005. "Multicultural Lawyering: Teaching Psychology to Develop Cultural Self-Awareness." *Clinical Law Review* 11:369–404.

Recommended Reading

Brett, J., Y. Doz, E. Meyer, and H. Gregersen. 2016. *HBR's 10 Must-Reads on Managing Across Cultures*. Boston, MA: Harvard Business Review Press.

Edmondson, A. 2019. *The Fearless Organization: Creating Psychological Safety in the Workplace for Learning, Innovation, and Growth*. Hoboken, NJ: John Wiley and Sons.

Livermore, D. 2015. *Leading With Cultural Intelligence: The Real Secret to Success*, 2nd ed. New York: AMACOM.

Morukian, M. 2022. *Diversity, Equity, and Inclusion for Trainers*. Alexandria, VA: ATD Press.

Steffey, D. 2018. *Destination Facilitation: A Travel Guide to Training Around the World*. Alexandria, VA: ATD Press.

Trompenaars, F., and C. Hampden-Turner. 2012. *Riding the Waves of Culture: Understanding Diversity in Global Business*, 3rd ed. New York: McGraw-Hill.

1.5 PROJECT MANAGEMENT

Analyzing and prioritizing elements of a learning initiative or talent solution helps to ensure a meaningful and relevant learner experience. Effective project management requires being able to plan, organize, direct, and control resources for a finite period to complete specific goals and objectives.

1.5.1 Knowledge of Project Management Principles and Processes

> **I. Project Management Principles**
> TD professionals should be knowledgeable about the need for a realistic, simple, and repeatable project management process to manage multiple projects with multiple stakeholders.

1.5.1.1 What Is a Project?

A project is a temporary endeavor with a clearly defined beginning and end in time, and therefore a defined scope and amount of resources. A project is unique because it is not a routine operation, but a specific set of operations designed to accomplish a single goal (PMI 2017). This is based on the standard Project Management Institute (PMI) definitions. Other component definitions add clarity to understanding project management (PM) relationships:

- **A process** is a standard list of tasks that are systematically repeated. For example, the payroll process works the same way every payroll cycle.
- **A program** is generally made up of related projects that are grouped together.
- **A task** is a single unit of work that can be completed by one person in less than half a day. Projects are made up of tasks.
- **Project management** is the application of knowledge, skills, tools, and techniques to address the requirements of the project.
- **A project management team** is the group of people who complete the tasks and support the project manager in completion of the project objectives. Project management teams may require collaboration between individuals who don't typically work together.

A project can become a process. For example, TD course developers analyze, design, and build learning solutions for a customer based on the learning objectives and requirements. This development, beginning to end, is a project. Once the project is completed, the program will be used over and over again until it is no longer useful. This ongoing use of a training program is a process. Both the project and the process are made up of tasks (single units of work).

1.5.1.2 Relationship of Project Management to Talent Development

Project management is critical to the TD professional's ability to deliver value to their organization. Being proficient in project management skills isn't optional in today's world; it is a basic requirement in almost every project. Implementing a systematic project management approach allows TD professionals to oversee and forecast completion dates for each project phase, ensuring that projects are completed on time, within budget, and within quality specifications. Project management practices can help TD professionals demonstrate the value of effective TD planning and execution.

Increased complexity of projects, greater speed and pacing of requirements, and increased use of technology have all placed demanding expectations on TD project managers. Therefore, a systematic approach is fundamental to their success; TD professionals can no longer improvise to complete projects with quality results.

1.5.1.3 Using Project Management in Talent Development

TD professionals should use a formalized project management approach when creating talent development solutions and new initiatives. These solutions could include anything from developing a single course to implementing a new competency-based development framework. Examples of projects include but are not limited to:

- Creating a certification program
- Designing a new leadership development initiative
- Converting a classroom course to an online or blended learning program
- Creating a process to systematically use subject matter experts (SMEs)
- Developing a new employee orientation
- Creating a job rotation process
- Standardizing a process for creating new job roles
- Creating a method for supervisors to coach their employees
- Creating a process and checklist that helps employees manage their own careers
- Establishing plans to leverage social learning in the organization
- Designing a process to consistently produce digital learning products

TD professionals should use a project management approach to fulfill their stakeholders' requests, develop new processes or services, improve current processes or services, and adjust to their organization's new technology or operational strategies.

1.5.1.4 When to Use Project Management

TD professionals will face various scenarios that may or may not be suited for project management practices. Sometimes, these scenarios will seem similar. Coaching is a good example—TD professionals may be asked to create a coaching process that can be used throughout an organization, which would be a likely candidate for project management. On the other hand, TD professionals may use coaching skills during interactions with their direct reports and internal customers, and external consultants may use coaching skills with their clients. Neither of those situations are considered a project management scenario.

TD professionals should know when to apply a broader set of processes and tools to a project management approach. Referring to the definition of a project, TD professionals can be assured they are discussing a project if it encompasses four things:

- **Temporary.** A project has a defined start and end date, and is intended to be completed within a specific timeframe.
- **Specific goal.** A project has a clear and targeted objective.
- **Unique.** A project has a specific set of objectives, activities, and resources that are differentiated from other projects.
- **Produces an output.** A project drives toward a specific end goal that produces something, such as a new product, service, or more broadly, an outcome or result.

Conditions are rarely ideal for every project: The due date is too soon, budget is too tight, scope is too broad, or timing is bad. Astute TD professionals are aware of this and will dig deep into their project management skills to do what's necessary during these times.

1.5.1.5 Preliminary Requirements to Ensure Project Management Success

To ensure success, project management requires clear roles and an agreed-upon approach. Project management professionals can choose from several project management models and frameworks. Although there are four to seven phases of project management, depending on the PM model used, most models share similarities in their presentation and required tasks. The shared phases of project management are:

- **Initiate** or start the project, including writing a charter.
- **Plan** or determine the schedule, required resources, and budget.
- **Manage**, execute, or control the work in progress, provide feedback, and resolve differences.
- **Close** or end the project, including documentation and holding a project review.

Project management requires roles of expertise. Various roles are required for successful project results. The levels of expertise can significantly lengthen or shorten the effort. "Expertise includes both the ability to do the task and the knowledge in the content area" (Russell 2016). Critical roles in project management include subject matter experts (SMEs) as well as those needed to complete the project, including, but not limited to:

- **Project sponsor.** The person or group of people who funded the project and are responsible for ensuring the project meets its goals.
- **Project manager.** The person acting as the steward of the project who is responsible for planning, organizing, and managing it.
- **Project stakeholders.** Anyone who has a vested interest in the project, including the project sponsor, project manager, and any team members needed to complete the project. The stakeholders give and receive information from the project manager and other stakeholders. The project manager may play the role of a stakeholder as well as the role of the project manager; however, this situation should be clearly defined so work is not accidentally forgotten.

> **II. The Project Management Process**
>
> A project management process is a template that suggests how to complete a project successfully. There are variations of project management processes, including those from the Project Management Institute in the United States (PMI.org) and PRINCE in other countries (PRINCE2.com).

1.5.1.6 Initiate
Initiate is the first PM phase and it results in developing and obtaining approval for the project charter. The phase includes these tasks:

- **Establish organizational objectives.** This references the goals or outcomes that are intended to be achieved as a result of a project. Objectives are typically aligned with the overall mission and vision of the organization and help guide the direction and priorities of the project.
- **Establish the project scope.** This includes all the tasks and work required to deliver the service or product defined by the project.
- **Identify project objectives.** These are the measurable deliverables that the project is supposed to produce.
- **Identify risks.** These are the potential events that could influence the objectives or the timeline.
- **Identify constraints.** These are the components that control the project, such as time, cost, and quality.
- **Identify stakeholders.** These are the individuals or groups that could affect or will be affected by the results of a project, such as customers and suppliers. Stakeholders are also anyone involved in the project, such as team members and the project manager.
- **Establish a governance plan.** Tailored to the organization and the specific project, the governance plan incorporates, but is not limited to, the policies, procedures, and relationships that create the rules guiding the oversight and authorization of the project.

The initiate phase kicks off the project to answer the questions, "Why are we doing this?" and "Why are we spending money on this instead of something else?" The initiate phase ends when the project team creates the project charter and outlines the requirements for the product, service, or process that will be created as the deliverables. TD professionals should hold a project charter briefing to determine whether the project moves forward. If the project is confirmed, the charter is approved by the project sponsor and the plan phase begins. Skipping this phase can be detrimental to a project. [See 1.5.2.1, 1.5.2.2, and 1.5.3.1]

1.5.1.7 Plan
Plan is the second phase in the project management process. A well-designed charter provides helpful information for this phase. Although the charter doesn't provide information about sequencing, it establishes expectations for what needs to occur, answering the questions, "What work needs to be completed and when?" and "How should we propose to design, organize, and execute the project?"

The output of this phase is a project management plan that integrates several subplans, including the outputs of these tasks:

- **Determine key milestones.** The dates that high-level goals (made up of a group of tasks) should be accomplished helps determine sequencing.
- **Establish a schedule.** The schedule is created by totaling the estimated completion time each task requires to reach a completion date. However, because projects often have due dates, scheduling may require working backward using similar estimations of each task. The schedule will also have sub-due dates for each task.
- **Assigning resources.** Resources include two components: team members and required physical items. Identifying and assigning task owners depends on determining the best choices by examining individuals' expertise, resource availability, and environmental factors, such as other unrelated responsibilities. Physical items might include equipment, software, or a specific space.

- **Create a budget.** Consider all expenses included in each project, such as labor time, supplies, training, meeting expenses, travel, conference calls, and any other additional related costs.
- **Create a communication plan.** The communication plan is critical for keeping all stakeholders informed. It should include a plan for proper messaging and a timeline for communicating based on deliverables and milestones.
- **Develop a risk management plan.** This plan identifies possible risks, such as time or cost estimates, work completed by inexperienced team members, changing requirements, and anything else that could need an adjustment plan. To evaluate risks that might occur, determine risk factors, their likelihood, their impact, if the risk can be prevented, and, if not, ideas for mitigation.
- **Develop a change management plan.** This will describe how change requests will be approved and assimilated into the overall plan. It should determine who has the right to make changes and to what extent. It is important to clearly outline in the change management plan who can:
  - Change the scope of the project.
  - Change the project budget.
  - Change the project timeline.
  - Change the people resources working on the project.

If the individuals who can change anything on the project are knowledgeable and accountable—and limited to a few people—the project team will be more efficient.

Constraints are an important part of planning. A constraint is any restriction that defines the project's limitations, such as the scope, resources, time, or a fixed budget. A knowledgeable TD professional in a project manager role understands how to prioritize and accept the constraints and keep moving.

The plan phase ends with a finished project plan and culminates in agreement of how the project will be completed and monitored by the project sponsor aided by the project manager. The project plan may also include, but is not limited to, the communication plan, risk management plan, schedule and timelines, stakeholder plan, resource plan, and change management plan.

The TD professional managing the project should accept that a project plan may change frequently. They can prepare by being flexible, considering how to adapt within the project constraints, and determining how to communicate changes to the team.

1.5.1.8 Manage

Manage is the third and likely the longest phase of the project. It uses inputs from the previous two phases (the charter, requirements, and project plan) and more resources are often added to help execute the work defined in the plan. During this phase, TD professionals in a project manager role monitor, manage, and execute the project plan. Their role often includes these tasks:

- **Control work in progress.** Tracking, reviewing, and reporting progress identifies a clear understanding of the project's current state.
- **Provide status and feedback.** Sharing the project's state with stakeholders ensures that they understand where the project stands regarding hitting time, budget, and the project objectives. It also provides a perspective for the future status of the budget, schedule, and quality forecasts.

- **Resolve conflict.** When a group of diverse people work together on a project, there are bound to be differences. When this happens, the project manager will need to align team members and stakeholders around achieving objectives and staying on schedule and other aspects related to project results.
- **Manage change.** Because it is impossible to anticipate everything that may occur during a project, it is helpful to have a process for how changes are addressed using the project governance and change management plans and the decisions made during the plan phase. Changes need to be approved, deferred, or denied, so they should be documented and communicated.
- **Leverage governance.** Using the governance plan created in the charter helps guide who decides what to do about requested changes.
- **Manage risk.** Although potential risks were identified in previous phases, it doesn't mean they will occur. The project manager must be alert to signs of risk and determine as soon as possible whether a mitigation plan should be implemented.

The TD professional should initiate the manage phase with a kick-off meeting to begin building team rapport and clarifying team member roles and responsibilities. The purpose of the kick-off meeting is to establish alignment on the project's goals, roles and responsibilities, and timeline, as well as ensure the project team understands what is expected of them.

A project rarely unfolds as planned; therefore, it's important for the TD professional in a project manager role to be flexible and have a clear plan for managing change. While change can occur in any phase, it is especially important to manage proposed changes appropriately during this one. Proposed changes, whether implemented or not, should always be documented—including any impact they have to the project's sub-plans.

All changes must be documented because they may require a revised task sequence, different completion dates, revised cost estimates, or different resource requirements, which may require changes to the project management plan. Only after proposed changes are formally approved should they be implemented.

The manage phase addresses the need to adapt to the unexpected. Although the charter doesn't change, the plan does, and it is adjusted throughout the project when events, expectations, and the environment changes. The manage phase spans the life of the project.

1.5.1.9 Close
Close is the last phase, finalizing all the project actions including these tasks:
- **Transition by turning over deliverables.** The project's services, products, and other results must be transferred to the appropriate team or organization for which the project was conducted. The project sponsor should also acknowledge whether all deliverables have been received and approved and whether the project is ready to be closed.
- **Hold a post-project review.** Multiple options exist to systematically review the project to determine what went well, what could be done differently, and what lessons were learned.
- **Finalize documentation.** Work with team members to create and complete the list of things that were not accomplished during the project, prepare a final budget report, and complete the final report. All project documentations and deliverables should be stored in a designated place.
- **Celebrate accomplishments.** Recognize the team and the contributions of everyone involved.

This phase addresses the need to learn how to be more effective in the next project and is captured in lessons learned. It may be one of the most relevant for TD professionals because it gives them the opportunity to learn through post-project reviews and share their experiences with the rest of the organization.

The close phase ends when the project team is finished as defined by the project manager; all actions related to the project's services, products, and other results are transferred to the appropriate groups; all project documents are finalized; the team celebrates its successes; and team members are formally released from the project.

1.5.1.10 Hybrid Methodology Choices

The project management approach presented here and other PM approaches use generally accepted practices that are applicable to most projects; this creates a foundation from which to start. Each industry has the option to build a hybrid PM approach on this foundation. When that occurs, the resulting system of techniques, procedures, guidelines, and rules is called a methodology.

There are several different TD methodologies, including ADDIE, Agile, rapid prototyping, and SAM; each is an adaption of an existing PM approach. TD professionals should understand the general difference between methodologies so they can select the right one or even combine methodologies to accommodate whatever the project requires.

1.5.2 Skill in Coordinating the Logistical Tasks Associated With Planning Meetings

> **I. The Roles of a Project Sponsor and Project Manager**
>
> TD professionals in a project manager role must be able to differentiate between the roles of the project sponsor and the project manager. The difference is critical, and the scope of the different roles and responsibilities must meld for project success. They must also coordinate the logistics for meetings with these two individuals and the rest of the stakeholders.

1.5.2.1 Project Sponsor Role

The project sponsor provides the time, money, and resources the project manager needs to complete the task and is also responsible for:
- Focusing on the ultimate project results
- Providing executive leadership of the project
- Collaborating with other executives and stakeholders
- Staying out of the details to focus on strategy
- Providing project constraints, including final due dates, staffing, budgets, and scope

The project sponsor's tasks include:
- Approving the budget, resources, and timeline (with details from the project manager)
- Intervening with peers and eliminating barriers to enable the project manager to complete the project
- Reviewing and approving final deliverables, as well as determining when the project is officially finished
- Signing the charter

While it is ideal for projects to only have one project sponsor, occasionally they require multiple sponsors. The project may require resources or expertise from multiple groups within an organization, each contributing in some way.

1.5.2.2 Project Manager Role

The organization depends on the project manager to be the steward of the project. The project manager plans, organizes, and manages the project workflow and is responsible for:

- Focusing on the schedule and work to be done
- Troubleshooting and managing the people, tasks, and due dates
- Providing regular status updates to the project sponsor
- Communicating frequently with key stakeholders
- Escalating complex problems by presenting multiple options to the project sponsor
- Collaborating with team members to drive trust and respect within the team
- Juggling project constraints, including schedules, resources, budgets, quality, and scope
- Planning, preparing, coordinating, and facilitating meetings [See 2.3]

The project manager's tasks include:

- Planning the project
- Managing change
- Organizing needed tasks
- Managing issues and challenges as needed

The project manager does not build anything. Instead, the role focuses on planning, organizing, and managing. However, the person who is the project manager may also play other roles.

1.5.2.3 Project Management Priorities

All projects balance five priorities:

- **Schedule**—milestones and the final date when the tasks and project will be completed
- **Cost**—budget required for project completion
- **Quality**—distinctive attributes or characteristics that define requirements
- **Scope**—all tasks and work required to deliver the service or product defined by a project
- **Resources**—people and physical items required to complete a project

Each priority is critical, and the project manager must decide which one requires the most attention at any given time. If any of these priorities are changed, all other parts of the project will be affected. For example, if the budget is reduced, the schedule may need to be adjusted, which would result in fewer resources or a lowered scope to produce fewer products or services. A reduced budget could also affect the quality.

1.5.2.4 Logistics to Facilitate Meetings

Many of the project manager's tasks are performed in meetings; therefore, they should know how to coordinate the logistics to plan and facilitate meetings. Planning logistics include:

- **Meeting room**—scheduling one that is the right size for the group
- **Seating**—planning for an arrangement that best accomplishes the meeting's goals

- **Equipment and visuals**—arranging what's required to accomplish the objectives, and completing an equipment check prior to the meeting
- **Agenda**—confirming all meetings have an agenda that identifies the objectives, time allotted for each, and who's responsible
- **Who, what, where, and when**—ensuring the right people are invited and that they know where and when the meeting is taking place
- **Expectations**—informing meeting attendees if they are required to complete prework so they have the information before the meeting in a timely manner
- **Virtual attendees**—ensuring that those who need it have an accurate dial-in number and all the materials that the in-person meeting attendees have [See 2.3.1.1, 2.3.1.15, and 2.3.2.3]

1.5.3 Skill in Evaluating and Prioritizing Implications, Risks, Feasibility, and Consequences of Potential Activities

> **I. Defining the Project Purpose**
>
> TD professionals managing projects must complete a project charter during the initiate phase, which is the critical first step to evaluate and prioritize the activities. This document summarizes the details of the project, and more importantly it formally authorizes the project and permits the use of resources for all project activities.

1.5.3.1 The Project Charter

The project charter is the outcome of the project's initiate phase. It presents the need for the project accompanied by a brief description of its deliverables and components, providing a short, high-level overview of the project and requirements for anyone involved. The charter is "a document issued by the project initiator or sponsor that formally authorizes the existence of a project and provides the project manager with the authority to apply organizational resources to project activities" (PMI 2017).

TD professionals should know the project charter's details, especially why the organization has undertaken the project. The charter provides continuous guidance for the TD professional, who may also be the project manager, and the team. It should outline the implications and consequences of the project.

The project manager and team usually draft the project charter for the sponsor to review and approve. The charter may be short, but it should convey clarity and quality. It is written in broad terms so that minor changes to the project can be managed easily without needing to change the charter.

The project charter introduces the feasibility of the project and includes a high-level introduction to several topics including, but not limited to, the:
- Justification, purpose, or need for the project
- Organizational and project objectives
- Cost-benefit analysis
- Key stakeholders
- High-level risks
- High-level constraints or boundaries
- Budget summary

- Critical milestones
- Criteria for success
- Authority for the project manager and others as required

TD project managers should use a project charter template (many are available on the internet) to easily develop the charter. Inputs to the charter may include:
- Documents, such as a business case for the project
- A statement of work
- Any contracts or agreements, such as memorandums of understanding, service-level agreements, emails, or other written communications
- Enterprise environmental factors, such as market conditions, regulatory requirements, or other constraints
- Any organizational standard policies and processes that might influence the charter

The charter is critically important because it provides a well-defined start to the project, including the project manager's name and authority, timelines, scope, and other big picture information. In addition, the charter develops a formal record of the project, provides clarity to the project manager, offers a rationale for acceptance of the project by senior leaders, and gives clear documentation of a common explanation of the project (Horine 2017).

The charter also signals the future end of the project by determining its goal. Because projects change, those adjustments are tracked through the change management plan, which is part of the project plan. What was conceived in the charter could differ from the result for many reasons. A change management plan helps address these changes.

Although it is tempting to skip the project charter and begin with the project plan, that is a mistake because the charter formally authorizes the existence of the project and the authority of the project manager. Without a charter, or if it is unsigned, officially, there is no project.

1.5.4 Skill in Developing Project Plans and Schedules That Integrate Resources, Tasks, and Timelines

> **I. Project Management Planning**
>
> TD professionals in a project manager role should develop a project plan to establish the project timeline based on the tasks and dependencies required.

1.5.4.1 The Project Plan

The project plan is the outcome of the plan phase. It determines how to plan, manage, and execute the project and has multiple components. To begin the plan, validate the charter, and ensure that everyone helping to develop the plan understands the project's intent and objectives, confirm nothing has changed since the plan was authorized. Once everyone agrees, the team can begin to design the parts of the project plan. There are four parts to consider when creating a project plan: [See 1.5.1.7]
- Determine what needs to be completed:

- Identify the logistical tasks, including meetings, required training, onboarding, and reviews.
  - Agree on criteria for acceptance.
  - Determine resource requirements and a plan to acquire them.
  - Assign resources, both team members and required physical items.
- Estimate the work and develop a schedule:
  - Begin with key milestone dates from the charter.
  - Identify the timeline's fixed due dates, and work backward to identify when each task must start and end.
  - Identify the skill sets necessary to complete the project, and then identify the best resource for each task.
  - Manage the timeline to ensure that the necessary person is available when their tasks are due.
  - Assign the person with the appropriate skill set to a specific task. The person assigned the task is the single owner of that task.
  - Finalize the schedule with the estimated completion time each task requires. The schedule may have sub-due dates for tasks.
- Identify project costs and budget:
  - Create a budget, considering all expenses included in each project, such as labor time, supplies, training, meeting expenses, travel, and conference calls.
- Create various subplans that ensure a smooth project implementation:
  - Develop change management plan.
  - Develop a communication plan.
  - Develop a risk management plan.

1.5.5 Skill in Adjusting Work Processes and Outputs in Response to or Anticipation of Changes in Goals, Standards, Resources, or Time

I. Project Management Implementation

TD professionals should leverage the project charter and project plan to more efficiently do the work that the project plan has identified. They should ensure that the customer receives the project results at the end of the manage phase.

1.5.5.1 The Project Progress

With the project plan completed during the plan phase, the team should be ready to begin the manage phase of the project. The project manager's flexibility is critical in this phase because the plan will likely never work exactly as originally written. Monitoring and tracking the actual conditions compared with the baseline plan, shifting resources, and identifying glitches are all part of this difficult and critical phase.

The manage phase implementation requires the project team to:
- Complete their work on time, within budget, and within scope while meeting the quality specifications.
- Alert the project manager to any issues or opportunities.
- Suggest potential solutions to the project manager if issues occur.

- Help other developers if there is an opportunity to do so.
- Collaborate with the customer team.
- Build training materials for the project transition.
- Accurately report status to track overall progress.

Assumptions used to create the project plan will change and so will the project schedule. To be successful, TD professionals in project manager roles must embrace schedule changes. Although the project schedule can be difficult and time consuming to build during the plan phase, creating the initial project schedule is well worth the effort. The tasks and dependencies must be carefully put in the right order to maximize the timeline—especially when the inevitable adjustments to the schedule occur throughout the project. The best defense against all change is a well-developed project plan, a flexible schedule, and a well-defined change control process.

The manage phase implementation requires the project manager to:
- Monitor progress and identify variances based on the project plan and schedule.
- Supervise the changes in time, cost, quality, and scope.
- Observe and develop the skills of the team members.
- Adapt to and prioritize project changes, including learning goals, business and project objectives, and milestones.
- Communicate status and progress to all stakeholders using a predictable schedule.
- Collaborate and communicate by adjusting work processes and outputs in response to changes required by the customer.
- Build a plan to transition the final deliverable to the customer.

When finished, the project manager obtains approval from the project sponsor to transfer the finished deliverable to the customer. The project sponsor is also responsible for reviewing each artifact with the key customer for approval. Only after the customer formally approves and accepts the outputs or deliverables is the project finished from the customer's perspective.

Project managers, however, have additional work to do in the close phase. They must close the project, transition the finished deliverables to the new owner (where maintenance will begin), and evaluate how to work more effectively next time.

1.5.6 Skill in Establishing, Monitoring, and Communicating Progress Toward the Achievement of Goals, Objectives, and Milestones

I. Assessing Project Management Progress

TD professionals in project manager roles must be able to monitor and communicate the progress of the project from start to end. They must always be alert to unexpected results by constantly watching for challenges and obstacles to mitigate them early.

1.5.6.1 Monitoring and Communicating Progress During Project Management

As part of the plan phase, the project manager establishes two critical people-influencing processes: monitoring the status of the project and communicating the status to those who need to know.

Monitoring the current status of the project involves reviewing, tracking, and documenting the progress to ensure that the work meets the objectives defined in the project plan. This is the role of the project manager. Monitoring is not possible without clearly defined and agreed-upon roles and responsibilities, which the project manager established in the project plan and schedule. The project manager might complete these tasks:
- Checking the status of individual tasks
- Comparing actual performance to the plan
- Updating current costs and schedules
- Assessing customer and stakeholder requests
- Ensuring continued alignment with the organization's objectives

Delivering ongoing communication keeps the customers, stakeholders, and project sponsor apprised of the project's progress. TD professionals who are fulfilling project manager roles should send timely and detailed status updates to the project sponsor. In the absence of a predictable update, the project sponsor may question their ability to lead the project team.

It is critical to establish a status update timeline, sending updates with a fixed frequency that fits the size of the project (for example, every two weeks). Project managers who share the project schedule or the parts that show which tasks are done, pending, added, or removed build confidence in everyone who sees it.

Project sponsors are focused on delivering the product or service to meet the defined goal. A TD project manager should send status updates that pertain to what the project sponsor wants to know, rather than what the project manager wants to share. The project manager should know what and how much information the project sponsor wants. [See 1.5.4 and 1.5.5]

A TD professional in a project manager role must create and deliver messaging that best serves the success of the project. A communication plan should include when and how each communication will be delivered and what the message will entail. While the project manager may be too busy to talk with all stakeholders, by designing and sending brief updates through social media, video, or email to the project team regularly, the project manager can ensure team members continue working confidently and collaboratively. The project manager should consider finding a communication campaign expert in the company to design this communication.

1.5.6.2 Bringing Projects to Closure

With the deliverables transferred to the customer, the manage phase ends and the close phase begins. It is the responsibility of the project manager to close the project. The developers and stakeholders are released after the project is delivered to the customer. This phase is often skipped, as staff move quickly to new projects. However, project managers must find the time to close the project appropriately, so the lessons learned are available for the future.

1.5 Project Management

When finished, the project manager shares the final results with the project sponsor, who is also responsible for following up with any customers. As the close phase ends, the project is finished from the project sponsor's perspective. The project manager alone is responsible for recording the strategic knowledge gained during the close phase. The project manager must conclude the project and document the project's evaluation. The close phase implementation requires the project manager to (Russell 2007):

- Meet with the project sponsor for project evaluation feedback.
- Work with the customer to clarify a roll-out timeline for their team.
- Deliver training (as needed) to the customer.
- Re-allocate staff to their next project.
- Publish a post-project review and meet with stakeholders to discuss ways to improve future project efficiency and effectiveness.
- Archive pertinent artifacts (such as the project charter and project plan) for use on future projects. Consider creating a shared project archive for the organization.
- Celebrate with the entire team.

REFERENCES

DeMarco, T., and T. Lister. 2013. *Peopleware: Productive Projects and Teams*, 3rd ed. Upper Saddle River, NJ: Addison Wesley.

Duncan, W.R. 1996. *A Guide to the Project Management Body of Knowledge.* Newton Square, PA: Project Management Institute.

Horine, G. 2017. *Project Management: Absolute Beginner's Guide*, 4th ed. Indianapolis: Que Publishing.

Lewis, B. 2006. *Bare Bones Project Management: What You Can't Not Do*. Eden Prairie, MN: IS Survivor Publishing.

PMI. 2021. *A Guide to the Project Management Body of Knowledge*, 7th ed. Newtown Square, PA: Project Management Institute.

Russell, L. 2007. *10 Steps to Successful Project Management*. Alexandria, VA: ASTD Press.

Russell, L. 2012. *Managing Projects: A Practical Guide for Learning Professionals*. Alexandria, VA: ASTD Press.

Russell, L. 2016. *Project Management for Trainers*, 2nd ed. Alexandria, VA: ATD Press.

Toenniges, L., and K. Patterson. 2005. "Managing Training Projects." *Infoline*. Alexandria, VA: ASTD Press.

Recommended Reading

Horine, G. 2017. *Project Management: Absolute Beginner's Guide*, 4th ed. Indianapolis: Que Publishing.

Russell, L. 2016. *Project Management for Trainers*, 2nd ed. Alexandria, VA: ATD Press.

1.6 COMPLIANCE & ETHICAL BEHAVIOR

Compliance and ethical behavior refer to the expectation that a talent development professional acts with integrity and operates within the laws that govern where they work and live. For talent development professionals, this may also require knowledge of and abiding by the regulations and laws related to content creation, accessibility, human resources, employment, and other public policies.

1.6.1 Skill in Acting With Integrity

I. Principles of the Ethical TD Professional

A TD professional should exhibit ethical behavior and must be aware of the compliance requirements related to talent development.

1.6.1.1 Comparing Compliance to Ethical Behavior

Ethical behavior means exhibiting good values and acting in ways that are consistent with the beliefs of society, an organization, and the profession. Ethical behavior defines an individual's moral judgment about right and wrong. It is based on decisions made by individuals or groups within an organization. It is often linked with compliance, although ethics is seldom mandated by an external agency or stipulated by a specific regulatory law.

Compliance is an action that is mandated by a law, agency, or policy outside an organization's purview. It is generally accompanied by a training program requirement. While compliance is mandatory, TD professionals must act with integrity because ethical behavior demonstrates respect for basic moral principles and they often set the tone for their organizations.

1.6.1.2 Necessity of Ethics and Compliance

Compliance and ethical behavior refer to the expectation that practitioners act with integrity and operate within the laws that govern where they work and live. TD professionals must also adhere to regulations and laws related to content creation, accessibility, human resources, employment, and other public policies.

Ethical behavior is based on decisions made by individuals or groups within an organization. It is good for business because it demonstrates respect for basic moral principles. Compliance, on the other hand, is mandated by law.

1.6.1.3 Sustaining Ethical Behavior in Today's Fast-Paced World

Maintaining an ethical approach is more difficult in today's business environment due to rapidly changing technology and increased competition. In addition, these rapid changes can lead to decreased quality or increased unethical practices. The fast pace, intense competition, and complexity may prevent time for reflection and gathering vital information before making decisions (Gino, Ordóñez, and Welsh 2014).

Harvard University offered the first course on business ethics in 1915, and many other business schools now offer them too. However, despite these courses, unethical behavior continues to happen in the workplace. TD professionals have a responsibility to prioritize ethics in their organizations. Ethical talent development practices and TD professionals' actions can pave the way for an organization's ethical culture and become a model in today's fast-paced world.

1.6.1.4 TD Professionals' Core Behaviors Representing Integrity

TD professionals inherently accept a personal obligation to the profession and to their organizations to demonstrate the core values and behaviors that represent integrity. Integrity comes from the Latin word *integritas*, meaning *one* or *whole*. To be whole, one must project values that are the same on the inside as they are on the outside. Integrity can mean many things, but at a minimum it includes the basic values identified by the American Bar Association and the American Arbitration Association:

- **Honesty**—a personal, objective, and constant commitment to being a witness to truth
- **Fairness**—impartiality in all business relationships, as evidenced by respecting the diversity of others in an equal and just manner
- **Lawfulness**—observance of both the letter and spirit of the laws governing commerce, individual rights in the workplace, and expectations of customers
- **Compassion**—response to the human needs of others in a personal and moral manner that recognizes the dignity of human life
- **Respect**—recognition that all human beings require an understanding of their thinking, the activities in their personal lives, and the individual beliefs that make them unique
- **Loyalty**—a sense of personal trust between people, among groups of employees, between employer and worker, or between a business and its clients
- **Dependability**—consistent personal behavior that meets or exceeds the expectations of all concerned parties

1.6.1.5 What Integrity Looks Like in Action

Integrity means doing the correct thing because it's the principled thing to do. How might integrity play out in the workplace? Consider these examples:

- Employees with integrity are truthful in all their interactions; they do not mislead or deceive others with selective omissions or partial truths. If an organization is facing a downturn or a future change, TD professionals would not make promises that couldn't be kept and would be completely transparent about the difficulties ahead.
- Employees with integrity are dependable and accountable. TD professionals meet deadlines and inform others as soon as they identify an issue that may delay producing a quality product in a timely manner.

- Employees with integrity are open about conflicts of interest. For example, TD professionals are open and upfront about personal relationships with potential vendors, perhaps recusing themselves from the final decision.
- Employees with integrity do not exercise power arbitrarily to gain an advantage. When working with colleagues, TD professionals are willing to assist others to accomplish more by sharing what they know—not holding back as others fail.
- Employees with integrity respect all other employees, maintaining dignity, autonomy, privacy, and their rights. TD professionals, for example, would be compassionate and courteous with argumentative supervisors who do not view developing their employees as a responsibility. The TD professional would continue to seek a rationale that would resonate with the supervisor (Hartman, DesJardins, MacDonald 2014).

1.6.2 Skill in Establishing, Maintaining, and Enforcing Standards for Integrity and Ethical Behavior in Self and Others

I. Creating a Culture of Ethics, Integrity, and Compliance

Effective compliance standards are strategic and aligned to the organization. TD professionals have a dual role of managing their personal ethical behavior and helping create a culture that demonstrates ethics, integrity, and compliance.

1.6.2.1 Establishing, Maintaining, and Enforcing Personal Ethical Behavior

Because the work that TD professionals do affects individuals and organizations, modeling ethics and integrity is critical. Applying organizational codes of ethics or conduct and standards for performance and integrity provides a framework for helping TD professionals resolve ethical dilemmas. Codes specifically serve as guides to support day-to-day decision making at work. They clarify values and principles and help practitioners put those values into practice.

However, there may be times when the code of ethics isn't specific enough. Ethical dilemmas will be different from industry to industry, although most will pose a conflict between:
- Short- and long-term concerns
- Principle and expediency
- Self-interest and community needs
- Truth and loyalty

Knowing how to make a thoughtful and responsible decision is helpful. The Coaching Association of Canada offers six steps for making a decision. TD professionals should:
1. Establish the facts.
2. Decide whether the situation involves legal or ethical issues.
3. Identify all options and any possible consequences.
4. Evaluate their options.
5. Choose the best option.
6. Implement their decision.

1.6 Compliance & Ethical Behavior

Ethical behavior is not about right or wrong but choosing between competing values. TD professionals can test a decision by asking:
- Can I defend my actions?
- How do I feel about the decision?
- Will it result in the greatest good for the greatest number of people?
- How would I feel if my family, colleagues, and friends learned about the decision?

TD professionals establish, maintain, and enforce standards for integrity and ethical behavior by leading by example, anticipating ethical conflicts, communicating with civility, listening, being consistent, standing by agreed boundaries, and having the courage to reset ethical boundaries when necessary.

1.6.2.2 Establishing, Maintaining, and Enforcing Organizational Standards

TD professionals are expected to help establish, maintain, and enforce organizational standards for ethical behavior. When compliance is not integrated into the organization's system and culture, the consequences could include legal action, penalties, damage to brand reputation, or other significant costs. TD professionals can help the organization avoid these issues. In his book, *Fully Compliant: Compliance Training to Change Behavior*, Travis Waugh (2019) provides a suggested process that TD professionals can use to establish an ethical and compliant culture (Waugh 2017; Chen and Soltes 2018):

- **Align compliance to organizational strategy.** An organization that establishes and enforces standards for ethical behavior can easily attract and retain talent and enjoys increased engagement and productivity. TD professionals may help alignment by addressing obstacles to traditional ethics and compliance enforcement.
- **Designate a compliance and ethics owner and committee.** TD professionals may begin by designating an ethics committee and, if appropriate, a champion or owner. TD professionals understand the skills team members require to identify goals, desired results, and measures and to ensure that they are aligned to the organizational strategy. Because TD professionals know who advocates for learning and who acts as informal leaders, they can recommend committee members. TD professionals know how to motivate individuals and keep team members involved, which is critical to establishing and maintaining an effective ethics and compliance plan.
- **Compile organizational standards, policies, and procedures into categories.** As the organization is establishing ethical standards, TD professionals can help recognize SMEs who are involved in ethical and compliance topics. They can partner with HR experts and assist the SMEs with identifying the standards that maintain a culture of ethics and compliance.
- **Document written standards and legal requirements for each category.** TD professionals may document laws and regulations and their specific requirements. Some laws identify who needs to receive training. Other laws specify the amount of time or the recurrence. TD professionals can use these requirements to plan for the training content, participants, and schedule.
- **Conduct a risk assessment for each category.** The risk assessment gives TD professionals an opportunity to align training and development with the issues that senior leaders view as the greatest risks. Addressing these risks with appropriate communication demonstrates talent development's contribution to achieving organizational goals.
- **Develop open communication and training where necessary.** TD professionals should deliver training that meets requirements by law, without being restrictive. Compliance subjects may include

ethical decision making, bystander intervention training, conflict of interest, or introductions to the organization's code of conduct or ethics policies. Good training leads to a cultural acceptance of compliance training and ultimately a more ethical organization.
- **Audit, monitor, and adapt as necessary.** To enforce the standards and change the culture, TD professionals should help shape employees' behaviors so that integrity is instinctive. The organization demonstrates value by objectively measuring behavior. TD professionals model appropriate behaviors and encourage others to do the same. Enforcement should be easier, but there is no guarantee that nothing will go wrong. When it does, TD professionals and the organization must respond consistently and appropriately to alleged offenses.

1.6.2.3 Establishing Codes of Ethics

TD professionals may also help their organizations maintain and enforce standards for integrity and ethical behavior by providing reminders to employees, which may be presented as a code of ethics. Developing an internal statement that summarizes the policies and procedures serves as a prompt to employees to consider compliance, ethics, and legal requirements. A code of ethics helps ensure that the workforce has knowledge of the organization's policies and procedures.

For example, ATD developed a code of ethics for its members to provide guidance for self-managed TD professionals. Developed by the profession for the profession, the ATD Code of Ethics is the public declaration of TD professionals' obligations to themselves, their profession, and society. It states that its members strive to:
- Recognize the rights and dignities of each individual.
- Develop human potential.
- Provide their employers, clients, and learners with the highest level of quality education, training, and development.
- Comply with all copyright laws and the laws and regulations governing their position.
- Keep informed of pertinent knowledge and competence in the TD field.
- Maintain confidentiality and integrity in the practice of their profession.
- Support their peers and avoid conduct that impedes practicing their profession.
- Conduct themselves in an ethical and honest manner.
- Improve the public understanding of talent development.
- Fairly and accurately represent their TD credentials, qualifications, experience, and abilities.
- Contribute to the continuing growth of the profession.

1.6.3 Knowledge of Laws, Regulations, and Ethical Issues Related to the Access and Use of Information

I. Laws, Regulations, and Ethical Issues Related to Data and Information
TD professionals require knowledge about laws, regulations, and ethical issues related to data and the use of information.

1.6.3.1 Sources for Appropriate Laws

As an organization grows, the regulations and laws it must follow related to information access become increasingly complex. In most cases, federal laws establish a baseline that organizations must adhere to. State and local governments may establish requirements that go above and beyond federal laws. For organizations outside the United States, TD professionals should determine where the final authority in their countries resides. In large organizations, human resource professionals and organizational attorneys usually serve as the source of knowledge for TD professionals.

1.6.3.2 Defining Common Information Types

Handling various kinds of information requires TD professionals to be meticulous, diligent, careful, and cautious to avoid inadvertently allowing the information to fall into the hands of someone who is not authorized to access it. This kind of information could include:

- **Intellectual capital**—such as employee expertise, organizational processes, or formulas
- **Personally identifiable information**—such as employee contact information
- **Patient information**—such as health information
- **Customer data**—such as the size of orders or customer contact information

1.6.3.3 Appropriate Uses of Information

TD professionals occasionally need to access proprietary data; for example, they may need to access personally identifiable information (PII) to register an employee for a college course, or they may use customer data when coaching customer service reps. TD professionals need to know how the information is stored, who has legitimate access, how sensitivity is classified, and how acceptable usage policies are defined. Mishandled information can cause real harm to:

- The organization's competitive advantage
- Employees
- Patients
- Customers' businesses or customer relationships (SHRM 2015)

1.6.3.4 Data Privacy Regulations

The European Union General Data Protection Regulation (GDPR) is a significant milestone in data privacy regulation. In effect since May 2018, GDPR is designed to harmonize data privacy laws across the European Union, protect and empower all EU citizens' data privacy, and reshape the way organizations approach data privacy.

Even though GDPR applies only to companies that do business with customers in the EU, many apply the policies globally because of the abundance of worldwide companies and relationships. These policies may have implications for TD professionals if they collect personal data from employees, including more transparency, stringent legal requirements for processing information, and increased accountability.

1.6.4 Knowledge of Laws, Regulations, and Ethical Issues Related to the Development of Instructional Content

I. Legal, Regulatory, and Ethical Requirements Related to Instructional Content

TD professionals require knowledge about laws, regulations, and ethical issues related to the design and delivery of instructional content. Instructional content presents several issues, including ethical behavior when working with other individuals in a coaching or change management setting. TD professionals also need to know appropriate copyright laws and accessibility requirements (Orey 2017; GSA 2017).

1.6.4.1 Sources for Appropriate Laws
Most large organizations have HR professionals who help TD professionals better understand accessibility requirements and workplace policies, as well as corporate attorneys who are knowledgeable about intellectual property and copyright laws.

1.6.4.2 Coaching Ethics and Standards of Conduct
TD professionals may find themselves acting as coaches to others in their organizations. When developing content and plans to coach others, they should follow coaching ethics and standards of conduct. Coaching associations have established ethical guidelines, which are focused on conflict of interest, privacy, confidentiality, and coaching relationship limitations. [See 2.7.8]

1.6.4.3 Change Management Ethics and Integrity
Change management can lead to various ethical issues, such as how a TD professional might address an executive who wants to manipulate data, a change that is based on a power relationship, a hidden agenda for a change, and how to address value conflicts. [See 3.6.2]

1.6.4.4 Copyright and Fair Use of Intellectual Property
The design and development of learning programs likely requires incorporating various sources of information, which means that TD professionals must follow copyright laws. Copyright, as defined by the US Copyright Office (2006), is a "form of protection provided by the laws of the United States for 'original works of authorship,' including literary, dramatic, musical, architectural, cartographic, choreographic, pantomimic, pictorial, graphic, sculptural, and audiovisual creations."

International copyright laws do not exist, so protection against unauthorized use depends on the laws of each country. The copyright laws mentioned here are relevant to the United States. Those who work outside the United States should consult the laws and regulations governing copyright in those regions. An organization's legal and human resources departments will likely have the most up-to-date information.

Copyright registration is a legal formality intended to create a public record of the basic facts of a particular copyright; however, registration is not a condition of copyright protection. According to the US Copyright Office (2006), "The use of a copyright notice is no longer required under US law, although it is often beneficial." Because prior law did contain such a requirement, however, the use of a notice is still relevant to the copyright status of older works.

TD professionals need to know when and how to obtain copyright permission. For example, copyright law protects the expression of an idea (but not the idea itself) in some tangible form (such as a book, magazine, video, film, MP3, or software). However, ideas, processes, procedures, methods of operation, concepts, principles, and discoveries cannot be copyrighted. Therefore, while the ideas in a book can't be copyrighted, the exact words, explanation, or illustration of them in a book may be copyrighted. TD professionals require written permission to reference exact words in another tangible form (Swindling and Partridge 2014).

In the United States, the Copyright Act of 1976 stipulated that copyright begins with the creation of the work in a fixed form from which it can be perceived or communicated. The exclusive rights of the author or owner are limited by the fair use doctrine, which states that brief excerpts of copyrighted material may be quoted verbatim for purposes such as teaching and research without the need for permission from or payment to the copyright holder. Whether a use is fair depends on several factors, including the:

- Purpose and character of the use, including whether the use of material is commercial or for nonprofit educational purposes
- Nature of the copyrighted work
- Amount, or substantiality, of the portion used in relation to the copyrighted work as a whole
- Effect on market potential for or value of the copyrighted work

Fair use standards may apply to training materials; however, each situation will be unique. TD professionals must request the permission of the copyright holder before making multiple copies of copyrighted works (ALA 2019).

1.6.4.5 Preparing for Research Issues

TD professionals may need to conduct research prior to developing instructional content, so they must be aware of participant rights and ethical issues related to research. Organizations that fund research often have an established researcher code of conduct (for example, the US Food and Drug Administration publishes an ethical research code). Most research codes of conduct include five ethical areas:

- **Informed consent** occurs when a person knowingly, voluntarily, and intelligently agrees to the research activities.
- **Protection** requires the researcher to resist probing questions when possible consequences outweigh the benefits to the research.
- **Anonymity and confidentiality** means that the subject's identity cannot be linked to the responses.
- **Objectivity** means bias in design, data analysis, or interpretation will be avoided to ensure measurement accuracy.
- **Openness** requires honest discussion of the research purpose before conducting research and truthful delivery of the results.

TD professionals can avoid ethical dilemmas by understanding their ethical obligations and what resources are available (such as their organization's code of ethics or values statement).

1.6.4.6 Accessibility Requirements

TD professionals who design and deliver training need to be aware of legislation affecting employers. For example, the US Americans with Disabilities Act (ADA) of 1990 prohibits discrimination in employment, public services, transportation, public accommodations, and telecommunications services against people with disabilities. Understanding the law's ramifications is especially important for talent development because the law requires that employees with disabilities have reasonable accommodations that enable them to function in their jobs. When designing and delivering learning solutions, TD professionals should consider aids that may be required, such as interpreters, magnifying glasses to aid reading, recorded text for those who are visually impaired, or instructional material with oversized lettering. In regions outside the US, check local laws for accessibility requirements (EEOC 2011; Sherbin and Kennedy 2017).

1.6.4.7 Role of Training Quality Standards

The industry currently lacks a true quality standard; therefore, the profession depends on International Organization for Standards (ISO) Guidelines, benchmarking, competencies, best practices, observed achievement, and input from participants and organizational leadership to measure quality.

Closely related to talent development is the ANSI/IACET standard. ANSI (American National Standards Institute) is a source for information on national, regional, and international standards; IACET's (International Accreditors for Continuing Education and Training) mission is to "advance the global workforce by providing the standard framework for quality learning and development through accreditation." The ANSI/IACET standard for continuing education and training provides a proven model to develop effective continuing education and training programs.

Even without a specific standard for talent development, TD professionals should attempt to achieve high-quality practices by establishing an internal governance group, determining curriculum review frequency, and striving for continuous improvement (Neal 2014).

1.6.5 Knowledge of Laws, Regulations, and Ethical Issues Related to Human Resources and Talent Development

> **I. Laws, Regulations, and Ethical Issues in Talent Development**
>
> TD professionals require knowledge about laws, regulations, and ethical issues related to human resources and talent development.

1.6.5.1 Sources for Appropriate Laws

The laws and regulations mentioned here are the most relevant US-based examples. Those who work outside the United States, or for an organization with offices outside the United States, should consult the laws and regulations affecting talent development in those regions. An organization's legal and human resources departments will likely have the most up-to-date information about hiring practices, testing, promotions, and other concerns related to employment law.

1.6.5.2 Hiring Practices and Testing

TD professionals will find themselves involved in hiring and promotion activities. Use of testing in hiring, promotion, or retention is an established and accepted practice. However, the potential for legal problems arise if a measure used for a significant employment decision is discriminatory. The question decided by federal courts states that procedures having an "adverse impact on the hiring, promotion, or other employment or membership opportunities of members of any race, sex, or ethnic groups will be considered to be discriminatory . . . unless the procedure has been validated" (29 CFR § 1607).

In general, this validation process requires the employer to confirm that the test criteria are directly related to job performance and that they measure those criteria. If testing is being used for hiring, promotion, employment placements of any kind, or certifications, the tests must be valid, reliable, and legally defensible. If the testing procedure has been validated in accordance with the US Equal Opportunity Commission (EEOC) guidelines, it will not be considered discriminatory.

Many industries require that employees have appropriate licenses and certifications. TD professionals may be responsible for offering courses, creating opportunities for licensing and certification, and maintaining a database that tracks all employees, their licensing status, test results, and compliance with any ongoing training and licensing renewals. TD professionals who live outside the United States should determine how hiring, testing, and job placement are regulated in their country.

1.6.5.3 Guidelines for Selection of Learners

TD professionals may be involved in selecting learners to participate in TD programs. For example, the EEOC regulations govern hiring, promoting, and training situations. Talent development–related examples include:
- Requiring training before job entry
- Selecting employees to attend internal and external programs
- Using measures in training as measures of job performance and retention
- Assigning jobs based on performance in the training program

The employer bears the burden of proof to demonstrate that any given requirement is related to job performance. TD professionals who live outside the United States should determine how selection of learners is regulated in their region.

1.6.5.4 Harassment Prevention Training Guidelines

Anti-harassment policies have received recent attention throughout the world. In June 2018, the National Academies of Sciences, Engineering, and Medicine (2018) released a report that compiled all available research on harassment prevention training. The data shows what works and what doesn't in anti-harassment training.

To be effective, harassment prevention training should:
- Focus on the desired behavior.
- Connect soft skills such as communication to harassment prevention.
- Introduce the topic during new-hire orientation.
- Provide bystander intervention training.
- Engage outside consultants to deliver the training for the executive audience.

Harassment prevention training should avoid:
- Emphasizing what not to do
- Spending time on understanding the law

- Trying to change participants' attitudes
- Delivering training without a live instructor

TD professionals are frequently asked to design and deliver ethical behavior and compliance training programs. The list of what worked and what doesn't provides a guide for effective training design. TD professionals outside the United States should investigate whether changes may have occurred in their regions.

1.6.5.5 Labor Relations

In the United States, two labor relations laws affect talent development: the Wagner and Taft-Hartley Acts. The Wagner Act prohibits discrimination against union employees regarding terms and conditions of employment, including apprenticeships and learning programs. The National Labor Relations Board considers training to be a condition of employment and a mandatory subject for collective bargaining. The Taft-Hartley Act permits noncoercive employer free speech, which may affect TD professionals. For example, in training, instructors should not use examples, case studies, or role plays that infringe on a person's philosophy or belief system. [See 1.6.3]

In the United States, TD professionals often work closely with local unions to:
- Define the type of training that should be provided.
- Determine safety training required to meet Occupational Safety and Health Administration (OSHA) guidelines.
- Maintain the records of those who have completed required training.
- Make recommendations for on-the-job training required for apprenticeship programs.

1.6.6 Knowledge of Laws, Regulations, and Ethical Issues Related to the Employment of Permanent, Contingent, or Dispersed Workforces

I. Laws, Regulations, and Ethical Issues Related to Employment

TD professionals require knowledge about laws, regulations, and ethical issues related to employment and safety of the workforce, whether it's permanent, contingent, collocated, or dispersed.

1.6.6.1 Sources for Appropriate Laws

TD professionals should consult their HR or legal department to learn more about employment laws regarding the employment of permanent, contingent, and dispersed workforces. The IRS is another resource for up-to-date content in the United States.

1.6.6.2 Legal, Regulatory, and Ethical Requirements Affecting the Permanent, Dispersed, and Contingent Workforce

Many organizations benefit by having a dispersed workforce, but there are challenges as well. A workforce can be classified into three general categories: collocated permanent employees, dispersed or remote employees, and contingent nonemployees. The challenges include managing the people, using technology securely, and protecting the brand across multiple locations.

1.6 Compliance & Ethical Behavior

Collocated permanent employees are the most common workforce members. Although laws vary greatly from country to country, in the United States organizations may be required to provide unemployment benefits, health insurance, paid vacation, paid sick days, or retirement. TD professionals may be involved in legal protections, such as maintaining regulations that protect against discrimination and harassment. [See 1.6.2 and 1.6.5]

The biggest ethical challenge for TD professionals regarding a remote workforce is that the results of the work performed must be measurable by some means other than observation. It is the responsibility of TD professionals to ensure that the collocated workforce has the tools and skills to work efficiently with a dispersed workforce, that everyone agrees the level of work is equitable, and that there are satisfactory ways to communicate on all issues.

Employees working from remote locations may experience limited management support. In addition, remote workers using mobile devices must be skilled in protecting sensitive data and adhering to the organization's cybersecurity guidance. TD professionals need to ensure that dispersed employees have effective training to comply with cybersecurity measures. Although there may be a few employment differences, remote employees generally enjoy the same benefits and legal protections as collocated employees.

Contingent or independent contractors usually present the greatest difference from a legal and regulatory perspective. The difference between an independent contractor and an employee often depends on the level of control the employer has over the person; the more control the employer has, the more likely the person is an employee. In the United States, the two types may be labeled as W2s (employees) and 1099s (consultants or contractors), which refers to the IRS forms used to document their income. When hiring a contingent worker for their expertise or to close a temporary skill gap, the organization typically provides few or no benefits or legal protections and is not obligated to provide developmental opportunities.

The legal ramification of hiring an independent worker is particularly significant to the TD function because they often use external consultants and facilitators. TD employees are likely to work side by side with contingent workers and may be responsible for their learning and development. Having an awareness of employment status is important because categorizing an external consultant or an internal employee incorrectly could have serious financial consequences, cause punitive damages, and result in penalties for the organization (OFCCP n.d.).

Talent development can help everyone work collaboratively and protect the organization's brand image. Challenges can be circumvented when TD professionals develop employees so they communicate effectively and build trust across dispersed teams. Everyone must understand the organization's values and how to implement them.

1.6.6.3 Workplace Safety and OSHA

Safety is an area of potential liability for TD professionals and their organizations. Safety infractions can occur because of:
- Injury to the person being trained, customers, or the general public
- Injury from an unsafe training facility or equipment
- Failure to train an employee who depends on the training

The US Occupational Safety and Health Act of 1970, which established the Occupational Safety and Health Administration (OSHA), requires employers to "furnish each of [their] employees employment and a place of employment which is free from recognized hazards that are causing or are likely to cause death or serious physical harm." Specific safety standards exist for each industry, and they have implications for TD professionals and those directing learning and development programs. Those who work outside the United States must learn what regulations guide their employees and what training they need to deliver to ensure regulations and laws are followed.

1.6.7 Knowledge of Regional and Market-Specific Education and Labor Public Policies

I. Global Laws and Regulations Affecting Talent Development
TD professionals whose work spans regions and countries have unique considerations. They must understand the laws and requirements of other countries and regions.

1.6.7.1 Ethical Differences Between Countries
Ethics vary widely between countries. Common international ethical differences may include working standards and conditions, workplace diversity and equal opportunity, child labor laws, supervisory oversight, human rights, religion, trust and integrity, bribery, and corruption. To learn more about the differences, TD professionals should:
- Gather data from their organization's HR department.
- Talk to someone from the country or culture.
- Read relevant books.
- Explore online news sources from the country or culture.
- Visit cultural centers.

1.6.7.2 IT Compliance
TD professionals are often asked to assist IT departments, which are mandated to adapt to emerging and rapidly changing information technologies, including improving the usability, reliability, and security of the organization's computer networks. National IT standards have been established to ensure that all systems and architecture work together. TD functions must provide access to courses and information to comply with these requirements. Talent development will work closely with the IT function to help it meet its legal requirements and, for example, to protect the organization against phishing and other hacking attacks. TD professionals may also help IT design, update, or enhance necessary training such as cybersecurity awareness training.

1.6.7.3 Data Act
Enacted in Sweden for all countries on May 11, 1973, the Data Act was the world's first data protection law. Since then, other data privacy laws have been passed in various countries, providing the foundational concepts for GDPR. The information privacy Data Act provided the basic principles of data protection including:
- There should be a stated purpose for all collected data.
- Information collected cannot be disclosed unless authorized by law or by the individual's consent.

- Records must be accurate and up to date.
- A mechanism must be available for individuals to review data about themselves.
- Data should be deleted when it is no longer needed.
- Transmission of personal information to locations where it cannot be protected is prohibited.

1.6.7.4 United Nations Convention

The first comprehensive human rights treaty of the 21st century was intended to serve as a human rights instrument. The Convention on the Rights of Persons with Disabilities (CRPD) and its optional protocol was adopted by the United Nations on December 13, 2006. It addresses a broad categorization of people with disabilities and reaffirms that anyone with any disability must enjoy all human rights and fundamental freedoms. It identifies areas where adaptations must be made for those with disabilities to effectively exercise their rights and where protection of rights must be reinforced. On the fundamental issue of accessibility, the convention required countries to identify and eliminate obstacles and barriers and ensure that those with disabilities could access their environment, transportation, public facilities and services, and information and communications technologies. The mandate for talent development is much like the ADA—to ensure accessibility for those in courses (UN 2006).

1.6.7.5 Region-Specific Laws and Regulations

Employment law, education, and labor regulatory requirements change from country to country. Some laws may also change from state to state.

REFERENCES

ALA (American Library Association). 2019. "Copyright: Distance Education and the TEACH Act." ALA, March 10. ala.org/advocacy/copyright/teachact/distanceeducation.

Bishop, W. 2013. "The Role of Ethics in 21st Century Organizations." *Journal of Business Ethics* 118:635–637.

Carroll, A., and A. Buchholtz. 2014. *Business and Society: Ethics, Sustainability, and Stakeholder Management*. Stamford, CT: Cengage.

Chen, H., and E. Soltes. 2018. "Why Compliance Programs Fail." *Harvard Business Review*, March–April.

EEOC (US Equal Employment Opportunity Commission). 2011. "Facts About the Americans With Disabilities Act." eeoc.gov/eeoc/publications/fs-ada.cfm.

Ferrell, O.C., J. Fraedrich, and F. Ferrell. 2017. *Business Ethics: Ethical Decision Making and Cases*, 12th ed. Boston: CENGAGE Publishing.

Gallo, A. 2010. "You've Made a Mistake. Now What?" *Harvard Business Review*, April 28. hbr.org/2010/04/youve-made-a-mistake-now-what.

Gino, F., L.D. Ordóñez, and D. Welsh. 2014. "How Unethical Behavior Becomes Habit." *Harvard Business Review*, September 4. hbr.org/2014/09/how-unethical-behavior-becomes-habit.

GSA (US General Services Administration). 2017. "Accessibility News: The Section 508 Update." section508.gov/blog/accessibility-news-the-Section-508-Update.

Hartman, L.P., J.R. DesJardins, and C. MacDonald. 2014. *Business Ethics: Decision Making for Personal Integrity and Social Responsibility*, 3rd ed. New York: McGraw-Hill/Irwin.

IACET (International Accreditors for Continuing Education and Training). 2012. "ANSI/IACET 2018-1 Standard for Continuing Education and Training." IACET. iacet.org/standards/ansi-iacet-2018-1-standard-for-continuing-education-and-training.

National Academies of Sciences, Engineering, and Medicine. 2018. *Sexual Harassment of Women: Climate, Culture, and Consequences in Academic Sciences, Engineering, and Medicine*. Washington, DC: The National Academies Press.

Neal, B. 2014. "How to Develop Training Quality Standards." *Infoline*. Alexandria, VA: ASTD Press.

Noe, R.A., J.R. Hollenbeck, B. Gerhart, and P.M. Wright. 2015. *Human Resource Management: Gaining a Competitive Advantage*, 9th ed. New York: McGraw-Hill.

Occupational Safety and Health Act of 1970, 29 USC § 654 (1970). osha.gov/laws-regs/oshact/section5-duties.

OFCCP (US Office of Federal Contract Compliance Programs). n.d. "Guide for Small Businesses With Federal Contracts." sba.gov/federal-contracting/contracting-guide.

Orey, M. 2017. "Designing Section 508 Compliant Learning." *TD at Work*. Alexandria, VA: ATD Press.

SHRM. 2015. "Complying with Employment Record Requirements." Society for Human Resource Management. shrm.org/resourcesandtools/tools-and-samples/toolkits/pages/complyingwithemploymentrecordrequirements.aspx.

Sherbin, L., and J. Kennedy. 2017. "The Case for Improving Work for People With Disabilities Goes Way Beyond Compliance." *Harvard Business Review*, December 27.

Steingold, F. 2013. *The Employer's Legal Handbook*, 11th ed. Berkeley, CA: NOLO.

Swindling, L.B., and M.V.B. Partridge. 2014. "The Legal Aspects of Training: Protect What Is Yours and Avoid Taking What Belongs to Someone Else." Chapter 18 in *ASTD Handbook: The Definitive Reference for Training and Development*, edited by E. Biech. Alexandria, VA: ASTD Press.

Treviño, L.K., and K.A. Nelson. 2013. *Managing Business Ethics: Straight Talk About How to Do It Right*, 6th ed. Hoboken, NJ: John Wiley and Sons.

UN (United Nations). 2006. "The Convention in Brief." From the Convention on the Rights of Persons With Disabilities (CRPD). United Nations, December 15. un.org/development/desa/disabilities/convention-on-the-rights-of-persons-with-disabilities/the-convention-in-brief.html.

Uniform Guidelines on Employee Selection Procedures, 29 CFR § 1607 (1978).

US Copyright Office. 2006. "Definitions (FAQ)." Copyright.gov. copyright.gov/help/faq/faq-definitions.html.

Waugh, T. 2017. "Building Compliance Training That Actually Matters." *TD at Work*. Alexandria, VA: ATD Press.

Waugh, T. 2019. *Fully Compliant: Compliance Training to Change Behavior*. Alexandria, VA: ATD Press.

Recommended Reading

Chesnut, R. 2020. *Intentional Integrity: How Smart Companies Can Lead an Ethical Revolution*. New York: St. Martin's Press.

Collins, D. 2019. *Business Ethics: How to Design and Manage Ethical Organizations*, 2nd ed. Thousand Oaks, CA: SAGE Publications.

Dalio, R. 2017. *Principles*. New York: Simon and Schuster.

Waugh, T. 2019. *Fully Compliant: Compliance Training to Change Behavior*. Alexandria, VA: ATD Press.

1.7 LIFELONG LEARNING

Lifelong learning is sometimes called continuous learning, agile learning, or learning drive. It is marked by traits such as self-motivation, insatiable curiosity, and intelligent risk-taking. TD professionals should model the value of lifelong learning by pursuing knowledge for personal and professional reasons. Taking ownership for one's own professional development signals to others that they can and should do the same.

1.7.1 Knowledge of How a Desire to Learn Can Lead to the Expansion and Development of Knowledge and Skills Over Time

> **I. Lifelong Learning**
> TD professionals should model lifelong learning for their organizations and clients by continuously seeking knowledge and being open to learning new skills.

1.7.1.1 Lifelong Learner Traits

Lifelong learner traits are associated with two learning theories: cognitivism and constructivism. [See 2.1.1.6] *Cognitivism* addresses learning by making sense of the relationship between what has been learned in the past and what is being learned. In fact, George Hallenbeck (2016) uses "sensemaking" in his model to describe learning from experience, a key element of lifelong learning. *Constructivism* theorizes that learning derives from many sources, including life experiences, and that what is learned depends on individual traits and how learners internalize what they have learned. [See 3.8.6.6 and 2.1.1]

ATD's 2018 report on lifelong learning found that "high performers are more likely to make developing lifelong learning behaviors a priority." According to the study, the traits and attributes of these lifelong learners include:
- Viewing learning as an exciting opportunity
- Self-motivation
- Self-awareness and knowledge of own interests
- Being open-minded
- Insatiable curiosity

1.7.1.2 Lifelong Learner Behaviors

Lifelong learners demonstrate many behaviors. ATD research found that the top required behaviors were:
- Asking questions
- Experimenting and trying new things
- Seeking resources and doing own research
- Applying new knowledge
- Sharing knowledge and teaching others

Lifelong learning does not depend on technology. In fact, tech savvy ranked last among the list of 13 potential attributes included in ATD's lifelong learning report. In contrast, responses showed that "lifelong learning relies more on an individual's mindset, determination, curiosity, and other characteristics" (ATD 2018). In other research, a Pew study found that digital technology played a very important role in the delivery of learning (Horrigan 2016). Although technology skills weren't necessary, using technology to learn was (for example, using a smartphone to watch a video or read an e-book).

1.7.1.3 Advantages to Employees

Lifelong learning has advantages for employees that are both personal and professional (ATD 2018; Horrigan 2016; Hallenbeck 2016).

Personal benefits:
- More opportunities to improve quality of life
- Boost confidence and self-esteem
- Challenge beliefs and opinions
- Achieve more satisfying life
- Increase personal development
- Less likely to derail their career

Professional benefits:
- Increases ability to adapt to change
- Less risk averse
- Improved job performance
- Improved levels of engagement
- Enhanced professional development
- Increased opportunities for advancement

1.7.1.4 Advantages to Organizations

Although individuals may seem to benefit most, organizations also reap value from investing in a culture that supports lifelong learning. ATD's 2018 research on lifelong learning found that the top five benefits to the organization were improved:
- Employee engagement levels
- Overall organizational performance
- Ability to retain talent
- Ability to meet changing organizational needs and objectives
- Organizational competitive ability

Learning organizations are places "where people continually expand their capacity to create the results they truly desire, where new and expansive patterns of thinking are nurtured, where collective aspiration is set free, and where people are continually learning how to learn together" (Senge 2006). *Harvard Business Review* describes the advantages of a learning organization as "improved innovation, agility, and organizational learning" (Groysberg et al. 2018). TD professionals should be prepared to provide evidence of the value of lifelong learning and examples relevant to the organization. [See 3.3.7]

1.7.1.5 Skills Lifelong Learners Need

According to George Hallenbeck (2016), "Learning agile individuals are distinguished by their willingness and ability to learn from experience." But he stresses that they must also excel at applying what they learn. He believes that something is not really learned until it is applied.

According to Hallenbeck, the skills required to become a lifelong agile learner fall into four categories and include, but are not limited to:

- **Seeking skills**—the ability to identify the boundaries of one's comfort zone, skills required to take risks, and the skill to expand one's network
- **Sensemaking skills**—the ability to identify learning opportunities, question one's own beliefs and perspectives, and prepare mentally and physically to learn
- **Internalizing skills**—the ability to reflect on and monitor progress, the capacity to pursue feedback, and the ability to identify experiences that promote self-awareness
- **Applying skills**—the skills to measure progress, the ability to identify connections and consistencies, and the skills to apply learning in planned and spontaneous situations

1.7.1.6 Opportunities

TD professionals should find ways to demonstrate to their leaders how lifelong learning and a culture of learning can provide opportunities for both individuals and the organization. For example, employers want employees who can solve problems, communicate, think critically, and collaborate with others; these skills are often a result of self-aware employees who are open to learning. ATD's research (2018) found that the top three benefits of lifelong learning to organizations were increased engagement, improved performance, and talent retention. [See 1.7.1.4]

Employees, on the other hand, want to learn, develop, and grow. A culture of lifelong learning leads to faster promotions and increased readiness for opportunities. For employees, successful job performance and career advancement are related to their desire to learn. [See 1.7.1.3]

1.7.1.7 Options for Learning

TD professionals should recognize how a desire to learn leads to the expansion and development of knowledge and skills over time. To take advantage of this, TD professionals should be prepared to offer learning opportunities, which fall into these four categories:

- **On-the-job,** such as accessing online tutorials, job shadowing, or completing a job rotation
- **Participating in courses, training programs, or certifications,** including taking an online course, attending an in-person learning event, or attaining a certification

- **Informal daily options,** such as joining a managers' networking group, mentoring an intern, or conducting research on a future project
- **Learning outside the organization,** including volunteering, speaking at a conference, or participating in an executive exchange

1.7.1.8 Maintain a Growth Mindset

A culture of learning requires a growth mindset, or the belief that people can increase their talent and ability through curiosity and learning. The growth mindset concept was pioneered by Carol Dweck (2013). Her research shows that employees with a growth mindset have a desire to learn and a tendency to embrace change, learn from criticism, and find inspiration in the success of others. [See 3.3.7.10]

A report by McKinsey and Company identified seven lifelong learning mindset practices that can help TD professionals and others become lifelong learners (Brassey, Coates, and van Dam 2019):

1. **Focus on growth** by ensuring employees have a growth mindset as defined by Dweck. TD professionals can help them see that there are no limitations to what they can learn.
2. **Become a serial master** by achieving mastery in several topics. As the world changes faster and people work longer, TD professionals should encourage employees to develop different areas of expertise to retain relevancy.
3. **Stretch outside their comfort zone.** TD professionals can encourage individuals to try new tasks, acquire new knowledge, and develop new skills.
4. **Build a personal brand and network** to understand what skills they need, set goals, recognize what they want to be known for, and their network. TD professionals can help others identify what differentiates them and prepare them for new opportunities.
5. **Own a personal development journey** by creating learning goals, measuring progress, working with mentors, seeking feedback, and making an investment. TD professionals can show others the skills required to take control of their own development.
6. **Discover *ikigai*** (Japanese for *reason for being*), which gives TD professionals four elements for an aligned future focus by discussing the intersection of doing what they love, what the world needs, what they are good at, and what they can be paid for.
7. **Stay vital,** which requires prioritizing health—including decisions about sleep, exercise, eating, meditation—and practicing a positive mindset.

1.7.2 Knowledge of Resources for Career Exploration and Lifelong Learning for Self and Others

I. Fundamentals of Career Exploration

Exploring personal growth and career options is a valuable skill for TD professionals. They should be knowledgeable about the fundamentals of career exploration to grow personally and help others learn and grow.

1.7.2.1 Role of Lifelong Learning in Career Exploration

To achieve results and attain goals, organizations must unlock the potential of their employees. A learning culture increases efficiency and employee satisfaction, develops a sense of ownership and accountability, creates a culture of knowledge sharing, and develops an enhanced ability for employees to adapt to change (Biech 2018). The role of lifelong learning becomes clear as both individuals and the organization benefit.

Organizations and roles are changing dramatically, and employees will require new skill sets and knowledge. To flourish, individuals must be in a continuous learning mode. Barbara Mistick and Karie Willyerd (2016) say that "tomorrow's workplace is being shaped by megatrends underway now." Their studies show that workers who are lifelong learners are prepared for the future and are the ones who thrive. [See 3.8]

According to Amanda Smith (2019), self-directed learning occurs when individuals "take complete ownership of their learning, from the needs assessment through goal-setting, active participation, and evaluation." She goes on to say that TD professionals must integrate a diverse range of learning opportunities to support and connect an individual's career to lifelong learning. When that occurs, the role of lifelong learning becomes a value to the individual and the organization. [See 1.7.1.3 and 1.7.1.4]

TD professionals should be able to balance others' career development desires with the future talent requirements of the organization. By understanding what the organization will be doing and what skills its leaders and employees will require to complete the work five years and beyond, they will be able to provide informed recommendations to employees (Biech 2018). TD professionals must be aware of career development theories to provide an approach and a way to measure results. Several theories will be presented in the next section. [See 3.4.14]

1.7.2.2 Career Development Theories and Approaches

Career development theories and approaches provide the basis for individual career development and link closely to organizational talent management. To be effective, TD professionals must have a working knowledge of various career development theories and approaches and how they best apply to the individual or organization.

Williamson's Trait-Factor Theory (Late 1930s)

This traditional approach to career decision making, based on work by Donald G. Paterson and E.G. Williamson, is still widely used. *Traits* refer to characteristics that can be measured through testing; *factors* are the characteristics required for successful job performance. The approach is based on the theory that people can be understood in terms of the traits they possess (such as intelligence, ambition, aptitude, and self-esteem). Factors are statistical representations of those traits. Trait-factor counseling is defined as matching people to jobs.

Super's Developmental Framework (1957)

D.E. Super based his theory of career development on the idea that careers move through five distinct stages and the choice of an occupation is influenced by each person's self-image and how this self-image maps to those already in a particular occupation. The five stages are:

1. **Growth stage.** As children, people develop interests and values through interactions at home, with friends, and in school.
2. **Exploratory stage.** From adolescence through their mid-20s, people's interests, aptitudes, and values solidify as they explore different roles and life situations.
3. **Establishment stage.** By their mid-20s, people achieve stable careers.
4. **Maintenance stage.** By age 45, most people are settled into their occupations.
5. **Decline stage.** Retirees who are most successful carry their vocational interests into retirement.

Personality or Typology Theory

Several theories help explain how individuals choose careers. For example, career choice content theory centers on the consistency of career choices and how realistic those choices are in matching an individual's core strengths and characteristics:

- Roe's 1956 theory of occupation includes eight groups of service and six decision levels. It is the basis for many tests that help determine one's best career choice based on interests.
- Holland's 1960 occupational congruency model matches individuals to their best career choice through interviews that address six work environments: realistic (motor coordination and concrete problem solving), investigative (ideas and intellectual activity), artistic (self-expression), social (interaction with others), enterprising (verbal and social skills), and conventional (rules and regulations).
- Psychodynamic theory is a tool used to help predict career success, choice, and behavior by trying to understand what motivates individuals and the internal conflicts that exist in humans.

Schein's Career Anchors Theory (1980s)

Edgar Schein identified what he calls "career anchors," which are a combination of competencies, motives, values, and attitudes that provide direction to an individual's career. These anchors become the drivers for an individual's choices. Schein's study found that as individuals learned more about themselves, their career choices were affected. Schein categorized the basic drivers of these career decisions into eight career anchors that fit all individuals: technical or functional competence, general managerial competence, autonomy or independence, security or stability, entrepreneurial creativity, service or dedication to a cause, pure challenge, and lifestyle. The tool helps individuals gain personal insight and make choices.

Behavioral Theory (1998-2002)

Behavioral career counseling is a scientific approach to career decision making that leverages psychology concepts. The approach notes that career-related behavior results from past events and can be broken down into its component parts so clients can understand their own behavior. Krumboltz, for example, has provided a direct link between social learning theory and career development and decision making. Krumboltz's model is known as the DECIDES model:

- **Define** the problem.
- **Establish** an action plan.
- **Clarify** values.
- **Identify** alternatives.
- **Discover** probable outcomes.
- **Eliminate** alternatives systematically.
- **Start** action.

1.7.2.3 Career Planning Process

The career planning process requires that TD professionals have several skills to assist others with career exploration. These skills include selecting assessment tools, interviewing and counseling individual employees, producing and interpreting reports based on assessments, and assisting individuals in developing realistic career plans. TD professionals should know where and how to locate resources and tools for career exploration opportunities, such as:

- Online databases—industry exploration websites and national repositories of occupational information (for example, the US Department of Labor's O*NET)
- In person—industry showcases and campus events
- Networks—people in the field or related to the field [See 2.3.7, 1.3.2.1, 1.3.2.2, and 2.5.9]
- Professional publications
- Career counselling professionals
- Competency models for specific professions
- Tools—such as occupation profiles, salary finders, and skills matchers

1.7.2.4 Lifelong Learning Web Resources
Knowledge of resources for career exploration is critical for TD professionals. Every TD professional should establish a menu of options that includes categories such as:
- Online courses
- Video lectures
- Streaming documentaries
- Open source learning
- Digital education guides
- Online conferences and learning events
- Education repositories

1.7.3 Skill in Acquiring New Knowledge Through Professional Development Activities for One's Self

> **I. Professional Learning Activities**
>
> TD professionals should have skills in identifying and procuring professional development activities for themselves and the clients they support.

1.7.3.1 Modeling Lifelong Learning and Professional Development
Learning is unavoidable and knowledge can be acquired anywhere at any time; however, TD professionals must have a set of mental tools they can use to model lifelong learning for others. According to Erika Andersen (2016), lifelong learners are self-aware, have a desire to learn, are curious, and are willing to be vulnerable.

TD professionals have the skills to identify what they need to learn and are willing to put themselves in uncomfortable situations to learn. They are honest with themselves, and can they assess their needs and establish professional development goals. They determine professional development needs by monitoring trends and future requirements and comparing their knowledge and skills to identify gaps. They may apply this information to their own needs or to those of others.

To model lifelong learning, TD professionals must be able to help others learn how they learn. Metacognitive control refers to the actions that learners take to manage their own learning and includes three basic components: planning, monitoring, and evaluation (Schraw 1998). TD professionals must practice critical and creative thinking to select tactics to meet a developmental need. They may select from numerous learning venues, such as conferences, reading, rotational assignments, stretch assignments, shadowing, mentoring, technology options, or social networking. [See 2.3.6.7]

1.7.3.2 Barriers to Lifelong Learning

TD professionals should also be aware of any obstacles that may prevent lifelong learning. ATD research (2018) identified five barriers to lifelong learning, with the most common being a personal "lack of motivation for non-required learning." The second most common was the organizational culture. If the culture did not support lifelong learning or leaders were not modeling lifelong learning, it became an underlying issue to encourage other employees to become lifelong learners.

The final three barriers as defined by ATD include the "difficulty quantifying the effects of lifelong learning on organizational results, a lack of accountability for non-job-related learning, and employees don't know how to self-direct their learning."

TD professionals should also be aware that socio-economic class, race, and ethnicity pose a challenge to lifelong learning. Pew Research found that some people are "less likely to engage in professional or personal learning and have less positive views of their impacts" (Horrigan 2016).

1.7.3.3 TD Strategies to Support Lifelong Learning

Peter Senge states, "Much has changed in the decades since I wrote the first edition of *The Fifth Discipline*. But one thing has not changed—the need for people in organizations to learn—individually and collectively" (Biech 2018). TD professionals should be able to tap into many strategies for themselves and for others, such as the ones suggested by ATD (2018):

- Accessing courses and assets
- Partnering with educational institutions
- Providing tuition assistance
- Creating individual development plans for employees and leaders [See 2.6.8.3 and 2.6.2.2]
- Making it easy for individuals to discover learning opportunities
- Offering learning assets (such as lists of in-person programs, webinars, and virtual workshops; libraries of self-paced courses; mobile learning; and microlearning assets)
- Encouraging knowledge sharing (such as supporting collaborative work practices, using a knowledge-sharing platform, and including time during meetings to share knowledge)

1.7.4 Skill in Developing, Maintaining, and Leveraging Networks Across a Range of People and Groups Inside and Outside the Organization

I. Networking Principles

TD professionals should hone their skills in developing and leveraging networks so they can leverage their own networks and help others develop their networking skills.

1.7.4.1 Professional Purpose of Networking

Networking takes place in many forms and places. TD professionals should consider their own needs for networking as well as the needs of other employees. Networks can be inside or outside the organization and can serve many purposes. To be effective, networks need to be developed, maintained, and leveraged. Networking requires an attitude of generosity—giving and helping first before expecting anything in return.

TD professionals should build networks inside their organizations and beyond. They can support members of their own networks by introducing them to others or sending them information they can use. TD professionals can define informal networks that serve different purposes, for example:
- **Advice networks** can be used to solve problems.
- **Trust networks** provide a location to share sensitive information.
- **Communication networks** are used to discuss work-related matters.
- **Information networks** focus on a need to transform or improve systems and procedures.
- **Influence networks** focus on organizational politics, the distribution of power, and cultural concerns.
- **Affect networks** are friends in the organization who help create the corporate culture.

Because organizations experience major changes, all employees should have networks they can leverage that span department boundaries so they are prepared if they must change positions, departments, or even locations. There are other advantages to internal networking as well. [See 1.7.4.3]

Individuals should also consider external networking outside their organization. The obvious reason is to prepare them for other job opportunities. But other reasons to do so include obtaining fresh ideas to solve problems on the job, advancing their careers, gaining new skills, raising their profiles by being visible, and learning about best practices that could transfer to the job.

Social media is now an integral part of networking. Experts generally recommend against individuals joining every social media network. Instead, they should choose specific networks to focus on based on which will be the most beneficial to them. Individuals should determine who they want to meet and on which social media platform they are likely to find them. [See 1.3.2]

Networking is also critical for TD professionals who consult or freelance and are not employed internally. TD consultants should find ways to optimize their social media presence to increase awareness of their services. They need to create a strategy, establish goals, and follow through on their plans. They also need to remember that the difference between them and employees is that they are networking to develop personally, enhance their careers, and grow their business. Networking may help consultants and freelancers generate referrals, demonstrate a positive influence, connect with more influential people, and meet potential partners, collaborators, and clients.

1.7.4.2 Personal Purpose for Networking

Building and maintaining connections is the underlying purpose of networking. TD professionals should know how to help individuals determine their personal purpose because networking won't be meaningful unless they see its value. The personal purpose an individual has for networking could include:
- Finding personal mentors
- Learning about other opportunities

- Providing a platform as a sounding board
- Practicing communication and social skills
- Making new friends

TD professionals can guide individuals to determine their personal need for networking by asking several questions:
- Are you networking for personal or professional reasons?
- What problem are you trying to solve?
- What are your career aspirations?
- Where do you see yourself in three years?

Then, TD professionals can use these questions to help guide the individual to determine where and how to focus their networking activities:
- What skills, knowledge, or experience does the ideal networking partner have?
- Where would you find this type of networking partner?
- Do you have someone specific in mind?
- How would you begin to connect with this networking partner? What do you have in common?

TD professionals can also plant the seeds of sincere networking. Individuals should recognize that networking can be most valuable when each party enters the relationship with authenticity, veracity, reliability, and a willingness to find mutual value. [See 1.7.4.6]

1.7.4.3 Benefits of Networking

The benefits of networking are many and varied. The beauty is that it can be anything anyone wants it to be. The benefits will align with networking's purpose—individuals benefit from networking personally and professionally.

Personal benefits include:
- Building self-esteem and confidence
- Expanding a support network
- Making connections
- Developing personal relationships
- Increasing visibility and recognition

Professional benefits include:
- Increasing chances for promotion
- Gaining professional skills and career advice
- Finding a more suitable job
- Creating a source to find answers to any question
- Providing a place to express and discuss industry-related options and opinions

Successful networkers know that sincere networking is mutually beneficial, so they should examine the benefits they can give as well as those they get. No one expects networkers to be altruistic, but helping others can be rewarding. For example, a networker can give these benefits:
- Creating an opportunity to help others begin their careers
- Providing a forum to discuss a charity or personal cause

- Developing new friendships
- Becoming a mentor to someone

1.7.4.4 Behaviors Required for Networking

TD professionals and others who choose to network must master several skills to be successful—especially during planned networking events:

- **Listen skillfully.** Because networking is a mutually beneficial relationship, it is more important to listen than to talk. Build trust by listening.
- **Display diplomacy and tact.** Model good networking skills with everyone. Be discreet, sensitive, and insightful. Use the six Cs of communication and, above all, avoid bragging. [See 1.1.1.3]
- **Demonstrate a positive attitude.** This should come through in the person's words, tone, body language, and outlook on life.
- **Keep moving.** Minimize time with each person. Don't monopolize anyone's time or become an annoyance.
- **Be a giver.** Focus on the other person and don't expect anything in return. Networking is not trading; it is building and maintaining connections for shared mutual gains. Help others succeed.
- **Plan strategically.** Just as a business makes investments to gain a return, investing in networking should deliver the return that is desired.
- **Practice authenticity.** No one should pretend to be someone they aren't; they will be discovered.
- **Remember names.** Networking is about building relationships for the future. Remembering names isn't easy, but there are tricks one can learn to improve name recall.
- **Ask interesting questions.** Networking is about getting the other person to talk. Ask questions that find the passion in others to learn what excites them, the best thing that's happened to them, what they're looking forward to, or what's important to them.
- **Follow up.** The best networking occurs after the networking event is over. Make the follow-up immediate and personal.

1.7.4.5 Establish Goals: Who, What, Where, When, and How

Like almost any successful endeavor, networking should start with a goal. Successful networkers have short-term and long-term goals—each increasing in difficulty and focusing on continued learning and development. Setting networking goals might be different from writing a SMART goal because they might be broken down into who, what, where, when, and how. Or they may just focus on one of those five questions.

TD professionals can use the who, what, where, when, and how questions to focus on their own goals or help others establish networking goals:

- **Who?** Perhaps the goal is to connect with an influential person. Because they may be approached frequently, determine how to connect with them and show gratitude. This question might also identify a group of people; for example, authors if the professional goal is to write a book or golfers if the personal goal is to join a country club.
- **What?** This question might conjure up questions about what the ultimate goal is, what problem needs solving, or even what is not known.
- **Where?** This question may require some research to determine if any company, community, team, club, or city-wide networking events are already scheduled. Learning where networking events occur is a good place to start.

- **When?** Some goals may be more adaptable as an individual begins the networking journey. The goal could simply mean scheduling one event each week or month to learn more about the activity.
- **How?** The goal might be to find a mutual connection, such as a location, a person, an interest, or something that connects them to their ultimate reason for networking.

For long-term goals, Rob Cross and Robert Thomas (2011) suggest beginning to build an effective network by following their four-step model:

1. **Analyze** what is delivered by the current network.
2. **De-layer** or remove energy-sapping relationships.
3. **Diversify** by adding people who will help achieve identified goals.
4. **Capitalize** by using the network.

They also recommend listing three results to achieve in the coming year and the people who could help.

1.7.4.6 Ensuring Networking Success

Once TD professionals have built a network, they should monitor who's in it, maintain its vibrancy, and leverage the network with integrity to continue accomplishing what it was originally intended for.

- **Monitor the network.** Networking may be difficult to start, but it can also get out of hand quickly. Individuals should ensure that they have solid goals in mind and that they focus on them. To maintain integrity in networking, they need to be certain that they are giving at least as much as they are getting (Zack 2010). Effective monitoring occurs when individuals screen those who are in their networks to determine if they still meet the intended goals. They may need to make hard decisions—people may need to be removed from the network due to limited time, or time may need to be minimized with people who take without giving, waste time, drain their energy, or create a negative atmosphere.
- **Maintain a vibrant network.** A vibrant network can be maintained by adding new people to take the place of those who were removed. The most successful networkers make it a priority to meet a diverse array of people. They schedule networking regularly to build and constantly maintain their network. Instead of only reaching out to others during a time of need, an individual who maintains a vibrant network has people available all the time. Maintaining a vibrant network requires both giving and asking. It means being available when someone wants to discuss an idea or asks for an introduction. Maintaining a network also occurs when an individual asks for support, ideas, or connections. Networking needs to be mutually beneficial.
- **Leverage networking with integrity.** Sometimes new networkers build a network but then don't use it. Adopting the right mindset—an abundance mentality—and finding the right balance makes networking beneficial for both parties. TD professionals may be concerned about giving and gaining mutual value, which is difficult—especially when one person is at a higher status. If the other person is at a higher status, they can consider what that person might find of value. It may be as simple as having the opportunity to invest in another person's career or reporting on the results of advice that was given. Remembering to say thank you is often the only value someone needs. Showing gratitude is a key part of leveraging networking with integrity (Azulay 2018).

REFERENCES

Andersen, E. 2016. "Learning to Learn." *Harvard Business Review*, March.

ATD (Association for Talent Development). 2018. *Lifelong Learning: The Path to Personal and Organizational Performance*. Alexandria, VA: ATD Press.

Azulay, H. 2018. "Networking With Integrity." *ATD Insights*, August 29. td.org/insights/networking-with-integrity.

Biech, E. 2018. *ATD's Foundations of Talent Development: Launching, Leveraging, and Leading Your Organization's TD Effort*. Alexandria, VA: ATD Press.

Brassey, J., K. Coates, and N. van Dam. 2019. *Seven Essential Elements of a Lifelong-Learning Mind-Set*. New York: McKinsey and Company.

Cross, R., and R. Thomas. 2011. "A Smarter Way to Network: Successful Executives Connect With Select People and Get More Out of Them." *Harvard Business Review*, July–August.

Dweck, C. 2013. *Mindset: The New Psychology of Success*. New York: Random House.

Groysberg, B., J. Lee, J. Price, and J. Cheng. 2018. "The Leader's Guide to Corporate Culture." *Harvard Business Review*, January–February.

Hallenbeck, G. 2016. *Learning Agility: Unlock the Lessons of Experience*. Greensboro, NC: Center for Creative Leadership.

Horrigan, J. 2016. *Lifelong Learning and Technology*. Washington, DC: Pew Research Center. pewresearch.org/wp-content/uploads/sites/9/2016/03/PI_2016.03.22_Educational-Ecosystems_FINAL.pdf

Mistick, B., and K. Willyerd. 2016. *Stretch: How to Future-Proof Yourself for Tomorrow's Workplace*. Hoboken, NJ: John Wiley and Sons.

Schraw, G. 1998. "Promoting General Metacognitive Awareness." *Instructional Science* 26:113–125.

Senge, P.M. 2006. *The Fifth Discipline: The Art and Practice of the Learning Organization*, rev. ed. New York: Currency/Doubleday.

Smith, A. 2019. "Self-Directed Learning Made Simple." *TD at Work*. Alexandria, VA: ATD Press.

Zack, D. 2010. *Networking for People Who Hate Networking*. San Francisco: Berrett-Koehler.

Recommended Reading

Hallenbeck, G. 2016. *Learning Agility: Unlock the Lessons of Experience*. Greensboro, NC: Center for Creative Leadership.

Hart, T. 2021. *Hardwired to Learn: Leveraging the Self-Sustaining Power of Lifelong Learning*. Chakra7 Press.

Mistick, B., and K. Willyerd. 2016. *Stretch: How to Future-Proof Yourself for Tomorrow's Workplace*. Hoboken, NJ: John Wiley and Sons.

Domain 2

Developing Professional Capability

2.1 LEARNING SCIENCES

Organizations with highly effective learning programs incorporate key principles from the learning sciences, the interdisciplinary research-based field that works to further the understanding of learning, learning innovation, and instructional methodologies. Talent development professionals applying best practices will understand and apply foundational learning theories, principles of adult learning theory, and cognitive science to design, develop, and deliver solutions that maximize outcomes.

2.1.1 Knowledge of the Foundational Learning Theories of Behaviorism, Cognitivism, and Constructivism

> **I. Foundational Learning Theories**
>
> TD professionals should be familiar with the foundational theories for learning: behaviorism, cognitivism, and constructivism. These theories, along with the techniques associated with them, should influence how TD professionals facilitate learning across the workplace.

2.1.1.1 Value of the Knowledge of Learning Theories to the TD Professional

TD professionals must be grounded in learning theory, which provides practitioners with a structure for making informed decisions about how to best help others learn. The best learning theories are based on years of research and debate, giving credibility to clients and stakeholders and confidence to practitioners. As Kurt Lewin (1943), a founder of modern organizational development, said, "Nothing is so practical as a good theory."

However, not all learning theories stand the test of time, so TD professionals need to understand each one; the values and presuppositions that underpin them; the techniques associated with them; how they are deployed in a learning ecosystem to support talent development; and their reliability as theories based on the research behind them.

2.1.1.2 Foundational Learning Theories

Talent development, which evolved from the world of training and adult learning, is based on numerous theories about learning and how it happens. These theories were informed by researchers, psychologists, practitioners, and thought leaders over the past 100 years about why, how, and when adults learn. Their work has culminated in three of the most influential learning theories:

- Behaviorism
- Cognitivism
- Constructivism

2.1.1.2.1 Behaviorism

Behaviorism concerns predicting and controlling behavior. It focuses on observable behaviors and suggests that learning happens when associations between stimuli and responses are strengthened or weakened. It was most influential in training and development in the first half of the 20th century, although elements of it still exist in training today through learning techniques and language.

The emphasis of behaviorism is the reward and in discovering the external controls that affect internal processes. The objective is to shape behavior through reinforcement until the learner internalizes it and the new behavior becomes rewarding itself. B.F. Skinner developed the theory of operant conditioning: the concept that behavior is shaped by the consequences of reinforcement or punishment. He used programmed learning, which divides information to be learned into small steps. As learners respond at each step, they are immediately told if their answer is right or wrong. Learners progress through the materials, and their behavior is gradually shaped until the objective is achieved.

Some of the advantages of behaviorism include that it:
- Establishes objectives that are clear and unmistakable
- Ensures behavioral practice, not just theory
- Works best for helping learners acquire behavioral skills
- Is highly specific
- Is observable (learners know when they have succeeded)

2.1.1.2.2 Cognitivism

Cognitivism considers how people think and remember and "tries to understand understanding" (Clark 1999). Cognitivism focuses on mental processes that involve how people perceive, think, remember, learn, solve problems, and attend to one stimulus rather than another. While behaviorist learning theory focuses almost exclusively on external events, cognitive learning theories address what is happening internally (Sink 2014). Behaviorists identify thinking as a behavior. On the other hand, cognitivists argue that how people think influences their behavior; therefore, thinking cannot be a behavior itself.

The cognitive approach is based on the principle that learning occurs primarily through exposure to logically presented information, and retrieval or rehearsal leads to retention. Cognitivism represents a shift from focusing on behavior to an interest in the organization of memory and thinking. For cognitive scientists, the basic model of the mind is an information-processing system. TD professionals use cognitive learning strategies to build on the behavioral approach, thus, expanding their repertoire of strategies and tactics for creating development options for learners.

Some of the advantages of cognitivism include that it:
- Treats people as adults
- Focuses on thinking skills
- Emphasizes foundational knowledge
- Builds a base of information, concepts, and rules
- Provides the rationale upon which action is based (Sink 2014)

2.1.1.2.3 Constructivism

Constructivism focuses on knowledge acquisition through experiences and interactions with the environment. According to Swiss developmental psychologist Jean Piaget, learners construct knowledge from assimilation and accommodation. When individuals assimilate, they incorporate a new experience into an already existing framework without changing that framework.

In contrast, when individuals' experiences contradict their internal beliefs, they may change their perceptions of the experiences to fit their internal beliefs. Based on this theory, accommodation is the process of reframing one's mental beliefs of the external world to fit new experiences. This is the mechanism by which failure leads to learning. Learning involves carefully designed experiential opportunities that are similar to what learners encounter in the real world. Constructivists focus on the learner and place the importance on the individual's culture, believing it influences how people learn. Constructivists also think that learners are motivated to learn only when they believe they can be successful.

Some of the advantages of constructivism include that it:
- Is discovery oriented
- Centers on learner understanding
- Builds learner understanding with real-world relevance
- Allows for differences in learner backgrounds and experiences
- Involves facilitators guiding learners through the learning process (Sink 2014)

2.1.2 Knowledge of the Principles and Applications of Cognitive Science for Learning

I. Principles of Cognitive Science for Learning

TD professionals should have knowledge of cognitive science because it provides a framework for understanding how learners make sense of their world and build their learning. At its heart is memory and cognition.

2.1.2.1 The Scientific Method

TD professionals should be familiar with the scientific method and why it is important to the profession. They need to be able to sort through all the information they observe daily.

Cognitive studies are based on the scientific method, which is a process used to examine observations and answer questions. This six-step problem-solving approach is used in all scientific fields:

1. Make an observation.
2. Formulate a question about the observation.
3. Construct a hypothesis describing the observation.
4. Make a prediction to test the hypothesis.
5. Analyze the data and draw conclusions.
6. Use the results to create new hypotheses.

2.1 Learning Sciences

TD professionals should be aware of cutting-edge research that improves how people learn, innovative products for their organizations, and state-of-the-art technology and tools. But everything they see may not be based on facts and data. If they are perusing research, they must clearly understand what constitutes a good study by looking at the methodology used and asking if the study would get the same results if it was repeated. If they are purchasing products, they should ask for data that supports the manufacturer's claims and who reviewed them. Taking a science-based approach to talent development means being up to date with current research and exercising critical discernment when making decisions. When TD professionals see too-good-to-be-true claims about new brain science, miracle leadership development programs, or the magical power of mobile learning, they need to assess the science behind the claims, perhaps using the six steps of the scientific method to explore further.

2.1.2.2 The Brain and Information Processing: How People Learn

There are many theories about how the brain makes sense of the world. Most address functions such as short-term memory and long-term memory. In the late 1960s, Atkinson and Shiffrin (1968) proposed the Multi-Store Model, which suggested that the brain processes information through three separate stages: the sensory register, short-term store, and long-term store. This model suggests that new information enters the sensory register, is processed in the short-term memory, and is stored indefinitely in the long-term memory when rehearsed or practiced (Figure 2.1.2.2-1).

Figure 2.1.2.2-1. Information Processing

SENSORY REGISTER → attention → SHORT-TERM MEMORY ⇄ (transfer / retrieval) LONG-TERM MEMORY

rehearsal (loop on SHORT-TERM MEMORY)

- Information enters the sensory register.
- Information is rehearsed in the short-term memory, which has a limited capacity.
- Rehearsed information is stored in the long-term memory. It has an almost limitless capacity.

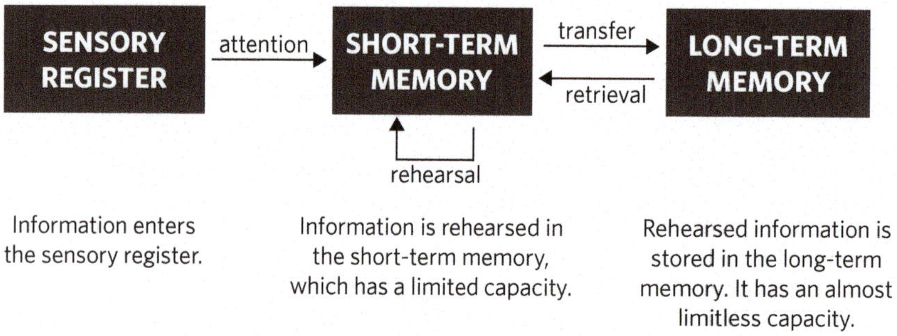

Like many theories, this model has been tested and criticized, but it has been influential on how memory and cognition are discussed, with many theories drawing on its structure and using its language. In simple terms, the working memory is where people make sense of what they've learned by manipulating existing memories with new information. It is a function of the brain and not a specific location within it. Molecular biologist John Medina (2008) describes working memory as "a collection of busy work spaces that allow us to temporarily retain newly acquired information." It is where learners hold and manipulate a few pieces of information, and then integrate it with existing knowledge in the long-term memory (Clark and Mayer 2016).

2.1.2.3 The Brain and Deliberate Practice

A key concept in cognitive learning is that long-term memories are strengthened through retrieval or rehearsal of information as it passes between the working memory and long-term memory. John Medina (2008) states, "If we don't repeat the information, it disappears." To ensure content is remembered and stored in the long-term memory, it needs to be practiced. Psychologist Anders Ericsson's research stresses that practice is critical, but not all forms lead to sustained memory retention. He uses the term deliberate practice to differentiate from other methods of practice (Ericsson, Krampe, and Tesch-Römer 1993).

Ericsson's studies show that it takes tens of thousands of hours of deliberate forms of practice to develop expertise. For example, he discusses classical musicians, who often study and practice for 15 years before gaining the expert level of skill to perform on the world stage. A recent replication of his 1993 study supports the idea that practice is critical but perhaps less so. The researchers found that practicing for any extended amount of time can make one an expert. In fact, they found that expert musicians actually practiced for fewer hours than the ones who were merely good (Macnamara and Maitra 2019).

Both studies examined deliberate practice to reach expertise; however, talent development in the workplace is more about proficiency than expertise. Deliberate practice techniques can help TD professionals deliver deeper learning that sticks and leads to better long-term retention:

- **Interleaving** describes when topics within instruction are alternated. For example, if nine hours are available to learn three skills, it would be tempting to spend three hours on a skill, move to the next for three hours, and then finish with the third skill. Interleaving suggests covering all three topics during each of the three-hour segments will lead to better results.
- **Spaced practice** occurs when learning is spaced over time with intervals between the practice sessions in which the learner may forget information. This technique is related to Ebbinghaus's Forgetting Curve and is similar to interleaving.
- **Elaboration** allows learners to put content into their own words and connect it with existing memories, such as skills or knowledge they already have.
- **Retrieval practice** asks learners to build retention by recalling a skill or piece of knowledge directly from memory rather than rereading a text or watching a demonstration (Brown, Roediger, and McDaniel 2014). [See 2.1.5.8 and 2.1.5.9]

2.1.2.4 John Sweller's Cognitive Load Theory

Cognitive load theory was developed by Australian educational psychologist John Sweller. It gives TD professionals greater clarity into how the brain processes learning and, most importantly, how to make learning experiences more effective. Cognitive load refers to the amount of effort needed to process new information in the working memory, which has a very limited capacity; some research shows it holds just three to five chunks of information (Cowan 2010). TD professionals need to design content so that it does not overload that capacity. There are three forms of cognitive load: intrinsic, extraneous, and germane (Sweller, Van Merriënboer, and Paas 1998).

- **Intrinsic cognitive load** refers to the amount of effort required of the learner based on the complexity of the content.
- **Extraneous cognitive load** is the effort required by the learner to make sense of content based on how it is presented. TD professionals need to create content that's easy to understand.
- **Germane cognitive load** refers to the work that the learner puts into building a schema or mental model in the long-term memory, such as with practice or rehearsal.

Cognitive load theory is concerned with how the brain works with schema and what TD professionals can do to create learning experiences that require less cognitive effort, or in other words, how to make learning easier. A key contribution to the field is the modality effect, which explains that the working memory processes information through an auditory and visual channel. It suggests that cognitive load is reduced when visual information is accompanied by auditory information, as opposed to when it is only visual.

2.1.3 Knowledge of Theories and Models of Adult Learning

> **I. Theories and Models of How Adults Learn**
>
> TD professionals should understand that philosophers, theorists, and researchers have proposed ideas and theories about how adults learn. This has influenced the fields of training, adult education, and now talent development. TD professionals who are familiar with the main influencers—John Dewey, B.F. Skinner, and Paulo Freire—going back as far as the 19th century understand better how talent development contributes to employee learning.

2.1.3.1 Malcolm Knowles's Adult Learning Theory

Malcolm Knowles was one of the most influential adult educators in America, promoting the idea that adults learn differently than children. This idea had been discussed for some time in Europe, where the word *andragogy* was used to differentiate teaching techniques used for adults from those used to teach children. The techniques associated with teaching children were referred to as *pedagogy*. The term andragogy was introduced in America in 1967 by Yugoslavian educator Dusan Savicevic. Knowles adopted it, writing an article the following year in *Adult Leadership* titled, "Andragogy not Pedagogy" (Knowles, Holton, and Swanson 2015). From there, he developed many of the concepts that influence training and human resource development today (which are summarized in Table 2.1.3.1-1).

Table 2.1.3.1-1. Characteristics of Pedagogical and Andragogical Learners

Learner Characteristics	Pedagogical	Andragogical
Self-concept of the learner	Is dependent	Is self-directed
Prior experience of the learner	Does not use experience	Uses experience as a resource for self and others
Readiness to learn	Is directly related to age and curriculum	Is developed from life experience
Orientation to learning	Is self-centered	Is task- or problem centered
Motivation to learn	Is based on external rewards and punishments	Is based on internal incentives and curiosity

Pedagogy

In Knowles's model, the pedagogic approach is based on the idea of teaching specific tasks to help children prepare to learn additional, more complicated tasks. For example, children are first taught to count so that they can later learn to add and subtract; later they are taught to multiply and divide; then they learn algebra, geometry, and so on. It is characterized by the traditional classroom. Key assumptions of pedagogy include:

- The instructor is the expert.
- The instructor is responsible for all aspects of the learning process.
- Instruction is content centered.
- Motivation is external.

Andragogy

Knowles's theory of andragogy altered many of the assumptions in pedagogy. It's characterized by classes in which the teacher and student are seen as equal, and learners have more control over how and when they learn. Knowles's andragogy theory is based on six key assumptions about adults:

- **The need to know.** Adults need to know why something is important and why they should invest time in a learning event. For this reason, learners must understand the purpose of training as early as possible. Participants need to know how this information or content will affect them, why they should care, and how it will make a difference.
- **The learner's self-concept.** People enter learning situations with their own perceptions of who they are; they see themselves as self-directing, responsible grown-ups and don't like taking directions from others. Consequently, helping adults identify their needs and direct their own learning experience is critical.
- **The role of the learner's experience.** Adults can draw from their life experiences to make sense of new knowledge. They have a great deal to contribute and should be recognized for this. Adult educators should look for ways to build on and make use of participants' hard-earned experiences and knowledge throughout group learning.
- **Readiness to learn.** Adults need to see how a learning experience is relevant to their needs. Seeing how the new knowledge will help them cope with daily life at work and in their personal life will increase their readiness to learn.
- **Orientation to learning.** Adults are practical and willing to devote energy to learning things they believe will help them perform better or solve problems. Adult educators should invest time in learning the needs and interests of people in their class so they can develop and adapt content in response to those needs.
- **Motivation.** Adults respond best to internal motivators such as job satisfaction, self-esteem, and quality of life. When a specific need arises that has intrinsic value or a personal payoff, adults are more motivated to learn. Therefore, andragogy practitioners should link learning with internal motivations.

2.1.3.2 Carl Rogers's Learner-Centered Instruction

American psychologist Carl Rogers (1951), considered one of the founders of the field of humanist psychology, believed that "We cannot teach another person directly; we can only facilitate his learning." He came to this conclusion by seeing therapy as a learning process and proposing the idea of a learner-centered approach to teaching. Rogers's theory of learner-centered instruction has variations depending on how one interprets his work. His theory supports the shift away from a teaching emphasis—when the learner is responsible for learning and the relationship between learners and facilitators is equal.

In a learner-centered approach, learners are involved from start to finish and can choose what to study. The TD professional's challenge is to include active-learning techniques that keep learners engaged and meet their needs. Rogers's key beliefs include the assumption that learners:
- Want to control what and how they learn
- Can be trusted to develop their own potential
- Should be encouraged to choose both the type and direction of their learning

Rogers presents a classical learner-centered approach with implications for facilitators:
- Establish the initial climate by clarifying the purpose of the session.
- Plan the widest possible range of resources to address needs as they arise.
- Limit lectures and incorporate activities that involve learners.

- Be prepared to show learners what's in it for them.
- Build in time for open discussion.
- Create a welcoming, friendly environment.
- Prepare discussion questions that help the facilitator be a guide, not an expert.

2.1.3.3 Abraham Maslow's Hierarchy of Needs

Abraham Maslow (1954) is known for his hierarchy of needs model (Figure 2.1.3.3-1). Motivation is a key component of learning, and TD professionals need to understand what motivates learners to want to learn. Maslow contended that people have complex needs that they strive to fulfill, and those needs change and evolve. Individuals achieve the next level of the hierarchy only after lower-level needs have been satisfied. Maslow categorized these needs into a logical hierarchy from physiological to psychological:

- **Physiological** needs include food, drink, sex, and sleep.
- **Safety** needs include freedom from fear and the need to be safe and stable.
- **Belongingness** is the need for friends and family.
- **Esteem** includes self-esteem and the need to be highly regarded by others.
- **Self-actualization** is the need to excel.

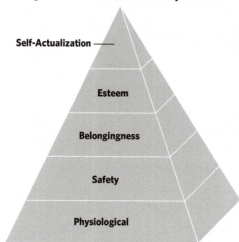

Figure 2.1.3.3-1. Maslow's Hierarchy of Needs

Source: Sharpe (1997).

Most jobs satisfy the needs of the four lowest levels of the hierarchy: wages or salaries to provide for physiological needs, a safe working environment, camaraderie for belongingness, and the respect of co-workers and peers for esteem. Needs related to self-actualization relate to the number and types of opportunities for growth and achievement. TD professionals who understand the learner and establish an appropriate climate and a sense of safety also satisfy these lower-level needs.

2.1.3.4 K. Patricia Cross's Adult Learning

K. Patricia Cross developed two conceptual frameworks that describe aspects of adult learning: chain of response and characteristics of adult learners. Much of her work was a synthesis of other research about adult learning, participation, and developmental stages.

2.1.3.4.1 Chain of Response
Cross (1981) described chain of response (COR) as a framework of adult participation in learning to "identify the relevant variables and hypothesize their interrelationships." Her relationships were based on situational characteristics (such as schedule, location, and mandatory versus voluntary) and personal characteristics (such as intelligence, life phases, and vocabulary) that resulted in these precepts:
- Motivation to participate is the result of a person's perception of both positive and negative forces. Certain personality types do not enjoy learning because of low self-esteem.
- Participation in learning events affects how individuals feel about learning and their outcomes.
- Higher-order needs for achievement and self-actualization can't be fulfilled until lower-order needs for security and safety are met.
- Expectations of reward are important to motivation.

2.1.3.4.2 Characteristics of Adult Learners
Cross described the differences between adults and children as part of her characteristics of adult learners (CAL) framework to allow for the development of alternative teaching strategies. By synthesizing the work of several adult education scholars, the CAL framework suggests that TD professionals should capitalize on participants' experiences and that adults should have maximum choices in what to learn. CAL also provides a means for thinking about the ever-changing adult in terms of developmental stages.

2.1.3.5 Neuroscience's Role in Talent Development
Neuroscience is a recent field of inquiry that has developed over the past 20 years and is becoming a significant influence on psychology and education. It is an interdisciplinary field that looks at thought, emotion, and behavior using sophisticated technology, such as brain-scanning devices, and then uses biology to describe what happens in the brain. For example, the theory that forming long-term memories involves retrieval and rehearsal between the working memory and the long-term memory prescribes important actions educators need to take to ensure learning success.

Developments in neuroimaging technology now enable scientists to more closely study the brain and how it functions. These images provide information about how the brain responds to different stimuli, such as threatening situations or pleasure. In some instances, they support what's been demonstrated in areas like cognitive studies and humanist psychology (Satel and Lilienfeld 2013).

An important neuroscience influence for TD professionals is the area of emotions and their influence on learning, such as the way the limbic system and the amygdala process and respond to events. For example, some studies suggest that a situation that threatens a person's sense of autonomy may cause the brain to redirect resources from the prefrontal cortex, where decision making and cognitive processing occurs, to the adrenal glands where fight or flight responses are performed. This limits a person's ability to process ideas and make decisions, which is a less than ideal state for someone to learn. This reinforces what thought leaders like Carl Rogers suggested in the 1950s. Research showing that memory is enhanced by firing neurons echoes the studies in cognitive learning that show retrieval and rehearsal lead to memory retention, which is similar to research from thought leaders John Sweller and Anders Ericsson.

The field of neuroscience is still in its infancy, and many of its findings need further study. TD professionals should use the scientific methods approach to determine whether something attributed to neuroscience is cognitive science (Shank 2016; Collins 2016). Exercise critical thinking and watch for new developments that may truly be insightful—although every concept may not be new or applicable, TD professionals can't afford to ignore neuroscience. [See 2.1.2.1]

> **II. Theories and Models of Design That Ensure Learning**
>
> Several theories and models help TD professionals design learning experiences that are both effective and efficient. Several of the most useful theories and models include those by Benjamin Bloom, Robert Gagné, Robert Mager, Hermann Ebbinghaus, and Albert Bandura.

2.1.3.6 Benjamin Bloom's Taxonomy

In 1956, Benjamin Bloom convened a committee of educators who determined that learning objectives fell into three significant domains and identified varying levels of complexity for objectives.

- **Cognitive domain** (also known as knowledge) involves the development of intellectual skills. Examples include understanding the principles of engineering, how to organize plants in a garden, or how to complete a series of steps in a task or process.
- **Psychomotor domain** (also known as skills) refers to physical movement, coordination, and the use of motor skills to accomplish a task. An example of a skill is the ability to operate a piece of equipment.
- **Affective domain** (also known attitude) refers to how people react to things emotionally, such as feelings, motivation, and enthusiasm. Although facilitators cannot change attitudes, they can influence them. TD professionals assist by selecting the right activities.

Bloom's Taxonomy gave rise to the common use of the acronym KSA (knowledge, skills, and attitude). Clarifying which domain a learning objective falls within helps TD professionals choose an appropriate instructional approach. For example, the techniques to teach a psychomotor skill, such as repairing a photocopier, typically come from a different toolkit than those used for facilitating a workshop on resistance in change management. Evaluation and assessment methods will also be different.

The taxonomy also categorizes learning into six levels of behavior: knowledge, comprehension, application, analysis, synthesis, and evaluation. This gives both the learner and facilitator greater clarity in learning and practicing a skill. In the late 1990s, Lorin Anderson, a former student of Bloom, revised Bloom's six levels, changing the category names from nouns to verbs and switching the order of evaluating and synthesis. She also changed the word *synthesis* to *creating*. The new terms for each level are remembering, understanding, applying, analyzing, evaluating, and creating (Figure 2.1.3.6-1).

2.1 Learning Sciences

Figure 2.1.3.6-1. Bloom's Revised Taxonomy

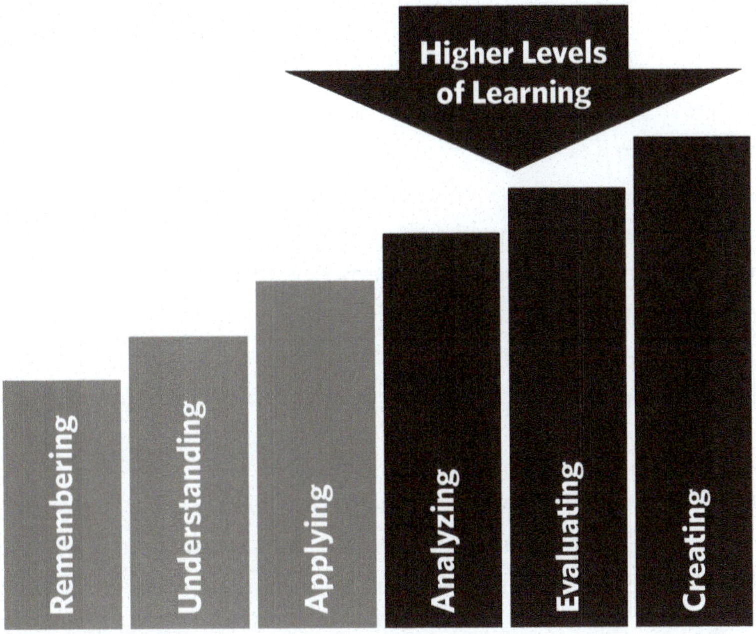

Higher Levels of Learning

Remembering | Understanding | Applying | Analyzing | Evaluating | Creating

Definitions and examples can be found in Table 2.1.3.6-1.

Table 2.1.3.6-1. Bloom's Revised Taxonomy Definitions and Examples

Remembering	Understanding	Applying	Analyzing	Evaluating	Creating
Recalling data or information	Constructing meaning from different types of information	Carrying out or using a procedure through executing or implementing	Breaking materials or concepts into parts, determining how the parts relate or interrelate to one another or to an overall structure or purpose	Making judgments about the value of ideas or materials	Putting parts together to form a whole, with an emphasis on making new meaning or structure
Increasing Level of Difficulty and Mastery→					
Define Describe Identify Label List Match Name Outline Recall Recognize Reproduce Select State	Comprehend Convert Distinguish Estimate Explain Extend Give an Example Infer Interpret Paraphrase Rewrite Summarize Translate	Apply Change Compute Construct Demonstrate Manipulate Modify Operate Predict Prepare Produce Show Solve Use	Analyze Compare Contrast Diagram Deconstruct Differentiate Discriminate Distinguish Identify Illustrate Infer Outline Relate Separate	Compare Conclude Contrast Criticize Critique Defend Describe Discriminate Evaluate Interpret Justify Relate Support	Combine Compose Create Devisew Design Generate Modify Organize Plan Reconstruct Reorganize Revise Rewrite Write

2.1.3.7 Robert Gagné's Five Types of Learning and Nine Events of Instruction

In the 1980s Robert Gagné, an American educational psychologist, outlined a broader spectrum of learning, which he divided into five types:

- **Intellectual skills** refer to learning concepts, rules, and procedures. In a sense, they are about knowing how to perform a task.
- **Cognitive strategy** refers to learners employing their own learning strategies for taking in information, remembering it, and applying it.
- **Verbal information** refers to information the learner can declare or state that they will use to make sense of new information.
- **Motor skills** refer to carrying out practical tasks or following a procedure.
- **Attitude** refers to the bias or values that influence a learner's action toward something.

The nine events of instruction is a model for lesson planning devised by Gagné (Table 2.1.3.7-1). Lesson plans are a sequential set of events that lead to a desired goal. They're important, especially when implementing the same course numerous times, sometimes in different places to conform to content and quality standards (Gagné, Briggs, and Wager 1988). Research shows that the teaching sequence enables learners to better retain concepts, skills, and procedures. Gagné's nine events of instruction join theory and practice in a way that can be used in most design situations.

Gangé's nine events have an instructional design component that is critical for the way learners process information. Because the events are based on empirical research, TD professionals should use them to ensure learning occurs.

Table 2.1.3.7-1. Gagné's Nine Events of Instruction

Event	Purpose	Examples
1. Gain attention.	Create a foundation for the lesson, set the direction, and motivate the learner.	Present a good problem or a new situation; use a multimedia quote; ask questions.
2. Inform learners of the objectives.	Allow learners to frame information.	State what learners will be able to accomplish and how they will be able to use the knowledge; give a demonstration.
3. Stimulate recall of prior knowledge.	Display how knowledge is connected; provide learners with a framework that helps learning and remembering.	Remind learners of prior knowledge relevant to the current content; ask for examples; guide discussion.
4. Present the stimulus (content).	Introduce learners to new content.	Use text, graphics, simulations, figures, pictures, and job aids; divide information into smaller pieces to enhance information recall; use techniques that appeal to all learning modalities.
5. Provide learning guidance.	Help with long-term retention.	Use case studies, examples, graphs, mnemonics, and analogies.
6. Elicit performance (practice).	Initiate responses from learners and allow them to confirm their correct understanding; repetition increases retention.	Learner uses content to practice skills or apply knowledge by solving a problem; practice keyboard skill; create a simulated product; deliver a presentation.
7. Provide feedback.	Show whether the trainee's response is correct; analyze learner's behavior; correct problems early.	Provide guidance with examples or verbal comments; practice reinforcement.
8. Assess performance.	Determine level of mastery and general progress information.	Use post-tests, demonstrations, and verbal assessments.
9. Enhance retention and transfer.	Ensure skills and knowledge are implemented.	Use job aids, online support, and help desk; assist supervisors with reinforcement ideas.

2.1.3.8 Robert Mager's Criterion-Referenced Instruction Approach

Robert Mager is known for the use of specific, measurable objectives that guide designers during course development, trainers during facilitation, and participants during the learning process. These instructional objectives, also known as behavioral or performance objectives, are synonymous with criteria-referenced objectives, which include provisions for measuring the ability of the learner to meet specific criteria upon completion of learning (Mager 1997).

Mager's central concept is that a learning goal should be broken into a subset of smaller tasks or learning objectives. He was one of the first to emphasize using specific verbs as opposed to vague language when writing objectives. By his definition, a behavioral objective should have three components (Mager 1997):
- **Performance** is the behavior written as a specific, observable action, described using a verb.
- **Condition** describes the setting under which the behavior is performed and should include the tools or assistance required.
- **Criteria** describes the level of performance and should be stated, including an acceptable range of allowable answers.

TD professionals can apply this concept by starting and ending most training and learning solutions with learning objectives. They use explicit terms to frame how a learner should be able to perform a task and provide a criterion to track the progress and measure final success.

2.1.3.9 Hermann Ebbinghaus's Forgetting Curve

One of the earliest thought leaders in the area of memory was German psychologist Hermann Ebbinghaus. He conducted a series of experiments in the 19th century showing that the process of forgetting or "memory decay" happens naturally and in a uniform way. This decay was illustrated on a graph now known as the forgetting curve, which shows that more than half of memory is forgotten within an hour (Ebbinghaus 1964). After that initial period, the rate of decay slows down.

While Ebbinghaus suggested that many factors including stress, sleep, and the difficulty of the content could affect the degree of forgetting, practical techniques could be used to arrest the rate of decay. In particular, he suggested the use of mnemonics and repetition. The process of repetition led to his spaced learning technique, in which learners retrieve a memory sequentially over a period of time with increasing spaces of time between each retrieval. Ebbinghaus's theory has been criticized—including that he was the subject of his experiments—but that doesn't mean the results were wrong. In fact, recent experiments have replicated Ebbinghaus's original findings (Murre and Dros 2015).

TD professionals can apply this concept to reduce memory decay by designing recall opportunities for learners over intervals of time. This might be within a classroom context; through microlearning, coaching, or innovative practices such as gamification; or by having supervisors follow up with learners.

2.1.3.10 Albert Bandura's Social Cognitive Theory

Leading psychologist Albert Bandura developed social cognitive theory, which evolved from social learning theory. He is best known for a series of experiments known as the Bobo Doll Experiments, which studied aggression and demonstrated that parental modeling influenced the behavior of children. Bandura drew on

B.F. Skinner's theory of operant conditioning, which states that effective learning depends on positive reinforcement (Knowles, Holton, and Swanson 2015).

Bandura's theory has been important in discussions about the influence that media such as films and television play in modeling behavior. Said to bridge behaviorism and cognitivism, social cognitive theory has prompted educators to incorporate modeling into their teaching to help participants learn new patterns or behaviors, known as the modeling effect, or reduce existing ones, known as the inhibitory effect (Bandura and Walters 1963). TD professionals can use modeling as a vehicle for reflection, such as modeling a behavior and then asking the learners to provide constructive feedback.

TD professionals can apply this concept by designing experiences that enable the facilitator to model ideal behavior. They can also create experiences when participants model behaviors or perform tasks in a way that offers an opportunity for other learners to watch and imitate.

2.1.4 Knowledge of Communication Theories and Models and How They Relate to Learning

> **I. Conceptual Models of Communication**
>
> TD professionals should be astute communicators, understanding communication theories and how they can be used to improve learning opportunities.

2.1.4.1 Claude Shannon–Warren Weaver's Communication Model

Mathematician Claude Shannon and scientist Warren Weaver developed one of the first models for communication in 1949 and used it to make radio and telephone cable communication more efficient. Their five-stage communication model was the first to suggest that noise or filters could interfere with good communication—something TD professionals need to consider. The five stages are: [See 1.1.1.4]

- **Information source**—the person who makes the message
- **Transmitter**—the person who encodes the message for the machine it is transmitted on
- **Noise source**—what interferes with the message such as static or environmental factors
- **Receiver**—the machine or person who decodes the message
- **Destination**—the person or place that receives the message [See 1.1.1]

2.1.4.2 David Berlo's Sender-Message-Channel-Receiver Model

In 1960, David Berlo further developed Shannon and Weaver's model by introducing dynamics to account for more personal aspects of communication. He described it as adding "a model of the ingredients of communication" (Croft 2004). The personal elements at each step of this model are:

- **Source**—communication skills, knowledge, attitude, culture, and social system
- **Message**—depends on the elements and structure, content, treatment, and encoding
- **Channel**—the five senses of seeing, hearing, touching, smelling, and tasting
- **Receiver**—same as the source: communication skills, knowledge, attitude, culture, and social system (James 2008)

TD professionals should underscore the emphasis that Berlo placed on the source and receiver of the model to ensure effective communication. [See 1.1.1.4]

2.1.4.3 Constructionist Model

The constructionist model of communication suggests that communication is not merely the transmission of a message, but a complex process of people building understanding or knowledge by drawing on internal paradigms. *Constructionism*, which was developed by Seymour Papert (a student of Piaget), is focused on the process of helping others construct meaning. It assumes complex factors influence communication such as social paradigm, linguistics, rhetoric, and conversational dynamics.

TD professionals who take a constructionist approach should provide opportunities for learners to increase their knowledge by creating an environment where they are engaged. Because TD professionals know that their presentation will be interpreted differently (no matter how perfect it is), many believe that the communication models proposed by Shannon and Weaver and Berlo are too simple. These models reduce communication to an unemotional process that fails to account for the rich experiences humans use to make sense of a message.

2.1.4.4 Communication Theories Related to Learning

TD professionals should recognize that communication is a key part of the learning process. Each of the following theories have direct applications for effectively communicating with others inside and outside an organization:

- **Cognitive dissonance** refers to situations when someone's attitudes, beliefs, or behaviors are in conflict (McLeod 2018). Most people prefer these to be in harmony, so when they collide, the tension leads to discomfort. Cognitive dissonance, proposed by psychologist Leon Festinger in 1957, may be experienced as learners are challenged to see things differently or explore processes from different perspectives.
- **Persuasion theory** is the study of how people can use messages to influence people. While general communication messages are delivered and left with the receiver to form a judgment or opinion, the intention of persuasion theory is to change the minds of the receivers and even encourage them to act. Many persuasion theories exist, and most are influenced by Robert Cialdini's 1980s research. The principles are reciprocity, consistency, social proof, authority, liking, and scarcity. [See 1.1.4.1]
- **Theory of reasoned action** looks at how to predict whether someone will act based on pre-existing attitudes and intentions (Doswell et al. 2011). Its purpose is to understand the liklihood that a listener or learner will change behaviors following a message (Colman 2015).
- **Diffusion theory** explains how the widespread adoption of a new idea or movement is accepted over time. It was developed in 1943 when Bryce Ryan and Neal C. Gross (1950) examined how long it took Iowa farmers to adopt hybrid seed. Originally applied to innovation, it's helpful for understanding the dynamics of change because it shows how few people initially adopt change. Diffusion theory reminds TD professionals that it takes time for new knowledge to be adopted. Diffused adoption is illustrated with a bell diagram showing the five stages of adoption (Kaminski 2011):
    - Innovators (2.5 percent)
    - Early adopters (13.5 percent)
    - Early majority (34 percent)
    - Late majority (34 percent)
    - Laggards (16 percent)

- **Machine learning** is an area of computer science that is closely related to artificial intelligence. The model of knowledge a computer has of someone or a topic of information is continuously extended by inputting new data. This is facilitated by algorithms such as decision trees, decision rules, and artificial neural networks. In online learning, it personalizes content and offers learners menus of predicted relevant learning material; automates time-consuming tasks such as scheduling and delivering content around learners' preferences; and provides somewhat personalized feedback (Lynch 2019).
- **Incremental theory,** the theory of how someone sees their own intelligence, was developed by Stanford psychology professor Carol Dweck. The way individuals see intelligence can affect how well they respond to difficult learning tasks. People who see intelligence as fixed and stable are often vulnerable to learned helplessness when faced with situations that are beyond their control or perceived as overly challenging—which is known as the entity view of intelligence. Alternatively, the incremental view of intelligence considers intelligence as something that can grow with learning and strategy. Learners who hold an incremental view of their intelligence adopt a mastery-oriented mindset that more often leads to success (David 2014).

2.1.4.5 Richard Mayer's Multimedia Theory

TD professionals create and curate digital content for many purposes that include classroom learning, microlearning, and distributed learning. They may use digital text, graphics, audio, and video independently or weave them together. The content needs to be structured and produced in a way that leads to knowledge transfer.

Richard Mayer's cognitive theory of multimedia learning is a series of key principles for effective multimedia learning based on cognitive research. This theory draws on John Sweller's work in cognitive load theory as well as Allan Paivo's dual encoding theory, which suggests that visual and verbal communication are two distinct systems within the working memory. In their book *eLearning and the Science of Instruction*, Mayer and Ruth Clark (2016) set out the key principles for effective use of multimedia:

- **Multimedia principle.** Use words and graphics rather than words alone.
- **Contiguity principle.** Align words to corresponding graphics.
- **Modality principle.** Present words as audio narration rather than onscreen text.
- **Redundancy principle.** Explain visuals with words in audio or text but not both.
- **Coherence principle.** Avoid adding extra material that can hurt learning.
- **Personalization and embodiment principle.** Use conversational style, polite wording, human voice, and virtual coaches.
- **Segmenting and pretraining principle.** Manage complexity by breaking a lesson into parts. [See 2.1.2.3 and 2.1.5.1]

When incorporating these key principles, testing learning programs for usability is critical. According to the Interaction Design Foundation, usability refers to the ease of access or use of a product or website that is part of the overall user experience (Soegaard 2019). In e-learning programs, for example, knowing how to find the program within the architecture of a learning management system (LMS) or how to use it within one's job is equally as important as the presented content (Norman and Nielsen 2019).

2.1.5 Skill in Applying Principles of Cognitive Science and Adult Learning to Design Solutions That Maximize Learning or Behavioral Outcomes

> **I. Applications of Cognitive Science in Adult Learning**
>
> TD professionals should be skilled in applying cognitive science to better understand how people learn. Cognitive science provides guidance on how to create content that is quicker and easier to comprehend, to help learners make sense of new content by activating existing memories, and to ensure content is remembered through deliberate practice.

2.1.5.1 Using Cognitive Science to Design Instructional Content

TD professionals can use these cognitive learning principles in instructional design:

- **Cognitive load.** Break content into chunks so it doesn't overload the working memory. Use both visual and verbal descriptions (dual encoding theory). Provide worked examples to help learners make sense of new information. [See 2.1.2.4]
- **Processing information.** Give learners opportunities to activate their own memories to make sense of new information. Allow time to reflect, discuss, and manipulate the memories.
- **Retention.** Incorporate regular opportunities for retrieval, including techniques like spaced learning, interleaving, and elaboration.
- **Metacognition.** Discuss the learning process and the strategies that will be used to support learning with learners.

2.1.5.2 Social Learning Theory

Social learning is the continuous process of learning from other people. This definition has been further elaborated to apply in the workplace. TD professionals should consider the value of social learning as they determine how to use cognitive science to develop talent, especially pertaining employees taking responsibility for their personal learning. [See 1.7]

Social learning theory, according to Albert Bandura, is sometimes viewed as complementary to both behaviorism and cognitivism. The theory demonstrates how modeling by facilitators and others helps learners succeed with new behaviors or by replacing existing ones (Bandura and Walters 1963).

TD professionals can design experiences that enable them to model ideal behavior in learning experiences and in the workplace. When done with intent by establishing rules that encourage learning, social learning enhances an organization's culture and fosters collaboration. People need to believe that they're part of a group, which includes supporting others and being supported in their learning efforts. Social learning can be supported for virtual employees or those working in other locations with videos, computers, webcams, and smartphones. As TD professionals consider their opportunities to enhance learning, they should determine how the content fits in their employees' everyday work and how they can take learning to where the work exists. [See 2.1.3.10]

2.1.5.3 Physiological Needs

Some people think of learning as merely the exercise of activating memories from the long-term memory with new visual and auditory stimulus and then processing them in the working memory to form new or more refined schemata. However, learning is also a physiological process that takes place at synapses where brain cells communicate and can be observed through brain imaging (University of California, Irvine 2008). Consequently, the brain can be affected by sleep, emotions, stress, and diet:

- Sleep has a significant impact on learning ability. Lack of deep sleep affects a person's ability to learn and perform, leading to poor memory formation, negative moods, poor abstraction, lack of ability to make judgments, and poor perception (Division of Sleep Medicine 2007). Disrupted deep sleep has also been shown to inhibit neuroplasticity (Sandoiu 2017). Good sleep, on the other hand, leads to better memory consolidation after a learning experience, better moods, and an overall better ability to learn.
- A learner's emotions can affect learning, especially attention levels and motivation (University of California, Irvine 2008). Emotions have been described as "relay stations between sensory input and thinking" (Lawson 2002). Anxiety, anger, and frustration affect a learner's ability to focus their cognitive processes.
- Negative stress has been shown to limit learning. However, not all stress is bad; moderate emotional arousal has been shown to promote memory formation. But when stress levels become too high, learning is inhibited (Lindau, Almkvist, and Mohammed 2016; Diamond et al. 2007). [See 2.1.5.7]
- Studies show that diet can affect the learning process. Although there are various views on which foods support brain function, there is little disagreement over the effect of alcohol. The consumption of alcohol leads to short-term memory loss and sometimes loss of control of physical functions (NIH 2004).

In summary, effective learning is more than just designing a good lesson plan or facilitating an engaging learning experience. Success also depends on the learner's physiological factors, which affect things like processing, memory consolidation, and motivation.

> **II. Maximizing Learning and Behavioral Outcomes**
>
> TD professionals should determine what they can do to maximize learning outcomes. Whether recognizing how to enhance memory, understanding what motivates learners, or determining the role that the appropriate level of stress plays in learning, they will be better equipped to achieve the outcomes they desire.

2.1.5.4 Dual Encoding Theory

Allan Paivo's dual encoding theory suggests that auditory and visual processing are two distinct systems within the working memory. Encoding is the process of entering information into the memory and is the first stage of the memory process. After information reaches the senses as stimuli, encoding allows the brain to change it so the information can enter the memory. Encoding occurs both automatically (unconsciously) and through specific effortful processing (when the observer or listener consciously tries to remember information). As the information enters the sensory memory, it changes into a form that can be stored. It can be encoded or changed as a visual, sound, or meaning. [See 2.1.4.5 and 2.1.5.1]

2.1.5.5 Information Storage and Retrieval, Memory, and Cognitive Load

TD professionals who can understand the memory process are more likely to be able to apply the principles of cognitive science and adult learning. Memory is the process used to acquire, retain, and retrieve information. The memory uses three domains of encoding, storage, and retrieval:

- **Encoding,** the first step to creating a new memory, begins with converting information to a relatable concept that is stored in the brain for later retrieval.
- **Storage** is how the brain places new information into memory.
- **Retrieval,** sometimes called recall, is how the brain accesses information that has been encoded and stored. [See 2.1.2.2, 2.1.2.3, 2.1.3.5, and 2.1.3.9]

2.1.5.6 Motivation

A person's motivation to learn has a significant influence on whether the learning experience is successful. TD professionals should have knowledge of the theories that explain motivation as well as what influences motivation in individuals. Several experts have created theories of motivation, including those that are most closely related to learning, such as Maslow, Cross, Knowles, and Dweck. Many of those theories present similar motivation factors and influence one another.

Adults' motivation to learn is influenced by many factors including their past experiences, acquaintances, stage of life, environment, and the culture in which they live and work. These factors produce reasons to learn, such as personal development, increased employment options, better job performance, curiosity, recognition, or simply a desire to learn or build social relationships (Merriam, Caffarella, and Baumgartner 2007; Solomon 2004). The reasons can be either intrinsically or extrinsically motivated.

TD professionals should recognize the need to balance intrinsic and extrinsic motivations:

- **Extrinsic motivation** causes a learner to engage in an activity or change behavior because it is driven by something from the outside. They may want to learn how to prepare for a promotion, avoid poor performance, or obtain a raise.
- **Intrinsic motivation** causes a learner to engage in a behavior because it is internally driven. They may want to learn how to explore a challenge, gain control over themselves or their environment, achieve a sense of accomplishment, or enjoy the pleasure of learning something new.

Human beings are multifaceted, and each person is unique; therefore, the science of motivation isn't straight forward or simple. For example, extrinsic motivation may be used to encourage individuals to learn new skills; once they internalize and begin to practice the skills, learners may continue to use them due to intrinsic motivation. On the other hand, when extrinsic motivators are offered for something that is already internally rewarding, the activity can become less intrinsically motivating. This is called the over-justification effect (Griggs 2016).

All individuals are unique, and intrinsic and extrinsic motivation are both important. Knowles's assumptions focus mostly on internal or intrinsic motivation of self-direction, readiness, and immediate application. They don't overtly consider the external social, familial, and cultural motivations that add complexity and are critical to learners. [See 2.1.3.1 and 2.1.3.4]

TD professionals may find providing motivation for every learner challenging because individuals are motivated for different reasons and have distinct perspectives on what motivates them enough to learn, change behavior, or continue to practice a new behavior. In addition, changing environmental or personal needs can cause individuals to change their attitudes about what they consider motivating. One solution is to balance intrinsic and extrinsic motivation factors. TD professionals can use these foundational principles to motivate adults to learn:

- **Inclusion and respect.** TD professionals should strive to create an atmosphere of respect and connection to ensure individuals believe they are part of an environment in which they can express themselves without fear of humiliation. This requires meaningful dialogue and a positive learner-facilitator relationship in all TD interactions.
- **Attitude and confidence.** TD professionals should encourage individuals to adopt a positive attitude and build their self-confidence. They can help learners see the value of development and learning by making interactions personally relevant, offering choices, and ensuring they have a growth mindset.
- **Autonomy and willingness.** TD professionals should ensure that individuals feel in control and encourage their desire to develop personally and professionally. Creating an engaging environment and ensuring participants see the relevance of their discussions and all learning events will connect them to their personal purposes.
- **Competence and experience.** Adults have an innate desire to be competent. TD professionals should create opportunities for individuals to demonstrate their competence and develop new skills accompanied with feedback and rewards. (Maslow 1954; Cross 1981; Knowles, Holton, and Swanson 2015; Dweck 2006).

2.1.5.7 Introduce Moderate Stress (Yerkes and Dodson Law)

TD professionals can help learners improve their performance by introducing a moderate amount of stress into the learning experience. The Yerkes and Dodson Law, coined by Robert M. Yerkes and John D. Dodson in the early 1900s, shows that a limited amount of stress (or arousal) leads to better performance, but then performance decreases once it exceeds a certain point (Yerkes and Dodson 1908). Stress and performance are related in an inverted U curve (Figure 2.1.5.7-1).

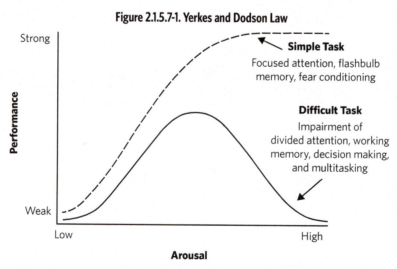

Figure 2.1.5.7-1. Yerkes and Dodson Law

Source: Diamond et al. (2007).

Studies have subsequently shown that the level of appropriate stress varies for different tasks (Diamond et al. 2007). Further studies in neuroscience have confirmed that too much stress (as shown by the release of stress hormones such as cortisol or glucocorticoid) can inhibit the production of long-term memory and learning, leading to the fight or flight mode, which reduces the amount of activity in the cortical areas where higher-level learning happens.

The stimulation to learn requires a moderate amount of stress (measured in the level of cortisol). A low degree of stress is associated with low performance. Moderate levels of cortisol (moderate stress) are beneficial for learning. Mild and extreme stress are detrimental to learning. Influences that affect stress include skill, personality, trait anxiety, and task complexity. [See 2.1.2.2 and 2.3.5]

2.1.5.8 Increase Retention Through Mental Rehearsal and Practice

A key goal of the learning experience is retention, which occurs with *practice* or *rehearsal*; these similar concepts have a slight difference:

- **Practice** is the cognitive or physical run-through of a skill or task including any verbalization or physical movement that is required.
- **Rehearsal** is an imagined practice of a skill or a task. Sometimes called visualization, the rehearsal is all in the mind rather than actual physical or verbal practice.

Practice is critical to developing expertise, which can take thousands of hours and involves the process of retrieving information from long-term memory and processing it in the working memory where the learner organizes it before transferring it back to the long-term memory (Ericsson, Krampe, and Tesch-Römer 1993). In addition, how learners practice matters. Ericsson suggests that deliberate practice, which involves techniques such as elaboration, interleaving, and spaced learning, is most effective. [See 2.1.2.3]

2.1.5.9 Increase Retention With Questions

Questions are a powerful tool for learning retention. Accordingly, they make up important parts of different philosophical approaches to learning, such as the Socratic method, dialogic learning (championed by Paulo Freiere), and Rogers's humanist psychology. There are some important concepts to remember about questions:

- Questions prompt learners to draw on their existing memories for making sense of new information and processing what they've learned. The third item of Robert Gagné's nine events of instruction and a key part of Malcolm Knowles's principles of adult learning involve experience. From a cognitive perspective, questions reinforce the notion that learners make sense of new information by accessing memories in the long-term memory.
- Questions improve retention through retrieval processes. They can be spaced or interleaved throughout a learning experience to help learners strengthen their memory.
- Questions honor the learner by showing that their opinions and ideas matter, thereby improving the learning experience. This supports Carl Rogers's principles of unconditional positive regard and that learning happens best in a safe environment.
- Questions create momentum through dialogue. Through effective facilitation, all members of a group will be engaged, and the facilitator can slowly withdraw and use the group's energy to sustain the learning conversation. [See 1.1.6.3]

To be effective, TD professionals should carefully craft the way they ask questions, respond to learner's responses, and answer questions that the learners ask. Good questions are carefully worded, whether they are open or closed, and adhere to appropriate structure and language. Nonverbal communication also affects how well questions work.

2.1.5.10 Metacognition

TD professionals can increase learning effectiveness by helping people understand the way they learn and explaining how activities and discussions that are facilitated in a face-to-face or virtual classroom or an online program will support that learning. Individual understanding of how they learn is referred to as metacognition, which means thinking about thinking.

In the early 1970s, educational psychologist John Flavell promoted metacognition, which is made up of two key elements (Mahdavi 2014):

- **Knowledge of cognition** comprises declarative knowledge (what is known about something), procedural knowledge (what is known about how to do something), and conditional knowledge (knowing when to apply cognitive strategies).
- **Regulation of cognition** refers to the actions that learners take to manage their own learning. It comprises three basic components: planning, monitoring, and evaluation (Schraw 1998). *Planning* means creating strategies to learn such as setting goals, reflecting, and managing time. *Monitoring* involves the learner testing their strategies to ensure they're achieving their goals. *Evaluation* is measuring each stage of learning, and it can prompt the learner to go back to planning if progress is not satisfactory.

A key part of metacognition concerns being self-aware about one's own ability, which is generally difficult, especially among people who have lower levels of competency. In 1999, psychologists David Dunning and Justin Kruger found that people with lower levels of competency often overestimated their competency level, which can lead to overconfidence.

Allowing learners to understand metacognition and the strategies that support it is useful for them as well as TD professionals, who should also be professional learners and apply metacognition to stay informed about the latest information on how to help people perform better. [See 1.7]

REFERENCES

Atkinson, R.C., and R.M. Shiffrin. 1968. "Human Memory: A Proposed System and Its Control Processes." In *The Psychology of Learning and Motivation*, vol. 2, edited by K.W. Spence and J.T. Spence, 89–195. New York: Academic Press.

AAS (Australian Academy of Science). 2017. "What Is Science?" *Australian Academy of Science*, November 14. science.org.au/curious/everything-else/what-science.

Bandura, A., and R. Walters. 1963. *Social Learning and Personality Development*. New York: Holt, Rinehart, and Winston.

Biech, E. 2017. *The Art and Science of Training*. Alexandria, VA: ATD Press

Bradford, A. 2017. "What Is Science?" Live Science, August 4. livescience.com/20896-science-scientific-method.html.

Brown, P.C., H.L. Roediger, and M.A. McDaniel. 2014. *Make It Stick: The Science of Successful Learning*. Boston: Belknap Press.

Cialdini, R. 2006. *The Psychology of Persuasion*, 2nd ed. New York: Harper Business.

Clark, R. 1999. "The Cognitive Sciences and Human Performance Technology." In *Handbook of Human Performance Technology*, 2nd ed., edited by H.D. Stolovitch and E. Keeps. Silver Spring, MD: ISPI.

Clark, R. 2019. *Evidence-Based Training Methods*, 3rd ed. Alexandria, VA: ATD Press.

Clark, R., and R. Mayer. 2016. *eLearning and the Science of Instruction*, 4th ed. Hoboken, NJ: John Wiley and Sons.

Cook, D.A., and A.R. Artino. 2016. "Motivation to Learn: An Overview of Contemporary Theories." *Medical Education* 50(10): 997–1014. ncbi.nlm.nih.gov/pmc/articles/PMC5113774.

Collins, S. 2016. "Neuroscience Under Scrutiny." *Training Journal*, June. trainingjournal.com/articles/feature/neuroscience-under-scrutiny-0.

Colman, A. 2015. "Theory of Reasoned Action." In *A Dictionary of Psychology*. New York: Oxford University Press.

Cowan, N. 2010. "The Magical Mystery Four: How Is Working Memory Capacity Limited, and Why?" *Current Directions in Psychological Science* 19(1): 51–57. ncbi.nlm.nih.gov/pmc/articles/PMC2864034.

Croft, R.S. 2004. "Communication Theory." Eastern Oregon University Computer Science Department. cs.eou.edu/rcroft/MM350/CommunicationModels.pdf.

2.1 Learning Sciences

Cross, P.K. 1981. *Adults as Learners: Increasing Participation and Facilitating Learning*. San Francisco: Jossey-Bass.

David, L. 2014. "Self-Theories (Dweck)." Learning Theories, July 22. learning-theories.com/self-theories-dweck.html.

Diamond, D.M., A.M. Campbell, C.R. Park, J.D. Halonen, and P.R. Zoladz. 2007. "The Temporal Dynamics Model of Emotional Memory Processing: A Synthesis on the Neurobiological Basis of Stress-Induced Amnesia, Flashbulb and Traumatic Memories, and the Yerkes–Dodson Law." *Neural Plasticity*, February. ncbi.nlm.nih.gov/pubmed/17641736?dopt=Abstract.

Division of Sleep Medicine, Harvard Medical School. 2007. "Sleep, Learning, and Memory." Healthy Sleep, December 18. healthysleep.med.harvard.edu/healthy/matters/benefits-of-sleep/learning-memory.

Doswell, W.M., B.J. Braxter, E. Cha, and K.H. Kim. 2011. "Testing the Theory of Reasoned Action in Explaining Sexual Behavior Among African American Young Teen Girls." *Journal of Pediatric Nursing* 26(6): 45–54.

Dweck, C. 2006. *Mindset: The New Psychology of Success*. New York: Ballantine Books.

Ebbinghaus, H. 1964. *Memory: A Contribution to Experimental Psychology*. New York: Dover. Originally published in 1885.

Ericsson, K.A., and W. Kintsch. 1995. "Long-Term Working Memory." *Psychological Review* 102(2): 211–245. doi.org/10.1037/0033-295X.102.2.211.

Ericsson, K.A., R.T. Krampe, and C. Tesch-Römer. 1993. "The Role of Deliberate Practice in the Acquisition of Expert Performance." *Psychological Review* 100(3): 363–406.

Festinger L. 1962. *A Theory of Cognitive Dissonance*. Stanford, CA: Stanford University Press.

Fiore, S.M., and E. Sales. 2007. *Towards a Science of Distributed Learning*. Washington, DC: American Psychological Association.

Fryer, B. 2006. "Sleep Deficit: The Performance Killer." *Harvard Business Review*, October. hbr.org/2006/10/sleep-deficit-the-performance-killer.

Gagné, R.M., L. Briggs, and W. Wager. 1988. *Principles of Instruction Design*, 3rd ed. New York: Holt, Rinehart, and Winston.

Griggs, R. 2016. *Psychology: A Concise Introduction*, 5th ed. New York: Worth Publishers.

Greer, W. 2013. "Intrinsic and Extrinsic Motivation: Abraham Lincoln as an Adult Learner." Master's thesis, Western Kentucky University. digitalcommons.wku.edu/cgi/viewcontent.cgi?article=2267&context=theses.

Halls, J. 2014. "Memory and Cognition in Learning." *Infoline*. Alexandria, VA: ASTD Press.

Halls, J. 2016. *Rapid Media Development for Trainers*. Alexandria, VA: ATD Press.

Halls, J. 2019. *Confessions of a Corporate Trainer: An Insider Tells All*. Alexandria, VA: ATD Press.

Huggett, C. 2013. *The Virtual Training Guidebook: How to Design, Deliver, and Implement Live Online Learning*. Alexandria, VA: ASTD Press.

James, R. 2008. "The Berlo Model of Communication: AKA Berlo's S-M-C-R Model." *Visual Language*, Fall. academia.edu/9134901/David_Berlos_SMCR_Model.

Kaminski, J. 2011. "Diffusion of Innovation Theory." *Canadian Journal of Nursing Informatics* 6(2). cjni.net/journal/?p=1444.

Knowles, M.S., III, E. Holton, and R. Swanson. 2015. *The Adult Learner: The Definitive Classic in Adult Education and Human Resource Development*, 8th ed. Burlington, MA: Elsevier/Butterworth-Heinemann.

Kruger, J., and D. Dunning. 1999. "Unskilled and Unaware of It: How Difficulties in Recognizing One's Own Incompetence Lead to Inflated Self-Assessments." *Journal of Personality and Social Psychology* 77(6): 1121–1134.

Lawson, C. 2002. "The Connections Between Emotions and Learning." The Center for Development and Learning, January 1. cdl.org/articles/the-connections-between-emotions-and-learning.

Lewin, K. 1943. "Psychology and the Process of Group Living." *Journal of Social Psychology* 17:113–131.

Lindau, M., O. Almkvist, and A.H. Mohammed. 2016. "Effects of Stress on Learning and Memory." In *Stress: Concepts, Cognition, Emotion, and Behavior: Handbook of Stress Series, Volume 1*, edited by G. Fink, 153–160. Cambridge, MA: Academic Press. sciencedirect.com/science/article/pii/B9780128009512000182?via%3Dihub.

Lynch, M. 2019. "4 Ways Machine Learning Can Improve Online Learning." The Tech Advocate, April 23. thetechedvocate.org/4-ways-that-machine-learning-can-improve-online-learning.

Macnamara, B.N., and M. Maitra. 2019. "The Role of Deliberate Practice in Expert Performance: Revisiting Ericsson, Krampe & Tesch-Römer (1993)." Royal Society Publishing, August 21. royalsocietypublishing.org/doi/10.1098/rsos.190327.

Mager, R.F. 1997. *Preparing Instructional Objectives*. Atlanta: Center for Effective Performance.

Mahdavi, M. 2014. "An Overview: Metacognition in Education." *International Journal of Multidisciplinary and Current Research*, May 20. ijmcr.com/wp-content/uploads/2014/05/Paper5529-535.pdf.

Maslow, A. 1954. *Motivation and Personality*. New York: Harper.

Malamed, C. 2017. "Graphics and Learning." In *Rapid Media Development for Trainers*, by J. Halls. Alexandria, VA: ATD Press.

McLeod, S. 2018. "Cognitive Dissonance." *Simply Psychology*, February 5. simplypsychology.org/cognitive-dissonance.html.

Medina, J. 2008. *Brain Rules*. Seattle: Pear Press.

Merriam, S., R. Caffarella, and L. Baumgartner. 2007. *Learning in Adulthood: A Comprehensive Guide*, 3rd ed. San Francisco: Jossey-Bass.

Murre, J.M.J., and J. Dros. 2015. "Replication and Analysis of Ebbinghaus' Forgetting Curve." PLoS One 10(7): e0120644. ncbi.nlm.nih.gov/pmc/articles/PMC4492928.

NIH. 2004. "Alcohol's Damaging Effects on the Brain." *Alcohol Alert*, October. pubs.niaaa.nih.gov/publications/aa63/aa63.htm.

Norman, D., and J. Nielsen. 2019. "The Definition of User Experience." Nielsen Norman Group, October 24. nngroup.com/articles/definition-user-experience.

Norris, D. 2017. "Short-Term Memory and Long-Term Memory Are Still Different." *Psychological Bulletin* 143(9): 992–1009. ncbi.nlm.nih.gov/pmc/articles/PMC5578362.

Rogers, C. 1951. *Client-Centered Therapy: Its Current Practice, Implications, and Theory*. London: Constable.

Ryan, B., and N. Gross. 1950. "Acceptance and Diffusion of Hybrid Corn Seed in Two Iowa Communities." *Iowa State College of Agriculture and Mechanic Arts Research Bulletin* 29(372). lib.dr.iastate.edu/cgi/viewcontent.cgi?article=1386&context=researchbulletin.

Sandoiu, A. 2017. "How Does Poor Sleep Affect Our Ability to Learn? Study Investigates." *Medical News Today*, May 23. medicalnewstoday.com/articles/317597.php.

Satel, S., and S. Lilienfield. 2013. *Brainwashed: The Seductive Appeal of Mindless Neuroscience*. New York: Basic Books.

Schraw, G. 1998. "Promoting General Metacognitive Awareness." *Instructional Science* 26:113–125. citeseerx.ist.psu.edu/viewdoc/download?doi=10.1.1.587.4353&rep=rep1&type=pdf.

Shank, P. 2016 "What Do You Know About Brain Science and Adult Learning" ATD Insights, April 14. td.org/insights/what-do-you-know-about-brain-science-and-adult-learning.

Sharpe, C. 1997. "Course Design and Development." *Infoline*. Alexandria, VA: ASTD Press.

Sink, D.L. 2014. "Design Models and Learning Theories for Adults." In *ASTD Handbook: The Definitive Reference for Training and Development*, 2nd ed., edited by E. Biech. Alexandria, VA: ASTD Press.

Soegaard, M. 2019 "Usability: A Part of User Experience." Interaction Design Foundation, December 12. interaction-design.org/literature/article/usability-a-part-of-the-user-experience.

Solomon, C. 2004. "Culture Audits: Supporting Organizational Success." *Infoline*. Alexandria, VA: ASTD Press.

Sweller, J., J.J.G. van Merriënboer, and F.G.W.C. Paas. 1998. "Cognitive Architecture and Instructional Design." *Educational Psychology Review* 10(3): 251–296.

University of California, Irvine. 2008. "Short-Term Stress Can Affect Learning and Memory." *ScienceDaily*, March 13. sciencedaily.com/releases/2008/03/080311182434.htm.

Washington & Lee University. 2013. "Formal Sciences." The Sciences at W&L, November 9. wlu.edu/the-sciences-at-wandl/formal-sciences.

Yerkes, R., and J. Dodson. 1908. "The Relation of Strength of Stimulus to Rapidity of Habit-Formation." *Journal of Comparative Neurology and Psychology* 18:459–482.

Recommended Reading

Biech, E. 2017. *The Art and Science of Training*. Alexandria, VA: ATD Press.

Brown, P.C., H.L. Roediger, and M.A. McDaniel. 2014. *Make It Stick: The Science of Successful Learning*. Boston: Belknap Harvard.

Quinn, C. 2018. *Millennials, Goldfish & Other Training Misconceptions: Debunking Learning Myths and Superstitions*. Alexandria, VA: ATD Press.

Shank, P. 2018. *Manage Memory for Deeper Learning: 21 Evidence-Based and Easy-to-Apply Tactics That Support Memory While Learning and Beyond*. Learning Peaks.

2.2 INSTRUCTIONAL DESIGN

Instructional design is an essential element of an effective learning effort. The creation of learning experiences and materials results in the acquisition and application of knowledge and skills. Talent development professionals follow a system of assessing needs, designing a process, developing materials, and evaluating effectiveness. Instructional design requires the analysis and selection of the most appropriate strategies, methodologies, and technologies to maximize the learning experience and knowledge transfer.

Foundational Principles of Design

2.2.1 Knowledge of Instructional Design Models and Processes

> **I. Learning Design Basics**
>
> TD professionals who have a solid foundation in learning theories design more effectively because they understand how adults learn best. They can identify the characteristics of learners and select appropriate instructional methods to create effective, targeted learning solutions that meet their needs and organizational goals.

2.2.1.1 The Role of Adult Learning Theories in Instructional Design

There are many different theories that TD professionals can draw from when designing learning solutions. These theories explain why some design techniques may work better than others. Although TD professionals refer to a theory by the name of the individual who first proposed it, such as "Maslow's Hierarchy of Needs," relating each theory's relevance to adult learning and incorporating it into the design is more important.

With a working knowledge of adult learning theories, TD professionals will be able to:
- Implement appropriate learning strategies, tactics, and experiences to create learning environments that support learners' needs.
- Connect the design of materials to the different ways adults learn.
- Assess designs to ensure they meet learners' needs.
- Demonstrate how learning theories can influence knowledge acquisition and retention as well as application of information to stakeholders.

2.2.1.2 Learning Theories

Learning theories, part of cognitive science, attempt to describe what is happening when people learn. Robert Gagné (1997) stated that learning theories "try to provide conceptual structures involved in the process of taking in information and getting it transformed so that it is stored in long-term memory and later recalled as an observable human performance. This entire process, or set of processes, forms the basis of what I refer to when I speak of learning theory."

Learning theories explain how knowledge is stored and retrieved in the brain—how learners acquire knowledge through thoughts, experiences, and the senses; process that information; and remember it. They also discuss how the input, short-term memory, and long-term memory interact. The three classic learning theories are behaviorism, cognitivism, and constructivism. [See 2.1.1]

2.2.1.3 Design Based on Malcolm Knowles's Adult Learning Theory
TD professionals should have a working knowledge of andragogy, which is one of the earliest and most cited learning theories. Popularized by Malcolm Knowles to distinguish adult learning from that of children, andragogy is the science of helping adults learn (Knowles 1984; Knowles, Holton, and Swanson 2005). [See 2.1.3.1]

2.2.1.4 The Whole-Brain Thinking Model
Learning happens using both sides of the brain. Although the two hemispheres of the brain process information differently, they use complementary processes. For example, when problem solving, the left side of the brain analyzes the problem while the right side develops solutions. To make a decision, the left side compares the solutions with the initial problem, and the right side evaluates the solutions related to the situation. Real power comes from combining the two; when the right and left sides of the brain work together, long-term learning occurs.

W.E. "Ned" Herrmann pioneered the study of how an individual's thinking preferences, or brain dominance, affect the way they work, learn, and communicate. He created a four-quadrant model in which each quadrant describes a type of information processing. TD professionals can apply a whole-brain experience based on the four quadrants by designing so learners can view the upcoming content, framing review concepts from a different quadrant perspective, and ensuring time is included to practice and reinforce what they have learned (Herrmann and Herrmann 2015).

2.2.1.5 Multiple Intelligences
Howard Gardner, psychologist and professor at Harvard University, has been challenging the basic beliefs about intelligence since the early 1980s. Gardner (2011) suggests that intelligence is multifaceted, and traditional measures, such as intelligence quotient (IQ) tests, do not accurately measure every facet. He also argues that intelligence is not fixed. In *Frames of Mind*, Gardner describes eight intelligences—musical, logical-mathematical, interpersonal, bodily-kinesthetic, linguistic, intrapersonal, spatial, and naturalistic—and says he anticipates the list to grow. Gardner asserts that while most people are comfortable in three to four of these intelligences, they avoid the others. Because it would be difficult for a TD professional to design for each learner's specific intelligence type, Gardner recommends pluralizing the teaching (or teaching the most important materials in multiple ways).

II. Instructional Systems Design (ISD) Models and Processes

TD professionals should have a working knowledge of ISD models to provide structure and meaning to the learning design. They will be able to visualize the interconnectedness of the requirements, content, materials, and application; separate the design into discrete and logical steps; and be equipped to create a holistic design.

2.2.1.6 The Purpose of ISD Models

A TD professional's process for building a course or program includes inputs (such as content and resources), an instructional systems design (ISD) process, and outputs (such as curriculum and materials). This combination of elements is called an instructional system. Anything from a lecture to online learning starts with the same fundamentals—models are essential for designing instruction.

2.2.1.7 ISD Models

ISD is a systems approach to creating instruction or learning experiences. It may also be called instructional development, curriculum development, instructional systems for training, learning experience design, or a variety of other terms. The differences among the many systems are usually modest in scope and tend to be linked to terminology and procedures. ISD is based on the idea that training is most effective when it provides learners with a clear statement of what they must be able to do as a result of learning and how their performance will be evaluated. The learning experience is designed to teach the skills through hands-on practice or performance-based instruction.

The advantages of using an instructional system are numerous; the most important is having the ability to design projects quickly, efficiently, and effectively. ISD works well because it produces observable, measurable, and replicable elements, including analytical methods, objectives, evaluation schemes, and design plans. Although ISD is a system, it is not so rigid that it lacks flexibility. In fact, the more experienced a TD professional is with ISD, the more they realize the many opportunities available to tailor the system to their needs. The following are some of the more well-known ISD models:

- **ADDIE.** The classic ISD model is the ADDIE model, or some variation of it, which provides the necessary structure for designing any curriculum, regardless of the instructional methods employed. ADDIE is based on and named for the five elements of ISD: analysis, design, development, implementation, and evaluation. These steps are the foundation for almost any learning design.
- **Seels and Glasgow.** The ISD process presented in Barbara Seels and Rita Glasgow's (1998) model assumes that design occurs within the context of project management. This model is an iterative design process in which feedback and interaction occur during the process. Design team members formulate and revise a project management plan—which establishes roles, tasks, timelines, budgets, checkpoints, and supervisory procedures—as necessary. Team members undertake the steps within the parameters of the project management plan, which is divided into three phases: needs analysis management, instructional design management, and implementation and evaluation management.
- **Dick and Carey.** The Dick and Carey ISD model was developed by Walter Dick and James Carey to describe the instructional design process from analyzing needs to identifying goals through writing objectives and evaluating instruction. They expanded the task analysis step to encompass instructional analysis, as well as analyzing learners and contexts (Dick, Carey, and Carey 2014). As a result, the analysis phase of this model focuses on the details of "what should happen."

- **Smith and Ragan.** The Smith and Ragan ISD model (2005) presents a three-stage process: analysis, strategy development, and evaluation. Patricia Smith and Tillman Ragan assert these three stages are common to most instructional design models. They qualify their model by cautioning that although TD professionals usually follow the stages in the order listed, circumstances can cause the designer to modify the sequence or complete steps concurrently. This model differs from others because test items are written within the analysis stage immediately after tasks are analyzed. Smith and Ragan also stress the iterative nature of design, which results in constant revision.
- **Successive Approximation Model (SAM).** This iterative and incremental development process allows requirements and learning solutions to evolve through collaboration between stakeholders. SAM fosters the creation of learning within real project constraints by making repeated steps (iterations) to continuously move closer to the best possible product with each milestone. SAM promotes adaptive planning, evolutionary development, and rapid and flexible responses to change.
- **Agile.** Originating from software development, Agile is a collaborative effort by cross-functional teams. As an iterative, incremental method of guiding designs, this model focuses on maximizing customer value. Highly flexible and interactive, Agile evolves solutions by enabling TD professionals to share preliminary elements with stakeholders, pilot partial solutions, and collect feedback at various stages throughout the process. In some situations, the decision to use Agile may be a requirement for digital learning.

2.2.1.8 Accelerated Learning

Based on cognitive science, accelerated learning is generally thought of as a delivery topic; however, to be effective, the TD professional should plan for it in the design. Accelerated learning involves the brain's right and left hemispheres, cortex, and limbic systems, which allows learning to become more natural. In the *Accelerated Learning Handbook*, Dave Meier (2000) describes techniques that stimulate all the senses to allow learners to learn faster. TD professionals should understand how the brain works so they can design with cognitive science in mind and use strategies to enhance memory, including:

- Promoting active discussion
- Using visuals and learning tools to improve understanding and recall
- Encouraging participants to find alternative patterns and solutions
- Ensuring participants can explain what they learned and put it into practice
- Guiding participants to explore and understand how content is connected
- Supporting reflection on the learning experience [See 2.3.5.7 and 2.3.6.3]

2.2.1.9 The Role of the Human Performance Improvement (HPI) Process

Prior to embarking on instructional design, TD professionals should understand how to use the human performance improvement process to determine the best solution. When a performance problem arises, stakeholders and sponsors often assume that training or development is the solution. However, a knowledge and skills gap that can be solved by learning is only one cause of performance problems in the workplace.

Training on its own does not always produce measurable changes in behavior because it only addresses one of the six drivers of performance (knowledge and skills). Employees may have the skills and knowledge to handle a task but still fail to perform the task effectively. In such situations, one or more of the other five drivers may influence performance:

- **Lack of motivation** can negatively affect performance, even if employees have the skills, knowledge, and resources to do their jobs.
- **Lack of tools or resources** may prevent employees from performing a task.
- **Inadequate or nonexistent structures, processes, or guidelines** may cause a disconnect between the goals and the measures that employees are rated on.
- **Lack of information** can create performance gaps.
- **Lack of health,** which could be something as simple as poor vision, must be addressed to ensure it's not the cause of the performance problem.

Solutions for improving performance that don't require training are called performance improvement solutions. Using this term often helps TD professionals consider different kinds of approaches. [See 3.5]

III. The ADDIE Model

The ADDIE model is the original ISD framework. The acronym represents the five phases for creating training and performance support tools: analysis, design, development, implementation, and evaluation. Most current ISD models are a variation of these five phases.

2.2.1.10 The Origin of ADDIE

The concept of ISD has existed since the early 1950s. The ADDIE model was created by the Center for Educational Technology at Florida State University for the US Army in 1975, and it was quickly adapted by the entire US military (Branson et al. 1975; Watson 1981). The five phases were based on a previous model developed by the US Air Force.

Initially, ADDIE was considered a linear model; however, it was not strictly linear because evaluations were performed throughout its life cycle so TD professionals could iterate and correct flaws found in the evaluation. By 1984, the model evolved into a dynamic approach with interrelated phases as displayed in Figure 2.2.1.10-1.

Figure 2.2.1.10-1. The ADDIE Model

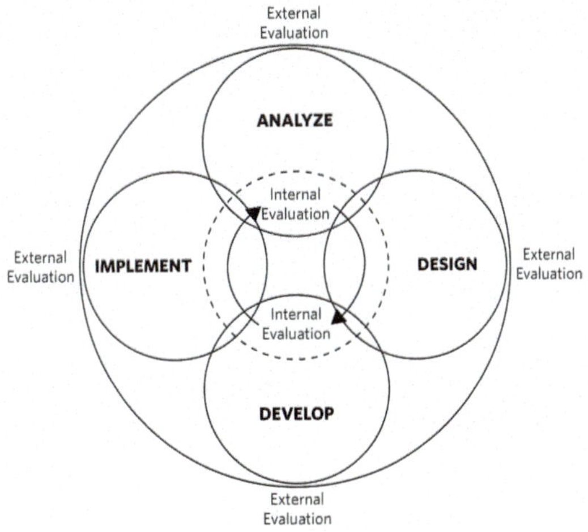

Adapted from US Army Field Artillery School (1984).

2.2.1.11 Phases of ADDIE

In the ADDIE model, analysis represents the input; design, development, and evaluation are the process; and implementation is the output. The elements overlap somewhat, depending on the project. ADDIE is sometimes called a process model, but TD professionals should consider using it as a guide to solve a design problem, adapting ADDIE to achieve the best results. For example, there may be times when TD professionals could incorporate other development models that better fit a problem. ADDIE is often displayed as a linear process, but TD professionals should use iterative steps and adapt it to their specific situations, using the original cyclical model. ADDIE is quite agile when used as it was intended (Figure 2.2.1.11-1).

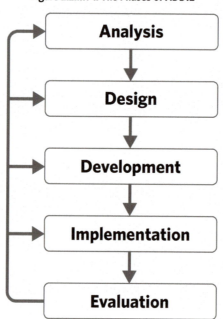

Figure 2.2.1.11-1. The Phases of ADDIE

2.2.1.11.1 Analysis

The first phase, analysis, is the process of gathering data to identify specific needs—the who, what, where, when, and why of the design process. This is how TD professionals determine what learners need to know to be successful, what the organization needs, and whether the initial diagnosis was accurate. It is necessary even if the project sponsors think they know what the problem is and what the solution should be. Their information might be correct; however, it might reflect an incomplete understanding of the learners or the content. [See 2.8.3]

Analysis allows TD professionals to verify the information and fill in any gaps. To get started, they need to understand the:
- Sponsor's requested outcome
- Organizational need or driver underlying the project
- Desired performance and tasks required
- Learners and what influences them
- Constraints on the project

TD professionals must gather information about the project before they consider anything else, which means that the first analysis question is critical: Can the problem be reasonably remedied by a development solution? This requires identifying the root cause.

Once training or learning is deemed an appropriate solution (or part of the solution), TD professionals can then determine the specific learning needs. In this phase, they will identify:
- Whether a performance problem exists that a development solution can address
- Potential goals and objectives
- Available resources
- The audience that requires the solution
- Any additional data needed to be successful

The analysis should also determine whether a formal, informal, or blended solution is recommended. Beyond the scope of the solution, TD professionals need to consider what resources are available, constraints that may create barriers, and how the solution is aligned to the organizational strategy. There are many potential methods for gathering and reviewing data, including surveys, focus groups, materials review, subject matter expert (SME) panels, and existing program reviews.

2.2.1.11.2 Design

During this phase, TD professionals create an outline of the specifications necessary to complete the training project. The foundation consists of goals, objectives, and evaluation tasks that must be developed. Then a sequence is determined with a structure based on the decisions regarding training platforms and other implementation questions. In this phase, the TD professional:
- Develops the outcome statement with input from the stakeholder or sponsor
- Writes learning objectives [See 2.2.4.1]
- Creates an evaluation plan [See 2.8.6.5]
- Recommends the modality that will be used to deliver content
- Outlines the sequence and structure of the course or program
- Prepares logic and objective maps
- Determines what materials are necessary and prepares draft copies of them

A key output of this phase is the project design plan, which guides development and lists:
- The objectives and additional items needed, including printed materials
- Scripts and storyboards for computer-based projects
- Evaluation materials including tests, quizzes, and other formal evaluations
- Lesson plans
- Assignments and responsibilities
- A project management plan with milestones and deadlines

The design phase may also require a report or summary of the analysis and design. This is a preliminary communication to the sponsors or stakeholders about current progress that provides an opportunity for suggestions and feedback. It helps ensure the solution will meet their expectations.

2.2 Instructional Design

2.2.1.11.3 Development

In this phase, the content and material move from conceptual design to deliverable. During the development phase, the designer may use pilot testing, prototyping, strawman lessons, or other iterative tools to test whether deliverables are accurate and effective. This allows the designers to make changes before the expenses associated with full-scale material development are realized. It also helps TD professionals feel confident that what they have designed is accurate. [See 2.2.13.4]

Some of the major development phase elements include these tasks:
- Participant and facilitator materials are prepared in draft form and reviewed by SMEs and TD professionals for accuracy.
- Nonprint media—such as audio, video, and computer-based content—are prepared and reviewed.
- Content is pilot tested, prototypes are completed, changes are incorporated, and final materials are modified as necessary.
- Programs are packaged and distributed in preparation for implementation.

2.2.1.11.4 Implementation

During this phase, the content is delivered using the chosen modality, such as an instructor-led course, a technology-enabled event, or a blended solution. The solution could be something as focused as an electronic performance support system (EPSS) or as broad as a leadership development effort. Whatever the effort, the goal is to achieve the objectives that were written in the design phase.

TD professionals should monitor the solution for any unexpected situations. For example, if facilitation is part of the solution, talent development can provide backup during the first delivery to offer support and feedback. They should also watch for any areas of the solution that need improvement, either now or in the future.

Because TD professionals must gauge the degree to which learners meet their objectives and facilitators or technologies deliver expectations, they should be prepared to:
- Evaluate the program or solution design.
- Review the effectiveness of how the materials are used.
- Determine the effectiveness for virtual users, user group size, format, and timing.
- State any modifications that need to be made before releasing the solution again.

All these are examples of evaluation actions that TD professionals may take during this phase.

2.2.1.11.5 Evaluation

Although it may appear to be the last element in the ADDIE model, evaluation should take place at every point throughout the ISD process to ensure sponsors and stakeholders are involved. Evaluation activities in each phase include:
- **Analysis.** The evaluation clarifies whether the organizational outcome aligns to the sponsor's requirements.
- **Design.** Evaluation helps determine useful questions for each evaluation level. TD professionals may conduct a preliminary evaluation of the plan to review with the sponsors and confirm that the goals meet their expectations.

- **Development.** The validated instructional plans require evaluation by SMEs. Evaluation at this stage may also examine whether all design elements have been met and the content is accurate.
- **Implementation.** The Level 1 (reaction) and Level 2 (learning) evaluations are completed during this stage to provide feedback to the facilitator, the learners, and the sponsors.
- **Evaluation.** In this phase, TD professionals measure Level 3 (behavior), the transfer of learning, and Level 4 (results), the degree to which the targeted outcomes are met. They should also evaluate whether the on-the-job environment supports the learning efforts.

TD professionals should communicate with the sponsors and stakeholders at each step, sharing the evaluation results to ensure they are meeting expectations. The final evaluation results may also be used by talent development to review lessons learned, identify process improvements, and measure results.

2.2.2 Knowledge of Needs Assessment Approaches and Techniques

I. Needs Assessment for Instructional Design

TD professionals should determine the need as the first step in the ISD process. Although needs assessment and needs analysis are often used interchangeably, there is a difference, and the two terms should be clarified:
- A **needs assessment** is used to identify, measure, and prioritize current gaps.
- A **needs analysis** is a process of synthesizing and reviewing the data and information after the needs assessment to determine the difference between the current condition and the desired future condition. [See 3.5.2.3]

It is critical to focus on needs assessment in instructional design to determine important design elements: Identify what should be happening, prove that there is a need, and provide a basis for evaluation.

2.2.2.1 Value of Needs Assessment

The needs assessment is a valuable part of instructional design because the results guide the TD professional and the rest of the ISD process. It can uncover the specific skill or knowledge gap, identify the best way to close the gap, gain support from stakeholders who are involved in the assessment, and build rapport with learners.

Beyond the obvious design aspect, the needs assessment can also be used as the basis for creating an evaluation strategy tied to the individual, the knowledge or skills learned, the performance on the job, and whether the training helped the organization reach its goals. A needs assessment confirms the presence of an organizational need and may also identify nontraining issues that affect the situation.

2.2.2.2 The Needs Assessment Process

The classic approach to determining needs or problems is identifying the discrepancy between the desired and actual knowledge, skills, or performance. That discrepancy translates into a learning or performance improvement need. A variety of methods—including interviews, observations, questionnaires, and tests—lead to the identification of needs. Using these methods effectively requires accurately gathering, analyzing, verifying, and reporting data.

2.2 Instructional Design

A needs assessment starts with identifying the organizational need. The goal in instructional design is to discover needs related to performance issues, which can include a broad variety of topics, such as processes, resources, and organizational structures. The needs assessment uncovers information to determine whether the performance deficit is a training problem. [See 3.5]

When implemented effectively, the needs assessment serves many purposes:
- It places the need or request in the context of the organization's needs.
- It validates or augments the initial issues presented by the sponsor or the client. Although sponsors and clients know the organization, they don't always know the cause of or the remedy for issues that involve human performance. The needs assessment can reveal new information, provide broader context, and offer different perspectives to the client's initial impressions.
- It ensures that the design of the solution supports employee performance and helps the organization meet its needs.
- It results in recommendations regarding nontraining issues that influence whether the desired organizational and employee performance goals are achieved.
- It establishes the foundation for back-end evaluation. Figure 2.2.2.2-1 illustrates how a needs assessment prepares for evaluation.

During needs assessment, measures may be taken in four areas: business needs, performance needs, learning needs, and learner needs. During evaluation (after delivery), those same items are measured, but they're now called the four levels of evaluation: reaction, learning, behavior, and results. The goal is to identify positive changes in each of the four needs assessment premeasures when they are measured during evaluation.

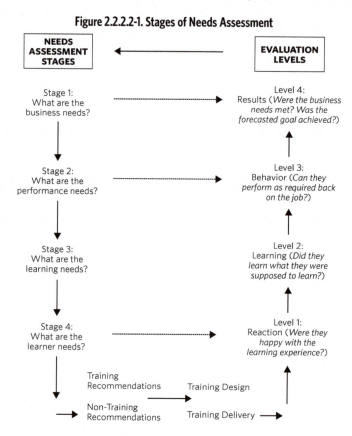

Figure 2.2.2.2-1. Stages of Needs Assessment

Source: Tobey (2005).

Sponsors may request TD support. They'll typically present a problem that needs solving and whether they suggest gathering data. In response, the TD professional may recommend the six steps used in a needs assessment.

2.2.2.2.1 Define the Purpose
TD professionals determine the purpose of the needs assessment, which could include:
- Identifying performance problems, deficiencies, and root causes
- Determining whether formal or informal development is a solution
- Securing the support and commitment of management
- Generating data that will be useful when measuring the effect of the solution
- Providing specific recommendations for design and delivery including scope, methods, frequency, cost, and location
- Identifying employees who need development
- Deciding on priorities for the upcoming year and long-range strategic planning
- Justifying spending to management by determining the value and cost—including calculating the expenses incurred or money lost by continuing with the same problems

2.2.2.2.2 Identify the Necessary Data
A thorough needs assessment requires information to identify the need, solution, and strategies. Knowing the nature and quantity of the information required is important for a useful assessment study. This information may come from opinions, attitude surveys, financial statements, job descriptions, performance appraisals, work samples, or historical documents from company archives.

2.2.2.2.3 Select the Data Collection Methods
TD professionals should know the advantages and disadvantages of each tool as they select or design a method to gather data. Structured or formal assessment methods are based on the data required and a comparison of each method's degree of effectiveness for gathering the required data. TD professionals should ensure that all tools (including questionnaires and surveys) are reliable and valid. [See 2.8.4.2]

2.2.2.2.4 Collect the Data
TD professionals should be able to gather information using each tool. Care must be taken when collecting data to ensure the proper sample size and representative sample population or study group. TD professionals should also be skilled at administering questionnaires, conducting interviews, observing performance, and other techniques. During the process, the TD professional should periodically report their progress to the sponsor. The report doesn't need to be formal; it can be sent in an email. If organizational changes occur, the sponsor may be able to provide access to alternative data sources. [See 2.8.6]

2.2.2.2.5 Analyze and Confirm the Data
To uncover problems and related trends or patterns, TD professionals should compare their data with previously collected information, confirm results, and check for accuracy by consulting with the people who originally provided the information.

2.2.2.2.6 Share Findings

TD professionals need to identify problems, needs, and weak areas, and then recommend strategies for improvement. They can then use tables, graphs, and other support data to share results in their final report to the sponsor or stakeholder. [See 2.8.7]

2.2.2.3 Levels of Needs Assessment

A needs assessment may occur at three levels: organizational, task, and individual.

2.2.2.3.1 Organizational Assessment: What Are the Organization's Needs?

An organizational assessment may be used if an organization is trying a new way of doing things, launching a new product line, considering succession planning, or improving engagement. As part of this assessment, TD professionals should include any knowledge or skills that employees will need in the future as the organization and their jobs change. Both formal and informal assessments of organizational needs are useful. To informally assess organizational needs, review the latest version of the organization's mission, goals, priorities, and recent survey data. Organizational projections may also be considered. For example, if new computer equipment or programs will be used within a few months, preparation for this change should be incorporated.

2.2.2.3.2 Task Assessment or Job Analysis: What Are the Performance Needs?

Task assessment or job analysis is defined as the systematic identification of the items necessary to perform any job, such as skills, knowledge, tools, conditions, and requirements. Task assessments can vary in complexity and scope. For instance, one could accurately document a simple set of tasks by interviewing current employees. Task assessments may also require data-gathering sessions to identify all the components of a complex job or a position undergoing change. Regardless of the level of complexity, task assessments share several fundamental steps:

- Identify the critical outputs of the job to understand the major tasks and task groupings.
- Divide the major tasks into subtasks or steps.
- Determine the type of tasks between knowledge and skills.
- Collect all the data necessary to document the tasks and subtasks.
- Validate the data, which is usually accomplished through direct observation.
- Obtain review and approval of task assessment from sponsors or other managers.
- Finalize the report and distribute findings to management for final approval.

2.2.2.3.3 Individual Assessment: What Are the Learning and Learner Needs?

An individual assessment focuses on how individuals complete their jobs. Individual assessments may be used for employee appraisals and to design developmental options. During this process, the TD professional focuses on individual employees and how they do their jobs successfully, pinpointing key activities that successful employees use to perform a job correctly. An individual assessment may also result in a development plan to help employees improve their performance.

2.2.2.4 Types of Data Collection Methods

Data collection methods include tools (such as questionnaires, checklists, and scales) that systematically gather data about individual groups or entire organizations. They indicate both weak and strong areas. To determine data requirements, consider some of these questions:

- What are the goals or expectations of the employees being studied? How do they relate to organizational goals?
- How will the organizational climate affect the need for anonymity, survey return rates, or the willingness of employees to be interviewed?
- Who will administer, score, and interpret the results?
- Does the use of the tools require special knowledge?
- Is the scoring objective?

These questions help TD professionals determine data collection needs and select the methods that best suit the project's requirements, time constraints, and budget. They need to be analyzed for their strengths and weaknesses so that potential methods can be identified for each data source.

2.2.2.4.1 Assessments and Tests

Assessments and tests gauge what the respondents know, can do, or believe in relation to the requirement being investigated. They include knowledge assessments through verbal or written responses to multiple-choice, true-or-false, fill-in-the-blank, or essay questions; actual performance of a skill while being observed; and analysis of work results, products, or output against quality criteria. The advantages of assessments and tests are that they're objective and identify the specific gap between the current and desired performance, knowledge, and skills. Disadvantages are that they can be time consuming and don't always examine the thought processes that support why an individual performed in a certain way.

2.2.2.4.2 Performance Audits

Performance audits or appraisals are useful when performance criteria are clear and sufficient data are available to measure the performance criteria. This method identifies employee efficiency and effectiveness. TD professionals may also use performance appraisals to review how well employees have performed in the past. The advantage of this approach is that the topics and goals are easier to determine because the designer can compare the gap between the criteria and actual performance. The disadvantage is that the data may be confounded by other variables, such as equipment downtime or external expectations.

2.2.2.4.3 Observation

In this method, an observer watches the job performer (experts or average performers) and documents each step they take to do the task, including movements, the amount of time for each step, and standards for successful performance. More advanced versions of this method include time-and-motion studies and human factors studies. Used to collect data on current and desired performance, observation is useful in two circumstances: when assessing a need for skill-based training or a program that changes behavior (such as serving customers or giving constructive feedback). An advantage to observation is that it may be used to create a step-by-step procedure (algorithm) that can be standardized for all learners as a flowchart, diagram, graphic, list of steps, or job aid. A disadvantage is some performers may not act as they normally would because they know they are being watched (which is known as the Hawthorne effect).

2.2.2.4.4 Interviews

Interviews or one-on-one discussions elicit the reactions of interviewees to a topic, yielding subjective data and illustrative anecdotes. They are most often used to collect data from a current performance situation or to gather organizational needs information from the client. Interviews are useful for clarifying ambiguous or confusing information obtained from documentation or observation. A positive, unintended outcome is that they often give participants ownership in the development process. Other advantages of interviews are that they provide rich details through a two-way conversation to clarify statements or ensure understanding of questions, and can be used to design a quantitative data collection tool. Disadvantages include that they can be time consuming and the interviewer must be careful to record exact responses and not interpret them.

2.2.2.4.5 Focus Groups

In a focus group, TD professionals identify five to 12 key individuals who can provide information about the need in a group setting. The group interview provides rich data regarding the job environment, current level of skill and performance, and perceptions of desired skill and performance levels. To be effective, focus groups should have two facilitators. One advantage of a focus group is that it can create deeper concepts as individuals build on one another's ideas. A disadvantage is that the group can be influenced by particularly verbal individuals, which gives the false impression of unanimity.

2.2.2.4.6 Surveys

Surveys are digital or paper-based questionnaires that ask a series of focused questions and are most often used for performance analysis and learner analysis. They can gather both qualitative and quantitative data and vary greatly in complexity and the amount of time and money needed to create them. TD professionals should choose a survey type that provides the needed data—not necessarily the one that's fastest, least expensive, or easiest to create. Advantages are that they are typically inexpensive, the results are easy to tally, they provide quick results, and they can reach people at a distance. The greatest drawback is that return rates can often be much lower than what a TD professional would like.

2.2.2.4.7 Work Samples

Work samples can include a manager's reports, a technician's equipment repair, or a programmer's software design. They may also be less tangible, such as observations of a TD professional facilitating a group or a manager conducting a meeting. TD professionals use work samples to identify problem areas that may require further analysis. Work samples may also be used to supplement other assessment methods, validate other data, or gather preliminary information for a study. The advantages are that they can be unobtrusive and provide direct data on actual work. Disadvantages are that the TD professional may need specialized content knowledge, and gathering and grading work samples can intimidate employees.

2.2.2.4.8 Extant Data

Extant data includes existing records, reports, and data that may be available inside or outside the organization, such as job descriptions, competency models, benchmarking reports, annual reports, financial statements, strategic plans, mission statements, staffing statistics, climate surveys, grievances, turnover rates, absenteeism, suggestion box feedback, and accident statistics. TD professionals often use extant data for organizational needs analysis and current performance analysis. Two advantages are that it provides exact numbers and measures that can enable an examination of trends and patterns over time. The biggest drawback is that extant data is usually collected for other purposes, so performance issues may need to be inferred from patterns in the data.

2.2.2.5 Qualitative and Quantitative Data

Data collection methods can be quantitative or qualitative or both. Quantitative methods are those that result in hard data, which is objective and measurable, whether stated in terms of frequency, percentage, proportion, or time. Qualitative methods yield soft data that is more intangible, anecdotal, personal, and subjective, such as people's opinions, attitudes, assumptions, feelings, values, and desires.

Quantitative and qualitative measures can be combined in a data collection process. For example, TD professionals can use a qualitative method (interviews) to collect anecdotes and examples. Then they can develop a quantitative method (a survey) using the collected anecdotes and examples as survey items, and measure how many respondents fit the examples and how frequently the examples fit the respondents. Conversely, a quantitative method can be used first to collect information on frequency and number of respondents. Then a qualitative method can be used to augment the survey items with richer details.

Qualitative and quantitative measures can also be combined in the same measurement tool. For example, items on a survey can be qualitative terms, such as feelings and opinions. How many times each is chosen (frequency) is a quantitative measure.

Objectives

2.2.3 Knowledge of Methods and Techniques for Defining Learning and Behavioral Outcome Statements

> **I. Designing to Meet Organizational Requirements**
>
> TD professionals should use the needs assessment results to define learning and behavioral outcome statements. They will want to ensure that the outcomes and objectives are aligned to the organization's strategy and goals. Organizations support TD departments to help them reach their goals and objectives.

2.2.3.1 Outcomes and Objectives

Although objectives and outcomes are written with similar guidelines, there are distinctions.

Outcomes are the specific outputs individuals are expected to achieve. They are significant and essential for making the changes the organization expects as a result of the investment in learning. Outcomes are more closely related to the organization and how the particular training is aligned to the business goal. Because they are more closely related to the organization, outcomes will be more meaningful to sponsors, stakeholders, and leaders.

Objectives are the skills and knowledge learners use to perform the tasks that lead to the outcome. They are written from the learner's perspective and are therefore more meaningful to them. Objectives identify what the learner will be able to do as a result of the learning or performance solution.

2.2.3.2 Partner With the Sponsor

To define outcomes, TD professionals start with the results of the needs assessment and work with the sponsor or stakeholder who has an investment and interest in the design of the learning or performance solution. Begin by sharing the results of the needs assessment to reach agreement on the consistency between the sponsor's original request and the results of the needs assessment.

The TD professional should keep the sponsor involved at every step of the needs assessment process, making sure to validate, augment, or disprove the initial issues presented by the sponsor. Consistent communication will make this discussion easier and more effective.

2.2.3.3 Ensure the Outcome Statement Is Aligned

The needs assessment should place the sponsor's request in the context of the organization's needs. Now the TD professional and the sponsor (or stakeholders) should discuss and confirm several aspects of the request in preparation for developing the outcome:

- Consider the organizational culture to ensure alignment.
- Review the behaviors that need to be changed to support the outcome the sponsor desires. The sponsor may have insight about how to reward people who accept the change and how to support those who do not—especially if the design is designated for the sponsor's function.
- Confirm a link between the TD solution and organizational drivers to ensure that the ultimate design supports employee performance and thereby helps the organization meet its needs.

2.2.3.4 Formulate the Sponsor's Outcome Statement

The sponsor's outcome statements may be in their performance goals or at least connected to them. TD professionals should use the sponsors' words as much as possible. However, TD professionals should clearly understand the sponsor before writing the learning objectives for the solution design. The sponsor should at a minimum define an outcome that clarifies intent using a verb, an adjective, and a noun; for example, "Migrate department's employees to the online support system." For more detailed statements, TD professionals can also write the outcomes using the same rules for writing objectives.

2.2.4 Skill in Developing Learning and Behavioral Outcome Statements

> **I. Writing Objectives**
>
> TD professionals should be able to write objectives. As one of the most important skills for instructional design, it enables them to state the outcome of a learning event.

2.2.4.1 Learning Objectives

Course objectives state what participants will be able to do differently as a result of training or other development. Every concept, skill, or behavior should be identified with an objective. TD professionals should understand the hierarchy of terminal and enabling objectives:

- **Terminal objectives.** Also known as performance objectives, these objectives represent what learners must master before completing the course. They're the final behavioral outcomes of

a specific learning event, describing the intended competencies for the unit, lesson, course, or program for which they were written.
- **Enabling objectives.** To master one terminal objective, learners must often master several subordinate ones, which are called enabling objectives. Enabling objectives support the terminal objectives by breaking them down into more manageable chunks. They are the building blocks providing the additional concepts or skills needed to meet the terminal objective.

2.2.4.2 Influence of Bloom's Taxonomy on Writing Objectives

Understanding Bloom's Taxonomy is vital to writing appropriate outcome statements. Benjamin Bloom's influence on learning objectives is based on the three domains he identified, which TD professionals often shorten to KSAs:
- **Knowledge** or cognitive learning involves mental processes and the acquisition of information.
- **Skills** or psychomotor involves manipulation of objects or machinery based on mental decisions.
- **Attitude** or affect involves motivation and perceptions.

Bloom's Taxonomy organizes these three domains in a hierarchy from the simplest behavior to the most complex: knowledge, comprehension, application, analysis, synthesis, and evaluation. When developing learning objectives, TD professionals should remember that there are different levels or outcomes of learning within each of the domains (Anderson et al. 2000). [See 2.1.3.6]

2.2.4.3 Mager's Model for Writing Objectives

According to Robert Mager (1962), a learning objective should include three components:
- **Behavior** or performance by the learner
- **Conditions** under which the learner must perform the behavior
- **Criteria** that measure the acceptable range of performance

Like many other learning experts, Mager contends that learning objectives should be specific and measurable to guide both the facilitator and the learner. He suggests using four A-B-C-D elements for writing objectives: audience, behavior, condition, and degree of mastery required. [See 2.1.3.8, 2.2.4.3, and 2.2.4.4.1]

2.2.4.4 Writing Learning Objectives

TD professionals need to frame measurable and observable objectives from the learner's perspective. While different formats for writing objectives exist, the two most recognized are Mager's A-B-C-D format and SMART objectives.

2.2.4.4.1 A-B-C-D Objectives

Mager's model is easy to remember:
- **Audience** is specified using the course title; for example, "Learners in Leading Meetings."
- **Behavior** provides a clear description about the anticipated performance; for example, "will be able to develop an agenda." The verbs must be observable and measurable.
- **Condition** states the support available to learners to complete the objective; for example, "using an agenda template."
- **Degree** indicates how close to perfection a learner must get to meet the objective; for example, "100 percent of the time" or "every time."

The complete example might be "Learners in Leading Meetings will be able to develop an agenda using the template every time."

2.2.4.4.2 SMART Objectives

SMART objectives are:
- **Specific.** Objectives need to clearly define what is expected.
- **Measurable.** Objectives must contain one or more defined standard (criteria) by which to gauge effective performance.
- **Achievable.** Objectives need to be difficult yet attainable by the learner.
- **Relevant.** Objectives need to be important to the organization and the purpose of the course.
- **Time Bound.** Objectives must include specific timeframes.

An example of a SMART objective is "By the end of this learning event participants will be able to write correct objectives using the SMART format 100 percent of the time."

2.2.5 Knowledge of the Criteria Used to Assess the Quality and Relevance of Instructional Content in Relation to a Desired Learning or Behavioral Outcome

> **I. Clarifying Desired Outcomes**
>
> Prior to developing content, TD professionals should review the objectives and compare them with existing content in the marketplace or within their organizations. If content already exists, they need to determine whether they can use it in the solution they are designing.

2.2.5.1 Review Objectives and Outcomes

During the needs assessment, TD professionals may focus on four areas: organizational needs, performance needs, learning needs, and learner needs. They should identify positive changes in each of the four needs assessment areas. These measures, written as objectives, relate to the outcomes and identify the skills and knowledge required.

2.2.5.2 Current Availability of Content

Once the objectives are confirmed, TD professionals should determine if content currently exists in the marketplace or within their organizations. If it does, they'll need to evaluate it and decide whether to use it or create new content instead.

Many members of the workforce desire more professional development than they receive. Artificial intelligence (AI) is one potential support option. As they prepare to use AI in learning, TD professionals will need to begin making decisions about whether to design new content or curate content that already exists. Learning experience platforms have begun to contextualize content, gathering it from millions of sources based on individual preferences, background, requirements, and skills. Whether through an automated or manual process, sourcing, evaluating, and selecting learning content as part of a curation process is an increasingly important aspect of the TD role.

Design

2.2.6 Skill in Designing Blueprints, Schematics, and Other Visual Representations of Learning and Development Solutions

> **I. The Design Process**
>
> TD professionals should be skilled in planning and designing their solutions using visual representations to establish the sequence and course map—both input to the development phase.

2.2.6.1 Basics of Course Design

Once TD professionals have refined objectives, they need to create a plan for the actual development of the learning solution. The design activities include:
- A final list of objectives
- Recommended modality
- Suggested module names
- Sequence of modules, topics, and activities (such as flow, transitions, and links)
- Practice opportunities
- Details about each objective:
    o Special teaching points
    o Suggested instructional methods
    o Media requirements
    o Testing requirements

After selecting the overall instructional modality, the TD professional will make general decisions about the methods and the media. Some questions to ask include "Will the course feature on-the-job training, classroom instruction, lab or workshop instruction, or self-instruction?" and "Will the course use participant materials, mobile devices, computers, audio, or video?" The selected methods should match the stated course objectives. TD professionals should also allot time for practice and may ask SMEs to examine the content.

After completing the analysis, writing the objectives, designing the test items, and considering the overall plan, the TD professional will know what to include in the program. The next step is to outline the information and develop a course map to identify the steps that lead to course completion. TD professionals may use visual representations to lay out the course map sequence.

2.2.6.2 Visual Representations of the Course Design

There are several different ways to visually present the course map:
- **Storyboards.** TD professionals may use a storyboard, which is a graphic organizer developed by the Walt Disney Studio in the early 1930s to help visualize the storyline of a movie. Storyboards can be intricate and time consuming, but they can also save TD professionals time by allowing them to move things around before much development has occurred. They provide an opportunity to experiment with changes at an early step in the process.

- **Wireframes.** Generally associated with the design of a website, wireframes are simple black-and-white layouts that outline the specific size and placement of page elements, site features, conversion areas, and navigation. They are devoid of color, font choices, logos, and any other real design element that takes away from purely focusing on the structure.
- **Mock-ups and prototypes.** These tools represent a way to present the final product. A mock-up looks like a finished product, but it is not interactive or clickable. A prototype provides partial functionality of the end results and enables testing. [See 2.2.13.4]

2.2.6.3 Types and Rationale of Sequencing

During the analysis phase, TD professionals identify certain types of relationships among job tasks. When designing and developing the solution, they use this information to identify the best sequencing of content. Some tasks are subordinate to others; some are equal in importance but must be performed in a particular sequence; others have a logical relationship but may be performed in any order; some tasks are unrelated to the others. Using the visual representations, TD professionals select a sequencing rationale. Sequence is important because it:

- Makes it easier for learners to follow
- Ensures a logical flow from one point to the next
- Allows for logical transitions from one chunk of information to the next

Here are a few ways to arrange learning objectives into a logical sequence:
- Job performance order
- Chronological order
- Simple content to complex
- Problem and solution
- General to specific
- Less risky to more risky
- Known to unknown
- Dependent relationship
- Supportive relationship
- Cause to effect

2.2.6.4 Course Map Plan and Modules

Similar to an outline, the course map lists the modules in sequence, and is accompanied by media selections and support requirements. Because adult learners respond best to small, organized units of learning, TD professionals should frame the course content into modules. A module represents the smallest unit of learning and provides content and practice based on the learning objectives. Each learning module contains:

- Objectives
- Knowledge content to enable the learner to complete the task
- Identification of facilitator and learner activities that will result in mastery of the objectives
- Practice activities to help reach the objectives
- An assessment mechanism (such as test items) to determine whether the objectives were achieved

Other factors to consider when creating learning modules include:
- Timing and breaks
- The amount of material to include
- Class or group size for activities
- Simulation of job conditions

2.2.6.5 Design Outputs
The design phase lays the groundwork for development. Outputs always include:
- A final recommendation about the modality that will be used to deliver the solution
- Required technology or special equipment

When using formal learning, outputs include:
- The sequenced design linked to the solution, outcomes, and objectives
- An evaluation plan
- Recommended methods and media
- Materials required with draft copies or mockups

When using an informal learning solution, outputs could include:
- Mock-ups of checklists or tip sheets for on-the-job learning
- A plan for how to tell employees about the resources
- Optional guidance for anyone using the informal learning solutions

2.2.7 Knowledge of Instructional Modalities

I. Instructional Modality Options
TD professionals should decide on the best modality as a part of the design phase.

2.2.7.1 Formal and Informal Approaches
Learning consists of two large categories:
- **Formal learning** is planned and derived from activities within a structured learning setting, including instructor-led classrooms, instructor-led online training events, certification programs, workshops, webinars, and college courses. There is a curriculum, agenda, and objectives that occur within a pre-established timeframe.
- **Informal learning** occurs outside a structured program, plan, or class. It occurs naturally in everyday life and on the job through observing others, trial and error, and talking and collaborating with others. It is usually spontaneous and could include massive open online courses (MOOCs), asynchronous options, multi-device learning, coaching, mentoring, stretch assignments, or rotational assignments. It can also include reading books and blogs, watching online video platforms such as YouTube, listening to podcasts, Googling content, and retrieving other digital content.

TD professionals often apply a blended learning approach, which is a combination of both formal and informal learning, using the modality that best addresses each objective. [See 2.2.7.5]

2.2.7.2 Formal and Informal Modality Examples

TD professionals should have a working knowledge of the modalities within both the formal and informal categories. Each modality has its own advantages and disadvantages. And TD professionals must decide which is most appropriate given scope, constraints, time to design and deliver content, cost, geographic location of learners, baseline knowledge of learners, technical skills required, and so on.

- **Formal modalities** include instructor-led classrooms, instructor-led online training events, certification programs, workshops, webinars, and lunch & learn sessions.
- **Informal modalities** include asynchronous options, planned rotational assignments, self-study, electronic or paper job aids, discussion forums, and performance support applications and tools.

Although some modalities may be used more frequently in either formal or informal settings, others are used in both formal and informal learning. For example, a learner may participate in a synchronous, virtual classroom on a mobile device and later access support materials from that same mobile device while performing a task. [See 2.3.6]

2.2.7.3 Advantages of Informal and Formal Approaches

The advantages of formal approaches include:
- Large numbers of employees learn the same information and processes at the same time.
- If properly designed, the content will be accurate and up to date.
- Employees who participate in formal training programs learn faster in new jobs.
- They can include a variety of methods to appeal to all learning preferences and conform to adult learning principles.
- They can be less costly to design.

The advantages of informal approaches include:
- They may occur in the workplace at the time learning is needed while learners are doing the job.
- They can be more effective in building proficiency than formal learning.
- They are natural ways to learn.
- They are highly relevant and occur in small steps.
- They can be less costly to deliver and more efficient due to the ubiquity of social media and mobile devices.
- TD professionals may experience less resistance with informal approaches than with formal training.

TD professionals typically make recommendations for the best modality in the design phase; however, that may be adjusted based on the iterative method guiding the design, recommendations from SMEs, or the discovery of sponsor discussions.

2.2.7.4 E-Learning Options

E-learning is a structured course or learning experience delivered electronically through various applications and processes (such as self-led or self-directed web-based, computer-based, and multi-device learning). This approach is often used for consistent, accessible delivery of content across a broad and sometimes geographically dispersed audience. One consideration for e-learning design is knowing how the content will be delivered, such as via the internet, users' mobile devices, an organization's intranet, or a shared computer network.

E-learning programs may be delivered through a learning management system (LMS) or learning experience platform and are frequently produced using commercially available authoring tools.

2.2.7.5 Blended Learning

Blended learning is the practice of using several modalities in one curriculum. It refers to the combination of formal and informal leaning events such as classroom instruction, online resources, and on-the-job coaching. [See 2.3.6.1]

According to Cindy Huggett (2022), "Blended learning journeys refer to a learning process with multiple cohesive components taking place over a designated period of time." Instead of a set of random learning events, they are "a thoughtfully planned set of experiences designed to help you learn." They use multiple delivery methods depending on what will be most efficient for the kind of content being designed.

There are several reasons to design a blended learning journey:
- Tailor the design to match each learning goal, objective, or performance need.
- Build evidence-based learning methods into the design—such as the spacing effect, chunking, and retrieval practice—for improved retention.
- Spread practice, collaboration, and discussion with peers throughout the experience.
- Make training a cohesive, sequential process rather than a singular event.
- Afford distributed workforces, who are not co-located, the ability to participate in learning with peers.
- Structure the material in a way that maximizes self-pacing and self-study options for learners.
- Minimize the disruption of work and schedules with learning solutions that fit into regular workflows.
- Reduce time and cost factors—such as travel and facility fees—sometimes associated with face-to-face classrooms.

Development

2.2.8 Knowledge of Methods and Techniques for Planning, Designing, and Developing Instructional Content

I. Methods and Techniques to Develop Content
TD professionals should have knowledge of the methods and techniques to develop content.

2.2.8.1 Basics of Course Development

Development is the process of creating, testing, and producing usable instructional materials. In the design phase, the TD professional defines the topic to be developed by creating topic content.

The development process is iterative as the TD professional works with SMEs, the sponsor, and others who are knowledgeable in the content area, instructional design, and evaluation. Content products will be reviewed and revised. TD professionals will use prototyping and pilot testing to check material and test instructional methods prior to delivery of the formal training program. The development phase uses the recommendations from the design phase, such as the sequencing and modality, and chooses a technique to plan the content. The outcome of the development phase is a formal or informal learning solution that is ready to implement.

2.2.8.2 Affinity Diagrams and Interrelationship Digraphs

Affinity diagrams gather numerous ideas and organize them into logical groupings based on the natural relationships between items. The *interrelationship digraph* shows cause-and-effect relationships among the groupings. They are best used when issues seem too complex and relationships among facts seem confusing, when thoughts or facts are ambiguous or chaotic, or when the TD professional and stakeholders need to discover the major themes contained in a great number of ideas.

Affinity diagrams and interrelationship digraphs help TD professionals gather ideas into related clusters, each with a clear title and with the relationship among the clusters clearly drawn. These groups can be placed in a logical sequence for developing content.

2.2.8.3 Outlines

When used for planning content, outlines should be designed following several helpful features:
- All headers should be parallel or of the same level and form.
- The outline should be presented in a logical flow. [See 2.2.6.1]
- Headers should be more general than the subheads.

2.2.8.4 Robert Gagné's Nine Events of Instruction

Although the steps in Robert Gagné's Nine Events of Instruction occur during instruction, TD professionals must plan for them during the design and development phases to ensure they are incorporated. The events are divided into three groupings:
- Preparation:
    1. Gain attention.
    2. Tell the learners the learning objective.
    3. Stimulate recall of prior learning (retrieval).
- Instruction and practice:
    4. Present the stimulus.
    5. Provide learning guidance.
    6. Elicit performance.
    7. Provide feedback.
- Assessment and transfer:
    8. Assess their performance.
    9. Enhance retention and transfer to other contexts (Gagné et al. 2004). [See 2.1.3.7]

2.2.8.5 ROPES Model

The ROPES model is an instructional design strategy to increase learning outcomes, presented as a logical sequence to enhance the learning process. The acronym stands for:
- **Review** is the transition from current knowledge to the new content by asking about the learner's familiarity with the new content.

- **Overview** is a general preview of the objectives, benefits, and importance of the content.
- **Presentation** is the description, discussion, and demonstration of the new content.
- **Exercises** are the activities that enable learners to practice and apply the new content.
- **Summary** is the review and reflection of the key points of the content and an invitation to ask questions about it.

2.2.8.6 Method Considerations for Developing Content

To meet organizational requirements, TD professionals should think beyond the learning event and expand the design expectations. Whether through an informal peer feedback group or a formal online class, TD professionals consider what must happen before the event to ensure participants are prepared and what must happen after the learning event to ensure it is contributing to the intended organizational goals.

These techniques help ensure that the content meets organizational requirements:
- Incorporate steps into the design that will occur prior to the learning experience to prepare participants for learning, such as a conversation with the participant's supervisor.
- Clarify with management what the participants are expected to do differently or better after the training, and how this aligns with organizational goals.
- Identify what action management will take to support these changes, such as reinforcement and feedback.
- Design both hard copy and online support materials that can be used after the training occurs.
- Ensure participants know how their efforts will affect organizational goals.
- Confirm participants know what is expected of them and how they will be held accountable.
- If facilitators are used, clearly identify their support and follow-up role.
- Verify participants know how to find assistance following the training program.

2.2.9 Skill in Eliciting and Using Knowledge and Information From Subject Matter Experts to Support or Enhance Learning

I. Using SMEs in Instructional Design

The most important part of every training program is its content. TD professionals must either already understand the core content, adeptly elicit appropriate content from SMEs, or thoroughly research topics from many different sources. When a project requires unique content, TD professionals should identify and gather information from SMEs.

2.2.9.1 Selection Process of SMEs

To be effective when working with SMEs, TD professionals need to understand the content as quickly as possible. One way to accomplish this goal is for the designer to interview the SME, seek clarification to questions, and then prepare the instructional materials. SMEs may not be aware of adult learning theories or instructional design techniques, so the TD professional needs to take responsibility for ensuring the integrity of the materials. If SMEs are effective communicators, they may mistake communication skills for instructional design skills.

Clarity is one of the most important keys to working with SMEs. Most experts like to have their knowledge or experience recognized and used. Working with TD professionals should be a positive experience for SMEs; once they realize the TD professional will provide the instructional framework, they can focus on the content.

Choosing the right SMEs is critical. TD professionals can guide SME selection using these tips:
- Only use SMEs with recent (one year or less) experience in the content area.
- Interview SMEs to screen for possible personality conflicts.
- Determine whether the SMEs have enough time to devote to the design process.
- Before starting, determine how SMEs will be incentivized, acknowledged, or compensated for their work.
- Determine whether the SME has instructional design experience (Hodell 2016).

Spending time finding the best SMEs early in the process may eliminate an irreversible error later in the project. Astute TD professionals will find ways to create partnerships with their SMEs.

2.2.9.2 Working With SMEs

TD professionals may find themselves collaborating with SMEs to design learning. SMEs are deeply knowledgeable about or experienced with the content. To be effective, SMEs must also understand the training program's objectives and how to achieve them. TD professionals fall into three kinds of roles in curriculum development with SMEs:
- The designer is also the SME and the only person involved.
- The designer has some content knowledge but works with a SME.
- The designer has little if any content knowledge and relies on the SME for assistance.

When working with SMEs, TD professionals should use questioning, analysis, data collection, and interviews to uncover content and determine what needs to be included in the learning experience. The relationship between a SME (who is the content expert) and a TD professional (who is the learning expert) is valuable, and clarifying the different roles and how to best work together at the start of the project is important. The SME's role is to:
- Provide expert testimony that can be translated into content.
- Check the accuracy of all content developed for the application.
- Work with the designer to ensure that the design and content are compatible.

2.2.9.3 Motivating SMEs

TD professionals should recognize that the most important factor about SMEs is motivation. There may be a problem if an assignment or reporting relationship assigned to a SME is undesirable; for example, if the assignment is not in their job description or development plan and they are concerned that they won't be rewarded for their efforts. For others, participation in the project may be viewed as a trivial, transitory, and unrewarded distraction from their real work. There are several ways to avoid this situation:
- Compensate the SME fairly.
- Give the SME's work increased exposure.
- Link the project to the SME's professional advancement.
- Establish a formal relationship, such as an official title.

If the SME is an internal resource, participation could be added to their job description, with benefits outlined up front and offered at the project's conclusion. If the SME is an external resource, the work could become a significant resume item. Consider making the SME a formal partner in the project, perhaps offering an important reporting relationship on the team.

2.2.10 Knowledge of Types and Applications of Instructional Methods and Techniques

> **I. Planning for Instructional Delivery**
> To ensure learning occurs, TD professionals should have knowledge of the dozens of optional instructional methods available as well as what factors will affect their choice.

2.2.10.1 Instructional Methods

The key purpose of any formal talent development program is to promote learning. Instruction promotes learning through a set of activities (or exercises) called instructional methods, which are developed to initiate, activate, and support learning. TD professionals use instructional methods to:

- Motivate learners.
- Help learners prepare for learning.
- Aid learners as they discover their own knowledge.
- Enable learners to apply and practice what they've learned.
- Assist learners in retaining and transferring what they have learned.
- Integrate learners' preferences with other skills and knowledge.

2.2.10.2 Factors That Influence Instructional Methods

Instructional methods are selected based on the needs assessment, the learning objectives, and the modality. TD professionals consider multiple factors when choosing instructional methods:

- **Instructional objectives.** Instructional methods or activities must match the objectives; determine if they involve cognitive learning (knowledge), psychomotor learning (skill), or affective learning (attitude).
- **Cost or budget.** TD professionals should understand costs when determining media and methods.
- **Lesson content.** Techniques and media must be consistent with the lesson content.
- **Learners' knowledge and expectations.** Learners will come from different age groups and backgrounds and have varying levels of experience and knowledge. TD professionals should understand the learner's level of comfort with different activities.
- **Time.** Expected duration of methods must fit realistically within time constraints.
- **Facilities, equipment, and material.** Constraints, such as fixed-row seating, will affect the choice of activities and should be considered in the design. Remote delivery also poses additional limits on instructional methods.

2.2.10.3 Experiential Learning Process

TD professionals must consciously plan ahead if they want to use David Kolb's experiential learning design in a course. Although it may seem like a simple process, experiential learning activities (ELAs) will fail without careful design because TD professionals must create a realistic scenario that duplicates analogously what will be learned and allow enough time for the learning to occur. Learners use inductive reasoning as they participate in ELAs through a four-stage process:

- **Experiencing** allows participants to complete a defined task that results in acquiring the intended knowledge, skill, or attitude.
- **Reflecting and processing** give learners an opportunity to reflect on and discuss what happened, why it happened, what they learned, and how they feel about it.
- **Generalizing** provides learners an opportunity to interpret the dynamics and connect them to the workplace; they may also identify how what they learned about the content and themselves relates to real life.
- **Applying** gives participants time to determine how they will transfer the knowledge to the workplace and their lives.

2.2.11 Skill in Selecting and Aligning Delivery Options and Media for Training or Learning Events to the Desired Learning or Behavioral Outcomes

> **I. Aligning Delivery Options to Objectives**
>
> Selecting delivery options requires TD professionals to have several key skills, starting with a clear understanding of how the delivery options link to the objectives.

2.2.11.1 Selecting Delivery Options Linked to Bloom's Taxonomy

TD professionals use different activities to ensure each objective is met. These objectives were determined in the analysis and design phases of the ADDIE Model. Different methods based on Bloom's Taxonomy are best for teaching knowledge or skills or to influence attitudes. For example, in a public speaking class, the learners need knowledge and skills, so the TD professionals might show a video to discuss techniques to gain knowledge and then provide role-play opportunities with feedback to gain skills.

Learners must be actively involved in the learning process to be able to retain knowledge. Depending on what a TD professional is trying to accomplish, one instructional method may be more appropriate than others. Many methods are available including discussions, role plays, case studies and critical incidents, action learning, demonstrations, skill centers, fishbowls, and experiential learning activities. [See 2.3.5.10]

Table 2.2.11.1-1 shows which learning methods are the best match for acquiring knowledge, enhancing skills, or influencing attitudes.

Table 2.2.11.1-1. Best Learning Methods: Knowledge, Skills, Attitudes

Learning Method	Knowledge	Skill	Attitude
Behavior modeling	K		
Brainstorming	K		
Case study or scenario	K	S	A
Debate	K		A
Demonstration	K		
Demonstration with practice	K	S	
Game, exercise, or structured experience	K	S	A
Group discussion		S	A
Guided note taking	K		
Hands-on practice		S	
Independent study	K		
Information search	K		
Interview	K	S	
Jigsaw (team teaching)	K	S	A
Lecturette	K		
Panel discussion	K		A
Polling			A
Reflection and self-assessment	K		A
Role play and skill practice		S	A

2.2.11.2 Selecting and Configuring Technology

Technology should be aligned to the objectives and be considered when selecting delivery options because it allows TD professionals to try new things in face-to-face and virtual classrooms. Knowing what technology is possible for their organizations and matching the appropriate choices to the objectives are important. However, to make an effective decision, TD professionals first need to determine the technology's capabilities:

- **Presentation** software enables them to embed videos, verbal files, customized animations, or high-resolution pictures to enhance a presentation beyond PowerPoint and Prezi.
- **Interactive presentation** software allows for more audience participation online or with live audiences through voting, quizzes, trivia, games, and creating word clouds.
- **Collaboration** tools allow TD professionals and participants to exchange documents online, provide feedback, and even project items on more than one screen.
- **Simulation** tools allow TD professionals to present experiential learning scenarios so learners can practice in a computer-generated setting.
- **Immersive** technologies such as augmented reality (AR), virtual reality (VR), or a combination allow learners to be immersed so that they are, or feel like they are, experiencing the actual learning environment.
- **Artificial intelligence** (AI) accommodates remote and on-the-go employees with a wide range of applications, including personalized and adaptive learning. TD professionals may use AI for content creation, voice-activated interfaces, and digital assistants. [See 2.4.10]

2.2 Instructional Design

- **Course management** tools allow TD professionals to support online components for pre-work, downloadable tools, assignments, and discussion boards. [See 2.3.1.3]
- **Video production** software adds additional audio and stylish fonts, highlights graphics, and incorporates other eye-catching tricks to customize any story.
- **Content-capture** tools allow TD professionals to record delivery and development discussions from their computers, which can then be uploaded for participants' future use. [See 2.4]

Criteria for selecting technology should include functionality, cost, ease of use, interaction, features, organizational compatibility, networking, and security. TD professionals should understand available learning technologies and their features and functionalities. They should also cultivate relationships with their company's IT professionals to share ideas about the possibilities in talent development. This will help TD professionals make the best decisions when designing learning content. [See 2.3.6.2]

2.2.11.3 Matching Media to the Learning Outcomes

Classroom training can occur with all participants in the same room or in rooms distributed around the world. Current technologies enable learning to take many forms outside the face-to-face classroom. To design effective programs, TD professionals must understand what is possible and when a specific medium is most effective. They will determine if the learning objective is a knowledge, skill, or attitude; how the objective will be assessed; and what constraints exist that prevent using a specific media. [See 2.4.4.3]

2.2.12 Skill in Designing and Developing Learning Assets

I. Creating Materials

Whether the course is online or in person, asynchronous or synchronous, the results will be enhanced with well-designed learning assets.

2.2.12.1 Facilitator Guides

A well-written facilitator guide—often called a producer's guide in virtual training—enables easier preparation and delivery for instructor-led courses. It helps ensure program consistency if more than one facilitator is used thanks to its descriptive titles and visuals that support the facilitation. Pages should be numbered to match the participant's guide if possible and should indicate where visuals, slides, and other facilitator assets are used; the timing; key learning points; questions to ask; transitions; and review checks.

The appendices should include any necessary facilitation tools along with additional participant materials (such as job aids, role-play scripts, and case studies). TD professionals can support the facilitator by including:
- A resource checklist and a background reading list
- Any required information or material, such as handouts, flipcharts, and media
- Integrators that link content to the participants' prior learning
- Administrative aids, such as participant rosters, maps, or name tags, if necessary
- An equipment and supply list for paper, media players, projectors, computers, charts, pointers, flipcharts, or markers

2.2.12.2 Participant Guides and Materials

Participant guides should have descriptive titles and visuals and could also include downloadable or fillable worksheets, especially for a virtual course. In addition to the participant guide, learner materials may include instruction cards or handouts for activities, assessments, or case studies. They may also include tangible items (a product, for example) so participants can judge quality or a physical tool they can use for practice. If instructions are included, ensure they are clear, complete, and correct and use step-by-step numbering with plenty of white space.

Participant-supporting materials include things such as the job aids, infographics, checklists, and templates they can use during the course as well as on the job. Standard infographic designs include top 10 list, history, defining details, how-to, comparing multiple ideas, and process types.

2.2.12.3 Media and Materials

During the development phase, media and materials are located, selected, or created. Off-the-shelf materials can be used or adapted. For example, if a video clip contains an excellent illustration of a procedure, but the sound doesn't fit the organizational climate, it may simply be shown without sound. Wall charts may be required, and in some cases, a model or representation may be needed.

2.2.12.4 Slide Development

Presentation slides are heavily leveraged across the major modalities—face-to-face, virtual classrooms, and e-learning programs. TD professionals should remember that when done effectively, visuals help minimize cognitive load and create room for learning. These basic guidelines will help ensure slides are effective and look professional:

- Use descriptive headings.
- Present one idea at a time.
- Use no more than two fonts and ensure they are both sized to read easily.
- Aim for more white space than content.
- Add graphics, pictures, charts, or other visuals that clarify the message.
- Use special effects only if they clarify and support the objective.

2.2.12.5 Designing Assessments to Test Learning

Common test formats include multiple choice, true/false, matching, completion, short answer or essay, and performance or hands on. If test results will have personnel consequences, use a formal validation process to document and store the test validity process. Typically, any test results reported outside the training session, such as to a supervisor or in a personnel folder, will require formal validation. TD professionals should check with human resources or legal staff regarding test validation procedures in their organizations. Other guidelines include:

- Provide clear instructions and resources.
- Only test what is required on the job.
- Keep information in questions brief and essential.
- Use key words, such as who, what, when, and where.
- Group questions by topic areas (Miner 2007). [See 2.8.4.2]

2.2.12.6 Evaluation Materials

Evaluation must be tied to objectives and it can be either formative or summative. *Formative evaluation* occurs continually throughout the analysis, design, development, and implementation phases. *Summative evaluation* occurs only after course completion. A plan for objective measures of success and written materials devised during the development phase should support both formative and summative evaluations.

A formative evaluation plan describes the means for improving a course and assessing learners' in-training progress and attitudes toward training. A summative evaluation plan describes measures such as post-training employee performance, turnover, and customer comments. An overall evaluation plan should document how and when information will be distributed and collected, as well as from and by whom.

Evaluation materials may be produced on paper or digitally. They should be reviewed and pilot tested prior to use to determine whether:

- They are grammatically correct.
- The rating scales measure what they are intended to measure.
- They are clearly written for the appropriate literacy level.
- The content is correct.
- The language is culturally appropriate for the employee. [See 1.4]
- They can be completed in a limited amount of time.
- There is a need to demonstrate skills in addition to knowledge.

2.2.12.7 Adaptive Learning

Adaptive learning is an approach that tailors the learning experience to the specific needs of the individual—and uses technology in a way that is scalable across a larger number of learners. The technology applies artificial intelligence to learning to optimize every moment and unlock individual and organizational performance. With adaptive learning, content adapts in real time to each learner's activity, so the right content is presented at the right time for each individual. Adaptive learning platforms help TD professionals respond to the fast-paced and disruptive work environment. By personalizing instruction content, TD professionals can create a learning tool that simulates a one-on-one instructor for every learner. Technologies related to adaptive learning include:

- **Artificial intelligence.** Computer systems perform tasks that normally require human intelligence. (Adaptive learning is AI applied to learning.)
- **Predictive analytics.** Existing data is used to determine patterns and predict outcomes. (Adaptive learning may incorporate this technology.)
- **Machine learning.** This is an application of AI that allows machines to learn from experience without human involvement. (Adaptive learning may incorporate this technology.)

TD professionals should consider using adaptive learning with learners who have a wide variety of experience. The immediate outcomes for employees include greater efficiency, effectiveness, and engagement. Organizations also experience improved performance. Adaptive learning methodologies can be integrated into an organization's learning content; for example, for salespeople in the field, for compliance courses that are required and could be completed quickly by those who know the content, or for helping learners achieve mastery in all areas.

Additional Design Approaches

2.2.13 Knowledge of How Design Thinking and Rapid Prototyping Can Be Applied to the Development of Learning and Talent Development Solutions

> **I. Using Design Thinking for Instructional Design**
>
> Prototyping is an integral part of design thinking, allowing TD professionals to test and improve ideas quickly. TD professionals can implement these methods and a bias toward action to support the rapidly changing world in which they operate.

2.2.13.1 Design Thinking Basics

Design thinking is a human-centered approach to innovation and problem solving that integrates the needs of people with the needs of the organization. It fosters creativity and innovation, focusing on finding the right solution rather than solving a problem.

2.2.13.2 Emphasis at Each Design Phase

Design thinking encourages the design team to challenge assumptions and explore new ideas. The design thinking methodology is based on five phases:

- **Empathizing** requires a clear and empathic understanding of the problem by consulting experts, engaging with people to understand their experiences, and immersing oneself in the environment to gain a deep personal understanding of the issues. Learning who is affected by the problem and what's at stake for them is important.
- **Defining** the problem requires compiling and synthesizing what was learned in the first phase. A part of the definition is to continue asking more questions and gather more data to stimulate ideas and solutions.
- **Ideating** begins once there is a clear understanding of the users and their needs, along with a solid background created by compiling the data. Like brainstorming, the goal is to formulate as many ideas or solutions as possible at the beginning of this phase. By the end of the ideation phase, investigate and test a couple ideas to find a good option.
- **Prototyping** requires the team to produce scaled-down versions of the solution. This is an experimental phase. Prototypes may be shared and tested within the team or outside the design team. The solutions or ideas are implemented within the prototypes, and each is investigated and accepted, improved, or rejected. This leads to understanding the constraints inherent to the problem.
- **Testing** is the final phase. Testing rigorously evaluates the final product. However, given the iterative aspect of the process, the results generated are often used to redefine the problem and inform the users (Glynn and Tolsma 2017).

Although design thinking seems like a linear process, in practice, it is more flexible and iterative. Ambiguity is inevitable, as the team experiments and pushes the limits.

2.2.13.3 Adapting Design Thinking
Implementing design thinking as an approach for instructional design would likely have the following results:
- Empathy, or the concern about people, can create a strong base for creating solutions.
- A large amount of data is gathered—probably more than in a typical analysis step in ADDIE—providing new ways of thinking about the data using frameworks and other tools to compile and display it.
- TD professionals should anticipate more back-and-forth exploration during the design and development phases.
- Presenting prototypes (which are less finished than usual) to stakeholders can be uncomfortable because most people are accustomed to striving for perfection.
- Stakeholders are likely to make suggestions for improving the prototypes. As a benchmark, test pilots are typically 90 percent complete, whereas a prototype is 65 to 75 percent complete (Glynn and Tolsma 2017).

2.2.13.4 Rapid Prototyping
Rapid prototyping is an iterative design-develop-evaluate process that enables stakeholders to view and provide feedback on the learning experience design throughout the design and development process, rather than waiting to see a finished product and incurring significant changes and cost. This iterative process begins with gathering information and concludes with the rollout of the finished product. The design and development processes are also iterative and provide successive products as the client and TD professionals search for and refine the best solutions. Typically, the design and development cycles both iterate three or four times. SAM (Successive Approximation Model) is one example of a rapid design model that borrows from software development models, such as Agile, which use iteration and short work cycles to produce quick results. [See 2.2.1.7]

2.2.13.4.1 Applying Rapid Prototyping to the Design Process
TD professionals should recognize prototyping as an important step in design because it saves resources and produces a better product. Storyboarding is an effective first step for gathering design ideas in a graphic format and determining if the design is appropriate. [See 2.2.6.2]

Prototypes are the physical proof or draft of the design concept and are often classified into three categories:
- **Low-fidelity prototypes** are paper prototypes or rough physical representations of the initial design.
- **Medium-fidelity prototypes** are wireframe prototypes, which are more polished and closer to the finished state.
- **High-fidelity prototypes** may be almost fully functioning working copies of the final design.

2.2.13.4.2 Rapid Prototyping for Gathering Feedback
Physical prototyping is a helpful tool to understand end users' feedback. By watching how individuals work within the interface and with specific elements, TD professionals can determine the effectiveness of the design. They should use a consistent method to explain the interface to users and what they hope to accomplish with the application. This will ensure that each user is starting with the same knowledge about the prototype. Inconsistency will skew the results of the testing and render the end-user feedback unusable. In addition, the

physical reactions of the end users will reveal what they think about the application and how easy it is (or not) for them to navigate from screen to screen.

2.2.14 Knowledge of How Formal and Informal Learning Experiences Influence and Support Individual and Group Development

> **I. Awareness of How Learning Influences Development**
>
> TD professionals know that the best organizations build a productive learning culture. They know how learning influences organizational success and how to support organizational learning.

2.2.14.1 Learning Begins at the Individual Level

Whether learning occurs formally or informally, it begins when individuals learn skills or ideas and implement or transfer the new knowledge to their work, perhaps increasing their productivity. They may or may not share their knowledge with others. However, when they leave the organization without sharing, the team and organization loses that knowledge. [See 2.5]

Most employees believe they have the technical and functional expertise required to do their jobs, but only a fifth rate their ability to learn as effective (CEB Research 2014). TD professionals should lead the way, ensuring that all employees are comfortable with behaviors that support their ability to learn, including:
- Asking for feedback
- Planning how to develop for the future
- Reinforcing a growth mindset [See 1.7.1.8]

2.2.14.2 Group Learning

Group learning occurs when individuals within a team acquire and share their experience and knowledge with other team members. If the group uses this information to modify future actions, group learning has occurred, which promotes teamwork. Senge (2006) defines the three dimensions of team learning as the ability to:
- Think insightfully about complex issues.
- Take innovative, coordinated action.
- Create a network that allows other teams to act.

2.2.14.3 Organizational Learning

TD professionals should help their organizations determine how to improve employees' learning capability. To begin, employees need to believe that their organizations want to create a supportive learning environment, but they also need to share that responsibility. TD professionals can lead this effort of shared responsibility by:
- Ensuring that leaders champion, recognize, and reward learning
- Instilling the value of lifelong learning in every employee
- Expecting managers to support employee development
- Inspiring employees to own their development

REFERENCES

Allen, M. 2016. *Michael Allen's Guide to eLearning*, 2nd ed. Hoboken, NJ: Wiley.

Anderson, L.W., and D.R. Krathwohl, eds. 2000. *A Taxonomy for Learning, Teaching, and Assessing: A Revision of Bloom's Taxonomy of Educational Objectives.* New York: Longman.

ATD (Association for Talent Development). 2011. *Developing Results: Aligning Learning's Goals and Outcomes With Business Performance Measures.* Alexandria VA: ATD Press.

ATD (Association for Talent Development). 2016. *Building a Culture of Learning: The Foundation of a Successful Organization.* Alexandria, VA: ATD Press.

Biech, E. 2009. *10 Steps to Successful Training.* Alexandria, VA: ASTD Press.

Biech, E., ed. 2014. *ASTD Handbook: The Definitive Reference for Training and Development.* Alexandria, VA: ASTD Press.

Biech, E. 2017. *The Art and Science of Training.* Alexandria, VA: ATD Press.

Branson, R.K., G.T. Rayner, J.L. Cox, J.P. Furman, F.J. King, and W.H. Hannum. 1975. "Interservice Procedures for Instructional Systems Development." Vol. 1–5. Ft. Monroe, VA: US Army Training and Doctrine Command.

CEB Research. 2014. "Building a Productive Learning Culture." Arlington, VA: CEB Learning and Development.

Clark, R.C. 2019. *Evidence-Based Training Methods: A Guide for Training Professionals*, 3rd ed. Alexandria, VA: ATD Press.

Clark, R.E. 1999. "The Cognitive Sciences and Human Performance Technology." Chapter 5 in *The Handbook of Human Performance Technology: Improving Individual and Organizational Performance Worldwide*, edited by H.D. Stolovitch and E.J. Keeps. San Francisco: Jossey-Bass.

Dick, W., L. Carey, and J. Carey. 2014. *The Systematic Design of Instruction*, 8th ed. Boston: Pearson Education.

Gagné, R.M. 1997. "Mastery Learning and Instructional Design." *Performance Improvement Quarterly* 10(1): 8–10.

Gagné, R.M., W.W. Wagner, K.C. Golas, and J.M. Keller. 2004. *Principles of Instructional Design*, 5th ed. New York: Holt, Rinehart, and Winston.

Gardner, H. 2011. *Frames of Mind: The Theory of Multiple Intelligences*, 3rd ed. New York: Basic Books.

Glynn, K., and D. Tolsma. 2017. "Design Thinking Meets ADDIE." *TD at Work*. Alexandria, VA: ATD Press.

Herrmann, N., and A. Herrmann-Nehdi. 2015. *The Whole Brain Business Book*, 2nd ed. New York: McGraw-Hill.

Hodell, C. 2016. *SMEs From the Ground Up*, 4th ed. Alexandria, VA: ATD Press.

Hofmann, J. 2018. *Blended Learning*. Alexandria, VA: ATD Press.

Kirkpatrick, D.L. 2006. *Evaluating Training Programs: The Four Levels*, 2nd ed. San Francisco: Berrett-Koehler.

Kirkpatrick, J., and W. Kirkpatrick. 2016. *Kirkpatrick's Four Levels of Training Evaluation*. Alexandria, VA: ATD Press.

Knowles, M.S. 1984. *The Adult Learner: A Neglected Species*, 3rd ed. Houston: Gulf Publishing Company.

Knowles, M.S., E.S. Holton III, and R.A. Swanson. 2005. *The Adult Learner: The Definitive Classic in Adult Education and Human Resource Development*, 6th ed. Burlington, MA: Butterworth-Heinemann.

Mager, R.F. 1962. *Preparing Objectives for Programmed Instruction*. Palo Alto, CA: Fearon.

McArdle, G.E. 2015. *Training Design and Delivery*, 3rd ed. Alexandria, VA: ATD Press.

Meier, D. 2000. *The Accelerated Learning Handbook: A Creative Guide to Designing and Delivering Faster, More Effective Training Programs*. New York: McGraw-Hill.

Miner, N. 2007. "The Art of Test Creation." *TD*, July.

Orey, M. 2017. "Designing Section 508 Compliant Learning." *TD at Work*. Alexandria, VA: ATD Press.

Piskurich, G. 2009. *Rapid Training Development*. San Francisco: Pfeiffer.

Rogers, C. 1951. *Client-Centered Therapy: Its Current Practice, Implications, and Theory*. Boston: Houghton-Mifflin.

Seels, B., and R. Glasgow. 1998. *Making Instructional Design Decisions*. Upper Saddle River, NJ: Prentice-Hall.

Senge, P.M. 2006. *The Fifth Discipline: The Art and Practice of the Learning Organization*, rev. ed. New York: Currency/Doubleday.

Silbermen, M., and E. Biech. 2015. *Active Training: A Handbook of Techniques, Designs, Case Examples, and Tips*, 4th ed. Hoboken, NJ: John Wiley and Sons.

Smith, P., and T. Ragan. 2005. *Instructional Design*, 3rd ed. Hoboken, NJ: John Wiley and Sons.

Tobey, D., and B. McGoldrick. 2005. *Needs Assessment Basics*. Alexandria, VA: ASTD Press.

US Air Force. 1970. *Instructional System Development (ISD)*. AFM 50-2. Washington, DC: US Government Printing Office.

US Army. 2011. *Army Learning Policy and Systems*. TRADOC Reg. 350-70. Washington, DC: US Government Printing Office.

US Army Field Artillery School. 1984. *A System Approach to Training*. ST-5K061FD92. Washington, DC: US Government Printing Office.

Watson, R. 1981. "Instructional System Development." Paper presented to the International Congress for Individualized Instruction, October. ED 209 239.

Recommended Reading

Dirksen, J. 2015. *Design for How People Learn*, 2nd ed. Berkeley, CA: New Riders Publishing.

Hodell, C. 2021. *Introduction to Instructional Systems Design: Theory and Practice*. Alexandria, VA: ATD Press.

Huggett, C. 2017. *Virtual Training Tools and Templates: An Action Guide to Live Online Learning*. Alexandria, VA: ATD Press.

Huggett, C. 2022. *The Facilitator's Guide to Immersive, Blended, and Hybrid Learning*. Alexandria, VA: ATD Press.

LaBorie, K., and T. Stone. 2022. *Interact and Engage*, 2nd ed. Alexandria, VA: ATD Press.

2.3 TRAINING DELIVERY & FACILITATION

Training delivery and facilitation are means for talent development professionals to help individuals improve performance at work by learning new skills and knowledge. The practitioner serves as a catalyst for learning by understanding the learner's needs, creating the right environment for learning, building rapport with participants, and using the appropriate delivery options and media to make learning engaging, effective, relevant, and applicable. Facilitating meetings means taking an objective approach to helping stakeholders discover new insights, achieve group outcomes, and work to make positive changes in the organization.

2.3.1 Skill in Coordinating the Logistical Tasks Associated With Planning Meetings or Learning Events

I. Planning and Coordinating Learning Events
Whether planning a meeting or learning experience, TD professionals should hone their organizing skills.

2.3.1.1 Prepare the Training Environment
TD professionals who facilitate learning events and meetings must consider many things to achieve the desired results.

2.3.1.1.1 Logistics for Facilitating Face-to-Face Training Programs
Even if someone else is responsible for preparing the room, the facilitator should arrive with enough time before the training begins to set up materials and tend to any last-minute crises. If no one else is able to take care of things, the facilitator may need to tidy the room, arrange furniture, set up and test equipment, and make final arrangements.

When choosing the room where the training will take place, avoid distractions or obstacles that could affect the participants' ability to learn. In addition, TD professionals should make sure that the room has:
- Adequate wall space for hanging posters or capturing content on flipcharts or whiteboards
- Seating arrangements that are appropriate for learning purposes (Table 2.3.1.1.1-1)
- Wi-Fi access and sufficient nearby restrooms
- Accessible for all, including people with limited mobility [See 1.6.4 and 1.6.7]

2.3 Training Delivery & Facilitation

Table 2.3.1.1.1-1. Seating Arrangements for Training Rooms

Name	Description	Example
Circle	A circle of chairs is often used to foster an intimate relationship among participants and with the facilitator, who occupies one of the chairs in the circle.	
Broken circle	This configuration offers the advantages of the full circle yet affords the facilitator a measure of control. The facilitator stands next to a flipchart.	
Circular table	This configuration takes advantage of a circle's informality but gives participants a place to put papers and books. The table also removes the sense of vulnerability some people feel in a plain circle of chairs. Studies show that people gathered at a round table participate more than people sitting in a plain circle of chairs.	
Square table	Square tables are a step toward a formal meeting arrangement. They are often used when there are sides to be presented. Research indicates that a square table seems to encourage conversation across the table.	
Rectangular table	At a rectangular table, no one can see the faces of all the people. Participants expect those at the ends of the table to control interactions. Rectangular tables can be effective for some kinds of training sessions, but they also highlight tensions felt by two sides facing each other.	
U-shaped table	This configuration is popular for seminars. A U-shaped table gives participants the sense that they are equal. The opening in the U is a position of power for a facilitator, note taker, or recorder.	
Classroom style	This configuration gives facilitators—especially if they stand on raised platforms—control, and people can't easily talk to anyone except those seated beside them. This arrangement accommodates many people in a small room and is effective for one-way communication.	

Table 2.3.1.1.1-1. Seating Arrangements for Training Rooms (cont.)

Name	Description	Example
Theater style	Theater or auditorium seating is used to maximize the number of people in one room. It's not a good arrangement for stimulating group discussion or participation.	ooooo ooooo ooooo ooooo ooooo ooooo

If a viewing screen is required, ensure the person sitting in the seat farthest from the screen still has good visibility. If a large group is expected, the facilitator may need a microphone, and they should also plan for a voice check prior to starting. Consider safety, and tape cords to the floor to avoid tripping hazards.

To maintain the highest quality participant experience, TD professionals should prepare any handouts and visual aids with enough time to have them thoroughly proofread. TD professionals must also decide how to share the materials; for example, will they be posted in a digital format?

2.3.1.2 Preparing for a Virtual Session

TD professionals electronically complete similar preparation steps for a virtual instructor-led training course or virtual meeting as they do for in-person events. However, materials may either be distributed to participants or placed in a central repository for them to download.

Last-minute preparation for a virtual event includes checking all technology connections, testing audio, loading polling questions, opening whiteboards, and verifying participant privileges. TD professionals may have the opportunity to work with a producer, who is a technical expert, for assistance during a live online session. Producers may specialize in technology-only assistance or co-facilitate sessions (Huggett 2013).

2.3.1.3 Preparing the Digital Environment

TD professionals should plan for any digital requirements to support the online components of a course. Many training courses include a learning portal, which is an intranet site that creates a gateway to the organization's resources. The portal may house pre-work assignments, ongoing course assignments, a discussion board, and downloadable tools. It is also a location where participants can submit their projects. TD professionals must remember to schedule time to review and update the learning portal prior to the learning event, when necessary. They'll need to:
- Determine the scope of content.
- Inform the participants of the location, when it will be available, and how to access it.
- Determine how to label and order the materials.
- Decide if the portal will include a social media aspect.
- Identify how it will be maintained and by whom.
- Decide how it will be branded.

If the portal has been used for other courses, TD professionals may need to confirm whether tools and resources are current or need to be updated or if new ones need to be created and uploaded to the site. Whether the portal is new or has been used for past courses, the TD professional should test it to ensure each element is working properly.

2.3.1.4 Communicating and Marketing

Sometimes TD professionals are asked to write an enticing course description or develop a series of announcements to generate interest in the course among potential participants. Whether the course is for internal employees or external clients, some effort should be put into marketing. Like with all product development efforts, marketing for training programs creates awareness in the target population and helps foster a culture of learning. Course names or descriptions might appear in promotional materials including a course catalog, a centralized registration system such as a learning management system (LMS), electronic ads on corporate websites or social networks, email announcements, flyers, or logo items such as pens, keychains, and buttons.

2.3.1.5 Planning for Emergencies

Well-prepared TD professionals should think through everything that could go wrong and know how to address emergencies. They should have an alternative plan—or a general idea—of what to do if the power goes out, an activity doesn't work, or learners have questions they can't answer.

2.3.1.6 Coordinating Administrative Tasks

Part of delivery involves coordinating a schedule and facility, determining LMS needs, and deciding how to administrate the program. The plan—whether for a single event or a large rollout—should identify who will do what, on what date, and how. It might also include how learners will register for training, how the TD professional will market and communicate with learners prior to class, how participant attendance will be tracked, when and how rooms will be reserved, and who will create course materials.

> **II. Facilitator Preparation**
>
> TD professionals should plan to invest ample time preparing to deliver any training event. They should review any assessment documents, understand how the content relates to organizational goals, learn something about the participants, master the content, and practice the delivery mechanics.

2.3.1.7 Training Needs Assessment Alignment

The individual responsible for delivering a training event should be aware of the needs assessment results, why the training event was created, and how it is related to organizational goals. They should understand how the needs assessment influenced the flow of the program, as well as the purpose behind it. [See 2.2.2]

2.3.1.8 Audience Analysis

TD professionals should learn as much as possible about the individuals attending the session so they can customize it. They should obtain a roster as soon as it is available to identify factors that will help them plan the session's level, pace, and focus. They should look for information such as participants' jobs in the organization, levels of responsibility and authority, understanding of the subject matter, location, reason for attending (for example, voluntary or mandatory, lack of performance, or new skills or role), and opinions about the training session.

2.3.1.9 Practicing Content to Gain Expertise

TD professionals should master the content of their training session or meeting by investing time in practicing. They may do this in several ways:

- Practice the activities with small groups to determine timing or whether the results garner intended responses.
- Practice the mechanics of the presentation, such as revealing something or determining the best time to provide additional handouts.
- Practice the theatrics aloud if telling a story or joke.
- Practice in the room where the session will occur, if possible.
- Practice speaking spontaneously.
- Record themselves and review the recording to determine what needs to be polished.
- Identify questions to ask at specific points.
- Anticipate questions participants may ask.
- Complete a dress rehearsal to determine how their planned outfit will be affected by movement and gestures.

2.3.1.10 Preparing for Delivery

Delivery is an opportunity for TD professionals to facilitate learning and improve workplace performance. Through careful preparation, facilitators can reduce and control nervousness; preparation is the most essential step in delivery. Here are some things TD professionals can do to prepare:

- **Learn the objectives.** Understand the learning objectives, which specify the performance (knowledge or skill) that is desired after training has been completed.
- **Review the needs assessment.** The needs assessment offers the rationale for the training.
- **Master the material.** TD professionals should master the training session's content. If they helped design and develop the course, they likely already understand the decisions that resulted in the final design.
- **Learn about the participants.** Before the session, the TD professional should learn as much as possible about the people who will be attending. In addition, they should gather background information about the business or performance need that motivated the session.
- **Create notes.** Effective notes aid the delivery preparation process and may also help the facilitator overcome nervousness. TD professionals should determine what note process works best for them. Some people like to facilitate from notes in a facilitator's guide while others write on a copy of the slides or develop their own notes.

> ### III. Prepare Participants and Their Managers
> TD professionals should realize that training delivery and facilitation will be more successful if they prepare participants and their managers. Participants will be more open to learning and change if they know how it will benefit them. Managers can support the effort by preparing their employees and reinforcing what they learn.

2.3.1.11 Preparing Participants for Learning

To prepare participants for the learning event, TD professionals may send out a welcome email with an agenda and a message relating the training content to their jobs, which will let them know what's in it for them. TD professionals may also include a roster of who will attend the session as well as specific logistics information. Communicate in advance with the participants, and make them feel welcome and comfortable.

2.3.1.12 Preparing Participants for Online Learning

Almost all the advice for in-person training also applies to online training. In addition, TD professionals need to consider how the technology-enabled learning experience will affect the learners. They may need to help participants set up their computers, test their access, and ensure appropriate software is downloaded. The critical element is ensuring that they do not wait until the last minute to engage. The participant must complete all setup or assignments in advance so they can be actively involved in online learning.

2.3.1.13 Strategies for Communicating With Managers to Coach Employees

If the participants have supervisors or managers, TD professionals should create a plan to communicate with the managers. Some managers may need guidance about their role to ensure transfer of learning:

- **Before a learning event,** TD professionals should meet with managers to discuss their expectations and how they can support the transfer of learning.
- **During a learning event,** TD professionals may invite managers to visit at a time that best supports the learners and their goals.
- **After a learning event,** TD professionals should encourage managers to reinforce what their employees have learned and find ways for them to practice their new skills. [See 2.7.3]

> ## IV. Planning and Coordinating Meetings
> In addition to facilitating learning programs, TD professionals should also be prepared to facilitate meetings. This requires planning and preparation.

2.3.1.14 Planning the Meeting Logistics

The first step in planning a meeting is to determine its purpose—why does the meeting need to be held? TD professionals should also consider whether an alternative option exists to reach the meeting's goal, such as a conference call, email, individual calls, a survey, or by adding time to another meeting. Once a meeting is determined to be necessary, other questions need to be answered:

- **Who?** Individuals in a meeting should all have a purpose for attending. Among other reasons, they may need the information, own the problem, have authority to make assignments or decisions, be directly affected by the topic, have input to the situation, or have a unique perspective.
- **What?** What will be addressed in the meeting and in what order? List everything that needs to be covered, assign priorities, and put the most important topics first—unless there is a logical sequence. Also, determine the type of meeting. Is it to provide information, identify an issue, solve a problem, create a plan, or train and educate?
- **When?** Meeting participants should have time to complete prework. Also, consider the timing for anyone joining the meeting virtually; they may be in another time zone or simply work during another shift. A meeting should be long enough to complete all meeting objectives but no longer.
- **Where?** Location should be determined by the proximity and ease of access for everyone and the importance of a neutral location. If people attend virtually, ensure the room has technology and equipment to accommodate them.

TD professionals should prepare thoroughly to achieve the desired meeting results. They should select a room that is free of distractions, conducive to discussion, located in a facility with the necessary communication and technology access for remote attendees, and accessible for all, including those with limited mobility. Seating arrangements should complement the meeting purpose. [See 1.6.4 and 1.6.7]

Everyone should know the location of the meeting well in advance, and if possible, a meeting agenda should be sent to participants 24 hours prior so they can prepare. The meeting agenda identifies the objectives, time allotted for each, and who's responsible. If there is a separate meeting leader, the facilitator may find it useful to be positioned either next to the leader so they can see the same thing or across from the leader so they can see cues the leader sends.

2.3.1.15 Setting Agendas

TD professionals should increase the value of a meeting by preparing an agenda that:
- Focuses the meeting and keeps it on track
- Helps participants prepare for the meeting
- Ensures everyone knows the expected outcomes
- Improves chances of achieving results in the meeting
- Establishes a timeframe for the meeting
- Demonstrates respect for all participants

While agendas vary in style and the amount of detail they include, the best ones provide:
- The date, time, and location of the meeting
- A list of everyone who will participate
- Meeting objectives
- A statement that each topic will be covered in priority order—most important first
- The amount of time allotted for each topic
- Who is responsible for each topic
- How each participant should prepare for the meeting

If a meeting is called on very short notice due to an emergency, the facilitator can build an impromptu agenda at the start of the meeting.

2.3.2 Skill in Facilitating Meetings or Learning Events in Face-to-Face and Virtual Environments

I. Facilitating Groups
TD professionals should hone their facilitation skills to add value to each facilitation event.

2.3.2.1 Role Differences for Learning Events Versus Meetings

Although they use many of the same tools and skills, there are differences between facilitating a learning event and facilitating a meeting:

- **Learning event facilitators** facilitate and deliver information and knowledge focused on what participants learn. They may be subject matter experts, have a point of view, and ensure learning occurs.
- **Meeting facilitators** enable discussion and focus on group outcomes by supporting processes and teams. They remain neutral and unbiased, helping the group build consensus, make decisions, and create next steps.

2.3.2.2 Differences Between Face-to-Face and Virtual Meetings

TD professionals follow the same best practices for facilitating face-to-face and virtual meetings. Virtual meetings need to avoid technical and time-zone scheduling issues and may enlist a producer to assist remote participants.

2.3.2.3 Methods and Tools to Support Facilitation

There are many methods and tools for creating effective meetings, depending on the purpose, including:
- **Giving information**—visuals, handouts, questions and answer periods, or guest SMEs
- **Discussing issues**—brainstorming, using nominal group technique, or playing devil's advocate
- **Solving problems and making decisions**—fact finding, solution/comparison grid, or an advantages/disadvantages table
- **Planning and setting a course of action**—Gantt charts, Pert charts, action planning, or force field analysis

As effective facilitators, TD professionals should create an open environment by:
- Encouraging people to participate
- Boosting participants' self-confidence
- Acknowledging participants' contributions
- Being honest about what they know—and don't know
- Recognizing when to end a discussion and move on

Several techniques are useful for helping move teams and groups through the team stages (forming to performing). [See 1.3.3.5.1] These include:
- **Listening** to understand issues
- **Following agendas** to keep everyone informed about next steps
- **Opening discussions** to identify objectives and purpose
- **Using a shared framework of understanding** to name expectations and outcomes
- **Summarizing** to validate speakers and clarify the message
- **Reframing** emotional statements into issues to help the group focus
- **Brainstorming** to help everyone expand the possibilities
- **Building consensus** through discussion, so everyone supports the decision verbally and actively
- **Reaching closure** by recapping agreements, outcomes, and action items

2.3.2.4 Facilitating Dialogue With Individuals and Groups

Dialogue is the flow of information among people with the intent of learning from everyone and making the best decision based on the total knowledge. To facilitate dialogue, a facilitator must remain neutral, have strong listening and reframing skills, and formulate good questions. [See 1.1.7 and 3.3.8]

2.3.2.5 Communication Considerations

Communication may be the most valuable skill a facilitator possesses. When facilitating groups:

- Establish clear communication methods and styles among group members and between the facilitator and the group to keep misunderstandings to a minimum.
- Establish agreement and maintain focus on the team's objectives, goals, and mission and their project or task. Members must believe that their relationship and role are clearly defined.
- Use communication to assist team members with relationship building by providing opportunities for group introductions, downtime, and celebrations.
- Become familiar with any cultural differences, and address these differences with individuals and the team to ensure that alternative opinions will be welcomed. [See 1.4]

II. Managing Effective Meetings

TD professionals should be skilled in and recognize the value of leading and managing effective meetings.

2.3.2.6 Managing Effective Meetings

Managing effective meetings requires the involvement of TD professionals before, during, and after the event.

Before the Meeting

Before a meeting is scheduled, the facilitator must decide if it is necessary: Is this the best way to meet the objectives, and will the results provide enough value to justify the time spent? If yes, the facilitator will then set objectives, determine who needs to attend, decide when and where the meeting will be held (including virtual connections), prepare an agenda, and communicate the purpose. [See 2.3.1.15]

During the Meeting

During the meeting, the facilitator starts on time, facilitates the group to generate ideas and make decisions, identifies and eliminates time wasters, and balances discussion. To close the meeting, the facilitator gains participants' commitment to act by creating an action plan that identifies who will do what by when. A closing should also include an evaluation—even if it's a short verbal pros and cons list to solicit ideas for how to improve future meetings. Facilitators should always end on time (or early), summarize the meeting verbally, thank participants, and close with a reminder of each person's responsibilities.

To maintain group dynamics, TD professionals can create a meeting code of conduct, which should include rules on how they will communicate, manage conflict, identify positions and roles, and outline consequences of commitment lapses; it should cover anything that team members may consider a good practice. Some codes of conduct include norms, such as a rule that all team members must take part in group discussions, members must not interrupt when another member is speaking, and all members will be punctual for meetings. TD professionals should be aware of groupthink, a term defined by Irving Janis to describe situations when groups make irrational decisions because individuals conform their stated opinions to the perceived consensus of the group. [See 1.2.8.3]

After the Meeting
After the meeting, the facilitator prepares and distributes a follow-up report that includes the items covered, decisions made, and actions to be taken with due dates and responsible individuals. A follow-up report reminds participants of their commitments, may include information that was not available during the meeting, and serves as a monitoring tool to ensure task completion. A facilitator should also evaluate the effectiveness of the meeting and make plans for continuous improvement.

2.3.2.7 Awareness of Meeting Task and Maintenance Roles
TD professionals should be familiar with the value that task and maintenance roles play in any group setting. The presence or absence of these behaviors can help facilitators understand whether their meetings are effective and why. Task and maintenance roles may arise naturally, especially in groups with recurring meetings. At other times, TD professionals may delegate these roles to individuals to help support meetings. Although the names of the roles have changed over the years, Kenneth Benne and Paul Sheats (1948) were probably the first to define this concept. In addition to task and maintenance roles, they also explored dysfunctional roles.

- **Task roles** supply the information, ideas, and energy necessary to accomplish the goals:
  - *Proposers* initiate new ideas or procedures.
  - *Seekers* ask for information, facts, ideas, opinions, or clarification.
  - *Coordinators* show the relationship, similarity, or differences of ideas.
  - *Clarifiers* compare ideas to standards or question the practicality of suggestions.
  - *Summarizers* bring ideas together, question the direction, or pursue completion.
  - *Energizers* prod the group to action or decision.
- **Maintenance roles** establish and preserve interpersonal relationships:
  - *Reconcilers* mediate differences.
  - *Compromisers* search for common elements.
  - *Motivators* praise and support others.
  - *Relaxers* reduce formality and bring out humor. [See 1.3.3.5]

2.3.2.8 Making Decisions
Several approaches are available for making team decisions, including consensus, a democratic vote, authority rule, expert decision, or minority control. [See 1.2.7.4]

2.3.3 Knowledge of Facilitation Methods and Techniques

> **I. Understanding the Role of Facilitation**
>
> Facilitation is a well-honed skill. When done well, the facilitator appears to be a natural who does not need to practice or prepare. However, TD professionals should know that facilitation requires rigorous preparation, refined skills, and a pleasant and personable demeanor.

2.3.3.1 Facilitating Versus Teaching Versus Presenting

TD professionals often deliver knowledge by facilitating, teaching, or presenting, and they may find themselves in all roles at different times. There are distinctions between each:

- **Facilitating** usually refers to taking less of a delivery role, being learner centered, and acting as a catalyst for learning. When a trainer uses facilitative methods, participants assume responsibility for their own learning.
- **Teaching** relates more to a teller or instructor who is distributing knowledge with limited learner involvement. This term is generally associated with a pedagogical process.
- **Presenting** typically denotes delivering a speech to a group of people with little two-way communication.

2.3.3.2 Identifying and Considering Facilitation Styles

In any presentation or facilitation scenario, how something is said is just as important as what is said. Experts have observed that the techniques used to communicate information often determine whether it is received and believed.

All TD professionals have a personal facilitation preference that is based on who they are, and each individual style will appeal to some people more than others. TD professionals should adapt their facilitation style to meet the needs of everyone in the group, as well as the formality of the audience, desire for a fast or slow pace, difficulty of content, and so on.

No one facilitation style is better than any other. Facilitators should be flexible and adapt to the needs of their audience, recognizing that it will be made up of different preferences.

2.3.3.3 Communicating As a Facilitator

TD professionals should be aware of the important role their communication plays when facilitating groups. They should focus on how they use their voice, open a session, and personalize their messages.

2.3.3.3.1 Using One's Voice Effectively

TD professionals should pay attention to how their voices sound. Projection—the pitch, volume, and rate of a voice—is crucial for effective delivery. A skilled TD facilitator varies these vocal qualities to emphasize key points. Incorporating voice inflection can capture and hold participants' interest, while a monotone voice may lose their attention. Facilitators should also pay attention to bad vocal habits, such as leaving long pauses between sentences or using filler words (such as *um*, *er*, or *like*). Facilitators must talk with, not at, participants using good two-way communication skills. Deliver key words and concepts slower. Less important material can be covered more quickly. [See 1.1.1.3 and 1.1.2.2]

2.3.3.3.2 Opening a Session

At the beginning of the session, TD professionals need to capture participants' attention and interest.

An effective opener or icebreaker is a great way to start. The first moments of the introduction set the tone, and a skilled facilitator will prompt the audience to want to know more about the topic. Examples of effective introductions include:

- Provocative statements
- Unique demonstrations

- An illustration of how the topic relates directly to work experiences
- Topic-related visuals
- Thought-provoking questions

2.3.3.3.3 Personalizing Communication

Facilitators should personally communicate with participants. They should learn how to pronounce and spell difficult or technical words and reinforce them. They accept and praise ideas offered by participants to keep them involved in the presentation, which ultimately encourages others to get involved and contribute. Facilitators can emphasize key points using relevant participant examples, questioning techniques, appropriate application activities, and the use of visuals. Sufficient and relevant examples help participants understand the presentation's subject. Facilitators also logically sequence topics and include smooth transitions between them.

2.3.3.4 Scanning for Learners' Reactions

TD professionals use eye contact to read participants' faces to detect comprehension, boredom, or lack of understanding. From the participants' standpoint, eye contact with the presenter is essential because it helps them feel as though they're part of the presentation.

When delivering live, online training, facilitators may need to use other techniques to keep participants involved. For example, a facilitator can still use questioning techniques such as waiting for a volunteer to answer or asking a specific participant to respond. They can also leverage tools available in web-based training, such as polling questions or raised hands, to immediately determine the group's understanding and ability to answer knowledge check questions correctly. These tools help gauge participants' comfort level and determine how many virtual learners are actively listening and understanding.

2.3.3.5 Addressing Disruptive Learner Behavior

The best approach to disruptive behavior is to prevent it from occurring in the first place. A TD professional's attitude and how they manage disruptive individuals will set the stage for how easy it is to manage the disruptions. Here are a few strategies for building trust with participants and creating a productive environment for all:

- Participants are more likely to self-manage behaviors if they establish their own ground rules.
- Create a climate in which participants feel free to give each other feedback.
- Build trust, reward appropriate behavior, and ignore inappropriate behavior.
- Model appropriate behavior.
- Be open to and invite individuals' comments, ideas, and disagreements.
- When someone disagrees, the facilitator should be professional and respectful, acknowledging that there are different ways to think about a topic.

Disruptions may still occur even after a facilitator tries to prevent them. However, TD professionals should give disruptors the benefit of the doubt; if it occurs again, let the participant know how their behavior is affecting everyone.

2.3.3.6 Mannerisms and Appearance

The effective use of body language and gestures contributes to communication—to emphasize, show agreement, and maintain participants' interest. Effective presenters should remember these points about body language:

- Use quick, positive, and energetic movements of the hands, arms, and head to maintain participants' attention.
- Coordinate movement and gestures with delivery.
- Avoid distracting mannerisms such as fidgeting, pacing, and jingling coins.
- Observe participants' body language, such as down-turned eyes, fidgeting, and slouching, and respond appropriately.
- Use positive facial expressions.
- Avoid sitting behind a desk or lectern because that establishes a barrier between the facilitator and participants.
- Move freely around the room and down aisles.
- Move toward participants as they respond to questions to encourage them to continue speaking.

When acting as facilitators, TD professionals should dress appropriately because how they look affects how participants perceive them; therefore, it can influence the presentation style. One guide suggests the facilitator should dress one step up from what they expect participants to wear and be comfortable, practical, and predictable. Credibility and respect are also conveyed through appropriate dress.

2.3.3.7 Participant Focus
TD professionals put the learner first—recognizing that focusing on the learner is their most important job. This idea was introduced by Carl Rogers's concept of "learner-centered learning." His approach is effective because it uses interactive techniques to engage learners, which improves retention, fosters collaborative learning, and makes learning more enjoyable (Rogers 1951). [See 2.1.3.2]

2.3.3.8 Building Credibility
TD professionals should recognize the value that credibility creates when facilitating training programs and meetings. They know that to gain credibility they must:
- Prevent a positive, welcoming attitude.
- Maintain tone of voice and body language that demonstrates confidence.
- Prepare in advance.
- Develop a peer-to-peer relationship with participants.
- Facilitate engaging meetings.
- Maintain neutrality during difficult discussions.
- Know the organizational culture.

2.3.3.9 Facilitation Techniques
Facilitation is a skill that requires practice and preparation with different techniques. It involves managing discussions while remaining unobtrusive, asking questions while pausing long enough for participants to answer them, and using silence and active listening effectively. Several useful techniques for facilitating include:
- Using active listening skills
- Giving clear directions
- Balancing participant involvement
- Checking for confirmation from the group
- Avoiding judgmental comments

- Maintaining focus on the process
- Planning transitions
- Summarizing key concepts
- Using silence to encourage participation
- Encouraging questions for clarity
- Sending welcoming nonverbal messages

2.3.3.10 Facilitating Discussion

A key to facilitating participant learning is managing discussions, including asking questions, generating ideas, and enabling decisions.

2.3.3.10.1 Ask Questions

Asking questions enables the TD professional to gather information, facilitate discussion, evaluate acquisition of knowledge, and promote learning. Critical skills for using questioning techniques include active listening, paraphrasing, and reflective questioning. TD professionals use all forms of questions and demonstrate a clear understanding of the advantages and disadvantages of each. Questioning techniques include:

- **Closed-ended questions** are used for obtaining specific facts or information, allowing for a specific fact, or eliciting a yes or no answer; they are preferable when the facilitator wants to limit information.
- **Open-ended questions** require more than a one-word answer; they are used to stimulate discussion and encourage individuals to apply their personal experience to the current situation or discussion.
- **Hypothetical questions** are used for prompting people to think freely in situations when many answers may be valid and allowing individuals and groups to consider different ways of handling a situation.
- **Socratic method** is named for Socrates, who believed that learners would arrive at their own conclusions through questions that examine the content. [See 1.1.6.3]

2.3.3.10.2 Generate Ideas

TD professionals should allow participants to generate ideas about the content in courses or about the agenda in meetings. Techniques that encourage this discussion include:

- Working in small groups
- Silent listing of ideas on paper
- Brainstorming
- Structured brainstorming
- Affinity diagrams

2.3.3.10.3 Enable Decisions

When decisions need to be made, TD professionals can use these techniques:

- Allow time for individual reflection so that all ideas are heard.
- Use small and large groups effectively to achieve consensus on decisions.
- Use prioritization techniques to arrive at top ideas quickly.
- Use the appropriate facilitation techniques to move the group to consensus.
- Summarize the areas of consensus to keep the group focused.

- Establish clear next steps.
- Allow participants with different behavioral styles to feel heard, understood, and included.

> **II. Engagement Methods and Techniques**
>
> Engaging participants is key to effective training delivery and facilitation. TD professionals should be aware of techniques they can use to increase learner participation.

2.3.3.11 Engaging Participants

To increase participation during facilitated learning sessions or meetings, TD professionals should use techniques and activities such as these:

- Organize the learners into small groups.
- Identify ways to engage those prone to silence.
- Use participants' names and make eye contact.
- Don't call on nonparticipators initially; build their comfort and self-confidence first.
- Acknowledge contributions, and encourage others to add to a response.
- Encourage participants to move and engage in discussions with other participants.

2.3.3.12 Managing Conflict

Hostility among meeting participants, training groups, or others that need to work together may occur occasionally. If the behavior is preventing the group from being productive, a TD professional may need to intervene using one of these techniques:

- Help participants differentiate the facts from assumptions.
- Remain unbiased.
- Stay calm and unemotional as the facilitator.
- Ask for clarification, or summarize to confirm the real issue.
- Ask the tough questions that nobody else will.
- Create a safe environment for discussion.
- If needed, pause or flex the agenda to resolve unexpected conflicts.
- In extreme cases, when TD professionals feel threatened, they may need to call security. [See 1.3.5, 1.3.6, and 2.3.3.15]

2.3.3.13 Understanding Context to Engaging Participants

To be good facilitators, TD professionals must understand the content, know the participants, implement basic adult learning theory, and be prepared for any unexpected actions that may occur during facilitation.

Facilitators need to understand the context in which they are working. They need to know what else is happening beyond the meeting or delivery of the content, including the participants' work environment; their relationship with each other; why they are in attendance; their expectations of the facilitator, the content, and others; their perception of the event or meeting; their biases and concerns; and a host of other things that make up the context.

Being aware of the context helps the facilitator direct the flow of the discussion and be an arbitrator. The specific context may shift as discussion continues. People will support positions, choose sides, participate, or

2.3 Training Delivery & Facilitation

stay quiet depending on what's going on in the room at any moment. If facilitators think someone is being excluded, they should ask the person or group, "What would you like to add about the issue?"

2.3.3.14 Online Learner Engagement

When delivering training content online, TD professionals should emphasize interactivity by creating exchanges between the facilitator and the learner, as well as among learners. TD professionals should be skilled in engaging online learners and using the tools available, such as chat, polling, and breakout groups. Cindy Huggett (2018) advises that "the trick to creating interactivity is to use these tools thoughtfully," which means using them to engage learners to help reach the learning goals. Huggett (2013) also suggests engaging participants every three to five minutes. In addition to using the technology available to drive interaction, TD professionals should consider these techniques:

- Use the time before the actual start time to engage learners by displaying a poll, posting a rolling set of quotes, or beginning a live chat with anyone who's logged on to the platform.
- Use a variety of response techniques; for example, switch between the chat window, a whiteboard, and the "raise hand" feature.
- Call participants by their names or incorporate them into the examples.
- Create a social aspect that starts by sharing the participant list, including brief introductions (verbally for a small group or in the chat window for a larger group).

2.3.3.15 Group Dynamics and Behavioral Styles

Individuals bring unique perspectives, skills, and ideas that contribute to learning. TD professionals must attend to participant engagement throughout the session. While participants are interacting in small group activities, TD professionals should move physically throughout the groups (or virtually if online) to observe individuals' behavior and interactions.

TD professionals need to understand behavioral styles because style differences can potentially create conflict. There are many models and style names, but most rely on four basic roles that reflect the styles of the participants:

- **A dominating, driving style** is direct and decisive. Candor and honesty are critical.
- **An influencing, expressive style** is positive and demonstrates enthusiasm for people. Having fun is important.
- **A steady, amiable style** is found in a true team player. Cooperation and sincerity are important.
- **A conscientious, analyzing style** is serious. Quality and accuracy are important. [See 1.1.4.2]

People who demonstrate each of these styles show different personalities, have different needs, and communicate differently. That means that there will be differences of opinions and conflicts among participants in a group setting. Most important, TD professionals should recognize these styles and be flexible enough to move into another's style comfort zone to communicate best.

2.3.4 Skill in Creating Positive Learning Climates and Environments

I. Creating Climates Conducive to Learning

TD professionals should know the importance of establishing an environment that is welcoming to all and be able to create a positive learning climate.

2.3.4.1 Engaging Facilitator Attributes

TD professionals should be engaging facilitators with a multitude of attributes that participants desire. For starters they are excellent communicators: clear, concise, complete, and considerate. They translate things that may be unclear or unrelated so everyone can understand. They care—truly care—about their participants. They select the right exercises for groups and always have a reason, which becomes clear through purposeful debriefs, for using an activity. They ask appropriate follow-up questions, remain a neutral catalyst, and challenge groups when necessary. They motivate groups and inspire individuals to be all they can be.

2.3.4.2 Get to Know Participants

To successfully create supportive learning environments, TD professionals become familiar with their participants. They learn about their professional lives by asking questions to better understand their skill level, knowledge, experience, and expertise. They also learn something about them personally to build a relationship.

2.3.4.3 Creating a Positive Environment Based on Adult Learning Principles

Adult learning researcher Malcolm Knowles said that being relaxed, trusting, mutually respectful, informal, warm, collaborative, and supportive, with openness, authenticity, and humility were the key factors in creating the right learning climate for adult learning (Biech 2015). Learning theorists consider these process elements, as defined in Knowles's process model of andragogy, to be crucial to adult learning.

Knowles believed that adults need to know why they should learn something before investing time in it (Knowles, Holton, and Swanson 2015). Therefore, TD professionals should share the purpose of the learning event and what's in it for the participants. In addition, they acknowledge that adults bring experiences and prior knowledge to learning settings and explain how that provides a solid foundation for what they will learn. [See 2.1.3.1]

According to Cindy Huggett (2018), most advice for face-to-face classroom facilitators remains true for virtual classroom facilitators. To create a positive learning environment, TD professionals must demonstrate knowledge of adult learning principles:

- **Create a safe haven for learning.** TD professionals can create a non-judgmental space for everyone by greeting participants at the door or online or sharing the objectives of the training early. Ensure confidentiality—what's said in the group stays in the group.
- **Create a comfortable environment.** Arrive online or at the training room early enough to help create a positive environment. In a virtual classroom, check all technology before the session, dial in 15 minutes before class, and ensure accuracy of all materials. Connect with everyone by using their names, and confirm they know how to use the technology. Arrive early to the face-to-face classroom. Turn the lights on, adjust the thermostat to a comfortable temperature, ensure the room looks organized, and confirm visuals can be seen by all.
- **Encourage participation.** Creating active and ample participation is important to enhance training. TD professionals should encourage everyone to meet others in the group and use small groups to overcome reluctance to share ideas or concerns. Use participants' names often.
- **Facilitate content.** At times, lectures are required, such as when rules or laws must be communicated verbatim or safety is an issue. For the most part, however, adults learn best through experiential learning activities facilitated by the TD professional.

2.3.5 Skill in Selecting and Aligning Delivery Options and Media for Training or Learning Events to the Desired Learning or Behavioral Outcomes

> **I. Ensuring Delivery Options Align With How Employees Learn**
> There are many delivery options that TD professionals can use to reach a learning event's goals and objectives. They should be skilled in selecting the appropriate ones.

2.3.5.1 Overview of the 70-20-10 Framework

Employees learn how to do their jobs while they are doing their jobs. In the 1980s, Morgan McCall Jr., Michael Lombardo, and Ann Morrison at the Center for Creative Leadership (CCL) examined how leaders learned the craft of leadership. Their research concluded that 70 percent was learned as hands-on experience on the job and directed by the individual's manager; 20 percent was learned through developmental interactions that some now call social learning; and 10 percent was learned through formal learning that consisted of classes, workshops, or reading. These findings came to be known as the 70-20-10 framework, which TD professionals use today.

Although 70-20-10 serves as a valuable guideline for using a wide variety of developmental options, the framework can be misunderstood. TD professionals should use it as a rough guide to think about how people develop, rather than an exact ratio. In addition, three essential ingredients must accompany the framework: challenging tasks, support from others that includes feedback, and a supply of new content. The best learning strategy draws on elements of all three categories (Lombardo and Eichinger 2011). Even though TD professionals are experts in the 10 percent category—delivering training or programs—they also need to focus on the other two.

2.3.5.2 Active Versus Passive Learning

When facilitating, TD professionals can use active training techniques to ensure participants take an active role in the content and construct personal meaning from it (Silberman and Biech 2015). Active training ensures participants are involved in the process, learning from one another in pairs and small groups. When used correctly, these techniques increase the longevity and relevance of the training. Passive learning, on the other hand, occurs when the learners are recipients of information. Table 2.3.5.2-1 compares several aspects of active and passive learning.

Table 2.3.5.2-1. Active and Passive Learning

	Active Learning	**Passive Learning**
Defined	Knowledge is acquired by learners	Knowledge is transferred to learners
Facilitator roles	Enables learning; guides learners	Presents information; tells learners
Learner roles	Responsible for their learning	Receiver of knowledge
Delivery methods	Small group activities, role plays, discussion, games, simulations	Recipients of lectures, reading, videos
Involvement	Learners engage in activities	Learners listen and observe
Kind of learning	Independent	Dependent
Experience assumptions	Learners have experience to contribute	Learners are inexperienced or uninformed
Objectives	Flexible	Predetermined and inflexible
Primary resource	Participants contribute to content	Facilitator is the content expert

Adapted from Biech (2015).

II. Learning Preferences

TD professionals should be aware that many theories acknowledge that individuals are unique and have different learning preferences. They should understand differences in learning and communication preferences based on organizational and cultural beliefs, behaviors, practices, and expressions.

2.3.5.3 Audience Variability

When delivering training content, TD professionals should plan for certain differences among learners. These considerations may have already been addressed in part through the instructional design process that led to the creation of the training program. Audience variability factors may relate to the content being taught, learners' level of prior knowledge or proficiency, desired learning outcomes, methods and media best suited to learning goals, and any requirements associated with the participants, such as accessibility needs, geographic location, and technology capability and availability.

While many learners may have a self-identified learning preference, there is no evidence to suggest that choosing a learning method based on a person's learning preference leads to better learning outcomes. Therefore, any requests from learners about such preferences should not be prioritized when delivering training material. Facilitators should, however, select effective learning strategies that consider the factors outlined above. All adults benefit from using multiple modalities to learn. Encourage participants to process, practice, and successfully learn material through multiple resources to deepen connections. For example, learners who are exposed to both auditory and visual representations of information experience dual coding, which reinforces the encoding process (turning information into memory) and supports learners' ability to retain and use the new information being taught.

Selecting and prioritizing training delivery approaches is also critical to addressing neurodiversity within the learner population. [See 1.4.4.1] Neurodiversity explains the variations of how individuals' brains learn or think, such as attention deficit disorder (ADD), dyslexia, and autism spectrum disorder. Research in brain science suggests that as much as 30 percent of the workforce is neurodiverse (Pisano 2017). Facilitators delivering training content may need to consider the ways it is being presented and how the pace of learning should be adjusted. Incorporating a variety of delivery techniques and activities into any adult learning experience will benefit neurodiverse learners. Planning to learn as much as possible about the participants and how much variability exists in the group will always help the facilitator create the most effective learning experience. [See 1.1.4.2 and 2.3.5.4]

2.3.5.4 Myers-Briggs Type Indicator

No matter what delivery choice TD professionals make, they are likely to have participants with a variety of personality types. The Myers-Briggs Type Indicator (MBTI) assessment, one of the most widely used personality instruments, measures the psychological preferences of how people perceive the world. Katherine Briggs and her daughter Isabelle Briggs Myers (1977) based their work on that of Swiss psychologist Carl Jung. The instrument they developed asks a person to self-report on individual preferences grouped into eight categories:

- Extroversion (E) or introversion (I)
- Perception by sensing (S) or intuition (N)
- Judgment by thinking (T) or feeling (F)
- Attitude of judgment (J) or perception (P)

The publishers of the MBTI assessment and other psychological tests and measures require that purchasers be properly accredited for using their products so their material is not misused. The MBTI assessment offers TD professionals one way to explore their participants' learning preferences. [See 1.1.4.2]

2.3.5.5 W.E. Herrmann's Whole Brain Approach

The Herrmann Brain Dominance Instrument is a method of personality testing developed by W.E. "Ned" Herrmann (1989), who is considered the father of brain dominance technology. The instrument demonstrates how people learn in terms of preferences for thinking in four modes based on brain function:

- **Left brain, cerebral**—logical, analytical, quantitative, factual, and critical
- **Left brain, limbic**—sequential, organized, planned, detailed, and structured
- **Right brain, limbic**—emotional, interpersonal, sensory, kinesthetic, and symbolic
- **Right brain, cerebral**—visual, holistic, and creative [See 2.2.1.4]

2.3.5.6 Multiple Intelligences

Although intake and learning preferences reflect how people prefer to receive information, intelligence reflects how they process that information. Howard Gardner (2011) suggests that intelligence is multifaceted, and traditional measures, such as intelligence quotient (IQ) tests, do not accurately measure all its facets. He also says intelligence is not fixed, and defines it as an aptitude that is:

- Measurable
- Used to create and solve problems
- Valued by the culture [See 1.2.1.1 and 2.2.1.5]

In *Frames of Mind*, Gardner (2011) describes the multiple intelligence theory and gives his initial list of intelligences.

2.3.5.7 Accelerated Learning Techniques and Principles

TD professionals should use delivery techniques that enable others to learn better faster. Accelerated learning is one of those techniques. It involves the right and left hemispheres, the cortex, and the limbic systems of the brain. A positive learning environment—which typically includes teamwork, collaboration, vivid colors on the walls, music, games, and activities—engages hemispheres of the brain, leading to a whole mind and body experience. Proponents of accelerated learning believe that knowledge is created rather than consumed, and this type of environment causes people to learn on many levels simultaneously by:

- Speeding and enhancing learning
- Reducing course design time
- Improving learning retention and job performance
- Creating healthier learning environments
- Involving learners at every stage (Meier 2000) [See 2.2.1.8]

2.3.5.8 Learning Rates

TD professionals should consider how learning rates might affect their chosen delivery option. As a group, adult learners vary widely in their education, background, experience, intelligence, emotional stability, and motivation for achievement. By setting goals and expectations, TD professionals help orient learners, motivate them, and leverage their experiences to make the connection between new knowledge and the background information they already have. Other factors that may influence the speed at which adults learn include their psychological, environmental, emotional, sociological, physical, intellectual, and experiential status.

2.3.5.9 Barriers to Communication

TD professionals should consider communication barriers as they select appropriate delivery options and media for learning events. Several to consider are culture, language and speech, the environment, psychology, nonverbal behaviors, proxemic zones, basic communications, and barriers to listening:

- **Culture.** Misunderstandings occur when members of one culture—whether that of another country or a minority group within a country—are unable to understand the differences in another culture's communication practices, traditions, and thought processes. To reduce intercultural communication problems, TD professionals need to be aware of their own culturally instilled ways of viewing the world. [See 1.4.2]
- **Language and speech.** Even when everyone speaks the same language, differences and misunderstandings can occur. The most-often cited difficulties include accent, linguistics, translation errors, and nuances. [See 1.1.1.6 and 1.1.1.7]
- **Environment.** Environment can create communication barriers including how people use personal space, technology advancements and skill, the friendliness of the physical space, distractions, temperature, and comfort.
- **Context.** The circumstances surrounding communication create the contextual level. High-context societies determine meaning from how a message is delivered and under what circumstances. Low-context societies are more literal—that is, more dependent on what's said or written.
- **Nonverbal behavior.** Nonverbal behavior such as appearance and body language can cause barriers to communication. Appearance clues fall into two categories: artifacts (items of appearance over which a person has control, such as jewelry and clothing) and physical traits (characteristics over which a person doesn't have control, including race, gender, body size, bone structure, and skin color). Differences in how people walk, talk, bow, stand, or sit occur not only between cultures but also between genders and subgroups within a culture.
- **Eye contact.** Eyes can convey several meanings, and those meanings vary from culture to culture:
  - *Cognitive eye movements* are associated with thinking. By looking away from a speaker, for example, a receiver indicates that no new information is being processed.
  - *Monitoring eye movements* are associated with understanding. The speaker in this case monitors the degree of eye contact from the listener.
  - *Regulatory eye movements* are associated with a communicator's willingness to respond. The speaker regulates the communication flow by making eye contact and allowing the receiver to indicate a desire for further communication.
  - *Expressive eye movements* are associated with the emotional responses of the people communicating.
- **Proxemic zones.** Proxemics is the relationship of people's physical positions. When people think someone is too close, they may feel threatened. On the other hand, if someone is too far away, they may think that person is unfriendly or cold. Facilitators from a different country than where they're conducting the training may encounter difficulties in communicating with people from other cultures because of this distance issue. [See 1.4.4.1]

2.3.5.10 Matching Learning Methods to Desired Outcome

During the design and development phases, TD professionals use the defined objectives to select a training event that will best achieve the objective. Selecting learning methods is primarily based on Bloom's domains and levels of learning. Depending on which domain and level of learning is required, certain methods work better than others. [See 2.1.3.6, 2.2.4.2, and 2.2.11.1]

To make the decision, the facilitator would ask:
- Are we addressing knowledge, skills, or attitudes?
- Who are the learners?
- What is the group size and experience level?
- What are the practical requirements?
- What logistics (time of day, amount of time available, facilities and materials available, and cost limitations) should be considered? [See 2.2.11.1]

III. Presentation and Training Tools

TD professionals should take advantage of the many tools that are available to enhance their facilitation and presentations.

2.3.5.11 Science of Using Visuals

Visuals make it easier for learners to acquire skills or knowledge and are an important element of learning in any modality. Ruth Clark, author of *Evidence-Based Training Methods* (2019), states that facilitators should use relevant visuals, keep visuals simple, explain complex visuals, and avoid visuals that are distracting to the learners. Visuals enhance learning retention and help people make sense of complex, abstract, or unusual content. At least 50 percent of the cortex is used for visual processing while only 10 percent is used for auditory processing (Snowden, Thompson, and Troscianko 2012).

2.3.5.12 Media Options

The best presentations have a mix of delivery methods, using verbal and nonverbal techniques as well as appropriate media to support the message. The media should reinforce the content while being easy to understand and high quality. TD professionals have numerous media choices available, and most training programs designate which media are appropriate and when to use them. Options include:
- Presentation software
- Videos
- Animations
- Polling software
- Collaboration software
- Smartboards
- Flipcharts and easels
- Whiteboards and magnetic boards
- Virtual and augmented reality [See 2.2.11]

2.3.6 Skill in Delivering Training Using Multiple Delivery Options and Media

> **I. Delivering Formal Learning**
>
> TD professionals should be skilled in delivering training using multiple delivery options. Delivery may be formal, informal, or a blend of both.

2.3.6.1 Types of Learning
Learning can be categorized several ways and overlap from one category to another. The following definitions can help TD professionals understand the differences.

2.3.6.1.1 Formal or Informal
- **Formal learning** is planned learning that derives from activities within a structured learning setting and includes instructor-led classrooms, instructor-led online training courses, certification programs, workshops, and college courses. A curriculum, agenda, and objectives occur within a pre-established timeframe.
- **Informal learning** is what occurs outside a structured program, plan, or class. It happens naturally in life and on the job when people observe others, use trial and error, and talk to and collaborate with others. It is usually spontaneous and could include coaching, mentoring, stretch assignments, or rotational assignments. It can also include reading books and blogs, watching online videos, listening to podcasts, searching the internet, and retrieving other digital content.

2.3.6.1.2 Classroom, Virtual, Online, Blended, and Hybrid Learning
TD professionals should know what determines whether classroom or online training is the best choice.
- **Classroom learning** is characterized by having a facilitator who is physically located in the same room as the participants.
- **Virtual classrooms** are an online learning space where participants and facilitators interact from different locations.
- **Online learning** describes technology-enabled training via computers, mobile devices, the internet, an intranet, or other technology. It is broader than a virtual classroom because it also includes synchronous and asynchronous training.
- **Blended learning** is the practice of using several modalities in one curriculum. It refers to the combination of formal and informal leaning events such as classroom instruction, online resources, and on-the-job coaching.
- **Hybrid learning** is a comprehensive approach to combining face-to-face and online learning simultaneously. Learners can participate live in-person or remotely using tools such as video conferencing hardware and software. All elements of the session need to be tailored to the hybrid learning format.

2.3.6.1.3 Synchronous and Asynchronous Learning
- **Synchronous learning** occurs when the facilitator and the learners participate in the training event at the same time.
- **Asynchronous learning** occurs when the facilitator and the learners do not participate simultaneously.

2.3 Training Delivery & Facilitation

2.3.6.1.4 Distance and Self-Directed Learning
- **Distance learning** is an educational delivery in which the instructor and participants are separated by time, location, or both. Distance learning can be synchronous or asynchronous.
- **Self-directed learning** is when the learner determines the pace and timing of content delivery. It occurs through a variety of media, print products, or electronically.

2.3.6.1.5 Instructor-Paced and Self-Paced Learning
- **Instructor-paced** refers to a course that adheres to a schedule set by the facilitator, including assignment due dates, tests, and other requirements.
- **Self-paced** describes any learning program based on learner response but without immediate feedback from facilitators. This type does not follow a predetermined schedule; instead, the learners complete assignments, exams, and other requirements at their pace. Generally, there is an end date for the course.

2.3.6.2 Evaluating and Staying Current With Technology
Methods for developing talent are constantly evolving. Technology breakthroughs have accelerated the need for TD professionals to stay up to date on cutting-edge technology resources so they can support the learning process. They should be prepared to assess, evaluate, and recommend new technology resources, which may ensure better learning outcomes, increase engagement, or support facilitators to make their jobs easier. TD professionals will need to stay ahead of trends like how performance support and social networks might shift learning to a more sustained and distributed model. In addition, they may need to determine how on-demand, mobile learning can support employees who need immediate access to information. And even though it's unlikely that TD professionals will purchase augmented reality (AR), virtual reality (VR), or mixed reality (MR) technology, they will buy applications that support their engineers' design skills or help supervisors recall a coaching process. By working with others in the organization's IT and knowledge management areas, TD professionals can identify and leverage the most innovative tools. [See 2.4]

> ## II. Applying Learning Science
> TD professionals should have a clear understanding of the cognitive processes of learning to deliver content that is retained and applied on the job.

2.3.6.3 Applying Learning Science to Delivery
Science gives TD professionals the ability to understand development, so they should take advantage of this knowledge to unleash workplace potential. Understanding how the human brain works isn't easy, but many studies have identified best practices to ensure content is presented and delivered in a way that takes advantage of this research. [See 2.1]

TD professionals need to learn all they can about cognitive science and adult learning theory to create effective learning experiences. People learn best when they hear it, see it, question it, discuss it, and do it. They may even want to teach it to someone else to solidify their understanding of the information or skill. Knowing the cognitive processes of learning and delivering training and other development options based on these cognitive processes will result in maximum learning, increased employee performance, and improved organizational results.

To ensure that participants learn, TD professionals should use delivery strategies grounded in cognitive learning science to enhance the brain's learning power. Strategies and supporting evidence that should be reviewed and incorporated into delivery and other development options include:
- Enhance learning with visual and verbal context (Clark 2019; Medina 2014).
- Require participation (Ericsson, Krampe, and Tesch-Römer 1993; Salas et al. 2012).
- Present content in bite-sized chunks (Miller 1956).
- Use movement for a cognitive boost (Medina 2014).
- Implement learning content immediately (Clark 2019).
- Design stimulating curriculum using stories, interactions, and visuals (Jensen 2008).
- Avoid playing music (Moreno and Mayer 2000; Jensen 2008).
- Give feedback (Clark 2019; Fleenor and Taylor 2005; Salas et al. 2012).
- Avoid cognitive overload (Ericsson, Krampe, and Tesch-Römer 1993; Medina 2014).
- Space practice and review (Rohrer and Taylor 2006).
- Allow choice (Salas et al. 2012).
- Involve multiple senses (Jensen 2008).
- Improve spacing (Ebbinghaus 1964; Clark 2019).
- Introduce moderate stress (Yerkes and Dodson 1908).
- Make it social (Maslow 1968). [See 2.1]

III. Exploring Informal Learning

TD professionals should be acutely aware of all the opportunities available to learners that occur while they are doing their jobs, having conversations with others, and even engaging in recreational activities. They should also understand how the organization can best support informal learning.

2.3.6.4 Definition and Examples

Informal learning is the term used to describe anything that's not learned in a formal program or class. It happens on the job through talking with or observing others, trial and error, collaboration, and seeking knowledge or information through social media. The broad category of informal learning includes social learning, but some instances of informal learning are not social—for example, studying and reading.

According to Jay Cross (2007), "Informal learning is the unofficial, unscheduled, impromptu way people learn to do their jobs." He compares informal learning to riding a bike (with the rider in control), while formal learning is like riding a bus (with the driver in control).

Formal learning is often part of a curriculum, course, or workshop and is estimated to comprise 10 to 20 percent of what people learn at work.

Informal learning, on the other hand:
- Occurs within the context of doing a job or in everyday life—not in the classroom
- May occur accidentally or through a series of purposeful activities
- Can happen instantly and intentionally, such as through an internet search

Informal learning examples may occur in several formats including:
- **Conversation**—storytelling, coaching, mentoring facilitation, giving feedback, modeling, reflecting, discovery, asking, observing, and trial and error
- **Communities of practice or virtual communities**—social networks, forums, virtual worlds, and knowledge management repositories
- **Digital content**—blogs and microblogs, wikis, intranet resources, search engines, frequently asked questions, and discovery

2.3.6.5 Talent Development's Role in Informal Learning

TD professionals know the important role informal learning plays in employee development. They should also know the role they play in advocating and supporting informal learning. TD professionals may coach employees and managers to accept and leverage informal learning. This can often be accomplished by:

- **Advocating for informal learning:**
    - Gain executive support for informal learning efforts.
    - Set clear expectations about informal learning among stakeholders.
    - Clarify goals and desired outcomes related to the organization's mission and vision.
    - Continually promote the availability of resources for informal learning.
- **Adding content and options:**
    - Curate an internal repository of content that can be leveraged for informal learning.
    - Work with knowledge management experts to identify resources and their locations.
    - Help employees locate independent study, research, and collaboration options.
    - Provide resources and guidance to managers and employees on informal learning options and link those to specific development opportunities.
- **Assisting learners:**
    - Create a path to help employees lead their own learning efforts.
    - Prepare employees with the skills required to learn and develop.
    - Coach supervisors to coach their employees. [See 2.7.3]
    - Help managers and employees identify gaps in their knowledge and skills.
    - Devise a plan for bridging skills gaps through informal learning.

2.3.6.6 Organizational Culture and Informal Learning

In their trusted advisor role, TD professionals help leaders recognize and enhance an organization's informal learning culture. Saul Carliner (2012) asserts that role is exhibited in four ways:

- A formal statement in support of informal learning activities
- Approval of funding for proposed projects related to informal learning
- Allowing the use of work time for informal learning activities
- Demonstrating support by participating in informal learning themselves

TD professionals can demonstrate the importance of informal learning and identify how leaders can support it. To influence the organization's culture, the TD professional should:

- Discuss the value of informal learning with organizational leadership, and remind them to discuss it with other leaders throughout the organization.
- Set clear expectations among stakeholders about what informal learning is and its capacity for supporting them in their work.

- Share a list of available informal learning opportunities.
- Ensure all supervisors understand the value of career discussions.
- Leverage employees' knowledge, and connect them with others.

2.3.6.7 Informal Learning Networks and Tools

TD professionals should identify the ways that informal learning can occur in their organizations. Many options are based on the theory of connectivism, which was developed by George Siemens (2005) and Stephen Downes (2010). It suggests that learners create connections and develop a network that contributes to their professional development and knowledge. Here are several informal learning tools:

- **Social networking tools** are podcasts, blogs, tags, wikis, communities of practice, and instant messaging services.
- **Personal learning networks** consist of the people a learner interacts with and derives knowledge from their environment. Individuals connect with others with the specific intent for some type of learning to occur.
- **Learning communities** are groups of people who share a professional interest or background and discuss opportunities, challenges, and feelings related to it. Communities can meet in person, online, or both. Clubs, professional associations, and affinity groups (people who share common demographics or interests) are examples of professional communities. Numerous groups use social media sites such as LinkedIn to participate in professional communities of interest. LISTSERVs or electronic bulletin boards are popular in academic institutions.
- **Online learning portals** are an organization's centralized repository for learning content and information, such as frequently asked questions (FAQs), job aids, online modules, and additional self-help resources. [See 2.2.7 and 2.3.1.3]

2.3.6.8 Work With the Organization

TD professionals should work with their organizations to determine their approach to informal learning. Initial questions to inform planning include:

- How prescriptive should the informal learning program be?
- Will it be evaluated?
- Is it part of an overall learning strategy or a separate part that helps build a culture of knowledge?
- Is this an organization-wide effort, or will there be a small pilot effort to test uptake and engagement?

The answers to these questions will help TD professionals determine an organizational strategy. Then they can help define informal learning, establish the roles of technology and knowledge management, determine a budget, decide how to provide developmental opportunities for everyone, and plan for evaluation and ongoing improvement.

IV. Self-Directed Learning Approaches

TD professionals should use various approaches and be prepared to support the workforce in their efforts to direct their own learning.

2.3.6.9 Learning On the Job

Because most learning occurs on the job, TD professionals should focus on how to support and encourage the kind of self-directed approaches that are important and most relevant to the workforce. Support for learning on the job may come from another person or an electronic or paper job aid.

2.3.6.9.1 Self-Directed Learning (SDL)

SDL is a general term that refers to self-paced training programs that use a wide variety of media, ranging from print products to web-based systems. SDL also can refer to less formal types of learning, such as team learning, knowledge management systems, and self-development programs. This is an appropriate option when:

- The group of learners is large, dispersed, or both.
- The subject matter is mostly cognitive.
- Learners have many individual needs.
- The resources for classroom-based training aren't available.
- Timely training is required.

2.3.6.9.2 On-the-Job Training (OJT)

OJT is an approach for developing skills in the actual work environment—using the tools, equipment, documents, or materials that employees will use in their normal work. It is typically a semi-structured process that is provided by an experienced colleague. To increase OJT success, TD professionals should have a checklist of critical knowledge details, a clearly defined work outcome, time for practice and discussion, and job aids (such as checklists, decision trees, a resource list, or step-by-step guides). OJT may be supported by other learning solutions such as peer coaching, mentoring, job shadowing, or job rotations. It is an appropriate option when:

- It's most useful to learn the skill in the actual environment where it will be practiced.
- The target learning group is small, and limited training resources are available.
- Immediate feedback on performance is helpful.
- OJT is delivered by people who are skilled at the job and given the time to deliver the training.
- TD professionals want to help people and understand cognitive techniques that make learning successful.
- Support materials, job aids, websites, and electronic performance support systems (EPSS) are available (Dillon 2017).

2.3.6.9.3 Electronic Performance Support Systems (EPSS)

An EPSS is software on a computer or other device that gives employees information or resources to help accomplish a task or achieve performance. It's essentially a comprehensive computer-based job aid. These systems deliver information on the job—timely, on-demand information, guidance, examples, and step-by-step dialog boxes—to improve job performance with minimum staff support. Potential EPSS applications include a calculator that simplifies or automates a procedure or an embedded tutorial that provides instruction for a work-related procedure. Use an EPSS application when:

- There's a performance problem caused by a knowledge or skills deficiency.
- Tasks related to the performance problem are relatively difficult to perform.
- Tasks are performed infrequently.
- Tasks don't have to be performed in emergency situations.

- There are serious implications if the tasks are performed inadequately.
- The performance environment accommodates the EPSS hardware.

2.3.6.9.4 Job Aids

A job aid serves the same need as an EPSS, but more simply and cost-effectively because it uses a paper format. A storage place for information that performers use while doing a task, job aids tell users when or how to perform a task, thus, reducing the amount of recall needed and minimizing error. Job aids help reduce training time and support learning. They have been developed for linear tasks, such as assembling equipment and filling out forms, and for complex tasks, such as medical diagnosis. A job aid may be one page or many volumes. Job aids work well for:
- A task performed with relatively low frequency
- A highly complex task with numerous steps
- A task with a high consequence of error
- A task with a high probability of change in the future

2.3.6.9.5 Mobile or Multidevice Learning

Mobile learning combines the use of tablets, laptops, smartphones, and other portable computing devices. When it's possible to access a learning program across multiple devices, it allows the program to extend beyond traditional learning spaces. TD professionals should consider the nuances that mobile learning presents, such as how content is displayed on smaller screens, features that may not be available on every device, and what devices employees have available to them. Mobile learning is unique because the device itself can provide a variety of purposes such as:
- Delivering asynchronous online learning content
- Delivering performance support content
- Supporting social and user-generated content and discussions
- Providing unique mobile content such as GPS and messaging

2.3.7 Skill in Designing or Developing Learning Assets That Align to a Desired Learning or Behavioral Outcome

I. Creating Course Materials

TD professionals know that even though materials are designed for the course before the delivery, there may be times when they must modify existing materials or methods or develop new ones without warning.

2.3.7.1 Considerations for Designing Assets

When a need for change arises, TD professionals should determine what needs to be designed or changed and why. They may find themselves enhancing their slide deck with more relevant content, designing wall charts to provide visual support, creating unique handouts to address learner needs, or adding or modifying activities based on the makeup of the group.

The reason a change occurs without warning is usually due to timing, relevance, or learning requirements:

- **Timing:**
  - Something has occurred in the workplace that is related to but not covered explicitly in the course.
  - The group size is different from what was expected.
  - Course objectives changed prior to the delivery.
  - The amount of available time has changed.
- **Relevance:**
  - Participants' supervisors requested an emphasis in one or more areas.
  - There is a need to add more real-world relevance for the group.
  - Participants require a different experience.
  - A unique problem exists in the workplace that affects most of the participants.
  - The assessment did not uncover the root cause, or something has changed since it was completed that changes the needs.
- **Learning requirements:**
  - Participants don't have the minimum skills for the content.
  - Participants require more advanced content and examples.
  - There is a broad division in the skill and knowledge level of the group.
  - Participants require more hands-on practice.
  - Participants require more depth in one or more topics.

2.3.7.2 Type of Learner Materials

When creating learning materials during the implementation phase, TD professionals should start with knowing what the objective is. The facilitator should then match the learning strategy, knowledge, skill, or attitude to the objective. Some examples include:

- If the participants need to gain knowledge about something, the facilitator could create a short presentation, diagram, problem-solving clinic, participant-led teach back, or internet research.
- If the participants need to be able to do something and acquire a new skill, the facilitator could create a case study, role play, practice session, job aid, or demonstration.
- If the participants need to change their attitude, values, or priorities, the facilitator could create a debate, exercises, self-assessments, feedback groups, or a brainstorming session.

2.3.7.3 Creating Required Materials

Design begins once the TD professional has decided on the kind of asset or learner material and activities that are needed. In some cases, the facilitator may have extra time to create the materials. If so, meeting with the participants' supervisors will yield some ideas about what to include. If the facilitator has to design an asset during the training event, it is best to create it over lunch or take a long break to get organized.

2.3.7.4 Participant-Created Learning Materials

TD professionals should recognize that program participants can provide a wealth of support if allowed to help with the design and learn in the process. For shorter online courses, these ideas could be used between sessions. For example, the facilitator could ask:

- Small groups to:
  - Research a topic online and then present what they learned.
  - Design short role plays or scenarios and exchange with other groups.
  - Create short case studies or critical incidents and then exchange them with other groups.
- The most experienced person in the group to provide a demonstration about the skill needed
- Individuals to create their own job aid and share it with the entire group
- The participants to form two groups and provide the parameters for a formal debate

TD professionals should have several preplanned activities that can be customized for a variety of situations. This should be simple to deploy on a flipchart, virtual whiteboard, or verbally.

REFERENCES

ATD (Association for Talent Development). 2016a. *2016 State of the Industry.* Alexandria, VA: ATD Press.

ATD (Association for Talent Development). 2016b. *Building a Culture of Learning: The Foundation of a Successful Organization.* Alexandria, VA: ATD Press.

Benne, K., and P. Sheats. 1948. "Functional Roles of Group Members." *Journal of Social Issues* 4(2): 41–49.

Biech, E. 2015. *Training and Development for Dummies.* Hoboken, NJ: John Wiley and Sons.

Biech, E. 2017. *The Art and Science of Training.* Alexandria, VA: ATD Press.

Biech, E., ed. 2022. *ATD's Handbook for Training and Talent Development.* Alexandria, VA: ATD Press.

Briggs, K.C., and I.B. Myers. 1977. *Myers-Briggs Type Indicator.* Palo Alto, CA: Consulting Psychologists Press.

Carliner, S. 2012. *Informal Learning Basics.* Alexandria, VA: ASTD Press.

Clark, R. 2019. *Evidence-Based Training Methods*, 3rd ed. Alexandria, VA: ATD Press.

Cross, J. 2007. *Informal Learning: Rediscovering the Natural Pathways That Inspire Innovation and Performance.* San Francisco: Pfeiffer.

Dillon, JD. 2017. "In Real Life: Don't Forget About On-the-Job Training." *Learning Solutions Magazine*, September 19.

Downes, S. 2010. "New Technology Supporting Informal Learning." *Journal of Emerging Technologies in Web Intelligence* 2(1): 27–33.

Ebbinghaus, H. 1964. *Memory: A Contribution to Experimental Psychology.* New York: Dover. Originally published in 1885.

Ericsson, K., R. Krampe, and C. Tesch-Römer. 1993. "The Role of Deliberate Practice in the Acquisition of Expert Performance." *Psychological Review* 100(3): 363–406.

Fleenor, J., and S. Taylor. 2005. *Closing the Loop: Getting the Most From 360-Degree Feedback.* Greensboro, NC: Center for Creative Leadership.

Gardner, H. 2011. *Frames of Mind: The Theory of Multiple Intelligences*, 3rd ed. New York: Basic Books.

Herrmann, W.E. 1988. *The Creative Brain.* Lake Lure, NC: Brain Books.

Huggett, C. 2013. *The Virtual Training Guidebook: How to Design, Deliver, and Implement Live Online Learning*. Alexandria, VA: ASTD Press.

Huggett, C. 2018. *Virtual Training Basics*, 2nd ed. Alexandria, VA: ATD Press.

Jensen, E. 2008. *Brain-Based Learning*, 2nd ed. Thousand Oaks, CA: Corwin Press.

Knowles, M.S., III, E. Holton, and R. Swanson. 2015. *The Adult Learner: The Definitive Classic in Adult Education and Human Resource Development*, 8th ed. Burlington, MA: Elsevier/Butterworth-Heinemann.

Lombardo, M., and R. Eichinger. 2011. *The Leadership Machine: Architecture to Develop Leaders for Any Future*, 3rd ed. Minneapolis: Lominger International: A Korn Ferry Company.

Maslow, A. 1968. *Toward a Psychology of Being*. New York: Litton Educational Publishing.

Medina, J. 2014. *Brain Rules*. Seattle: Pear Press.

Meier, D. 2000. *The Accelerated Learning Handbook*. New York: McGraw-Hill.

Miller, G.A. 1956. "The Magical Number Seven, Plus or Minus Two: Some Limits on Our Capacity for Processing Information." *Psychological Review* 63(2): 81–97.

Moreno, R., and R.E. Mayer. 2000. "A Coherence Effect in Multimedia Learning: The Case for Minimizing Irrelevant Sounds in the Design of Multimedia Instructional Messages." *Journal of Educational Psychology* 92(1): 117–125. doi.org/10.1037/0022-0663.92.1.117.

Orey, M. 2017. "Designing Section 508 Compliant Learning." *TD at Work*. Alexandria, VA: ATD Press.

Pisano, G. 2017. "Neurodiversity as a Competitive Advantage." *Harvard Business Review*, May–June. hbr.org/2017/05/neurodiversity-as-a-competitive-advantage.

Rogers, C. 1951. *Client-Centered Therapy: Its Current Practice, Implications, and Theory*. London: Constable.

Rohrer, D., and K. Taylor. 2006. "The Effects of Overlearning and Distributed Practice on the Retention of Mathematics Knowledge." *Applied Cognitive Psychology* 20:1209–1224.

Rosenberg, M.J. 2001. *E-Learning: Strategies for Delivering Training in the Digital Age*. New York: McGraw-Hill.

Salas, E., S. Tannenbaum, K. Kraiger, and K. Smith-Jentsch. 2012. "The Science of Training and Development in Organizations: What Matters in Practice." *Psychological Science in the Public Interest* 13(2): 74–101. pdfs.semanticscholar.org/0181/b9aa533fd262df009ff113ac42a887afdf95.pdf.

Silberman, M., and E. Biech. 2015. *Active Training: A Handbook of Techniques, Designs, Case Examples, and Tips*. Hoboken, NJ: John Wiley and Sons.

Siemens, G. 2005. "Connectivism: A Learning Theory for the Digital Age." *International Journal of Instructional Technology and Distance Learning* 2(1): 3–10.

Snowden, R., P. Thompson, and T. Troscianko. 2012. *Basic Vision: An Introduction to Visual Perception*, 2nd ed. Oxford: Oxford University Press.

Yerkes, R., and J. Dodson. 1908. "The Relation of Strength of Stimulus to Rapidity of Habit-Formation." *Journal of Comparative Neurology and Psychology* 18:459–482.

Recommended Reading

Halls, J. 2014. "Memory and Cognition in Learning." *Infoline*. Alexandria, VA: ASTD Press.

Huggett, C. 2018. *Virtual Training Basics*, 2nd ed. Alexandria, VA: ATD Press.

Huggett, C. 2022. *The Facilitator's Guide to Immersive, Blended, and Hybrid Learning*. Alexandria, VA: ATD Press.

Silberman, M., and E. Biech. 2015. *Active Training: A Handbook of Techniques, Designs, Case Examples, and Tips*. Hoboken, NJ: John Wiley and Sons.

2.4 TECHNOLOGY APPLICATION

Disruption via technology will continue to be a reality for organizations and talent development functions. TD professionals must have the ability to identify, select, and implement the right learning technologies to serve the best interests of the organization and its people. Practitioners should be able to identify opportunities to adapt and leverage the right technologies at the right time to meet organizational goals.

Administering a Learning Technology Ecosystem

2.4.1 Skill in Selecting, Integrating, Managing, or Maintaining Learning Platforms

> **I. Selecting, Integrating, Managing, and Maintaining Learning Platforms**
>
> TD professionals should understand how technology relates to the learning and support needs of their audience and make informed selections and recommendations. After a technology has been acquired but before it is fully implemented with the intended audience, TD professionals should determine how the technology will be administered and maintained over the life of the platform. However, they may not own all these tasks if their organization has a technology or learning technology department.

2.4.1.1 Platform Functionality

TD professionals should complete an in-depth organizational needs assessment to identify the functionality required in a new learning and development technology. This should include a detailed exploration of the intended audience's work experience, skills, and needs, as well as a summary analysis of other components in the organization's existing technology ecosystem. Once the needs assessment is complete, TD professionals should document their technology requirements in sufficient detail to evaluate existing technologies or enable the supplier selection process for new technologies. This documentation should include clear explanations of:

- The problem they are trying to solve with technology
- How the technology will interact and integrate with other organizational platforms or systems
- User stories that summarize the common tasks users will need the system to perform and how they expect to interact with the system
- The features and capabilities required to execute the desired end-user experience, ranked in order of priority need
- Stakeholders and partners who will play a role in the selection process

- An assessment of any initial obstacles to adoption, which will need to be considered throughout the project as part of ongoing change management
- The process and timeline for technology identification, selection, testing, and implementation

2.4.1.2 Supplier Relationship Management

Vendor relationship management is critical for TD professionals. Many ecosystems are a blend of internally developed and externally acquired tools. If a tool is acquired or managed by the TD function, the team is also responsible for developing and maintaining a positive relationship with the supplier. This should include regular touchpoints between a designated vendor contact and the TD professional responsible for managing the relationship or platform. In addition, clear guidelines should be established for systems training, troubleshooting, planned enhancements and version control, downtime administration, and disaster recovery. Maintaining regular contact with a supplier may also help TD professionals acquire preferential terms for future contracts and participate in future planning. Engaged TD professionals should ensure that the development road maps of vendors and suppliers align with the real needs of the technology users, benefiting their organizations and the wider TD community.

2.4.1.3 Talent Development's Partnership With IT

Talent development exists within the organization's larger technology ecosystem. Therefore, TD professionals should align with established IT regulations and processes. They should forge an effective partnership with IT, gain an understanding of how they operate, and clarify which functions should own the tasks associated with the learning platform and other TD technologies before requesting support. This is even more important with an expanded remote workforce. TD professionals should develop their technology review, acquisition, implementation, and support processes to align with—and benefit from—existing IT guidelines. Although TD professionals should leverage IT expertise to make sure all applied technology is secure and functional, they should not defer responsibility or decision making. IT professionals are the technology experts, but TD professionals are responsible for delivering a right-fit learning and support experience to end users.

2.4.1.4 Troubleshooting and Downtime Administration

TD professionals should develop a consistent, scalable process for maintaining all learning technologies, including responsive troubleshooting and downtime management. Technology users should have a simple way to report technology challenges, such as a contact email, phone number, or online submission form. Service level agreements (SLAs) should be established for each platform based on how critical the technology is to the working experience so users understand how quickly specific problems will be resolved. Escalation processes should also be established to determine when to involve different internal and external partners in troubleshooting to avoid unnecessary expense, effort, or duplication of work. TD professionals should include these processes within all technology supplier contracts to ensure consistency and reliability. They should also regularly report to stakeholders and vendor partners regarding any downtime or functionality issues that are negatively affecting the end-user experience.

2.4.1.5 Administration Processes

All TD professionals who apply technology in their work should have a thorough understanding of the technology's features and functionality. This should be recognized within the context of the intended audience, the organization, and the broader IT ecosystem. Their understanding should be supplemented by technical documentation, which the supplier may provide, or augmented by internal experience, testing, and knowledge sharing. The supplier may also provide formal training during the implementation process, which should be leveraged by the TD professionals who will be held most responsible for administration of the tool.

TD professionals should define clear, scalable processes to perform all the basic functions of the technologies they implement for both administrative tasks and audience use cases. These processes should be designed to maximize the value of the technology, enhance adoption, and protect the end-user experience while also ensuring the consistent availability of key TD data, such as usage analytics and completion records. All processes and procedures, including an accountable stakeholder for each tool, should be documented in a shared location and regularly reviewed and updated as the technology ecosystem evolves.

2.4.1.6 Upgrade Process Management

TD professionals may be administrators for some learning technologies and should establish maintenance and upgrade processes for each. For hardware, this includes documenting the expected device life cycle and replacement plans. For software, they need to consider the supplier's regular update schedule. Due to the increased application of cloud technology, upgrades tend to take place more frequently and require less effort from administrators. Updates may even happen passively, without requiring any administrator action, sometimes without notice. When changes happen, administrators and other stakeholders must work together to analyze the scope of the updates and the potential impact. If necessary, they should prepare testing and change management plans to ensure a seamless transition.

2.4.1.7 Content Upload, Testing, and Management

TD professionals should ensure the quality and usability of all content that is created, revised, and delivered via technology platforms beginning with the initial upload and deployment and continuing through any technology changes or content updates. They should establish content testing and revision processes that fit the needs of their organization. Although testing should involve a variety of participants—including TD professionals, subject matter experts, stakeholders, and end users, when appropriate—processes should not be overly administrative or burdensome. TD professionals must recognize how to balance when a solution is "good enough" to avoid more investment than justified. Crafting quality control measures pragmatically will ensure acceptable standards are maintained within the constraints of available time and resources and errors are acknowledged and corrected when appropriate.

The life cycle of the content will vary based on topic and use, but steps should be taken to create a process for ensuring that outdated information or references are regularly removed or updated. Careful design and development should focus on content that has the longest shelf life with embedded links that will not go out of date.

2.4.1.8 Data Standards and Integrations (Such as SCORM, AICC, and xAPI)

TD administrators should work with organizational partners, including IT, HR, and other relevant groups, to determine integration opportunities for technology platforms. This is especially important for a learning delivery tool—such as a learning management system (LMS) or learning experience platform (LXP)—to ensure a simplified user and administrator experience that is consistent and scalable over time. Initial integration opportunities may include concepts such as single sign-on authentication and user provisioning.

2.4 Technology Application

Additional opportunities may include content delivery and aggregation, data record keeping, and user interface and experience elements. Integrations also help talent and development maintain a prominent role in the organization by embedding real-time data from the learning delivery systems into other high-impact processes. For example, integrations can allow managers to easily review learning records or recommend new learning programs within their routine processes for performance management or succession planning. All potential benefits should be balanced with the long-term technical support required to maintain the integration (if applicable).

TD professionals should maintain awareness of the content and data standards that are applied within their technology ecosystem. This may include a range of standards, such as:
- SCORM—Shareable Content Object Reference Model (1.2 or 2004)
- AICC—Aviation Industry Computer-Based Training Committee
- xAPI—Experience Application Programming Interface
- cmi5—computer managed instruction, fifth attempt

A range of coding formats, such as MP4, AVI, and MOV, may also be used for video-based content. TD professionals should apply formats that provide the desired user experience and work seamlessly with the audience's default hardware, software, and skills. All implemented technology should be interoperable to avoid unnecessary complexity or conflicts between systems. TD professionals should also maintain awareness of technical developments within the industry that may lead to the wide-scale adoption or decommissioning of a particular standard, such as Adobe Flash Player.

2.4.1.9 Reporting Tools and Processes

Before selecting a tool, TD professionals should develop a reporting strategy based on the needs of their organization. TD professionals should partner with internal experts in the business intelligence and operations departments to understand how their organization uses data. They should look for opportunities to integrate people analytics, including training completion, compliance, knowledge development, and behavior change metrics, with existing key performance indicators (KPIs). An effective reporting strategy should provide actionable data and recommendations to the right stakeholders at the right time. This strategy may include several considerations, including the impact of TD programs on organizational results, risks and compliance requirements, and user engagement statistics and feedback after learning activities. Reports may be provided to stakeholders in several ways—they can be integrated with existing organizational dashboards or leveraged as their own tools. In each case, data may be visualized or exported into a spreadsheet, document, or presentation for analysis and sharing.

TD professionals must be aware of privacy issues regarding user data. Data privacy and security issues largely depend on the type of data collected, how it will be used, and who will have access to it. The General Data Protection Regulation (GDPR) unifies data privacy laws across the European Union. In effect since 2018, it requires businesses to protect the personal data and privacy of EU citizens by keeping all customer information secure and confidential. It gives individuals more control over what personal data is collected by organizations, including the right to access, correct, and remove the data, as well as the right to restrict the processing of their data. Even if an organization has policies in place related to data privacy and GDPR, TD professionals need to be aware of the risks and requirements associated with compliance as they oversee technology administration and collect user data. [See 1.6.3]

2.4.1.10 Accessibility

TD professionals should consider a person's ability to access and properly engage with technology. Many disabilities are not easily observed or known; therefore, TD professionals should do their best to stay updated on accessibility standards and practices, including formal regulations, which vary around the world, as well as additional tactics that ensure talent development opportunities are available to everyone. In the United States, Section 508 of the Americans With Disabilities Act (ADA) requires that both employees of the federal government and members of the public with disabilities who are seeking information or services from a federal agency have "comparable access to and use of information and data as (do these groups) without disabilities, unless an undue burden would be imposed on the agency." Although it can be challenging to apply technology that is accessible to everyone, including people with cognitive, sensory, or mobility limitations, a learning and development platform should be accessible to all employees who need to use it. TD professionals should partner with accessibility experts to develop guidelines for identifying, developing, applying, and maintaining high-quality technology experiences for every user. [See 1.6]

Assessing, Selecting, and Implementing Learning Technology

2.4.2 Skill in Identifying, Defining, and Articulating Technology System Requirements to Support Learning and TD Solutions

> **I. Identifying, Defining, and Articulating Technology System Requirements**
>
> When defining learning technology system requirements, TD professionals should avoid the urge to focus on the new technology's features and marketing. Instead, they should begin with a thorough understanding of the desired user experience, content strategy for the tool, and learning outcomes.

2.4.2.1 Marketplace Awareness

Marketplace awareness is a critical factor in selecting a right-fit learning technology. With the speed of technological innovation, the marketplace may have changed considerably since TD professionals last explored new tools. Therefore, TD professionals with strategic oversight of their organization's learning technology ecosystem should dedicate time to following the latest industry advancements by attending webinars and conferences, reading publications and blogs, and networking with external peers. Many technology companies offer free trials of tools, which allow TD professionals to conduct hands-on evaluations of how a new technology could solve existing needs or enhance the end-user experience.

2.4.2.2 Organizational Needs Assessment

TD professionals should conduct an in-depth organizational needs assessment before exploring potential suppliers. This assessment must include a detailed exploration of the intended users' work experience. TD professionals should ask:

- What roles do the users perform within the organization?

- In what types of physical environments do they complete their work?
- How much time is available for learning and support activities in the typical workday?
- What tools, resources, and devices do they use when completing their work?
- What challenges do they face in performing their roles?
- What technological knowledge and skills are they expected to possess?
- How are they commonly supported from a talent development perspective?
- What content delivery tools and formats have they used in the past?
- How is their performance measured?

The results of this assessment should be used to identify functionality requirements and establish the scope of the technology evaluation effort. Needs assessments might lead TD professionals to consider developing custom solutions in-house if the necessary resources are available. They may decide to run small, targeted experiments to validate a new concept before starting a formal technology evaluation project. Rather than waiting for the opportunity to formally pilot a potential tool, they could quickly run an experiment using existing tools or prototypes with small sample audiences. Feedback gathered during these experiments can help shape the direction of the larger technology project and clarify feature requirements in an iterative process. [See 2.8.2]

2.4.2.3 Scope and Requirements Management

TD professionals who are responsible for managing technology evaluation should identify and document the scope of the project as well as the functional and technical requirements for any tool that will be considered:

- **Functional requirements** (or specifications) define what the system must do. They are based on business needs, focusing on what the user expects of the technology.
- **Technical requirements** (or specifications) define how the system works. They are based on how a business need can be achieved with the technology, focusing on the technical details and how the technology needs to be configured to meet the business requirements.

Depending on the scope of the need and tool being selected, requirements documentation can be complex. These considerations must be used throughout the project to ensure clarity and consistency. Otherwise, scope creep (the uncontrolled growth of a project) may take place, and the resulting technology decision may not meet the true needs of the organization. Scope creep may also cause the project to run over time and over budget. TD professionals should keep everyone involved in the project—including suppliers and internal stakeholders—aligned regarding the agreed-upon requirements. If a stakeholder wishes to expand the project's scope and introduce new requirements, TD professionals should engage the entire project team and reach a new agreement on scope before considering additional technology options.

Once a thorough analysis has been completed, TD professionals should document the project requirements in sufficient detail to enable the supplier selection process. This documentation should incorporate the same explanation that was used to define the platform functionality. [See 2.4.1.1] In addition, it should incorporate the change management plan for implementation. [See 3.6]

2.4.2.4 Project Management

Technology evaluation is a considerable responsibility that requires interaction with several potential suppliers and internal stakeholders. A new tool will likely cost an organization a considerable amount of money, time, and effort during contracting and implementation. Therefore, TD professionals who lead technology evaluation processes should have solid project management skills. They must effectively identify and coordinate the participation of people from across the organization, including peers, department stakeholders, subject matter experts, executives, and end users. They should gather all input and establish requirements before engaging with potential suppliers. During the process, they should involve the right people at the right time while maintaining the pace of the project to ensure the desired technology is implemented on time and on budget.

TD professionals should decide early in the project which project management model best suits their organization's needs. This might mean following a traditional, linear model through which a tool is carefully designed, cautiously developed, and implemented in its final desired state. In many cases, a more iterative approach is required to keep pace with technology advances. In an iterative model, technology is designed and delivered quickly, with further rounds of development happening concurrently to audience use. This allows the organization to benefit from core functionality more quickly and may lead to better technology solutions by incorporating user feedback while development is ongoing. However, the iterative approach requires more frequent communication between all stakeholders to ensure fixes are made quickly and the evolving product continues to work for everyone's needs. [See 1.5]

2.4.2.5 Stakeholder Management

Technology evaluation should include detailed interviews with stakeholders from the intended audience, including operational partners, senior management, and end users. Interviews help TD professionals understand organizational goals beyond learning and development. They also determine how the effectiveness of any new learning technology or initiative will be measured. It's important that the right stakeholders are included when gathering requirements to ensure they are aligned with the final selection and implementation plan. IT will be a key stakeholder in any organizational technology project and must be included early in the process. [See 1.3.2, 3.2.2, and 3.2.3]

2.4.2.6 User Technology Experience Design

Talent development technology is part of an organization's larger technology ecosystem. People use a variety of tools to do their work, and learning and support tools are part of the overall technology ecosystem. Employees are interacting with more technology than ever to conduct their work, communicate, collaborate, and learn, especially when they are in a remote or hybrid work environment. Therefore, TD professionals should consider the overall design of the user's technology experience when selecting new tools.

To start, TD professionals should consider whether existing tools could be used in lieu of new technology. An organizational needs assessment can help identify gaps in the desired TD experience, which can then be used to evaluate current processes and consider more efficient and effective uses of existing technology to address those gaps. If TD tools are needed, they should fit within the larger technology ecosystem—whether they're formally integrated with existing technologies or simply work alongside them through a less formal experience design. The learning technology ecosystem likely extends beyond tools that were implemented by TD

2.4 Technology Application

professionals or with the distinct purpose of delivering structured training, and may include social media platforms, a company intranet, chat functions, and other technologies both inside and outside the organization.

In addition to the user experience, TD professionals should understand the technological capabilities of their organization. A strong, ongoing partnership with IT will help them become familiar with the technology infrastructure into which any new learning platforms would be introduced, including considerations such as available IT support, regulations, processes, hardware and software options, integration requirements, accessibility guidelines, Wi-Fi availability, mobile device usage, and network bandwidth. TD professionals should stay apprised of IT's future improvement plans, including any infrastructure or device updates in their short- or long-term technology road map.

2.4.2.7 Data Integrations

Integrations are an important consideration when designing a modern talent development experience. Therefore, integration requirements should be included in any technology assessment process. Integrations may include data-based integrations (such as user provision, recordkeeping, and single sign-on) and content integration (which allow objects to move across platforms to facilitate ease of use and administration). Technical integrations may require custom development work, which needs to be clarified with all technology suppliers and properly included in the project scope and budget. It's also important to consider accessibility and IT regulations and processes when selecting any TD technology. [See 2.4.1.8 and 2.4.1.10]

2.4.2.8 Procurement and the RFI or RFP Process

A request for information or proposal (RFI or RFP) process is common when looking for right-fit technology providers and products. Such requests should be based on the requirements identified in the organizational analysis and focus on the desired end-user experience rather than a list of unnecessary features. TD professionals should use this request to challenge prospective suppliers on their ability to execute the desired end-user experience. Although they should be open to alternative approaches, TD professionals should also remain steadfast regarding the core problems they are trying to solve through technology. These requirements can be used to guide supplier discussions, pitches, and demonstrations, as well as stakeholder and user feedback to make the ultimate decision regarding platform selection.

2.4.3 Knowledge of Criteria and Techniques for Evaluating and Selecting E-Learning Software and Tools

I. Evaluating and Selecting E-Learning Software

E-learning is an important part of a modern digital learning strategy, especially within large organizations with geographically dispersed workforces. E-learning is a structured course or learning experience delivered electronically through a wide set of applications and processes, including web-based, computer-based, and multi-device learning. It usually refers to self-led or self-directed learning. TD professionals should establish clear criteria for selecting tools that support the development of high-quality digital learning content. These tools may also be used by partners outside the TD department to write content specific to their areas of expertise. [See 2.2.7.4]

When TD professionals select e-learning software and tools, they should remember several requirements, although they're not specifically detailed in this capability:

- **Marketplace awareness**—stay current with changes. [See 2.4.2.1]
- **Workplace context**—understand the end user's day-to-day context. [See 2.4.3.3]
- **Accessibility**—consider accessibility requirements. [See 2.4.1.10]
- **Reporting and compliance**—validate that a potential development tool can capture and export the required data before implementation. [See 2.4.1.9]
- **Impact**—have a clear idea of the behavior the tool is intended to change or the knowledge it is intended to transfer.

2.4.3.1 Instructional Design Knowledge

To properly leverage e-learning design tools, TD professionals should understand instructional design principles and establish a methodology that aligns with the needs of their organization. These standards should be established before implementing the technology to ensure the selected tool can execute all content requirements. TD professionals should also recognize the skills available within their organization to properly use a new authoring tool, including both formal instructional design and developer roles as well as subject matter experts who may be expected to use a tool to develop digital content. They should select a tool that balances their organization's design process, quality requirements, and skill level. [See 2.2.1]

2.4.3.2 Content and Training Modalities

Training can be delivered in many modalities, including digital modules (e-learning), videos, classroom sessions, job shadowing, games and simulations, and reference materials. When TD professionals select tools to build and deliver training, they should consider the mix of modalities needed throughout their organizations. They should also consider existing content and whether to maintain the legacy format or redevelop it using a more modern platform. Format compatibility for both work and delivery files must be considered when selecting a new authoring platform.

2.4.3.3 Delivery Technology

An effective e-learning strategy often requires multiple, well-aligned tools. When selecting an e-learning platform, TD professionals should consider which delivery tools their intended audiences will use to access digital content. The authoring tool must be capable of building and exporting content formats that can be uploaded and accessed by existing (or new) delivery technologies. For example, if the delivery platform is an LMS that is commonly accessed via users' mobile devices, an authoring tool must allow for the development of output files that can be accessed easily via a mobile device. TD professionals should ensure all desired formats—such as HTML5, SCORM (1.2 or 2004), AICC, xAPI, or cmi5—can be exported from the selected tool with publish settings that are compatible to their hosting systems.

2.4.3.4 E-Learning Authoring Software Accessibility

TD professionals should implement e-learning authoring software that allows them to develop and output content that aligns with accessibility regulations and best practices. They should work with their suppliers and internal partners to ensure all content developed with a potential tool meets these standards before implementation. New training content should be designed considering accessibility from the start, which often generates a better learning experience for every participant. [See 2.4.1.10 and 1.6]

2.4 Technology Application

2.4.3.5 Experimentation

E-learning authoring software is commonly licensed by the supplier to an individual user, often with free trial periods. Therefore, the TD professionals are able to experiment with multiple tools quickly and with limited expense before deploying them to the entire organization. A limited number of content developers should be tasked with testing potential tools using a defined process that includes creating new content and editing existing modules (if applicable). Experimental content can be published to test users through all potential delivery technology to ensure everything functions as expected. TD professionals can also experiment with new tools released to the marketplace even if they are not considering a new implementation.

2.4.3.6 User Testing

The intended audience for e-learning content developed with a new authoring tool should be included in the testing process, even though they will not use the tool themselves. TD professionals should provide sample content from the new authoring tools to a testing group through their standard delivery platform and request feedback regarding key elements of the learning experience. This will help them make a more informed, user-focused decision regarding potential technology additions. If people outside the TD department will be expected to use the software to develop their own digital learning content, additional user testing should be conducted.

2.4.4 Skill in Identifying, Selecting, and Implementing Learning Technologies

> **I. Identifying, Selecting, and Implementing Learning Technologies**
>
> When identifying, selecting, and implementing a learning technology, TD professionals should focus on what their organization needs and the user experience they want to create. They should establish assessment criteria based on the proven needs of the organization, ensuring all technology is selected and implemented with a clear purpose.
>
> When TD professionals define learning technologies, they should remember several requirements, although they're not specifically detailed in this capability:
> - **User technology experience**—consider the overall design of the user's technology experience. [See 2.4.2.6]
> - **Workplace context**—understand the end users' day-to-day context. [See 2.4.3.3]
> - **Stakeholder management**—include detailed interviews with stakeholders to understand the goals of the organization beyond the basics of learning and development. [See 2.4.2.3 and 2.4.2.5]
> - **Accessibility**—consider accessibility requirements. [See 2.4.1.10]
> - **Reporting**—validate compliance and whether a potential development tool can capture and export the required data before implementation. [See 2.4.1.9]
> - **IT regulations**—align with established IT regulations and processes, and partner with them to develop an understanding of how they operate before requesting project support. [See 2.4.1.2 and 2.4.1.3]

2.4.4.1 Aligning Learning Technology to Instructional Content

Training can be delivered in many ways, including digital content (e-learning modules, videos, and reference materials), job training, and classroom sessions. TD professionals should consider the mix of modalities that will be of greatest value to their intended audiences when selecting and implementing learning technology.

Although the tools may or may not be formally integrated, they all serve as part of a learning ecosystem and must complement one another within the organization's talent development strategy. For example, even though an authoring tool may primarily be used to build digital content, this content may also be used as part of a blended experience that includes performance support tools or stand-alone communications. TD professionals should also consider legacy tools and content modalities when introducing new technology. They should decide whether to retire these elements, maintain them in their legacy format, or rebuild them using the new technology.

2.4.4.2 Reporting and Compliance Requirements

Selected tools must be able to capture and export the information required to meet all data strategy and record-keeping requirements. This data may be exported from a learning content object to a delivery system (such as an LMS) or another database (such as a data warehouse or LRS). For example, a self-paced course may send a score or completion status back to the hosting system. TD professionals should also consider technology reporting capabilities, including data visualizations, dashboards, and exports. Reporting must meet both internal and external regulatory requirements and provide the desired ease of use when sharing information with stakeholders. [See 3.7.5]

2.4.4.3 Matching the Correct Tool to the Intended Outcome

Selecting technology tools for learning is similar to selecting instructional design methods. TD professionals should recognize that selecting the correct tool begins by determining if the objective is to gain knowledge, acquire a skill, or influence an attitude, ensuring that the technology is selected and implemented with a clear purpose. They must also consider how the tool supports the ability to assess if the objective has been achieved, including whether the tool will allow for assessments throughout, whether pretests would be useful, and what other assessments are necessary to measure knowledge transfer or behavior change. Finally, before matching the correct tool to the intended outcome, TD professionals should explore constraints that dictate what can or cannot be achieved. Constraints can be categorized as:

- **Organizational**—such as employees on different shifts, heavy travel schedules, or remote locations
- **Individual**—such as a wide variation in technology skills or language variations
- **Managerial**—such as lack of support or limited communication channels
- **Technological**—such as limited equipment or home office employees using personal computers
- **Resource-specific**—such as a limited budget for technology or an understaffed workforce

2.4.5 Knowledge of Methods and Techniques for Testing the Usability and Functionality of Learning Technologies and Support Systems

I. Methods and Techniques for Testing Usability

The purpose of usability testing is to provide more effective learning and development experiences for the end users. Usability testing refers to "evaluating a product or service by testing it with representative users" (Usability.gov 2013a). Within talent development initiatives, usability testing may be applied to hardware devices, software platforms, or training content during initial implementation or version updates. TD professionals should define testing requirements for all hardware and software tools, which will ensure that problems are identified and resolved before they can negatively affect the intended users.

2.4.5.1 Establishing Success Criteria

TD professionals should establish clear success criteria for all technology evaluation processes. The foremost factor to consider is user experience—technology should be acquired to implement a user-friendly talent development ecosystem that fits the needs of employees now and into the future. Additional requirements to consider include:

- **Workplace context.** Technology should fit the end users' day-to-day work realities.
- **Accessibility.** Hardware and software must meet all regulatory and organizational requirements regarding accessibility for all potential users.
- **Integrations.** New tools should integrate with existing technology in formal and informal ways.
- **Format and data interoperability.** Content and data should be easily shared between new and existing tools whenever possible.
- **Objectives.** Content should meet the desired knowledge transfer or behavior change objectives for the intended audience. Many technology systems include analytics and reporting that can be used to assess the effectiveness of the tools.
- **Reporting and compliance.** Validate compliance and whether a potential development tool can capture and export the required data before implementation. [See 2.4.1.9]

The evaluation success criteria should be documented and shared with all project participants to ensure alignment and scope management.

2.4.5.2 Project Management

TD professionals who test the usability and functionality of learning technologies and support systems should have solid project management skills. They should be able to identify and coordinate the participation of people from across the organization, including peers, department stakeholders, subject matter experts, executives, and end users. They should be well-versed in multiple project management models and be able to use the model that best suits the needs of the project and their stakeholders. [See 1.5 and 2.4.2.4]

2.4.5.3 Test Script Development

TD professionals should ensure that technology testing processes cover the full range of situations in which the technology will be used. Depending on the tool and intended use, this may require the creation of scripts, which guide participants to complete specific tasks during an evaluation. Test scripts are a line-by-line description of each step (and the expected result) that is performed to validate the system under consideration. They should be aligned with the established success criteria and reflect the real-world use of the tool. Scripts should provide enough detail to direct the test user to complete the desired function. The test environment should simulate a realistic experience; therefore, the script should not provide more guidance than will be available to the standard user when the technology is implemented. Test scripts can be used during initial technology evaluation as well as during future upgrade processes.

2.4.5.4 Testing Processes

The testing process should be clearly outlined based on the established success criteria as well as internal technology standards and requirements. Testing should take place within a realistic setting that is similar (if not identical) to the context in which the product will ultimately be used. If software or content is being tested, the test should be run on the same devices that participants will use during full deployment.

TD professionals may approach a technology evaluation and implementation using different methods. In every case, however, they should first establish clear processes, responsibilities, timelines, and measures of success. Evaluation and implementation can be:

- **Immediate.** If the technology is the result of extreme vetting or leverages an existing technology that is proven within the organization, it may be implemented with the full audience immediately without additional testing.
- **Piloted.** When a technology is implemented to a test group for a period of time, it's called a pilot. Upon the completion of the pilot period, the project team reviews the results and determines whether it makes sense to continue with a larger implementation.
- **Phased.** A phased implementation plan for the full user audience is created through a series of evaluation milestones. The technology is then implemented with a select audience, and project success criteria are reviewed once the first milestone is reached. However, unlike a pilot, the implementation does not stop during the review. If the technology is deemed successful, it then expands to the next audience and the milestone review process continues until the full implementation is complete or the project is halted.

TD professionals can collect usability testing data in many ways. Depending on the product being tested, they can collect data directly from the platform or device to analyze how users complete tasks. They may also deploy surveys or conduct feedback discussions after testing is complete to gather anecdotal feedback. Testing can also be used to observe real users interacting with the system in unguided testing sessions. TD professionals should analyze all the collected data to make decisions regarding the next steps toward implementation.

2.4.5.5 Stakeholder Testing

Usability testing should incorporate detailed interviews with stakeholders within the intended audience, including operational partners, senior management, and end users. Testing should ensure that what was built aligns to their needs. If it does not align, TD professionals should work with the tester, the technology provider, and other internal stakeholders to determine what needs to change. This will help them understand the needs of their organization beyond talent development. Further testing should be planned, as needed, to validate any changes.

2.4.5.6 Tester and User Management

A test group should include a range of participants from within the project group, with users from the intended audience being among the most important. These testers should represent the general audience population and not be hand selected by management. The testing group may also include stakeholders who are actively participating in the technology project as well as other TD and IT professionals. Test group participation should include representation from all key audience groups and stakeholders, but the number of individual testers should be kept to a minimum to avoid slowing down the project.

Building a Workplace Technology Ecosystem

2.4.6 Knowledge of Existing Learning Technologies and Support Systems

I. Existing Learning Technologies

In most cases, one technology cannot provide all the support a workforce requires. Therefore, TD professionals should have a strong knowledge of learning technologies and be able to apply them. These tools make up an organization's learning technology ecosystem and enable the overall working and learning experience for each person.

When TD professionals are involved with existing learning technologies, they should remember several requirements, although they're not specifically detailed in this capability:

- **User technology experience**—consider the overall design of the user's technology experience. [See 2.4.2.6]
- **Workplace context**—understand the end user's day-to-day context. [See 2.4.3.3]
- **Accessibility**—consider accessibility requirements. [See 2.4.1.10]

2.4.6.1 Purposeful System Selection and Integration

Learning technologies can be sorted into categories based on intended use, including:

- **Development.** These tools are used by TD professionals to create learning content in many modalities, including e-learning programs, videos, documents, and imagery.
- **Delivery.** User-facing hardware or software are used for accessing learning content and include LMSs, learning experience platforms (LXPs), virtual reality applications, virtual classrooms, remote sites, and mobile devices.
- **Management.** Administrative tools are used to manage the storage and execution of learning activities, such as content management systems and administrator portals.
- **Social.** User-facing tools enable sharing, access, and discussion of workplace information and learning content.
- **Virtual collaboration.** Physically disconnected and distributed workers require tools that allow for synchronous and asynchronous communication, video conferencing, collaboration, reporting, and document management. [See 3.8.4.3]
- **Adaptive.** These tools use data and user interactions to intelligently assign content and resources based on the unique needs, knowledge, and skills of each individual user.
- **Analysis.** These platforms are designed to collect, store, and analyze data, such as an LRS, data visualization tool, database, or data warehouse.

Other technologies that weren't acquired or managed by the TD department may also be used to support talent development initiatives. These may include intranets, point-of-sale systems, customer relationship management tools, survey tools or other resources to support evaluating the impact of learning, and existing social media platforms.

Tools should be added to the organizational learning ecosystem with purpose. New resources should complement, rather than duplicate or complicate, existing resources. The ecosystem should be consistently re-evaluated based on the changing needs of the organization and end users as well as improvements in the marketplace.

2.4.6.2 Learning Technology Ecosystem Architecture

TD professionals should work with their organizational partners to help users get the most value from their overall technology ecosystem. This includes establishing a clear purpose for each implemented technology and integrating tools in ways that will create the simplest end-user experience. [See 2.4.2.6]

2.4.6.3 Strategic Tool Selection and Application

Technologies should be selected and implemented with a clear purpose, including user-facing technologies (such as LMSs) and TD tools (such as content authoring software). As the needs of their organization change, TD professionals should continuously evaluate the learning ecosystem to make sure each tool's intended purpose remains viable. Over time, some tools may take on new or additional value while others are no longer necessary.

Like consumer technology, workplace technology evolves at a rapid pace. Therefore, TD professionals should maintain constant awareness of new products and capabilities, even if they are not able to acquire or implement new technology. This will help organizations identify when new technology can solve existing obstacles and deliver a better overall experience for end users, while reducing the chance of content outages and technical issues due to obsolete formats.

2.4.6.4 Modality Options

TD professionals should remain well versed in the variety of content modalities that can be used to enable performance. This includes digital content (such as e-learning modules, videos, podcasts, virtual reality applications, adaptive support tools, toolkits, and knowledge sharing) as well as other experiences (including classroom sessions, job training, and mentoring). Although not all modalities may apply within a single organization, TD professionals should consider all options based on their workplace context, objectives, and instructional design methodology. As learning technology evolves, new modalities will continue to emerge and provide new opportunities for talent development.

2.4.6.5 Data Collection and Reporting

The potential for TD professionals to leverage data in new ways often evolves alongside related technologies. Therefore, they should maintain awareness of new data and reporting capabilities, even if they are not able to introduce them within their organizations right away. These capabilities may help them build a case for investing in new technology, especially if they can provide clear value to the organization and improve the user's learning experience. Stakeholders and regulators are asking for more sophisticated evidence that demonstrates the effectiveness of TD initiatives. A strong knowledge of the latest data reporting options allows TD professionals to design and implement content with measurement in mind from the start.

2.4.6.6 Delivery and Access Options

TD professionals often need to leverage hardware devices that are already being used within the organization for training delivery. This may include desktops or laptops, company-issued mobile devices, workplace systems, and personal mobile devices. TD professionals should work with IT and platform administrators to

2.4.6.7 User Behavior, Motivation, and Preferences

stay updated on their organization's technology ecosystem and related guidelines. This will help them make more informed decisions when evaluating new learning technologies. They should also keep a record of issues encountered by users when accessing certain forms of content. This is helpful when working with IT to determine if any changes can be made to correct access issues.

2.4.6.7 User Behavior, Motivation, and Preferences

Technology is a ubiquitous part of everyone's life. TD professionals can learn from how people interact with their everyday tools, even if the same technologies are not applied within the workplace. They should stay abreast of consumer technology trends, including best practices for user engagement, behavior, and motivation. Many of these concepts come from well-researched studies in the field of cognitive psychology and are applied in practice more quickly in consumer tools. Similar tactics may become applicable within an organization, especially if they are introduced to support learning and performance. However, TD professionals should always take care to apply their workplace context to these concepts and not assume that because something works in everyday life, it will work the same way within the workplace. They must also balance a wider range of ethical implications when considering user behavior. A practice may be known to drive engagement or online activity, but if it is detrimental to the overall goals of the organization or the well-being of the individual users, it should not be implemented. [See 3.3.10]

2.4.7 Knowledge of Human Resources Systems and Technology Platforms and How They Integrate With Other Organizational and Business Systems and Processes

I. Integrating Human Resources Systems and Technology Platforms With Other Systems

Human resources teams, especially within larger organizations, use a variety of technologies to support the employee life cycle, including tools dedicated to talent acquisition, performance management, payroll administration, and engagement. Because talent development is part of the overall HR technology ecosystem, TD professionals should understand how these components fit together to provide a high-value HR experience.

When TD professionals integrate HR systems and technology with other organizational systems and processes, they should remember several requirements, although they're not specifically detailed in this capability:

- **User technology experience**—consider the overall design of the user's technology experience. [See 2.4.2.6]
- **Learning technology ecosystem architecture**—include all HR tools that people use to support their continued development. [See 2.4.6.2 and 2.4.6.3]
- **Accessibility**—consider accessibility requirements. [See 2.4.1.10]
- **Reporting and compliance**—validate compliance and whether a potential development tool can capture and export the required data before implementation. [See 2.4.1.9]
- **IT regulations and processes**—align with established IT regulations and processes and partner with IT to understand how they operate before requesting project support. [See 2.4.1.2 and 2.4.1.3]

2.4.7.1 Purposeful System Selection and Integration

All technologies should be implemented and integrated with clear purpose. Some HR tools are part of a suite of systems from one supplier. However, rather than automatically implementing each tool because it is part of an overall package, TD professionals should vet each one individually to ensure it is the right system and meets the needs of the organization. To avoid confusion among users, steps should be taken to streamline access options by avoiding redundant applications, buttons, or views that don't serve a unique purpose. Technical integrations often require additional internal IT resources and can slow down the implementation process. Therefore, this additional effort should only be made if there is clear value to the organization or end user. For example, establishing integration between HR and TD systems for provisioning user access can simplify the user experience and reduce administrative work. TD professionals should also follow all established internal guidelines and external regulations regarding data governance and privacy when integrating systems. [See 3.1, 1.6.3, and 1.6.5]

2.4.7.2 Data Integration and Reporting

TD professionals may explore a variety of data integrations to reduce administrative tasks and improve the user experience. In some cases, TD tools (such as an LMS) are bundled within a larger HR software suite to simplify integration and increase the ability to share data and content. A common integration is single sign-on, which allows users to access HR systems with a common login. Integrations may also provide user demographic data or security and authentication tools to maintain a list of active and qualified employees or automate audience selection for targeted TD initiatives. TD professionals must abide by data privacy and security regulations when collecting and using personal data. [See 1.6]

TD professionals should understand their organization's reporting requirements—including internal stakeholder reporting, audience identification, and record-keeping requirements for external auditors and regulators—before determining how to integrate HR and TD tools. Integration may help TD professionals leverage organizational and employee data to provide better learning opportunities that align with established needs. TD professionals should work with organizational partners, including IT, HR, and other relevant units, to determine integration opportunities. They should follow all established reporting processes and guidelines. [See 3.2]

2.4.8 Knowledge of Communication Technologies and Their Applications

I. Communication Technologies and Their Applications

Communication tools are an important part of the workplace learning and support experience. Employees use tools to communicate and collaborate within the workplace, which provides opportunities for informal learning. TD professionals may use similar tools to communicate with their audiences and should select tools that ensure effective message delivery as well as meaningful participant engagement. Instead of creating a new social media platform for a TD project, for example, it may be more effective to add TD content to an existing platform that employees are already using on a frequent basis. TD professionals should understand the platform features and design learning experiences that fit the capabilities of the technology.

When TD professionals apply communication technology, they should remember several requirements that are not specifically detailed in this capability:
- **User technology experience**—consider the overall design of the user's technology experience. [See 2.4.2.6]

- Workplace context—understand the end user's day-to-day context. [See 2.4.3.3]
- Accessibility—consider accessibility requirements. [See 2.4.1.10]
- IT regulations and processes—align with established IT regulations and processes and partner with IT to understand how they operate before requesting project support. [See 2.4.1.2 and 2.4.1.3]

2.4.8.1 Types of Communication Tools

TD professionals can leverage workplace communication tools to support talent development activities. They should always develop content that fits the specific means of delivery. For example, video and web-conferencing tools are commonly used as online classrooms for synchronous virtual events, which can reach a remote or distributed audience with a consistent, engaging message. These platforms may be selected specifically for learning purposes or used for meetings and other virtual events across an organization. TD professionals should leverage interactive features such as chat, polls, emojis, and whiteboards, when appropriate, to involve participants more directly in the experience. They should design the online experience based on the participants' context, including available time, technology, familiarity, and bandwidth. Traditional classroom content should not be transferred directly to an online setting unless it was designed for both purposes.

TD professionals may also leverage technology in the classroom to facilitate message delivery and audience engagement. Presentation software is a ubiquitous part of the classroom learning experience; however, like any other technology, it should be used only when it adds to the participants' experience. Visual design principles—such as color selection, slide layout, and font sizing—should be applied to all presentations. Rather than using slides as a handout, TD professionals should leverage visual presentations to support facilitated delivery and provide separate documentation for ongoing reference. Depending on their audience and the needs of their organization, TD professionals should consider delivering any support guides or documentation in a digital-first format, which avoids unnecessary environmental waste, streamlines updating and maintenance, and allows participants to retrieve and use key information in the moment of need. [See 2.2]

2.4.8.2 Applications for Communication Tools

TD professionals should consider how users traditionally engage with communication tools for existing use cases and tasks. When possible, TD professionals should align with existing use cases rather than expecting users to change their behavior or learn new functionalities. [See 2.4.3.3]

2.4.8.3 Instructional Design

When leveraging communication tools to support learning, TD professionals should balance the established or intended use of the tool with their established instructional design practices. Tools should not be forced into a predefined instructional model. Rather, TD professionals should consider how they can expand their instructional practices by leveraging familiar, right-fit tools to communicate important messages and reinforce the desired knowledge transfer or behavior change.

2.4.8.4 User Preferences

TD professionals should take established user preferences and behaviors into account when leveraging a workplace communication tool to support learning activities. They should conduct research to determine how a tool is being used and explore existing user feedback. During design, they should take advantage of the technology's capabilities while also aligning with established user expectations, which supports adoption of the tool for the new purpose and simplifies the user experience so they can focus on the message being delivered. [See 2.2]

2.4.8.5 Delivery and Access for Devices

The TD professional often needs to leverage technology that is already in use within their organization to deliver talent development solutions. A common example is when existing communication tools are employed to support talent development activities. [See 2.4.6]

Building Learning Technology Tools

2.4.9 Knowledge of Principles of User Interface Design

> **I. User Interface Design Principles**
>
> A user interface (UI) is how an individual interacts with a technology platform or content module. This typically involves a combination of hardware and software to facilitate user input. TD professionals should apply good UI design principles when building custom platforms, creating new integrations, customizing off-the-shelf platforms, or developing interactive digital content.
>
> When TD professionals are involved in UI design, they should remember several requirements, although they're not specifically detailed in this capability:
> - **Accessibility**—consider accessibility requirements. [See 2.4.1.10]
> - **Delivery and access to devices**—remember to leverage communication technology software that is already in use within the organization. [See 2.4.6]

2.4.9.1 User Interface Design Principles

The elements of a good UI include but are not limited to:
- **Input controls**—buttons, text fields, dropdown lists, toggles, and natural language processing
- **Navigation**—breadcrumbs, search fields, icons, pagination, and virtual environments
- **Information**—icons, progress indicators, notifications, text, videos, audio, and scenarios

To properly apply these elements, TD professionals, possibly in collaboration with UI design experts, should understand the users, including their goals, knowledge, skills, and preferences. An interface should be simple and avoid the need for additional instruction or extra labels. TD professionals may consider leveraging familiar concepts and best practices from everyday technology and content experiences, such as popular websites and social media applications. An interface should also be consistent, meaning that once a user learns how to do something, they can use this knowledge elsewhere in the experience. All color, text, texture, and imagery decisions should maximize readability and attention. Finally, a good UI communicates with the user and makes sure they understand where they are within the platform or content and how their actions are interacting with the system.

TD professionals who aren't familiar with UI design principles or do not have the skill available in-house should consult with subject matter experts or engage an external designer for support to ensure a high-quality technology and content experience.

2.4.9.2 User Experience Design

User interface (UI) and user experience (UX) design are evolving practices, much like the overall technology marketplace. TD professionals, especially those responsible for the design of technology and content experiences, should be aware of new developments in the UX discipline, which will allow them to bring familiar concepts into their learning experience designs. They may also partner with internal or external UI and UX experts to support their continued learning and awareness of the topic.

2.4.9.3 Design Thinking

Design thinking is a process for creative problem solving that focuses on the human experience (IDEO U 2018). This approach combines the needs of people, the capabilities of technology, and the requirements of the organization to arrive at a right-fit solution. TD professionals can leverage design thinking to develop technology and content experiences that best fit the real-world needs of their audiences. Although design thinking is not a linear process, it typically involves several fundamental features:

- **Frame the question.** Focus on the question driving the need for a learning solution.
- **Identify the needs of the target audience.** Gather feedback and information about those who will be most affected.
- **Gather inspiration.** Explore related solutions and concepts to potentially inspire a new idea.
- **Generate ideas.** Consider a wide range of possibilities to avoid the obvious, potentially less-effective solutions.
- **Make ideas tangible.** Experiment with basic prototypes.
- **Test to learn.** Gather feedback from stakeholders and end users through rapid testing.
- **Share the story.** Frame the chosen solution in terms of the human story and real-world application.

2.4.9.4 Prototyping Tools and Processes

UI and UX designers can use prototypes to rapidly test with users and stakeholders. Rather than building a fully functioning application, designers can focus the test on key components of the user experience, such as navigation, interactions, and look and feel. Prototypes can be built with a variety of tools, including online applications with an array of built-in designer options and feedback collection options. TD professionals may also leverage existing tools, such as presentation software, to build basic prototypes for quick sharing and review. Prototypes can be sketched on paper or portrayed in simple shapes, as long as the visual representation allows the relevant stakeholders to understand the concept and share meaningful feedback. Prototypes are useful during early iterations of technology design and testing. [See 2.4.5.3 and 2.4.5.4]

2.4.9.5 App Development Tools and Processes

UI and UX design principles are especially important for TD professionals who design custom applications. Off-the-shelf learning technologies often have limited customization options. Similarly, training content typically fits within the UI and UX of the delivery technology with minimal design requirements. However, even small decisions in publish settings and content presentation can have a meaningful impact on the user experience, so it is essential to consider the audience's needs and preferences and to pursue user experience testing when appropriate. Custom applications require a more comprehensive design effort because they can stand alone and involve many design decisions from concept to execution.

2.4 Technology Application

Depending on the desired functionality and available skills, applications may either be custom built using a programming language or with digital authoring tools that require little to no coding knowledge. TD professionals should consider the expected life cycle of an application, along with the amount of continued maintenance requirements, when deciding how to develop the program. If their organization doesn't have the skills or resources needed, TD professionals may contract a third-party developer to create the program. Like new technologies and content modules, applications should be tested using well-documented and managed review processes. [See 2.4.5.3 and 2.4.5.4]

2.4.9.6 Ensuring Accessibility Through UI and UX Designs
UI and UX design are critical parts of ensuring accessibility standards and requirements are met for all intended users. [See 2.4.1.10]

2.4.9.7 Testing UI and UX Designs
Just as with any other new piece of content or technology, UI and UX designs should be tested under realistic conditions with representative users. Minimal additional instruction should be provided to ensure the test mirrors real-world use. TD professionals should observe users as they navigate the UI and collect feedback at the end of the test period. Designers can then apply relevant responses to improve the experience before the UI is fully implemented. [See 2.4.5.3 and 2.4.5.4]

2.4.10 Skill in Developing Artificial Intelligence, Machine Learning Algorithms, Augmented Reality, Virtual Reality, and Mixed Reality Tools That Are Ethical and Free of Bias

> **I. Developing AI, Machine Learning Algorithms, AR, VR, and Other Mixed Reality Tools**
>
> TD professionals should have a clear understanding of new technology with a specific focus on the ethical issues surrounding AI, AR, VR, and other mixed reality tools.
>
> When TD professionals develop AI, machine learning, AR, VR, and mixed reality tools, they should remember several requirements, although they're not specifically detailed in this capability:
> - **User experience design**—study the overall design of the user's technology experience. [See 2.4.2.6]
> - **Accessibility**—consider accessibility requirements. [See 2.4.1.10]
> - **IT regulations and processes**—align with established IT regulations and processes and partner with IT to understand how they operate before requesting project support. [See 2.4.7]
> - **Delivery and access to devices**—remember to leverage technology that is already used within the organization to deliver talent development solutions. [See 2.4.7]

2.4.10.1 Artificial Intelligence Concepts, Definitions, and Use Cases
AI is typically defined as "the ability of a machine to perform cognitive functions that are associated with human minds, such as perceiving, reasoning, learning, interacting with the environment, problem solving, and even exercising creativity" and includes two critical subdomains (Chui, Kamalnath, and McCarthy 2018):
- **Machine learning algorithms** "detect patterns and learn how to make predictions and recommendations by processing data and experiences, rather than by receiving explicit programming instruction."

- **Deep learning** is a type of machine learning "that can process a wider range of data resources, requires less data preprocessing by humans, and can often produce more accurate results than traditional machine-learning approaches."

AI-enabled tools are quickly being introduced within a variety of industries and functions. TD professionals should have a fundamental understanding of how AI and automation affect their organizations so they can adjust their training programs to enable new types of work. Knowledge of AI and machine learning also open TD professionals to new learning and support strategies. They may leverage AI through a wide range of applications, including personalized and adaptive learning, video and content creation tools, content recommendation engines, natural language processing, translation services, voice-activated interfaces, digital assistants, and advanced data analysis. TD professionals should partner with internal AI experts as well as external suppliers to determine how they can best leverage AI in their training strategies.

2.4.10.2 Augmented Reality Concepts and Use Cases

AR overlays digital information onto real-world environments using a mobile or head-mounted device. This information may include navigation directions, location information, schematics and product details, translations, or many other location-based details. AR is valuable for TD professionals as a means of performance support because targeted information can be displayed in context without requiring the user to stop their work.

Although AR can be accessed with a typical smartphone or tablet, it is increasingly applied using purpose-built devices, such as smart glasses and helmets, which are a natural fit for the working environment. Several AR software tools are available for developing custom applications, and familiar TD tools are increasingly introducing AR capabilities as well.

2.4.10.3 Virtual Reality Concepts and Use Cases

VR uses a head-mounted display or headset or a 2D device like a smartphone or computer screen, to immerse a user in a 3D environment. Users can explore this fully rendered digital environment and manipulate objects using handheld controls, voice commands, or their keyboard or other input devices. VR is valuable for TD professionals when delivering learning content that's dangerous or hard to replicate, such as emergency response events or heavy equipment simulations. With VR, users can learn through realistic application, failure, and receive immediate feedback with minimal risk to themselves, others, or property.

The metaverse—in which humans, as avatars, interact with one another in a virtual space—also promises new opportunities to meet and collaborate in virtual words using either advanced VR headsets or simple browser applications. TD professionals can host live experiences in these environments to enhance onboarding sessions and enable learning cohorts to collaborate in new ways. These activities are a good way to build networking relationships in remote work environments, which do not allow individuals opportunities to interact in-person, and they can also add value to traditional workplaces as part of a blended learning approach.

VR often requires custom hardware, software, and content, although the barriers to entry are lowering. VR headsets are becoming more powerful and affordable, popular applications allow participation in virtual worlds from 2D smartphones or computers, and rapid authoring tools are emerging that allow even novice users to begin building virtual content and worlds. However, the most immersive content still requires considerable investment and skill to develop. TD professionals should monitor the latest trends to identify opportunities to effectively apply various levels of virtual technology within their resource constraints.

2.4.10.4 Assessing AI and Mixed Reality in the Workplace

AI and mixed reality technologies may represent new components of the workplace experience for many people. Therefore, TD professionals should assess how these tools will alter the way people work and learn. They should also determine how to best articulate the value of these tools to motivate people to adopt the technology and adjust their behavior accordingly.

2.4.10.5 AI and Machine Learning Tools

AI is quickly becoming a foundational capability within many TD technologies, including content delivery tools and those used for needs analysis and measuring TD effectiveness. TD professionals should work with their partners and suppliers to understand how AI is being applied within the systems they are already using so they can determine how to best leverage those capabilities.

2.4.10.6 Data Collection and Analysis Methods

AI and machine learning tools require an extensive amount of data to function. Therefore, TD professionals should improve their data collection and analysis practices to provide the data necessary for AI to establish a use case, such as personalized learning, content recommendation, or impact measurement. TD professionals should work with internal data experts to understand what data is available within their organization and how it may be applied to support AI-enabled talent development practices. Properly categorizing and tagging data ensures TD professionals are ready to implement new AI tools when they become available. To improve their data practices, they should consider applying the five Vs of big data:

- **Volume.** Huge data sets must be evaluated to establish connections and identify patterns that were previously invisible to human analysts.
- **Velocity.** Data must be continuously collected and analyzed at the pace of performance.
- **Variety.** Structured and unstructured data can be analyzed to improve decision-making practices.
- **Veracity.** Data must be trustworthy and reflect reality.
- **Value.** Collected data must lead to insights related to the desired goal.

TD professionals cannot always predict which types of data will reveal useful correlations, but they should only collect and keep what they believe they will use. They should make informed decisions about which metrics are most relevant to their audience and organizational goals and use that data for deeper processing.

2.4.10.7 Developing and Training Machine Learning Algorithms

Machine learning models must be continuously trained to accurately recognize patterns and provide meaningful results. TD professionals should work with their internal data partners, IT professionals, and technology suppliers to understand the data requirements of their AI tools and find the data needed to train the application. This often necessitates a high level of individual engagement in the early stages of development, with subject matter experts continuously interacting with the tool and providing feedback on the results. This time reduces significantly as the tool becomes more familiar with the key inputs and outputs, allowing it to continue learning from its own experience. However, unattended tools can become prone to bias or glitches over time. Machine learning models should be reviewed on a regular basis to ensure continued accuracy.

2.4.10.8 Open-Source AI Tools

Although AI and machine learning applications require considerable domain expertise to develop independently, rapid authoring tools are emerging that apply AI and machine learning algorithms to many use cases. Large consumer technology companies are constantly developing open tools in the marketplace. TD professionals should stay up to date with these advancements so they can properly apply them within their solutions. They should also partner with their organization's data science and business intelligence teams to identify additional opportunities to develop and apply custom AI and machine learning tools. Depending on the application, this may require considerably more data than is made available through traditional training evaluation.

2.4.10.9 AR Development Tools

AR development tools are becoming more readily available for consumer and workplace use, and large technology companies are making it easier to build AR applications. TD professionals should explore these easy-to-use and cost-effective tools to determine their potential application within the workplace. Rapid development tools within the TD industry are also starting to introduce basic AR capabilities, which present a more familiar option for experimentation and delivery.

2.4.10.10 VR Development Tools

High-quality VR development can require considerable expertise. Although TD professionals can experiment with these powerful tools, they may require a considerable time investment if TD professionals do not already have the necessary skills. Less immersive formats—such as 360-degree videos and virtual events in off-the-shelf VR environments—can be developed quickly and used to introduce basic VR use cases to a talent development experience. Introductory VR development capabilities are also being added to rapid development tools, which provide a more familiar option for experimentation.

2.4.10.11 AI Bias and Ethical Considerations

Bias is a growing concern for AI applications because a system is only as effective as the data it is given. Therefore, TD professionals should carefully select which data feeds power AI applications. This data, along with the outputs from any AI applications, should be continuously assessed to ensure the impact of inherent bias in the data is effectively mitigated. For example, if AI is used to identify candidates to be considered for promotion, a human reviewer should regularly check to ensure it is not excluding segments of the population. Historical data, sometimes based on historical bias, can create data outliers that are difficult for machines to recognize and classify. As a result, human review and input remains a key component of any AI-driven process. TD professionals should work with their data, HR, legal, and IT partners to share how AI is being used within the workplace. Employees should have an opportunity to learn and influence how their data is being used to change the way they are supported at work. [See 3.2 and 1.4.6]

Applying Learning Technology

2.4.11 Skill in Using E-Learning Software and Tools

I. Using E-Learning Software and Tools

E-learning is a common tool for training delivery, especially within large and geographically dispersed organizations. E-learning content can be developed quickly and accessed on demand to ensure a consistent experience across a large audience. Therefore, TD professionals should know how to properly leverage e-learning content as part of their talent development strategy.

When TD professionals use e-learning software and tools, they should remember several requirements, although they're not specifically detailed in this capability:

- **Accessibility**—consider accessibility requirements. [See 2.4.1.10]
- **Device compatibility**—leverage communication technology software that is already used within the organization to deliver talent development solutions. [See 2.4.8.5]

2.4.11.1 Results-First Approach

Like any TD activity, e-learning content should be developed and implemented with a results-first approach. The focus should not be on the content itself; rather, TD professionals should design the right e-learning experience to achieve a clear, measurable goal for their organization. The desired result and related knowledge and skill requirements must be identified before any e-learning content is developed, and TD professionals should identify in advance the metrics that will be used to evaluate the effectiveness of the learning experience.

2.4.11.2 Platform Functionality

E-learning programs usually refer to self-directed web-based learning and include a several content objects, such as interactive modules, simulations, videos, animations, quizzes, and narrated or text-based presentations. E-learning programs represent one type of online learning, which is a broader category of digitally offered development solutions that can be created using many tools—from professional media development software to rapid authoring tools designed for workplace learning. There are several factors to consider when deciding on the right tool for content development, including:

- Organizational and regulatory requirements for user accessibility
- Desired end-user experience
- Audience engagement
- Output format requirements for content delivery platforms (including SCORM, AICC, and xAPI)
- Data collection requirements
- Delivery device specifications
- Available team skills for content design, development, and ongoing maintenance
- Alignment with instructional design methodology, including the desired objectives
- Initial purchase and ongoing licensing fees
- The timeline for content development and implementation

Once these requirements are determined, TD professionals can select the best tool for the content development.

2.4.11.3 Instructional Design

When developing e-learning content, TD professionals should apply their organization's established instructional design practices and guidelines, as well as principles, methodologies, and commonly accepted practices from the talent development field. A tool should not dictate a solution's design; rather, evidence-based instructional principles should be applied to show how the tool is used to develop a right-fit learning solution. [See 2.2]

2.4.11.4 Media Development

E-learning content may include multiple media formats, such as images, text, video, audio, interactive elements, games, and animation. TD professionals should consider several factors when deciding which media elements to use within an e-learning module, including the development timeline, available skills, delivery technology, and user context and environment. For example, TD professionals may design a VR module, but users cannot benefit from the experience if VR headsets are not readily available in the workplace. Videos can add style and audience engagement to some topics, but for others, like processes with many steps, simple text may provide a more efficient and effective learning experience. TD professionals should try to use the simplest solution to solve a performance problem and avoid unnecessarily using media-rich content or the latest technology features.

2.4.11.5 Visual Design

Although some TD teams may include professionals with visual design experience, they won't all be designers. Regardless, TD professionals should always try to apply solid visual design principles when building e-learning content. Quality visual design aids the learning process and helps users focus on the intended message. These concepts include but are not limited to space, typeface, color, balance, contrast, scale, framing, alignment, and texture.

If possible, TD professionals should leverage internal design expertise from partner teams in marketing or communications to improve their capabilities and ensure brand consistency for their organization. This also helps increase adoption because audience members are more likely to recognize the relevance and authenticity of e-learning content if it looks and feels like other messages they receive from an organization. Visual design is another important part of ensuring e-learning content meets accessibility standards. [See 2.3.5.11]

2.4.11.6 UI and UX Design for E-Learning

UI and UX designs are important considerations for e-learning development. Although e-learning content is often delivered via another platform (such as an LMS, mobile device, or internet browser), it still includes a variety of UI and UX elements within the hosted content, which are determined by the e-learning designer. These may include navigation features, interactions, buttons, and inputs. Therefore, TD professionals who develop e-learning content should have at least a basic understanding of UI and UX design principles. [See 2.4.9.1]

2.4.11.7 Assessment Writing

Assessments are an important part of a digital learning experience because they provide users with the opportunity to apply their knowledge and test their understanding. They can also offer important insights into knowledge transfer and behavior change if the assessments are designed and delivered in a format that can be tracked. [See 2.4.11.10]

Assessments are commonly used as approval gates, requiring a minimum score before a module is marked complete. They may also be used to qualify a user for a job role or task. Questions and scenarios help reinforce key knowledge points long after training occurs. TD professionals should develop assessments that are easy to understand, appropriately challenging, and focus on practical knowledge application. Assessment content must align with the objectives of the learning content and should be developed early to clarify how users will be required to apply new knowledge after the learning experience. [See 2.2.2]

2.4.11.8 User Motivation and Behavior
Digital content is ubiquitous in everyday life, so TD professionals should leverage familiar content experiences and expectations in their development. Many of the design principles applied in consumer technology are based on well-researched cognitive psychology. Similar tactics may be applied to simplify the user experience within an e-learning module. However, TD professionals should apply their workplace context to these concepts and not assume that because something works in everyday life, it will work in the same way within the workplace.

2.4.11.9 Data Specifications (SCORM, AICC, and xAPI)
E-learning content should use data aligned with an organization's data specifications. This will ensure all required information is properly tracked, stored, and reported upon completion of the program. [See 2.4.1.8]

2.4.11.10 Reporting Requirements for E-Learning Content
TD professionals should design e-learning content that meets all established reporting requirements. This includes internal data and reporting needs as well as external regulatory record-keeping guidelines. Content developers should understand how data will be retrieved from the content and tracked within the system of record, such as an LMS or LRS, which may include simple completion records and aggregate scores, detailed question level data, or even the amount of time spent on each component within the course. The required data for an instructional design model and objectives will determine which data standards to follow during development and inform the selection of e-learning development tools.

2.4.11.11 Content Management
TD professionals should keep long-term content management in mind when developing e-learning programs. The expected life cycle of the content should be clarified during the needs analysis and design process, and content should be designed with these factors in mind. If the content will be used indefinitely, TD professionals should include content management considerations to reduce long-term administrative effort. For example, they should avoid referencing information that is known to change frequently, thereby requiring constant updates to the material. Instead, the e-learning course can focus on the underlying principles with links to external content that are easy to update over time. Upon completion and release, the content should be included in the TD department's ongoing content management process and revisited both at scheduled intervals and as needed based on organizational changes.

2.4.12 Knowledge of Functions, Features, Limitations, and Practical Applications of the Technologies Available to Support Learning and Talent Development Solutions

> **I. Functions, Features, Limitations, and Application of Available Technology**
>
> TD professionals should understand the technologies available within their organization that may be used to support learning and development solutions. These may include tools that are administrated by TD professionals as well as those that are managed by partners but leveraged for similar purposes.
>
> When TD professionals are involved in technology application, they should remember several requirements, although they're not detailed in this section:
> - **Workplace context**—understand the end user's day-to-day context. [See 2.4.3.3]
> - **Learning technology ecosystem architecture**—include all HR tools people use to support their continued development.
> - **Accessibility**—consider accessibility requirements. [See 2.4.1.10]
> - **Reporting**—validate that compliance and reporting capabilities are adequate.
> - **Delivery and access to devices**—leverage communication technology software that is already used within the organization for the delivery of talent development solutions. [See 2.4.8.5]

2.4.12.1 Consider the Outcome

As TD professionals apply technology to support talent development initiatives, they should begin with a clear and measurable organizational outcome. Rather than delivering training for the sake of training, they determine the KSAs required to achieve the outcome. Then, they can make an informed recommendation regarding the technology they should use to support employee learning and development as related to the stated goal. This approach also helps TD professionals measure the results of their initiatives.

2.4.12.2 Platform Functionality

TD professionals should understand the full capabilities of the tools available to support their learning activities, including features that are currently used as well as those that may not yet have been introduced. This understanding will help them make informed decisions regarding their application and avoid unnecessary technology evaluation processes and potential duplication of functionality.

2.4.12.3 Purposeful System Selection and Integration

TD professionals should understand the purpose of each component of their organization's technology ecosystem. For example, one platform may serve multiple purposes based on how it is leveraged by the end users. TD professionals should align their application of available technology with this established purpose to avoid confusing users or complicating the learning experience. If they're expanding the purpose of an existing technology, TD professionals should collaborate with all applicable partners in IT to ensure the tool is being used correctly and does not conflict with or duplicate another part of the ecosystem. Change management strategies and tools should be used to ensure successful adoption of the new features. [See 3.6]

The same concept applies to technology integration, which often requires additional administrative resources to establish and maintain and should only be created when there is a clear, long-term value for users and administrators that cannot be achieved without integration.

2.4.12.4 User Technology Experience Design

When considering the application of a specific technology, TD professionals should understand the role that technology plays within the overall user experience and how users and data will move between technologies in a seamless environment. They should try to align with the existing experience whenever possible rather than attempting to introduce new user expectations and behaviors. [See 2.4.2.6]

2.4.12.5 Learning Technology Ecosystem Architecture

TD professionals should understand their organization's complete learning technology ecosystem, which includes tools that were purpose-built for talent development (such as the LMS) and other hardware and software that are used within the TD workflow or broader organization. They can then expand their options and leverage the right tools to identify and address performance challenges regardless of how the platform was acquired or administrated. This understanding will also inform future search and acquisition efforts, eliminating redundancy and preserving resources.

It is unlikely that a single technology will be able to support every organizational need. Although a limited number of tools should be used whenever possible, designing a technology ecosystem with purpose will help users easily move between platforms without confusion.

2.4.13 Skill in Using Human Resource Technology Systems to Store, Retrieve, and Process Talent and Talent Development–Related Information

> **I. Using Technology to Store, Retrieve, and Process Talent Information**
>
> TD professionals leverage technology to handle two different categories of information: content and data. Each comes with its own unique considerations, and TD professionals should leverage HR technology to apply the information in ways that support individual development and organizational goals.
>
> When TD professionals are involved in leveraging HR technology, they should remember several requirements, although they're not detailed in this section:
>
> - **Learning technology ecosystem architecture**—understand the organization's complete learning technology ecosystem, which includes tools that are purpose-built for talent development (such as the LMS) as well as other hardware and software that are used within the user audience workflow. [See 2.4.12.5]
> - **Accessibility**—consider accessibility requirements. [See 2.4.1.10]
> - **Reporting**—understand the reporting capabilities in the technology ecosystem. [See 2.4.1.9]
> - **Delivery and access to devices**—leverage communication technology software that is already in use within the organization to deliver talent development solutions. [See 2.4.8.5]

2.4.13.1 Planned System Selection

TD professionals should understand the need for HR systems that will store and process the right information based on the needs of their organization. They should collaborate with HR to prevent conflicts between systems and data sets. [See 2.4.12.3]

2.4.13.2 Data Integration

TD professionals should understand the capability of their HR technology tools. HR systems may store a variety of people data (including employee demographics, job histories, and role details), performance data, and learning data (including training completions, assessment scores, certifications, and performance observations). TD professionals should work with HR to explore ways to integrate HR and TD technologies and other business tools, such as any additional systems or dashboards used to track employee performance and organizational metrics. They should only pursue integration if a clear, long-term value exists.

2.4.13.3 Content Management

All information stored within HR and TD systems should be regularly reviewed based on an organization's established content management and record-keeping processes. Unnecessary information, including training content and employee data records, should not be stored any longer than legally required. Saving data that is no longer needed makes it more difficult to navigate systems and retrieve useful information. In addition, it may expose the organization to unnecessary risk. All content management practices must meet external regulatory requirements.

2.4.14 Knowledge of Techniques and Approaches to Leverage Social Media Platforms and Tools to Support Knowledge Sharing, Idea Exchange, and Learning

I. Techniques and Approaches That Leverage Social Media Platforms

Nearly 75 percent of US adults use at least one social media site, and this technology has fundamentally changed how people share information in their everyday life (Pew Research Center 2019). Similar technology has been introduced into the workplace, but it's not always effective or adopted. TD professionals should understand the potential and capabilities for social tools to support learning and performance.

When TD professionals are involved in using social media techniques, they should remember several requirements, although they're not detailed in this section:
- **Learning technology ecosystem architecture**—understand the organization's complete learning technology ecosystem, which includes tools that are purpose-built for talent development (such as the LMS) and other hardware and software that are used within the user audience workflow. [See 2.4.12.5]
- **Accessibility**—consider accessibility requirements. [See 2.4.1.10]

2.4.14.1 Social Media Tools for Talent Development

Social media platforms are an increasingly common part of the learning technology ecosystem. Although TD platforms may include social capabilities, enterprise social media software is often managed by other teams, such as operations or communications. TD professionals should consider how to leverage these tools as part of their instructional design approach. Social media platforms may not be integrated with more traditional learning tools, but TD professionals should still consider including social engagement in blended experiences.

2.4.14.2 Social Media Platform Functionality

Social media platforms can help TD professionals enable and scale peer-to-peer learning and performance support and are more important than ever with a large remote workforce. These tools may be used as part of programmatic training deliveries through features like discussion boards within a learning delivery platform; however, in many cases, they are most effective when used within a workplace context, not as a structured training activity. For example, social tools that are available within the workflow can help team members ask questions and engage in discussions with a large pool of subject matter experts from anywhere in the world. These tools also provide the opportunity for people to "work out loud" and share their insights and experiences for collective benefit. [See 2.5.9]

To leverage social technology that is as close to the workflow as possible, the TD department may have to partner with other teams that own the specific platforms, such as IT, HR, communications, or marketing. Integrating social technology into the working experience should therefore be a collaborative effort with TD professionals helping partners focus on the learning and enablement potential of the tools. TD professionals should evaluate whether they can leverage existing and familiar tools before implementing custom social media platforms used only for talent development purposes.

Consumer social technology platforms still play a role in talent development, even if they cannot be used formally within an organization. These tools can help TD professionals continuously improve their knowledge and skills by developing a personal learning network of fellow practitioners outside a typical peer group to share constantly evolving research and content trends and provide design inspiration to use as learning content. Through thoughtful observation, TD professionals can use social media to access new ideas and resources at minimal cost and effort.

2.4.14.3 User Motivation, Behaviors, and Engagement

When applying social technology, TD professionals should remain aware of the 1-9-90 rule, which asserts that only 1 percent of internet users actively create new content while 9 percent edit it and 90 percent view it (Arthur 2006). The rule does not necessarily apply directly within organizations, and the numbers should not be taken literally, but it is a reminder that people will not share information or engage in discussions simply because they have the opportunity. Instead, people are more likely to engage at varying levels based on their interest in and the perceived value of the interaction. TD professionals can motivate users to engage by enabling simple, easily accessible tools like one-click course rankings and content sharing, instead of online activities like surveys and text review that require larger investments of time and interest.

2.4.14.4 Curation

Because social technology is defined by a user's ability to find, share, and discuss information in a digital format with other users, they can engage by commenting, adding new information, generating new threads, or distributing information to additional users rather than simply accessing on-demand content. Individual users shape the conversation and the content available on the system. User-generated content may be synchronous or asynchronous and take on a variety of formats, including content posts, comments, file uploads, and audio or video clips. These interactions may be synchronous or asynchronous.

Information moves quickly across these social channels, proliferating and making it difficult for users to notice and use the most relevant content. Therefore, TD professionals should consider applying curation tactics that balance user engagement with some level of content validation. They may use curation to collect, organize, delete, or share information to best address clear organizational needs. However, to scale information sharing at the speed of the modern workplace, TD professionals should enable contributors across their organization to curate information within their domains of expertise. [See 2.5.5, 2.5.6, and 2.5.7]

However, TD professionals must also be aware of the legal risks of content curation to avoid potential fines and penalties. For example, if a TD professional decides to incorporate an article found online in a learning experience, but their organization does not hold a license to use the content, the article's author could take legal action.

2.4.14.5 Community Management

TD professionals should work with organizational partners (including legal, compliance, HR, and IT) to establish guidelines for online sharing and user-generated content. These guidelines should align to general employee guidelines and organizational values and not introduce new risks. TD professionals may opt to initiate a community management process to oversee online social interactions and ensure everyone follows the rules. They should not discourage open, honest discussion; rather, community managers should protect the overall user experience, help people find the information they need, and ensure everyone is treated with fairness and respect. Community managers should also follow an escalation process if someone violates a community guideline.

2.4.14.6 Access Devices

Digital social tools require consistent engagement and scale to provide value to users. Therefore, TD professionals should ensure people have continued access to social tools so they can use them as part of their everyday work. A critical consideration for engagement is the access device, which should be positioned as close to the working environment as possible. TD professionals should collaborate with their internal partners to make sure social tools are easily accessible on the same devices people use to do their work.

2.4.14.7 Legal and Compliance Requirements

Social media creates a record of human interaction. In the workplace, these records may introduce additional risks to the organization if they're not managed correctly. Therefore, TD professionals should work with their legal, compliance, and HR partners to establish community guidelines that all social media users are expected to abide by. These guidelines should include escalation processes for potential violations and state clear accountability standards for individual users. They may also include restrictions regarding how external social tools are used to conduct organizational business. TD professionals should balance the legal requirements of their organization with information sharing opportunities.

Advancing the Learning Technology Ecosystem

2.4.15 Knowledge of Artificial Intelligence, Machine Learning Algorithms, Augmented Reality, Virtual Reality, and Mixed Reality Trends That Are Ethical and Free of Bias

> **I. Knowledge of AI, Machine Learning Algorithms, AR, VR, and Mixed Reality Trends**
>
> TD professionals should maintain a practical awareness of new technology trends, especially those that will have an immediate influence on the workplace. AI and mixed reality tools are quickly changing the way work is done. They have immediate applications within talent development and should therefore become growing areas of focus for the profession.
>
> When TD professionals are involved in advancing learning technology, they should remember several requirements, although they're not detailed in this section:
> - **User technology experience**—consider the overall design of a user's technology experience. [See 2.4.2.6]
> - **Accessibility**—consider accessibility requirements. [See 2.4.1.10]
> - **IT regulations and processes**—align with established IT regulations and processes and partner with IT to understand how they operate before requesting project support. [See 2.4.1.3]
> - **Delivery and access to devices**—leverage communication technology software that is already used within the organization for the delivery of talent development solutions. [See 2.4.8.5]
> - **VR concepts and use cases**—have users explore a digital environment, especially when training in a dangerous or hard to replicate situation. [See 2.4.10.3]
> - **AI and machine learning tools**—plan to leverage several open tools in the marketplace that large consumer technology companies are constantly developing. [See 2.4.10.5]
> - **AR concepts and use cases**—use AR as a means of performance support; targeted information can be displayed in context without requiring a user to stop working. [See 2.4.10.2]

2.4.15.1 Staying Current With Technology

The rapid evolution of consumer technology is always creating opportunities for TD professionals to introduce new tools within the workflow. As technology continues to quickly evolve, TD professionals should also remain informed so they can offer the best possible learning experiences within their organizations. AI is already a common fixture in consumer technology, generating entertainment recommendations, interacting with humans via voice-enabled assistants, and driving autonomous vehicles. Likewise, mixed reality technology is becoming more commonplace through AR mobile applications and VR entertainment offerings. TD professionals should maintain awareness of evolving consumer and workplace trends with mixed reality technology to identify potential learning and performance applications. They should pay special attention to the emergence of rapid authoring tools that make these technologies easier and possibly more affordable to adapt to organizational needs. They should also take advantage of demonstrations and free trials to continuously evaluate these possibilities.

2.4.15.2 Existing Workplace Technology Applications

Talent development is not the only workplace function that can take advantage of AI and mixed reality technologies. For example, AI is a growing feature of workplace automation, and mixed realities are commonly used in safety-critical environments. They may also be used externally in customer-facing capacities. Thus, TD professionals should collaborate with teams that are exploring these potential use cases to establish foundational guidelines to leverage for future learning applications. Collaboration can lead to new applications being adopted by more users, who may only be comfortable using a new technology in simple, frequently repeated ways. TD professionals should also work with IT to understand the requirements for introducing AI and mixed reality technologies into the workplace, especially if other teams have not already paved the way.

2.4.15.3 AI Concepts and Definitions

Several types of AI models can help TD professionals make better decisions based on data analysis. Generative AI models that use large data sets to create text, images, videos, and scripts hold the most promise for learning. TD professionals can use generative AI to create high-quality learning content and personalization. AI can track and analyze learner behavior to create personalized learner journeys for their specific needs. TD professionals must understand the risks and ethical implications associated with generative AI models. Staying informed and updated on the latest advances will help ensure understanding of the capabilities and limitations of this technology.

2.4.15.4 AI and Mixed Reality Delivery and Access to Devices

Hardware is a vital consideration for TD technology strategy. Some AI and mixed reality tools can be delivered using existing devices, such as desktops or laptops, company-issued mobile devices, workplace systems, and personal mobile devices. Others, including many VR applications, require specific devices with high-speed computing infrastructure, such as 5G, that may not be available in the workplace. These may include head-mounted headsets, haptic wearables and garments, or AR glasses. TD professionals should stay up to date on advances made with these devices, which improve accessibility in mixed reality, and device requirements must be considered when selecting and implementing new technology strategies. TD professionals should work with platform administrators and IT to stay up to date on their organization's technology ecosystem and related guidelines.

TD professionals should also remain informed about the changing technology landscape, including the next evolution of the internet. Although still in its early stages, Web3 is the decentralization of the internet and provides a personalized and interactive experience while giving users more control over their personal data and privacy. It is built on blockchain technology and could affect published e-learning content and how it is distributed to learners. A *blockchain* is a distributed database that allows for secure, transparent, and tamper-proof transactions that include the buying, selling, and transferring digital assets, such as courses, credentials, certifications, and nonfungible tokens (NFTs). NFTs are digital assets (videos, graphics, courses, or books) encoded using the same software as cryptocurrency, granting the author immutable rights.

2.4.15.5 User Experience Design

TD professionals should understand the role technology plays within the overall user experience. This is especially true for AI, which is often a less visible component of user-facing systems. Most AI tools can be integrated into existing interfaces with minimal changes in use for the average user. TD professionals should try follow the existing experience whenever possible, rather than attempt to introduce new user expectations and behaviors. [See 2.4.2.6]

2.4.15.6 Data Integrations
AI tools may require a considerable amount of data to function. This can greatly exceed the information that is typically available within a TD or HR platform. Therefore, TD professionals should work with their internal data experts to identify potential data sources that can be leveraged in support of AI applications. This may include several data types, such as user demographics, learning records, performance metrics, and business results. Technical integrations should be considered if they can provide the necessary data and limit ongoing administration requirements.

2.4.15.7 Device Procurement and Maintenance
Many mixed reality technologies require investments in hardware in addition to software and content. Although AR can be accessed using a typical smartphone or tablet, it is commonly applied using purpose-built devices, such as smart glasses and helmets, that fit the needs of the working environment. VR headsets and associated gear are also becoming more powerful and affordable. TD professionals should work with their IT and procurement partners to explore viable device options for mixed reality use cases. In addition to initial purchase costs, processes must be established for the ongoing cleaning, maintenance, and replacement of mixed reality devices, as well as the potential training costs for users and system administrators to fully leverage the new features.

2.4.15.8 User Safety
Long-term impacts of these emerging technologies are still unknown, but TD professionals should monitor the latest evidence to ensure that how they are using these tools remains safe and positive for users' well-being. TD professionals should only use these systems for the right purposes—considering environmental factors and establishing safety requirements for each application. For example, a second person should be present while an employee is using a VR headset in case an emergency occurs. TD professionals should also consider developing secondary solutions for users who physically cannot endure or choose not to participate in a mixed reality experience, especially during the technology's initial implementation.

2.4.15.9 AI Bias and Ethical Considerations
TD professionals should be aware of potential bias and ethical considerations when using AI. Bias can be inadvertently encoded into algorithms because the data itself may be biased (due to the ongoing legacy of past biased decisions and practices). In some settings, TD professionals must make complex ethical judgements about whether AI is making the right decisions. For example, if an AI algorithm can select high-performing employees for enhanced talent development opportunities, TD professionals must decide if making a development or promotional decision solely based on this data is fair. Because most individuals will not be able to navigate the specific algorithms that drive AI recommendations, TD professionals must work with HR, legal, and IT to spot and evaluate potential dilemmas and unintended consequences as they arise. AI can be a useful tool to find useful trends in massive sets of data, and TD professionals fulfill an important role by using these outputs ethically, balancing the needs and rights of individual users with the goals of their broader organization. [See 1.6 and 2.4.10.11]

REFERENCES

ADA.gov. 2010. "The Current ADA Regulations." Information and Technical Assistance on the Americans With Disabilities Act. ada.gov/2010_regs.htm.

Arthur, C. 2006. "What is the 1% Rule?" *The Guardian*, July 19. theguardian.com/technology/2006/jul/20/guardianweeklytechnologysection2.

ATD (Association for Talent Development). 2018. *2018 State of the Industry*. Alexandria, VA: ATD Press.

Chui, M., V. Kamalnath, and B. McCarthy. 2018. "An Executive's Guide to AI." McKinsey and Company, February 9. mckinsey.com/business-functions/mckinsey-analytics/our-insights/an-executives-guide-to-ai.

IDEO U. 2018. "Design Thinking." ideou.com/pages/design-thinking.

Pew Research Center. 2019. "Social Media Fact Sheet." Pew Research Center Internet and Technology, June 12. pewinternet.org/fact-sheet/social-media.

SAP Insights. n.d. "What Is a Technology Platform?" sap.com/insights/what-is-a-technology-platform.html.

SCORM.com. 2011. "SCORM Explained 201: A Deeper Dive Into SCORM." scorm.com/scorm-explained.

Stepper, J. 2015. *Working Out Loud: For a Better Career and Life*. Ikigai Press.

Taylor, D.H. 2017. *Learning Technologies in the Workplace: How to Successfully Implement Learning Technologies in Organizations*. New York: Kogan Page.

Udell, C., and G. Woodill. 2019. *Shock of the New: The Challenge and Promise of Emerging Learning Technologies*. Alexandria, VA: ATD Press.

Usability.gov. 2013a. "Usability Testing." usability.gov/how-to-and-tools/methods/usability-testing.html.

Usability.gov. 2013b. "User Interface Design Basics." usability.gov/what-and-why/user-interface-design.html.

Wikipedia. 2020. "Technology Adoption Life Cycle." en.wikipedia.org/wiki/Technology_adoption_life_cycle.

Recommended Reading

Dillon, JD. 2022. *The Modern Learning Ecosystem: A New L&D Mindset for the Ever-Changing Workplace*. Alexandria, VA: ATD Press.

Hugget, C. 2018. *Virtual Training Basics*, 2nd ed. Alexandria, VA: ATD Press.

Huggett, C. 2022. *The Facilitator's Guide to Immersive, Blended, and Hybrid Learning*. Alexandria, VA: ATD Press.

Meacham, M. 2020. *AI in Talent Development: Capitalize on the AI Revolution to Transform the Way You Work, Learn, and Live.* Alexandria, VA: ATD Press.

Rogers E. M. 2003. *Diffusion of Innovations*, 5th ed. New York, Free Press.

Taylor, D. 2017. *Learning Technologies in the Workplace: How to Successfully Implement Learning Technologies in Organizations.* New York: Kogan Page.

Udell, C., and G. Woodill. 2019. *Shock of the New: The Challenge and Promise of Emerging Learning Technologies.* Alexandria, VA: ATD Press.

2.5 KNOWLEDGE MANAGEMENT

In a knowledge economy, lost institutional knowledge can cost organizations real money in the form of turnover, recruitment, and training costs. Knowledge management is the explicit and systematic management of intellectual capital and organizational knowledge as well as the associated processes of creating, gathering, validating, categorizing, archiving, disseminating, leveraging, and using intellectual capital for improving the organization and the individuals in it.

Knowledge Management

2.5.1 Knowledge of Principles of Knowledge Management

I. Principles of Knowledge Management

TD professionals should understand the principles and elements of managing organizational knowledge, the advantages of doing so for the organization, and how to apply those principles and elements to the development of talent.

2.5.1.1 Knowledge Management Defined

Knowledge management (KM) is a systematic approach to achieving organizational goals by creating, capturing, curating, sharing, and managing the organization's knowledge to ensure the right information flows to the right people at the right time.

The concept of knowledge management as a distinct discipline arose from the increasing need for organizations to effectively manage information and knowledge assets in an economy that's shifting from industrial to service. In the past, industrial workers relied primarily on the machinery of industry as the means to deliver value. As the shift to services occurred, things like decisions, understanding based on experience, and application of concepts to action became the value creation engine. Workers could no longer be trained to perform a discrete task on a piece of machinery and execute that activity without change for the next several decades. Instead, activity became varied and fluid, requiring workers to make many more decisions based on changing information that was increasingly dispersed across the organization.

This shift was evident as early as 1966 when Peter Drucker coined the term *knowledge worker* in his book *The Effective Executive* while discussing the differences between manual workers and knowledge workers.

2.5 Knowledge Management

Managing knowledge begins by differentiating between the components of knowledge management. To understand and effectively apply KM, TD professionals need to understand what constitutes knowledge based on these definitions:

- **Data** represents the "facts of the world," which are specific but unorganized. Data has no context, and is limited by direct experience or interaction. Thierauf (1999) defines data as "unstructured facts and figures that have the least impact on the typical manager."
- **Information** is data that is contextualized, categorized, calculated, and condensed (Davenport and Prusak 2000); it is data with relevance and purpose (Bali, Wickramasinghe, and Lehaney 2009). Information may uncover trends or indicate a pattern of business in a particular period. According to Ackoff (1999), information is found "in answers to questions that begin with such words as who, what, where, when, and how many."
- **Knowledge** is associated with action and implies understanding. "The knowledge possessed by each individual is a product of his experience and encompasses the norms by which he evaluates new inputs from his surroundings" (Davenport and Prusak 2000).

2.5.1.2 Different Types of Knowledge

In addition to understanding the difference between data, information, and knowledge, TD professionals should understand and be able to distinguish between the different forms of knowledge that can exist in an organization. For example, while knowledge can be easily shared if it is captured in a document or set of reports, managing the knowledge gathered over years by experts and stored only in their heads requires a different approach.

Within KM, there are two types of knowledge:

- **Explicit knowledge** is typically captured in information systems. Sometimes referred to as *know-what* (Brown and Duguid 1998), it is easy to identify, store, and retrieve. For this reason, explicit knowledge is aligned with and managed by KM systems, which store, retrieve, and control versioning of documents and text. Explicit knowledge is found in databases, memos, notes, documents, and so forth.
- **Tacit knowledge,** which was originally defined by educator Michael Polanyi, is sometimes referred to as *know-how* (Brown and Duguid 1998). Tacit knowledge is primarily experience based and intuitive; it only resides in individuals' memories and minds and is hard to define and communicate. It is the most valuable source of knowledge because it is based solely on successful experience and performance, not broadly disseminated, and not usually shared or understood by many. Many KM experts believe it is the most likely type of knowledge to lead to breakthroughs in an organization (Wellman 2009). Further, Gamble and Blackwell (2002) link the lack of focus on tacit knowledge directly to the reduced capability for innovation and sustained competitiveness. Knowledge stakeholders (holders of tacit knowledge assets) hold knowledge about cultural beliefs, values, attitudes, and mental models, as well as skills, capabilities, and expertise (Botha, Kourie, and Snyman 2008).

TD professionals should understand the role that KM plays in talent development, because it is another enabler in their toolkit to improve individual and organizational performance. In the discipline of human performance improvement (HPI), knowledge (and skill) represents a sixth of the potential factors affecting performance (Gilbert 2007). Knowledge alone, therefore, does not accomplish performance outcomes; it needs to be combined with skill.

Finally, a distinction must be made between information management and knowledge management. Information management seeks to use technology to organize large quantities of data; for example, IT systems allow us to catalog and contextualize data—to store our *facts*. Knowledge management, on the other hand, is focused on *people* and capturing what they know, which is information that is actionable and contains context, know-how, and experience. Information systems may be used to support KM efforts, but they are not themselves knowledge management. Think of information systems as the hardware and software that might be used to house data and information (data and context), whereas knowledge management systems are the maps that make connections, allow for application, and demonstrate the location of the elements necessary for successful performance.

When individuals talk about managing data in their information system, they are referring to the facts they store—for example, an employee's age. An employee can be either 35 or 45, but not both. This is the nature of facts. Information is how facts are cataloged—it's a point-in-time data storage. So, in the employee's case, the system could have the wrong information (that they are 35 and 45), but the data itself would not be wrong because data is always the fact. The information could be wrong because it is contextualized and stored. Knowledge allows the person to understand that a human cannot be both 35 and 45 and to apply the correct action.

2.5.1.3 KM Concepts, Philosophy, and Theory

Because improving performance is a central goal of the TD professional, knowledge must be connected to job accomplishments. In other words, the real indicator of the value of knowledge to an organization is performance and the relationship of knowledge to performance. Understand that the purpose of KM is to harness the right knowledge to enable people to perform at a higher level. Not all knowledge is created equal, and not all knowledge leads us to better outcomes and improved results.

Therefore, the real trick for the TD professional to execute KM effectively is to determine how it relates to performance excellence. It is not sufficient to gather all knowledge relative to a task or job accomplishment and attempt to somehow transfer this to the performer. The goal needs to be to present the knowledge in the form, format, quantity, and context necessary to the performer in the service of achieving higher levels of performance. Determining what that knowledge is, and how and when it should be delivered, is central to the mission of KM.

For example, think about a racecar driver who needs to understand the braking system of the car. They could learn a lot about the system—brake fluid hydraulics, friction, heat dissipation, and so forth; however, to win the race, the driver only *needs* to know when to press the brake, and for how long, when going into and coming out of a turn.

2.5.1.4 Types of KM Systems

KM systems have evolved to several forms. Systems like Microsoft SharePoint, for example, are used by many organizations for collaboration and sharing. Increasingly, as organizations have realized that knowledge can be a competitive advantage, more and more systems have sprung up to support efforts to manage that knowledge. In short, any IT system that supports knowledge, enables collaboration, catalogs knowledge sources, captures and uses knowledge, or supports or enables the KM process is by default a KM system.

Some examples of KM systems include:
- **Groupware systems**—software that supports multiple users working on related tasks in local and remote networks
- **Intranet and extranet**—intranets are internally shared networks; extranets may be accessible to others outside the organization
- **Data warehousing, data mining, and online analytical processing**—generally considered business intelligence, these systems allow rapid analysis of large data sets
- **Decision support systems**—systems that support judgements or courses of action for an organization
- **Content management systems**—systems that warehouse and manage large quantities of digital content
- **Document management systems**—systems to track, store, and manage documents
- **Artificial intelligence tools**—tools and systems that support the search, optimization, and evaluation of knowledge and information
- **Simulation tools**—tools that allow for simulation of performance events where knowledge elements are deployed
- **Semantic networks**—systems that map connections between ideas or concepts in an organization (Bali, Wickramasinghe, and Lehaney 2009)

2.5.1.5 KM Elements

TD professionals should be familiar with the range of elements that cover the KM life cycle, such as identifying the right knowledge and where it exists, connecting those knowledge sources to specific initiatives and systems, and arranging and curating knowledge content. The elements include:
- **Creation and capture** refers to where the knowledge is created and how it can be captured so that it can be shared and reused. Knowledge mapping is one technique for this element.
- **Curation, enrichment, and sharing** concerns how the accuracy of the knowledge elements can be confirmed, what additional context is required, and where the knowledge is needed.
- **Storage and retrieval** includes the appropriate mechanisms for storing captured knowledge, including IT systems.
- **Knowledge dissemination** describes the embedded processes and mechanisms for disseminating knowledge, including collaboration, communities of practice, and peer networks.

2.5.1.6 Advantages for the Organization

Effective knowledge management provides many organizational advantages. As the economy values intangible or nonphysical resources, these assets have become a source of competitive advantage (Mitrović, Maksimović, and Tešić 2008). Documented advantages of effective KM include:
- Improved employee performance, productivity, and job satisfaction
- Reuse of knowledge with confidence
- Increased innovation and agility
- Improvements in speed and responsiveness to organizational needs
- Enhanced shareholder and customer value

2.5.1.7 Advantages to TD Professionals

Knowledge management holds numerous advantages for TD professionals:

- **Embeds learning in the organizational information chain.** KM allows knowledge to be a part of the knowledge ecosystem and incorporated into a variety of solutions.
- **Improves quality and productivity.** A validated and easily referenced source of knowledge, KM enables TD professionals to provide timely quality services and solutions.
- **Ensures higher value TD products and solutions.** TD professionals can ensure that products and solutions are targeted to optimize performance and value.
- **Creates confidence in knowledge resources.** Capturing, mapping, validating, codifying, and curating knowledge needs, elements, and sources increases confidence in the available knowledge.
- **Lowers costs of learning.** TD professionals can focus less time and fewer resources on sharing available knowledge.

2.5.1.8 KM's Relationship to Learning and Performance

Knowledge is a differentiator between average or poor performance and key or exemplary performance (Holloway and Mankin 2004). By drawing knowledge or knowledge sources into the development process, TD professionals can examine the work in a way that only a small portion of the workforce is able to discover on its own because the knowledge often resides in isolated pockets until TD professionals bring it to the attention of the broader workforce. Through this identification, mapping, and inclusion of knowledge and knowledge sources, the TD professional can leverage KM as a way to enhance learning and improve performance.

To ensure organizational consistency, TD professionals should strategically link KM with learning and performance and deliver a coordinated organizational approach. Managing and delivering knowledge through TD solutions are not two separate and discrete activities. By interweaving talent development and knowledge management, TD professionals can create an explicit connection between what knowledge performers need, where that knowledge resides, and how they can access it. Once this condition is established, TD professionals should know whether the knowledge is internalized or external:

- **Internalized (learned reference) knowledge** is stored in the performer's memory. It is necessary when immediate access to the information is required.
- **External (accessed reference) knowledge** is stored elsewhere, for example in a system or other storage option. It is useful if the performance requirements allow more time for knowledge retrieval and access.

Determining where the knowledge is stored relies on a combination of factors:

- **Speed of performance.** How fast does the performer need to respond to a particular signal to perform?
- **Frequency of performance.** How often will the knowledge be accessed during the performer's daily activity?
- **Consequence of error.** How significant are the consequences of making a mistake in the performance of the activity?

TD professionals also need to know when in the performance sequence the person will need the knowledge. This provides the necessary context to effectively embed knowledge elements within solutions.

2.5.1.9 Organizational Knowledge Sources

Knowledge can exist on several levels:

- **Individual knowledge** is personal; it is often tacit and held by individuals as expertise or particular know-how. It can be explicit if it is closely held but tacit if stored in files, notebooks, or other locations.
- **Group and community knowledge** is held by a group but not shared with the rest of the organization.
- **Structural knowledge** is embedded in the DNA of the organization's routines, processes, and culture.
- **Organizational knowledge** is the sum of accessible knowledge in the organization when other knowledge elements are combined to form new knowledge.
- **Extra-organizational knowledge** exists outside the organization. [See 3.5.7.5]

2.5.1.10 Organizational Learning

Organizational learning is the creation, retention, and dissemination of knowledge within an organization to ensure improvement over time. It is based on a systematic implementation of best practices throughout the entire organization, and governance bodies are often created for each function to oversee these efforts. KM can be a key enabler of effective learning organizations by identifying, documenting, and making all tacit and explicit knowledge available for knowledge sharing. [See 3.3.7.2]

2.5.2 Knowledge of Methods and Techniques for Capturing and Codifying Knowledge

> **I. Knowledge Mapping**
>
> TD professionals should be aware of the methods and techniques for capturing and codifying knowledge.

2.5.2.1 Develop the Organizational Knowledge Map Based on Performance Requirements

Knowledge mapping is a visual representation that connects knowledge requirements to knowledge sources, the type of knowledge element, and the nature of the requirement. Mapping enables TD professionals to decide how to use these connections when developing client solutions.

Knowledge mapping is one of the most effective means of understanding the organization's knowledge landscape. Well-developed knowledge maps help identify intellectual capital, socialize new employees, and enhance organizational learning (Liebowitz 2003; Wexler 2001). To be effective in this approach, TD professionals should understand the key factors and constraints of knowledge mapping:

- **Knowledge is transient.** It develops, is passed on, and expires according to organizational needs and cycles.
- **Knowledge must be connected to organizational value.**
- **Knowledge often has boundaries.** Whether real or perceived, it is important to understand these boundaries from the individual's perspective. For example, revenue formulas or pricing decisions may be held by only a few people and are therefore out of the boundaries of others.
- **Knowledge is not always known;** some will need to be identified before it can be mapped.
- **Knowledge exists in many forms** in the organization; it can be tacit, explicit, or embedded.

The American Productivity and Quality Center (2018) identifies seven types of knowledge maps in three broad categories:

- **Expertise knowledge maps:**
  - *Strategic overview maps* are the largest in scope. They outline the knowledge required for each strategic focus area, how critical that knowledge is to achieving the organization's goals, whether the needed knowledge currently exists in the organization, and where any existing knowledge resides.
  - *Expertise overview maps* provide a broad understanding of what knowledge an organization has in various parts of the organization and what may be at risk.
- **Cross-functional knowledge maps:**
  - *Expertise tacit maps* are used to identify specific experts and their areas of expertise. They usually work best inside an organizational unit or a division with similar units.
  - *Technical or functional knowledge maps* help an organization more clearly understand its strengths and gaps within specific technical or functional knowledge domains (such as ship design or component assembly).
- **Process- and role-based knowledge maps:**
  - *Process-based maps* identify specific knowledge needs, as well as the sources, recipients, locations, and formats of that knowledge within a process or domain. They are particularly useful for establishing a baseline for KM solutions, such as communities or mentoring.
  - *Job- or role-based maps* inventory the knowledge required for various jobs or roles. They are similar to the functional or technical knowledge map, but include the specific knowledge each job role needs.
  - *Competency or learning needs maps* explicitly articulate the learning or competency needs associated with a business process or job role.

2.5.2.2 Knowledge Mapping Considerations

The goal of knowledge capture in KM is to understand the answers to these questions:

- What knowledge is required to successfully get work done?
- Who has that knowledge, or how can it be accessed?
- When and where is that knowledge needed? (APQC 2018)

Because knowledge is most often scattered across the organization and can exist in different domains and serve different requirements or needs, the knowledge collection activity must be appropriately broad and consider knowledge sources across an array of potential categories. Typical sources include individuals, groups, and communities—structural, organizational, and extra-organizational (KMT 2010). [See 2.5.1.5]

TD professionals may capture knowledge through interviews, focus groups, document review, stories, decision trees, and data mining. They start with an understanding of how knowledge flows in the organization, and those involved must have sufficient understanding of the organization's strategic goals and processes.

2.5.2.3 Creating Taxonomies

The captured knowledge must be codified and ordered in some meaningful way before it can be useful. One of KM's goals is to make the organization's tacit and embedded knowledge (knowledge that is assumed in the organization's structures, processes, and shared memory) explicit and shareable (or reusable). Codification is a means of translating that knowledge into content.

Codifying knowledge relies on the application of some system of order in the form of a taxonomy. This taxonomy focuses on enabling the efficient retrieval and sharing of knowledge, information, and data across an organization. It is built around work processes and knowledge needs in an intuitive structure (Lambe 2007; Malafsky 2008).

Creating a KM taxonomy should be viewed as a unique project within the broader context of the knowledge management program. TD professionals should consider the content domain (what general area of skills, activities, and abilities the knowledge relates to), metadata strategy (the words and ideas that the typical person would search for when looking for the knowledge), location of and availability of SMEs, and organizational knowledge lexicon (definitions of organizational knowledge terms and where they are found). Ultimately, taxonomies need to reflect the organization's working environment and culture. And, because working environments change continually, taxonomies should also be flexible and adapt to the changing environment (Pellini and Jones 2011).

TD professionals should tie taxonomy development to the overall mechanisms of the KM program and systems. This should involve:

- **Senior leadership support.** For the taxonomy to be successful (as with many programs) it must have unwavering commitment from senior leadership.
- **Effective scoping and analysis.** The analysis should include a clear description of why it is being undertaken, who will be involved, how it will be implemented, and a reasonable cost estimate. The scoping should also account for key stakeholders, required skills for the team, and specific requirements from the organization.
- **Synthesizing information captured from multiple sources.** A taxonomy must be designed to allow for the recognition of different knowledge sources that may address requirements in subtly or in distinctly different ways.
- **Appropriate design.** Complexity is a key consideration in the design. It requires a decision about how complex (or simple) the taxonomy needs to be to meet the purpose.

2.5.2.4 Using Tools

TD professionals should be aware of the range of tools that can support KM activities. There are seven tool categories that support the KM effort:

- **Content repository.** These tools allow users to manage and share knowledge content. Document management systems have historically dominated this category, but organizations have recently begun to engage tools that can manage a broader range of content. Examples include content management systems (CMS), enterprise content management (ECM), and cloud content management (CCM).
- **Knowledge search.** Search is an essential function that allows users to find what they need.
- **Communication tools.** This category includes email, chat, instant messaging, VoIP (Voice over Internet Protocol), speech recognition, video conferencing, and collaboration tools.
- **Social software.** Tools that support the social sharing of knowledge are increasingly embedded in enterprise software like enterprise resource planning (ERP) and customer relationship management (CRM) systems.
- **Knowledge visualization.** These tools are used to visually communicate knowledge, such as PowerPoint and 3D data representation systems.

- **Decision support.** These tools allow users to discover patterns of knowledge in large volumes of data.
- **Big data.** These tools store, manage, and explore high velocity, variety, and volume data, including structured (database tables) and unstructured data (documents and conversations).

2.5.3 Skill in Designing and Implementing Knowledge Management Strategy

I. Designing and Implementing a KM Strategy

TD professionals should be skilled in designing and implementing a KM strategy that effectively supports talent and learning for organizational objectives.

2.5.3.1 Understanding Business Processes That Support Knowledge Exchange

TD professionals should connect the organization's knowledge needs and sources with how the work gets done. They can overlay the KM map with the work process map (a visual representation of the work process) for the workgroup in question. This is not as complicated as it sounds—it is simply comparing work process maps to knowledge needs and sources according to the KM map. This will require some work to ensure that all needs are accurately identified and linked. The combined deliverable clearly shows knowledge needs at the point in the work process when they are required then connects the associated knowledge source that can satisfy it. [See 3.5.2.5 and 3.5.5.3]

Further, because all work processes are not equal in complexity or contribution to overall organizational value, TD professionals should use the map to highlight critical processes where knowledge elements are key. This is done by connecting business drivers to job outcomes and mapping them to the associated work processes that have been connected to the knowledge sources. The result is a prioritization framework for understanding the value contribution of both the knowledge and its application in support of the workflow.

2.5.3.2 Corporate Culture and Leadership

Knowledge management is more about people than systems. For KM to succeed in an organization, it must be valued as a strategic asset and recognized as a core cultural element. Leadership should encourage and reward collaboration, the public sharing of information, and any other processes that create and scale knowledge. It is, therefore, a requirement of the TD professional to engage leadership early in the process, share observations and findings, make recommendations for required improvements, and maintain effective communication throughout the process. [See 2.5.3.1]

2.5.3.3 Attitude of Management

Management's attitude toward knowledge management and the implementation of KM systems and strategies is paramount to the success of any KM effort, program, or initiative. TD professionals should enlist the support of management early on, and that support must be continuous, demonstrable, and provide more than budget and approval. Management should be actively engaged through messaging, oversight, and review and accountability. TD professionals should help managers develop a mantra of "Document, participate, and, when in doubt, participate and document." (Documenting effort and progress and active participation are two of the most important facets of management participation.) When managers encourage and become champions of the KM effort, employees will be more likely to view it as something that makes their jobs easier, not more difficult.

2.5.3.4 Rewards and Incentives

Driving the right behavior is central to the success of a KM system and strategy. Establish measures for participation, and create reward programs linked to measurable action:

- Revise job descriptions and review process so that contributing to the KM system is required; for example, staff might be required to contribute three KM articles per quarter.
- Conduct periodic appraisals and award spot bonuses based on participation.
- Link awards for outstanding performance to KM contribution.
- Use gamification to challenge and reward participation and sharing.

2.5.3.5 Align KM With TD Needs

KM supports one of talent development's central goals: the application of knowledge to accomplish organizational objectives. This is accomplished by identifying, mapping, capturing, codifying, and sharing knowledge that was previously unknown or known to only a few people. TD professionals apply this work by creating solutions to connect competencies, skills, and knowledge. The common denominator is knowledge.

TD professionals should understand what knowledge is required by each role and level of responsibility in their organization to accomplish organizational objectives. The KM system should provide a clear line of sight to the knowledge needs by role and level, and to the knowledge required to accomplish the objectives.

2.5.3.6 Identify the Efficient and Effective Application of Knowledge

Huang, Lee, and Wang (1999) identified 10 strategies for the successful implementation and application of knowledge:

- **Establish a KM methodology.** Decide on policies, rules, techniques, and procedures that prescribe how work is to be performed and provide proven ways to do so successfully. This may be organic in nature (developed entirely within the organization), rely on established methodologies from the broader KM community, or a combination of both.
- **Designate a point person.** Appoint a chief knowledge officer to promote and manage KM activities in the company.
- **Empower knowledge workers.** In any organization, knowledge originates from knowledge workers. Thus, it's critical to empower and support knowledge workers by making them a key component of the KM system. This could be as simple as giving them explicit permission to participate and share.
- **Capture customer-centric knowledge.** TD professionals should assist organizations in strengthening their position in a competitive environment not only by emphasizing customer satisfaction but also by focusing on both learning about and learning from their customers and incorporating this into the overall KM approach.
- **Manage core competencies.** Identify and understand what the organization is good at. Core competencies can vary based on the benefits organizations provide their customers by combining human capital, intellectual and intangible assets, processes, and technologies. Thus, the core competencies of one firm may not be easily replicated by other firms.
- **Foster collaboration and innovation.** Organizations can nurture collaboration by accentuating the importance of teamwork, learning, sharing, trust, and flexibility. Developing an appropriate reward structure for innovation also fosters high creative potential among individuals. Collaboration is a key element of KM—without it, the SECI cycle (socialization, externalization, combination, and internalization) breaks down through failure of the first two elements.

- **Learn from best practices.** By recording and sharing best practices, organizations can prevent reinvention and encourage reuse of the best ideas and methods, which makes them more efficient and effective. In the past, firms shared and learned about best practices through symposiums, conferences, and seminars. Now, web-based approaches are becoming the norm.
- **Extend knowledge sourcing.** Knowledge sourcing is the successful retrieval of information and dissemination of knowledge. It can be extended through different media such as the internet, intranet, and extranet. Organizations can use these mechanisms to retrieve and deliver knowledge.
- **Interconnect communities of expertise.** Links between internal and external communities can be created using formal virtual communities and teams and through electronic libraries with whitepapers or knowledge banks. Internal experts aid in problem solving, while external experts are generally connected with senior management for advice on specific areas.
- **Report the measured value of knowledge assets.** Organizations must measure how knowledge management contributes to the organization. It is a difficult but important task to validate the development and use of a knowledge management system, as is true for any information system.

2.5.3.7 Knowledge Management Support

TD professionals should provide support for the KM contribution and efforts of the employees. This can take several forms:

- **Peer KM champions** are local KM champions assigned to provide troubleshooting and support for KM issues.
- **KM self-help** is a knowledge base or frequently asked questions (FAQs) for support.
- **Help desk** provides phone support (typically through the IT help desk or customer care).

2.5.3.8 Effects of Knowledge Management

KM can have a significant positive influence on organizations:

- **Introduction and implementation of metrics.** Because TD professionals are managing knowledge, they can measure its use, effectiveness, and access. Rather than allowing knowledge to be an unknown asset (in terms of measurable value), KM offers a way to connect and measure that knowledge.
- **Improved quality of information.** Knowledge systems provide the ability to track and review the knowledge assets, allowing the knowledge sources to improve through review, feedback (from consumers of the knowledge), and curation by the knowledge manager.
- **Information updates.** Information and information systems can be mined for other hidden elements using data analytics and machine learning.
- **Cost and productivity benefits.** Knowledge and best approaches are shared and embedded in structural knowledge, which means that costs in hours worked (as represented in cost per output) may be reduced. By reducing the amount of time spent seeking knowledge and applying better knowledge to the performance, both measures can be lowered.
- **Improved customer metrics.** Higher-quality knowledge access and sources may enable staff to better serve the customer, resulting in improved customer metrics.
- **Improved staff morale.** Valuable employees can become dissatisfied with their jobs if they don't have ready access to the knowledge they need to be successful.

2.5.3.9 The Value of Knowledge Management

The TD professional should be prepared to discuss the strategic and tactical benefits and values of knowledge management.

KM helps organizations increase their strategic benefits by:
- Enhancing decision making based on facilitated access to expertise knowledge and practices
- Improving innovation and collaboration across disconnected parts of the organization
- Reducing loss of expert knowledge by formally capturing explicit and tacit knowledge
- Exploiting market opportunities through building strategy and planning on current validated knowledge

Knowledge management helps at the tactical level by:
- Enabling performers to safely share best practices
- Capturing work process innovation for reuse
- Increasing efficiency and productivity and reducing rework and reinvention
- Reducing time to competence by creating targeted onboarding and providing access to knowledge

2.5.4 Knowledge of Methods, Techniques, and Structures for Disseminating and Sharing Knowledge Across Individuals, Groups, and Organizations

> **I. Techniques to Establish Knowledge Sharing**
> TD professionals should be aware of the methods for disseminating and sharing knowledge across the organization.

2.5.4.1 Determine Organizational Preferences for Knowledge and Information Sharing

TD professionals should be aware of and account for their organization's preferences for knowledge sharing in three areas:
- How well the organization's culture supports the concept of sharing and transferring knowledge
- The organization's strategy for using knowledge resources to support organizational goals and objectives
- Information systems that are available to support knowledge dissemination

Of the three, culture is the dominant factor because it often informs strategy and is therefore a precursor to it. KM systems are an investment or expense (depending on the point of view) that is made in alignment with corporate needs, values, and culture. The long-term success of any KM program requires TD professionals to determine the cultural influences on knowledge creation, sharing, and learning. If the organization doesn't currently have an effective culture of learning and knowledge sharing, TD professionals should begin in this area or any other efforts are likely to fail.

Fortunately, the cycle of knowledge is well documented, and there are several models that address this aspect of KM. The SECI model or SECI KM Spiral is one of the most referenced (Nonaka and Takeuchi 1995). This model identifies four distinct areas, or quadrants, as knowledge moves from tacit to explicit (Figure 2.5.4.1-1).

2.5 Knowledge Management

Figure 2.5.4.1-1. The SECI KM Spiral

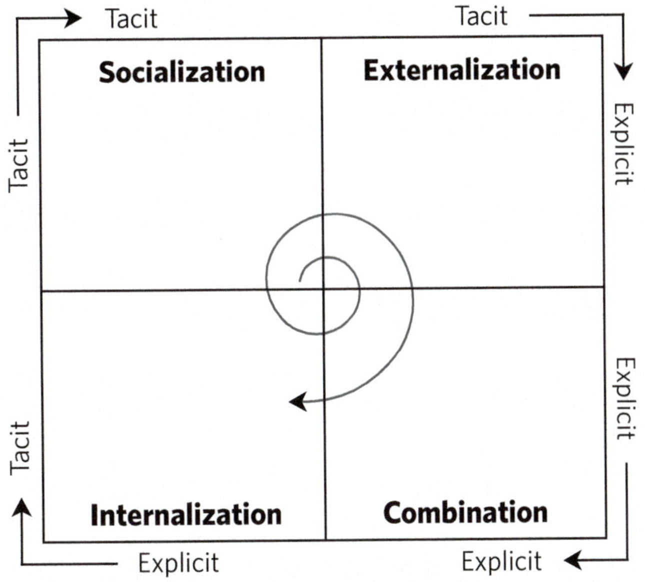

	Tacit	Tacit	
Tacit	Socialization	Externalization	Explicit
Tacit	Internalization	Combination	Explicit
	Explicit	Explicit	

Source: Nonaka and Takeuchi (1995).

In this model, tacit knowledge (held by the individual) is socialized in some way, which externalizes the knowledge and results in it becoming explicit (rather than tacit). As knowledge is never static, the new explicit knowledge is combined with new perspectives and experiences, resulting in an internalization of discovery—the formation of new (and now tacit) knowledge. The cycle then repeats, thus the term *SECI spiral*.

An organization's culture can influence how effectively it leverages this cycle. In cultures that weaponize knowledge for personal gain, for example, TD professionals may find moving knowledge from the tacit to socialized extremely difficult. Recognize the status of cultural elements in advance to execute against the SECI model, and determine if specific cultural initiatives should be introduced first.

The TD professional's challenge is to effectively support and operationalize this cycle in the service of learning and development. After identifying where the knowledge exists, invest deliberate effort in encouraging socialization and supporting externalization through systems and solutions. The result of those efforts can then be monitored as *new* knowledge is created and internalized. [See 3.3.3.2, 3.3.7, 3.3.8, and 3.3.9]

2.5.4.2 Techniques to Share Knowledge Across Organizations

TD professionals must use explicit methods to operationalize the SECI spiral and not leave it to chance. They should ensure that this knowledge can be effectively shared, consumed, and operationalized. Methods to achieve this goal fall into three categories:

- **Peer-to-peer (informal).** Also thought of as decentralized, solutions in this category are directed toward enabling users to interact directly as opposed to through an intermediary knowledge curator or capture system. While powerful for collaboration, they can be limiting in how broadly the knowledge is disseminated. These methods are one-to-one (me to you) or many-to-many (us to them). Social collaboration sites or social networks are typical solutions in this category.

- **Structured (formal).** Also thought of as centralized, solutions in this category are collected and curated. There is specific governance and control over the addition, maintenance, and expiration of knowledge assets. These methods are one-to-many.
- **Reference sources (IT based).** These methods are characterized by the technology systems in which they exist. Document repositories and content management systems are typical methods deployed.

Each method comes with benefits and challenges as well as specific tools to support. For example, peer-to-peer methods offer immediacy and access to other experts in the organization but can lack structure, consistent participation, and validation of what is shared. On the other hand, structured methods and reference sources benefit from curation and can be maintained on a consistent basis; however, they are often more costly to maintain and lack some of the immediacy and intimacy of the peer-to-peer method. TD professionals should determine which approach (or set of approaches) most effectively aligns to the goals of the KM activity and the organization's culture and preferences.

2.5.4.3 Ensuring Reliability and Validity of Knowledge

TD professionals should establish mechanisms to ensure that knowledge is trusted, valued, and consumed once shared. They should be deliberate about the value of the knowledge, which requires a process that involves:

- **A formal review cycle** should include recognized experts (by peers) in the knowledge areas being shared.
- **Establish methods for contributing new and incremental knowledge** because participation and use will generate even more participation. The KM approach will fail if it is limited to the organizational elite (that is, any segment of the organization generally perceived to receive special treatment).
- **Grant easy access to knowledge sources.** Too many calls, requests, or clicks will create obstacles for use and cause overall rejection of the KM efforts.

2.5.4.4 How Knowledge and Information Support Daily Actions

Knowledge management supports work in daily processes through:

- **Decision making.** KM systems and processes must be aligned to the need and support the ability to make the necessary (optimal) decisions for the organization.
- **Analysis.** KM efforts must support ongoing analysis in the service of organizational strategy formation and execution.
- **Operations.** Awareness of current best practices and expertise, as well as expansion of tacit knowledge, must be embedded in a cycle of continuous improvement for organizational operations.

2.5.4.5 Support Typical Functions

TD professionals should focus on embedding KM efforts in multiple systems and functions to derive maximum benefit for the organization. Some examples include:

- **Sales and marketing**—best practices, techniques, and competitive analysis
- **Manufacturing**—process innovations, safety procedures, and cost savings approaches
- **Service departments (HR, IT, contracts, and accounting)**—service improvements and risk mitigation
- **Research and development (R&D)**—innovation and new product and service creation
- **Supply chain**—knowledge process outsourcing, up-chain efficiency, and information accuracy
- **Management and supervision**—strategy, organizational performance, productivity improvements, and engagement

Curation

2.5.5 Skill in Identifying the Quality, Authenticity, Accuracy, Impartiality, and Relevance of Information From Various Sources

> **I. Establish Governance for Content Curation**
>
> TD professionals should be knowledgeable about curation and the methods for establishing effective governance for content curation in KM systems. Curation is the process of identifying, gathering, organizing, and preparing to disseminate related content or information.

2.5.5.1 Content Curation Governance

Successful curation requires effective governance. TD professionals should establish proper curation guidelines and oversight to ensure the success of the KM program over time. This means determining what model is most effective for the needs and culture of the program and organization.

Rohit Bhargava (2011) identified five distinct curation models, which serve different sources and purposes:

- **Aggregation** is the act of curating the most relevant information about a particular topic into a single location.
- **Distillation** is the act of curating information into a more simplistic format, sharing only the most important or relevant ideas.
- **Elevation** refers to curation with a mission of identifying a larger trend or insight from smaller daily musings posted online.
- **Mash-ups** are unique, curated juxtapositions that merge existing content to create a new point of view.
- **Chronology** organizes historical information based on time to show an evolving understanding of a particular topic.

TD professionals should incorporate more than one of these five curation models when developing a governance structure. The different knowledge content sources (internal or external) and knowledge consumption needs will determine which models to use. Further, because content is not knowledge, curation requires active participation from the knowledge sources to maintain accurate context. While the content objects can be managed by a traditional library function, an effective knowledge curation system requires the input of knowledge experts.

To establish an effective curation process:

- **Determine who owns the curation function.** The owner typically acts in an oversight capacity to ensure that contributors, reviewers, and approvers meet their functional obligations and that the system remains healthy (from a knowledge content perspective).
- **Establish processes for content intake, review, maintenance, and removal.** This includes who can contribute, what content must be reviewed, who the reviewers are, and where approvals are required (for inclusion and deletion). It also outlines the process to support. (For example, is there a transition period between when content is marked for removal and when it's removed or archived?)

- **Ensure the quality, authenticity, impartiality, and relevance of information.** This requires TD professionals to establish measures by content type or source outlining the minimum acceptable levels for these criteria (for example, specific credential requirements for expert sources, attributions, or age of content).
- **Design a governing structure and cadence for ongoing oversight.** This addresses who has responsibility at each level, frequency of reviews, and corrective actions for knowledge content breaches (such as poorly curated, incorrect, or expired data).

2.5.5.2 Identify the Quality, Authenticity, Impartiality, and Relevance of Information

Curation of both internal and external knowledge sources is important. KM programs will fail quickly if members doubt the veracity, quality, or timeliness of the shared knowledge. TD professionals need to account for the quality of the content and create a process to address the essential content attributes. They need to determine if the content is:

- Accurate
- Authentic
- In the correct context
- From a credible creator
- Complete and comprehensive
- Just enough (so it's not overwhelming)
- Bias free
- High priority
- Easy to find, learn, and use
- Reinforcing, not contradicting, other content
- Copyright protected or owned elsewhere
- Recent or removed when expired [See 3.7.1.1]

2.5.6 Skill in Organizing and Synthesizing Information From Multiple Sources

> **I. Map Information From Knowledge Sources to Application**
>
> TD professionals should understand the methods for mapping knowledge sources to the appropriate application of that knowledge for organizational outcomes.

2.5.6.1 Use the Performance Chain As an Organizing Framework

Once mapped, knowledge content, much like information, can seem overwhelming in quantity and total volume to the person accessing it. This is particularly true if similar or complementary knowledge sources serve the same need. TD professionals should be able to organize content in a way that is accessible and actionable.

Because their primary focus is in service of accomplishing measurable business or organizational results, TD professionals' focus should be performance. By using an HPI approach, they can align the knowledge sources along the performance chain to the appropriate point and level of need. For example, a knowledge element is required to decide the sequence of tasks in a work process, or a knowledge element is necessary to recognize key facilitators or barriers in the production of an individual performance outcome. Using an HPI approach allows TD professionals to move backward from the desired job outcomes to the work processes and assign or align knowledge sources to the specific point of need. Decisions can then be made on whether those needs are met through internalization or external reference.

Synthesis is another important element in the organization process. Simply arranging many similar versions of the same information creates confusion rather than minimizing it. Synthesis in KM separates the signal from the noise—or makes sense of several sources brought together to present the knowledge concept in a condensed and actionable form. This process is increasingly important to the successful adoption and effectiveness of KM systems, because the quantity of available knowledge content is growing exponentially. [See 2.5.5]

The process of synthesis involves five steps:
1. **Frame the knowledge element.** What need is being served by this knowledge content?
2. **Gather material from different sources.** What are the sources of this content?
3. **Fit the parts together.** Where do the sources overlap, conflict, converge, or diverge?
4. **Achieve synthesis.** Which source (based on curation governance criteria) takes precedence in a conflict, and how will similar information be merged? [See 2.5.5.1]
5. **Unify.** How will the knowledge elements come together into a unified and consumable knowledge content source?

2.5.7 Skill in Curating Instructional Content, Tools, and Resources

> **I. Curating Content, Tools, and Resources for Knowledge Management**
>
> TD professionals should be knowledgeable about the methods, tools, and resources that support KM curation efforts.

2.5.7.1 Curate All Organizational Content

TD professionals should evaluate the appropriate instructional and learning elements from various sources to support knowledge requirements in the broader knowledge system. They should assess learning content, both internal and external to the organization, against the knowledge map to determine where there is appropriate application. This is an ongoing activity that falls into the cadence established under the KM program governance. [See 2.5.5.1]

Evaluation and curation apply to all organizational learning content, including:
- **Instructional content**—review cycles, shelf life, and applicability, as well as reviewing against current knowledge needs
- **User-generated content**—SME or expert review, timing, approvals, retiring of content, and notification processes
- **SME-generated content**—secondary review, approval process, notifications, retiring of content, archiving, and access
- **Public domain content**—inclusion decisions, access, and disclaimers
- **Third-party content**—review and acquisition cycles, applicability to performance review, and legal and usage review

2.5 Knowledge Management

Applying KM in Talent Development

2.5.8 Skill in Identifying the Type and Amount of Information Needed to Support TD Activities

> **I. Identifying Information for Talent Development**
> TD professionals recognize that knowledge, performance, and development are linked and must continuously identify and clarify the relationship between elements.

2.5.8.1 What Knowledge and Information Is Necessary at Discrete Levels of Development

By undertaking the KM process through the lens of performance—establishing the knowledge requirements by role that are necessary for organizational success—TD professionals can create a clear hierarchy to manage the talent development process.

This allows for the direct application of the knowledge needs to the various levels and solutions deployed in talent development, such as:

- **Courses.** TD professionals can instruct learners in knowledge requirements, how to acquire subsequent knowledge from the expert sources, and where to find it.
- **Curricula.** TD professionals can group and balance subjects and courses to develop talent according to knowledge progressions.
- **Career progression.** Knowledge needs, sources, and contributions vary by level and are mapped accordingly. TD professionals can determine and measure how well the performer is able to leverage knowledge to the production of outcomes and how much knowledge is created and contributed.
- **Succession planning.** Knowledge forms the basis for decisions around succession because needs and capabilities can be examined by role and level and measured by performer. This provides further leverage in determining the appropriate developmental paths for succession.

2.5.8.2 Connect Sources to Requirements for Effective Talent Development

In the past, the notion of knowledge management in an organization was that of the gatekeeper: individuals held the secrets necessary to achieve the results. These secrets could be internal, like best practices and process innovations, or external, like key suppliers or information sources. Often, talent management efforts were targeted at identifying these individuals and focusing on developing their successors.

For TD professionals, the fusion of talent management and knowledge management holds important competitive implications. The successful generation, capture, transfer, and dissemination of knowledge heavily depends on and is intimately entangled with the effective management of talent. Specifically, the support of a consistent set of management practices is needed to capture, codify, and share knowledge and know-how as well as ensure they are fully used to achieve organizational objectives. The goal is to identify the knowledge requirements at each level in the TD process and embed that information in the TD approach.

2.5.8.3 Need to Integrate Knowledge Solutions Directly in the Workflow

One of the best applications of knowledge is to embed it directly in the workflow. The knowledge need not be referenced or called upon through recollection of learning by the performer; rather, it is embedded in the structural knowledge of how things are done.

2.5.9 Skill in Developing, Managing, Facilitating, and Supporting Knowledge Networks and Communities of Practice

> **I. Develop and Manage KM Networks and Communities of Practice**
>
> TD professionals should understand how to form, develop, and manage communities of practice in service of KM initiatives.

2.5.9.1 Identify and Leverage Formal and Informal KM Systems in the Organization

Both formal and informal KM systems exist in most organizations. Typical examples include knowledge networks and communities of practice. Knowledge networks are informal, such as a group of geographically dispersed people who use communications technology to connect and create, share, and disseminate knowledge; communities of practice are more formal—a group of people with a shared interest or concern who interact regularly in a structured format. Knowledge networks and communities of practice are important factors in the long-term viability of and engagement in a KM system. As such, TD professionals should ensure the appropriate steps are taken to sustain these structures.

There are important distinctions between communities of practice and knowledge networks. Etienne Wenger (1999), a global leader in community of practice development, described three important dimensions:

- **Domain.** People organize around a domain of knowledge, which gives members a sense of joint enterprise and brings them together. Members identify with the domain and joint undertaking that emerges from this shared understanding of their situation.
- **Community.** People function as a community through relationships of mutual engagement, which bind members together into a social entity. They interact regularly and engage in joint activities that build relationships and trust.
- **Practice.** People build capability in practice by developing a shared repertoire and resources, such as tools, documents, routines, vocabulary, symbols, and artifacts that embody the community's accumulated knowledge. This shared repertoire serves as a foundation for future learning.

Knowledge networks are based on need, and relationships are always shifting and changing as people connect around specific knowledge requirements. These networks develop and exist primarily in informal structures with the sole purpose of collecting and passing along information and knowledge. They tend to be more informal because no joint enterprise holds them together, as opposed to a community of practice, which requires a sense of mission or shared accomplishment or understanding.

2.5.9.2 Considerations for Establishing KM Systems

TD professionals should be involved if their organizations establish a KM system, and they should help make decisions about various elements, including:

- **Organization structure.** KM systems can be formal or informal, and this structure will affect how knowledge flows across the broader organization. Formal structures, while easier to control and measure, can affect the free flow of knowledge. Informal structures, while harder to control, can be managed through project or cross-functional teams, teamwork, or peer networks.
- **Staffing.** In a formal KM system, staffing must be accounted for. Will the KM system will be a discrete function or an additional set of responsibilities?
- **Roles and responsibilities.** There are some roles within the KM system that can be filled depending on the size of the organization, the formality of the system, and the extent of the knowledge being managed. Typical roles include chief knowledge officer (CKO), KM program manager, KM project manager, KM director, operations KM director, KM author, KM lead, KM liaison, KM specialist, KM system administrator, knowledge engineer, knowledge architect, KM writer, knowledge manager, and KM analyst.
- **Incentives.** The system is only effective if it is consistently and continuously used. Rewards and incentives are required to encourage participants to use the system by contributing, applying and using the information, reviewing and updating content, and performing any other tasks associated with the system's health and maintenance.
- **Standards, processes, and metrics.** To be effective, the system must have effective processes and standards, which should be designed to ensure the fidelity of knowledge assets and sources, veracity of current knowledge under management, and routine and the agreed-upon disposition of both current and retired knowledge elements. All systems and processes should be continually measured for access, availability, and use to ensure they are healthy and functioning according to standard.
- **Advocacy.** The program should establish communication channels and designate champions across the organization to advocate for participation in and use of the knowledge system.

2.5.9.3 Critical Success Factors for Communities of Practice

While having an organic quality about them, communities of practice require specific effort targeted at a defined set of success factors and a deliberate approach to formation and governance. Some critical success factors for communities of practice include:

- **Peer identification.** Allow and encourage members of the emerging community to identify peers for membership. Help establish clear criteria to ensure the selection process is fair and encourages development and participation. Peers place a great deal of trust in the *best* among them; leveraging this trust helps the community succeed.
- **Value to user.** Clarify the purpose. Members should understand and support the community's mission, activities, and purpose. Establishing clear value to the user can drive adoption.
- **Easy to use.** Make it easy—if participants must work to join or participate, many will forgo the extra effort. Identify and procure tools to support the community for communications, remote meetings and collaboration, knowledge capture, polling, voting on ideas, and so on.
- **Make it special.** Create a system of nomination, approval, and rewards for the community. Even small rewards can drive big changes in behavior.
- **Community leadership.** Rotating leadership through the community and allowing members to contribute broadly creates a sense of shared ownership and responsibility.
- **Support from the top.** Ensure that leadership is fully supportive and present in the community. Schedule periodic leadership involvement through community updates or readouts.

- **Minimal oversight.** Allow the community to be self-administered and self-sustaining to the extent possible.
- **Trusting culture.** Ensure continuous emphasis on an open and trusting mutual exchange of ideas and knowledge.

2.5.9.4 Development Stages for Communities of Practice

With these factors in mind, TD professionals should consider five stages of development when creating communities of practice (Wenger 1999). Each stage requires a different set of activities and opportunities for support:

1. **Potential.** At this stage there is a loose network of people with similar issues and needs. People need to find each other, discover common ground, and prepare for a community.
2. **Coalescing.** At this stage people come together and launch a community. They find value in engaging in learning activities and designing a community.
3. **Maturing.** The community takes charge of its practice and grows. Members set standards, define a learning agenda, and deal with growth. By now, they are engaging in joint activities, creating artifacts, and developing commitment and relationships.
4. **Active.** The community is established and goes through cycles of activities. They need ways to sustain energy, renew interest, educate novices, find a voice, and gain influence.
5. **Dispersing.** The community has outlived its usefulness and people move on. The challenges are about letting go, defining a legacy, and keeping in touch.

2.5.9.5 Looking to the Future of KM for Talent Development

There has been a recent trend in the TD world to talk about the death of KM. People make broad pronouncements about knowledge management fading from the organizational landscape or being a forgotten fad. To deny that KM has had and continues to face challenges would be disingenuous. There have certainly been challenges as well as many abandoned initiatives and there's less interest in (and fewer internet searches on) the topic. For example, Bain's *Management Tools and Trends* survey didn't list knowledge management in the top 25 tools for their most recent survey in 2023 (Rigby, Bilodeau, and Ronan 2023).

TD professionals must help their organizations overcome common KM challenges and promote the continued need for a deliberate approach to identify, catalog, and connect knowledge to performance.

The need for KM initiatives to prevent redundant efforts, avoid repeated mistakes, and take advantage of the expertise and experience of others in the organization will be around for some time, even in the face of competing approaches and evolving technologies. TD professionals should connect KM programs with the needs of their target audience and the associated benefits. They should also continue to focus on connecting the intangible assets embodied as organizational knowledge to the organization's talent.

REFERENCES

Ackoff, R.L. 1999. *Ackoff's Best: His Classic Writings on Management*. New York: John Wiley and Sons.

APQC (American Productivity and Quality Center). 2018. "Getting Started With Knowledge Mapping." Whitepaper. American Productivity and Quality Center, June 29. apqc.org/resource-library/resource-listing/getting-started-knowledge-mapping.

Bali, R., N. Wickramasinghe, and B. Lehaney. 2009. *Knowledge Management Primer*. Routledge Series in Information Systems. New York: Routledge.

Bhargava, R. 2011. "The 5 Models of Content Curation." Rohit Bhargava, March 31. rohitbhargava.com/2011/03/the-5-models-of-content-curation.html.

Botha, A., D. Kourie, and R. Snyman. 2008. *Coping With Continuous Change in the Business Environment, Knowledge Management and Knowledge Management Technology*. Oxford: Chandos Publishing.

Brown, J.S., and P. Duguid. 1998. "Organizing Knowledge." *California Management Review* 40(3). doi.org/10.2307/41165945.

Davenport, T.H. 2015. "Whatever Happened to Knowledge Management?" *The Wall Street Journal*, June 24. on.wsj.com/1IySHT2.

Davenport, T.H., and L. Prusak. 2000. *Working Knowledge: How Organizations Manage What They Know*. Boston: Harvard Business School Press.

Gamble, P., and J. Blackwell. 2002. *Knowledge Management: A State-of-the-Art Guide*. New York: Kogan Page.

Garfield, S. 2015. "Is Knowledge Management on Life Support in Most Organizations?" LinkedIn Pulse, June 29. linkedin.com/pulse/knowledge-management-life-support-most-organizations-stan-garfield.

Gilbert, T. 2007. *Human Competence: Engineering Worthy Performance*. San Francisco: Pfeiffer.

Graef, J. 2002. "Ten Taxonomy Myths." *Montague Institute Review*, June. montague.com/review/articles/myths.pdf.

Holloway, M., and D. Mankin. 2004. *Performance DNA*. Alexandria, VA: ASTD Press.

Huang, K.T., Y.L. Lee, and R.W. Wang. 1999. *Quality Information and Knowledge*. Upper Saddle River, NJ: Prentice Hall.

KMT (Knowledge Management Tools). 2010. "KM from A to Z." knowledge-management-tools.net.

Lambe, P. 2007 *Organising Knowledge: Taxonomies, Knowledge and Organisational Effectiveness*. Oxford: Chandos Publishing.

Liebowitz, J. 2003. *Addressing the Human Capital Crisis in the Federal Government: A Knowledge Management Perspective*. Oxford: Butterworth-Heinemann.

Malafsky, G.P. 2008. *Knowledge Taxonomy*. Fairfax: TechI.

Mitrović, V., R. Maksimović, and Z. Tešić. 2008. "The Application of Balanced Scorecard Methodology in Small Business." *Total Quality Management & Excellence* 36(1–2): 339–346.

Nonaka, I. 1994. "A Dynamic Theory of Organizational Knowledge Creation." *Organization Science* 51:14–37.

Nonaka, I., and H. Takeuchi. 1995. *The Knowledge-Creating Company: How Japanese Companies Create the Dynamics of Innovation*. New York: Oxford University Press.

Pellini, A., and H. Jones. 2011. "Knowledge Taxonomies: A Literature Review." Overseas Development Institute, May. odi.org/sites/odi.org.uk/files/odi-assets/publications-opinion-files/7123.pdf.

Rigby, D.K., B. Bilodeau, and K. Ronan. 2023. *Management Tools & Trends 2023*. Boston: Bain and Company. bain.com/insights/management-tools-and-trends-2023.

Robertson, J. 2007. "There Are No 'KM Systems.'" Step Two. steptwo.com.au/papers/cmb_kmsystems.

Thierauf, R.J. 1999. *Knowledge Management Systems for Business*. Santa Barbara, CA: Praeger.

Wenger, E. 1999. *Communities of Practice: Learning, Meaning, and Identity*. Cambridge: Cambridge University Press.

Wellman, J.L. 2009. *Organizational Learning*. London: Palgrave Macmillan.

Wexler, M.N. 2001. "The Who, What and Why of Knowledge Mapping." *Journal of Knowledge Management* 5(3): 249–263.

Recommended Reading

Davenport, T. 1997. *Working Knowledge: How Organizations Manage What They Know*. Boston: Harvard Business School Press.

Edmondson, A. 2012. *Teaming: How Organizations Learn, Innovate, and Compete in the Knowledge Economy*. San Francisco: Jossey-Bass.

Leonard, D., W. Swat, and G. Barton. 2015. *Critical Knowledge Transfer: Tools for Managing Your Company's Deep Smarts*. Boston: Harvard Business Press.

Pentland, A. 2014. *Social Physics: How Good Ideas Spread—the Lessons From a New Science*. New York: Penguin.

2.6 CAREER & LEADERSHIP DEVELOPMENT

Creating a culture of career development in an organization can be a competitive advantage. Being effective at career and leadership development requires the ability to create planned processes of interaction between the organization and the individual that allow an employee to grow within the organization. Understanding the specific skills and capabilities an organization needs now and in the future is important when developing assessments, programs, and pathways to advance employees within the organization.

Career Development

2.6.1 Knowledge of Career Models and Paths

I. Career Models and Paths

Career development planning involves assessing an employee's interests and capabilities and encouraging development that fulfills their aspirations and meets the organization's needs.

Organizations experience many of the benefits of a healthy career development plan, including a skilled workforce, a filled succession plan, and prepared future leaders. But the benefits of career development also include acquisition of the best talent, increased retention, increased engagement, and a workforce that is as motivated, productive, and innovative as possible. The power has shifted in employees' favor and the absence of career development is discouraging for many in the workforce.

TD professionals should have knowledge of their organizations' career development plans and the models and paths that assist employees with their career planning and development.

2.6.1.1 Career Models and Paths

TD professionals use career models and paths, which are designed by the organization to help employees with their development goals. Organizational models are beneficial because they establish the capabilities the organization needs and values today and in the future. But organizations must be transparent with their plans for career progression. There are many different paths a career can follow:

- **Vertical** describes the traditional path that moves in an upward progression. Each advancement represents increased responsibility and authority.

- **Horizontal** represents a career move that is accompanied by a desire for more variety in tasks or challenges. It will include broader experience but does not include a promotion.
- **Career lattice** crisscrosses the career path through an organization and offers opportunities to experience different jobs or departments while learning more about the organization.
- **Matrix** attempts to make each milestone meaningful by ensuring that individuals learn specific content before advancing. The matrix path will likely have two or more tracks, required competencies, and defined roles.
- **Cyclical** is made up of a succession of spirals in which the individual moves from home base to another location to gain knowledge or skills and then cycles back to home base, which can be accomplished through either a permanent position or a temp agency (Williams and Reitman 2013).

2.6.1.2 Alternative Learning Paths

In addition to some of the more traditional career models, learning paths may also support an individual's career progression. Two examples are stackable credentials and apprenticeships:

- **Stackable credentials** are "part of a sequence of credentials that can be accumulated over time to build an individual's qualifications and help them to move along a career pathway or up a career ladder to different and potentially higher-paying jobs" (Collins 2018).
- **Apprenticeship programs** combine on-the-job training with related classroom instruction. The employee learns the theoretical aspects of a highly skilled occupation in the classroom and the practical elements while being supervised by a journey-level crafts person or a trade professional on the job. Although apprenticeships typically focus on manual labor and hands-on fields, they are expanding into other industries such as telecommunications, finance, and information technology (Ellis 2019). [See 2.6.6]

2.6.1.3 Challenges Associated With Career Planning

TD professionals should try to prevent or resolve these common career planning challenges:

- **Investment in employee development.** Organizations may struggle with showing the return on investment for career development because gathering the required data hasn't been a priority. With the advent of people analytics, this should become easier. As TD professionals use analytics to understand what and how learners learn, they can use dashboards and AI to help leaders see how talent development contributes to the bottom line. [See 3.7 and 2.8]
- **Generational differences.** In the United States and Canada, there are currently five generations working side by side. Each generation has its own preference about how development and advancement should be addressed (Meister and Mulcahy 2016):
  - Traditionalists were born prior to 1946.
  - Baby Boomers were born between 1946 and 1964.
  - Generation X was born between 1965 and 1980.
  - Millennials were born between 1981 and 1996.
  - Generation Z was born after 1997.
- **Gender stereotyping.** Cultures that reward behaviors and strategies used primarily by one gender create issues for other genders. The entire workforce is affected when some employees are not satisfied with developmental opportunities or advancement options. The organization suffers, the brand suffers, and a risk of lawsuits occurs when valuable talent leaves.

- **Multicultural influences.** Because organizations are multicultural, racial and cultural issues cannot be ignored in terms of career development. Bringing a diverse workforce together through recognition and celebration of differences is key and an important legal responsibility as well.

2.6.2 Skill in Facilitating the Career Development Planning Process

I. Supporting Individual Lifelong Learning and Career Development

TD professionals should be able to facilitate a process to support employees with their development and plan their careers while, at the same time, aligning with organizational needs as shown in Figure 2.6.2-1. Doing so helps TD professionals discuss career development with employees. The goal is to identify the target area that meets all aspects and determine the individual development required.

Figure 2.6.2-1. Align Skills and Interests With Organizational Needs

Source: ATD's Integrated Talent Management Certificate Program.

2.6.2.1 Facilitating the Career Development Process

Career development planning is:
- Assessing an individual's interests, values, and capabilities
- Exploring their options
- Establishing goals
- Encouraging employee development to fulfill their aspirations and meet the organization's needs

The career development process may be initiated by an employee, an employee's manager, or a TD professional. A career development process map, which shows the learning and development experiences necessary to move from one level or job to the next, guides the planning.

TD professionals may use a career development process map by following typical steps:
1. Help employees articulate career aspirations.
2. Objectively assess strengths and development needs; this may require using assessment tools. [See 2.6.3]
3. Help employees identify needs and gaps.
4. Provide options for career goals looking at what the individual needs and what the organization needs, such as competency requirements or future role needs. [See 2.7.3.3]
5. Help employees develop a realistic individual development plan, which typically offers the necessary actions—set goals, list actions, identify resources, and establish target dates. [See 2.6.2.2]
6. Implement and follow up with employees. Identifying critical items in a development plan helps employees stay focused on what's most important. (Hosmer 2015; Williams and Reitman 2013).

2.6.2.2 Individual Development Plans

An individual development plan (IDP) is a plan for personal improvement in a current job or for job advancement. Developing an IDP is an important step in the career development conversation. Helping employees stay on track is equally important. While most organizations have their own IDP format, they all should include these components: long- and short-term goals, success criteria, target dates, resources required, and actions that assist with reaching the goals. Goals should be written using SMART guidelines that stretch employee development. The IDP should also represent a variety of actions and learning opportunities on the job, outside the job, independently, and through interactions with others. Reflection and feedback should be built into the plan.

TD professionals who manage others should schedule IDP discussions with their employees. They should find ways to empower employees to continue their developmental journey. Using an IDP helps ensure that employees are prepared for job opportunities and the organization has a pipeline of people available to fill roles (Hosmer 2015). [See 2.7.3.3]

TD professionals should confirm that managers are discussing career goals with employees and using IDPs to plan their employees' development. IDPs are especially useful because they record and track goals and development, tying personal development to the organization's strategic goals. Table 2.6.2.2-1 shows who has responsibility for each step (Hosmer 2015).

An IDP complements an employee's goals and should include several basic components:
- A link to the organization's or department's strategies and goals
- The individual's development needs
- Completion dates
- Personal and professional needs as related to department and organizational needs
- Space to document learning opportunities, schedules, and costs
- Space for supervisory comments
- Employee's long- and short-term goals (Biech 2018)

Table 2.6.2.2-1. Manager and Employee Responsibilities

Manager Responsibilities	Employee Responsibilities
☐ Initiate the process.	☐ Provide responses to career-related questions.
☐ Use company-provided frameworks for career planning.	☐ Self-reflect to identify career and development goals.
☐ Explain the IDP process and its purpose.	☐ Evaluate skills and interests openly.
☐ Provide an atmosphere of trust and open communication for employees to discuss their careers and progress.	☐ Draft an IDP with input from managers.
☐ Guide the career and progress discussions.	☐ Be open to feedback and taking on new challenges.
☐ Ask questions and listen.	☐ Implement and own the plan.
☐ Identify potential career opportunities for employees.	☐ Assess progress and initiate follow-ups.
☐ Identify learning resources and activities.	
☐ Provide constructive feedback.	

Source: Hosmer (2015) as shown in Biech (2018).

2.6.2.3 The Employee's Role

TD professionals should motivate and empower employees to take active ownership of their own career development. They should know how to help learners be self-sufficient and encourage them to make decisions about what to learn and when. Employees need to manage their own career development by setting goals, drafting an IDP with input from their managers, using development approaches to reach their goals, documenting progress, and gathering evidence of their performance. TD professionals can encourage them to learn from team members and regularly ask for feedback and support from their managers (Hart 2018).

2.6.2.4 Talent Development's Role in Fostering Employee Development

TD professionals should encourage employees to see their career as a point in time on a path that combines short-term and long-term goals. They can show employees how to document their progress and identify actions that help them learn and meet their goals. TD professionals can also put employees in touch with mentors and coaches, and recommend courses, online classes, and digital resources. They can show employees the benefits of networking and provide encouragement.

At times, employees may want to follow a career plan that does not include the organization. For example, they may want to work in a different industry or start their own business. TD professionals who support these employees will benefit in the long run. The organization is likely to retain them as employees longer than if they were not getting support; they are also more likely to share their positive experience with others, which will enhance the organization's reputation and encourage others to apply. TD professionals can support these individuals by sharing articles or books that address their interests, introducing them to people who can support their career moves, and encouraging them to discuss their plans. They can also help them identify what they have to offer and how to share it with others before leaving (Kaiden 2015; Cast 2018).

TD professionals also should encourage discussions between employees and their managers. Regular conversations are meaningful and valuable, and TD professionals should ensure that everyone knows continuous learning is a priority.

2.6.3 Skill in Developing, Administering, and Debriefing Results of Assessments of Intelligence, Aptitude, Potential, Skill, Ability, or Interests

I. Using Assessments for Career Development
TD professionals should be skilled in developing, administering, and debriefing various assessment instruments.

2.6.3.1 Assessment Options
TD professionals should be aware of appropriate uses of assessments as well as the ethical and legal issues involved in selecting and administering assessments in the workplace. This list includes some of the major assessment types:

- **Intelligence assessments** typically consist of language and math questions to assess general intelligence and problem-solving skills.
- **Personality assessments** ask preferential questions and assess aptitudes and personality style. Some target specific job categories (such as sales) or competency areas (such as leadership).
- **Aptitude assessments** ask questions to determine if an individual has the potential to complete a specific role without prior knowledge, experience, or training. Employers may use them to make hiring decisions.
- **Skill or ability assessments** provide an objective evaluation of an individual's ability to complete a job or task. The assessment measures current skills.
- **Interest assessments,** sometimes called career assessments, help individuals match preferences to specific jobs, job categories, or professions.
- **Multi-rater assessments,** sometimes called 360-degree reviews, collect feedback from multiple reviewers including the individual, the manager, co-workers, and sometimes customers to gain insight into the development needs of an individual. [See 1.6.5]

2.6.3.2 Best Practices in Administering and Debriefing
TD professionals should understand the importance of administering and debriefing an assessment tool.

When administering an assessment, TD professionals should:
- Ensure that the instrument is reliable and valid and will measure the right skills.
- Take time to properly explain the purpose and how the data will be used.
- Assure the individual that no breaches of confidentiality will occur.

When debriefing assessments, TD professionals should:
- Have clearly defined objectives and expectations.
- Provide written reports in person initially.
- Tailor the results to the individual.
- Provide a thorough interpretation accompanied by reports that are easy to use.
- Ensure that enough time is allowed for a thorough debrief, or schedule a follow-up meeting.
- Link results to development options when possible.

- Discuss next steps.
- Offer to follow up.

2.6.4 Knowledge of Career Development Methods and Techniques

I. Development Approaches for Key Roles and Jobs

TD professionals should explore the development opportunities available, create and invent new options, and assign those that align best with the individuals and what they need to learn or experience.

2.6.4.1 Approaches to Career Development

Organizations need to focus on developing employees for key roles, which means being knowledgeable about the many development methods available. An environment in which people have access to the tools, resources, professional support, and experiences to develop these skills will broaden their perspectives, ensure their long-term career growth, and provide opportunities to add value to the organization in key roles.

There are myriad approaches TD professionals can use to develop employees for roles and jobs in an organization, including:

- **Formal learning programs**—certifications, courses, academic assignments, advanced degree education, immersive classes
- **Informal development**—coaching, mentoring, online personal development courses
- **Job-related opportunities**—stretch assignments, committee and task force involvement, action learning
- **Outside the job, but in the organization, opportunities**—rotational assignments, attending meetings in other departments as an observer, job shadowing
- **Volunteering**—instructing at a community college, providing community service, loaned executive program, an opportunity to gain experience working in another organization (usually a nonprofit)
- **Self-study**—research projects, reading, study groups
- **Networking activities**—professional associations, online and social-supported networks

2.6.5 Skill in Conducting Individual and Group Career Planning Sessions to Provide Guidance Across Career Phases

I. Supporting Employees' Career Cycle

TD professionals should be skilled in career planning by providing guidance throughout employees' careers, whether one-to-one or in a group.

Although past career development approaches have been tied to career development theories and the phases they promote, such as D.E. Super's five development phases, the 21st-century approach is to focus on the individual. The world is less predictable, work is subject to change, and individuals have limited control over their jobs. To address these concerns, career development has become less linear and more dependent on the individual's desires and the environment's influences (Bright and Pryor 2011). TD professionals should be prepared to provide individual or group planning sessions throughout an employee's career journey. [See 1.7.2.2]

2.6.5.1 Career Development Opportunities During an Employee's Career

During an employee's time with an organization, they are likely to change jobs and even careers. Several key career development points may occur, including onboarding, moving into supervisory roles, or transitioning from one job to another; moreover, during an organizational change, their role, title, or department may change, which would also require further development.

2.6.5.1.1 Onboarding Efforts

An effective onboarding experience sets the stage for future career development and is beneficial to the employee and the organization. Employees gain a deeper appreciation for the organization when they are involved in onboarding. When employees feel valued from the outset, they are less likely to leave; more than half of employees who leave their jobs do so within the first 12 months (Forbes Coaches Council 2017). However, formal onboarding increases the chance that new employees will stay for at least three years by 69 percent (Lombardi and Laurano 2013).

Onboarding will be different in every organization based on what the company and individuals need; therefore, the entire process may take three to six months. Onboarding should introduce the foundational elements employees need for success to build their careers with the organization (Dávila and Piña-Ramírez 2018; Biech 2018). Gallup suggests five questions must be answered during onboarding:
- "What do we believe in around here?"
- "What are my strengths?"
- "What is my role?"
- "Who are my partners?"
- "What does my future here look like?" (Clifton and Harter 2019)

2.6.5.1.2 New Supervisor Preparation

Becoming a supervisor is one of the biggest career changes an employee will make. They should be as prepared as possible before making the move. New supervisors go from doing the work to ensuring that the work is done. Previously they were only accountable to their immediate supervisor, but now they are also responsible to their direct reports. The new role requires them to lead others and guide their work, coach employees' performance, lead change, be a liaison to other departments, create budgets, and complete many other new actions (Scisco, Biech, and Hallenbeck 2017).

2.6.5.1.3 Transition to a New Job

People entering the workforce can anticipate making five to eight career changes in their lifetime. TD professionals should support employees and help them prepare for their next position or career. Then, when an opportunity arises, they can work with employees to create a transition plan, regardless of whether the new position is internal, external, local, or international. If the role is internal, TD professionals can make introductions, suggest pretransition development, provide support to manage feelings of insecurity, arrange a turnover plan, and perform other actions that will make the transition as smooth as possible for the employee and the organization.

2.6.5.1.4 Organization Change

TD professionals should increase their organization's agility by fostering change-ready employees, creating change leaders at all levels, and preparing employees for job and career changes. Career development is important, and it becomes even more critical during periods of change. Talent development may need to support other individuals and departments through job modification, downsizing, reorganizations, organizational mergers, or acquisitions. TD professionals should keep employees informed, prepare them for new jobs, and support their ability to identify new roles.

2.6.5.2 Group Career Planning

TD professionals should support group career planning by conducting career planning sessions, providing guidance across career phases, or initiating self-sustaining peer mentoring groups.

Advantages of group career planning include:
- Reach more employees at the same time.
- Use the social aspects of work and learn from one another.
- Create a less threatening environment in which employees are with their peers.
- Offer more opportunities for employees to learn by practicing skills in activities such as role plays.
- Prepare employees for more intensive one-on-one planning.

Conducting group career planning sessions can be helpful when individuals would like to learn from others. Group sessions can also efficiently address more than one person. TD professionals can use this time to provide action planning templates, help individuals establish goals, and offer developmental opportunity ideas. They should obtain group participation to share their ideas and cover agenda items such as:
- Align skills and interests with organizational needs (Figure 2.6.2-1) and learn how to find the target area for development.
- Identify various developmental opportunities.
- Practice completing an IDP.
- Review the employee experience and phases of development.
- Discuss the organization's future needs (short-term and long-term goals).

Initiating peer coaching is a way to provide a "low-cost, high-impact, customizable way to promote professional and personal growth, develop leaders, and influence positive organizational culture" (Johnson 2019). Peer coaching is conducted in pairs or small groups to encourage personal or professional leadership development by supporting, challenging, and coaching one another. It can be part of formal training, a follow-up to formal training, a stand-alone program, or a support group for entrepreneurs or consultants (often called master mind groups). Groups develop their own norms and define their success. TD professionals should provide training in coaching skills for members of the group.

2.6.6 Knowledge of How to Develop and Implement Qualification Programs

I. Develop and Implement Qualification Programs
TD professionals should know the basic steps of developing and managing qualification programs.

2.6.6.1 Defining Qualification Programs

Qualification programs are important because they identify the competencies that must be mastered to ensure employees have the skills and knowledge to perform specific tasks. This is particularly important when safety is a priority, such as in healthcare, chemical processing, and electrical systems. Qualification programs may be academic, vocational, or skills-related efforts. TD professionals should be familiar with the following terminology:

- **Qualification** is determined based on achieving narrowly defined content with specific learning objectives. A qualification program may be delivered as a classroom experience followed by a knowledge exam. There is no recertification component. A qualification may be valid for life or require the learning experience to be repeated.
- **A certificate** is earned by acquiring knowledge. Course attendance is often the only requirement, although a test or project may be required. Individuals receive a certificate that never expires; however, they are not "certified," which is a designation only bestowed on those who are in a practice, such as a Certified Public Accountant (CPA).
- **An assessment-based certificate** is more rigorous than a certificate. This non-degree granting program delivers training and evaluates participants' acquisition of skills, knowledge, and competencies. It is awarded to only those who "meet performance, proficiency, or pass standards for the assessment(s)" (Hirt 2019).
- **Certification** refers to a program that is administered by a non-governmental organization and assesses whether an individual has the knowledge and skill to perform a role measured against a set standard. The administering body grants individuals a credential for a specific time period. Certification is available to those who meet predetermined, standardized criteria, and the knowledge required to pass an assessment is learned through classes, self-study, and experience. The assessment is independent of a class or training program. To retain the credential, recipients must meet renewal requirements.

2.6.6.2 Requirements for Qualification and Certification Programs

A key difference between qualification and certification programs is that qualification programs are often a job requirement to ensure employees remain competent, especially in roles that concern safety or people's lives. Conversely, certification is generally voluntary.

Essentials of a qualifications program include:
- It is based on narrowly defined content taught in a course and measured by an assessment.
- It tests specific knowledge or skills based on the learning objectives.
- A qualification is awarded if the standards, such as a passing score, are met.
- The process has limited rigor and discipline.
- Facilitators are aware of the test scores and may conduct the assessment.
- Credential holders retrain and retest at the end of a time period unless the qualification is valid for life.

Essentials of a certification program are specific and include:
- It is based on a broad body of knowledge.
- It is independent of any education or training program.
- Assessment is based on a body of knowledge, not specific learning outcomes.
- Recertification is required to maintain the credential, such as continuing education opportunities.

- It prohibits those who train the content from conducting the assessment.
- Guidelines prohibit the release of exam questions to anyone teaching or developing prep courses (Institute for Credentialing Excellence n.d.).

2.6.6.3 The Need for Qualification Programs

The main reason for establishing a qualification program, and in some cases a certification program, is to ensure that an organization's employees have the appropriate skill sets. Deciding between a qualification or certification program depends mostly on the investment the organization is willing to make in time and money. The key reasons for implementing either program are that they:

- Build capacity for the organization's talent needs.
- Attract qualified candidates to become employees.
- Provide training and development.
- Offer individuals recognition of achievement.
- Address a regulatory requirement.
- Meet the requirement to be legally defensible.
- Address the industry requirements for a license, certification, or other qualification program.

2.6.6.4 Successful Program Design

TD professionals should know how to design and develop a qualification program. With a few differences, designing a qualification or certification program is similar to designing most instructor-led training programs. Start with completing due diligence, which is included in steps one through four:

1. **Establish goals.** These may include increasing competencies of employees, validating skills, being recognized as an industry leader, creating a more qualified talent pool, or addressing a regulatory requirement.
2. **Analyze the audience** by projecting the size and location of the group that will participate.
3. **Analyze the jobs or roles** to decide which types will be certified and what skills and knowledge need to be learned and assessed. This information is important for the assessment.
4. **Prepare a budget, finance model, and pricing structure** for the program. Decide if the program will be a profit or cost center. If the certification or qualification decision has not been made, remember that a certification effort requires a much larger investment. The budget may need to include exam development, training development, and learning management system (LMS) add-ons.
5. **Determine a model,** framework, and features for the program. This includes the name of the program and credential, the paths available to candidates, how the program will be introduced, whether there will be stackable exams, and the exam format. If the decision hasn't been made, talent development must decide if the program will be a qualification or certification program.
6. **Assess training** that is available to determine if it needs to be created or redesigned, as well as materials for training or self-study that may need to be created.
7. **Determine a timeline** that includes a launch date, marketing plan and design, first cohort selection, unveiling the credential name, and other key initiatives.
8. **Develop the training delivery and exam** using several subject matter experts to create a bank of questions. Remember that questions for the certification need to be kept secure.
9. **Check all legal concerns** and have nondisclosure agreements signed (Moorhead 2016; Manijak 2016; Institute for Credentialing Excellence n.d.).

2.6.6.5 Talent Development's Responsibilities for Qualification Programs

Once the design is completed, TD professionals have responsibilities and decisions to make that include:
- Determine whether to run a test pilot study.
- Plan a marketing campaign for the program.
  - Begin collecting testimonials.
  - Write a blog post.
  - Get senior-level leaders involved.
- Determine a plan for keeping exam questions secured.
- Create a specific email address for the program.
- Develop an update plan to ensure the program keeps pace with the industry and other world changes.

TD professionals may also be responsible for ongoing efforts such as:
- Offering courses related to the qualification or certification program
- Maintaining a database that tracks employees who have applied, are enrolled, and have completed the program
- Managing how learners access self-paced materials, reference documents, or job aids
- Creating reports for their stakeholders

Finally, TD professionals should look for ways to continue improving the program and discuss any plans with their stakeholders.

Leadership Development

2.6.7 Knowledge of Leadership Development Practices and Techniques

> **I. Understanding Leadership Development**
>
> Leadership development is an overall organizational plan that increases the capacity of employees to perform in leadership positions and may include individualized development opportunities such as coaching, mentoring, internal and external courses, new experiences, stretch assignments, or other development opportunities. TD professionals should be knowledgeable about what is available to develop the organization's leaders so they can support them with the required resources.
>
> In today's information-saturated, digitally fluent workplace, ubiquitous leadership is required. No longer does information reside only with senior leadership, so fostering leadership at every level is critical. TD professionals must find ways to distribute leadership throughout the organization and build a foundation for every employee to become a leader.

2.6.7.1 Evolution of Leadership Models

In designing leadership development programs, TD professionals should understand the evolution of leadership models. Current models can be split into two chronological time periods: the industrial and postindustrial. Industrial leadership models arose during the industrial revolution and are largely hierarchical and authoritarian, with leaders directly telling their followers exactly what to do and how to do it. Industrial leadership models see leadership and management as identical concepts. Industrial-era leaders were managers and senior managers who led by command-and-control structures. Examples of industrial leadership models include:

- **Behavioral theory** focuses on the actions of leaders such as democratic, autocratic, and laissez-faire leaders.
- **Great man theory** assumes leaders are born, not made.
- **Trait theory** assumes people are born with inherited traits, some of which are suited to leadership.

Postindustrial leadership models recognize that work environments have changed and are no longer factory-based systems in which people are as interchangeable as parts of a machine. These models account for factors like complexity of organizations, the widespread availability of information, the speed of change, and new expectations of knowledge workers. In postindustrial leadership models, leadership behaviors are anticipated at every level of an organization, not just senior managers. Examples of postindustrial leadership models include:

- **Contingency theory** suggests that there is no one correct leadership type.
- **Situational theory** is related to contingency theory, which means leaders choose the best action.
- **Participative theory** proposes that the ideal style includes other's input.
- **Management or transactional theory** focuses on the role of supervision and group performance.
- **Relationship or transformational theory** focuses on the connections formed between leaders and followers.
- **Adaptive leadership framework,** introduced by Ronald Heifetz and Marty Linsky (2017), is the ability to adapt and thrive in challenging environments based on four principles (emotional intelligence, organizational justice, development, and character). [See 1.3.10]

2.6.7.2 Leadership Styles

Leadership styles are not independent from leadership theories; instead, they are the theories in practice. Leadership styles are the manner and approach of providing direction, implementing plans, and motivating people.

The following classification of leadership styles can help TD professionals recognize not only the various leadership styles in an organization but also their own leadership styles, which enables them to adapt their own styles as needed. Although the list of leadership styles is vast, most fall into several categories:

- **Directive leaders** give specific advice to the group and establish ground rules and structure by clarifying expectations and specifying or assigning certain work tasks to be followed.
- **Supportive leaders** promote good relations with the group and show sensitivity to employees' needs.
- **Participative leaders** base decisions on consultation with their group; they share information with the group.
- **Achievement-oriented leaders** set challenging goals and encourage high performance to show confidence in the group's ability.
- **Transformational leaders** encourage and motivate employees following the four Is: inspirational motivation, idealized influence, individualized consideration, and intellectual stimulation.
- **Situational leaders** adopt a different style depending on the requirements of the situation and the development level of everyone being addressed.
- **Charismatic leaders** are generally driven by their commitment to their cause; they derive their influence from their charm and persuasiveness.

- **Servant leaders** lead from a desire to better serve others, not to attain more power; they see themselves as servants of their followers.
- **Transactional leaders** focus on practically managing the work and rewarding performance; they are most effective in crisis and emergency situations.

No matter what roles leaders hold in an organization, their success depends on the leadership style they adopt and their ability to use the best style for any given situation. By understanding these styles and their effects, TD professionals can know more about the leaders they interact with and develop themselves into more flexible, better leaders.

2.6.7.3 Comparing Leadership to Management

Postindustrial leadership models distinguish between leadership and management as separate concepts: *management* focuses on administrative processes (such as an organization's annual performance review process) while *leadership* relies on behaviors and characteristics (such as leading a team through a change initiative).

Managers, by definition, have employees and a position of authority that focuses on carrying out the organization's goals efficiently. The manager's job is to plan, organize, and coordinate. Leaders influence others (followers) in the organization to achieve greater effectiveness and fulfillment of the organizational purpose and goals. The leader's job is to inspire and motivate—they may or may not have employees as direct reports.

2.6.8 Skill in Sourcing, Designing, Building, and Evaluating Leadership Development Experiences

> **I. Designing a Leadership Development Initiative**
> TD professionals should be skilled in designing and developing leadership development programs.

2.6.8.1 Need for Leadership Development

Leadership development benefits an organization by aligning learning and development initiatives to its mission, goals, and performance expectations. Leadership behaviors affect employee engagement, turnover, and ultimately the bottom line. One research study of more than 2,600 organizations in 74 countries found that organizations with the highest quality leaders were 13 times more likely to outperform their competition in key bottom-line metrics such as financial performance (Boatman and Wellins 2014). The study also showed that organizations with higher quality leadership were up to three times more likely to retain employees and had more than five times the number of highly engaged leaders. Another study showed that 70 percent of the variation between great workplace engagement and low workplace engagement could be explained by the quality of the manager or team leader (Clifton and Harter 2019).

2.6.8.2 Create the Organization's Leadership Development Foundation

TD professionals create leadership development programs by coordinating with many key stakeholders. Senior leaders set the organization's vision, mission, and direction; therefore, they must have a key role in designing a leadership program. Development begins by engaging leaders from the outset on three topics: the organization's readiness, corporate drivers for increasing leadership development, and leadership's values and beliefs about leadership development.

Organizational Readiness

TD professionals should involve their leaders in discussions about the organization's readiness to invest in leadership development initiatives. Six key factors distinguish organizations that have successful leadership development programs:

- **Future focused.** Organizations should ensure that their leadership development programs are strategically driven. They should look for the skills required for future success.
- **Leadership responsibility.** Organizations should have fully engaged senior managers who recognize leadership gaps as an obstacle to the execution of strategy.
- **Leadership quality.** Organizations should recognize the importance of having a pipeline of experienced, high-quality leaders to fill positions, because having a vibrant succession plan may be better than hiring from the outside.
- **Results oriented.** Organizations should institute standards and establish, track, measure, and evaluate goals.
- **Value learning and development.** Organizations should value learning and development for all employees, not just leaders. It should be a learning organization that begins development early.
- **Long-term, aligned systemic approach.** Organizations should align the leadership development program with other aspects of the organization and take a systemic approach to developing leaders who are prepared to cope with the challenges of the future.

Corporate Drivers

To ensure alignment of the leadership development initiative to the organization's strategy, TD professionals should focus their discussion on how leadership development will support the strategy, defining how leadership development will support corporate drivers and the organization's vision, mission, and goals. Leaders should also articulate what defines success and how it will be measured.

Values and Beliefs About Leadership Development

Discussing what leaders believe about leadership development will focus the effort's direction. The results could reveal whether everyone or only high-potential employees should have access to leadership development as well as whether development should begin upon employment or only after an employee has spent a certain amount of time in the organization.

Ensuring Leadership Development Success

TD professionals should help their organizations determine what they hope to accomplish with a leadership development program and how they will measure the results. They can help organizations understand how to optimize formal and informal learning by integrating it into daily work (Gurdjian, Halbeisen, and Lane 2014). In addition, according to a 2016 article in *Harvard Business Review*, for leadership training to be successful, "it's important to attend to organizational design and managerial processes first and then support them with individual development tools such as coaching and classroom or online education" (Beer, Finnström, and Schrader 2016). The overall organization—including systems, policies, and processes—needs to support and sustain the desired leadership behaviors or the program will not be successful.

II. Build a Leadership Development Plan

Leaders who are skilled and knowledgeable are essential to ensuring organizations achieve their strategic imperative. TD professionals should help build leadership development plans so that existing and future leaders acquire the skills and development they need to support their organizations.

2.6.8.3 Analyze Development Needs

Many organizations have competency models that identify skills their leaders require today and in the future. When such a model does not exist or when the organization's compentency model is lacking, TD professionals should begin with the organization's desired results and how its leadership views leadership development. TD professionals can then conduct an analysis of what needs to be included in the program's design. They should compare current leadership behaviors against desired leadership behaviors to uncover the gap.

When an organization does not have a competency model, identifying leadership requirements for the future involves a different analysis than what TD professionals may use. If the organization has implemented a system that uses data and predictive analysis, the answers may be easier to find. If not, TD professionals can ask questions to help determine the competencies future leaders will need, including:

- What are the top three business issues the organization will face in the next five to 10 years?
- What external changes (technology, competition, regulatory, industry, and demographic) or internal changes (employee base, strategy, and product line) will alter the requirements of leadership in the organization?
- What emerging issues and problems will require unique leadership skills? How well prepared are current leaders to address them?
- How will leadership competencies need to change to meet the organization's future needs?
- What attributes might be lost with upcoming retirements? [See 3.7.1.1 and 3.7.4.4]

2.6.8.4 Clarify the Purpose and Establish Goals

Discussions with leaders and analyzing any gaps uncovered helps TD professionals clarify the purpose and establish goals for the leadership development initiative. Clearly defined goals enable evaluation and measurement. Leadership development program goals fit into one of three categories:

- **Operational or programmatic goals** are related to the details required to start and implement the leadership development effort, such as scheduling the date the program will be deployed or completing an action like identifying all eligible employees.
- **Interim goals** are indicators of final goals and progress to the end result. An interim goal could be "80 percent of all leadership development program components are completed by end of year" or "Each participant will complete one project that spans at least two departments." Progress on specific competencies can be shown using 360-degree instruments.
- **Outcome goals** are based on the needs of the organization and the expectations of senior leaders, and measure the results an initiative has on organizational goals. They could be related to leadership preparedness, such as "Promote from within 80 percent of the time," or they could relate to resolving an organizational goal, such as "Reduce turnover by 50 percent within 18 months."

2.6.8.5 Determine Design Features

The purpose and goals of the leadership development program provide TD professionals with enough information to begin deciding on fundamental design features, such as overall program design, content, and delivery alternatives.

2.6.8.5.1 Overall Program Design

The design will be based on the organization's overall philosophy about leadership development and includes decisions about design issues, such as:
- Who is eligible to participate and how will high potentials be identified and selected?
- Who will champion the program and what administration is required?
- How will success be measured?
- What is leadership's responsibility?
- What is the tuition reimbursement policy?
- What opportunities will be available for leadership development candidates?
- How will leadership development align with other development efforts?
- How does the leadership development program complement other initiatives, such as succession planning? (Cremo and Bux 2017)

2.6.8.5.2 Content

Content will address the skills and knowledge the organization needs to reach its goals and include skills that are crucial for most executive positions such as results orientation, strategic focus, collaboration and influence, team leadership, developing organizational capabilities, change leadership, and market understanding (Fernandez-Araoz, Roscoe, and Aramaki 2017). TD professionals should look to the future to determine the likelihood that their leaders will need skills to lead through more complexity and ambiguity, lead remotely, or manage humans and machines, as well as what will be most important to their organizations (Volini et al. 2019).

Content will also include specific skills and knowledge based on the gap analysis and specific future competency requirements of the organization. For example, the current organizational culture may not place enough emphasis on accountability, so that may be an important developmental area. Or the organization may require reskilling to use data and analytics to analyze and predict future trends.

2.6.8.5.3 Delivery

TD professionals have multiple opportunities for delivering skills. Formal leadership development courses may be designed and available to all employees and may include customized leadership development courses, specified virtual and digital courses, or self-study courses. Because most development occurs on the job, they should tap into the wide variety of learning experiences available to develop future leaders. Supervisors must also understand their roles in helping to develop their employees. On-the-job experiences could comprise committee or team assignments, job rotations, stretch assignments, and interim appointments. Other options include making mentoring and coaching available, taking an active role in a professional association, getting 360-degree feedback, or shadowing a leader. External development may also be a part of the design, such as taking college courses, attending conferences, participating in certification programs, offering tuition reimbursment, or promoting community volunteer experiences.

2.6.8.6 Designing Blended Leadership Development Experiences

Leadership development often occurs on the job, as a leader experiences real-world situations. Diverse learning experiences help develop leaders and broaden their exposure to other leaders, issues, and styles across an organization.

TD professionals should use a blended approach as their basis for leadership development. Many organizations sponsor formal leadership learning programs, and competency models may be used to develop leaders. Experience helps develop specific competencies. Employees should be assessed not just for their current competencies but also for their potential to learn from experience. Leadership placement isn't just about finding the most talented employee for the job; it's about finding who can be stretched and developed for the next challenge.

To use development experiences, TD professionals should ask:
- Which experiences matter and what will be learned?
- Who should have what relevant experience?
- How can employees be moved across department and location lines effectively?
- How can leaders ensure that the correct lessons are learned? (McCauley et al. 2014)

Leadership development should mix formal learning and practical experiences. To enhance the formal learning curriculum, TD professionals can recommend experiences at different structure levels that are embedded in the employees' work environment, such as:
- **Semi-structured leadership development** experiences could include a community of leaders joining a book club discussion, discussing a speaker's message, watching videos, observing meetings, or enrolling in internal and external courses based on a recommended list.
- **Structured leadership development** could include a list of annual recommended courses, short-term projects or processes that build skills without great disruption to current job responsibilities, stretch opportunities with feedback, learning through hardships, or mentoring.
- **Highly structured leadership development** could include a structured curriculum and last several years. Potential activities within that curriculum include job rotation programs, international job assignments, a loaned executive program (volunteering in a nonprofit to broaden leadership skills), and coaching from an external consultant.

2.6.8.7 Candidate Eligibility, Referral, and Selection

TD professionals should be prepared to help their organizations determine the best way to identify leadership development candidates. When organizations maintain a current and active succession plan, they're better informed and able to identify candidates. Other organizations may have different avenues. [See 3.4.10]

Some organizations train leaders at all levels while others solicit candidates from several referral options. In some cases, leaders can self-nominate and sign up to participate. Other organizations may require leaders to be nominated by their supervisor or other credible source, or they may determine eligibility based on tenure; for example, all managers must participate within their first 12 months of promotion.

Candidate referral systems should have a clear nomination process that includes an application, supporting documentation, deadlines, required approvals, and supervisory signatures. Referral systems provide an opportunity to expand diversity in an organization's leadership ranks. While there is no one best way to select candidates for leadership development, the selection process must be fair and accurate. It may include a weighted evaluation of applications, assessment instruments, interviews with a selection committee or senior executives, or a committee assessment.

At higher levels of the organization, participants are often evaluated and selected by several different methods:
- Nomination by a manager
- Cumulative data from performance management systems or past talent review discussions
- Individual assessments and custom developmental plans based on their outcomes
- Participation in an assessment center exercise
- Behavior or structured interviews (Phillips, Phillips, and Ray 2015)

2.6.8.8 High Potentials

High-potential employees (also known as HiPos) are consistent, superior performers who have the potential and the desire to develop and succeed more effectively in the organization than other employees. TD professionals should know the value of identifying HiPos and communicating expectations to them. Furthermore, "organizations that formally identify their top talent are less likely to lose valuable people" (Smith and Campbell 2014). [See 3.4.16]

To identify HiPos, TD professionals need to help their organizations establish promotion criteria defining high-potential behaviors and achievements, based on transparent, objective performance assessments. The process needs to focus on potential, not just past or current performance. It should also include factors such as:
- Alignment with organizational values and culture
- Ability to build strategic partnerships and influence others
- Ability to build teams and lead them to success
- Capacity to deal with pressure, adversity, and setbacks with poise

Once identified, HiPos should have the opportunity to develop the required skills for future promotions; without this opportunity, they could fail to advance professionally. The word *potential* indicates that they are not fully developed and require additional experiences and talent development.

2.6.8.9 Sustaining and Evaluating Leadership Development Progress

Because many leadership development initiatives are complex, multiyear programs, TD professionals should create a set of processes to sustain and evaluate each program.

Sustaining

Organizations are dynamic entities; therefore, they should periodically review their leadership development initiatives to ensure the program grows and changes to continue meeting organizational needs. Topics addressed during a leadership program review should include:
- **Leadership succession plans,** such as gaps in key areas or predictions for outside talent recruitment
- **Leadership development requirements,** including changes in future competencies and trends in development requirements
- **Future planning** for addressing increases in diversity or reviewing what has changed

- **Review recommendations for new candidates,** including their readiness and commitment, as well as organizational needs
- **Operational discussions** to review the budget and whether progress is on target

Evaluation

TD professionals should apply standard strategies when evaluating leadership development initiatives, which should be tied to the organization's strategic imperatives. Common evaluation strategies include:

- Kirkpatrick's Four Levels of Evaluation
- Brinkerhoff's Success Case Method
- The Phillips ROI Methodology [See 2.8]

REFERENCES

Beer, M., M. Finnström, and D. Schrader. 2016. "Why Leadership Training Fails—and What to Do About It." *Harvard Business Review*, October. hbr.org/2016/10/why-leadership-training-fails-and-what-to-do-about-it.

Biech, E. 2018. *ATD's Foundations of Talent Development: Launching, Leveraging, and Leading Your Organization's TD Effort*. Alexandria, VA: ATD Press.

Boatman, J., and R. Wellins. 2014. *Ready-Now Leaders: 25 Findings to Meet Tomorrow's Business Challenges*. Global Leadership Forecast 2014|2015. Pittsburgh: Development Dimensions International.

Bright, J.E.H., and R.G. Pryor. 2011. "The Chaos Theory of Careers." *Journal of Employment Counseling* 48(4): 163–166.

Cast, C. 2018. "6 Ways to Take Control of Your Career Development if Your Company Doesn't Care About it." *Harvard Business Review*, January 19.

Clifton, J., and J. Harter. 2019. *It's the Manager: Gallup Finds the Quality of Managers and Team Leaders Is the Single Biggest Factor in Your Organization's Long Term Success*. Omaha, NE: Gallup Press.

Collins, B. 2018. "Develop Your Career With a Professional Certification." *TD at Work*. Alexandria, VA: ATD Press.

Cremo, A., and T. Bux. 2017. "Developing a Leadership Pipeline." *TD at Work*. Alexandria, VA: ATD Press.

Dávila, N., and W. Piña-Ramírez. 2018. *Effective Onboarding*. Alexandria, VA: ATD Press.

Ellis, R. 2019. "Primed for Apprentices." *TD*, September. td.org/magazines/td-magazine/primed-for-apprentices.

Fernandez-Araoz, C., A. Roscoe, and K. Aramaki. 2017. "Turning Potential Into Success: The Missing Link in Leadership Development." *Harvard Business Review*, November–December.

Forbes Coaches Council. 2017. "Seven New Onboarding Strategies You'll See This Year." *Forbes*, January 30. forbes.com/sites/forbescoachescouncil/2017/01/30/seven-new-onboarding-strategies-youll-see-this-year/#1cc872007b4d.

Gurdjian, P., T. Halbeisen, and K. Lane. 2014. "Why Leadership Development Programs Fail." *McKinsey Quarterly*, January. mckinsey.com/featured-insights/leadership/why-leadership-development-programs-fail.

Hart, J. 2018. "How to Become a Modern Professional Learner." Sidebar in *ATD's Foundations of Talent Development: Launching, Leveraging, and Leading Your Organization's TD Effort*, edited by E. Biech, 351–353. Alexandria, VA: ATD Press.

Heifetz, R., and M. Linsky. 2017. *Leadership on the Line, Staying Alive Through the Dangers of Change*, revised ed. Boston: Harvard Business Review Press.

Hirt, M. 2019. "Credentialing Terminology Job Aid." Association for Talent Development.

Hosmer, D. 2015. "The Manager's Guide to Employee Development." *TD at Work*. Alexandria, VA: ATD Press.

Institute for Credentialing Excellence. n.d. "Promoting Best Practices for the Credentialing Community." credentialingexcellence.org.

Johnson, S. 2019. "Peer Coaching: The Wave of the Future." *TD at Work*. Alexandria, VA: ATD Press.

Kaiden, S. 2015. "Keeping Your Career on Track." *TD at Work*. Alexandria, VA: ATD Press.

Lombardi, M., and M. Laurano. 2013. *Human Capital Management Trends 2013: It's a Brave New World*. Waltham, MA: Aberdeen Group. deliberatepractice.com.au/wp-content/uploads/2013/02/8101-RA-human-capital-management.pdf.

Manijak, P. 2016. "Create Your Own Certification Program: Step-by-Step Instructions (Part 1)." *Certification Magazine*, December 6. certmag.com/create-certification-program-step-step-instructions-part-1-2.

McCauley, C., D. Derue, P. Yost, and S. Taylor. 2014. *Experience-Driven Leader Development*. Hoboken, NJ: John Wiley and Sons.

Meister, J., and K. Mulcahy. 2016. *The Future Workplace Experience: 10 Rules for Mastering Disruption in Recruiting and Engaging Employees*. New York: McGraw-Hill.

Moorhead, C. 2016. "7 Steps for Building a Credible Certification Program." SecurityInfoWatch.com, December 20. securityinfowatch.com/video-surveillance/article/12289208/7-steps-for-building-a-credible-certification-program.

Phillips, P.P., J.J. Phillips, and R. Ray. 2015. *Measuring the Success of Leadership Development*. Alexandria, VA: ATD Press.

Scisco, P., E. Biech, and G. Hallenbeck. 2017. *Compass: Your Guide for Leadership Development and Coaching*. Greensboro, NC: Center for Creative Leadership.

Smith, R., and M. Campbell. 2014. *Talent Conversations: What They Are, Why They're Crucial, and How to Do Them Right*. Greensboro, NC: Center for Creative Leadership.

Volini, E., J. Schwartz, I. Roy, M. Hauptmann, Y. Van Durme, B. Denny, and J. Bersin. 2019. "Leadership for the 21st Century." Deloitte Insights, April 11. deloitte.com/us/en/insights/focus/human-capital-trends/2019/21st-century-leadership-challenges-and-development.html.

Williams, C., and A. Reitman. 2013. *Career Moves: Be Strategic About Your Future*. Alexandria, VA: ASTD Press.

Yohn, D.L. 2018. "2018 Will Be the Year of Employee Experience." *Forbes*, January 2. forbes.com/sites/deniselyohn/2018/01/02/2018-will-be-the-year-of-employee-experience/#9e0b5951c8f.

Recommended Reading

Bennis, W. 2009. *On Becoming a Leader*, 4th ed. Philadelphia: Basic Books.

Kaye, B., L. Williams, and L. Cowart. 2017. *Up Is Not the Only Way: Rethinking Career Mobility*. Oakland, CA: Berrett-Koehler.

Tate, D., M. Pantalon, and D. David. 2022. *Conscious Accountability: Deepen Connections Elevate Results*. Alexandria, VA: ATD Press.

Treasurer, B. 2022. *Leadership Two Words at a Time*. Oakland, CA: Berrett-Koehler.

Zenger, J., and J. Folkman. 2019. *The New Extraordinary Leader: Turning Good Managers Into Great Leaders*. New York: McGraw-Hill.

2.7 COACHING

Coaching is a discipline and practice that is an essential capability for any TD professional, and it has the power to catalyze breakthroughs to enhance individual, team, and organizational performance. Coaching is an interactive process that helps individuals explore possible future scenarios, develop more rapidly toward a preferred future state, produce results, set goals, take action, make better decisions, and capitalize on their natural strengths. It requires using active listening skills, asking powerful questions, evoking awareness, and creating action plans.

2.7.1 Knowledge of Organizational Coaching Models

I. Coaching Basics
TD professionals should be knowledgeable about the practice of coaching and its various models.

2.7.1.1 Coaching Defined

Coaching is a developmental process through which an experienced person (the coach) offers guidance and advice to a learner, team, or group (the client) focusing on the skills and actions they require to achieve personal or professional goals. The close relationship between coaches and clients inspires and motivates clients to set higher goals and make remarkable improvements in their personal and professional lives.

The International Coaching Federation (ICF) defines coaching as "partnering with clients in a thought-provoking and creative process that inspires them to maximize their personal and professional potential." Although coaching is always about individual development, TD professionals should understand the difference between client-directed and coach-guided coaching. *Client-directed coaching* occurs when the client leads the way, and it may result in minimal directives. However, when coaching is *coach-guided*, the coach provides performance knowledge and motivation, broader perspectives, resources, and process knowledge. This is often the case when a manager or supervisor is using coaching skills. A common element to all types of coaching is working toward an individual's goals (DiGirolamo and Tkach 2019).

Organizations, groups, and individuals can leverage many types of coaching, including executive, leadership, career, life, accountability, or team, as well as coaching related to specific roles such as a sales or consultant coach. Coaching conversations can be used by supervisors to develop their employees, and coaching may be used by external consultants to assist clients inside an organization.

2.7.1.2 Organizational Coaching Models

Many organizations have a defined coaching model, which, when used consistently, reinforces the concepts and language. A defined model also ensures that a step is not missed and that the coach has considered all necessary parts before moving on. It also means the coach and client have identical expectations and follow a process that works.

A coaching model is helpful for defining a clear process, identifying objectives, and creating a focus to stay on track. It follows a specific and repeatable process because it has been proven to be effective. Many coaching models exist, but they all follow similar steps and anticipate an iterative experience with steps naturally crossing over and blending into one another. The steps may be combined or separated to create four to eight steps. As practitioners gain expertise and experience, the process becomes more fluid and conversations more dynamic.

ATD Coaching Model

The ATD Coaching Model follows six steps (Figure 2.7.1.2-1):

1. Clarify an agreement.
2. Create a working partnership between the coach and the client.
3. Collect and analyze data to assess the needs and situation.
4. Construct a development plan that includes setting goals.
5. Collaborate with an iterative process in which the client gains skills, coaches and clients identify new development challenges, and the development plan is upgraded. (Steps 4 and 5 are repeated until all parties agree that clients have reached their goals.)
6. Conclude soon after coaches and clients agree that the goals have been met; due to the supportive relationship that is built during the process, coaches and clients may mark the end of the formal relationship with a celebration. Even if the formal coaching has been completed, the client can continue to develop in other ways.

Figure 2.7.1.2-1. The ATD Coaching Model

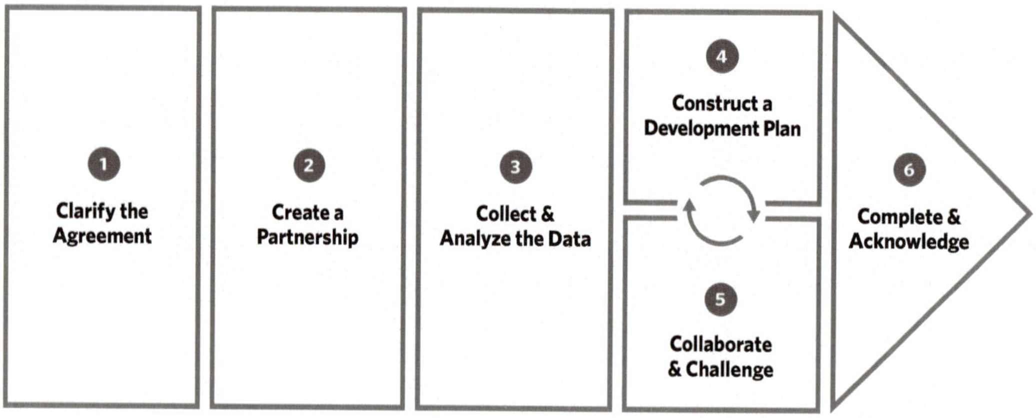

1. Clarify the Agreement
2. Create a Partnership
3. Collect & Analyze the Data
4. Construct a Development Plan
5. Collaborate & Challenge
6. Complete & Acknowledge

Source: Biech (2018b).

GROW Model of Coaching

The GROW Model of Coaching was developed in the 1980s by John Whitmore and Max Landsberg for coaching managers and became a blueprint for how coaching is structured in almost every model that followed (Whitmore 2009). The technique originated with sports coaches and was influenced by Tim Gallwey's book

The Inner Game of Tennis. GROW, following a specific structure and relying on skillfully worded questions, is an acronym that stands for:
- **G**oal
- **R** for current reality
- **O**ptions or obstacles
- **W**ill or way forward

CLEAR Coaching Model
The CLEAR Coaching Model, developed by Peter Hawkins in the 1980s, adds more definition to the GROW model (Hawkins and Smith 2013). It stands for:
- Contracting
- Listening
- Exploring
- Action
- Review

ACHIEVE Model
The ACHIEVE Model is a coaching tool developed by Sabine Dembkowski and Fiona Eldridge (Dembkowski, Eldridge, and Hunter 2006). It provides greater flexibility to GROW's goal setting and problem-solving stages. In the model, ACHIEVE stands for:
- Assess the current situation.
- Creatively brainstorm alternatives.
- Hone goals.
- Initiate options.
- Evaluate options.
- Validate an action program design.
- Encourage momentum.

2.7.1.3 Coaching May Occur Beyond the Models
Informal coaching can occur one-on-one or in groups, as well as face-to-face or virtually. In some cases a specified coach is involved, but peer coaching can also be helpful (Johnson 2019). Even though coaching often occurs through a formal coaching engagement, TD professionals should use coaching skills in every interaction with learners, clients, and those they supervise.

For coaching to be helpful, it needs to relate to something the client wants to accomplish. It is not counseling, mentoring, training, or giving advice. Instead, coaches focus on their clients and the goals they want to achieve.

2.7.1.4 The Difference Between Coaching and Mentoring
TD professionals should know that coaches and mentors serve different needs in employee development and that both are necessary.

Although mentoring and coaching are often used interchangeably, they are not the same. *Mentoring* is a process that helps people with their career development and occurs between mentors and their clients. It typically generates motivation, connections, and advice, and it is less focused on performance improvement.

2.7 Coaching

Coaching, on the other hand, is a professional partnership between a coach and an individual or team that uses a structured approach to achieve specific goals or objectives. The coach may be a professionally trained and qualified individual or a supervisor or manager who provides on-the-job constructive advice and feedback to improve an employee's performance. Use the Table 2.7.1.4-1 to help differentiate the two.

Table 2.7.1.4-1. The Difference Between Mentoring and Coaching

	Mentor	Coach
Focus	Conversations for professional development	Establishes goals toward professional development
Approach	Learner-led discussions	Learner-led process
Time period	Usually long term	Short term
Role	Expert sharing wisdom and knowledge	Facilitator focused on learner goals
Experience	Highly experienced senior-level person	Professional coach or manager using coaching skills
Manager relationship	Discussions are confidential	Manager may be the coach as skills are applied
Discussion topics	Career and personal development	Usually work-related development
Important tool	Mentoring agreement	Coaching agreement; various assessments and skill guides
Learner's emphasis	Let me learn from your experience	Help me achieve my goals by asking me questions

Source: Biech (2018a).

2.7.2 Skill in Helping Individuals or Teams Identify Goals, Develop Realistic Action Plans, Seek Development Opportunities, and Monitor Progress and Accountability

> **I. The Coaching Process**
>
> Coaching is an essential discipline and practice for every TD professional; however, TD professionals know they must demonstrate specific skills and in some cases be certified to conduct coaching.

2.7.2.1 When Talent Development Uses Coaching Skills

TD professionals should use coaching skills in many situations, most often informally, but also in more explicit formal situations:

- **Informal coaching discussions** are used more frequently by TD professionals and managers. TD professionals use coaching as a conversation focused on helping employees move forward relative to their goals, hopes, and future plans. Informal coaching uses some of the same skills and tools but may not follow a model's steps. For example, TD professionals may use a coaching approach implicitly in conversations with employees or when coaching learners during or after formal training sessions. One of TD professionals' most important roles is to coach managers to support and develop their employees. These informal situations are considered a style of management that often occurs naturally once a manager learns the skills.
- **Formal coaching** describes the process used when the coach and client are engaged in and committed to a formal one-on-one coaching process. It usually occurs during scheduled meetings when both the coach and client are invested in and following the parameters of the coaching process. Specific

training is required to become a coach who leads formal coaching engagements. Coaches can obtain certification through several organizations including the International Coaching Federation (ICF).

2.7.2.2 Coaching Competencies

To conduct formal coaching activities, TD professionals should be proficient in the competencies used in coaching. A nonprofit organization that sets standards and provides certification for coaches, ICF develops individuals to be proficient coaches and presents the required skills in four clusters of eight competencies:

- **Foundation**
    1. *Demonstrates ethical practice.* Understand and consistently apply coaching ethics and standards of coaching. [See 2.7.8.2]
    2. *Embodies a coaching mindset.* Develop and maintain a mindset that is open, curious, flexible, and client centered.
- **Cocreating the relationship**
    3. *Establishes and maintains agreements.* Partner with the client and relevant stakeholders to create clear agreements about the coaching relationship, process, plans, and goals. Establish agreements for the overall coaching engagement as well as those for each coaching session.
    4. *Cultivates trust and safety.* Partner with the client to create a safe, supportive environment that allows the client to share freely. Maintain a relationship of mutual respect and trust.
    5. *Maintains presence.* Be fully conscious and present with the client, employing a style that is open, flexible, grounded, and confident.
- **Communicating effectively**
    6. *Listens actively.* Focus on what the client is and is not saying to fully understand what is being communicated in the context of the client's systems and to support their self-expression.
    7. *Evokes awareness.* Facilitate client insight and learning by using tools and techniques such as powerful questioning, silence, metaphor, or analogy.
- **Cultivating learning and growth**
    8. *Facilitates client growth.* Partner with the client to transform learning and insight into action. Promote client autonomy in the coaching process.

Coaching focuses on identifying and clarifying the client's goals—emphasizing action, accountability, and follow through. The client drives the professional relationship by making final decisions and initiating appropriate actions. The client is also responsible for abiding by a system of accountability. Factors such as the organizational culture and structure, available resources, and the organizational business objectives will also influence the plan.

2.7.2.3 The Purpose of Coaching

Coaching is usually part of a larger strategy designed to help individuals, units, systems, and organizations make major improvements in performance. The demand for culture change is often associated with larger performance initiatives. Coaching is a tool for creating performance improvement and culture change. Unlike traditional face-to-face training, one-on-one coaching allows the coach and the client to focus on issues the client is facing. It is just-in-time, personal attention that often occurs on the job or during a coaching conversation.

Coaching expert Robert Hargrove (1995) asserted, "The primary methodology of masterful coaches is transformational learning." His focus on transformational learning has strong parallels with the single- and multiple-loop learning theory originally developed by Chris Argyris (2005) and popularized by Peter Senge (2006):

- **Single-loop learning** occurs when people learn and use new skills for necessary incremental change. Learning how to create a project plan is an example of single-loop learning.
- **Double-loop learning** focuses on a fundamental change in thinking patterns and behaviors. People often refer to this as reframing or changing the context. An example of double-loop learning is learning and practicing effective planning habits, which may be initiated due to coaching.
- **Triple-loop learning** happens when individuals make fundamental shifts in how they view themselves, and then willingly alter their beliefs and values about themselves and the world (a transformational act). Becoming an inspirational leader who creates and reinforces a culture of planning and execution is an example of triple-loop learning.

A skilled coach supports employees and the organization by moving easily among the three loops, or levels, of learning using communication techniques, dialogue, active listening, and targeted questioning skills. [See 1.1.2]

2.7.2.4 The Role of the Coach

TD professionals should be prepared for their role as a coach, which helps employees become better performers. Individuals are effective coaches when they know how to build trust, evoke awareness that helps clients create their own learning, and inspire clients to continually grow. The coach must ensure there is complete understanding and agreement during the contracting process. Their role entails:

- Encourage the client.
- Help the client define and clarify goals.
- Keep discussions focused and moving.
- Ask stimulating questions.
- Summarize and clarify discussion topics.
- Help the client develop an action plan.
- Offer resources or tools to improve the client's self-awareness or skills.
- Review progress toward goals.
- Facilitate the client's willingness to explore coaching.
- Vocalize agreements about next steps and follow-up.
- Demonstrate interest in helping the client achieve their goals.

2.7.2.5 Role of the Client

To be effective, the client must be willing to experience coaching. TD professionals should be able to sense whether their clients are excited about getting feedback, will make coaching a priority, are open to making improvements, and are interested in learning more about how to develop their skills. The client's role is to:

- Demonstrate accountability.
- Seek development opportunities.
- Monitor their own progress.
- Complete tasks and assignments on time.
- Share goals, desired outcomes, and hopes.
- Openly discuss frustrations, problems, setbacks, questions, and successes.
- Discuss assumptions, opinions, and points of view relative to their goals.

- Participate in creating and implementing action plans.
- Take ownership of asking for coaching and follow-up.
- Review progress to goals.
- Be open to exploring new ideas and approaches.
- Share setbacks and barriers.
- Be open to suggestions and willing to explore alternatives.

> **II. Following a Coaching Process**
>
> TD professionals should understand the benefit of using a model with a specific and repeatable process. They should follow the model chosen by their organizations as much as possible. Using a consistent approach reinforces the coaching language and supports the coaching environment the organization is trying to create.

2.7.2.6 The ATD Coaching Process

All coaching models, whether they have four or eight steps, follow a series of generic steps. This is true whether the coaching is between a supervisor and an employee or a coach from outside the reporting chain and a client. Most models are presented linearly, even though the process is iterative. The following lists what the coach does during each step of the ATD Coaching Model (Biech 2018b).

1. **Clarify the agreement**
   - Build a relationship with the client.
   - Determine whether the client is ready for coaching.
   - Establish a coaching agreement.
   - Determine if the coach and client are a good match.
   - Initiate a cooperative relationship.

2. **Create a partnership**
   - Determine the needs of the client or the situation.
   - Model being a good partner.
   - Review the data available, such as multi-rater surveys.
   - Decide what other data is required.
   - Analyze all available information.

3. **Collect and analyze the data**
   - Provide client feedback.
   - Discuss the data candidly and caringly.
   - Ask the client for observations about the data.
   - Isolate specific issues to improve.
   - Help the client determine what to improve.

4. **Construct a development plan**
   - Guide the client to generate development options.
   - Brainstorm options.
   - Create a results-oriented action plan or development plan.
   - Assist the client to identify required resources.
   - Help identify how to measure results.
   - Set measurable objectives.

5. **Collaborate and challenge**
    - Keep the client focused and on track.
    - Ask powerful questions.
    - Challenge the client to accomplish all that is possible.
    - Monitor milestones and track results.
    - Support movement toward the goal.
    - Be available for the client during setbacks and celebrations.
    - Motivate and inspire employees to do more than they think they can.
6. **Complete and acknowledge**
    - Reach agreement with the client that it is time to end the relationship.
    - Reflect on successful results.
    - Teach the client to practice self-coaching.
    - Discuss ways the client can continue to grow.
    - Create a list of next steps.
    - Bring closure to the formal relationship.
    - Identify ways to celebrate success.

2.7.3 Skill in Coaching Supervisors and Managers on Methods and Approaches for Supporting Employee Development

I. Coaching Managers to Support Improved Performance and Employee Development

TD professionals should recognize that the most important role their organization's managers have is to develop their people. Because regular coaching conversations between managers and employees increase employee productivity and engagement, TD professionals should support managers in becoming more effective.

2.7.3.1 Linking Coaching to Engagement

Performance management has evolved, and daily coaching conversations are replacing the annual performance review. TD professionals should know how to develop managers as coaches to create a learning culture that is supported by coaching. A manager's most important role is to develop their employees; those who do so have more productive and engaged employees (DiGirolamo and Tkach 2019). Talent development professionals can support managers as they develop and coach their employees. [See 2.7.2.3 and 3.3]

However, before they begin developing managers as coaches, TD professionals should lay the groundwork for an environment that is motivating, engaging, and enhances employee development. Gallup research found several links between coaching and engagement:

- Managers must establish expectations to ensure that employees know what is expected of them. When employees are involved in setting goals, they are four times more likely to be engaged.
- Managers must coach constantly and provide feedback based on understanding the individuals, their strengths, and their career goals. When employees receive daily feedback and coaching, they are three times more likely to be engaged.

- Managers must create accountability by holding progress reviews several times each year. Although similar to past performance reviews, progress reviews should ensure employees know why they do what they do and connect this purpose to current achievements and future development.
- Managers need to connect an employee's performance and accountability measures to their individual development plans. These conversations should include a discussion about their career goals, their future plans, and a strategy to reach them, which will ultimately lead to clear and aligned expectations (Clifton and Harter 2019).

2.7.3.2 Developing a Manager's Coaching Skills

TD professionals should help managers use coaching conversations to improve employee performance. Managers who want their employees to be productive and engaged need to actively coach them. For a successful conversation to occur, managers should know three things:

- What the organization needs from the employee
- What each employee is capable of
- Each employee's career goals

Research shows that once managers and leaders learn coaching skills, they usually weave them into all their conversations (DiGirolamo and Tkach 2019). To start, TD professionals should ensure that managers have skills in three basic coaching conversation topics:

- **Plan for coaching conversations.** Help managers understand what's important when approaching the coaching conversation, such as clearly articulating the current situation, planning the conversation in advance, and being a good listener.
- **Discuss strengths and development.** Mangers should be able to talk about the employee's career growth, know what learning opportunities are available, and explain what a stretch opportunity is.
- **Deliver constructive feedback.** Managers need to understand how to start from a positive place, be specific, be timely, and allow for responses during their coaching conversations.

When TD professionals are confident that the manager has the basics in place, they can share an easy-to-remember approach to individual coaching meetings, which will help the manager be successful as a first-time coach. TD professionals should use a predefined process, such as the C-O-A-CH conversation process designed by Virginia Bianco-Mathis, Cynthia Roman, and Lisa Nabors (Bianco-Mathis and Nabors 2016). The four steps in the C-O-A-CH process are:

- **C**urrent situation—describe and explore data, feedback, and the client's perspective.
- **O**bjectives—define coaching goals, desired results, and measurable objectives.
- **A**lternatives—explore alternative approaches and ideas for how to reach the designated objectives.
- **CH**oices—provide support as the client makes choices for action.

TD professionals should tell managers that being prepared for any discussion with an employee increases the probability of productive outcomes. This helps managers cope with their anxiety and builds their confidence, especially if they do not have much experience with coaching discussions. Being ready with forethought and materials sets them up to conduct the coaching meeting in an organized manner and saves time. Being prepared also sends a message that they care enough to be prepared for something that's important to the employee.

Developing people, closing skills gaps in the workforce, and increasing knowledge are enhanced by a partnership between TD professionals and managers. TD professionals can use a similar coaching process with managers that managers use as coaches with employees. This is a meta-coaching process because they are coaching the managers to be coaches. Here are some ideas for how TD professionals can guide managers:

- Help managers learn how to think about developing their employees as they plan work assignments.
- Work with managers to analyze which skill improvements would best fulfill the employee's ability to accomplish their goals.
- Help managers rethink how they delegate work.
- Encourage managers to have a growth mindset.
- Help managers see the value in sharing information about current operations and opportunities across the organization.
- Demonstrate the value of career discussions.
- Show managers how to complete an individual development plan.
- Ensure that managers are aware of available resources (Axelrod and Coyle 2011).

TD professionals should help managers realize that coaching cannot solve all performance issues. For example, coaching may be an appropriate solution if an employee doesn't understand expectations or priorities or needs help learning to complete a task to reach performance standards. However, coaching will not solve performance problems due to obstacles (such as a lack of resources, unrealistic expectations, or too many responsibilities) unless the manager adjusts these factors.

2.7.3.3 Introducing Managers to Resources and Approaches

Every approach that is available to TD professionals is also available for managers to use with their employees. TD professionals should ensure that managers are aware of these approaches. Resources can take a variety of forms, including people, information, abstract concepts (time or ideas), and materials. The approaches might be formal or informal, on-the-job or beyond, and include job shadowing, job rotations, stretch assignments, mentoring, social media, access to senior management, time to take on a new assignment, conferences, internal or external volunteering, training, self-development options, online learning, and networking. TD professionals should consider creating a list of these approaches to share with managers (Hosmer 2015). [See 2.6.4]

2.7.3.4 Manager Involvement in Formal Learning

An important role that TD professionals should exercise is connecting with managers when their employees attend formal training events. TD professionals can tell managers how they can be involved throughout the process. [See 2.3.1.13]

TD professionals might consider doing the following:

- **Before a learning event**—meet with managers to discuss their expectations and how they can support the transfer of learning.
- **During a learning event**—invite managers to visit at a time that best supports the learners and their goals.
- **After a learning event**—encourage managers to find ways for their employees to practice their new skills.

2.7.4 Skill in Creating Effective Coaching Agreements

> **I. Establishing a Coaching Engagement**
> To establish a coaching engagement, TD professionals should measure the client's readiness, uncover the client's expectations, and be prepared to help the client create the coaching agreement.

2.7.4.1 Skills Required to Create Coaching Agreements

To develop effective coaching agreements, TD professionals should recognize that they occur in a formal coaching situation. The skills needed to create a coaching agreement include excellent communication skills:
- Identify the client's communication style to lay the foundation for the rest of the discussion.
- Listen for understanding; every comment has at least two messages (the content and the intent).
- Ask pertinent and thought-provoking questions.
- Determine a client's readiness.
- Convey self-confidence without arrogance.
- Project a professional image.
- Demonstrate flexibility.
- Clarify expectations.

To establish and maintain effective agreements, the coach must also:
- Explain what coaching is (and is not) and describe the process.
- Reach agreement about what is appropriate in the relationship, what is being offered, and the responsibilities of the client and relevant stakeholders.
- Reach agreement about the guidelines and specific parameters of the coaching relationship, such as logistics, fees, scheduling, duration, termination, confidentiality, and inclusion of others.

TD professionals should also partner with the client to:
- Establish an overall coaching plan and goals.
- Determine client-coach compatibility
- Identify or reconfirm what the client wants to accomplish in the session.
- Define what the client believes they need to address or resolve to achieve what they want to accomplish in the session.
- Define or reconfirm measures of success for what the client wants to accomplish in the coaching engagement or individual session.
- Manage the time and focus of the session.
- Continue coaching in the direction of the client's desired outcome unless the client indicates otherwise.
- End the coaching relationship in a way that honors the experience (ICF 2022).

2.7.4.2 Creating Effective Coaching Agreements

TD professionals should craft a coaching agreement. Depending on the situation, this can be a written and signed document, a summary agreement, or a verbal acknowledgement for an informal coaching engagement. The type and content of the agreement depends on whether the coaching is formal, less formal, or informal.

It also depends on whether the coach is internal or external or a manager or a colleague. Common agreement content areas include:
- Logistics, such as schedule, length of the engagement, and protocol for canceling or changing meetings
- Communication processes during and between meetings
- Desired outcomes (such as objectives and goals, performance expectations, and measures of accomplishment)
- Action plan documentation
- Roles during and between meetings
- Plans to address problems
- Confidentiality agreement

2.7.4.3 Client Readiness

Clients' readiness for coaching means that they are open to new ideas, willing to discover their strengths and weaknesses, inclined to explore new goal areas, and ready to devote the time required by the coaching process. TD professionals should be able to determine most clients' degree of readiness during the first meeting.

There are certain clues to look for while creating the coaching agreement. Behaviors and dialogue that might signal readiness include:
- Client actively engages in discussions, asking questions about the coaching process.
- Client is open to gathering data or information about their perceived strengths and challenges.
- Client appears to be excited about getting feedback and open to making improvements or exploring changes.
- Client is willing to prioritize coaching.
- Client is ready to try new methods and practices on the job.

2.7.4.4 Using a Coaching Agreement to Identify Expectations

TD professionals should try to agree on basic expectations during the first meeting. Some coaches rely on talking about these topics while others capture decisions in writing. The dialogue should lead to decisions that are documented in the coaching agreement. Example expectation topics include:
- Logistics, such as meeting location, length, and frequency
- Expected outcomes and measures that may be used
- Format and expectations for documenting actions and progress
- Confidentiality regarding data, discussions, and all other issues
- Commitment expected, including time commitment and meeting cancelations
- Communication desires for the client and the coach, such as candor or how to communicate between meetings
- Role clarification

These decisions may be captured in a standard organizational format or an original document drawn up with each client, depending on the organization's expectations.

2.7.5 Knowledge of Methods and Techniques to Evaluate the Effectiveness of Coaching

I. Evaluating a Coaching Engagement
TD professionals should have knowledge of the various ways to evaluate a coaching engagement.

2.7.5.1 Incorporate Outcomes Into the Coaching Agreement
TD professionals should document the client's goals, measure outcomes, and compare the results. A coach can plan for these measurements in the beginning when crafting the coaching agreement. When establishing the client's action plans, TD professionals should identify measurable goals and include dates for comparison at the end of the coaching engagement. Data gathered prior to the coaching engagement could come from client data, such as a multi-rater survey, performance reports, supervisory input, or self-assessments.

2.7.5.2 Creating an Action Plan
As coaching partners, TD professionals balance supporting their clients and challenging them to push beyond their comfort zones. An action plan may be required to move the client toward a goal. An action plan is a written acknowledgment of the current situation; it expresses specific goals with steps to attain them, and identifies timelines, expected outcomes, and the coach's role. The action plan should be a living document that is reviewed, reflected on, and updated periodically. It will be used throughout the coaching engagement to gauge accomplishments and evaluate success.

The coach and client create the action plan, which may include:
- Premeasures (when possible)
- Ideas for change or action
- Connecting the client with others in similar situations
- Role-playing scenarios to provide practice
- Assignments that invite the client to enter difficult situations or perform at a higher standard
- Dates, outcomes, and tactics to achieve the goal
- Help with contingency planning

2.7.5.3 Measuring Results
TD professionals should measure results from multiple perspectives. They can compare the coaching agreement and the client's action plan with what the client accomplished. They can also evaluate individual client progress using pre- and postcoaching surveys, interviews, and self-assessments.

In addition, because a coaching initiative often supports specific organizational objectives, TD professionals should link these objectives to metrics that provide a measurable comparison, especially when measuring results against organizational performance. To create measurable objectives, the coach determines the expected outcomes and ties them to the program's goals. Potential organizational results can be tangible or intangible (Phillips, Phillips, and Edwards 2012).

Tangible organizational results include:
- Increased productivity
- Improved quality
- Improved retention
- Increased sales or revenue
- Reduced turnover
- Increased customer service ratings
- Decreased production time
- Increased market share
- Decreased absenteeism

Intangible organizational results include:
- Improved working relationships
- Stronger image and reputation in the community
- Improved teamwork
- Increased job satisfaction
- Increased organizational commitment
- Increased confidence
- More productive meetings
- Improved development of direct reports

2.7.5.4 Debriefing and Reflecting on the Coaching Experience

In the final phase of the coaching process, TD professionals and clients agree to end the relationship and decide how to debrief and reflect on the experience.

Signs it is time to end the coaching engagement include:
- The agreed-upon end date or progress has been reached.
- The client has met all identified goals.
- The client and coach have become friends and find themselves discussing personal things more than organizational objectives.
- The coach determines that the client needs a coach with a different skill set.
- One or both believe it is time to end the experience.

The coach and the client should end their relationship by doing five things:
1. Reach a mutual agreement that the end has come. Discuss observations about progress or ask, "Are we still making progress?"
2. Identify next steps as well as what the client still needs; don't leave a client without support.
3. Review how far the client has come, and help the client identify ways to maintain their new skills and behaviors.
4. Outline any incomplete actions, agree on a way to complete them, and set a target date.
5. Acknowledge and celebrate the ending; consider sharing a personal note or gift.

2.7.5.5 Addressing Next Steps

TD professionals should end the engagement when clients have mastered the expectations originally identified. However, there is always more to learn. TD professionals should ensure that the client has a plan to continue to learn, grow, and improve. Link coaching efforts to other aspects of organizational learning so the client understands the range of learning opportunities available.

2.7.6 Skill in Establishing an Environment That Fosters Mutual Respect and Trust With Coaching Clients

> **I. Creating an Environment That Supports Coaching**
>
> TD professionals have a responsibility to create an environment that supports coaching throughout the organization. The coaching environment must begin at the top with senior leaders who model mutual respect and trust with employees and value time that managers spend coaching their employees.

2.7.6.1 Defining the Coaching Environment

The fundamental philosophy behind coaching is that individuals have the knowledge within them to be successful in their roles. In their purest form, coaches do not teach, tell, or provide advice; instead, they ask questions or bring awareness in other ways to help facilitate thinking. Employees must understand the distinction between coaching and telling or giving feedback.

Internal coaches, in addition to their one-to-one professional coaching engagements, frequently promote a coaching environment, creating a natural opportunity for more people to hear the language of coaching, experience coaching behaviors, and see the results. These results are based on respect, trust, and support, which make up the basis of coaching. Behaviors that define a coaching environment include:
- People are challenged to be their best while at the same time supporting others.
- Everyone reaches higher levels of performance than they thought possible.
- People's best emerges as a result of being supported and respected.
- Trust-based communication is used, such as open dialogue, questioning, active and empathetic listening, and reflection. [See 1.1.2.1]
- Increased self-awareness, personal responsibility, and accountability are valued.

To support a coaching environment, leaders and the organizational infrastructure must facilitate and reward everyone to learn, practice, and grow. Coaching behaviors are exhibited everywhere. Leaders must believe that mindful coaching conversations accomplish the goal of helping employees reach both personal and professional development and success.

2.7.6.2 The Value of a Coaching Environment

Coaching creates an environment that supports a proactive approach to developing employees, enhancing engagement, improving team performance, and more. In the recent past, the performance focus was on enhancing an employee's current skills or acquiring new skills. Research by the Conference Board shows that this focus is shifting toward expanding capabilities and preparing for the future; providing leaders with greater self-awareness through multi-rater assessments; and focusing on performance to reduce gaps and build capabilities (Abel, Ray, and Nair 2016). A coaching environment can benefit the organization, the TD function, the individual, and the coach.

2.7.6.2.1 Benefits to the Organization

When all managers are experienced in using coaching skills with their employees, the organization experiences many benefits including:

- Promoting organizational consistency when using the common coaching language
- Furthering leadership development
- Reducing turnover as individuals see that the organization wants to invest in them
- Ensuring leadership succession by transmitting corporate values and behaviors to the next generation of leaders
- Improving performance and productivity of both coaches and clients
- Improving the organizational climate by helping employees understand their impact on others and organizational success
- Increasing employee commitment and engagement
- Creating an organization that not only talks about development but actively supports and values learning
- Creating trust and building better professional relationships
- Integrating the corporate strategy and leadership philosophy into individual goals by promoting commitment and engagement

2.7.6.2.2 Benefits to Talent Development

When managers use coaching skills to develop their employees, they become an additional resource for developing talent. Talent development benefits from a coaching environment in several ways because internal coaches:

- May be less costly than external coaches, giving talent development a way to maximize its budget
- Equip talent development with flexibility to serve employees who may need a different approach
- Give talent development access to a different developmental resource to improve performance
- Require less onboarding time because they are already familiar with the organization's landscape.

2.7.6.2.3 Benefits to the Client

The benefits to clients are easy to enumerate; after all, the focus is on them and enhancing their capacity. Some benefits include:

- Individualized professional development, especially in the specific needed area
- Feedback about personal strengths and style
- Career enhancement and better preparation for other jobs within the organization
- A better sense of the organization's culture and what it takes to succeed
- Being a recipient of the coach's expertise and experience
- Increased self-awareness and confidence
- Gaining knowledge, skills, and competencies, including approaches and techniques they can use to coach their own employees
- Enhanced cross-department understanding

2.7.6.2.4 Benefits to the Coach
There are many reasons why TD professionals may want to focus on coaching. Among those, coaches:
- Are viewed by others as contributors to organizational success
- May contribute to making decisions about policies such as the organization's succession planning processes
- Increase their own capacity for leadership
- Have the organization's respect as developers of leaders, managers, and employees
- Review, renew, and upgrade their own professional skills when they coach others
- Have an opportunity to advance their own career, both internally and externally
- Gain intrinsic rewards for contributing to employees and the organization
- Receive open appreciation for the work they do with clients

Coaching is a valuable skill, and coaches should be clear about their reasons for focusing on it. Coaching is goal oriented and benefits the organization, talent development, the individual clients, and the coach.

2.7.6.3 Attributes That Lead to a Coaching Environment
TD professionals acknowledge that the coaching environment begins with the coach-client relationship; when successful, it expands to create an organizational coaching environment, which means establishing respect and trust and providing support.

Building a coaching organization requires a total systems approach by incorporating learning and organization development concepts such as emotional intelligence, employee engagement, strategic planning, constructive feedback, and change management (Bianco-Mathis and Nabors 2016). Developing a coaching environment requires three building blocks: [See 1.1, 1.2, and 1.3]
- All employees need to learn and practice basic coaching skills.
- The organizational culture promotes the use of coaching skills in all conversations.
- The infrastructure provides access to coaches.

Establishing Respect
A strong relationship between the coach and client is required. In establishing respect, the coach can improve the process by having deep and meaningful conversations with the client.

Establishing Trust
The effectiveness of coaching can be hindered if coaches and clients are uncomfortable with being open and candid with one another. When coaches create a contract with their clients, both parties agree on how to handle confidential or sensitive topics. This relationship of trust can be a building block of an organizational culture of trust.

Providing Support
For development to occur, coaches need to deliver feedback and other support. By building on trusting relationships, coaches can more constructively share feedback as well as difficult messages. This kind of support also permeates the organization's culture, eventually leading to a coaching environment. [See 1.1.3]

2.7.6.4 Communicating Expectations

When establishing a coaching environment, TD professionals should clearly communicate expectations, including some general guidelines:

- Align the effort with management and organizational goals.
- Develop a plan that highlights the strategic alignment, goals, timeline, budget, and measures of success.
- Create a launching plan that includes who will serve as a coach, how they will gain skills, and how they will be selected and recruited.
- Identify highlights of the coaching design, such as schedules and key attributes including confidentiality.
- Determine how success will be measured and reported.

2.7.6.5 Engaging Senior Leadership

If TD professionals want to establish a cadre of trained internal coaches, they should obtain the C-suite's support to lead and model a coaching initiative by creating a vision, identifying the benefits, designing and selling the plan to key stakeholders, identifying roles and responsibilities, and navigating politics that may cause a roadblock. TD professionals should encourage managers to endorse and fund the effort and give coaches and clients time away from their jobs to meet and form relationships. They should also document the progress of coaching using evaluation instruments, meeting notes, reports, and logs. This documentation can also be used to recommend maintaining, expanding, or eliminating the coaching effort.

2.7.6.6 Build a Coaching Environment

TD professionals should create a clearly defined plan and budget that demonstrates value and strategic alignment, linking the coaching effort to the stakeholders and their agendas. They should also assess the political climate within the organization and plan for how to use formal and informal support networks. A coaching environment is built on behaviors such as:

- Demonstrating the value and power in dialogue
- Offering multi-rater feedback to everyone with coaching support
- Encouraging leaders to act as positive role models
- Creating informal coaching that flows in all directions
- Developing a common coaching method and language

2.7.7 Skill in Recruiting, Training, and Pairing Coaches and Mentors With Employees

> **I. Fostering an Active and Enduring Coaching Initiative**
>
> TD professionals should be able to recruit and train coaches to foster a permanent coaching environment.

2.7.7.1 Recruiting Additional Coaches and Mentors

Most organizations begin a formal coaching practice by creating a core group of TD professionals. Eventually the organization will add additional coaches and determine which approach they will use to assign coaches (such as application, nomination, sponsorship, or assignment).

Regardless of the process, TD profession should determine specific criteria for identifying what makes a good coach in the organization, including:

- **Credibility.** Credibility could be based on a solid and positive reputation, a successful track record, how long a person's been with the organization, and whether people trust them.
- **Commitment.** Coaching requires commitment and passion, which may mean going beyond the actual coaching role to include things such as development or sharing and contributing to a community of practice. Another consideration is whether the potential coach's supervisor is committed to allowing the additional time away from the job.
- **Interpersonal skills.** Coaches should have interpersonal skills that include sensitivity, excellent communication, flexibility, influencing, and appropriate assertiveness.
- **Capacity.** Depending on whether the internal coach works full time or part time, they must make time for any additional responsibilities that coaching will bring. The TD function should determine the number of hours that will be expected of coaches who aren't in the role full time.

2.7.7.2 Maintaining Coaching Momentum

TD professionals should maintain momentum once a coaching effort has started by:

- Communicating to keep people interested in the effort, such as through coaching tips or a newsletter
- Rewarding and recognizing special things that coaches or a client-coach partnership accomplished
- Providing development through job aids or lunch & learn sessions
- Implementing a reliable matching process
- Leading by example by becoming a coach

2.7.7.3 Providing Coaching Training or Certification

TD professionals should be sure that the organization provides all coaches with the tools required to be effective in their role. With appropriate role modeling, training, facilitation, and support systems, all employees in an organization can begin applying a coaching model to conversations—thus raising the performance of the entire organization.

2.7.8 Knowledge of Professional Standards and Ethical Guidelines for Coaching

> **I. Professional Standards and Ethical Guidelines for Coaching**
>
> The relationship between the coach and client makes coaching a potentially powerful method for enhancing development in organizations. TD professionals should understand, value, and adhere to the professional standards and ethical guidelines that govern this powerful relationship.

2.7.8.1 Professional Coaching Organizations

The International Coaching Federation (ICF) is the leading global organization dedicated to advancing the coaching profession. Other professional coaching organizations include:

- European Mentoring and Coaching Council (EMCC), which exists to develop, promote, and set the expectation of best practices in mentoring, coaching, and supervision for the benefit of society.

- International Association of Coaching (IAC), which offers certification that goes "beyond an intellectual understanding of coaching."

The Center for Credentialing and Education also offers the Board Certified Coach certification.

2.7.8.2 International Coaching Federation

As the largest organization dedicated to the coaching profession, ICF sets professional standards, provides certification, and has created a worldwide network of trained coaching professionals. To ensure that talent development practices are ethical, TD professionals must be conscious of the effects their products, services, and actions have on an organization's employees. Coaching is one of those services.

ICF (2022) developed a code of conduct and ethics guidelines for practitioners, which TD professionals acting in a coaching capacity must abide by. The details of the 28 ethical standards can be found on ICF's website and include things such as:

- Being open about any conflict of interest
- Honoring all contracts and agreements made in the context of the coaching relationship
- Maintaining a client's confidentiality
- Maintaining, storing, and disposing of records
- Providing only the best advice and coaching
- Refusing any personal, professional, or monetary advantages
- Respecting the client's right to terminate
- Setting clear, appropriate, and culturally sensitive boundaries governing physical contact
- Terminating the coaching relationship when someone else could offer better services

2.7.8.3 Aligning Coaching Expectations

TD professionals serving in a coaching capacity must align to the expectations of the client and the organization. These expectations may include maintaining privacy and confidentiality, avoiding conflicts of interest, or establishing relationship limitations.

2.7.8.3.1 Privacy and Confidentiality Expectations

Privacy and confidentiality are required in a coaching arrangement. TD professionals who are coaching must interact with clients in private, without interruption. They should select locations for coaching sessions that offer a maximum amount of privacy. Confidentiality ensures that all information discussed in the coaching session remains private, which is essential for the client to fully trust the coaching relationship. Without trust, no development takes place, and the process will be a waste of time and money.

2.7.8.3.2 Conflict of Interest

A conflict of interest arises when a TD professional acting as a coach has an interest that impedes or interferes with their ability to act in the best interest of their client, such as when the coaching relationship is used for inappropriate personal gain or when personal interests conflict with the coaching agreement. The personal and professional information they learn must be held in strictest confidence; therefore, coaches should avoid even the appearance of a conflict of interest.

2.7.8.3.3 Relationship Limitations

Coaches begin to build a relationship with their clients from the first interaction, so that is the time to establish an agreement about expectations and boundaries. The coach cannot do the work for the client and is not responsible for the client's progress; however, the coach must manage and confront a lack of progress by following up on deadlines. In addition, a coach or client may choose to end a coaching relationship early for a variety of reasons.

Clients may wish to terminate a coaching relationship because:
- Their needs are not being met.
- Their personal or professional priorities change.
- Improved performance reduces the need for coaching.
- The coaching process does not meet expectations.
- They are uncomfortable with the coach's style, approach, or personality.
- Funding for the coaching program is eliminated or decreased.

Coaches may wish to terminate a coaching relationship because:
- The client is no longer benefiting.
- The client's needs fall outside the jurisdiction of the definition of coaching.
- The client is disinterested, unavailable, negative, or resistant.
- The coach thinks someone else could be more beneficial for the client.
- The coach believes the client has moved beyond the need for more coaching.

TD professionals should remember that coaching can only solve certain problems. It is not a panacea or the right solution for every performance challenge or opportunity.

REFERENCES

Abel, A., R. Ray, and S. Nair. 2016. *Global Executive Coaching Survey 2016: Developing Leaders and Leadership Capabilities at All Levels.* New York: The Conference Board.

Argyris, C. 2005. "Double-Loop Learning in Organizations." Chapter 13 in *Great Minds in Management: The Process of Theory Development*, edited by K.G. Smith and M.A. Hitt. New York: Oxford University Press.

ATD Education. "ATD Coaching Certificate Program." Association for Talent Development. Alexandria, VA: ATD Education.

Axelrod, W., and J. Coyle. 2011. *Make Talent Your Business: How Exceptional Managers Develop People While Getting Results.* San Francisco: Berrett-Koehler.

Bianco-Mathis, V., and L. Nabors. 2016. "Building a Coaching Organization." *TD at Work*. Alexandria, VA: ATD Press.

Biech, E. 2018a. *ATD's Foundations of Talent Development: Launching, Leveraging, and Leading Your Organization's TD Effort.* Alexandria, VA: ATD Press.

Biech, E. 2018b. *ATD's Action Guide to Talent Development: A Practical Approach to Building Your Organization's TD Effort.* Alexandria, VA: ATD Press.

Clifton, J., and J. Harter. 2019. *It's the Manager.* New York: Gallup Press.

Dembkowski, S., F. Eldridge, and I. Hunter. 2006. *The Seven Steps of Effective Executive Coaching.* London: Thorogood.

DiGirolamo, J.A., and J.T. Tkach. 2019. "An Exploration of Managers and Leaders Using Coaching Skills." *Consulting Psychology Journal: Practice and Research* 71(3): 195–218.

Fournies, F.F. 1987. *Coaching for Improved Work Performance.* New York: Liberty Hall Press.

Hargrove, R. 1995. *Masterful Coaching: Extraordinary Results by Impacting People and the Way They Think and Work Together.* San Diego: Pfeiffer.

Hawkins, P., and N. Smith. 2013. *Coaching, Mentoring and Organizational Consultancy*, 2nd ed. Berkshire, UK: Open University Press.

Hosmer, D. 2015. "The Manager's Guide to Employee Development." *TD at Work*. Alexandria, VA: ATD Press.

IAC (International Association of Coaching). n.d. "Overview." certifiedcoach.org/about.

ICF (International Coaching Federation). n.d. "ICF Core Competencies." coachingfederation.org/credentials-and-standards/core-competencies.

ICF (International Coaching Federation). 2015. "ICF Code of Ethics." coachingfederation.org/ethics/code-of-ethics.

ICF (International Coaching Federation). 2022. "About ICF." coachfederation.org/about.

Johnson, S. 2019. "Peer Coaching: The Wave of the Future." *TD at Work*. Alexandria, VA: ATD Press.

Kouzes, J.M., B.Z. Posner, and E. Biech. 2010. *A Coach's Guide to Developing Exemplary Leaders: Making the Most of The Leadership Challenge and the Leadership Practices Inventory (LPI)*. San Francisco: Pfeiffer.

Morris, B. 2000. "Executive Coaches: So You're a Player: Do You Need a Coach?" *Fortune*, February.

Phillips, P.P., J.J. Phillips, and L. Edwards. 2012. *Measuring the Success of Coaching*. Alexandria, VA: ASTD Press.

Senge, P.M. 2006. *The Fifth Discipline: The Art and Practice of the Learning Organization*, 2nd ed. New York: Currency/Doubleday.

Whitmore, J. 2009. *Coaching for Performance: GROWing Human Potential and Purpose: The Principles and Practice of Coaching and Leadership*, 4th ed. Boston: Nicholas Brealey.

Recommended Reading

Bianco-Mathis, V., and L. Nabors. 2017. *Everyday Coaching: Using Conversation to Strengthen Your Culture*. Alexandria, VA: ATD Press.

Bungay Stanier, M. 2016. *The Coaching Habit: Say Less, Ask More & Change the Way You Lead Forever*. Toronto: Box of Crayons Press.

Edwards, L. 2014. "Creating an Internal Coaching Program." *TD at Work*. Alexandria, VA: ATD Press.

Greiner, N. 2018. *The Art of Executive Coaching: Secrets to Unlock Leadership Performance*. Alexandria, VA: ATD Press.

Greiner, N., and B. Davis. 2024. *The Executive Coaching Playbook: How to Launch, Run, and Grow Your Business*. Alexandria, VA: ATD Press.

Haneberg, L. 2016. *Coaching Basics*, 2nd ed. Alexandria, VA: ATD Press.

Zenger, J., and K. Stinnent. 2010. *The Extraordinary Coach: How the Best Leaders Help Others Grow*. New York: McGraw-Hill.

2.8 EVALUATING IMPACT

Evaluating the impact of talent development programs is correlated with learning and business effectiveness. Talent development professionals should be able to implement a multilevel, systematic method for gathering, analyzing, and reporting information about the effectiveness and effort of learning programs. Collecting data relevant to business strategies and goals helps decision making, improves learning programs, and increases the value proposition of learning in the eyes of senior leaders and business stakeholders.

2.8.1 Knowledge of Models and Methods to Evaluate the Impact of Learning and Talent Development Solutions

> **I. Assessing and Evaluating the Impact of TD Solutions**
>
> TD professionals should be familiar with a variety of methods to evaluate the impact of talent development solutions as well as basic features of evaluation that affect all methods.

2.8.1.1 Purpose of Evaluating Talent Development Solutions

Evaluation is a multilevel, systematic method for collecting, analyzing, and interpreting data to confirm the effectiveness of talent development initiatives. Successful TD professionals know that their efficacy depends on demonstrating the value of the talent development investment. Evaluation is one way to document whether the investment in talent development achieved the desired outcomes. Programs are based on objectives specifying what they must accomplish and in what timeframe.

TD professionals should base their decisions about program additions, changes, or deletions on the data they collect through evaluations. These results can also be used to prioritize needs at the organizational level. In addition, decision makers can shift financial and other resources from efforts that are found to have a small effect on corporate goals to those that have greater influence.

TD professionals should consider these purposes of evaluation:
- Calculate business impact, cost-benefit ratio, and the ROI for the solution.
- Determine whether the objectives of the solution were met and how well.
- Assess the effectiveness and appropriateness of the content and instructional strategies.
- Reinforce learning concepts by using a test or similar performance assessment.
- Provide feedback to the facilitator.
- Provide feedback to participants about what they learned.
- Assess the on-the-job environment to support learning retention.

2.8.1.2 Benefits of Evaluating TD Solutions

Evaluating learning experiences confers several advantages to talent development and the organization, because it:

- Secures client support and confidence to build client relationships (discussing the evaluation plan demonstrates that the TD professional has a structured approach to ensure quality and continuous improvement of training efforts)
- Allows the TD professional to see whether the results of the program were consistent with the organizational opportunity analysis and needs assessment
- Validates performance gaps and learner needs
- Helps TD professionals determine whether training was the solution to a performance gap
- Helps the management team meet its objectives as TD professionals become partners in the organization's success

Evaluation measures will be most beneficial when TD professionals incorporate them into the design of the solution from the beginning and relate them to the learning objectives. Monitoring the measurement process helps ensure value is being created for the organization throughout the program.

2.8.1.3 Assessment

TD professionals use well-defined needs assessment statements as a first step in the process of designing and developing a solution. The results of the needs assessment are used to create the evaluation plan and initiate the measurement process. [See 2.2.2]

2.8.1.4 Ralph Tyler's Goal-Attainment Method

In 1949, Ralph W. Tyler presented one of the earliest design processes incorporating evaluation based on the objectives. His goal-attainment method is a process for evaluating the success of a curriculum that includes "objectives, the ends of instruction, [which] are first identified. The content of instruction is identified to address the objectives, and the various instructional elements, the means, are then designed to assist learners in obtaining the objectives" (Herschbach 1992; Tyler 1949).

Tyler's model poses four questions:

- What objectives should learners achieve?
- What learning activities will assist learners to achieve these objectives?
- How should the curriculum be organized?
- How should learner achievement be evaluated?

2.8.1.5 Measurement Process

A *measure* is a standard used to evaluate the degree or quality of the results of a solution. *Measurement*, a part of research, is the process of quantifying assessment data and providing the necessary information to make sound decisions about an issue or situation. Measurements define or quantify specific attributes of an observation. Using assessment data, TD professionals should identify the desired outcomes before designing an evaluation plan. They can gather, summarize, and interpret the data generated by the assessment process to determine the root cause, which could be the process; a lack of resources, information, or motivation; poor health; or a need for knowledge, skills, or affective (attitude) learning (KSAs). Based on these results, TD professionals will determine the best solutions and write objectives. [See 2.2.2, 2.2.4, and 3.5.5.2]

TD professionals should consider the nature of the solution, the characteristics of the learners, and the outcome focus to select the best measurement process. Most evaluation process models begin like Tyler's goal-attainment method by determining the outcomes, goals, or objectives for the solution:

- Use the assessment data to identify evaluation outcomes and goals.
- Develop an evaluation design and strategy.
- Select and construct measurement tools.
- Analyze data.
- Report data.

2.8.1.6 Output Models

A program is a set of resources and activities directed toward one or more common goals, typically under the direction of a single manager or management team. It may consist of a limited set of activities in one organization, a complex set of activities that are implemented at many sites to two or more levels in an organization, or activities developed by a set of in-house, public, nonprofit, or private providers.

Program evaluation is the systematic assessment of program results and, if possible, the assessment of how the program caused them. Results may occur at several levels: reaction to the program, what was learned, what was transferred to the job, and the impact on the organization. Evaluation includes ongoing monitoring of programs as well as one-time studies of program processes or effects. The approaches are based on social science research methodologies and professional standards. Two categories of evaluation provide different information and help ensure that the program generates impact:

- **Program evaluation** assesses the effect of a learning program.
- **Learning transfer evaluation** measures the participant's ability to use what they've learned on the job.

2.8.1.7 Formative Versus Summative Evaluation

One of the key challenges of preparing a learning program is ensuring that it accomplishes the objectives for which it was developed. TD professionals use the terms *formative* and *summative evaluation*:

- **Formative evaluation** occurs throughout the design of any talent development solution. Its purpose is to improve the draft learning program and increase the likelihood that it will achieve its objectives. TD professionals should conduct a formative evaluation while the learning program is being developed and use this information to revise the program immediately to make it more effective. During formative evaluation, TD professionals should ensure the learning program is understandable, accurate, current, and functional. Formative evaluation could include pilot testing, beta testing, technical reviews with SMEs, production reviews, and stakeholder reviews.
- **Summative evaluation** occurs after a talent development solution has been delivered and focuses on the results or impact of the solution to provide evidence about the program's value. This type of evaluation could measure participant reactions, the effect on organizational goals, the initiative's costs, and stakeholder expectations. A summative evaluation measures the outcome and could include standardized tests, participant reaction forms, stakeholder satisfaction surveys, and final return on investment.

II. Evaluation Methodologies

TD professionals have several evaluation methodologies available to systematically apply to talent development initiatives. They should be most familiar with Kirkpatrick's Four Levels of Evaluation, the Phillips ROI Methodology, the Brinkerhoff Success Case Method, and the Balanced Scorecard Approach.

2.8.1.8 Kirkpatrick's Four Levels of Evaluation

Kirkpatrick's Four Levels of Evaluation model was first published by ASTD in 1959. Throughout the years, it has been refined, identifying four levels of evaluation:

- **Level 1: Reaction** measures the degree to which participants find the program favorable, engaging, and relevant to their jobs.
- **Level 2: Learning** measures the degree to which participants acquire the intended knowledge, skills, attitudes, confidence, and commitment.
- **Level 3: Behavior** measures the degree to which participants apply what they learned during the program when they are back on the job.
- **Level 4: Results** measures the degree to which targeted outcomes occur as a result of the program (Kirkpatrick and Kirkpatrick 2016).

Level 1 evaluates a learner's reaction. Reaction sheets, sometimes called smile sheets, are the most popular mechanism for conducting this level of evaluation. This is usually requested at the end of a program and may also include word-of-mouth feedback to the instructor, managers, or other employees about how much a participant enjoyed a session.

Level 2 evaluates a learner's mastery of the program content. Knowledge or performance tests are used to determine their ability to demonstrate the knowledge or skills. Observation of skills or behaviors may also be used to measure changes by the learner.

Level 3 evaluates a learner's transfer of knowledge and skills to the job and the extent to which they have applied what they learned. This level of evaluation is characterized by comprehensive, continuous performance monitoring based on the behaviors taught in the program. There are many ways to measure the desired behavior including observation, manager assessment, and self-assessment.

Level 4 evaluates whether targeted outcomes occur, which is often viewed as a program's organizational effect. This evaluation seeks to measure quantifiable changes in key performance measures and can be accomplished only if well-defined targeted outcomes are identified prior to designing the program. TD professionals can consider productivity and production measures, cost or expense measures, financial or direct output measures, employee turnover, or engagement ratings.

Table 2.8.1.8-1 provides a summary of Kirkpatrick's Four Levels of Evaluation.

Table 2.8.1.8-1. Evaluation Worksheet

Level	When to Measure	What to Measure	How to Measure
1	• During the program (end of day) • End of program	• Reactions • Pace and sequence • Relevance (content) • Instrument strategies • Interaction • Facilitator's style • Level of discussion • Objectives met • Environment • Facilitator's knowledge level • Participant interaction • Registration process	• Questionnaire or surveys • Individual responses in class • Follow-up interviews • Observation checklists
2	• Before the program • During the program • After the program	• Learning and extent of learning • Teaching of content • Knowledge of participants	• Knowledge tests (which may be paper-and-pencil based), oral questions, and answers • Performance tests, role plays, case studies with evaluation or feedback sheets • Monitored skill demonstrations • Checklists • Product tests
3	• A few weeks to three months after the program	• On-the-job change	• Performance records • Performance contracts • Action plans • Interviews • Surveys or questionnaires • Direct observation with checklists • Supervisor interviews
4	• Three months to one year after the program	• Effect on organization	• Action plans • Interviews • Questionnaires • Focus groups • Performance contracts

2.8.1.9 The Phillips ROI Methodology

TD professionals should be able to determine the return on investment (ROI) of their talent development programs and solutions. ROI can demonstrate accountability.

To calculate ROI, TD professionals must first isolate the effects of the training using business measures. Then, they need to convert those business impact measures to monetary values and compare them with program costs, which requires placing a value on each unit of data connected with the program. Several techniques are available to convert data to monetary values depending on the type of data and the situation.

The Phillips's process for determining the ROI of performance yields six types of data:
- Level 1: Reaction and planned action
- Level 2: Learning
- Level 3: Application and implementation
- Level 4: Business impact
- Level 5: Return on investment
- Intangible measures (Phillips and Phillips 2016)

To convert measures to monetary values, the ROI Methodology uses:
- Standard values, which are those that are already accepted in the organization
- Historical costs, which represent what the measures being converted have cost the organization in the past (such as the cost of an unexpected absence)
- Input from internal or external experts on a particular measure
- Participant estimates when necessary
- Supervisor and manager estimates when appropriate
- Links to other measures that have already been converted to monetary value, like placing value on customer and employee satisfaction (Sasser, Schlesinger, and Heskett 1997)
- Talent development staff estimates when credible

The ROI Methodology also includes a step for isolating the effects of training programs, which answers the question: How do we know our training program caused the results? Using a control group is one way to answer this question, although that's not always feasible. Other approaches include using trend line analysis, forecasting methods, and experts. Table 2.8.1.9-1 summarizes the Phillips ROI Methodology, including when to measure, what to measure, how to measure, and how to convert the monetary value of program effects. To calculate ROI, compare the monetary value to the fully loaded program costs.

Table 2.8.1.9-1. ROI Worksheet

	When to Measure	What to Measure	How to Measure	How to Convert to Money
ROI	• Three months to one year after the program	• Monetary value of the effect of training	• Control groups • Trend line analysis • Participants' estimates • Supervisors' estimates • Management's estimates • Use of experts • Extant data • External studies	• Standard values • Historical costs • Input from experts • Participant estimates • Manager estimates • Links to other measures • Talent development estimates

2.8.1.10 The Brinkerhoff Success Case Method

The Brinkerhoff Success Case Method (SCM) involves identifying the most and least successful cases in a program and examining them in detail. This approach was developed by Robert Brinkerhoff to assess the impact of organizational solutions, such as training and coaching, although it's not limited to this context. SCM is a useful approach for documenting stories of impact that can then be shared with stakeholders and used to develop an understanding of the factors that enhanced or impeded program success.

The five key SCM steps are:
1. Focusing and planning a successful case study
2. Creating an "impact model" that defines what success should look like
3. Designing and implementing a survey to search for best and worst cases
4. Interviewing and documenting success cases
5. Communicating findings, conclusions, and recommendations (Brinkerhoff 2003)

2.8.1.11 The Balanced Scorecard Approach

Using a balanced scorecard is a way for organizations to evaluate effectiveness with more than financial measures (Kaplan and Norton 1996). This model consists of measuring effectiveness from four perspectives:

- **The customer perspective.** Did the solution, initiative, or practice meet the customer's need or expectation?
- **The innovation and learning perspective.** Did users gain the needed skills or knowledge?
- **The internal business perspective.** Did the solution, initiative, or practice influence the job?
- **The financial perspective.** Did the solution, initiative, or practice have a financial payoff?

The balanced scorecard approach involves an entire organization, not just talent development.

2.8.1.12 Additional Evaluation Approaches

TD professionals should be familiar with the evaluation methodologies already discussed, but they should also be aware of other approaches such as:

- **Cost-benefit analysis** measures monetary gains and losses; it can be traced to 1667 when it was used to calculate the public health costs of combatting the Great Plague of London at a ratio of 84:1 (Kearsley 1982).
- **Culturally responsive evaluation** is a holistic framework for centering evaluation in culture (Frierson et al. 2010).
- **Developmental evaluation** approaches are useful in complex or uncertain environments such as innovation, radical program redesign, or crises (Patton 2010).
- **International Society for Performance Improvement's Human Performance Technology (HPT) evaluation model** stresses an analysis of present and desired levels of performance, identifies the causes for the gap, and offers a range of solutions.
- **Six Sigma** is a disciplined, data-based approach to eliminate defects in processes; it was popularized by the Motorola Company.
- **Lean Six Sigma** combines eliminating waste with Lean practices and quality improvement from Six Sigma.
- **Predictive learning analytics** is a systematic methodology for predicting learner outcomes and actions.
- **Return on expectations** is a Kirkpatrick approach in which stakeholders identify the TD value in terms of how it contributes to their goals.
- **Robinson's training for impact** helps achieve organizational goals, gives people the skills and knowledge they require, and produces measurable results that can be traced on the job.
- **Total quality management (TQM)** focuses on improving quality and productivity; it was pioneered by Walther A. Shewhart, W. Edwards Deming, and Joseph M. Juran.

2.8.1.13 Meta-Evaluation

Meta-evaluation is an evaluation of an evaluation. According to David J. Basarab and Darrell K. Root (1992), "These evaluations are conducted to provide assurances of the quality of an evaluation, to provide, when necessary, credibility to the evaluation, and to improve subsequent evaluations." TD professionals should analyze each step to evaluate the evaluation.

2.8.2 Knowledge of Qualitative and Quantitative Data Collection Methods, Techniques, and Tools

> **I. Qualitative and Quantitative Data Collection Methods**
> TD professionals should have a basic understanding of statistics that allows them to use both qualitative and quantitative data collection methods to determine the impact of talent development solutions.

2.8.2.1 Overview of Statistics

Statistics is the collection, analysis, display, interpretation, and presentation of data. Sometimes called data analysis, statistics allows data to be organized and summarized in a way that makes it possible to reach a conclusion. TD professionals can use statistics to document current levels of performance (individual, group, or organizational), measure the effect of TD initiatives, and offer data-based feedback for change. This section is designed to serve as a primer on statistics.

For many TD professionals, the use of statistics is onerous—but it shouldn't be. Software applications can perform necessary calculations; however, TD professionals must understand several essential concepts and principles. They should be prepared to use statistics for three purposes:
- Summarize large amounts of data.
- Determine the relationship between two or more items.
- Compare the differences in performance.

The two types of statistics are *descriptive* and *inferential statistics*.

Descriptive statistics summarizes the data numerically or graphically in four ways:
- **Measures of frequency** show how often something occurs (count, percent, or frequency) and are used to show how often, for example, a response is given.
- **Measures of central tendency**, or averages, locate the distribution at specific points (mean, median, and mode) and are used to show the most common responses.
    - *Mean*, sometimes called the average, considers the quantitative value of each number. The mean equals the sum of all numbers divided by the number of values that make up the sum.
    - *Median* is the middle of a distribution arranged by magnitude—half the items are above the median and half are below. The median is less sensitive to extreme scores than the mean. To determine the median, order the numbers from smallest to largest. The median in a distribution of odd numbers is the middle number; in a distribution of even numbers it is the calculated average of the two middle numbers.
    - *Mode* is the most frequently occurring score in a distribution; accordingly, it is also used as a measure of central tendency. Because it is subject to sample fluctuations, mode is not recommended for use as the only measure of central tendency. Some distributions have more than one mode, which is called multimodal.
- **Measures of dispersion or variation** show the spread of the numbers by stating them in intervals (range or standard deviation). They are used to show the data spread.
    - *Range* is the two highest and lowest numbers.
    - *Standard deviation* is the difference between the number and the mean.

- **Measures of position** describe how numbers relate to one another and are used to compare a number to a predetermined norm. Most common are:
    - *Percentile* is one of 100 equal groups that a total population can be divided.
    - *Quartile rank* is one of four equal groups that a population is divided into; the rank is 1, 2, 3, or 4.
    - *Standard score* is the number that has the same mean and standard deviation for comparing what is normal for a defined population.

Inferential statistics uses analysis to infer data about a larger population than was actually sampled; it then models the relationships within the data. There are several categories of inferential statistics, including:
- **Estimation** uses numbers to approximate the data and relate it to the larger population.
- **Modeling** uses mathematical equations to describe the relationships between two or more variables.
- **Hypothesis testing** is used to determine whether the data supports the hypothesis.

Additional terms TD professionals should know include:
- **Control group** is the group that does not receive treatment, benefit, or training to represent a reference point for comparison in any study or initiative.
- **Correlation** is the association or relationship between two or more variables.
- **Data isolation** is the data control that determines when and how a change to the data made by one action becomes visible to another. The goal is to allow numerous transactions at the same time without influencing one another.
- **Frequency distribution** is a list, table, or graph that shows the frequency of numbers or items in a sample. The numbers may be summarized using graphs and summary numerals. A frequency distribution can show the actual number of observations falling in each range. In the case of percentage of observations, the distribution is called a relative frequency distribution.
- **Normal distribution** is a way in which observations tend to gather around a certain value instead of being spread evenly across a range of values. It is generally most applicable to continuous data, and is best described graphically by a bell-shaped curve.
- **Outlier** is a data point that's further from the others in the data set, meaning it's an unusually large or small value compared with the others. An outlier might be the result of an error in measurement, which distorts interpretation of the data and has an undue influence on many summary statistics (for example, the mean).
- **Skewness** is asymmetry in the distribution of sample data values. In other words, values on one side of the distribution tend to be farther from the middle than values on the other side.

2.8.2.2 Overview of Quantitative and Qualitative Methods
Data-collection methods use quantitative or qualitative measures:
- **Quantitative methods** yield hard data, which is objective and measurable and can be stated in terms of frequency, percentage, proportion, or time. TD professionals can use quantitative data to measure the problem or opportunity numerically and apply statistical analysis to validate a hypothesis. Quantitative data provides the facts that inform decisions about whether a problem is real or just someone's perception.
- **Qualitative measures** yield soft data, which is intangible, anecdotal, personal, and subjective, as in opinions, attitudes, assumptions, feelings, values, and desires. Qualitative data may be difficult

to express in specific numbers because the analysis is often descriptive. Data is typically collected through focus groups and interviews or other sources, such as observer notes and survey comments. The analysis of qualitative data identifies common themes and atypical data, which is then categorized by specific topics.

Both types of data are important. For example, knowing how employees feel (qualitative measure) about a skill is just as important in a program's final design as knowing how well (quantitative measure) they perform the skill. Qualitative data can provide the context to the problem; it can put a human voice to the objective numbers and trends in the results. Incorporating the human element helps to highlight information that numbers will not uncover.

2.8.2.3 Techniques Used for Quantitative and Qualitative Data Collection

Many data collection techniques are available to TD professionals, who should select one that meets their needs but also avoids problems during the collection. [See 2.8.3 and 2.8.4]

Quantitative data sources include:
- Surveys and questionnaires
- Analytics from technology platforms
- Examinations and assessments
- Self-evaluations
- Simulations and observations
- Archival or extant data (existing records, reports, and data)

Qualitative data sources include:
- Focus groups
- Interviews
- Comments from surveys and questionnaires
- Notes from observations
- Benchmarking
- Impact analysis

2.8.2.4 Choosing the Right Method

TD professionals should combine quantitative and qualitative measures in a data collection process to ensure the results are both useful and accurate. For example, they can collect anecdotes and examples using a qualitative method (interviews) to support or design a quantitative method (such as a survey). Qualitative and quantitative measures may also be combined in the same measurement tool. For example, items on a survey can be qualitative terms, such as feelings and opinions; how many times each item is chosen (frequency) is a quantitative measure.

2.8.2.5 Planning for Data Storage

TD professionals should be aware of options for storing and displaying evaluation data, including spreadsheets, databases, and tables. Using a computer application to manage data simplifies data analysis, and the spreadsheet and database applications on most computers are suitable for the task. These applications often include a data entry table or form, automatic calculation tables, and automatic charts for reporting. Statistics may be used in conjunction with charts and graphs to provide a simple way to visualize trends:

- **Automatic calculations table.** The cells in an automatic calculations table contain formulas that extract and calculate information from the data entry table.
- **Automatic charts.** Data analysis includes presenting data in various charts, such as bar charts and line charts, to find trends.

TD professionals should value data management and security and keep evaluation data confidential to protect the anonymity of respondents. Specifically, they should plan how long to retain collected data, decide on standard naming conventions for spreadsheet files or databases for later retrieval, and determine how to ensure that the system storing the information is secure.

2.8.3 Skill in Identifying and Defining Individual and Organizational Outcome Metrics Based on Evaluation Strategy or the Business Objectives of a Solution

> **I. Identifying Outcome Metrics**
>
> TD professionals should begin evaluation early in the process and use the information from the needs assessment, business goals, and course objectives to identify outcome metrics.

2.8.3.1 Incorporate Needs Assessment Into the Evaluation Strategy

As the first step in an evaluation strategy, TD professionals should conduct a needs assessment to measure four areas of need: business, performance, learning, and learner needs. TD professionals can build an evaluation strategy by converting these pre-program measures to evaluation measures, which are also known as the four levels of evaluation: learner reaction, knowledge and skill mastery (learning), behavior, and results. The goal of the solution should be to identify positive changes in each of the four needs assessment pre-program measures when they become postprogram measures during evaluation. [See 2.2.2]

2.8.3.2 Examine Data Collection Techniques

TD professionals have many choices for data collection techniques. This section examines several of these methods, when they might be useful, and a sample of issues TD professionals need to consider when designing measurement instruments. [See 2.8.1]

2.8.3.2.1 Surveys and Questionnaires

Surveys are paper-and-pencil, online, or email questionnaires that ask respondents a series of focused questions. They vary widely in complexity and the amount of time and money they require. TD professionals should choose the type of survey that best provides the data needed—not necessarily the one that's fastest, cheapest, or easiest. They also need to consider whether they should conduct more than one type of survey to collect different kinds of data about the same topic.

TD professionals can use surveys to gather both qualitative and quantitative data, and use various questioning options and rating scales, such as multiple-choice, Likert scale, forced-choice, and open-ended questions.

2.8 Evaluating Impact

The advantages of surveys are that they can be inexpensive and their results are easy to tally. They also provide quick results. The challenges are that the wording of questions must have the same meaning to all respondents (reliability) and produce the information that's sought (face validity). Sometimes obtaining a large enough sample to make the data reliable can be difficult.

2.8.3.2.2 Analytics From Technology Platforms

TD professionals can gather data that is routinely stored on a server. These tracking files automatically record things such as what was done and how long something was used. TD professionals can collect, compile, and analyze the data produced and make inferences about it.

2.8.3.2.3 Examinations, Assessments, and Tests

Examinations, assessments, and tests gauge what respondents know about, can do with, or believe about the content being investigated. Types of assessments and tests include:

- Knowledge assessments through verbal or written responses to multiple choice, true-or-false, fill-in-the-blank, or essay questions
- Observations of a person's performance of a job skill
- Analysis of work results, the product, or output against quality criteria

TD professionals should use examinations, assessments, and tests to gauge current learner knowledge, skills, or performance levels. They should formulate questions and measurement criteria carefully to ensure an accurate interpretation. A pilot examination, assessment, or test should be conducted with a small sample of the population to gauge face validity and reliability.

The advantages of these techniques are that they can be objective and focus on a specific gap. The drawbacks are that they don't reveal the reason for a lack of performance and time constraints can make it challenging to include both knowledge and skill examinations. Also, tests may not be constructed properly to legally justify how the results are used.

2.8.3.2.4 Self-Evaluations

Participants can complete self-assessment tests or checklists to evaluate how comfortable they are with performing certain functions and where they need more remediation to ensure they can complete the tasks.

An advantage of self-evaluations is that they can be easily compiled. A disadvantage is that participants may inflate their level of competence.

2.8.3.2.5 Simulations and Observations

An instructor's or manager's observations of on-the-job performance in a work simulation indicate whether a learner's skills have improved.

The advantage is the ability to observe and evaluate firsthand the demonstrated skills and knowledge. The drawback is that this is time consuming, and the Hawthorne effect may cause learners to perform differently because they know they are being watched. [See 2.2.2.4.3 and 2.8.6.2.4]

2.8.3.2.6 Archival or Extant Data

Archival data—also known as extant data—may be available inside or outside an organization. Examples include job descriptions, competency models, benchmarking reports, financial statements, strategic plans, staffing statistics, climate surveys, performance appraisals, grievances, turnover rates, absenteeism, suggestion box feedback, and accident statistics.

The advantage of archival data is that it provides reliable data, trends, and patterns that are usually collected for purposes other than evaluation. The drawback is that TD professionals cannot control the methodology used to collect the data, so it might be mixed with data that is extraneous to the purpose.

2.8.3.3 Document Needs Assessment Results

The final step in conducting a needs assessment that is useful to the evaluation process is presenting the results. By organizing information and discussing interpretations from analysis, TD professionals can succinctly and clearly show stakeholders how the proposed plan will solve the identified problem and respond to management's request. TD professionals should know how to communicate the results in writing and in a presentation. This communication also provides an opportunity to encourage the client to take ownership of other issues and recommendations.

The final report defines and documents the findings of the needs assessment process and summarizes the problem statement, the analyses used to determine the development need, and a proposed module design. The final report should discuss how the findings relate to the organization's overall strategy and goals and how the proposed change or plan will benefit the organization and the employees. The results of a needs assessment should:

- Explain the current state by outlining the organization's goals and its effectiveness in reaching those goals.
- Provide baseline data to determine the gap and measure whether progress is made in the future.
- Envision the future state by describing the vision and gathering hard metrics and data to measure.
- Explain the gap between current and future states by including root causes for suboptimal performance.
- Identify issues that will support, distract, deter, or prevent success.
- Describe the most appropriate solutions to close the gap.

2.8.3.4 Determine the Appropriate Solution

Based on the needs assessment results and feedback from the client, TD professionals should determine the appropriate solution. The solution should be tied to business needs and, when possible, use business metrics to measure the ultimate objectives. TD professionals should recognize that the appropriate solution may not be entirely training; perhaps training isn't the appropriate solution at all. They can use their knowledge of performance improvement to make this decision. [See 3.5]

2.8.3.5 Develop an Evaluation Strategy

TD professionals need to know how to design research methods to develop an evaluation strategy. Expertise in this knowledge area benefits TD professionals by providing a foundation for implementing measurement and evaluation. When embarking on an evaluation strategy, TD professionals should first determine which results to measure and how to measure them. They should select the measures before designing and developing the evaluation strategy. The methodology should clearly show why a method or procedure was selected.

It is critical for TD professionals to define and validate the business drivers to accurately establish measures for an evaluation (Barksdale and Lund 2001). Business drivers are the internal and external forces that direct an organization's strategy, goals, and business and performance needs. Internal business drivers are generated by internal decisions and can include technology; a change in system, process, or key policy; shareholder or financial drivers; human resources; and new product generation. External business drivers can include economics, government policy, public perception, and market or customer drivers.

Once TD professionals have identified the business drivers and performance needs, they can choose the evaluation method. As mentioned, potential methods include Kirkpatrick's Four Levels of Evaluation, the Phillips ROI Methodology, the Brinkerhoff Success Case Method, or another model that focuses on the effectiveness and efficiency of learning related to organizational goals. It is feasible to have three to five measures and corresponding approaches for the evaluation strategy. When TD professionals consider specific evaluation approaches, they should determine how the specific approach relates to the evaluation measures. This means that they may use a variety of methodologies to ensure that measurement and evaluation show the impact of a solution. [See 2.8.1.10]

2.8.3.6 Data Analysis

Analysis is the process of discovering and interpreting meaningful relationships in data and summarizing empirical results. The levels of analysis typically include individuals, workgroups, functions, and organizations. Specific analysis techniques summarize the effects of programs or solutions. Knowledge in this area allows TD professionals to explore data comprehensively, inform decision making, and determine the value of the outcome metrics.

Data analysis determines the impact of the solution. Level 4 of Kirkpatrick's Four Levels of Evaluation, for example, provides information about what affects the organization's environment and influences outcomes. Models for measuring learning also look at business results, which are important when designing large and expensive programs or determining whether an expansive company-wide initiative should be implemented.

Data analysis also determines if the outcome metrics were achieved. This level of evaluation should provide closure on a full-circle approach, starting with the business need and ending by quantifying the solution's effect on that business need. Table 2.8.3.6-1 shows this approach and how questions asked during the assessment can define the business need. Defining the business need in the planning stage identifies what should be quantified and what questions should be answered in a Level 4 evaluation.

Table 2.8.3.6-1. Preassessment for Level 4 Evaluation

Question Asked in Assessment	Question Answered in Level 4 Evaluation
What is the business need?	Was the business need met as desired?
What are the specific outcomes desired?	Were the specific outcomes realized?
What are the benefits of providing this service, product, or solution?	Were the desired benefits of providing this service, product, or solution achieved?
What are the objectives?	Were the objectives met?

2.8.3.7 Analysis Methods

To identify outcome metrics, TD professionals should be familiar with several methods of analysis including ROI, cost-benefit analysis, benefit-cost ratio, and utility analysis.

2.8.3.7.1 ROI Analysis

Return on investment (ROI) is a financial metric that compares the monetary benefits of a program with its cost. Program benefits and costs are defined using the same terms—money—allowing TD professionals to compare the two and demonstrate the direct financial impact. When learning is positioned as an investment, the TD professional can help executives see how it aligns with business needs. ROI presents the economic contribution of a program. However, reported alone, the ROI analysis does not show stakeholders how the program achieved the reported ROI, which means practitioners can't improve programs, and tangible benefits can't be highlighted.

TD professionals should use ROI in conjunction with impact objectives. A chain of impact occurs as people are involved in programs and projects. Figure 2.8.3.7.1-1 illustrates the chain of impact in the context of the five levels of evaluation. ROI does not need to be calculated for all programs, and TD professionals should know which programs will most benefit from ROI analysis, such as those with a long life cycle that are important in meeting operational goals or those that are closely linked to the organization's strategic initiatives.

Figure 2.8.3.7.1-1. The Chain of Impact

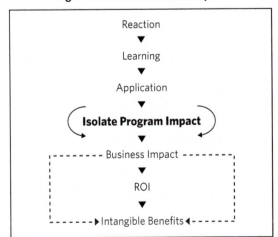

Source: Phillips and Phillips (2019).

2.8.3.7.2 Cost-Benefit Analysis

Cost-benefit analysis is a framework for considering a range of costs and benefits in monetary terms. It provides several analytical tools to quantify and monetize hard and soft data measures to reflect the value of learning. When performing this type of analysis, TD professionals should calculate all costs (including time away from work, travel, materials, and overhead costs) as well as lost opportunity costs (such as failure rates, downtime, rework, and accident costs). TD professionals should also calculate benefits-solution savings, including increased productivity, new accounts generated, reduced overtime, items sold, and on-time shipments. Some results are difficult to monetize; however, cost-benefit analysis is useful for showing overall benefits, comparing relative magnitude of specific costs and benefits, and prioritizing alternatives.

2.8.3.7.3 Benefit-Cost Ratio

Benefit-cost ratio (BCR) is the output of the cost-benefit analysis and is the ratio of the monetary benefits of a program relative to the costs. It is grounded in welfare economics and public finance, whereas return on investment (ROI) is based in business and finance.

ROI compares the net monetary benefits of a program to the cost of the program, and the output of the formula is a percentage. Historically, BCR was used to determine the economic feasibility of investing in a program or project, but today it is often used to indicate the actual results. ROI, on the other hand, was used historically to indicate the return on what was previously invested, but today, the common practice is to forecast the ROI for programs and projects.

The two metrics are similar, yet different. For example, a BCR of 1:1 indicates the same as an ROI of 0 percent. A BCR of 1:1 indicates that for every $1 invested, $1 is returned. The ROI of 0 percent indicates that for every $1 investment, the dollar is returned and there are no additional benefits. Both ratios tell a program owner that it broke even. A BCR of 2:1 indicates that for every $1 invested, $2 were returned. This translates to an ROI of 100 percent, telling the program owner that for every $1 invested, the dollar was returned along with an additional dollar in benefit (Phillips 2017).

2.8.3.7.4 Utility Analysis

Utility analysis measures a program's economic contribution according to how effective the program was in identifying and modifying behavior and, therefore, the future service contribution of employees. It differs from ROI in that it places a value on new skills, disregarding the actual effect of those skills in the workplace.

TD professionals can use the Brogden utility estimation equation to estimate the dollar value of a training program:

$$U = N \times T \times dt \times SDy - c$$

Where:
- **U** = Total change in utility in dollars after implementing a learning solution
- **N** = Number of employees developed
- **T** = Duration, in number of years, of a program's effect on performance
- **dt** = True difference in job performance between the average trained and average untrained employees in units of standard deviation
- **SDy** = Standard deviation of job performance of the untrained group in dollars
- **c** = Cost of training per employee (Brogden 1946)

2.8.3.8 Forecasting

Using a different approach, TD professionals may use forecasting to define outcome metrics. This is a process for predicting future outcomes based on current and past data, usually by analyzing trends. The prediction is derived from trend data plus additional influences that may affect the results, and it creates a statement about the future. Forecasting is more challenging if more than one additional influence needs to be considered because that may require more sophisticated statistical techniques and software for multiple variable analyses. Even then, the data may not be a good fit for the model.

2.8.4 Skill in Creating Data Collection Tools

I. Steps for Creating Evaluation Instruments

TD professionals must focus on what should be measured and included in the evaluation process and then select a tool that will meet the desired criteria.

2.8.4.1 Steps to Create Data Collection Tools

TD professionals should determine the purpose of the evaluation instrument and what will and will not be included in it. There are many possible data components to assess. In addition to deciding on the type of evaluation to use, TD professionals should decide how to isolate the data to make valid comparisons, determine control groups, get management support, and overcome any barriers. To develop evaluation instruments, TD professionals should determine:

- The purpose the tool will serve
- The format or media that will be used to present and track results
- What ranking or rating scale will be used (Likert or a different scale)
- What demographics are needed
- How comments and suggestions should be captured
- The degree of flexibility that the tool needs
- How the tool will be distributed (email or in person at the end of the program)
- The timeframe
- How the results will be tracked, monitored, and reported
- How the results will be communicated
- How to reach a high level of return

2.8.4.2 Creating Exams, Assessments, or Test Evaluation Instruments

Exams, assessments, and tests are instruments that test knowledge and the ability to perform on the job; however, they may not be the best way to ensure a skill was learned. When testing is related to employment decisions, such as hiring, promotions, or pay increases, the test requirements may fall under professional standards, regulatory body guidance, or laws that vary from country to country. [See 1.6.5] Tests used for these purposes require more rigor to ensure validity and reliability (ACT 2014). Understanding validity and reliability concepts helps TD professionals construct better evaluation instruments.

2.8.4.2.1 Validity

Validity means the evaluation instrument measures what it was intended to measure. TD professionals can solicit feedback from SMEs to verify the validity of an evaluation instrument. This is important because it ensures that all learning participants interpret the meaning of a test question the same way. According to Jack Phillips (1997), there are three ways to determine whether an instrument is valid:

- **Content validity** is the extent to which the instrument represents the program's content.
- **Construct validity** is the degree to which an instrument represents the construct it's supposed to measure. The construct is the abstract variable that the instrument is intended to measure, such as knowledge or skill.
  - **Convergent validity,** a subcategory of construct validity, tests that constructs expected to be related, are, in fact, related.
  - **Discriminant validity,** a subcategory of construct validity, tests that constructs that should have no relationship are, in fact, not related.
- **Criterion validity** is the extent to which the assessment can predict or agree with external constructs. It is determined by looking at the correlation between the instrument and the criterion measure.

- **Concurrent validity,** a subcategory of criterion validity, is the extent to which an instrument agrees with the results of other instruments administered at approximately the same time to measure the same characteristics.
- **Predictive validity,** a subcategory of criterion validity, is the extent to which an instrument can predict future behaviors or results.

Test validity is based on several test result considerations:
- The test should be reasonably reliable and free from measurement errors; a test that is developed correctly reduces the amount of measurement error (ACT 2014).
- The test should include all the content that is needed to perform the job safely and competently.

2.8.4.2.2 Reliability

Reliability is the ability of the same measurement to produce consistent results over time. Certain types of data are inherently reliable. Other, more subjective types of data can be much less reliable. Scientifically determining an instrument's reliability requires that it be administered to a sample of participants and undergo statistical analysis. Without this, TD professionals can still improve reliability by wording questions and evaluating responses over time. Generally, tests with reliability coefficients at or above 75 percent ($p = 0.75$) are considered adequate.

2.8.4.2.3 Test Difficulty

Test reliability and validity are maximized if the level of difficulty for answering most test items is more than just a lucky guess and, at the same time, the degree of difficulty is not too high. If a test is too easy, it will result in high grade averages, which may translate into poor job performance, on-the-job accidents, or damage to expensive equipment.

Test scores can mean many things. A test or question that appears to be easy could mean the information was well taught, answers were cued in some way, or participants already knew the information. If a test or test item is too difficult, perhaps information wasn't presented adequately in person or in reading materials, or maybe the item was so difficult that only the most knowledgeable person could answer it correctly.

There are several ways to test the reliability of a test:
- **Split-half reliability** splits one test into two shorter ones. Test items are randomly assigned to one test half or the other; each half is scored, and the correlation between the two halves is calculated. The participants then take the other half of the test for their retest, which overcomes the memory bias in a test-retest approach.
- **Test-retest check of reliability** is an approach in which the same test is administered twice to the same group of people. The scores are then compared. However, timing is a critical issue in a test-retest check: If the period between tests is too short, a participant could simply remember the test items, but if the period is too long, other variables enter the equation, such as exposure to new information.

2.8.4.3 Creating Surveys, Questionnaires, or Interview Evaluation Instruments

When the evaluation is linked to a needs assessment, TD professionals might use instruments other than exams. They should gather the most valid and reliable data possible. Considering several elements is important when creating surveys, questionnaires, and interview guide instruments:

- Be certain that the test items are directly connected to the measurement plan.
- Determine whether any definitions or other standards exist that need to be clarified.
- Decide whether reading ability or a second language is a concern.
- Explore whether to use a pilot test on the instrument.

These data collection methodologies have additional cautions (which are detailed in other sections) that TD professionals should heed. [See 2.2.2.4, 2.8.3, and 3.2.4.3]

2.8.4.3.1 Surveys or Questionnaires

Generally, surveys and questionnaires are inexpensive, but the test items need to be worded carefully so that everyone understands them in the same way. To ensure effectiveness when creating surveys, TD professionals should consider these suggestions:
- Keep the survey or questionnaire as short as possible.
- Identify ways to obtain a high return rate.
- Be sure the instructions are clear.
- Select the question type that best meets the purpose (for example, multiple choice, multiple answer, ranking preferences, open-ended, or scaled). [See 2.8.6.1.2]
- Decide if anonymity is required and how it will be addressed.
- Avoid leading questions.
- Use simple language.
- Avoid asking more than one question at a time.

2.8.4.3.2 Interviews

When creating one-on-one discussions, TD professionals can probe for additional information, but they should always start with a list of consistently worded questions. In addition, they should:
- Determine the specific information that is needed.
- Pilot test the interview.
- Train the interviewers.
- Ensure the interviewers can clearly explain the instructions to the interviewees.
- Plan a statement about anonymity and how the results will be used.

2.8.4.3.3 Observations

Observations are good for measuring skill ability. The instrument used most often to observe whether on-the-job performance has improved is a checklist. When creating a checklist:
- Include room to add additional comments.
- Clearly define each behavior.
- Train observers to avoid interpretations.

2.8.5 Knowledge of Research Design Methodologies and Types

> **I. Research Methods and Design**
>
> TD professionals should understand how to design a research plan for learning analysis or measurement and evaluation.

2.8.5.1 Research Design: The Overall Structure of a Study

TD professionals should know how to implement measurement and evaluation research methods, assess proposed methods, and make recommendations for how to implement a measurement and evaluation study.

To create solutions and measure their effectiveness, TD professionals should identify what learners need to be able to do and what metrics or measures will show whether the outcomes have been realized. To begin the process, they should determine which research methods will meet the constraints of their timeframe, cost, population, and so on. There will be trade-offs regarding the breadth and depth of information they can acquire. The research methods must be appropriate for the objectives of the research, and the methodology should also discuss any problems that occurred and how the influence was minimized.

2.8.5.2 Research Methods

TD professionals should understand research design methods, which are the techniques or processes used to collect data or evidence for analysis to uncover new information or create better understanding of a concept. Different types of research methods use different tools for data collection. TD professionals should have a working knowledge of these concepts:

- **Experimental design** includes a controlled factor or group that is given special treatment for purposes of comparison with a constant or controlled group.
- **Correlational research** is a type of nonexperimental research in which the measures of two variables are assessed for the statistical relationship (correlation) between them. Correlation is a measure of the relationship between two or more variables; if one changes, the other is likely to make a corresponding change. If a change moves the variables in the same direction, it is a positive correlation; if a change moves the variables in opposite directions, it is a negative correlation.
- **Meta-analytic research** is the statistical procedure for combining data from multiple studies. When the influence is consistent from one study to the next, meta-analysis can be used to identify a common effect.
- **Longitudinal research** involves repeated observations of the same variables, such as people, over short or long periods of time.
- **Cross-sectional research** involves groups of people who differ in the specified variable but share other characteristics, such as socioeconomic status, educational background, or ethnicity.
- **Quasi-experimental research designs** occur when a treatment is administered to only one of two groups whose members were randomly assigned.

2.8.6 Skill in Selecting or Designing Organizational Research

I. Designing Organizational Research

TD professionals should be familiar with research design concepts so that they know about available options when they want to measure the effect talent development and other solutions have on the intended outcomes.

2.8.6.1 Research Concepts

TD professionals should be knowledgeable about basic research concepts and what to consider when selecting tools, defining populations, and collecting data for both talent development and organizational research. [See 3.7]

2.8.6.1.1 Dependent, Independent, and Extraneous Variables

In research experiment design, the evaluator controls the independent variable. Participants are split into different groups, with each group associated with a different treatment (or value) of the independent variable. The treatment can simply be to identify what group a participant is in, or it can be associated with a numeric value. The independent variable is the influencing variable; the dependent variable is the one being influenced and the one that is measured.

Extraneous variables are undesirable because they influence the relationship between the variables an evaluator is examining. Although these variables influence an experiment's outcome, they aren't actually the variables of interest, which adds error to an experiment.

2.8.6.1.2 Research Questions

TD professionals should word questionnaires precisely because questions that are open for interpretation could invalidate the research. Question formats include:

- **Multiple-choice questions** are used when all responses to questions can be included, when exclusivity can be constructed, and when bias resulting from forced selection is insignificant.
- **Multiple-answer questions** do not have exclusive answers.
- **Ranking questions** ask respondents to indicate, in order, their personal preferences and reveal the relative importance of the answers.
- **Open-ended questions** allow respondents to answer without prompting.
- **Scaled questions** are used to determine opinions or attitudes by measuring degrees (negative to positive) and intensity (strongly negative to strongly positive).

2.8.6.1.3 Experimental Design

TD professionals should organize an experiment properly to ensure that the right type of data, and enough of it, is available to answer the questions as clearly and efficiently as possible. This process is called experimental design.

TD professionals should clearly identify the specific questions an experiment is intended to answer before completing the experiment. They should also attempt to identify known or expected sources of variability in experimental units because one of the main goals of a designed experiment is to reduce the influence of variability on answers to questions of interest. Focus on designing experiments that improve the precision of the answers.

2.8.6.1.4 Statistical and Design Control of Variables

TD professionals should know what options are available when a control group is needed. The control group includes the participants in an experiment who are equal in all ways to the experimental group except that they do not receive the experimental treatment. The TD professional will need to know the independent variable that differentiates the two groups to determine if the solution produces the results that were forecasted and to what degree. The most common experimental design models include one-way analysis of variance, two-way analysis of variance, completely randomized design, or completely randomized block design.

2.8.6.1.5 Sampling

A sample is a portion of the population that a TD professional is interested in collecting data from. To ensure that all characteristics of the population are represented in a sample, TD professionals should include some employees at every level. When testing a specific solution, the sample population should consist of those directly affected by the solution. Sampling concepts include:

- **Random sampling** means that each person in the population has a known and equal chance of being chosen for the sample.
- **Random selection** is the process of drawing the sample of people for a study from a population.
- **Random assignment** is the process of assigning the sample to different groups or treatments in the study. It's possible to have both random selection and random assignment, as well as to have neither random selection nor random assignment.
- **Stratified random sampling** occurs when the population is divided into constituent parts, and then sample members are chosen randomly from those. This method produces a more representative sample than random sampling because it considers important differences in the population such as age, education level, or department.

2.8.6.1.6 Sample Size Estimation

The size of the sample needed depends on the size of the population, the desired accuracy of results, and the level of confidence that the results were not caused by chance. TD professionals should decide how confident they want to be that the findings are real and not caused by chance. A 95 percent confidence interval is generally acceptable; this means that 19 times of 20, or 95 percent of the time, there is confidence that the findings from the sample lie within the estimated value plus or minus the error. In some cases, an evaluator may decide that the findings were caused by chance one time in 10; that is, a 90 percent confidence interval. Once the size of the population is known, an acceptable error rate has been decided, and a level of confidence has been established, TD professionals can determine how large a sample is needed to meet those criteria.

2.8.6.1.7 Power Analysis

When designing experiments, TD professionals should perform power analysis in addition to sample size estimation. These calculations ensure that the sample size will be on target rather than too high or too low, which would result in unreliable answers and wasted time and resources. Some power analysis software programs use graphical and analytical tools to precisely evaluate the factors affecting power and sample size. For the study to be cost effective and scientifically useful, the information gained from these programs will be invaluable.

2.8.6.2 Sources of Measurement Error and Bias

Because measurement is part of research, the development of research methods and instruments is subject to measurement errors and bias at all levels of evaluation. TD professionals should recognize these types of bias.

2.8.6.2.1 Sampling Bias

Selecting specific individuals may be easy, but it can result in tainted data. TD professionals should always conduct surveys or interviews with participants selected on a random basis.

2.8.6.2.2 Selection Bias
Selection bias distorts a statistical analysis by intentionally selecting the samples. This process typically causes measures of statistical significance to appear much stronger than they are, but it can also cause completely illusory artifacts. Selection bias can result from scientific fraud, which means manipulating data directly, but more often it's unconscious or caused by biases in the observation instruments.

2.8.6.2.3 Insufficient Sample Size
TD professionals should ensure the sample size is large enough by using sample size guidelines. [See 2.8.6.1]

2.8.6.2.4 Observation Bias
The more visible the observation process, the less reliable the data is. When an observer is not trained or given proper instruments, the data becomes more unreliable. Therefore, TD professionals should conduct observations in the least obtrusive manner while still getting the needed information, preferably by multiple observers. The Hawthorne effect is a well-documented phenomenon that influences many research observations. In addition, observers should receive training and some sort of a checklist to aid their work. [See 2.2.2.4.3, 3.7.4.2, and 2.8.3.2.5]

2.8.6.2.5 Bias in Interviews and Focus Groups
Interviews and focus groups can provide high-quality information. However, to be most useful and avoid bias, the interview design must ensure that:
- The sample is representative of the population.
- Participants understand the questions.
- Participants are willing (their participation is not mandatory).
- The interviewer is trained in interviewing techniques and knows how to record the information accurately.
- A protocol for consistency in questioning is in place.
- The method used to evaluate interview results is objective.

2.8.6.2.6 Central Tendency Bias
When filling out a survey, some people may avoid committing to either end of a scale, and instead indicate responses near the middle. This behavior is called the central tendency bias. TD professionals can address this bias by developing a scale with no middle value (such as 1 to 4), but it's also important to gather evidence that a scale with a middle position isn't working before dropping the value. This conclusion is best determined through a pilot test of the survey.

2.8.6.2.7 Administrator Bias
TD professionals should be aware of facilitator or administrator bias toward test participants or the subject being evaluated. For example, if administrators think that one group of people will score the solution lower than other groups, or won't perform as well as another group, they may be inclined to dismiss or exclude the data or they might adjust the scale to account for lower scores from a certain population.

2.8 Evaluating Impact

2.8.6.2.8 Emotional Bias
Emotional bias affects reaction level evaluation data (or smile sheets) to the greatest extent. This bias occurs when participants allow their feelings (like or dislike) for the facilitator to sway their ratings. If these emotions go unchecked, they may contaminate the ratings.

2.8.6.2.9 Restriction of Range or Range Error
Some respondents to a survey or questionnaire may engage in the error of restriction of range. This occurs when respondents or raters restrict their ratings to a small section of the rating scale—whether positive (leniency) or negative (severity). In some cases, this phenomenon is an unconscious bias on the part of the rater.

2.8.6.3 Ethics and Participants' Rights
When preparing for research, TD professionals must protect the confidentiality and privacy of the data and respondents, as well as the data and its proprietary nature. Guidelines include:
- **Keep responses anonymous.** Anonymity allows participants to be open with comments that can be helpful and constructive.
- **Have a neutral person collect feedback forms.** This increases the objectivity of the input.
- **Explain the purpose of the evaluation.** Restating the process in terms of the flow and use of data clarifies the use of feedback data. [See 1.6]

2.8.6.4 Identifying Research Issues
Several tools are available to identify what to research prior to evaluating and measuring learning. These tools include Lewin's force field analysis, cause-and-effect (also known as Ishikawa or fishbone) analysis, and hypothesis testing.

2.8.6.4.1 Force Field Analysis
Kurt Lewin (1890–1947) is sometimes referred to as the founding father of organization development because of his profound effect on the field. His force field analysis helps identify the forces maintaining the organization's status quo and clarify approaches needed to facilitate change. In evaluation, the force field analysis could help TD professionals identify issues that may prevent performance, uncovering root causes that are unrelated to the solution. [See 3.5.2]

2.8.6.4.2 Cause-and-Effect Analysis
A cause-and-effect diagram is used to identify, explore, and display the possible causes of variation. This diagram was developed by Kaoru Ishikawa, a pioneer of quality management processes, so it's sometimes called an Ishikawa diagram; it's also called a fishbone diagram because of its shape. Cause-and-effect analysis can help identify problems with the evaluation process or the solution. [See 3.5.2]

2.8.6.4.3 Hypothesis Testing
The purpose of inferential statistics is to test a hypothesis and then accept or reject it. Generally, TD professionals should always test a null hypothesis—stating that they expect no difference between the treatment group and the control group.

2.8.6.5 Preparation for Research Design

TD professionals use evaluation data to ensure that their solutions meet the needs of learners and client organizations. Focusing attention on the planning phase of the evaluation process and defining the future use of data avoids unused data and yields important benefits. A comprehensive plan defines the what, why, how, and who of the evaluation planning and implementation process.

TD professionals should follow these eight steps to ensure comprehensive evaluation planning:

1. **Determine the purpose.** TD professionals should pinpoint the evaluation's objectives to choose the right data to collect and identify the right audience for the final report.
2. **Determine stakeholders.** The needs of critical stakeholders typically drive the evaluation's purpose. Four basic stakeholder groups are decision makers, program sponsors or clients, program participants, and providers.
3. **Determine the level.** To select the appropriate level of evaluation, TD professionals should consider stakeholders' needs, which are defined in the program objectives in a front-end analysis. Another way to determine the level of evaluation is to compare the program with a set of criteria. The closer the program comes to meeting the criteria, the higher the level of evaluation to pursue.
4. **Identify program objectives.** These drive the evaluation planning process, ideally reflecting the stakeholders' needs based on a thorough needs assessment.
5. **Plan data collection.** TD professionals should connect program objectives with each level of evaluation planned, describe the measures or data descriptors to use for each objective to determine whether an objective has been met, specify the data collection method for each level, select sources of data, determine timing of data collection, and designate responsibilities.
6. **Plan data analysis.** Planning the process of analysis is especially important in Level 4 and ROI evaluations.
7. **Plan communication.** Often a neglected step in evaluation planning, the development of a communication plan highlights issues that may influence the evaluation.
8. **Develop a project plan.** Project management is a matter of keeping a project's scope, schedule, and resources balanced.

2.8.7 Skill in Analyzing and Interpreting Results of Data Analyses to Identify Patterns, Trends, and Relationships Among Variables

I. Analyzing and Interpreting Results

TD professionals should be able to interpret and report the data so it is easy to understand.

2.8.7.1 Interpret Results by Analyzing Whether Goals Were Met

One goal in talent development is to identify positive changes in each of the four pre-event needs assessment measures when they are measured during evaluation.

TD professionals should interpret results by referring to the needs assessment and the TD solution's original goals. The needs assessment established the foundation for back-end evaluation when the TD professionals created measures and established objectives for business, performance, and learner needs. During evaluation, the corresponding measurements are taken: learner reaction, knowledge and skill mastery (learning), behavior or job transfer, and results.

TD professionals should determine if the data answers these questions:
- Were the learner needs met according to Level 1 evaluations?
- Were learning needs met according to Level 2 evaluations?
- Were performance needs met according to Level 3 evaluations?
- Were business needs met according to Level 4 evaluations?

2.8.7.1.1 Analyzing
When analyzing data, TD professionals have three major tasks:
- **Sorting data** shows whether the information has been collected correctly.
- **Tabulation** is the process of extracting and categorizing data from the instruments used to gather it. It is used to review and understand the data by reducing it from its raw state into a quantified format without changing the meaning.
- **Comparing the raw data** with the condensed data ensures that it hasn't been distorted.

2.8.7.1.2 Interpreting
After the condensed data is stable (that is, it reflects the raw data accurately), it is ready to be interpreted. TD professionals should examine the data from several aspects:
- **Content analysis** requires an analysis of the meaning of the data and whether a reliable data pattern has emerged.
- **Process analysis** examines whether any variables influenced the process and what interdependencies existed.
- **Quantitative analysis** reviews how the data can be measured, whether anything is missing, and how the results can be interpreted.

2.8.7.2 Use Visualization Tools to Identify Patterns, Trends, and Relationships Among Variables
TD professionals should use good judgment when analyzing survey results and question anything that doesn't seem right. Once TD professionals are satisfied with the data's integrity, they can use charts and graphs to make each question's result evident.

The primary tools for presenting quantitative evaluation are charts and graphs, such as line graphs, pie charts, scatter charts, bubble charts, time series charts, ranking comparisons, year-over-year comparisons, distribution of individual data points, and word clouds. TD professionals can also use crosstab tables to show a pictorial comparison of the results of two or more questions. These tables can help evaluators analyze cause-and-effect and complementary relationships. [See 3.7.5]

Two guiding principles for these tools are scaling and integrity. *Scaling* shows proportions and relationships. *Integrity* focuses on the presentation's truthfulness and accuracy. Edward Tufte (2001) states that graphics show the data best if their graphs encourage viewers to think about the substance and encourage the viewer to compare different pieces. The data should be displayed at several levels of detail, from a broad overview to the fine structure. Graphics should clarify the message quickly.

2.8.7.3 Developing Recommendations

When TD professionals have finished interpreting the data, they are ready to list the results by key findings. This enables deeper interpretation by comparing the analysis results with business drivers and identified needs.

When evaluators have invested effort in creating or supporting evaluation, they can easily become biased about the results. Accordingly, TD professionals should follow these guidelines for good evaluation reporting:

- Be aware of personal biases and filter them from findings, conclusions, and recommendations.
- Accept what the findings say because negative results can still provide opportunities for improvement.
- Begin to generate options and views from multiple perspectives while reviewing the data. This process stimulates recommendations and next steps.
- Order data in different ways, such as by demographics, process, or issues.
- Analyze data from the perspective of a case study.
- Link data from the evaluation tool to the business need, measures, content of a solution, and the practice of talent development.

2.8.7.4 Provide a Professional Report

Evaluating data and producing a successful outcome are meaningless unless TD professionals promptly and properly communicate their findings to stakeholders so they can act accordingly. Preparing and communicating evaluation results are two sensitive yet critical steps toward making improvements and satisfying the needs of various stakeholders.

TD professionals' communications about evaluation results should be objective, credible, and accurate. Consider these suggestions while reporting:

- Focus on the solution and not the program.
- Briefly address the evaluation methodology to give credibility to the findings.
- Clarify data sources and explain why they are credible.
- State any assumptions made during the analysis and reporting and clarify why they were made.
- Be pragmatic—only make claims that are supported by the data.

2.8.7.5 Communicate to Stakeholders

TD professionals should carefully and thoroughly plan how to communicate the evaluation results to stakeholders. They should provide timely communication, target it to specific audiences, and use effective media to convey the message. The communication should be unbiased, modest, and consistent with past practices.

Be prepared when communicating with key client groups. Plan the information presentations around each group's individual needs. In some cases, the presentation should be brief and general; other groups will want detailed information or a report on interim results, and still other groups will need to see results that have been screened for confidential and sensitive issues. TD professionals must safeguard information and only use it as agreed upon. Communication with client groups should deliver what they require.

2.8.7.5.1 Know the Content

Because TD professionals analyze evaluation report data, they must be familiar with it as they plan how to communicate and report the information. TD professionals can consider these suggestions to help with this process:

- Summarize data to be succinct yet maintain the key message.
- Interpret the data according to what is meaningful to the stakeholders.
- Relate various parts of the data to other parts; for example, show cause and effect, contrasting views, or complementary results.
- If the data came from more than one source (such as interviews, questionnaires, or corporate data) determine the relationships between each piece.
- Identify examples that will enhance the presentation.
- Provide clients with all the data they need to make good decisions.

2.8.7.5.2 Know the Audience

TD professionals should know what the audience will expect. Will they want a summary or narrative? Will they want to view the entire data set or a portion of it? Will they want a report or a slide presentation? Answering these questions will help design the presentation.

2.8.7.5.3 Know the Presentation

TD professionals should plan for a successful presentation following these guidelines:

- Start with the methodology but include only enough information to make the audience confident in the approach.
- Include the strengths and limitations of the approach.
- Present a summary without interpretation—provide the data and the analysis only.
- Focus on the data that provides answers to the situation.
- Include a clearly marked section that delivers recommendations and ties them to the data.
- If appropriate, provide several recommendations from which the audience may select.
- End with next steps, which might include asking the audience to make a decision.

REFERENCES

ACT. 2014. *ACT Test Design and Delivery Certificate Program*. Alexandria, VA: ASTD Press.

Barksdale, S., and T. Lund. 2001. *Rapid Evaluation*. Alexandria, VA: ASTD Press.

Basarab, D.J., and D.K. Root. 1992. *The Training Evaluation Process: A Practical Approach to Evaluating Corporate Training Programs*. New York: Springer.

Biech, E. 2015. *Training and Development for Dummies*. Hoboken, NJ: John Wiley & Sons.

Bloom, B., T. Hastings, and G.F. Madaus. 1971. *Handbook on Formative and Summative Evaluation of Student Learning*. New York: McGraw-Hill.

Brinkerhoff, R. 2003. *The Success Case Method*. San Francisco: Berrett-Koehler.

Brogden, H.E. 1946. "On the Interpretation of the Correlation Coefficient As a Measure of Predictive Efficiency." *Journal of Educational Psychology* 37(2): 65–76. doi.org/10.1037/h0061548.

Frierson, H.T., S. Hood, G.B. Hughes, and V.G. Thomas. 2010. "A Guide to Conducting Culturally Responsive Evaluations." Chapter 7 in *The 2010 User-Friendly Handbook for Project Evaluation*, edited by J. Frechtling, 75–96. Arlington, VA: National Science Foundation.

Herschbach, D.D.R. 1992. "Technology and Efficiency: Competencies As Content." *Journal of Technology Education* 3(2): 15–25.

Kaplan, R., and D.D. Norton. 1996. *The Balanced Scorecard*. Boston: Harvard Business Press.

Kearsley, G. 1982. *Costs, Benefits & Productivity in Training Systems*. Reading, PA: Addison-Wesley Publishing.

Kirkpatrick, D.L., and J.D. Kirkpatrick. 2006. *Evaluating Training Programs: The Four Levels*, 3rd ed. San Francisco: Berrett-Koehler.

Kirkpatrick, J.D., and W.K. Kirkpatrick. 2016. *Kirkpatrick's Four Levels of Training Evaluation*. Alexandria, VA: ATD Press.

Marshall, V., and R. Schriver. 1994. "Using Evaluation to Improve Performance." *Technical and Skills Training*, January: 6–9.

Patton, M. 2010. *Developmental Evaluation Applying Complexity Concepts to Enhance Innovation and Use*. New York: Guilford Press.

Phillips, J.J. 2016. *Handbook of Measurement and Evaluation Methods*, 4th ed. New York: Routledge.

Phillips, J.J., and P.P. Phillips. 2019. *ROI Basics*, 2nd ed. Alexandria, VA: ATD Press.

Phillips, J.J., P.P. Phillips, and T. Hodges. 2004. *Make Training Evaluation Work*. Alexandria, VA: ASTD Press.

Phillips, P.P., ed. 2010. *The ASTD Handbook of Measuring and Evaluating Training*. Alexandria, VA: ASTD Press.

Phillips, P.P. 2017. *The Bottomline on ROI*, 3rd ed. West Chester, PA: HRDQ Press.

Phillips, P.P., C. Gaudet, and J.J. Phillips. 2003. "Evaluation Data: Planning and Use." *Infoline*. Alexandria, VA: ASTD Press.

Phillips, P.P., and J.J. Phillips. 2014. *Measuring ROI in Employee Relations and Compliance*. Alexandria, VA: SHRM.

Phillips, P.P., and J.J. Phillips. 2015. *Making Human Capital Analytics Work*. New York: McGraw-Hill.

Phillips, P.P., J.J. Phillips, and B. Aaron. 2013. *Survey Basics*. Alexandria, VA: ASTD Press.

Sasser, E.W., L.A. Schlesinger, and J.L. Heskett. 1997. *The Service Profit Chain*. New York: Free Press.

Scriven, M. 1967. "The Methodology of Evaluation." In *Perspectives of Curriculum Evaluation*, vol. 1, edited by R.W. Tyler, R.M. Gangé, and M. Scriven. Chicago: Rand McNally.

Tufte, E.R. 2001. *Visual Display of Quantitative Information*. Cheshire, CT: Graphics Press.

Tyler, R. 1949. *Basic Principles of Curriculum and Instruction*. Chicago: University of Chicago Press.

Wholey, J.S., H.P. Hatry, and K.E. Newcomer. 2004. *Handbook of Practical Program Evaluation*, 2nd ed. San Francisco: Jossey-Bass.

Recommended Reading

Kirk, A. 2019. *Data Visualization: A Handbook for Data Driven Design*, 2nd ed. Thousand Oaks, CA: SAGE Publications.

Kirkpatrick, J.D., and W.K. Kirkpatrick. 2016. *Kirkpatrick's Four Levels of Training Evaluation*. Alexandria, VA: ATD Press.

Phillips, P., and J. Phillips. 2019. *ROI Basics*, 2nd ed. Alexandria, VA: ATD Press

Robinson, D., J. Robinson, J.J. Phillips, P.P. Phillips, and D. Handshaw. 2015. *Performance Consulting: A Strategic Process to Improve Measure and Sustain Organizational Results*. San Francisco: Berrett-Koehler.

Vance, D., and P. Parskey. 2020. *Measurement Demystified: Creating Your L&D Measurement, Analytics, and Reporting Strategy*. Alexandria, VA: ATD Press.

Domain 3

Impacting Organizational Capability

3.1 BUSINESS INSIGHT

To add the most value to an organization, talent development professionals should understand business principles and the specific business or organization in which they work. Business insight is the understanding of key factors affecting a business, such as its current situation, influences from its industry or market, and factors influencing growth. It also includes understanding how an organization accomplishes its mission or purpose, earns and spends money, and makes decisions, as well as the internal processes and structures of how work gets done. Having business insight is essential to strategic involvement with top management and ensuring talent development strategies align with overall business strategy.

3.1.1 Knowledge of Business and Organizational Processes, Operations, and Outputs

> **I. Organizational Insight**
>
> TD professionals should have a working knowledge of the business and its makeup. Understanding various aspects of the organization builds leadership's confidence in the TD professional and ensures that talent development strategies align to best support the organization.

3.1.1.1 General Business Knowledge

A business model is the method organizations use to plan how to generate revenue and profits, identify and serve customers, and produce services and products. Whether the organization is nonprofit or for-profit, the business model involves both strategy and implementation. The business model's key levers are price and cost; an organization can either raise prices or reduce costs, such as labor and supplies. The model determines how an organization:

- Selects its customers, users, or members
- Differentiates its product offerings
- Creates value for its customers
- Acquires and keeps customers
- Promotes and distributes its products and services
- Defines the tasks to be performed
- Configures its resources
- Captures profit

3.1 Business Insight

Business models vary by industry and in complexity and describe how an organization functions. Models include direct sales, brick-and-mortar stores, franchising, and hybrids, such as combining a brick-and-mortar store with an online retail outlet. Defining the type and state of the business helps determine whether it will be successful. To be a valued business partner in the organization, the TD professional should understand the:

- Business model
- Business objectives or annual goals
- Factors that affect growth
- Strategic drivers or forces shaping the organization and the industry
- Industry landscape and competition
- Success measures

TD professionals should understand business metrics and how the organization defines and measures success. These factors drive how talent development departments create and link learning programs and services to business goals and objectives.

Other general business knowledge includes topics such as culture and value systems, organizational environment, organizational structure, and governance.

3.1.1.1.1 Organizational Culture

The organizational culture represents the underlying beliefs, values, and assumptions employees have about their work and their feelings toward the organization. To understand an organization's culture, TD professionals should review the organization's history, mission, goals, strategy, tactics, vision, and plans.

3.1.1.1.2 Organizational Environment

The organizational environment is influenced by a variety of factors including:

- **Internal factors**—technology, new products, shareholder influence, financial performance, and changes in systems, processes, or policies
- **External factors**—economic changes, human resource and skill shortages, government decisions, public perception, and market or customer requirements
- **Employee factors**—labor shortages or shortages in the number of employees with a certain skill set, union demands, and employees' needs to balance time between family and work
- **Contractual factors**—contracts for full- or part-time employees, agreements with a contingent workforce, and agreements with suppliers for services and raw materials

3.1.1.1.3 Organizational Structure

The organizational structure defines department functions, roles, and responsibilities; relationships among departments; and reporting structures. The organization's layout, flow, and exchange of information, documents, and other resources is also determined, along with the workflow network—the formal structure supporting the workflow for business processes (Guerra-López and Hicks 2015).

3.1.1.1.4 Governance

Governance is the system that directs and controls an organization. Corporate governance typically refers to what the board of directors (or board of governors) does. While management is responsible for implementing the policies and procedures within the organization, its board is responsible for oversight of the governance process. Components of a governance operating model may include structure, oversight, culture, and infrastructure. The board should receive operational, financial, risk management, and reporting information so that it can implement effective governance without unnecessarily hindering business units from accomplishing their work (Baret et al. 2013).

3.1.1.2 Define Outputs: Products and Services
Organizations exist to produce products and services:
- **Products** are usually the tangible or visible items that are made and placed on the market for consumer acquisition or consumption.
- **Services** are the intangible (or invisible) items that are also available for consumer use.

Products and services are often combined in one package. For example, a car is clearly a product, but the extras that accompany its purchase, such as oil changes or tire warranties, are services.

3.1.2 Knowledge of Business Strategies and Factors That Influence an Organization's Competitive Position in the Industry

> **I. Understand What Makes an Organization Successful**
>
> TD professionals should be knowledgeable about factors that affect their organization's competitive position so that they develop required talent and deliver effective training.

3.1.2.1 What Defines Business Success
Business success depends on the type of organization and its vision, mission, and goals. TD professionals should be able to define their organization's strategic imperative—how it defines success. A for-profit company generally defines success based on financial drivers such as growth in earnings, operating margins, return on equity, and sales growth. Publicly held companies are also interested in satisfying their stakeholders and the dividend payout ratio.

Nonprofit organizations generally define their success by how well they achieve their mission. Although they may not be revenue-driven, nonprofits that sell products or services still use earnings as a success factor. Nonprofits also consider other factors that are critical to achieving their mission, such as how well they manage resources, how satisfied their members are, whether they have developed a sustainable business model, and how effectively they collaborate with the community they serve (Haddad 2018).

Success for a government agency is even less defined than nonprofits—agencies depend on their mission and can be local, state, or federal. Success may be measured by how their products or services improve quality of life, a judgement of whether the value delivered is worth the cost of delivering, or the relative influence over others in the world (Eder 2015). In general, government agencies are there to provide services as stewards to and representatives of taxpayers.

3.1.2.2 Business Needs
Business needs may represent broader strategic goals or more specific tactical objectives, which determine what an organization needs to do to achieve its goals or deliver on its mission. TD professionals should know

how they can assist and support these business needs through the development of the organization's talent. Business needs may include:
- Reaching identified objectives and goals
- Providing products or services
- Serving those in need
- Entering a defined market
- Delivering on a stated mission

Business needs might also include improvements such as:
- Reducing expenses
- Increasing sales
- Reducing time to market

3.1.2.3 External Factors That Affect Organizational Performance

External systems affect organizational performance and an organization's talent development requirements. TD professionals who understand how external factors affect the organization are more likely to become strategic partners and valued members of the organization. Conducting an environmental scan and a strengths, weaknesses, opportunities, and threats (SWOT) analysis helps TD professionals understand the current environment and gain insight into the corporate strategic plan, which defines where the organization aims to be in the future (Brodo 2018).

An environmental scan is an inventory of the political, economic, sociological, cultural, global, technological, and employment forces that influence the way an organization functions. These factors relate to internal and external influences. The scan involves analyzing the current environment and the trends that may affect it to assess customer needs and stakeholder expectations. There's no standard for conducting environmental scans. TD professionals should strive to collect as much information as possible on factors that could influence the organization's direction, including:

- **Economic factors**—effects of employment rates and interest rates on gross domestic product, consumer price index, disposable income, and inflation
- **Political influences**—level of privatization in governmental services, political trends affecting suppliers and customers, and level of partisanship in governmental bodies
- **Sociological factors**—worker skills, corporate responsibilities and ethics, population shifts, immigration, migration, age, gender, generational differences, minority groups, and nontraditional labor, such as contingent or contract labor
- **Cultural influences**—effects of national and local cultures on employees and organizations as well as the influence of corporate cultures on departments, regions, and the organization
- **Global influences**—effects of multinational organizations, wage comparisons, trade agreements, and globalization
- **Technological factors**—effects of technology advances on skills and process changes
- **Employment factors**—effects of recruitment and unions on unemployment, turnover, and relocation
- **Legal, regulatory, and ethical requirements**—laws that control how organizations conduct business [See 1.6]

3.1 Business Insight

In addition to understanding external environmental factors influencing the organization, TD professionals should understand the external relationships with customers, suppliers, competitors, the community, and charities. Partnerships are a type of external relationship and can greatly affect organizations. [See 3.2.7]

3.1.3 Knowledge of How Organizations Provide Customer Service

> **I. Customer Service Fundamentals**
>
> TD professionals should understand how organizations provide customer service so they can develop TD solutions that support organizational goals, such as increased sales, better customer relationships, faster response times, increased customer satisfaction, and more repeat orders.

3.1.3.1 Meeting and Exceeding Customer Expectations

Organizations should know what their customers expect from them, including the level of quality, the cost, how fast they can acquire products or services, and the features included in each product. Some organizations even strive to go beyond or exceed what their customers expect.

All organizations should have a deliberate customer strategy, which should change along with their customers' expectations. Organizations must also weigh the additional cost required to exceed customer expectations to determine the return on investing in exceeding expectations.

3.1.3.2 The Value of Customer Loyalty

Customer loyalty is important to every organization, and occurs when people choose one organization's products or services consistently over its competitors. This leads to repeat business and referrals.

Acquiring new customers can cost five times more than satisfying and retaining current customers (Forrester 2019). A survey by Harris Interactive, commissioned by RightNow, found that 86 percent of consumers would pay more for a better customer experience and 89 percent began doing business with a competitor following a poor customer experience (Oracle 2012).

3.1.3.3 Understanding the Customer Value Proposition

A key component of the business model is the value proposition. The term *value proposition*, which comes from the field of marketing, describes a company's promise to deliver value when customers buy its product. The customer value proposition is made up of all the benefits an individual (or a business in a business-to-business transaction) receives in exchange for purchasing the product or service. [See 1.1.8]

TD professionals should understand how to develop customer value propositions that address the benefits to customers by understanding their needs and strengths. In their role as trusted advisors to the organization's leaders, TD professionals should also know how the customer value proposition differentiates the organization from its competitors so they can provide informed advice to leadership.

3.1.3.4 Customer Service Goals

TD professionals should understand their organizations' customer service goals. They should also contribute ideas that support their organizations in accomplishing these goals and improving the customer experience. Typical guidelines for customer service might include:
- Clearly understand the need or question.
- Respond promptly.
- Convey knowledge and credibility.
- Ensure quality.
- Establish relationships and deliver quality exchanges by friendly staff.
- Respond to and resolve problems as quickly as possible.
- Evaluate customer service.
- Use analytics to adjust quickly (Oracle 2012; MacDonald 2019).

3.1.3.5 Customer Success Criteria

Businesses should be designed around delivering excellent customer service. In their annual evaluation of customer satisfaction for companies and industries, Forrester (2019) recommended that organizational leaders leverage strategic learning to ensure employees have the skills to "deliver stellar customer service experiences."

TD professionals can help their organizations master superior customer service by developing a talent pool of employees who:
- Decrease response time.
- Increase the overall resolution rate.
- Increase the percent of first contact resolution rates.
- Increase call or ticket volumes.
- Increase customer satisfaction ratings.
- Increase customer loyalty.

Poor customer service can drastically hurt an organization, and executives are taking a stronger interest in customer service than ever before. The brands performing in the top 20 percent of the same 2019 Forrester study had higher stock price growth and returns than the companies in the bottom 20 percent.

3.1.3.6 Customer Experience Management

Customer experience management is the action required to manage customer interactions through the touchpoints that lead to customer loyalty. Customer experience is important to organizations because it directly affects the bottom line (Nicastro 2018; Forrester 2019). PwC's Digital IQ report found that 65 percent of respondents viewed customer experience as critical to advancing business performance (Clarke and Kinghorn 2018).

Although the customer experience is generally focused on external customers, TD professionals should also consider the experience their internal customers receive. They can follow external customer experience management guidelines, which include these actions:
- **Personalizing** all internal customer interactions requires knowledge of customers' businesses so each customer can receive focus and appreciation in the context in which they operate.

- **Maintaining customer profiles** means recognizing that the more a company knows about its customers, the more relevant support it can offer them, which builds a partnership.
- **Anticipating customer needs** means delivering the right information to the right people when they need it. This is possible if TD professionals use what they learn in the first two guidelines to create their own customer experience.

3.1.4 Knowledge of How Talent Development Contributes to an Organization's Competitive Advantage

> **I. Understanding Talent Development's Contribution to Organizational Outcomes**
>
> TD professionals should be able to articulate how talent development contributes to an organization's success. Having business acumen, industry knowledge, and the ability to link TD initiatives to organizational goals will demonstrate this contribution. The TD manager plays an important role to ensure organizational outcomes.

3.1.4.1 The Role of the TD Manager

Depending on the type and size of the organization, the TD manager's role may vary. In a one-person TD department, the manager may be responsible for everything. In other instances, they may have a large in-house staff and several supplier relationships to meet the organization's needs. In this case, the TD manager may oversee the department and focus on future strategies. All TD managers, regardless of function size, should focus on:

- Defining their relationship to the corporate mission and vision
- Demonstrating how talent development contributes to the organization's competitive advantage
- Tracking the external and internal forces that affect the organization and the industry
- Determining specific training development activities
- Figuring out how much of the organization's budget will be spent on talent development
- Communicating the value of talent development to senior-level employees
- Aligning TD plans to organizational goals
- Implementing the processes and procedures for providing TD services or products
- Identifying the resources and technology required to support TD activities

3.1.4.2 Talent Development Is Part of a System (Recruitment to Reward)

Organizations are more effective when they view acquiring, developing, and deploying their talent as a system. Integrating the practices and functions that produce an organization's capability is the focus of integrated talent management (ITM). TD professionals can help their organizations bring these talent management elements together to determine how to maximize their organization's contribution to its goals and mission (Rath 2011). [See 3.4.1]

To better achieve their goals, organizations have more closely integrated their TD and HR processes, which maximizes efficiency and effectiveness (Oakes and Galagan 2011). This approach should also be integrated with experts from line departments (Ulrich 2011).

3.1.4.3 Talent Development Contributes to the Organization's Outcomes

TD professionals should think holistically about their role and how they can collaborate across the organization to help the workforce learn, grow, and achieve success. For example, they can assist with:

- **Talent acquisition and recruiting.** TD professionals understand job responsibilities and know how to define job tasks and write objectives, which support recruiting and acquiring talent.
- **Onboarding.** TD professionals may be responsible for ensuring that new employees understand the organization's culture, values, and mission; learn what they need; and are able to perform their roles.
- **Career development.** TD professionals can support individual development with practices that go beyond training, such as assessment, succession planning, mentoring, coaching, and performance management.

TD professionals can contribute in a meaningful way by engaging stakeholders throughout the organization. To encourage these collaborations and demonstrate what talent development functions can contribute, Robert Brodo (2018) recommends using a process to engage in business dialogues with key stakeholders:

- Prepare for the dialogue to determine the business context.
- Schedule business dialogues with stakeholders.
- Identify desired business outcomes with the stakeholder and challenge assumptions and beliefs.
- Solve the business challenges discussed with the stakeholder by linking TD strategies to the organizational strategy.

3.1.4.4 Measure Contributions With Quantitative Data

TD professionals can demonstrate their contribution by measuring specific quantitative outcomes, such as:

- Increased engagement scores
- Decreased turnover
- Increased customer satisfaction
- Reduced numbers of accidents
- Increased numbers of sales closed [See 2.8]

TD professionals should attempt to identify and measure the impact of training on the business despite the many variables and external influences. [See 2.8.2]

3.1.4.5 Measure Contributions With Qualitative Data

TD professionals can demonstrate their contribution to organizational outcomes with qualitative data. These statements may be more intangible, anecdotal, personal, and subjective, as in opinions, attitudes, assumptions, feelings, values, and desires. Qualitative data characterizes results and is not measurable. Although some of these examples could be assigned a numerical value and converted to quantitative data, they are not measurable as written here. Examples of qualitative data include:

- Satisfied and productive employees
- Motivated employees
- Efficient processes
- Creative and innovative solutions
- Consistency in attracting high-quality employees
- Maintaining competitive skills [See 2.8.2]

3.1.4.6 Increasing Talent Development's Contributions to the Organization

TD professionals have many opportunities to increase their contributions so the organization can accomplish its goals (Van Velsor 2013). These include:

- Coaching the TD team to support the organization [See 3.4.1.6]
- Challenging assumptions and beliefs about talent development
- Anticipating and assessing the organization's needs
- Meeting quality standards for services
- Evaluating and improving customer satisfaction
- Linking TD strategies to ensure the organization achieves its strategy [See 3.2.2.5, 3.3.7.9, and 3.4.8]

3.1.5 Knowledge of Financial Management Principles

> **I. Business Acumen: Critical Concepts for TD Professionals**
>
> TD professionals should demonstrate business acumen so they have a clear understanding of their organization's strategy and how to best support it from a strategic and financial perspective.

3.1.5.1 The Importance of Business Acumen

TD professionals require an understanding of business acumen, such as the ways that resources are allocated in organizations and how the environment affects the business. The ability to describe learning initiatives in appropriate business terms helps TD professionals position the talent development function as a strategic business partner.

3.1.5.2 Financial Terminology

TD professionals should have a clear understanding of the basic financial terms that are most relevant to their organization and be able to use them in conversation. These terms represent the language of business and of the organization's leadership, so TD professionals should use them to communicate talent development's value credibly to senior management:

- **Assets** refer to economic resources—what a company owns—which may be expressed in monetary terms.
- **Liabilities** are the debts or expenses a company owes.
- **Equity** is the value of the owners' or shareholders' portion of the business after all claims against it are calculated.
- **Balance sheet** is a statement of the organization's financial position, including assets, liabilities, and equity (liabilities + equity = assets).
- **Income statements** explain revenues, expenses, and profits over a specified time period (revenues − expenses = net income).
- **Chart of accounts** is the list of account lines maintained in a general ledger.
- **General ledger** is a document that contains all the organization's accounts.
- **Cost-benefit analysis** is a comparison that weighs the costs against the outcomes achieved; it is performed to determine the ROI.
- **Expenses** are the costs incurred in the process of earning revenues and conducting business.

- **Incurred expenses** are expenses for which obligations have been fulfilled but not paid.
- **Operating expenses** are expenses that relate directly to business operations, not to developing and providing products or services.
- **Revenue** is the money a company earns by providing goods and services to its customers.
- **Financial statements** show the end results of an organization's financial condition; there are four different statements: balance sheet, income statement, statement of cash flows, and statement of owners' equity (Novak 2012; Cope 2014).

3.1.5.3 Financial Management Principles

TD professionals should have a basic understanding of financial management principles as they undertake work that involves pricing, contracts, budget preparation, accounting, forecasting, and reporting (Tracy 2009). Actions to take include:
- Practice ethical behavior to maintain the highest quality standards.
- Address all tasks and transactions in a timely manner.
- Establish realistic, sound budgets based on thorough analysis.
- Ensure a reasonable justification for all project goals and adhere to all federal guidelines.
- Make sure all expenditures comply with the organization's policies and procedures.
- Provide sufficient documentation and retain and organize it to withstand an audit.
- Ensure all documents that require a signature have received the authorized signatures. [See 3.1.6]

3.1.6 Skill in Managing Budgets and Resources

> **I. Budgeting, Accounting, and Financial Management**
>
> TD professionals create strategic plans outlining the activities that aid the organization's ability to achieve its goals. This plan is then used to establish a budget showing how the talent development department invests its time and resources.

3.1.6.1 Strategic Plan Development

Strategic planning is the process of systematically organizing plans; leaders use past experience as a filter for future decisions. TD professionals should develop a strategic plan linking the department to the organization's business strategy. The strategic planning process includes developing these elements:
- **TD vision**—focuses on future goals
- **Mission statement**—defines the purpose of talent development, its reason for existing, and its direction
- **Value statements**—describe the value talent development brings or proposes to bring to the organization
- **Strategic goals**—statements that define broad TD accomplishments based on the organization's needs
- **Objectives**—statements that identify how to achieve the strategic goals by dividing them into sets of specific tasks
- **Action plans**—steps that address how the strategic plan will be implemented, who is involved, the completion timeline, required resources, and how success will be measured

TD professionals link new learning programs to existing programs and systems, as well as current and future business needs. While organizational priorities should be their focus, TD professionals should also think beyond these priorities, using their knowledge of workplace, workforce, and population trends to demonstrate the connection between business strategy and employee development while also determining the department's future focus.

3.1.6.2 Budget Management

TD professionals should organize and oversee their departments like businesses, demonstrating as much planning and fiscal responsibility as any other unit in the organization. By managing their department like a business, TD professionals can gain credibility with organizational leaders and command more responsibility.

A budget is a working plan that guides fiscal decisions. Whether TD professionals are tasked with making an improvement or bringing new expertise into the organization, understanding the value of the investment requires a budget's financial data. Budgeting is part of a larger, three-step accounting system:
- Budget design and development
- Budget execution (such as expense tracking, monitoring, and managing)
- Reporting and reconciliation

In an optimal planning process, TD professionals will design budgets based on the business plan to fund the plan or previous spending levels. The assumption is that business goals justify the expenditures. Preparing and managing budgets involves four major steps:
- **Analysis and research** examines the past TD plan, historical records, baseline funds, the previous year's budget accuracy, benchmark data, and the success rationale for previous projects. TD professionals should remember that they never drive the budget process; finance does. Thoroughly researching budgets can be informative and helpful.
- **Planning** determines the programs, projects, and activities for the upcoming year. TD professionals create an annual plan that includes any existing programs and services that will continue to be provided as well as proposed new programs. The plan should be clearly tied to the business needs. In most planning processes, TD professionals gather information from two directions—senior leaders (which may depend on the access they have to high-level organizational data) and needs assessment data and feedback from clients and participants.
- **Budget review** comes after a budget draft is complete. This is when the budget is shared for review and approval with the TD professional's immediate supervisor up to various senior levels, depending on the organization's size. It does not matter how critical the funding need is; unless the TD professional presents the proposed budget in a logical, concise manner that shows how projects and programs link directly to the organization's success, the budget will be subject to revisions and cuts.
- **Budget management** requires the TD professional to track and manage the budget on an ongoing basis. Budgets provide details on accounts and forecasted expenses, so once they are approved, TD professionals need to track their expenses, document deviations from the budget, and perform periodic budget reviews.

3.1.7 Skill in Creating Business Cases for Talent Development Initiatives Using Economic, Financial, and Organizational Data

> **I. Business Cases for TD Initiatives**
>
> TD professionals should be skilled in creating business cases to show the value of TD initiatives and develop confidence in talent development. A business case is a presentation of the rationale and justification for initiating a project or task.

3.1.7.1 Communication Strategies

TD professionals should create communication strategies that incorporate the information about a program or initiative, determine the audience, identify methods available, and establish a timeline for delivering the information. A communication strategy will also include an action plan and the economic, financial, and organizational data necessary for buy-in. A business case may be part of a communication strategy. [See 3.4.7]

3.1.7.2 Creating Business Cases to Gain Buy-In for TD Initiatives

A business case serves a key purpose—gaining buy-in from stakeholders. Creating a business case requires TD professionals to gather data, define a rationale, and deliver supporting arguments. A business case includes a definition of the situation, the benefits, the costs, a timeline, and the impact on the organization—which can help convince leaders to support the initiative, even if they don't initially. Although a business case is often written for the senior leadership team, it's also a useful communication tool for other stakeholders.

Five steps are required to create a business case:

1. **Examine the organization's strategic priorities** and clearly define the situation, the need, and the opportunity for the initiative in terms of those priorities.
2. **Identify possible solutions** and how talent development can contribute. TD professionals should quantify the benefits and forecast the costs that may be involved for potential solutions. They should incorporate financial, economic, and organizational data and determine any risks or issues for each solution.
3. **Analyze and compare all solutions.** TD professionals should base the analysis on predetermined criteria and document the data and analysis.
4. **Select the best solution and determine the details required to make the recommendation.** TD professionals should define metrics that support the initiative's influence on the organization's top and bottom lines. They should also determine where the most impact will occur, and create an approximate budget to balance the success metrics. No one expects exact numbers in a business case.
5. **Describe the implementation plan.** TD professionals may want to tap into their network to obtain data and examples to use as benchmarks for the initiative. A general rule is to only present projects with a positive value.

The TD professional must present information in a way that the organization's financial leaders will understand. It is important for every organization—nonprofit and for-profit alike—to demonstrate talent development's impact or ROI. This means that the business case needs to focus on how the initiative will create organizational value.

The presentation of the information is an important consideration. A business case is generally organized in a similar format with the following components:
- Executive summary
- Current situation
- Initiative description
- Environmental analysis and alternatives
- Business and operational impacts
- Preliminary risk assessment
- Cost-benefit analysis
- Implementation timeline and strategy

3.1.8 Skill in Communicating Business and Financial Information to Different Audiences Using Appropriate Terminology and Relevant Examples

I. Communicating Business and Financial Information

TD professionals should be able to engage in an appropriate business dialogue with leaders and key stakeholders using accurate terminology.

3.1.8.1 Techniques to Communicate With Executives and Other Audiences

To effectively communicate with an organization's leadership, TD professionals should understand the business strategy as well as each operating function. They should also understand how organizational success is measured. This provides the basis for understanding how TD professionals can help the organization and its stakeholders achieve their goals.

To represent talent development at all levels of the organization, TD professionals should be able to think and present strategically to senior leaders. According to Dianna Booher (2017), "A big part of strategic thinking involves sorting the significant from the trivial." That means occasionally setting aside the talent development function's concerns to focus on the bigger picture—the entire organization.

Once TD professionals understand the business strategy and how success is measured, they need to learn and practice accurate terminology. These skills provide the basis for developing business and financial communications for various stakeholders within the organization. [See 3.1.2.1 and 3.1.5.2]

Booher (2014) provides these suggestions to craft a message that will be accepted and respected:
- Begin by reviewing what is most important to each stakeholder and at what level.
- Ensure the messages are clear, succinct, and strategic.
- Present a specific position supported by facts, data, and relevant examples.
- Keep the message at a high level, beginning with the ultimate outcome.
- Follow through with memorable points supported by facts that tell a story.
- Allow time to ask questions.
- Answer questions focusing on the significant items supported by data.
- Ask thought-provoking questions. [See 1.1.6.1]

3.1.8.2 Techniques to Present Business and Financial Information

TD professionals should state the ultimate outcome up front to help the audience focus immediately, and ensure they are using accurate terminology. Because business and financial information will likely have numbers and statistics, TD professionals should use graphs, charts, tables, and other methods for displaying data to allow stakeholders to easily and immediately comprehend the information. These tools help listeners focus on the substance of the message by revealing data at several levels of detail and presenting a clear argument. [See 2.8.7.3]

3.1.8.3 Varying Messaging for Different Audiences

To better connect with different audiences, TD professionals should determine the best format for each situation, confirm that any content they are using is current, and provide examples that are relevant to the situation. Robert Brodo (2018) suggests that senior leaders will engage with TD professionals if they believe the discussion adds value. By using business acumen skills and customizing messages for different audiences, TD professionals can gain credibility.

To successfully engage with different audiences, TD professionals should understand the specific business needs of each, engage in meaningful dialogue, proactively suggest talent development solutions, and link measurable TD results to organizational needs. Providing this thoughtful, compelling content requires an investment of time by TD professionals. [See 1.1.3]

REFERENCES

Baret, S., E. Hilda, S. Hatfield, N. Sandford, and J. Vazirani. 2013. *Developing an Effective Governance Operating Model: A Guide for Financial Services Boards and Management Teams*. Deloitte. deloitte.com/content/dam/Deloitte/global/Documents/Financial-Services/dttl-fsi-US-FSI-Developinganeffectivegovernance-031913.pdf.

Bell, C. 2017. *Kaleidoscope: Delivering Innovative Service That Sparkles*. Austin: Greenleaf Book Group Press.

Booher, D. 2014. "Securing Executive Support." Chapter 38 in *ASTD Handbook: The Definitive Reference for Training and Development*, 2nd ed., edited by E. Biech. Alexandria, VA: ASTD Press.

Booher, D. 2017. *Communicate Like a Leader: Connecting Strategically to Coach, Inspire, and Get Things Done*. San Francisco: Berrett-Koehler.

Brodo, R. 2018. "Business Acumen Basics for Talent Development." *TD at Work*. Alexandria, VA: ATD Press.

Clarke, D., and R. Kinghorn. 2018. *Experience Is Everything: Here's How to Get It Right*. PWC. pwc.com/future-of-cx.

Cope, K. 2014. "Building Your Business Acumen." In *ASTD Handbook: The Definitive Reference for Training and Development*, edited by E. Biech. Alexandria, VA: ASTD Press.

Eder, P. 2015. "How Do You Measure the Effectiveness of Government?" *Government Executive*, July 15. govexec.com/management/2015/07/how-do-americans-measure-effectiveness-government/117814.

Forrester. 2019. *Light on the Horizon: The State of Customer Experience Quality*. Cambridge, MA: Forrester Research. go.forrester.com/wp-content/uploads/2019/07/Forrester-Light-On-The-Horizon.pdf?

Guerra-López, I., and K. Hicks. 2015. "Turning Trainers Into Strategic Business Partners." *TD at Work*. Alexandria, VA: ATD Press.

Haddad, F. 2018. "How Do You Measure Nonprofit Success?" NonProfit PRO, November 16. nonprofitpro.com/post/how-do-you-measure-nonprofit-success.

MacDonald, S. 2019. "Five Ways to Deliver Excellent Customer Service." SuperOffice, November 18. superoffice.com/blog/five-ways-to-deliver-excellent-customer-service.

Nicastro, D. 2018. "What is Customer Experience Management?" CMS Wire, November 29. cmswire.com/customer-experience/what-is-customer-experience-management.

Novak, C. 2012. "Making the Financial Case for Performance Improvement." *Infoline*. Alexandria, VA: ASTD Press.

Oakes, K., and P. Galagan, eds. 2011. *The Executive Guide to Integrated Talent Management.* Alexandria, VA: ASTD Press.

Oracle. 2012. *Customer Experience Impact Report.* Redwood Shores, CA: Oracle Corporation.

Rath, T. 2011. "Foreword." In *The Executive Guide to Integrated Talent Management,* edited by K. Oakes and P. Galagan. Alexandria, VA: ASTD Press.

Tracy, J.A. 2009. *How to Read a Financial Report.* Hoboken, NJ: John Wiley and Sons.

Ulrich, D. 2011. "Integrated Talent Management." In *The Executive Guide to Integrated Talent Management,* edited by K. Oakes and P. Galagan. Alexandria, VA: ASTD Press.

Van Velsor, E. 2013. *Broadening Your Organizational Perspective.* Greensboro, NC: Center for Creative Leadership.

Recommended Reading

Booher, D. 2017. *Communicate Like a Leader: Connecting Strategically to Coach, Inspire, and Get Things Done.* San Francisco: Berrett-Koehler.

Cope, K. 2018. *Seeing the Big Picture: Business Acumen to Build Your Credibility, Career, and Company.* Orem, UT: Acumen Learning. Kindle.

Guerra-López, I., and K. Hicks. 2017. *Partner for Performance: Strategically Aligning Learning and Development.* Alexandria, VA: ATD Press.

Haines, S. 2019. *The Business Acumen Handbook: Everything You Need to Know to Succeed in the Corporate World.* New York: Business Acumen Institute.

3.2 CONSULTING & BUSINESS PARTNERING

Being seen as a valued business partner should be a goal for talent development professionals. Consulting and business partnering use expertise, influence, and personal skills to build a two-way relationship that facilitates change or improvement in the business. Clients may be internal or external. Successful consulting and business partnering requires skill in needs assessments, data analysis, communication, systems thinking, problem solving, negotiation, facilitation, and coaching.

3.2.1 Skill in Establishing and Managing Organizational and Business Partnerships and Relationships

> **I. Talent Development's Role As a Trusted Advisor**
>
> TD professionals should act as trusted advisors to members of the C-suite who face rapid change, environmental complexities, a competitive global market, and evolving technology. An organization's leaders depend on TD professionals to help them make strategic decisions, create solutions, and implement change to achieve the outcomes the organization requires. In their role as trusted advisors, TD professionals should build relationships and partner with stakeholders throughout the organization to proactively use their expertise to deliver problem-solving guidance (Biech 2018).

3.2.1.1 Defining Partnering and Consulting

The trusted advisor role is ongoing, which means becoming a strategic business partner to combine what the TD function knows about people and cognition to help organizations reach their strategic goals. Although TD professionals require similar skills to partner and consult, there is one key difference: Partnering is an ongoing role, whereas consulting is defined by a start and finish that follows a process outlined by the consultant or the client. The client can be any internal business unit or department; if the consultant is external, the client could be the entire organization.

3.2.1.1.1 Partnering

Partnering is proactively establishing a long-term relationship based on mutual trust and each partner's expertise to reach a successful common goal. TD professionals should work in partnership with learners, clients, stakeholders, and others to help address talent development needs and solve problems. Partnering requires continuous engagement with all levels, and TD professionals show support by helping clients identify originating causes and articulating the actions needed to resolve issues. This requires a collaborative decision-making process that involves TD professionals and the stakeholders, and it may require working with specialists in their areas of expertise. Partnerships require good listening skills, trust, and respect for one another's knowledge and expertise. Through the partnering process, TD professionals gain the credibility needed for clients to agree to a solution that will achieve organizational results.

3.2.1.1.2 Consulting

Consulting is the short-term, defined process of solving problems and helping individuals, groups, or organizations move from a current state to a desired state. It is an extension of partnering that occurs when supporting other functions in the organization requires a more defined process. At this point, TD professionals take on the role of consultant, using their expertise to facilitate change or achieve a stated outcome requested by a client. Consultants can be internal or external to the organization and usually focus on one project. In this consulting role, they rarely have formal authority to implement any recommendations.

In the role of consultant, TD professionals will follow one of many specific processes. Although these processes vary in number of steps required, they all follow a similar chain of events:

- Defining the issue
- Gathering and analyzing data
- Presenting findings and deciding on next steps
- Implementing the solution
- Evaluating the results

3.2.1.2 Foundations of Consulting Theory and Roles

TD professionals should know theories and models, which provide a foundation for current consulting practices. There are many early experts in the field of consulting. The following list highlights a few experts, along with their key contributions:

- **Edgar Schein,** author of the book *Process Consulting: Its Role in Organization Development,* introduced the concept that consultants should focus on adapting a solution to the organization as opposed to presenting a packaged solution.
- **Richard Beckhard,** author of *Organization Development: Strategies and Models,* helped define organization development as it is known today: an organization-wide, planned process initiative that is managed from the top to increase organizational effectiveness.
- **Chris Argyris** introduced the concept of single-, double-, and triple-loop learning and contributed to the development of organizational and experiential learning, the reflective model, and the ladder of inference. Each of these concepts can be used by consultants for effective results.
- **W. Edwards Deming,** an engineer, statistician, and consultant, brought his 14 points and process improvement concepts first to Japan and then the United States. He popularized the plan, do, check, act (PDCA) cycle for continuous process improvement, showing the benefits that occur when all employees are involved in making incremental quality improvements.
- **Peter Block's** book *Flawless Consulting: A Guide to Getting Your Expertise Used* is currently used by most consultants and has been recognized by the OD Network as the most influential book for organization development practitioners in the past 40 years. His five phases of consulting provide the basis for most current consulting models.

As a consultant, a TD professional may play many roles, including those defined by Ruth McCambridge (2007), who wrote about how to ensure an effective consulting engagement. This was an extension of the roles first introduced by Edgar Schein (1988) as a pair of hands, an expert, and a partner. McCambridge identifies four roles consultants can play with varying complexity:

- **The expert** role occurs when the consultant takes a directive role. The consultant is generally viewed as the authority; they provide advice, but the implementation is often conducted by others.
- **The facilitator** role means the consultant is in a neutral position and serves to facilitate meetings or teams that address process improvement, team building, or other actions to draw the answers out of a group.
- **The process consultant** examines processes, systems, interactions, traditions, culture, funding sources, and other interfaces to determine their effect on one another and the results. This role is generally the longest from a time perspective and the broadest from a range of topics and relationships.
- **The other pair of hands** generally refers to a consulting role focused on analyzing, planning, and rolling out the project. As the name implies, the consultant plays a supporting role, and the client is in charge of the outcome. This works best for short-term projects with few stakeholders.

3.2.1.3 Partnering and Consulting Are Natural Roles for TD Professionals

It is natural for TD professionals to partner with stakeholders in other departments and provide consulting services because they potentially interact with every employee at every level in the company at one time or another. TD professionals should also be skilled in processes that require partnering and consulting, such as teamwork, collaboration, communication, problem solving, performance improvement, and project management.

Consulting uses some of the same tools as TD work, such as risk assessment, needs assessment, planning, communication plans, vision statements, mission statements, and guiding principles.

3.2.1.4 Importance of Credibility and Credibility Requirements

TD professionals should build credibility with clients so they can be valuable partners. They should:

- **Be proactive:**
  - Partner with key leaders to identify the organization's issues.
  - Get involved with new projects, improvement teams, and task forces.
  - Anticipate corporate needs.
  - Propose initiatives that address current business issues.
  - Take initiative in the organization's strategic planning process.
- **Focus on organizational success:**
  - Spend time doing what the senior management team values.
  - Demonstrate the TD function's relevance by tying it to the bottom line.
  - Anticipate corporate needs and discuss them with senior leaders.
  - Establish a reputation for recognizing that the business must come first.
  - Think and act strategically.
- **Apply business acumen:**
  - Learn more about all aspects of the organization.
  - Further explore the industry the organization is in.
  - Read the same journals as senior leaders.

- o Learn more about the organization's competitors.
- o Investigate what strategic challenges the organization will face in the next few years.
- o Complete an organizational scan focusing on the trends that will affect the organization in the future.
- **Participate and communicate:**
  - o Network, especially with influential leaders—both formally and informally. [See 1.7.4]
  - o Attend or review senior leaders' presentations.
  - o Learn more about customers, their expectations, their issues, and what gives them satisfaction.
  - o Read the senior leader meeting minutes.
- **Deliver value:**
  - o Complete tasks even when unsure how to do it; someone will be able to help.
  - o Learn about organizational politics without allowing them to affect results.
  - o Establish credibility as a results-oriented player.
  - o Exhibit a positive can-do demeanor.
  - o Remain professional, honest, and ethical.

3.2.1.5 The Consulting Process

All consulting processes generally follow the same distinct phases. Although they may have different names, these processes all accomplish the same thing in sequence: diagnosing the current state and the desired state, taking action to improve, and managing the improvement. The five-phase process outlined here accomplishes all three. [See 3.3.1.3 and 3.3.2.1]

3.2.1.5.1 Phase 1: Assessing the Need

The first phase of the consulting process is used to define the need. It is also called the contracting phase, and it is when TD professionals begin to understand the client's organization, department, and needs. They should use an exploratory meeting to develop a consultant-client relationship and agree on their roles. They should also discuss the expectations and actions each will be responsible for. Most importantly, the consultant and client should agree on the expected goal, deliverables, and outcomes (Landers 2018).

3.2.1.5.2 Phase 2: Understanding the Issue

The second phase of a consulting process is used to discover and analyze the data. TD professionals should begin to collect data to better understand the issue and the environment in which it exists. Collecting data serves multiple purposes because it:

- More clearly defines the problem and the need
- Uncovers the potential causes of the problem
- May determine the preferred or desired future state
- Provides a baseline or starting point for comparison
- Identifies the content and scope of the solution
- Could increase individual and organizational support

TD professionals can use many different data collection methods; however, they should determine the criteria before selecting a method. Criteria may include:

- **Time.** What is the turnaround time?
- **Cost.** How much money is available for the assessment?
- **Comfort level and trust.** What is the organizational atmosphere? Will the data be reliable?
- **Size of the population to be surveyed.** How many people need to be involved in the assessment?
- **Confidentiality.** Is confidentiality an issue for individuals being surveyed?
- **Reliability and validity.** To what extent is this critical? How will the assessment methodology affect reliability and validity?
- **Culture of the department or organization.** What have employees used in the past, and how might different methods be perceived?
- **Location of those to be surveyed.** Are many people located remotely?

Once they determine the criteria, TD professionals can consider which method to use based on the advantages and disadvantages of each as outlined in Table 3.2.1.5.2-1. They may even combine tools depending on the situation and requirements. Once the data is collected, TD professionals analyze it to better define the issue and prepare to develop recommendations. [See 2.8.3.2 and 3.2.4]

Table 3.2.1.5.2-1. Understanding the Issue

Method	Advantages	Disadvantages
Surveys	<ul><li>Inexpensive</li><li>Results are easy to tally</li><li>Participation is easy</li><li>Can be both qualitative and quantitative</li></ul>	<ul><li>Constructing questions and selecting an appropriate scale must be done carefully</li><li>Words may mean different things to different people without an opportunity to clarify</li><li>Questions may not allow for free expression</li><li>Response rates may be low</li></ul>
Interviews	<ul><li>Provides rich detail because the interviewer can probe</li><li>Generates in-depth information</li><li>Uses the same wording and interview protocol to produce consistent data</li><li>Can be conducted in person, by web video conferencing, or by telephone</li></ul>	<ul><li>Can be time consuming and labor intensive</li><li>Interviewees must represent the target population</li><li>Interviewer must take care to not interpret responses</li></ul>
Focus groups	<ul><li>Able to observe nonverbal behaviors</li><li>Able to interview more people in a shorter timeframe</li><li>More ideas can be generated when participants build on each other's ideas</li></ul>	<ul><li>Time and resource intensive</li><li>Verbal members may be influential, whereas quiet members may not give a viewpoint</li></ul>
Observations	<ul><li>Creates a step-by-step procedure that should be standardized</li><li>Job environment conditions may make a difference and be incorporated in the solution</li><li>Provides a realistic view of the situation</li></ul>	<ul><li>Difficult to identify when one portion begins or ends</li><li>Performers may act differently when being watched (Hawthorne effect)</li><li>Only indicates the behavior, not the reasons for the behavior</li></ul>
Self-assessments	<ul><li>Enables ability to obtain candid information</li><li>Provides foundational information on which to build</li></ul>	<ul><li>May be biased</li><li>Unlikely this data can stand on its own</li></ul>
Extant data	<ul><li>Source of hard data</li><li>Enables ability to examine trends over time</li><li>Offers consistent measurements that lead to reliable data</li></ul>	<ul><li>May not be exactly the raw data required</li><li>Little control over methodology used to record the data</li><li>May need to sift through extraneous data</li></ul>

3.2.1.5.3 Phase 3: Present Findings and Interpretations

The third phase of the consulting process is used to deliver the findings and decide on next steps. In this phase, TD professionals provide the client with findings, interpretation, and recommendations. Together TD professionals and the client decide the next steps and, if necessary, adjust the goals and deliverables. They will also agree on an approach. TD professionals should know how to:

- Frame the findings or issues.
- Create effective feedback agendas.
- Conduct feedback meetings.
- Determine next steps.
- Manage sensitive information.
- Address resistance.

3.2.1.5.4 Phase 4: Developing and Implementing a Solution

The fourth phase of the consulting process is used to design the solution and implement it. Using the approach that was agreed on in phase 3, TD professionals design a solution that incorporates all components of the system and takes all stakeholders into consideration. TD professionals should create a transition strategy and may support the client as they're implementing the changes or new plan. In the consultant role, TD professionals may act as a coach, facilitator, leader, or guide during the implementation. Ongoing communication, as well as buy-in among stakeholders, is especially critical during this phase. TD professionals should know how to:

- Use a team approach.
- Create a transition strategy.
- Create an implementation plan.
- Work across organizational boundaries.
- Provide feedback to leaders.
- Gain buy-in.
- Share credit.
- Document the solution.

3.2.1.5.5 Phase 5: Completing the Project and Evaluating the Results

The final phase of the consulting process is used to end and review the process. If the project has ended, TD professionals will evaluate the results, identify lessons learned, and create a monitoring plan. There may be other times when the project is extended due to issues that were uncovered in the process, or they may need to cycle back to phase 2 or 3 to gather additional data or redesign the solution. Thus, in this phase, TD professionals should know how to:

- Bring closure to a project.
- Identify lessons learned.
- Create a monitoring plan.
- Address any uncovered issues.
- Evaluate the consulting process.

3.2.2 Skill in Partnering With Other Organizational Units to Provide Guidance on Departmental or Organizational Talent Requirements

> **I. Partnering Across the Organization**
>
> TD professionals should be skilled in working across departments and functions to provide guidance for all organizational talent requirements.

3.2.2.1 Opportunities for Partnering

TD professionals have multiple opportunities for partnering with all organizational units to provide guidance on departmental or organizational requirements. Partnering options may include:

- Evaluating talent requirements
- Advising on talent acquisition strategies
- Leading engagement surveys
- Designing, organizing, and conducting an onboarding plan
- Coaching managers to develop people
- Establishing mentoring programs
- Selecting high-potential candidates for leadership development efforts
- Increasing innovation
- Leading a focus group to gather data
- Supporting performance efforts
- Administering personality and leadership assessments

3.2.2.2 Interpersonal Partnering Skills

TD professionals should have the interpersonal skills necessary to successfully conduct partnering efforts. These include communication (both speaking and writing), collaboration, emotional intelligence, and leadership skills. [See 1.1, 1.2, and 1.3]

Solid partnerships between business and talent development ensure that the organization thrives. TD professionals can build this partnership by:

- Building a relationship with the leadership team
- Using business language
- Gaining a clear understanding of the organization's strategic imperatives, goals, and plans
- Understanding and helping solve organizational challenges
- Demonstrating collaboration, accountability, and timeliness
- Becoming a systems thinker to show understanding of how changes in one part of the organization will affect the rest of the organization
- Promoting positive change
- Exhibiting enthusiasm and pride in talent development work

3.2.2.3 Requirements for Partnering With Business Units

To build and sustain organizational relationships with the business units, TD professionals should have a clear understanding of the organization as well as the business or agency's mission and industry. They should take a systems perspective and think strategically and critically. They should have business acumen, financial knowledge, and marketing skills. [See 3.1]

3.2.2.4 Requirements to Work Across Departments

One of the opportunities TD professionals have is to partner across departments. This role, commonly called boundary spanning, describes employees who communicate with one another and share information across department lines. The term *boundary spanning* was coined by Michael Tushman (1977) at the Harvard Business School. Organizational requirements to support boundary spanning include:

- Defining boundaries to create safety
- Creating understanding of boundaries to foster respect
- Connecting to suspend boundaries and build trust
- Reframing boundaries to develop community
- Interlacing boundaries to advance interdependence
- Cross-cutting boundaries to enable reinvention (Ernst and Chrobot-Mason 2011)

3.2.2.5 Align Talent Management to Organizational Talent Requirements

By partnering with leadership, TD professionals develop a strategy that meets the organization's needs and is aligned with its goals and objectives. The ability to think differently is required for the TD professional to align to the organization. These skills include:

- Systems thinking
- Strategic thinking
- Critical thinking
- Collaboration (Guerra-López and Hicks 2015) [See 3.4.1.7 and 3.4.2]

Ingrid Guerra-López and Karen Hicks (2015) identify four levels of alignment and the influence they have on organizations. In addition to aligning for organizational results, employee results, and work processes, they suggest that aligning for external value to the organization's clients represents the highest level of strategic impact. Guerra-López and Hicks suggest that this alignment "can add value to customers and society at large, and in turn positively affect organizational stability."

3.2.2.6 Benefits of Employee Development

Talent development benefits the organization by creating development opportunities for employees. Organizations that support employee development reap the benefits of that effort in many ways, such as:

- Increasing retention
- Enhancing morale
- Improving the ability to match a person to the job
- Maintaining current skills
- Flexibility
- Aligning talent with organizational strategy [See 3.4.9]

3.2.2.7 Meet Organizational Requirements

TD professionals facilitate the process as specific requirements flow down from the organization's objectives to talent strategy to talent management objectives. To align the process, TD professionals should complete a workforce plan for their clients, identifying critical roles and gaps between the current population and what is needed. [See 3.4.14]

3.2.2.8 Offer Development Options
Many development options exist to ensure that employees enhance their skills and stay abreast of organizational changes. Here's a partial list, and more are outlined in several other capabilities:
- Advanced degree education, executive and management courses, and certificate programs
- Cross-functional or cross-country job rotations
- Committee and task force involvement, on-the-job coaching or training, and mentoring programs
- Loaned executive programs (that is, executives are temporarily loaned to another organization)
- Retreats, sabbaticals, immersive management development classes, and adventure learning
- Shadowing or understudy efforts
- Replacement or academic assignments
- Self-development opportunities, professional associations, and opportunities to present at a conference or workshop [See 1.7 and 2.3.6]

3.2.3 Skill in Managing Stakeholders on an Ongoing Basis to Sustain Organizational or Business Relationships

> **I. Building and Managing Stakeholder Relationships**
>
> Whether TD professionals are internal or external, they should manage stakeholder relationships to become trusted as consultants and partners. They should be excellent communicators, consider the entire system, and avoid and manage potential problems.

3.2.3.1 Involve Stakeholders
TD professionals should work with stakeholders on an ongoing basis to sustain their relationships. They should begin by discussing the stakeholder's needs and identifying their pain points. Only after they learn about needs should they initiate discussions about how talent development can support them. Once they reach agreement, they can learn more about the reporting structure, and clarify the roles of the client's supervisor or other senior managers who might be involved in any of the initiatives.

TD professionals should initiate a discussion that incorporates the entire organization. When a discussion reaches the planning stages, they should agree who in the department, unit, or function will participate. Then they should expand the discussion to clarify the roles of other relationships, including stakeholders, customers, or vendors.

The key is to keep stakeholders involved as TD professionals maintain the relationship and demonstrate how they can help other functions throughout the organization.

3.2.3.2 Communicate Clearly and Completely
The most trusted advisors in every profession are not those who have all the answers but those who can ask pertinent questions and facilitate conversation. This is also true with talent development too. TD professionals should: [See 1.1.1.3, 1.1.2, and 1.1.1.5]

- Determine what to communicate.
- Dictate the frequency of the communication.
- Decide who the primary communicator will be on a project.
- Select appropriate communication vehicles, such as emails, text messages, or critical meetings.

3.2.3.3 Build a Relationship

The skills required to build a stakeholder relationship are no different than those used to build other relationships. If TD professionals demonstrate that they truly care about supporting stakeholders, building and sustaining the relationships becomes easier and more accepted. Authenticity is critical to ensuring successful relationships. TD professionals should:

- Identify the stakeholder's communication preference and use it.
- Listen for understanding.
- Ask pertinent and thought-provoking questions.
- Provide feedback and coaching.
- Remember and use names.
- Learn something personal about the client and use that for another discussion focus.
- Exude self-confidence without arrogance.
- Project a professional image.
- Be flexible.
- Share credit.
- Do what's right.

3.2.3.4 Decision Making

TD professionals should ensure that the decision-making process is well thought out and appropriate for each project. For smooth decision points, stakeholders and TD professionals should agree on:

- Who has what level of decision-making authority?
- Who will be involved in key decisions?
- How will differences be resolved?

The decision-making process may change from project to project. [See 1.2.7 and 1.2.8]

3.2.3.5 Seek and Provide Additional Information or Knowledge

Communication is the biggest thing that can go wrong in a client partnership or during a consulting process. To avoid miscommunication, TD professionals should focus on clarity as well as complete and timely information sharing.

TD professionals should ask questions to learn additional information and probe when there may be something more behind the answer; open-ended questions gather the most information. TD professionals should also identify areas where stakeholders need additional knowledge about talent development and how it can help or support the department's mission and goals. [See 1.1]

3.2.3.6 Use a Systems Perspective to Work Across Organizational Boundaries

Both internal and external consultants need to demonstrate a systems perspective (that is, viewing the organization and its processes as one entire organization). A systems perspective requires TD professionals to know the business, discuss the broader implications of any project, and explore organizational systems and structures related to the stakeholder. Topics the TD professional and stakeholder could explore about the stakeholder's department include (Scott and Barnes 2011):

- How are department strategies linked to the organization's strategy?
- What is the relationship of the department's mission to the rest of the organization?
- Who comprises the department's internal and external customers and suppliers?
- How is performance measured?
- What measures are in place for cross-functional participation?
- What performance gaps exist, and has the stakeholder identified causes?
- What process activities are in practice?

3.2.3.7 Learning Organization Roles

Sometimes people do not know the benefits of a learning organization. If the TD professional is working toward creating a learning organization atmosphere, they should explain the concept (without jargon) to stakeholders. TD professionals may also want to share the rationale, which includes financial benefits and these basic actions:

- Create a shared understanding of the importance of learning.
- Agree to set aside time periodically to exchange information.
- Commit to feedback and reflection on what is learned. [See 1.1 and 1.3]
- Plan to create processes and structures for organizational learning (Burkett 2017).

3.2.4 Knowledge of Needs Assessment Approaches and Techniques

> **I. Designing Organizational Needs Assessments**
>
> TD professionals should be knowledgeable about assessment options so they can select and design methods that are appropriate for the data required in each unique situation.

3.2.4.1 Planning Data Collection

Data collection is important when it is used properly because it provides a path to clarify problems and identify solutions. The analysis of the data provides support for choosing the best solution. Data collection may serve other purposes for the TD professional, the stakeholder, and the organization by:

- Placing the training need or request in the context of the organization's needs
- Validating or dispelling the initial issues presented by a manager or leader
- Providing executive management support for a new idea or project
- Ensuring that the solution design supports employee performance and organizational needs
- Uncovering the cause of the problem
- Potentially validating other financial data by applying a methodology to track and report cost avoidance, savings, or return on investment
- Resulting in recommendations regarding nontraining issues that may be interfering with the achievement of desired organizational and employee goals
- Establishing a foundation for evaluation (Biech 2018)

3.2.4.2 Engaging Stakeholders

TD professionals should create a plan for the data collection to answer these questions:
- What is the objective of the data collection?
- What data is needed?
- What methodology will be used? [See 3.2.1.5.2 and 3.2.4.3]
- From a systems perspective, who will this project affect and what data do they own?
- Who should data be gathered from?
- Who should gather the data?
- What's the timeline required for the results?

As TD professionals create the data collection plan, they should take a systems perspective and determine what data will be valued by the department they are serving, as well as the organization as a whole. Then, they should ensure that they tie the data to the strategic initiatives. If that is not possible, they may want to reevaluate the project's relevance.

In all cases, they should discuss the plan with the stakeholders and incorporate their ideas whenever possible to ensure that the partnership is sustained.

3.2.4.3 Methods to Uncover Requirements and Gather Data

TD professionals have many options for how to gather data and uncover requirements. Accepted practices that apply to data collection methods include: [See 2.2.2.4, 2.8.2, 2.8.4, and 3.2.1.5]

- **Questionnaires and surveys.** This method is used to collect specific information from a large or widely dispersed group when confidentiality is not a requirement. Many people can be included and the results are easy to discern. Questionnaires and surveys are used to gather both qualitative and quantitative data. They may use various questioning options (forced-choice, multiple-choice, or open-ended questions) and rating scales (Likert or semantic differential scales). Good questions without errors and typos will lead to quality data. TD professionals should first test a new questionnaire on a small group of people.
- **Interviews.** TD professionals can use this method by identifying the audience who can provide the needed information and then interviewing them. An interview provides an opportunity to obtain candid, in-depth information about the problem and others' ideas about how to handle the situation. TD professionals should create a list of questions before the interview, establish appointments with the individuals, meet with them, and ask the questions, while taking notes and clarifying responses. They should hold the interviews in a neutral location where disruptions can be minimized.
- **Focus groups.** Somewhat like interviews, focus groups should include people TD professionals and the client have identified who can provide information about the need. However, instead of interviewing them individually, they are interviewed in groups to facilitate participant interaction to build on one another's ideas. A focus group generally lasts one to two hours and consists of eight to 12 people. Focus group members are chosen for their knowledge or experience in the topic area. If more than one group is conducted, TD professionals should ensure that questions are phrased in exactly the same way for each group. Two people should facilitate a focus group—one to work the group dynamics and a second to take notes. Organizations use focus groups for other purposes too, such as testing the market for a new product.

- **Observation.** This technique is used to view, record, and measure skills. It is useful under two circumstances: when assessing the need for skill-based training and when conducting a program that changes behavior (for example, customer service). TD professionals should clearly define what they are observing based on the consulting requirement. The observation is usually recorded on a tally sheet to compile specific behaviors; it can only indicate behavior, not the reasons behind the behavior or action. Consultants need to be aware of the Hawthorne effect—the fact that the mere presence of an observer may change the way people act. Also, because this is an interpretation of what the consultant sees, bias must be considered.
- **Extant data.** This method is used when existing records, reports, and data are available. It is an appropriate choice when it is critical to have data points and sufficient data can be obtained. The reports may come from inside or outside the organization. Examples include competency models, benchmarking reports, job descriptions, meeting documentation, financial reports, strategic plans, climate surveys, performance appraisals, grievances, absenteeism rates, turnover rates, suggestion box feedback, and accident statistics. TD professionals should take care that the data is not confounded by other variables, such as equipment downtime or external expectations.

3.2.4.4 Data Collection Pitfalls

Whether acting as internal or external consultants, TD professionals should be aware that the data gathering stage poses stumbling blocks.

Internal consultant pitfalls include:
- Becoming too familiar and accepting of the status quo
- Avoiding difficult employees when gathering input
- Not looking deep enough to get to the origin of the cause
- Not gathering data due to an assumption of already having the information and knowledge
- Losing objectivity
- Doing only what the client wants when it may be incorrect or inadequate

External consultant pitfalls include:
- Lacking criteria for interviewee selection
- Being less attentive after seeing or hearing repetitive information
- Underestimating the influence the organization's culture has on behaviors
- Getting caught in organizational politics
- Not being sensitive to the pace of change within the organization
- Doing only what the client wants when it may be incorrect or inadequate

3.2.4.5 Compiling and Analyzing Data

Once the data is gathered, TD professionals search for themes and relationships so the data can be presented in a cohesive, logical way. TD professionals should note these themes and review them to identify duplication. If a model was used, determine if it fits the themes. Models that are frequently used include:
- **Weisbord's Six Box Model**—purpose, rewards, relationships, leadership, structure, and helpful mechanisms [See 3.3.3.2]
- **Appreciative Inquiry Model**—discovery, dream, design, and destiny [See 3.6.1.11]

- **7 S Model**—skills, strategy, structure, systems, style, staff, and shared values
- **SWOT Analysis**—strengths, weaknesses, opportunities, and threats [See 3.1.2.3 and 3.4.2.1]
- **Value Chain Analysis**—nine primary and support activities
- **PIPE**—procedures, information, people, equipment

After the themes are listed, review the data one more time, looking for any additional themes. TD professionals may arrange the themes in a sequence or a diagram to display the information. Review the data to extract phrases and quotes that further establish the themes. Finally, TD professionals should identify recommendations.

An alternative exists for TD professionals who want the customer to be more involved in establishing recommendations. They may organize the data and provide examples in the feedback meeting so the team can identify their own themes and recommendations. This process helps participants take ownership of the data, and is particularly useful when conducting a team-building exercise.

3.2.4.6 Framing the Data for the Client

The boundary TD professionals place around the problem is called framing, which is a way of structuring or presenting the data. A model could frame the data, or TD professionals could simply describe the context of the situation and pose it to reflect the beliefs of the audience. Framing is important because it provides an opportunity to influence how the customer understands and perceives the data. The goal is to ensure they are focused on the picture the TD professional is presenting. They should include the successes and strengths related to the issue because those allow the customer to see how positive contributions lead to a positive future, which is called positive reframing. If the TD professional presents opportunities for improvement, the customer will view the issue as something that can be solved.

3.2.5 Skill in Synthesizing Information to Formulate Recommendations or a Course of Action to Gain Agreement, Support, and Buy-In From Stakeholders

> **I. Gain Agreement, Support, and Buy-In From Stakeholders: Synthesizing Information**
>
> Whether internal or external, TD professionals should be adept at gaining agreement toward a plan of action based on data that is easy to comprehend and recommendations that are clearly presented.

3.2.5.1 Know the Client

Formulating recommendations and actions that garner buy-in requires TD professionals to know their audience and begin to assess them from the start. They should begin by determining the client's readiness to take on a project, which will help TD professionals determine what they need to do to prepare, uncover issues that may affect the project's results, anticipate problems along the way, and gain agreement from the client. There are three things to consider about the client in preparation for making recommendations:

- **The client's role** in the project addresses whether they are the decision makers or the resource owners and whether they are ultimately responsible for the results.
- **The client's opinions** address how positive they are, how ready they are to move forward, and whether they have a sense of urgency and a willingness to partner on the implementation.

- **The client's priorities** examine what is most important to them; clients should have a mix of business needs and personal motivation; while gaining improvements is important, clients also need personal rewards such as recognition or a sense of achievement.

3.2.5.2 Establish Credibility

Credibility as a consultant is based on reputation, relationships with management, success with past projects, length of time in the organization, and how the TD function and the consulting roles are viewed. Credibility helps TD professionals readily gain agreement and support from their stakeholders. It can be established while building relationships through many small efforts such as being respectful of the client and always doing good work. TD professionals should build relationships at all levels and across department lines. [See 3.2.1.4]

3.2.5.3 Identify Barriers in Advance

At times, TD professionals will work with someone who exhibits negativity or creates obstacles. Most often, this happens when the information and recommendations are presented. Sometimes there is little that can be done, but TD professionals can watch for early warning signs that might include:
- Withdrawing commitment from parts of the project
- Failing to provide information as promised
- Being slow to approve work
- Changing direction in the middle of the project
- Requesting that information be omitted or changed
- Seeming to have a hidden motive

TD professionals should address these behaviors as soon as they occur. Ignoring them will only let things get worse or appear at an inopportune time.

3.2.5.4 Synthesize Information in Presentation Methods

Using their knowledge of framing and formatting data, TD professionals should consider how to present information. They must follow excellent presentation skills and methods to make choices about reports, case studies, charts, graphs, tables, diagrams, pictures, and visual aids or videos. [See 1.1.5 and 2.3]

3.2.5.5 Use Communication Tactics to Influence

TD professionals can influence the way the client accepts and buys into a recommendation. According to Beverly Scott and Kim Barnes (2011), "Successful influence begins with understanding the balance between expressive (sending) and receptive (receiving) communication." TD professionals can use both to influence the client. Scott and Barnes define these tactics:
- **Use expressive influencers:**
    - **Tell.** Communicate the desired action by making suggestions or expressing needs.
    - **Sell.** Convince the other to commit to action by offering reasons or referring to goals and benefits.
    - **Negotiate.** Give the other a vested interest in taking the action by offering incentives or describing consequences.
    - **Enlist.** Create enthusiasm and alignment through envisioning or encouraging success.

- **Use receptive influencers:**
  - **Inquire.** Get information and guide thinking by asking open-ended questions or drawing out answers.
  - **Listen.** Learn about, reinforce, or expand the other's thinking through checking understanding or testing implications.
  - **Attune.** Build trust or increase openness through identifying with the other or disclosing information.
  - **Facilitate.** Help the other to accept responsibility for taking action through clarifying issues or posing challenging questions.

3.2.6 Skill in Conveying Recommendations or a Course of Action to Gain Agreement, Support, and Buy-In From Stakeholders

> **I. Gaining Agreement, Support, and Buy-In From Stakeholders: Communicating Recommendations**
>
> Whether internal or external, TD professionals should be able to communicate recommendations, actions, and changes confidently to ensure buy-in from their stakeholders.

3.2.6.1 Determine the Best Format

TD professionals can communicate recommendations in a report, an executive summary, or even a fully formed product that represents the recommendation. They should know their clients and how and when they'd prefer to receive information and documentation. Timing of meetings, whether to share information in advance or during the meeting, and the kind of discussion or feedback requested are important considerations.

Another format decision is whether to use visuals, which are useful to ensure clarity and provide summaries. A large amount of numerical data should be summarized on a graph or in a table [See 2.8.7]. No matter the format, Benjamin Estes (2018) asserts that presenters must consider three steps:

- **Suggest.** Paint a clear picture of the recommendation.
- **Demonstrate.** Share reactions and what this will do when confronted with such a picture.
- **Elaborate.** Explain why this reaction is reasonable.

3.2.6.2 Presenting Recommendations

TD professionals should start with the bottom line and then stay focused on what is significant to the message. Sifting the trivial out from what is important is a skill that can be learned and practiced. Plan a well-thought-out design before the presentation. Start with the bottom line, and then build the rationale with facts presented in a logical sequence. Strengthen the message with analogies and short stories.

TD professionals should know the role they are playing before presenting their data. Depending on the situation, they may want to:

- **Take a point of view.** Make a recommendation if the consulting role was an expert. In this case the recommendation should be backed by data and what organizational goal it contributes to, such as improving performance or retaining talent (Booher 2014).

- **Be impartial.** Present the data clearly when the role is as a facilitator or "pair of hands." The data should be reported objectively so that the stakeholders or group can make recommendations or decisions. [See 3.2.1.2]

TD professionals should know the message a stakeholder wants to hear and focus on that significant message. If there is any uncertainty, they should err on the side of the more strategic, big picture considerations. Generally, the higher up the stakeholder is in the organization, the more strategically they'll think. A strategic message is apparent when it meets these criteria:
- A central common vision is offered.
- A long-term concern is presented.
- The presentation is about *why* to do something, as opposed to *how*.
- It is focused with a plan.
- It's about structure (Booher 2014).

3.2.6.3 Ask Thought-Provoking Questions

Staying focused on the message is critical, but it's equally important to be prepared with questions that create the kind of discussion that will gain support and buy-in from the stakeholder.

As the questions are formulated, TD professionals should ask themselves what they are trying to accomplish. They should guide the stakeholders into thinking about the best conclusion. The questions should also demonstrate how the presenter thinks. (Are they a strategic, creative, or systems thinker?) These question starters often produce good, thought-provoking questions:
- What if. . . ?
- How would it be different if. . . ?
- What would change if we could. . . ?
- Suppose that. . . ?

TD professionals should always test their thought-provoking questions before using them in a significant presentation.

3.2.6.4 Make the Finale Memorable

TD professionals should use a powerful opening and begin their recommendation with the bottom line. They then build support through logically presented data and facts that tell a story, making their points memorable and asking thought-provoking questions. They also need to end with a powerful and memorable message; for example:
- Returning to the opening to bring it full circle
- Ending with a question—perhaps one of those thought-provoking questions like, "Are you ready to accept the challenge of. . . ?"
- Addressing an objection that may be lingering
- Telling a story related to what happened during the data gathering stage or some other part of the process
- Ending with a quote, a repetition, or a dramatic call to action [See 1.1.6.1 and 3.1.8.1]

3.2.7 Knowledge of Methods and Criteria for Sourcing, Establishing, and Managing Partnerships

> **I. Establishing External Partnerships**
>
> TD professionals should know what external sources are available to ensure they are obtaining the most effective, efficient, and cost-effective services. They form external partnerships for many reasons including:
> - Extending expertise beyond what's available internally
> - Adding to or supplementing the workforce
> - Gaining a new perspective
> - Getting access to alternative resources
> - Gaining access to a new audience
> - Saving costs or sharing services

3.2.7.1 Identifying Potential Partners

TD professionals may spend much of their time securing the services and products the organization needs. In many cases, they must determine whether to use internal or external resources. For example, what resources are available in-house? Seasoned employees may be perfect candidates to take on coaching or mentoring roles. Likewise, how can external partners solve organizational problems? TD professionals should consider these sources to support talent development efforts:

- Expert thought leaders
- Vendors and suppliers
- Talent development consultancies
- Universities
- Professional associations
- Nonprofit organizations
- Workforce development agencies

3.2.7.2 Rationale for Using External Resources or Outsourcing

TD professionals may need to leverage external resources in various ways to deliver service and solutions. For example, when the organization:

- Has multiple diverse development needs
- Needs technology expertise that would take too long to develop in-house
- Only requires short-term or temporary TD needs
- Is not able to provide required services because of budget, time, or talent constraints
- Has a large initiative that requires more resources than are available
- Has learners who are globally dispersed

3.2.7.3 Making Sourcing Decisions

Whether the TD function decides to create or buy services and products, these decisions will have numerous repercussions. TD professionals should consider cost, alignment to the organization, available internal expertise, ability to customize the content, time available, speed with which it is needed, how often the product or service will be needed, production technology, and credibility of the vendor. Considerations around whether to use internal or external resources include those outlined in Table 3.2.7.3-1.

Table 3.2.7.3-1. Making Sourcing Decisions

Use Internal Resources	Use External Resources
☐ Qualified and credible experts are available.	☐ The best expertise is available external to the organization.
☐ Specific knowledge is only available internally.	☐ An objective or fresh perspective is required.
☐ Building credibility with sponsors is desired.	☐ Time is of the essence.
☐ There is time to guide SMEs.	☐ Staff are not available to dedicate time to the project.
☐ Time is available to test the products and services.	☐ Budget is available.
☐ Budget constraints exist.	☐ The organization lacks the technology or ability to produce quality materials.
☐ An experienced instructional designer and OD expert are available.	☐ Relevant, credible materials and programs are available.
☐ Quality materials can be produced quickly and inexpensively.	☐ Outside authorities have more credibility.
☐ Relevant data is only available internally.	
☐ A mistrust of not-invented-here mentality exists in the organization.	

Source: Biech (2018).

3.2.7.4 Working With External Consultants

TD professionals may use external consultants who can be very helpful to the organization and serve a valuable role. The organization benefits the most when a partnership is formed and all parties work together with a common investment to achieve the best results. Beverly Scott and Kim Barnes (2011) share suggestions for forming a partnership and working more successfully with external consultants. To ensure a project goes smoothly, TD professionals should:

- Encourage a partnership with the external firm. Present a specific proposal that defines expectations and proposed roles; manage the scope of the project carefully.
- Ensure that management understands the value and expertise of internal consulting before an external firm is brought in.
- Help external consultants understand the dynamics of organizational politics.
- Ensure clear communication and discuss how talent development can best support the external consultants. Also, clarify what is needed following the project.
- Allow the external consultants to take the credit they need to be seen as successful in the project.
- Define expectations for the external and internal partners in the project.

3.2.8 Skill in Identifying, Minimizing, and Overcoming Organizational Barriers to Implementing Talent Development Solutions or Strategies

I. Overcoming Barriers and Resistance to TD Solutions

TD professionals should be knowledgeable about the barriers and skilled in addressing resistance that might prevent the implementation of TD solutions or strategies.

3.2.8.1 Identify Possible Barriers

TD professionals should be aware of possible barriers to implementing what may seem like practical and necessary solutions. Before even suggesting a solution, they should ensure it is aligned with the organization's needs and understand that they may collide with other higher-priority organizational needs. If the barrier is limited resources or a short-term focus, building a business case is a possible deterrent to show how the solution is an investment that saves time or money. [See 3.1.7]

TD professionals should be aware of the maturity level of their organization's learning culture. If the culture is undeveloped, there may be an assumption that learning is different from work, departments may not have an organizational perspective because they work in structural silos, or leadership may not recognize that continuous learning should be leveraged as a competitive advantage. In addition, an organization may not view learning as a strategic asset. In that case, TD professionals should influence and educate the leadership team (Burkett 2017). They must demonstrate how creating a learning culture throughout the organization can increase collective learning and problem solving to improve the organization's ability to accomplish its mission.

Sometimes there is a general resistance to change because individuals fear the unknown. There may be a fear of losing power, control, or influence. TD professionals can learn the reason for the resistance by ensuring that:
- It is safe to express disagreement.
- Other options are shown to the resistor.
- The origin of the cause of the problem has been identified.

3.2.8.2 Preventing Organizational Barriers to Implementation

Even though TD professionals may have gathered data, created a business case, and had a positive strategy that demonstrates a return on investment, they may still experience barriers and resistance to their solutions and strategies. TD professionals can minimize and prevent these barriers from occurring with several actions including:
- Anticipate objections; include them in the presentation or be prepared when they arise (Scharlatt 2008).
- Demonstrate alignment to organizational needs.
- Provide clarity on how the solution supports organizational goals, using data when appropriate.
- Determine appropriate stakeholders and communicate the right message at all levels.
- Continuously engage with all organizational levels to sustain partnerships.
- Build long-term relationships and avoid waiting until a need arises to identify support.
- Use the organization's informal communication network (or "grapevine") judiciously to lay the groundwork for future communication. *Note: Even though it may be a fast way to transfer information, TD professionals should not depend on this tactic due to the risk of inaccuracies.*

REFERENCES

Biech, E. 2018. *ATD's Foundations of Talent Development: Launching, Leveraging, and Leading Your Organization's TD Effort*. Alexandria, VA: ATD Press.

Block, P. 2011. *Flawless Consulting: A Guide to Getting your Expertise Used*, 3rd ed. San Francisco: Pfeiffer.

Booher, D. 2014. "Securing Executive Support." Chapter 38 in *ASTD Handbook: The Definitive Reference for Training and Development*, 2nd ed., edited by E. Biech. Alexandria, VA: ASTD Press.

Burkett, H. 2017. *Learning for the Long Run: 7 Practices for Sustaining a Resilient Learning Organization*. Alexandria, VA: ATD Press.

Cohen, S. 2017. *Building and Growing a Talent Development Firm*. Alexandria, VA: ATD Press.

Ernst, C., and D. Chrobot-Mason. 2011. *Boundary Spanning Leadership: Six Practices for Solving Problems, Driving Innovation, and Transforming Organizations*. New York: McGraw-Hill.

Estes, B. 2018. "How to Present a Recommendation." Distilled, March 6. distilled.net/how-to-present-recommendations.

Guerra-López, I., and K. Hicks. 2015. "Turning Trainers Into Strategic Business Partners." *TD at Work*. Alexandria, VA: ATD Press.

Landers, A. 2018. "7-Phase Consulting Model for Change Projects." *TD at Work*. Alexandria, VA: ATD Press.

McCambridge, R. 2007. "Ensuring a Successful Consulting Engagement." *Nonprofit Quarterly*, December 21. nonprofitquarterly.org/ensuring-a-successful-consulting-engagement.

Scharlatt, H. 2008. *Selling Your Ideas to Your Organization*. Greensboro, NC: Center for Creative Leadership.

Schein, E. 1988. *Process Consultation: Its Role in Organization Development*, 2nd ed. Upper Saddle River, NJ: Prentice-Hall.

Scott, B., and B. Barnes. 2011. *Consulting on the Inside: A Practical Guide for Internal Consultants*. Alexandria, VA: ASTD Press.

Tushman, M. 1977. "Special Boundary Roles in the Innovation Process." *Administrative Science Quarterly* 22(4): 587–605.

Recommended Reading

Block, P. 2011. *Flawless Consulting: A Guide to Getting Your Expertise Used*, 3rd ed. San Francisco: Pfeiffer.

Scott, B., and B. Barnes. 2011. *Consulting on the Inside: A Practical Guide for Internal Consultants*. Alexandria, VA: ASTD Press.

3.3 ORGANIZATION DEVELOPMENT & CULTURE

To remain relevant, organizations must continually develop capability and capacity. Organization development (OD) is an effort that focuses on improving an organization's capability through alignment of strategy, structure, management processes, people, rewards, and metrics. Organizational culture encompasses the values and behaviors that contribute to the social and psychological environment of a business. Understanding an organization's culture, norms, formal and informal relationships, power dynamics, and hierarchies informs the planning of initiatives to develop systems, structures, and processes to improve effectiveness.

Organization Development

3.3.1 Knowledge of Organization Development Concepts

> **I. Organization Development Basics**
>
> TD professionals should comprehend organization development concepts because organizational systems reflect the environment and context that influence talent attraction, retention, and engagement, as well as learning transfer.

3.3.1.1 Body of Knowledge and Practice Used

OD can be viewed as the use of organizational resources to improve efficiency and productivity in the workplace. It involves an ongoing, systematic, long-range process of improving an organization's problem-solving capabilities and its abilities to cope with changes in the external and internal environment.

OD is both a field of applied behavioral science and a field of scientific study and inquiry. It is interdisciplinary, with research rooted in social psychology, adult education, anthropology, social work, human resource management, change management, individual psychology, group dynamics, theories and models of change, organization behavior, research analysis and design, culture, and innovation, among others.

A core foundation of OD is its emphasis on systems theory and systems thinking, which pervades all theory and practice on the topic from diagnosis to solution implementation to evaluation. Systems thinking is a conceptual framework that looks at a problem or issue from a holistic perspective to understand how the links and interactions between system "components" influence one another and the whole system (Senge 2006).

A *system* is an arrangement of interrelated parts that represent interdependency and interconnectedness as well as a set of elements that constitute a holistic, identifiable whole. All open systems take in input from the environment in the form of energy, information, money, people, raw materials, and so on. For example, an open system may take in input from customers through surveys or market research and then channel that input with throughput processes that are converted to outputs meant to influence the environment. Outputs, in this example, might be advertising, marketing, or lobbying activities.

Other characteristics of open systems that influence organization development include:
- **Boundaries.** An open system has a permeable boundary that allows the exchange of information, resources, and energy between the system and the environment.
- **Feedback mechanisms.** An open system has feedback mechanisms through which it imports information from the environment.
- **Integration and coordination.** Every system must provide mechanisms, processes, and procedures for integrating and coordinating its various parts.
- **Homeostasis.** Systems strive to achieve a steady state of equilibrium when faced with disruptive forces, whether internal or external. The basic principle is preservation of the system.

Organizations—much like the human body or other biological systems—are living systems with interrelated and interdependent parts that make up the whole. A systems approach increases awareness of the larger environment in which a project, issue, or challenge is operating, and it helps TD professionals understand that activities, initiatives, or changes in one part of the system influence other parts as well as the entire organization.

3.3.1.2 OD Competencies and Capabilities: The Global OD Practice Framework

The Global OD Practice Framework defines the competencies needed for TD professionals who work as OD practitioners and represents the knowledge, skills, and behaviors they require. The framework was developed through research by the Organization Development Institute and is endorsed by OD thought leaders. Foundation competencies include interpersonal skills, consultation skills, business acumen, collaboration, problem solving, conceptualizing, project management, technological savvy, and presentation skills.

These competencies are broad, inclusive skills that describe how OD professionals can carry out their responsibilities and succeed in their roles. Competence is a prerequisite for having a capability—for instance, capability involves the use and deployment of competencies to accomplish professional or organizational goals.

The five major capabilities for OD professionals are:
- **Systems-change expert.** This capability includes competencies as a systems-change leader, culture builder, and innovator. It requires knowledge of system dynamics; theories and models of change; organization behavior, design, and research; analysis and diagnosis; group dynamics; individual psychology; culture; and innovation.
- **Efficient designer.** This capability includes competencies as an efficient designer, process consultant, and data synthesizer. It requires knowledge of data collection; data analysis; designing and selecting appropriate initiatives or solutions; and collaboration.
- **Business advisor.** This capability includes competencies as a strategic catalyst, results-oriented leader, and trusted advisor. It requires knowledge of developing client relationships; managing the consulting process; project management; and evaluating organizational change.

- **Credible strategist.** This capability includes competencies as a credible influencer, collaborative communicator, and globally diverse integrator. It requires knowledge of strategic planning; communication; developing client capability; and managing the consulting process.
- **Informed consultant.** This capability includes competencies as an exemplary consultant, emotionally intelligent leader, and lifelong learner or practitioner. It requires knowledge of business acumen; group facilitation; process consultation; and managing conflict. It also includes awareness of emotional intelligence and how personal bias can influence interactions. [See 1.2]

Implications for TD Professionals

Because TD professionals apply, develop, and deploy their skills and talents in organizational systems, they should understand how OD competencies and capabilities are defined, distinguished, and supported by the capabilities outlined in ATD's Talent Development Capability Model. Integrating OD skill sets with learning and development, performance improvement, and talent management capabilities will increase professional and organizational effectiveness.

Keep in mind, however, that it would be challenging for any one person to develop proficiency in all possible OD or TD capabilities. Therefore, it's best for TD professionals to focus on a few vital skills and knowledge sets that will most influence success in a specific role and to leverage the experience and expertise of leaders, subject matter experts, team members, and professional networks for additional support.

3.3.1.3 Integrating Organization Development

Organization development is the act, process, or result of promoting or advancing the growth of an organization. TD professionals must understand the consulting process that characterizes OD work, primary tasks, and common types of OD solutions they can use.

3.3.1.3.1 Consulting Process

Most consulting processes follow distinct phases; the OD consulting process has three:
- **Diagnosis** is a collaborative process between the organization's members and the TD professional to collect data about the total system and its processes, culture, or other areas of interest. It stems from two needs—the need to know the current state of "what is" and the need to know "what should be." [See 3.6.4.1]
- **Action** includes the activities and solutions designed to improve how the organization functions.
- **Program management** involves activities designed to ensure the success of OD strategies or solutions; for example, project management, managing relationships, stakeholder expectations, change or project teams, communication strategies, implementation plans, goal setting, and risk mitigation plans (French and Bell 1999). [See 3.2.1]

3.3.1.3.2 Tasks

During change management, TD professionals move the organization from the "what is" to the "what should be." TD professionals must focus on three primary tasks when designing and implementing OD strategies:
- Help the client system generate valid data.
- Enable the client system to have free, informed choice.
- Aid the client system as it generates internal commitment to the choices made (French and Bell 1999).

3.3.1.3.3 Types of Initiatives
OD initiatives are typically categorized as:
- **Human process initiatives**—team building, interpersonal and group process approaches, and coaching
- **Techno-structural initiatives**—restructuring organizations, such as mergers and acquisitions, flexible work design, downsizing, business process engineering, total quality management (TQM), quality of work life (QWL), Six Sigma, and Agile
- **Human resource management initiatives**—employee engagement, performance management, succession planning, coaching, mentoring, career development, and diversity awareness
- **Strategic initiatives**—organization transformation, culture change, leadership development, and attraction and retention initiatives

Most initiatives have elements of each category. TD professionals should ensure that any OD solution is aligned to specific strategic objectives.

3.3.2 Skill in Designing and Implementing an Organization Development Strategy

> **I. Designing and Implementing an OD Strategy**
>
> TD professionals should understand how to design and implement an OD strategy to successfully lead and support initiatives focused on increasing organizational effectiveness. When implementing OD strategies, the target of any solution is the organization as a whole system, while learning-oriented strategies target individuals or groups within the system.

3.3.2.1 Five Phases to Designing and Implementing an OD Strategy
TD professionals should integrate OD skills with the growing number of L&D, performance improvement, and talent management solutions focused upon increasing organizational effectiveness. The process used by OD practitioners to design and implement an OD strategy is structured in five phases:

1. **Entry** represents the initial contact between consultant and client where they present and explore the problem, opportunities, or situation. The output of this phase is generally an engagement contract or project plan that establishes mutual expectations and preliminary agreements on project scope (such as time, money, and resources).
2. **Diagnosis (assessment)** represents the fact-finding phase. It is a collaborative data collection process between organizational stakeholders and the consultant in which relevant information about the presenting problem is gathered, analyzed, and reviewed.
3. **Feedback** represents the return of analyzed information to the client or client system; exploration of the information for understanding, clarity, and accuracy; review of preliminary agreements about scope and resource requirements; and the beginning of ownership of data by the client. The output of this phase is typically an action plan that outlines the change solutions to be developed, along with defined success indicators based on the information and data analysis.
4. **Solution** represents the design, development, and implementation of the solution or set of solutions meant to correct problems, close gaps, improve or enhance performance, or seize opportunities.

Outputs may include a role-and-responsibility matrix, a training curriculum, or a training, communication, implementation, risk management, evaluation, or change management plan.

5. **Evaluation** represents the continuous process of collecting formative and summative evaluation data to determine whether the initiative is meeting the intended goals and achieving defined success indicators. Outputs generally include an evaluation report with recommendations for continuous improvement.

3.3.3 Knowledge of Theories and Frameworks Related to the Design, Interaction, and Operation of Social, Organizational, and Informational Systems

I. General Theories Supporting Organization Development

TD professionals should understand general OD theories to determine which theory and approach is best suited for the problem, opportunity, or change request.

Effective solutions depend on marshaling the appropriate theory and practice for a given situation. Because theories have been vetted, there is a good chance for success when they are used in the correct situations. Different theories are better suited to different areas of need or practice. Understanding the advantages and disadvantages of respective theories helps TD professionals select the best approach.

3.3.3.1 OD Theories

TD professionals should be familiar with these OD theories:

- **Systems thinking** is based on the concept that the component parts of a system can best be understood by examining their relationships with one another and with other systems rather than in isolation. The holistic view is important to change initiatives because small changes to any part of a system affect the whole system based on their level of interconnectedness. [See 3.1.1]
- **Open systems theory** refers to how organizational structure affects the flow of information and interaction internally and with the external environment. It is characterized by input-throughput-output mechanisms. Open systems planning involves scanning the environment to determine the demands and expectations of external stakeholders; developing scenarios of possible organizational futures; and developing action plans to ensure that a desirable future occurs. This kind of thinking is a requirement for creating learning organizations (Senge 2006). [See 3.3.1.1]
- **Complexity theory** defines an organization as a complex, adaptive system that needs to respond to the external and internal environment by remaining on the edge of chaos while also self-organizing and continuously reinventing itself. In complexity theory, the future is unknowable, so the ability to learn is critical to ongoing organizational effectiveness. Application requires experimentation and innovation to develop new operations patterns.
- **Chaos theory** is an interdisciplinary theory that says there are underlying patterns, constant feedback loops, repetition, and self-organization, even in the apparent randomness of chaotic, complex systems. The *butterfly effect* describes how a small change in one state of a system can result in large differences in a later state, meaning there is sensitive dependence on initial conditions.

- **Social network theory** represents how people, organizations, or groups interact with others inside their network. Networks comprise actors and the relationships between those actors, who are referred to as nodes and can be individuals, organizations, or companies. Actors are always the smallest single unit inside a network.
- **Action research,** a term first coined by Kurt Lewin in 1944, is also known as participatory research. It is learning by doing in the sense that a group of workers—or teams as part of a community of practice—identifies a problem, develops a resolution, implements the solution, and then analyzes the results. Transformative change occurs through the simultaneous processes of taking action and doing research, which are linked by critical reflection.

3.3.3.2 Planned Change Models

Organization development is an ongoing, systematic process of implementing positive and effective organizational changes. Change models that influence OD practice include:

- **Kurt Lewin's Force Field Analysis** (1947) is based on the premise that what is occurring at any point in time is the result of forces pushing in opposite directions. Lewin suggests that change is a three-stage process of unfreezing the old behavior, moving to a new level of behavior, and refreezing behavior at the new level. [See 3.6.1.2]
- **William Bridges's Transition Model** (1991) describes planned change as situational and transition as psychological. This model focuses on transitions and letting go versus planned change. Bridges describes three phases of transition: ending, neutral zone, and new beginning. [See 3.6.1.6]
- **W. Warner Burke–George H. Litwin Model** (1994) identifies the variables involved in creating first-order (transactional) and second-order (transformational) changes. It distinguishes between organizational climate and organizational culture:
  - *Climate* represents individuals' collective assessment of an organization in terms of whether it is a good or bad place to work
  - *Culture* represents the collective assessment of an organization based on deeper, relatively enduring, often unconscious values, norms, and assumptions.
  - *Transformational change* and fundamental culture shifts are produced by solutions that are directed toward leadership, mission, strategy, and organization.
  - *Transactional change* or changes in climate are produced by solutions directed toward management practices, structure, and systems.
- **Congruence Model** (1997) was developed by David A. Nadler and Michael L. Tushman and describes a seven S approach for examining how interdependent, organizational subsystems scan and transform input from the external environment to outputs in the organization across individual, group, and total levels. The seven Ss are strategy, structure, systems, shared values, skills, style and culture, and staff.
- **Peter Senge's Fifth Discipline Model** (2006) describes organizations as organisms, challenging the concept of the top-down, hero-leader, and large-scale change. Senge advises small, incremental change through five disciplines of organizational learning. [See 3.3.7.1]
- **Prosci ADKAR Model** (2003) is a goal-based change management model used to guide both individual and organizational change. It is different from many other change management models because it focuses on guiding change at the individual level through five distinct phases: awareness (A), desire (D), knowledge (K), ability (A), and reinforcement (R). [See 3.6.1.5]

- **Marvin Weisbord's Six Boxes Model** (1976) is a research-based OD model that tells practitioners where to look and what to look for when diagnosing organizational problems. It categorizes six critical areas as leverage points for influencing organizational success and achieving maximum impact. The model is used to teach leaders, managers, and performance professionals how to think systemically when identifying factors that currently enable or obstruct organizational behavior.

TD professionals should recognize that there is no single, uniform approach to applying OD theories to talent development. However, understanding different OD theories and their unique value will help TD professionals determine which approach is best suited to specific business needs or organizational change requests. [See 3.6.1 and 3.6.4.1]

3.3.4 Skill in Identifying Formal and Informal Relationships, Hierarchies, and Power Dynamics in an Organization

I. Understanding Organizational Relationships, Hierarchies, and Power Dynamics

TD professionals should understand organizational relationships, hierarchies, and power dynamics so they are better equipped to influence and drive talent and organization development strategies.

3.3.4.1 Knowledge of Relationships in Organizations

TD professionals should be able to identify, establish, and maintain strong, trusting relationships with clients and organizational stakeholders to:
- Identify business needs, performance gaps, and change opportunities.
- Gain support for organizational change initiatives.
- Align solutions to strategic business priorities.
- Promote participation and collaboration with solution design, development, implementation, and evaluation.
- Identify risks and barriers to solution implementation.
- Determine follow-up mechanisms to reinforce and sustain change progress.
- Establish credibility as a strategic change agent and business advisor.

3.3.4.2 Identifying Relationships and Organizational Charts

An organizational chart illustrates the structure of an organization and the relationships and relative ranks of its parts and positions. It is an overall picture of company hierarchy and personnel reporting relationships and provides insight to TD professionals seeking to identify relationship structures.

However, organizational charts only show formal relationships and do not recognize the pattern of human (social) relationships or managerial styles that influence organizational culture. To go beyond this, TD professionals can use several tools to identify how relationships work formally and informally, such as a stakeholder analysis, an environmental scan, or a network diagram. TD professionals should seek to identify, build, and influence relationships across all organizational levels.

3.3.4.3 How Relationships Support Organization Development

There are many benefits to building healthy working relationships with clients, teams, and stakeholders. These people have a stake in the success of OD efforts, can secure resources for projects, and help projects stay on track. TD professionals cannot expect to practice and promote OD as a participatory, problem-solving process without modeling collaborative behaviors and mindsets. Healthy working relationships include:

- **Trust,** which means others can rely on the character, ability, strength, or truth of someone or something
- **Mutual respect,** which means taking time to understand and value the opinions and ideas of others
- **Mindfulness,** which means being intentional and responsible for words and actions
- **Welcoming diversity,** which means accepting diverse people and opinions
- **Open communication,** which means communicating authentically, transparently, and candidly

Building and maintaining healthy working relationships not only increases engagement and commitment when identifying issues and developing solutions but can also open doors to key projects, career opportunities, and potential coaches or mentors.

3.3.5 Knowledge of the Principles of Organizational Management

> **I. Principles of Organizational Management**
>
> TD professionals should understand how the principles of organizational management influence the lines of authority and responsibility for OD efforts.

3.3.5.1 Organizational Systems

An organizational system defines how a company is set up; its structure dictates how each business division is aligned, the hierarchy of who reports to whom, and how communication is meant to flow throughout the organization. There are five main types of organizational structures:

- **Functional organizational structures** are a traditional hierarchy common in larger corporations that feature several specialized divisions with division heads who report to senior management. Because of these specialized divisions, employees also tend to become specialized. This structure provides clear reporting lines and a more obvious path for promotion and growth.
- **Divisional organizational structures** divide the organization into teams based on the projects employees are working on. Each project team has a director or vice president and exercises a certain level of autonomy within the organization. This structure allows employees to become familiar with other skill specialties and their team member's work.
- **Matrix organizational structures** are a cross between a functional and a divisional structure. This structure is set up with a traditional hierarchy and specialized divisions, with each division then split into projects and smaller teams. It encourages cross-collaboration by exposing employees to other departments and projects.
- **Horizontal or flat structures** flatten much of the hierarchy and allow employees more autonomy over their work. This setup may consist of temporary teams, although they don't usually have formal structures. While top-down dynamics are minimal, at least some level of senior leadership is typically involved. This structure has been adopted by many startups and tech companies because it encourages

innovation and employee input. It also increases communication across teams and eliminates some of the communication issues that can happen when messages travel up a top-down structure.
- **Network structures** are less hierarchical but also more decentralized and flexible than other structures because they outsource noncritical, specialized workers. This structure depends on open communication and reliable internal and external partners. It is viewed as more agile than other structures because it has more control and bottom flow of decision making. It also eliminates unnecessary departments and minimizes administrative costs.

3.3.5.2 Evolution of Organizational Structures

Today's organizations must adapt to evolving changes around how they work, how they lead, and how they are structured. In *The Future of Work* (2015), Jacob Morgan introduced 14 principles of the future organization, which were based on the growing shift away from hierarchical command structures. These principles emphasized the need for flatter, more collaborative and adaptive structures where any employee could act as a teacher or student and learn from colleagues anytime and anywhere. His predictions have become the current reality—these 14 principles of future organizations apply to organizations today:
- Globally distributed with smaller teams
- Connected workforce
- Intrapreneurial (that is, the practice of employees who work internally but are expected to act using entrepreneurial attributes)
- Operates like a small company
- Focuses on wants instead of needs
- Adapts to change faster
- Innovation everywhere
- Runs in the cloud
- More women in senior management roles
- Flatter structure
- Tells stories
- Democratizes learning
- Shifts from profits to prosperity
- Adapts to the future employee and the future manager

The evolution of organizational structures has led to these recommendations for high performance:
- Push responsibility down to employees operating in flatter organizations.
- Increase the emphasis on line managers to support tasks traditionally handled by HR.
- Instill learning as a priority in all organizational systems.
- Decentralize decision making to autonomous units and employees.
- Link performance measures for employees to financial performance indicators (Cascio 2012).

3.3.5.3 Principles of Organizational Management

Henri Fayol pioneered the five functions of management and is considered the founding father of concepts such as the line and staff organization. His ideas and strategies remain useful tools for forecasting, planning, process management, organization management, decision making, coordination, and control. Fayol's five functions of management are:

- **Planning** involves looking ahead. According to Fayol, drawing up a good plan of action is the hardest function because it requires active participation of the entire organization and available resources must be linked to and coordinated on different levels.
- **Organizing** is necessary because an organization can only function well if it is well organized. This means that there must be sufficient capital, staff, and raw materials to run smoothly and build a good working structure with the appropriate division of functions and tasks.
- **Commanding** involves clear working instructions that allow employees to know exactly what is required of them. Successful managers can motivate a team and encourage employees to take initiative with a participatory approach.
- **Coordinating** all resources and activities allows the organization to be at its best. Coordination also aims at stimulating motivation and self-discipline within teams.
- **Controlling** verifies whether activities are carried out according to a plan. This takes a four-step process:
    1. Establish performance standards based on organizational objectives.
    2. Measure and report on actual performance.
    3. Compare results with performance and standards.
    4. Take corrective or preventive measures as needed (van Vliet 2014).

The five functions are key to management in all levels and functions linked to one another.

3.3.5.4 Political Dynamics

Organizational politics refers to a variety of activities associated with the use of influence tactics to improve personal or organizational interests. Political dynamics consist of the implicit norms, hidden assumptions, and unspoken processes and guidelines that define how things are done in an organization. Organizational politics vary from one company to another, but all organizations have some sort of internal political dynamic that can help or hurt its effectiveness.

To deal with these dynamics, TD professionals should be aware of the players, rules, and landscape of their organization's political dynamics; the company's organizational chart will provide some insight into the political landscape. Gaining and leveraging political savvy has important benefits for TD professionals. Studies show that individuals with political skills tend to do better in gaining more personal power as well as managing stress and job demands than their politically naive counterparts. They also have a greater impact on organizational outcomes (Jarret 2017).

3.3.6 Knowledge of Work Roles, Relationships, and Reporting Structures Within an Organization

I. Organizational Reporting Structures

TD professionals should understand organizational reporting structures to determine the relationship between structure and culture, assess the impact of structure on organizational performance, and identify who and where to go to for support when leading or supporting OD efforts. Organizational structure, roles, and relationships provide guidance and clarity on specific HR issues, such as managerial authority and resource allocation, and must continually adapt to meet the evolving needs of the workplace and workers. [See 3.3.5.3]

3.3.6.1 Purpose of Reporting Structures
Reporting structure refers to the authority relationships in a company—who reports to whom—and is created by these authority boundaries. Reporting frameworks establish who is in charge of different tasks, departmental areas, and the organization as a whole.

3.3.6.2 Current Reporting Structures
There are four common types of reporting structures:

- **Vertical** means that authority increases incrementally up to the top of the reporting structure, stopping at the owner or CEO, creating a power hierarchy. Operational, middle, and top management have line authority over those they directly supervise. Employees only have the authority to do their individual jobs and are at the bottom of the hierarchy.
- **Horizontal** establishes peer and lateral relationships; individuals and groups from across the organization must coordinate efforts to achieve goals. This structure lays out each manager's span of control, which is the number of people reporting to them.
- **Staff authority** occurs when staff workers are empowered to advise line managers and functions (such as production and sales). Their role is to create, develop, collect, and analyze information, which flows to line workers in the form of advice. Line managers retain authority over those who report directly to them, while staff have advisory authority.
- **Functional authority** provides some staff managers with authority over certain procedures or tasks. For instance, a human resources manager may have created procedures that all managers must follow to prevent discrimination. Managers from across the company report their compliance to the human resources manager, who holds functional authority over the procedures.

Culture

3.3.7 Knowledge of Strategies and Techniques for Building, Supporting, or Promoting an Organizational Culture That Values Talent and Learning as Drivers of Competitive Advantage

> **I. Fostering a Learning Organization**
>
> TD professionals should understand the characteristics of a learning culture and be able to leverage their role as learning leaders to help organizations build and sustain a culture of continuous learning.

3.3.7.1 Origins of the Learning Organization
Organization-wide learning can be traced back to research from the 1940s when companies like Shell Oil, General Electric, Pacific Bell, Honda, and Johnsonville Foods began to realize the potential for increasing organizational performance and competitive advantage (Marquardt 2011).

However, it was Peter Senge's seminal work *The Fifth Discipline: The Art and Practice of the Learning Organization* that brought the concept of organization-wide learning to the forefront of organization development.

Learning organizations are places "where people continually expand their capacity to create the results they truly desire, where new and expansive patterns of thinking are nurtured, where collective aspiration is set free, and where people are continually learning how to learn together" (Senge 2006). As shown in Figure 3.3.7.1-1, Senge proposed the use of five component technologies or disciplines to shape an organization's overall capability to harness learning for continuous growth and revitalization:

- **Systems thinking** involves the ability to see the big picture and distinguish patterns instead of conceptualizing change as isolated events.
- **Personal mastery**, considered the cornerstone of a learning organization, begins when individuals commit to lifelong learning and continuously achieve results that are important to them.
- **Mental models** begin with self-reflection, unearthing deeply held beliefs, assumptions, and mindsets to understand how they dramatically influence actions and world views. Mental models are used to stimulate "learningful" conversations that support reflection and inquiry.
- **Building shared visions** involves finding commonly shared ideas about the future that foster genuine commitment rather than mere compliance.
- **Team learning** is the process of developing a team's ability to come together, share goals, and create desired results.

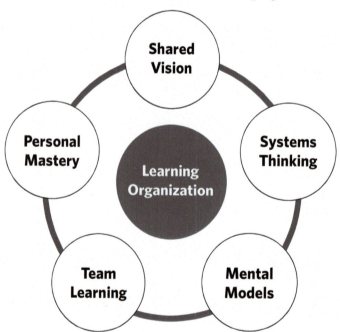

Figure 3.3.7.1-1. Senge's Five Disciplines of a Learning Organization

Source: Zeeman (2017).

Senge's five disciplines are all interrelated and focus on long-term organizational growth. While it may be more manageable for organizations to focus narrowly on one or two disciplines while working incrementally on the others, it's the use and integration of all five that ultimately leads to long-term growth.

3.3.7.2 Characteristics of a High-Performing Learning Organization

The focus on organizational learning and performance is what distinguishes a learning culture from a training culture. In a learning culture, the focus is less on training and more on creating a space where "employees continuously seek, share, and apply new knowledge and skills to improve individual and organizational performance" (ASTD 2014). In these cultures, learning is embedded as a "way of life" in everyday activities and is an organizational value that permeates all aspects of an organization.

Since Senge's pioneering efforts, many groups have conducted research on the characteristics of high-performing learning organizations and what they do differently. Table 3.3.7.2-1 lists the hallmarks of these organizations based on collective research findings (Burkett 2017).

Table 3.3.7.2-1. Characteristics of High-Performing Learning Organizations

From This	To This
Learning is focused on isolated, episodic events for individual audiences.	Continuous, collective, and daily learning occurs across all organizational levels.
Learning is focused on facilitating interaction and engagement among training groups.	Learning is focused on facilitating connection and engagement across boundaries.
Learning leaders function as facilitators and gatekeepers.	Learning leaders function as strategic business advisors.
Learning is driven by the learning organization.	Learning is self-directed and driven by employees and managers on their own.
Learning leaders assess individuals' learning progress or skills gained and provide feedback.	Learners, managers, and peers are constantly involved in feedback loops about one another's learning progress or skills gained.
The learning function is unable to demonstrate its contribution to the business.	Learning provides qualitative and quantitative measures of business impact.
Learning is a stand-alone function.	Learning is an integrator of strategy, talent, and knowledge.
Learning is isolated and vulnerable to environmental influences.	The learning function is continuously interacting with and influencing the environment.

Source: Burkett (2017).

3.3.7.3 A Learning Culture Is an Organizational Imperative

As automation and robotics improve, globalization increases, and workplaces become more complex, multigenerational, and diverse, the only competitive advantage for today's organization is to learn faster than the competition (Volini et al. 2019). Continuous learning is a necessary resource for closing skills gaps, building change capabilities, and fueling the innovation needed to survive and thrive in an age of disruption.

Organizations with a learning culture are better able to:
- Attract top talent.
- Develop leaders at all levels, which is essential in succession planning.
- Improve employee retention.
- Develop employees who readily embrace and adapt to change.
- Promote growth mindsets and high performance.
- Learn at a rate faster than change.

From an employee perspective, learning organizations are better environments because they:
- Encourage independent thought.
- Increase change readiness.
- Increase productivity.
- Increase job satisfaction and commitment.

- Provide opportunities for continuous learning and development.
- Increase employability due to the focus on upskilling.

Learning cultures have been proven to improve employee engagement, lower turnover, increase employee satisfaction, encourage problem solving among employees, and increase employee retention. Employees want an environment that's conducive to continuous learning and growth; if they aren't learning, they're leaving (Asghar 2014).

3.3.7.4 Help Managers Create a Learning Culture

TD professionals should recognize that managers are the most important factor in building a learning culture. They should provide managers across all levels—as team leaders, managers of other managers, or executive leaders—with challenging experiences that engage them and develop their strengths (Biech 2018). Managers are much more likely to inspire big-picture, cross-team cooperation and knowledge sharing among their employees when they are also engaged. Companies that include high-impact coaching as a component of a learning culture outperform their peers, according to studies conducted by the Human Capital Institute (HCI) and the International Coaching Federation (ICF). High-impact coaching practices include leveraging external coaches, a cadre of trained internal coaches, or leaders and managers as coaches to accelerate learning and development. [See 2.7.6]

3.3.7.5 Build Effective Partnerships

Learning cultures start at the top with leadership and are driven by middle managers. To ensure executive support of a learning culture, TD professionals should partner with leaders and organizational units who own the business need and have authority to make decisions and allocate resources toward learning and performance solutions (Skibola 2011).

Promoting partnerships across all organizational levels helps TD professionals improve their knowledge of the organization and identify areas where the learning organization can help solve real problems in real time. For example, partnerships ensure that TD professionals can properly identify the:
- Best solution to meet identified needs
- Context in which learning solutions will be used
- Extent of environmental support available to reinforce learning transfer and application of knowledge and skills on the job
- Specific performance and impact measures for assessing the success of learning and performance improvement solutions [See 3.2]

TD professionals should also partner with leaders, managers, and teams to keep the perspective of the modern learner in mind when assessing needs and designing and delivering solutions (Hart 2019). This means ensuring that solutions focus on providing relevant learning experiences (versus learning events) and making sure that learners have a choice and personal responsibility for their development. Taking time to strengthen alliances and understand the needs of the organization from multiple customer perspectives will establish credibility and trust for TD professionals (Robinson et al. 2015). [See 3.2.1.1, 3.2.1.3, and 3.2.2]

3.3.7.6 Engaging With Leaders to Learn About the Business

The sustained success of a learning culture depends on the support of leaders who own the business need, have the authority to put learning on the agenda, and make decisions about how learning resources will be allocated (Dearborn 2015). Most leaders recognize that they need the support of the TD function to address pressing performance challenges, yet many hesitate to engage the learning organization because TD professionals may view the world through a learning lens versus a business lens.

TD professionals should engage senior leaders' support by establishing credibility as business partners who are focused more on the performance that results from learning than on the learning itself. Understanding and speaking the language of the business shows stakeholders that TD professionals are interested in helping leaders get the results they want to succeed; additionally, helping stakeholders get the results they want is the best way to get the kind of leadership support and commitment that TD professionals need to grow the learning culture. A mature, high-impact learning organization is one that aligns business executives and employees throughout the organization around continuous learning (both formal and informal), which is aided by the adoption of strategic tools for L&D and a flexible, agile structure with processes, practices, and programs that are fully optimized to support a range of development needs that shift over time. Achieving optimal levels of process maturity is a transformative process characterized by distinct, iterative phases of development. While learning organization maturity levels may not be absolute, they do give leaders a strong sense of where their companies are and what they need to do to move forward. Four commonly used levels are recognition, resistance, refinement, and renewal (Burkett 2017). [See 3.2.1 and 3.2.3.3]

3.3.7.7 Show Value

Clients and managers who approve TD budgets need evidence that TD efforts are worth the investment of time, money, and resources. The elusive seat at the executive table must be earned through a strategic, results-oriented focus. A learning organization can demonstrate a results-oriented focus by using evidence-based data to show business leaders how it has achieved results that are important to them. While impact measures are valuable, some managers may simply want to know whether initiatives are on track, meeting targets, and achieving strategic goals.

In general, systematically showing the value of learning organization initiatives helps TD professionals and stakeholders determine whether:
- The right strategy is driving the right issue.
- Strategy execution is happening according to plans and timelines.
- The right tools and resources are being provided in the right way, at the right time, and to the right people.
- Organizational constraints or cultural barriers are interfering with learning, performance, and business objectives.

Using evidence-based data as a form of storytelling has also been shown to win funding and sponsor support, gain added commitment of stakeholders, inform decision making about program investments and resources, and help identify improvement opportunities (Biech 2018).

3.3.7.8 Challenge Organizational Assumptions and Beliefs About Talent Development

Many leaders have long thought of employee learning as something that happens in a classroom, delivered by a trainer away from the worksite, with content and activities selected by an instructional designer. Managers, as well as many TD professionals, have also come to believe that good training can solve any performance problem. However, the workplace has changed, and beliefs about learning need to change with it. In an age of automation and disruption, an organization's competitive advantage will be in the application of its collective knowledge and expertise, not in how many courses it offers. This means that organizations need to transition from a training culture to a learning culture (Burkett and Holliday 2018).

Building a learning culture begins by examining the deep underlying beliefs and assumptions along with the values and principles that influence organizational action (Schein 2010; Gill 2017). Critical beliefs and assumptions that distinguish training from a learning culture are listed in Table 3.3.7.8-1.

Table 3.3.7.8-1. Beliefs and Assumptions of a Learning Culture

Training Culture Beliefs and Assumptions	Learning Culture Beliefs and Assumptions
Instructor centered—assumes that responsibility for employee learning resides with instructors and training managers, who drive learning	**Learner centered**—assumes that responsibility for learning resides with employees, managers, and teams, who are expected to seek knowledge and skills and apply learning when and where it is needed
Event based—assumes that the most important learning happens in events, such as workshops, courses, e-learning programs, and conferences	**Continuous**—assumes that learning happens all the time, not just during events but also on the job, socially, through coaches and mentors, from action learning, on smartphones and tablets, and by experimenting with new processes
Centralized—assumes that learning resources are controlled by the chief learning officer (CLO) or the HR or TD departments	**Decentralized**—assumes the entire organization is engaged in facilitating and supporting learning resources inside and outside the workplace
Siloed—assumes that departmental units in the organization compete for information and that information should be hoarded	**Shared**—assumes that information and resources are shared freely among units with everyone to drive success and knowledge across the organization
Delivery—assumes the L&D function is evaluated on output measures like delivery of programs and materials	**Results**—assumes results are less about outputs and more about outcomes—how knowledge and skills are acquired, applied in the workplace, and contribute to strategic goals and priorities

Executive Leadership

Executives approve or sponsor TD projects or programs because of their promise to add value and meet business needs. To serve senior leaders, TD professionals should be ready to:
- Use data-driven approaches to communicate the value of learning strategies or solutions.
- Continuously improve leadership development programs to build critical capabilities.
- Establish and demonstrate expertise as a learning leader, organizational consultant, performance improvement professional, or talent manager. [See 3.3.1.2]

Managers

Middle and frontline managers are usually tasked with executing strategic initiatives, identifying and allocating resources (time, material, and people), and establishing priorities to support project implementation. Managers are critical to successful execution of projects and have the most influence on how learners transfer skills and knowledge back on the job. In general, serving managers' needs involves:
- Sharing tools and resources to prepare managers for new roles, including coaching roles

- Providing performance support to ensure managers' participation before, during, and after project implementation
- Having managers identify enablers and barriers to learning transfer
- Supporting managers in their efforts to improve team performance (Biech 2018)

3.3.7.9 Link TD Strategies to Organizational Strategy

Studies show that companies that align learning with business priorities significantly improve company revenue (Carter, Ulrich, and Goldsmith 2004). In broad terms, a learning strategy identifies what a learning organization wants to accomplish, how it will add overall business value, and how it will achieve and support organizational goals.

TD professionals need to be aware of internal and external factors that influence their organization's success. They should be skilled in conducting environmental scans to identify current and emerging trends in society and the environment. [See 3.8.2]

This information will help them know when to adapt, pivot, or reverse course with a TD strategy that supports what the organization requires. By continually reviewing strategic needs and objectives that reflect organizational priorities, TD professionals can:

- Better position the learning organization as a catalyst for business success.
- Lay the foundation for effective program evaluation by identifying critical measures of success.
- Help create shared ownership of learning results. [See 3.4]

3.3.7.10 Factors That Contribute to a Learning Culture

Although there is no ideal approach to developing a learning culture, key factors and focus areas have been proven to help facilitate, reinforce, and advance the transformation process. They include:

- **Leadership.** Commitment to a learning organization must start at the top, with the active involvement of CEOs in such roles as leader-teachers, executive advisors, or mentors. Mid-level and frontline supervisors also play an important role as coaches, developers, and managers of multigenerational, dispersed work teams (Mitchell, Ray, and van Ark 2014).
- **Alignment.** Higher-performing learning cultures are more likely than their lower-performing counterparts to have strategies that are aligned with strategic business objectives. An aligned learning strategy is one that engages leaders in defining relevant performance requirements.
- **Measurement.** High-performing learning cultures monitor the impact of learning to determine whether processes are adding value and achieving desired results. They regularly measure the success of their learning strategies and use results to identify improvement opportunities (Prokopeak 2013).
- **Collaboration.** In high-performance learning organizations, employees share knowledge through communities, social networks, and technology-based, collaborative learning tools. Meaningful connections drive innovation and engagement and boost the value of the learning organization (Kelly and Schaefer 2015).
- **Change capability.** Mature learning organizations build change readiness by integrating change capabilities with leadership development and management training, using disciplined change management processes and leveraging employee networks to build change capability across an enterprise (Anand et al. 2019). [See 3.3.7.6, 3.4.2.2.8, and 3.6.4.5]

- **Integration.** Sustainable learning organizations build and leverage integrated talent management processes (recruiting, onboarding, engagement, rewards, performance management, knowledge management, and learning) to demonstrate an organization's commitment to learning (Oaks and Galagan 2011). TD professionals should audit human capital practices for alignment and consistency. [See 3.4]
- **Innovation.** What sets mature, sustainable learning cultures apart is their commitment to continual innovation and their ability to renew or reinvent themselves and their organizations as new conditions and demands emerge (Burkett 2017). They hire for and reward innovation, link incentives to creative solutions and innovative behaviors, and approach innovation as a core capability and learnable skill.

Adopting these factors is not a single accomplishment but a continuous evolution of growth and maturity.

3.3.8 Skill in Creating a Culture That Encourages or Creates Opportunities for Dialogue and Feedback Between Individuals and Groups

> **I. Learning Cultures Encourage Dialogue, Feedback, and Collaboration**
>
> TD professionals should know how to build learning strategies that emphasize dialogue, continuous feedback, collaboration, and social learning to foster knowledge sharing, increase innovation, and improve employee engagement.

3.3.8.1 Elements of a Learning Culture

Becoming a viable learning culture is about learning, which can be viewed as the process of absorbing knowledge or skills through experience or study to make use of it in various contexts. To remain agile and responsive to rapid workplace changes, knowledge acquisition needs to be built into what employees do every day. This means creating an environment where they can acquire knowledge or skills through continuous, accessible, and progressive learning experiences designed to accelerate skill development, engagement, and innovation. The focus is on creating meaningful learning experiences.

The drive to seek learning experiences comes from a growth mindset, which is an essential element of any learning culture. With a growth mindset, people believe that their most basic abilities can be developed through dedication, deliberate practice, and hard work—brains and talent are just the starting point. This mindset creates a love of learning and a resilience that is essential for accomplishment. Individuals are not discouraged by failure—rather than seeing themselves as failing in those situations, they see themselves as learning (Dweck 2007).

TD professionals should assist their organizations to foster a growth mindset by systemically building continuous learning into daily work with short, frequent pull-versus-push bursts of information that are readily accessible and available to all employees at the time and place of need. Other elements of modern learning organizations include:

- Strategic plans that address the capabilities employees require to achieve corporate goals
- Budgets that support a dedicated learning function
- Mission and value statements that reference growth for the economy, customer, and employees
- Organizational values that incorporate the purpose of learning and development

- Forward-thinking leaders who accept responsibility for developing their employees
- Collaborative environments that encourage diversity of thought, innovation, and open communication across boundaries
- Lifelong learning mindsets of all employees
- Knowledge sharing that supports individual and team learning

Transforming from a training culture to a learning culture means that learning is repositioned from a business cost to a true business driver, from a tactical nice-to-have to a strategic must-have. TD professionals should frame a learning culture as the glue that connects the organization and attracts and engages the talent needed to grow strategic capabilities and fuel innovation.

3.3.8.2 Create a Culture That Encourages Collaboration

Collaboration occurs when two or more individuals, teams, or organizations work together toward a common goal. A collaborative culture is one that works across boundaries to build connections and shared purpose. Employees at all levels have increased demands for collaborative cultures and supportive peer networks, projects that connect with their strengths, and managers that challenge them through team-based training and development (Jaramillo and Richardson 2016). Beyond the increased demand from workers, jobs simply require more collaboration among people from different units and supervisory levels than they did in the past. The ability and flexibility to collaborate and connect with others has a proven impact on employee satisfaction and retention, as well as organizational performance and innovation.

While most organizations recognize that collaboration makes good business sense, many expect employees to work well together without properly showing them how or defining what collaboration looks like in daily practice and behavior (Ashkenas 2015). In addition, collaboration often fails because it's viewed as an activity instead of a skill or it is a mandated performance requirement focusing on compliance instead of commitment. TD professionals can help promote collaboration as a cultural value by teaching leaders and teams new processes for working together, resolving conflicts, providing constructive feedback, and making decisions. They can also foster collaboration by leveraging technologies that break down silos and enable information sharing across boundaries.

Today's workplace poses additional challenges for TD professionals beyond helping leaders and teams learn to collaborate. Collaboration often occurs among individuals who are not in the same workspace, who may not even be in the same time zone or on the same continent. Collaboration is an ongoing event that doesn't have physical boundaries but also does not recognize time boundaries. TD professionals should be aware of the tools that will be most effective for their organizations and be able to assure their leaders that they will have the right data available when they need it.

3.3.9 Skill in Articulating and Codifying Talent and Leadership Principles, Values, and Competencies That Guide the Organization's Culture and Define Behavioral Expectations

I. Defining and Articulating an Organization's Culture

TD professionals should know how to assess, build, and maintain workplace cultures that promote continuous learning and high performance and engagement.

3.3.9.1 Defining a Culture

Culture is the collective assessment of an organization based on enduring, often unconscious, values, norms, and assumptions. The informal elements of a company's culture include the distinguishing sights, sounds, atmosphere, and work environment. Culture represents the sense of cohesion and shared identity among employees—the "secret sauce" that carries organizations through eras of change (de Geus 2002). [See 3.3.7.3 and 3.3.7.10]

A clear organizational culture keeps everyone pointed in the same direction, provides employees with a shared meaning and purpose about their work, and empowers engagement and performance, despite organizational changes (Clow 2015).

3.3.9.2 Principles of Shaping a Culture

Despite increased emphasis on culture as a competitive advantage, global executives consistently cite culture and engagement as top challenges and very important organizational problems (Deloitte 2015). Senior leaders are increasingly turning to TD professionals as partners in transforming cultures. They should consider these factors:

- **Culture is every day.** Culture is created, sustained, or changed by daily behaviors, interactions, and overall business practices.
- **Culture does not change overnight**—it evolves over time. Deeply embedded assumptions, beliefs, or values cannot be replaced with simple upgrades or even major overhauls. Growing a mature learning culture may take years, and it requires large-scale alignment of people, structures, systems, processes, tools, and technology, as well as an intentional, future-focused growth mindset from all people leading the charge.
- **Culture is not one-size-fits-all.** Valuable information can be gained by researching other learning cultures, but it's more important to focus on the values and behaviors that work best for a TD professional's current business or industry.
- **Culture can always improve.** A culture does not have to be toxic to warrant nudges forward. TD professionals should consider driving their culture where it needs to go.
- **Culture change doesn't guarantee success.** A great culture is no guarantee of sustained excellence or success. It's not something that can be imposed.
- **Culture literacy is key.** TD professionals should understand what culture is, how it's assessed, and how it affects employees' motivation, performance, and engagement. Culture change must favor positive cultural traits embedded in an organization and minimize negative ones (Burkett 2017).

3.3.9.3 Articulate and Codify Principles That Guide an Organization's Culture

The mission and values of an organization create a shared understanding of what the organization is trying to achieve and how employees should try to achieve it. They are meant to convey a sense of purpose and meaning for employees and customers.

The *mission* defines the direction of the organization and, to some extent, describes what an organization will and will not do. *Values* are an important supplement to a mission statement because they define the specific behaviors and principles the organization wants to lead. Values help the culture take shape and provide the everyday context for how employees should act. When an organization's mission and values are clearly stated and aspirational, employees can connect to a higher purpose and find more meaning in their work.

Engagement

3.3.10 Knowledge of How Employee Engagement and Retention Influence Organizational Outcomes

> **I. Employee Engagement and Retention**
>
> TD professionals should understand how a learning culture influences employee engagement and retention so they can position learning as a catalyst for driving engagement and retention strategies.

3.3.10.1 Defining Engagement

Employee engagement can be defined as "a heightened emotional and intellectual connection that an employee has for his/her job, organization, manager, or co-workers that, in turn, influences him/her to apply additional discretionary effort to his/her work" (Ray et al. 2015).

Gallup's 2016 research across 230 organizations in 49 industries and 73 countries describes three levels of employee engagement:

- **Engaged.** Employees who willingly go the extra mile, work with passion, and feel a profound connection to their organization are engaged. Engaged workers stand apart because of the discretionary effort they consistently bring to their roles.
- **Not engaged.** Employees who are likely to do just enough to fulfill their job requirements and have essentially checked out are not engaged. Converting this group into engaged workers is an effective strategy to increase performance.
- **Actively disengaged.** Employees who want to damage a company and undermine whatever engaged employees do, such as solve problems, innovate, and create new customers are actively disengaged (Reilly 2014).

3.3.10.2 Job Elements That Influence Engagement

TD professionals should know that the job elements that influence engagement the most are "autonomy, mastery, and purpose" (Pink 2011):

- **Autonomy** is how much freedom employees have while working. Higher levels of autonomy tend to increase job satisfaction and engagement.
- **Mastery** is the urge to get better at something that matters. It begins with flow—when job challenges are matched with abilities. Flow must be coupled with a growth mindset to achieve mastery. Employees with growth mindsets are more likely to seek improvement opportunities.
- **Purpose and meaningful work** ensure that employees know their work matters (Sinek 2011). Having a direct connection that shows how work contributes to organizational performance is a key driver of engagement (Ray et al. 2015).

Other job factors that help drive engagement include career growth opportunities, job-, and person-fit factors, task variety, feedback, and workload balance (McCormick 2016).

3.3.10.3 Retention Strategy

Organizations known for their engaging cultures consistently outperform their peers in productivity, profit, and customer satisfaction, attracting, retaining, and engaging employees. TD professionals can help organizations develop retention strategies by incorporating several best practices.

3.3.10.3.1 Foster an Inclusive Workplace

Organizations that prioritize inclusion strategies are eight times more likely to achieve better business outcomes (Bourke 2018). While an inclusive culture includes a commitment to workplace diversity, it also includes a climate that cultivates respect, equity, and positive recognition of differences.

To foster inclusion, TD professionals should help leaders address and overcome their unconscious biases, create open forums for discussion, and ensure that leaders and managers view diversity and inclusion as business imperatives. [See 1.4.5 and 1.4.6]

3.3.10.3.2 Foster Respect in the Workplace

Job seekers value respect in prospective employers (Casserly 2013). Encouraging mutual respect in the workplace can reduce workplace stress and conflict, improve communication between colleagues, encourage teamwork, and increase productivity and knowledge.

TD professionals can foster a culture of respect by promoting feedback, rewards, and recognition as well as encouraging creativity and collaboration. Improving communication skills is a critical element. TD professionals should help employees learn how to engage in respectful discourse to encourage knowledge sharing and collaboration.

3.3.10.3.3 Earn Employees' Trust

A lack of trust and transparency from leaders can drive employees to seek new employment. Trust is earned when employees have confidence in their leaders' decisions, when they believe that leaders are on their side, and when they know they will be treated fairly. Aligning leaders' words and actions is a key pillar for building workplace trust and increasing engagement and retention.

TD professionals can foster organizational trust by encouraging leaders at all levels to walk the talk and consistently model the behaviors they seek. They must also emphasize that building trust involves conscious, intentional effort over time—and once trust is lost, it can be very difficult to recover.

3.3.10.3.4 Encourage Employee Creativity

Although many companies say they value creativity, they don't necessarily have any initiatives or policies in place to support it. TD professionals should help organizations foster creativity by setting up innovation teams or idea-funding programs and linking compensation to innovation to signal the value of creative solutions.

3.3.10.3.5 Challenge Employees in a Balanced Way

Finding the balance between challenge and support is rarely easy because every employee is different, and what one might find rewarding, another might find tedious and too complex. Best practices include:
- Express belief in employees.

- Push people out of their comfort zone, giving them a chance to take risks.
- See failure as a learning opportunity; process failure together by learning from it.
- Encourage a growth mindset—reward effort, not just results or talent.

3.3.10.3.6 Offer a Competitive Base Salary or Hourly Wage

Employees want to believe the effort they put into work is worth their time. When it comes to employee retention, money isn't everything, but offering a competitive wage can help people feel like their work and time are valued.

3.3.10.3.7 Establish Work-Life Balance

Work-life balance is a harmonious arrangement between personal and professional activities. Several factors influence whether individuals believe they have balance. Flexible scheduling and work-from-home opportunities play a major role in an employee's decision to take or leave a job—almost 70 percent of employees want flexible work schedules (Gallup 2017). Other elements that affect whether employees think they have work-life balance are based on having time to engage in leisure and personal care, limiting the number of hours spent in meetings, aligning with corporate culture, and ensuring effective technology use.

3.3.10.3.8 Focus on Meaningful Work

TD professionals should focus on supporting employees' work-life balance by making work meaningful and providing a sense of belonging and trust in the workplace. Organizations must "change from a culture of paycheck to a culture of purpose" (Gallup 2017).

3.3.10.4 Engagement and Retention Influence Organizational Outcomes

Employee engagement can have significant organizational benefits. For example, Gallup research supports a well-established connection between employee engagement and key performance outcomes, including customer ratings, profitability, productivity, safety incidents, shrinkage, absenteeism, safety incidents, quality, and turnover (Reilly 2014).

Turnover can cost an average of six to nine months of an employee's salary, including the negative financial impact of the cost to recruit, hire, and train their replacement. Despite the documented costs of poor retention and employee turnover, however, many organizations are more apt to invest in recruiting new employees than retaining existing talent. Other significant barriers preventing organizations from improving engagement and retention outcomes include:

- **Budget constraints.** Budget is a primary obstacle to improving employee retention and the biggest hurdle to implementing technology that would reduce manual or administrative work.
- **Conflicting priorities.** HR leaders may not be able to adequately focus on attraction and retention as critical issues because of competing priorities and perpetual emergencies.
- **Outdated technology.** Poor automation or manual processes detract from acting strategically.
- **Lack of support.** A lack of executive support and organizational vision prevent addressing retention (HR.com 2019).

Armed with these findings, TD professionals should plan to implement employee retention strategies that are driven from the top and visibly supported across all organizational levels. [See 3.3.11 and 3.3.12]

3.3.11 Skill in Assessing and Evaluating Employee Engagement

> **I. Assessing and Evaluating Employee Engagement**
>
> TD professionals should know how to assess and evaluate employee engagement initiatives to determine whether the right strategy is driving the right issue and whether engagement strategies are achieving targeted learning, performance, and business objectives.

3.3.11.1 Organizations Must Measure Engagement to Determine the Value

Organizations can only drive engagement if they know how it is measured. Successful ones use these best practices to determine the value of engagement efforts (Reilly 2014):

- **Define engagement goals in realistic, everyday terms.** Leading organizations make engagement goals meaningful to employees' day-to-day experiences and describe what success looks like using powerful descriptions and emotive language. TD professionals should weave engagement into daily interactions.
- **Coach managers and hold them accountable for their employees' engagement.** Managers are primary drivers of their employees' engagement. TD professionals should provide coaching to managers on building engagement plans with their employees, holding managers accountable, and tracking their progress.
- **Invest time and resources.** Top organizations invest in integrated processes and internal or external expertise to make sure that the right engagement criteria are being targeted and that targeted measures are making the right impact on strategic outcomes. They also invest in a dedicated workforce to identify key insights from data (Ray et al. 2015).
- **Use ongoing measures.** Leading organizations apply a regular cadence for collecting and analyzing ongoing measures of engagement versus relying exclusively on a rear-view annual engagement survey (Brown 2018).

3.3.11.2 Measuring and Tracking Engagement Outcomes

Measuring and tracking engagement outcomes is a fundamental element to a successful engagement culture. There are three common ways of measuring employee engagement:

- **Use an employee engagement survey provider.** Incorporating constructs provided by the organization—such as engagement factors, organizational commitment, or job satisfaction—the provider designs a survey to measure each construct through several questions and manages the logistics and software. The survey's results are reported to the company on a high level.
- **Measure employee engagement internally.** When measuring engagement internally, organizations can own their data, include engagement data in tactical and strategic reporting, and use results from previous years to improve questionnaire design.
- **Adopt a hybrid approach** in which annual engagement is measured by the survey provider while pulse engagement surveys are given by the company throughout the year. Hybrid approaches include surveys, pulse polls, or questionnaires for specific employee segments. These are done in addition to the annual survey and specific analyses; for example, to assess sales performance or analyze reasons for absenteeism in a specific department (van Vulpen 2018).

New solutions are emerging to help organizations adopt an "always on" approach to tracking and increasing engagement. For instance, companies can leverage a new generation of pulse survey tools and open anonymous feedback systems that employees use to rate managers, executives, or workplace issues on a near-real-time basis. The thoughtful use of such tools can create a true listening environment for employees while giving leaders critical insight into what's working and what's not on an operational level.

Engagement, retention, and employee productivity are complex, multifaceted issues, and merely measuring engagement is not the whole answer. The primary task around engagement is not simply to have an engagement index but to address the broader, more significant challenge of building an engaging culture. [See 3.3.8.1 and 3.3.12.1]

3.3.11.3 Common Mistakes

Even the most well-aligned, well-designed, and well-implemented engagement survey has limitations. TD professionals should understand the advantages and disadvantages of the various assessment tools, methods, and processes used to collect and analyze engagement data. Using multiple modes of assessment provides the greatest insight and perspective. A basic requirement for any assessment system is that it is progress oriented, trustworthy, easy to work with, and individualized. While there is an increasing amount of nudge technology to remind and motivate managers to monitor or track the right things, tools shouldn't become nag technologies that are ignored.

In a typical evaluation process, organizations deploy annual surveys to benchmark a company's level of employee engagement or satisfaction from year to year. Potential problems with this approach include:
- No strategy for aligning and leveraging engagement data
- Poorly constructed survey instruments
- Lack of decisions about how survey data will be used and who will see it
- Concerns about confidentiality or anonymity in providing feedback
- Failure to communicate results
- Failure to support managers to act on results
- Poor follow-up and follow through with recommended actions.

TD professionals should recognize when it may be appropriate to leverage external resources for assistance in designing, collecting, or analyzing engagement data.

3.3.12 Skill in Designing and Implementing Employee Engagement Strategies

I. Designing Employee Engagement Strategies

TD professionals should be able to lead the design and implementation of employee engagement strategies for their organizations.

3.3.12.1 Elements of an Engaged Culture

Culture represents a system of values, beliefs, and behaviors that influence how work is accomplished within an organization. Engaging cultures start with a clear set of values and a compelling mission supported by strategies, policies, and performance-based practices that allow employees to reach their full potential at work. Eight common elements of highly engaging cultures and barriers to them are outlined in Table 3.3.12.1-1.

Table 3.3.12.1-1. Elements of Highly Engaged Cultures

Common Elements	What They Look Like	Common Barriers
Alignment of business and engagement strategies	Highly engaged cultures articulate the relation between business objectives and employee engagement, leading to strong alignment between the two. The focus on engagement as a key business driver and performance indicator leads these organizations to invest resources for engagement initiatives. [See 3.3.7.9]	Obtaining adequate time, money, and other resources for engagement efforts can be difficult, especially if TD professionals do not demonstrate the link between engagement and strategic business outcomes.
An organization philosophy that emphasizes a core purpose	Highly engaged cultures ensure their mission, vision, and values take precedent. These organizations integrate engagement into mission-focused business initiatives.	Viewing engagement as a stand-alone program or something to be measured once a year. Some organizations struggle to shift from being profit driven to mission driven.
Formal programs and policies that drive the engagement agenda	Highly engaged cultures establish formal programs and policies that promote employee engagement and communicate it as a priority. This includes integrating it with leadership development and diversity programs and recognizing and rewarding valued behaviors. [See 3.3.10.2]	Organizations may treat engagement as an afterthought or as an addition to other practices or programs, rather than designing a specific formal effort.
Open proactive, leader-driven communication about engagement	Highly engaged cultures communicate with employees to meet informational needs and encourage open, transparent dialogue with leadership throughout the enterprise.	Organizations may communicate only on a "need to know" basis and do not give ample opportunities for employees to provide input or ask questions.
A workplace and organizational structure that promotes collaboration and inclusion	Highly engaged cultures embrace and enable diversity, inclusion, and collaboration through better work-life balance, flexible working arrangements, open workplaces (physically or virtually), and a supportive organizational structure. [See 1.4.5, 3.3.8.2, and 3.3.10.2]	Organizations may have a narrow focus on performance, rigid work schedules, unclear strategic direction, or redundant responsibilities that hinder collaboration and inclusion.
A regular cadence for assessment and follow-up	Highly engaged cultures drive engagement if they know how it is measured and monitored on an ongoing basis to provide relevant, timely, and actionable data.	Poorly constructed, administered assessment tools; unclear measurement goals; no plan for using results; not communicating results in a timely, transparent manner; and not supporting leaders and managers to act on results can prevent effective assessment and follow-up.
Leaders who are expected and empowered to build engagement	Highly engaged cultures require leaders and managers to have clearly defined performance measures and outcomes related to engagement.	Organizations may struggle to define who is responsible for engagement, fail to provide proper guidance to managers about their role, or fail to empower frontline employees to innovate or execute daily tasks.
Demonstration of the impact of engagement	Highly engaged cultures take time to understand the value of implementing targeted engagement initiatives. Leaders and managers define every decision related to engagement in terms of its business impact.	Organizations may not have standard measures of success in place for engagement initiatives and are challenged to allocate enough resources for tracking the business value of engagement-related activities. They may lack the right level of data or analytical skill needed to link engagement scores to business outcomes.

Source: Ray et al. (2015).

In general, TD professionals can best create the conditions for employee engagement by helping leaders elevate employee engagement from an isolated, stand-alone program to a core business strategy.

3.3.12.2 Compensation and Rewards

While compensation is an important factor in employee satisfaction, increasing it does not directly increase engagement. The company's total rewards package (such as salary or compensation, benefits, work-life flexibility, performance, recognition, growth, and development) is the most important factor.

Recognition, in particular, is a core component of an organization's total reward system and a key engagement driver. Companies with a culture of recognition might have social reward systems (tools that give people points or ways to reward others), regular thank-you activities, and an unspoken mantra of appreciating everyone from top to bottom. TD professionals should be aware of how to create a social environment where recognition can flow from peer to peer, freeing managers from being solely responsible for employee recognition. [See 3.3.10.2]

3.3.13 Knowledge of the Principles, Policies, and Practices Associated With Programs and Initiatives Designed for Organizational Well-Being

> **I. Well-Being for Organizational Success**
>
> To effectively build engagement cultures, TD professionals should understand how essential elements of well-being influence individuals' motivation, capability, and learning capacity.

3.3.13.1 Essential Elements of Well-Being

In partnership with leading economists, psychologists, and scientists, Gallup studied elements of well-being through a comprehensive global study of more than 150 countries representing more than 98 percent of the world's population (Rath and Harter 2010). Based on this research, Gallup defined five broad categories of well-being:

- **Career well-being**—how individuals occupy their time or simply like what they do every day
- **Social well-being**—whether individuals have strong relationships and love in their lives
- **Financial well-being**—how effectively individuals manage their economic life
- **Physical well-being**—how individuals maintain good health and the energy to complete tasks on a daily basis
- **Community well-being**—how individuals maintain a sense of engagement with where they live

Struggles in any one of these domains damage a person's well-being and wear on their daily life. From an engagement perspective, each element of well-being has the potential to spark or diminish their motivation and capacity to exert the discretionary effort that characterizes engagement. Employee engagement recognizes that all the basic well-being needs must be met for a person to perform effectively (Volini et al. 2019).

Additional research by Gallup shows that the global cost of turnover and lost productivity due to lack of well-being at work was more than $322 billion—mostly due to burnout (Clifton and Harter 2021). In contrast, Gallup also found that employees who believe their employer cares about their overall well-being are 69 percent less likely to search for a new job, 71 percent less likely to report experiencing burnout, three times more likely to be engaged, and five times more likely to strongly advocate for their organization as a place to work.

Elements related to physical well-being have gained prominence as a critical human capital and engagement issue due to the increased prevalence of employee burnout. The World Health Organization (WHO) describes three characteristics of burnout:
- Feelings of depleted energy or exhaustion
- Increased mental distance from one's job or negativity or cynicism about one's job
- Reduced professional efficacy (Borysenko 2019)

For example, according to Deloitte researchers, 95 percent of human resource leaders say employee burnout is one of the biggest threats to retention, with some saying it causes more than 50 percent of annual workforce turnover (Bourke 2014). They have also cited the "overwhelmed employee" as a global business concern as a result conditions like information overload and the always connected 24/7 work environment.

TD professionals should recognize the importance and impact of the burnt-out, overwhelmed, hyper-connected employee on learning, job performance, and engagement. After all, the message of a perfectly aligned, designed, and delivered development initiative will be lost if employees are too fatigued and checked out to hear it. TD professionals must partner with organizational and HR leaders to shape the kind of flexible, employee-centric work climate that promotes well-being and engagement. This includes making the right information easier to find, simplifying processes and systems, keeping teams small, and making sure leaders provide time for employees to think, reflect, and practice self-care.

3.3.13.2 Elements of Well-Being That Transcend Countries and Cultures

Although the elements of well-being are universal across faiths, cultures, and nationalities, people take different paths to increase their individual well-being. Some individuals may say that faith is the most important facet of their lives and the foundation of their daily efforts, and spirituality drives them in all areas of well-being. For others, a deep mission, such as protecting the environment, is what inspires them each day.

Although it's important to recognize that what motivates an individual may differ greatly from one person to the next, the engagement outcomes related to an employee's overall well-being do not. Specifically, engagement strategies that emphasize career development (career well-being), social connections (social well-being), total rewards and recognition (financial well-being), work-life balance (physical well-being), and organizational values and cultures that promote a sense of community and purpose (community well-being) are more likely to create the kind of positive employee experience that drives engagement, retention, and high performance.

REFERENCES

Anand, A., S. Merchant, A. Sunderraj, and B. Vasquez-McCall. 2019. "Growing Your Own Agility Coaches to Adopt New Ways of Working." McKinsey Digital, August. mckinsey.com/business-functions/mckinsey-digital/our-insights/growing-your-own-agility-coaches-to-adopt-new-ways-of-working.

Asghar, R. 2014. "What Millennials Want in the Workplace and Why You Should Start Giving It to Them." *Forbes*, January 13. forbes.com/sites/robasghar/2014/01/13/what-millennials-want-in-the-workplace-and-why-you-should-start-giving-it-to-them/#75267452fdfb.

Ashkenas, R. 2015. "There's a Difference Between Cooperation and Collaboration." *Harvard Business Review*, April 20. hbr.org/2015/04/theres-a-difference-between-cooperation-and-collaboration.

ASTD (American Society for Training & Development). 2014. *Change Agents: The Role of Organizational Learning in Change Management*. Alexandria, VA: ASTD Press.

ATD (Association for Talent Development). 2016. *Building a Culture of Learning: The Foundation of a Successful Organization*. Alexandria, VA: ATD Press.

ATD Staff. 2015a. "Building Talent: The Very BEST of 2015." *TD*, November. td.org/magazines/td-magazine/building-talent-the-very-best-of-2015.

ATD Staff. 2015b. "Haworth Inc." *TD*, November. td.org/magazines/td-magazine/haworth-inc.

Bersin by Deloitte. 2014. "Meet the Modern Learner." Infographic. 2syt8l41furv2dqan6123ah0.wpengine.netdna-cdn.com/wp-content/uploads/2015/10/unnamed.png.

Bersin, J. 2015. "Becoming Irresistible: A New Model for Employee Engagement." Deloitte Review, January 27. deloitte.com/us/en/insights/deloitte-review/issue-16/employee-engagement-strategies.html.

Biech, E. 2018. *ATD's Foundations of Talent Development: Launching, Leveraging, and Leading Your Organization's TD Effort*. Alexandria, VA: ATD Press.

Borysenko, K. 2019. "Burnout Is Now an Officially Diagnosable Condition: Here's What You Need to Know About It." *Forbes*, May 29. forbes.com/sites/karlynborysenko/2019/05/29/burnout-is-now-an-officially-diagnosable-condition-heres-what-you-need-to-know-about-it/#2d9692a42b99.

Bourke, J. 2014. "The Overwhelmed Employee: Simplify the Work Environment." Deloitte Research, October. deloitte.com/au/en/pages/human-capital/articles/overwhelmed-employee-simplify-environment.html.

Bourke, J. 2018. "The Diversity and Inclusion Revolution: Eight Powerful Truths." *Deloitte Review*, January 22. deloitte.com/us/en/insights/deloitte-review/issue-22/diversity-and-inclusion-at-work-eight-powerful-truths.html.

Brown, A. 2018. "Why Is Employee Engagement So Important?" Engagement Multiplier, December 5. engagementmultiplier.com/blog/why-is-employee-engagement-so-important.

Burkett, H. 2015. "The Talent Manager as Change Agent." Chapter 20 in the *ATD Talent Management Handbook*, edited by T. Bickham. Alexandria, VA: ATD Press.

Burkett, H. 2016. "From Making It Stick to Making It Last: Seven Practices for Sustaining a Resilient Learning Organization." *TD*, September.

Burkett, H. 2017. *Learning for the Long Run: 7 Practices for Sustaining a Resilient Learning Organization*. Alexandria, VA: ATD Press.

Burkett, H. 2018. "Valuing a Learning Culture." Sidebar in *ATD's Action Guide to Talent Development*, by E. Biech, 7–12. Alexandria, VA: ATD Press.

Burkett, H., and T. Holliday. 2018. "Can Government Organizations Really Be a Magnet for Talent?" *TD*, June.

Carter, L., D. Ulrich, and M. Goldsmith. 2004. *Best Practices in Leadership Development and Organization Change*. San Francisco: Pfeiffer.

Cascio, W. 2012. *Managing Human Resources*, 9th ed. New York: McGraw-Hill Education.

Casserly, M. 2013. "Top Five Reasons Employees Will Quit in 2013." *Forbes*, January 2. forbes.com/sites/meghancasserly/2013/01/02/the-top-five-reasons-employees-will-quit-in-2013/#a36c6d3109e3.

Clifton, J., and J. Harter. 2021. *Wellbeing at Work: How to Build Resilient and Thriving Teams*. Washington, DC: Gallup Press.

Clow, J. 2015. *The Work Revolution*. New York: Wiley.

De Geus, A. 2002. *The Living Company*. Boston: Harvard Business Review Press.

Dearborn, J. 2015. "Why Your Company Needs a Learning Culture." *Chief Learning Officer*, June 3. clomedia.com/2015/06/03/why-your-company-needs-a-learning-culture.

Deloitte. 2015. *Global Human Capital Trends 2015*. Deloitte University Press. deloitte.com/content/dam/Deloitte/au/Documents/human-capital/deloitte-au-hc-global-human-capital-trends-2015-301115.pdf.

Deloitte. 2016. *Global Human Capital Trends 2016*. Deloitte Insights. deloitte.com/us/en/insights/focus/human-capital-trends/2016.html.

Duncan, R.D. 2014. "How Campbell's Soup's Former CEO Turned the Company Around." *Fast Company*, September 18. fastcompany.com/3035830/hit-the-ground-running/how-campbells-soups-former-ceo-turned-the-company-around.

Dweck, C. 2007. *Mindset: The New Psychology of Success*. New York: Ballantine Books.

French, W., and C. Bell. 1999. *Organization Development: Behavioral Science Interventions for Organization Improvement*, 6th ed. Upper Saddle River, NJ: Pearson.

Gallup. 2017. *State of the American Workplace*. Gallup. gallup.com/workplace/238085/state-american-workplace-report-2017.aspx.

Gill, S. 2017. "From a Training Culture to a Learning Culture." ATD Insights, January 10. td.org/insights/from-a-training-culture-to-a-learning-culture.

Hart, J. 2019. *Modern Workplace Learning 2019*. Centre for Modern Workplace Learning.

HR.com. 2019. *The State of Employee Engagement in 2019*. HR Research Institute, hr.com/en/resources/free_research_white_papers/hrcom-employee-engagement-may-2019-research_jwb9ckus.html.

Jaramillo, S., and T. Richardson. 2016. *Agile Engagement: How to Drive Lasting Results by Cultivating a Flexible, Responsive, and Collaborative Culture.* Hoboken, NJ: John Wiley and Sons.

Jarret, J. 2017. "The 4 Types of Organizational Politics." *Harvard Business Review*, April.

Kelly, K., and A. Schaefer. 2015. *Creating a Collaborative Organizational Culture.* Chapel Hill, NC: UNC Executive Development.

Lawton, G. 2018. "Nine Strategies to Increase Employee Engagement and Retention." HR Software, August 2. searchhrsoftware.techtarget.com/feature/Nine-strategies-to-increase-employee-engagement-and-retention.

Marquardt, M.J. 2011. *Building the Learning Organization*, 3rd ed. Boston: Nicholas Brealey Publishing.

McCormick, H. 2016. *7 Steps to Creating a Lasting Learning Culture.* Chapel Hill, NC: UNC Executive Development.

Mitchell, C., R. Ray, and B. van Ark. 2014. *The Conference Board CEO Challenge 2014: People and Performance.* New York: The Conference Board.

Mitchell, C., R. Ray, and B. van Ark. 2015. *The Conference Board CEO Challenge 2015: Creating Opportunity Out of Adversity.* New York: The Conference Board.

Morgan, J. 2015. *The Future of Work: Attract New Talent, Build Better Leaders, and Create a Competitive Organization.* Hoboken, NJ: John Wiley and Sons.

Oaks, K., and P. Galagan. 2011. *The Executive Guide to Integrated Talent Management.* Alexandria, VA: ASTD Press.

Phillips, P.P. 2017. *Bottom Line on ROI*, 3rd ed. West Chester, PA: HRDQ.

Pink, D.H. 2011. *Drive: The Surprising Truth About What Motivates Us.* New York: Riverhead Books.

Prokopeak, M. 2013. "DAU: Keeping Above the Fiscal Fray." *Chief Learning Officer*, May.

Rath, T., and J. Harter. 2010. "The Five Essential Elements of Well-Being," Gallup Workplace, May 4. gallup.com/workplace/237020/five-essential-elements.aspx.

Ray, R., D. Dye, P. Hyland, J. Kaplan, and A. Pressman. 2015. "How to Build a Culture of Engagement." Chapter 7 in the *ATD Talent Management Handbook*, edited by T. Bickham. Alexandria, VA: ATD Press.

Reilly, R. 2014. "Five Ways to Improve Employee Engagement Now." *Gallup Business Journal*, January 7. gallup.com/workplace/231581/five-ways-improve-employee-engagement.aspx.

Robinson, D.G., J.C. Robinson, J.J. Phillips, P.P. Phillips, and D. Handshaw. 2015. *Performance Consulting: A Strategic Process to Improve, Measure, and Sustain Organizational Results*, 3rd ed. San Francisco: Berrett-Koehler.

Schein, E. 2010. *Organizational Culture and Leadership.* San Francisco: Jossey-Bass.

Senge, P.M. 2006. *The Fifth Discipline: The Art and Practice of the Learning Organization*, rev ed. New York: Currency/Doubleday.

Sinar, E., R.S. Wellins, R. Ray, A.L. Abel, and S. Neal. 2014. *Ready-Now Leaders.* Bridgeville, PA: Development Dimensions International; New York: The Conference Board. ddiworld.com/DDI/media/trend-research/global-leadership-forecast-2014-2015_tr_ddi.pdf?ext=.pdf.

Sinek, S. 2011. *Start With Why: How Great Leaders Inspire Everyone to Take Action*. New York: Penguin.

Skibola, N. 2011. "Leadership Lessons From WD-40's CEO, Garry Ridge." *Forbes*, June 27. forbes.com/sites/csr/2011/06/27/leadership-lessons-from-wd-40s-ceo-garry-ridge/#619a22ca1fae.

van Vliet, V. 2014. "Five Functions of Management (Fayol)." Toolshero, June 23. toolshero.com/management/five-functions-of-management.

van Vulpen, E. 2018. "Measuring Employee Engagement the Right Way." AIHR Analytics. analyticsinhr.com/blog/measuring-employee-engagement.

Volini, E., J. Schwartz, I. Roy, M. Hauptmann, Y. Van Durme, B. Denny, and J. Bersin. 2019. *2019 Deloitte Global Human Capital Trends*. Deloitte Insights. deloitte.com/content/dam/insights/us/articles/5136_HC-Trends-2019/DI_HC-Trends-2019.pdf.

Zeeman, A. 2017. "Senge's Five Disciplines of Learning Organizations." Toolshero, November 7. toolshero.com/management/five-disciplines-learning-organizations.

Recommended Reading

Burkett, H. 2017. *Learning for the Long Run: 7 Practices for Sustaining a Resilient Learning Organization*. Alexandria, VA: ATD Press.

Clifton, J., and J. Harter. 2021. *Wellbeing at Work: How to Build Resilient and Thriving Teams*. Washington, DC: Gallup Press.

Senge, P.M. 2006. *The Fifth Discipline: The Art and Practice of the Learning Organization*, rev. ed. New York: Currency/Doubleday.

Stallard, M. 2020. *Connection Culture: The Competitive Advantage of Shared Identity, Empathy, and Understanding at Work*, 2nd ed. Alexandria, VA: ATD Press.

3.4 TALENT STRATEGY & MANAGEMENT

For an organization to realize its potential, talent development should be integrated into all components of talent strategy and management. Talent strategy and management are the practices used to build an organization's culture, engagement, capability, and capacity through the implementation and integration of talent acquisition, performance management, employee development, and retention, ensuring these processes are aligned to organizational goals. Depending on organizational context and structure, broad partnerships with HR and line leaders will be needed.

3.4.1 Knowledge of Talent Management Functions

> **I. Integrated Talent Management Functions**
>
> TD professionals should have a broad understanding of talent management functions and how they are integrated so they can align TD goals with those functions and foster a talent-based culture that benefits both the workforce and the organization. [See 3.3.9.1]

3.4.1.1 Strategic Workforce Planning Defined

Strategic workforce planning (SWP) is the six-step process an organization uses to analyze its current workforce and plan for future staffing needs:

1. Understand the three-to-five-year business strategy.
2. Assess current workforce capabilities.
3. Create models of future workforce needs.
4. Analyze and validate the talent gaps.
5. Build the strategic workforce plan.
6. Monitor and adjust the plan annually.

SWP is the first step in developing a talent strategy. It refers to the practice of forecasting the types of talent that will be needed to meet organizational goals and assessing those needs against current capabilities or gaps. It occurs as organizational strategy is being developed, when new strategic objectives are set, or on a regular basis as conditions change. [See 3.3.5 and 3.4.14.2]

3.4.1.2 Sourcing Talent Defined

Sourcing talent is the acquisition, recruitment, and selection of talent. It entails recruiting for the organization through internal or external sources, attracting talent to the organization and role, and selecting the best candidate for the organization and role. [See 3.4.14]

Most organizations use an SWP process to analyze their workforce and determine the steps needed to meet current and future staffing needs. This process also involves determining the most efficient and cost-effective methods to recruit and retain talent. In essence, SWP helps ensure that the right people with the right skills are hired at the right time at the right cost.

Based on priorities identified through SWP, a talent acquisition strategy is developed to describe where and how candidates will be sourced and who the target audience is for various roles. A thorough talent acquisition strategy should also align with the organization's DEI objectives so that vacancies are efficiently, effectively, and equitably filled. [See 1.4]

Although employee onboarding typically occurs after external talent has been hired, it may be part of the acquisition process to ensure that external hires reach productive levels quickly. A formal onboarding process goes beyond orientation on the first day—it begins during the acquisition phase and is typically completed between one and three months after hire, although it can last for six months or longer.

3.4.1.3 Talent Development Defined

Talent development refers to the efforts that foster individual and team learning and development to drive organizational growth and performance, productivity, and results. A talent development strategy is based on an organization's strategic objectives and a strategic workforce plan that targets developing specific roles and skills. The strategy may include opportunities for learning, development of critical roles, and career development. [See 3.4.15]

Learning solutions typically focus on an employee's current role, while development solutions focus on long-term initiatives that enhance an organization's capabilities (for example, a leadership development program to prepare employees for leadership roles). These solutions can include formal and informal resources, such as knowledge management databases, communities of practice, and artificial intelligence. Many of these solutions are designed to help employees learn in the flow of work instead of stopping what they're doing to partake in a formal learning solution.

TD professionals should create an aligned talent development strategy in partnership with leadership that meets the needs of their organization. This strategy, which is a natural flow down from the talent strategy, should also consider other talent management practice areas so all objectives are integrated and silos are reduced.

3.4.1.4 Performance Management Defined

Performance management is the ongoing communication between supervisors and employees to establish expectations supporting an organization's strategic objectives, including clarifying expectations, setting objectives, providing feedback and coaching, and reviewing results.

Management typically manages individual employee and team performance. Managers recognize and reward employees and teams when expectations and goals are accomplished, while also providing learning opportunities to meet development goals and help fill performance gaps (which could be skills or knowledge based). [See 3.4.16]

3.4.1.5 Compensation and Reward Management Defined

Compensation and reward management refers to the financial and nonfinancial rewards given to employees for work provided. Although compensation is important, an organization's total rewards package matters more. This package includes salary or compensation, bonuses, benefits, health insurance, 401(k) plans, paid time off, work-life flexibility, recognition, growth, and development. Flex time and the ability to work remotely are two other important parts of a reward package.

Compensation and rewards tend to make up a large part of an organization's costs. A total reward package starts with the pay strategy—that is, where in the marketplace does the organization want to target its pay? Above market, at market, or below market? This decision is based on the workforce plan and availability of talent. It also allows the organization to determine what makes up the rest of its rewards package. For example, if the organization is having difficulty hiring or retaining talent in a critical role, it may decide to pay above market for that job and offer hiring bonuses. If the organization hires contingent workers for short-term assignments, it may decide to pay at market and provide scaled-down benefits.

Compensation and rewards professionals typically manage the job classification structure, pay plans and salary structures, raise pools, promotion criteria, employee benefits and vendors, 401(k) plans, and other benefits or perks their organization offers. [See 3.3.12.2]

3.4.1.6 The Role of Talent Development in an Integrated Talent Ecosystem

Most companies have two groups focused on organizations and systems: human resources and talent development. These groups must work in parallel to identify the skills needed for current and future business success and to create the opportunities and support structures to build needed capabilities. An integrated talent management ecosystem is an essential foundation of this alignment. A talent management ecosystem has several elements including competency and skill matrices, growth pathways, assessment mechanisms, talent sourcing tools, learning resources, and a dynamic curriculum.

Integration points in the system represent spaces where one talent management practice area overlaps with another area to present a program, process, activity, or tool that focuses on the capability needs. Talent management practice areas that are integrated with others throughout the employee life cycle include workforce planning, sourcing, selection and hiring, onboarding, employee development, performance, and recognition and reward. Although TD professionals may not require in-depth knowledge or experience in all practice areas, understanding how components work together is important.

Many organizations seek integration by first aligning development and performance management practices. When learning and development needs are identified through the performance management process, they can be linked to learning programs. In addition, if the processes are automated through a talent management platform, learning needs can be added to the learning management system (LMS) and employees can be

3.4 Talent Strategy & Management

enrolled in the appropriate programs. However, these integration activities do not need a talent management technology platform to be achieved; manual processes work as well.

Talent management functions can be integrated in several ways:
- The competencies developed through the workforce planning process can be used to develop role-based learning and learning paths.
- The competencies raised through the workforce planning process can be used to develop individual development plans and as part of the performance management process.
- Talent development may support the creation of assessment instruments for recruitment and selection, succession planning, and identifying high-potential employees.
- TD programs can train and coach managers to enhance their management skills, leading to better engagement and development among employees. [See 3.3.12 and 2.6.8.1]
- Development needs identified through the succession and talent review process can form the basis of leadership and other development programs.
- Achievement of specific career or individual development goals can be recognized and rewarded.

3.4.1.7 Skills Required to Align Talent Management to Organizational Strategies

Alignment ensures that talent management policies, practices, and priorities are effectively linked to business needs and strategic objectives. The skills necessary to properly align practice areas include:
- **Systems thinking** is based on the idea that the component parts of a system can be best understood by examining relationships with each other and other systems, rather than in isolation. This holistic view is important for change initiatives because small changes to any part of the system can affect the whole system, depending on the level of interconnectedness.
- **Strategic thinking** is a form of analysis that generates insights and opportunities to help differentiate an organization and make it more competitive. It can be part of an organization's strategic planning process, and individuals can use it to help achieve a goal.
- **Critical thinking** is a form of analysis that helps people evaluate an issue to form a logical and well-thought-out judgement. They do not accept all arguments and conclusions without question when thinking critically. Rather, they want to see the evidence that supports the argument or conclusion. Many skills comprise critical thinking, including analytical thinking, open mindedness, problem solving, and decision making. [See 1.2.8.1]
- **Creative thinking** is a way of looking at problems or situations from a fresh perspective that suggests unorthodox solutions. Creative thinking can be stimulated both by an unstructured process, such as brainstorming, and by a structured process, such as lateral thinking (Business Dictionary 2007).
- **Design thinking** "is a human-centered process that provides a means for defining problems from multiple perspectives, brainstorming possible solutions, prototyping those solutions, and then testing and iterating to optimize the best approach. It focuses on the balance between organizational needs, user needs, and technology or environmental constraints" (Boller and Fletcher 2020). [See 2.2.13 and 2.4.9.3]
- **Collaboration** occurs when two or more individuals work together with equal opportunity to participate, communicate, and collectively complete projects and goals. During conflict, collaboration facilitates both parties working together to develop a win-win solution.

- **Industry awareness** involves understanding what is changing or is new in an organization's trade, commerce, or business area.
- **Business acumen** is a combination of knowledge and skill informed by experience—knowledge about key business issues, the skill to apply that knowledge, and the confidence to act. It includes the ability to provide a big picture view of a situation and influence both strategic decisions and decision makers.

3.4.2 Skill in Creating and Aligning Talent Development Vision and Strategy With Organizational and Business Vision and Strategy

> **I. Aligning Talent Strategy to Organizational Strategy**
>
> TD professionals should have a clear understanding of how to create and align a TD vision and strategy to their organization's vision and strategy to support its strategic imperatives.

3.4.2.1 Developing a Talent Strategy

A talent strategy identifies how talent will be used to support an organization's goals. Without one, each talent management function is left to determine which objectives to develop. Although those objectives can be linked to organizational objectives, a siloed approach reinforces the notion that each talent management function operates independently. Having an overarching talent strategy forces the integration of talent management functions to ensure the achievement of a broad set of organizational objectives.

If their organization is small, a TD professional might develop both the talent strategy and the TD strategy alone or with line leaders. If their organization is large, the TD professional must work with other talent management professionals to ensure their strategies are aligned and integrated to support their organization's overall talent needs. The strategic planning process is identical to the process organizations use to create long-term objectives.

A robust talent management strategy represents the highest-level plan of action for optimizing employee talent and performance. It allows the TD function to focus resources on key strategic initiatives, increasing departmental performance and the ability to adapt to future challenges. A talent strategy shows TD professionals:
- What learning and development is needed to achieve organizational goals
- What skills and capabilities are required
- How it will have a measurable impact on attainment of organizational goals
- The value TD adds to the organization

To summarize, a *talent management strategy* determines which skills and capabilities are necessary to achieve an organization's objectives. A *talent development strategy* is used to narrow the view by mapping the training and career paths needed to help individual employees advance and contribute to business success.

3.4.2.1.1 Aligning Talent Strategy to Organizational Strategy

A talent strategy should be developed from an organization's strategic requirements and key performance indicators, which are quantifiable measures used to evaluate the organization's success in meeting its objectives. A thorough talent strategy describes how an organization will harness its potential to meet current and future needs and outlines the specific activities each talent management function should undertake.

3.4 Talent Strategy & Management

The same tools organizations use to build strategic plans can be leveraged to create a talent strategy, including:
- **SWOT analysis** on talent looks at the strengths and weaknesses (internal to an organization) and opportunities and threats (external to an organization). The output of this analysis is placed on a 2x2 matrix to make further determinations of what can be leveraged or changed. The results can be used to help develop strategic talent objectives. [See 1.2.8]
- **Scenario planning** looks to the future and imagines what events are likely to happen, what would happen if these events occurred, and how to respond or benefit from them. Scenario plans form the basis of strategic objectives.
- **Environmental scans** broadly examine the impacts to future success that are outside the organization, including economic, sociological, political, and technological considerations and forecasted changes. [See 3.8.2]
- **Industry scans,** including benchmarks from research, broadly focus on the impacts to an organization's industry and how those might affect future success.
- **Senior leader interviews** may be used to validate an analysis conducted using the mentioned tools or to gain additional insights about an organization's strategic objectives.
- **Employee interviews or surveys** may be used to inform talent objectives based on performance gaps or career development needs.

The talent management requirements resulting from strategically analyzing internal and external factors and scenarios create a picture of how talent can help an organization meet its objectives. These requirements are further refined through the SWP process.

3.4.2.1.2 Create a Strategic Workforce Plan

A foundational step in creating a talent strategy is to create a strategic workforce plan. This activity begins by examining the key roles the organization needs to meet its future demand, as well as the competencies needed to fulfill those roles. Next, an assessment of the existing talent is conducted using:
- Data from performance management processes
- Output from talent reviews or other assessment processes
- Assessment instruments
- Individual development plan data
- Assessments by leaders on the perceived gaps
- Other organizational processes that may yield talent gaps (such as proposal bids for work) [See 3.4.1.1]

Once gaps are identified, talent management professionals can determine whether a talent segmentation approach is most appropriate. A talent segmentation strategy identifies present gaps in an organization's critical roles and defines strategic objectives for filling those gaps. This allows TD and talent acquisition professionals to identify and develop plans needed to fill the roles either through acquisition of talent or development of internal resources. [See 3.4.2.1]

Other outputs of an SWP process are job analyses that describe a role's key tasks, duties, and responsibilities, and job descriptions that describe the competencies each job needs.

The talent strategy developed in conjunction with a strategic workforce plan creates talent management strategies that each area refines and flows down. As new talent needs emerge, new strategies and goals can be set. For example, if a new job family is being developed, TD professionals can establish a goal to develop role-based learning for the new role.

3.4.2.1.3 Talent Management Strategies

Talent management strategies drive whether talent will be acquired from outside an organization, developed through internal learning and development programs, or found through a combination of approaches. This may be done through an analysis of the six Bs (buy, build, borrow, bound, bounce, or bind). [See 3.4.15]

For example, if an organization is targeting a new customer or market, it may discover it does not have the proper skills mix to execute that strategy, so it may decide to buy (or recruit and hire externally) the talent it needs from the external marketplace. Once these goals are established, the talent acquisition strategy can determine the overall implementation plan, whereas the TD strategy might simply contain an associated subgoal. The talent management strategic objectives give rise to the various talent management strategies that are subsequently developed.

To ensure consistency and fairness, the same competencies that are identified for each role in a strategic workforce plan should be used to hire and develop talent.

3.4.2.1.4 Talent Management Measures

As talent management strategies and subsequent flow-down objectives are developed, talent management measures should be developed concurrently based on measures an organization deems acceptable. These measures need top-level support and agreement before any activity is undertaken to support them.

Before beginning work on the goals, TD professionals need to develop talent management metrics for each objective and reach an agreement with stakeholders. Some questions to ask when determining the proper measures include:

- Why do you want to measure? (What are the strategic objectives you are measuring?)
- What should be measured? (What outcome measures will show that strategic objectives have been met?)
- How should they be calculated? (How often and by whom?)
- How should they be reported?
- How should the measures and reports be used?
- What is a successful recruit?

Measures specific to talent development initiatives could include:

- **Effectiveness measures** address the quality of a program, effort, or activity. Typical TD effectiveness measures are reaction and satisfaction, learning, application, organizational impact, and return on investment.
- **Efficiency measures** review time, quantity, and costs. Typical TD efficiency measures include the number of participants, hours of training, how quickly programs are designed and developed, and the total costs of the learning programs.
- **Outcome measures** are the results or impact of a learning program or TD initiative on desired objectives. Typical TD outcome measures include the results of a training program, such as how a leadership development program has affected succession plans.

Measures specific to talent management more broadly might specify learning and development goals, succession planning goals, performance management goals, and other goals that support the development of talent, including compliance training measures, onboarding, speed to productivity, and basic employee skills needed for daily operations. L&D departmental goals could also be evaluated, such as reducing cost per learner or decreasing the design and development time for learning programs. Different measures will be collected for different audiences and strategic questions the organization is asking.

3.4.2.2 Talent Strategy Alignment Challenges

Talent development efforts succeed when the objectives are aligned with organizational objectives and measured to show impact. Several barriers can cause misalignment, and TD professionals can benefit from understanding them (Biech 2018).

3.4.2.2.1 Indirect Reporting Structure

An indirect reporting structure in which the TD department does not have a direct reporting relationship to the CEO or another senior leader can hamper communication and cause misalignment with strategic goals. A stronger alignment occurs when learning activities are reported directly to a senior leader. TD professionals, whose alignment is not always direct, may not be able to change their organizational reporting relationship; however, looking for opportunities to engage with senior leadership may keep talent development visible and supported by them.

3.4.2.2.2 Limited Understanding of an Organization and Its Strategies

TD professionals must understand the model in which they operate. The way their organization is structured, how it makes money, how it defines an expense, and how it views data is fundamental to the TD professional's ability to create organizational impact. A lack of understanding will show up in unaligned activities, programs, and objectives, and eventually lead to senior leaders questioning the viability of talent development.

3.4.2.2.3 Failure to Relate to Stakeholders

TD professionals who do not understand their organization will struggle to identify or develop relationships with key stakeholders, including HR, who influence talent strategy and drive organizational success. Without this knowledge, they cannot become trusted advisors who help leaders solve their problems.

3.4.2.2.4 Lack of Focus on Organizational Strategies

Understanding the connection between an organization's strategies, mission, and vision is the first step to aligning TD objectives to the organization. Only with this understanding of organizational strategies can TD professionals align their initiatives. Every TD objective, program, or activity should be able to answer the question, "What organizational objective is this serving?"

3.4.2.2.5 Not Having a Talent Strategy

Many organizations do not have an explicit talent strategy that is documented and communicated. However, they may have specific strategies for talent management or HR that can help ensure those areas are operating as effectively as possible.

3.4 Talent Strategy & Management

3.4.2.2.6 Lack of Accountability

In certain organizations that do not see talent as an asset, talent development may be viewed as an expense rather than an investment in people. In these instances, TD activities may only be seen as keeping the organization in compliance or providing basic skills training, and true accountability for developing talent isn't required. Over time, this will diminish the organization's view of the TD function's ability to add value to the organization or be worthy of strategic investment. When talent development is viewed this way, it can become subject to budget cuts or even elimination during financial downturns. TD professionals should ensure that their initiatives are visible to stakeholders by sharing strategies and post-implementation results from their programs, or stakeholders may never see the value of TD efforts.

3.4.2.2.7 A Lack of Measures of Success

If stakeholders are not expecting to see results, TD professionals may not measure or analyze data to show results. Measures of success are part of the strategy development process and are determined in connection with stakeholder agreement. Without predefined measures, it can be difficult to evaluate a strategic objective, program, or activity after-the-fact. [See 3.4.2.1]

3.4.2.2.8 Constant Change

Organizations currently operate in a volatile, uncertain, complex, and ambiguous (VUCA) world with disruption representing the new normal. *VUCA*—a well-established, common term in HR, talent development, and OD fields—describes an environmental condition and business climate issue that greatly influences change readiness and capability (Bennett and Lemoine 2014). TD professionals must ensure that their talent strategies continually evolve to match the changing business conditions and address critical skill gaps that could hinder organizational success.

3.4.2.2.9 Limited Resources

TD professionals are often challenged to do more with less. They should determine where limited resources can have the biggest impact and focus scarce discretionary resources on talent initiatives that will drive strategic organizational goals.

3.4.3 Skill in Developing a Talent Strategy That Aligns to Organizational Strategies to Positively Influence Organizational Outcomes

I. Talent Development's Role in Influencing Positive Organizational Outcomes

TD professionals should be able to align their goals and objectives with organizational objectives and demonstrate results that measure impact on organizational outcomes.

3.4.3.1 Linking TD Goals to Organizational Strategy

Each TD goal flows from an organizational objective and describes how the objective will be achieved by developing the talent involved. Goals have specific measures that state how to evaluate whether they were achieved and are agreed upon upfront with stakeholders. [See 3.4.2.1]

Part of the TD goal-setting process is to define the results required for critical roles that have a performance gap. TD professionals should conduct a job analysis to identify the competencies necessary to perform each role. Then, they should undertake a task analysis, which is the process of examining a single task within a job and breaking it into smaller steps. They should continue deconstructing each task from the job analysis until each one is thoroughly described. [See 3.4.13]

The task analysis describes the competencies a role requires for successful execution. TD professionals can use this information to identify which role-based knowledge, skills, and attitudes (KSAs) should be developed. From this analysis, they can establish and communicate specific TD goals. [See 3.4.8]

3.4.3.2 Ensuring Organizational Alignment

TD professionals should ensure alignment between their strategic goal-setting processes and their organization's needs by understanding those needs and working with stakeholders to set TD goals that properly address them.

Depending on the size of their organization, TD professionals may or may not be part of this organizational goal-setting process; however, they do have multiple options for customizing alignment:

- Prepare by reading the organization's strategic plan, business plans, or any other documentation available. Take notes to confirm understanding and identify questions.
- Meet with senior executives and stakeholders to discuss the organization's strategic objectives and how TD programs may help achieve those objectives.
- If there is a talent strategy, become part of that process. If that is not possible, read and understand the strategy to align TD objectives with it.
- Begin analyzing the information from interviews with any executives and stakeholders. Meet with other TD professionals to determine which strategic objectives TD initiatives could positively influence. Determine the internal capabilities the TD department has and whether outside assistance would be required.
- Review recommendations with the stakeholders to confirm understanding of the goals and receive feedback on the approach.
- Once confirmed, decide on the measures for each goal (Biech 2018).

By being proactive, TD professionals can avoid receiving direction from multiple stakeholders who have no clear priorities. Having a TD strategy that is aligned with organizational needs ensures that the organization's objectives are being served.

TD professionals manage a variety of programs, initiatives, activities, and resources to successfully achieve their objectives. Aligning these goals to organizational strategy typically includes the full range of requirements for learning and development:

- **Help the organization comply with regulations.** TD professionals may provide learning solutions that keep the organization in compliance with relevant laws and regulations.
- **Deliver basic capability.** TD professionals should provide basic skills training and information to quickly assimilate new employees and reduce the time it takes them to learn their new job.
- **Replicate the organization's success model.** Over time, organizations find ways to get things done more efficiently. Especially in times of growth or retrenchment, TD professionals' most important work is

to replicate those models of success through ongoing efforts, like development programs, or ad hoc solutions, such as when an organization opens a new location and entire systems must be replicated.
- **Provide tactical support.** TD professionals may be called upon to provide learning and development opportunities when new initiatives or activities are planned; for example, in a new system implementation, the information is included in the implementation project plan and the TD activities are viewed as integral to the successful completion of the project.
- **Develop strategic partnerships.** By getting a "seat at the table," TD professionals can ensure strategic TD objectives are included in their organization's strategic planning process. Partnering involves aligning with and supporting the strategic initiatives the organization has developed.
- **Engage in future proofing.** TD professionals should help their organizations prepare for the future. [See 3.8.1.3]

3.4.3.3 Execute Strategy and Gather Results

Once a TD strategy is developed, all relevant stakeholders must agree with it, and TD professionals should define specific goals and milestones. The goals may be further defined on a team or individual basis. This process helps ensure alignment at every level to keep prioritized activities in the forefront.

Many TD products and services involve projects and should be planned and executed. [See 1.5] Project plans can be used to track execution of a strategy, as well as the measures established to complete them successfully. Determining these measures should follow the same process as establishing strategic objectives. [See 3.4.2.1] They represent the effectiveness and efficiency of L&D programs, activities, and initiatives, as well as their impact on the organization. The measures also represent the efficiency and effectiveness of the TD function. [See 3.4.2.1.4]

Any measures can be thoroughly examined at the end of a project to explain its outcomes, successes, and lessons learned. They can also be used to demonstrate the TD function's influence on the organization, build a business case for additional resources, discover ways to enhance the quality of programs, make the TD function more efficient, and support decision making.

3.4.3.4 Ensure Continued Alignment

TD professionals should ensure that daily TD activities are closely aligned to organizational objectives. In the face of constant organizational changes, TD professionals may find themselves focusing on new initiatives or requests that detract time and attention from organizational goals, such as responding to a request for training just because the training already exists and it won't take much time to provide.

TD professionals should know their TD objectives and measures and understand how they align with organizational objectives. Their individual goals should also be aligned with the strategic TD objectives and measures. TD managers should provide continuous coaching and feedback to ensure continued alignment and quick course correction if problems arise. Using individual development plans, TD professionals may be able to develop their current skills or learn new ones to ensure successful completion of individual objectives. By confirming that every manager's request will solve the root cause of their problem, TD professionals can ensure their solutions align with organizational priorities.

3.4.4 Skill in Designing and Implementing Strategic Plans for Talent Development Projects, Programs, and Functions

> **I. Planning for Talent Development Work**
> TD professionals should understand how talent development projects, programs, and other offerings are aligned with strategic objectives so that priorities are established and executed.

3.4.4.1 Steps to Design and Implement TD Strategic Plans

The TD function's strategic objectives and vision and mission statements guide its work. They also inform the TD professional's approach when setting up a department.

3.4.4.1.1 Develop a Vision and Mission Statement for Talent Development

A *vision statement* is an aspirational description of the future, while a *mission statement* defines the purpose of a TD department, its reason for existing, and its direction.

Vision statements answer the question, "What do we want to be as an organization in X years?" They provide a clear picture of how an organization will look when the strategic objectives that support the vision have been accomplished. [See 3.1.6.1 and 3.4.2.1] The mission is more focused on the present. Mission statements answer the questions, "What is our purpose?" and "Why do we exist?" They can also be inspirational.

The vision and the mission statements drive the TD department's values and strategy, which address how the vision and mission will be accomplished. These strategies are measured with key performance indicators and flow down as departmental and individual goals. The department's vision and mission should align with the organization's stated vision, values, and strategy to ensure total alignment.

3.4.4.1.2 Determine Strengths and Improvement Opportunities

Like an organizational strategic plan, a TD department needs to conduct an environmental review to determine its strengths and opportunities for improvement. A SWOT analysis—which identifies strengths, weaknesses, opportunities, and threats—is good tool for performing an environmental review. TD professionals can use this information to compensate for constraints and weaknesses using the TD department's available strengths and opportunities. [See 3.4.2.1]

3.4.4.1.3 Planning for Action

TD professionals should develop strategic goals, objectives, and an action plan:
- **Strategic goals** should align with the organization's business goals and clearly support its critical issues. TD departments need the capabilities, funding, and information required for their strategies to succeed. The risks should be clear and there should be plans to avoid or minimize them.
- **Objectives** focus on details and provide more specific tasks that must be accomplished. Both goals and objectives should be specific and measurable.
- **Action plans** take the planning process one step closer to reality by providing the critical details to achieve the department's strategies. They identify who will do what and by when, as well as key programs and initiatives, a timeline, and resources to tasks.

3.4.4.2 Beyond the Strategic Plan

TD professionals must understand their organization's vision, mission, strategy, and goals. To support those priorities, they must be trusted advisors who know what problems will arise and what changes will occur.

3.4.4.2.1 Know What Talent Development Stands For

TD principles can provide guidance to an organization and its employees. In addition, TD professionals can help employees and their organization understand what talent development represents through a value statement. The statement might proclaim what the TD function values, such as supporting employees, teamwork, collaboration, or development. A simple proclamation can be a guiding principle that helps employees relate to TD activities.

3.4.4.2.2 Anticipate and Plan for Change

TD professionals should return to their SWOT analysis to review problems that may affect TD initiatives. Organizational priorities constantly shift and learning requirements change regularly, which may cause resource reallocations or other problems and constraints for TD initiatives. Anticipating what could happen during the performance period is necessary to ensure an agile approach to change. In large organizations, a learning governance council may effectively respond to needs as changes arise. In small organizations, TD professionals must work in partnership with senior leaders so they can be aware of any shifting priorities that may affect them.

3.4.4.2.3 Establish Priorities

The established TD objectives are the basis for the TD department's priorities. TD professionals should also have a process for establishing other priorities that evolve throughout the planning period, including how new requests will be handled. Some TD professionals partner with stakeholders to establish a vetting process for prioritizing TD initiatives according to their value to organizational outcomes and ease of implementation.

3.4.4.2.4 Maintain Compliance

The TD department, in partnership with other stakeholders, is frequently involved in ensuring organizational compliance. TD professionals should know which compliance programs are required by law or statute for their country, region, state, or locale, and plan for the fulfillment of those requirements. Fulfillment entails understanding the needs of all learners to verify that TD activities comply with applicable laws and ensure accessibility. [See 1.6]

3.4.4.3 Planning for Major Programs

When planning major TD programs, initiatives, or events, TD professionals should use basic project management approaches to ensure successful completion. Even if large initiatives are planned, developed, or scheduled, they may be cancelled or changed to something else midstream. Depending on the organization's size, TD professionals may need to use contingent hires to meet deadlines, so it's good to be prepared. [See 1.5]

3.4.5 Skill in Identifying Anticipated Constraints or Problems Affecting Talent Development Initiatives

> **I. Identifying and Overcoming Constraints and Problems With TD Initiatives**
> TD professionals should be able to forecast potential barriers and constraints to TD initiatives and determine ways to reduce the likelihood of occurrence.

3.4.5.1 Tools to Predict Problems
Many tools exist to help forecast problems and barriers to achieving objectives. Many problem-solving tools begin with brainstorming and then sorting or categorizing the output. Potential tools include:
- **Cause and effect diagram,** also known as a fishbone diagram, represents the relationship between an effect and all of its possible causes. Such diagrams are drawn to illustrate the causes in major categories.
- **Five whys** can be used to determine the cause of a problem by asking "why?" five times. This helps ensure the problem has been correctly identified instead of listing symptoms.
- **Force field analysis** looks at the factors that are influencing movement toward and away from a goal. [see 3.5.5.2 and 3.6.3.2]
- **Nominal group technique** is a brainstorming method that involves individuals generating their own ideas and then collectively creating ideas based on the convergence of opinion.
- **Pareto charts** are vertical bar charts that determine which problems to solve in what order.
- **Scenario planning** uses trends and uncertainties to create possible future scenarios so they can be prepared.
- **Impact assessment** defines how proposed changes in skills, knowledge, processes, or systems may affect target audiences as they transition from the current to target state of talent development. [See 3.5.2.6]

3.4.5.2 Conduct a Constraints Analysis to Identify Limiting Factors
A constraints analysis identifies the project's limiting factors, which may include budget, time available, scheduling, space, resource availability, resource expertise to conduct the analysis, and competing organizational priorities. This analysis should also detail all factors required to design a successful initiative and all resources needed to effectively plan, design, and develop communications and change management initiatives to support the solution implementation and resulting behavior change.

All potential constraints and issues should be discussed in the initial planning process. All risks can be identified in the project plan, and a risk mitigation plan can be developed.

3.4.5.3 Anticipate, Avoid, and Mitigate Common Problems
Many TD projects involve teams of subject matter experts, instructional designers, and others to execute the tasks. Common problems associated with projects and project teams include:
- **Talent shortages** occur when organizations struggle to find enough workers and skilled candidates to fill an ever-increasing number of high skilled jobs (Burner et al. 2019).

- **Role uncertainty.** If the roles on the project team are not clearly articulated, it may cause gaps or overlaps in work assignments. A clearly defined team charter can specify team roles and responsibilities and who has decision-making authority.
- **Lack of support.** Key initiatives that are not visibly supported can lose momentum over time. TD professionals should ensure each initiative is aligned with a TD strategic objective and has a key customer who visibly supports it.
- **Shortage of resources.** A lack of resources to adequately address the project's expected results can lead to failure. TD professionals should only start a project once the resources have been committed.
- **Unreasonable deadlines.** Sometimes schedules are set too aggressively. TD professionals should negotiate with sponsors for more realistic timeframes or reduced project scope.
- **Missing deadlines.** The schedule may not account for unexpected problems or changes. TD professionals should create a schedule with space to address problems and changes to ensure high-quality results completed on time.
- **Lack of communication.** Sometimes TD professionals work without visibility or communication with stakeholders. They should schedule regular check-ins on the project plan to ensure they continue to be supported and visible.
- **Technology challenges.** Technology or platform issues may arise and negatively affect TD efforts and initiatives. TD professionals should speak to the developer or vendor or find additional resources to customize the most critical deficiencies either now or in the future.
- **Change fatigue** is characterized by exhaustion, brain fog, and mental distance from one's job. Often confused with resistance, TD professionals should continually assess the impact of change fatigue upon employee's performance, motivation, and engagement. [See 3.3.10]

When executing any project plan, unplanned changes and problems are likely. By monitoring the project plan and schedule, it is possible to avoid big problems if minor adjustments are made as soon as a problem is identified.

3.4.6 Skill in Establishing and Executing a Marketing Strategy to Promote Talent Development Activities

I. Creating a TD Marketing Strategy

TD professionals should be able to market their value proposition, initiatives, and programs. A marketing strategy is defined as a set of goals, tactics, systems, and processes that identify offerings, communicate key messages to help users select what they need, and enable customers to find and obtain their services.

3.4.6.1 Clarify the Purpose of the Marketing Strategy

In developing a clear purpose for a marketing strategy, TD professionals should begin with the end in mind. What is the ultimate result? TD professionals should plan for two marketing efforts. The first is creating an overall learning culture—a culture in which employees are continuously learning and passing that knowledge on throughout the organization. TD professionals begin by building relationships with leaders throughout their organization. This is likely their most important marketing charge.

The second marketing effort is to ensure that the entire organization comprehends the products and services the TD function offers, such as learning platforms, management or leadership experiences, courses, and tools and resources. TD professionals should realize that the target audience experiences these services in their own unique ways, and they decide whether the TD value proposition demonstrates what it has stated based on those experiences. [See 3.4.8.4]

Ask these questions to help clarify the TD marketing strategy's purpose:
- How relevant are TD programs and practices?
- Who are the customers of TD products?
- How is the TD function and its value perceived by its customers?
- How committed are the stakeholders and customers to continuous learning?
- How is the TD function adding market value to the organization?
- How are TD programs and practices enhancing attraction and retention of talent?
- Does the TD brand need to evolve to meet changing needs?

Aligning the TD function to an organization's strategy is essential. A valuable part of a well-formulated marketing plan is to state how TD professionals help their organization achieve its goals.

3.4.6.2 Create a Marketing Strategy

The TD strategy should form the basis for the marketing strategy. The key is to focus on marketing the value of the learning culture. Marketing material may be broadly communicated to an entire organization, or a specific service or program might be narrowly targeted to a specific audience. The marketing strategy includes defining the target audience for services and products, developing messaging, identifying goals, and establishing the message.

3.4.6.2.1 Define the Target Audience

When marketing efforts are not focused on an entire organization, having a well-defined target audience helps TD professionals direct communication to those who are more likely to use TD offerings. To assess the target audience for a unique offering, TD professionals may ask:
- Who are the current customers?
- What talent segments is this TD initiative supporting?
- Which specific audiences will benefit from this offering?
- Are there specific demographic commonalities for this offering?
- Is the TD department responsible for external audiences like customers, contingent employees, or seasonal workers?

Once they've clearly defined the target audience, TD professionals can determine where and how to market individual offerings.

TD professionals must always keep their key message in focus: Create a learning culture in which everyone learns and grows and the organization achieves its goals. A marketing effort is essential for creating awareness around the benefits TD activities offer individuals and organizations. [See 3.3.7 and 3.3.8]

3.4.6.2.2 Develop Effective Messaging

Advertising and promoting requires TD professionals to craft messages that articulate what they're offering, the benefits for their targeted audience, and the necessary information about where, when, and how to access the offering. Through careful analysis of the audience and its needs and the marketing options available, TD professionals can ensure their initiatives are visible and not lost amid all the other competing messages. They may even determine that different audiences require different approaches; for example, role-based training may only be marketed to employees in those roles.

3.4.6.2.3 Identify Objectives

The marketing objectives should support the TD program's goals and establish the criteria for measuring marketing effectiveness. TD professionals can use Mager's A-B-C-D process for developing objectives:

- **Audience**—the who
- **Behavior**—the performance; what the person is expected to be able to do, stated as specifically as possible
- **Conditions**—the environment under which the behavior is completed, including the tools or assistance provided
- **Degree**—the criterion of acceptable performance that the person should exhibit, such as time limits, accuracy, and quality [See 2.2.4.4]

The marketing metrics should be established at the same time as the goals. Using Mager's A-B-C-D process, TD professionals can weave the measures of effectiveness into a statement. For example, Leaders (audience) will enroll in the leadership development program (behavior) by submitting the nomination form (condition) no later than August 31(degree). The measure of effectiveness could be the number of leaders who submit the nomination form by August 31.

3.4.6.2.4 Establish a Clear and Memorable Message

Even if they might otherwise be interested, overwhelmed employees may ignore these marketing efforts. To prevent this, TD professionals should create very clear and memorable marketing messages. One approach is to use the six Cs of communication to objectively evaluate the effectiveness of different forms of communication, what's working, what isn't, and why:

- **Clear.** Choose audience-appropriate words that are precise and descriptive.
- **Correct.** Select accurate words, use correct grammar, and avoid using the wrong words.
- **Complete.** Articulate comprehensive messages that include all the details.
- **Concise.** Choose short, specific sentences and phrases.
- **Coherent.** Maintain consistency, select simple sentence structures, and present information in an easy-to-follow order.
- **Courteous.** Use words that are friendly, positive, gender-neutral, and sensitive to form messages that are respectful and authentic. [See 1.1.1.3]

TD professionals should also target messages to the right audience and be credible. Employees want to be convinced that there are personal benefits, and management wants to know the strategic value of initiatives. TD efforts should be positioned as strategic activities that are essential to reaching organizational goals, and TD professionals should use every opportunity to raise awareness about the value their efforts bring to the organization.

3.4.6.3 Identify Marketing Tactics

Marketing tactics use financial resources to maximize the effective promotion of products and services and allow TD professionals to deliver messages that result in customer engagement and satisfaction. Marketing tactics include:

- **Written communications**—such as brochures, case studies, direct mail, newsletters, press releases, or emails
- **Social media**—such as blogs, podcasts, videos, forum boards, or landing pages
- **Personal connections**—such as through special events, referrals, presentations, crowdsourcing, or testimonials

3.4.6.4 Establish a Marketing Budget

A detailed budget of expected marketing expenses helps TD professionals devote appropriate resources to the plan. Although the total expenses may be summarized as a line item in the TD budget, the marketing objectives and tactics can include cost estimates and priorities. [See 3.1.6]

These steps are essential when creating a marketing budget:
1. Understand how TD programs are funded and how budgets are established.
2. Know all costs associated with the TD function and its operations.
3. Review trend data such as spend rate for the past few years.
4. Set a marketing budget based on TD goals and objectives.
5. Consider plans for growth.

3.4.6.5 Implement the Marketing Plan

As the plan is implemented, TD professionals should collect measures and track them against objectives. To determine the effectiveness, they should ask:

- Are the objectives being met?
- Is performance improving?
- Has communication improved? [See 3.5]

3.4.6.6 Ultimate Marketing Achievements

TD professionals should recognize that an excellent TD marking plan can reach audiences inside and outside an organization. Internally, TD professionals can demonstrate the results of their marketing efforts and the value achieved for their organization.

Marketing can also have positive effects outside an organization by improving its reputation for supporting a learning culture and developing its people. A good reputation can enhance recruitment efforts for a talented workforce.

3.4.7 Skill in Designing and Implementing a Communication Strategy to Drive Talent Management Objectives

I. Creating a TD Communication Strategy

TD professionals should be able to communicate about talent development offerings and activities so their availability is widely known.

3.4.7.1 Determine Critical Information and Data

A communication plan helps TD professionals market TD offerings, new initiatives, and other relevant learning and development information to target audiences. It also helps keep learning visible and accessible to stakeholders.

Organizational objectives and TD objectives, activities, and results (as well as the marketing strategy) all inform the communication strategy's content. As new organizational initiatives arise, TD professionals should clearly identify and communicate learning initiatives associated with them. By determining what information needs to be communicated, TD professionals can craft the key messages to deliver. The communication plan also keeps the messages consistent with the established TD brand. It will be easier to recognize where the communication originates if the brand is part of the message.

3.4.7.2 Determine the Audience: People Who Need to Know or Want to Know

TD professionals should identify target audiences for specific objectives and key messages. They should also consider that there may be more than one audience for a key message when building a communication plan. Specific elements of the message should be targeted to each audience's needs or interests. For example, stakeholders and executives have different communication needs than all other employees, but they still need to hear the same key message; therefore, TD professionals should understand how to communicate with the C-suite. [See 3.1.8]

3.4.7.3 Identify Available Methods

There are many methods available for communicating with stakeholders, including reports, written messages, presentation-based briefings, and discussion-based meetings. TD professionals should understand that a message sent once is not sufficient to garner attention or comprehension. Deciding on the best communication method may be easier to do after the key messages and audience are determined. [See 1.1.5]

3.4.7.4 Identify a Timeline

A timeline for communicating key messages to target audiences is developed in context with an organization's timeline. For example, if people are typically on vacation during the summer months, TD professionals should consider delaying communications about major new initiatives until the fall. If an organization has an organization-wide calendar, it can help shape the timeline for TD communication events.

An organization-wide calendar can also inform the release of TD results. For example, if an organization has an annual planning process—with goals established at the beginning and results communicated at the end—TD professionals can follow that guidance when releasing their results. They can schedule meetings and reports with executives well in advance to communicate the TD department's annual results.

The TD communication timeline should include redundancy—key messages should be sent several times using several different methods to ensure they are received.

3.4.7.5 Create a Communication Plan
A communication plan includes dates, key messages or events, target audience analysis, a timeline, methods or media, responsible staff members, and any other notes that staff should be aware of. It could also include other activities planned by the TD department and any other functions that coincide with the timeline.

3.4.7.6 Engage Stakeholder Review
Getting feedback on messages is essential for knowing whether they have been received as intended. Feedback can be obtained by counting page clicks online, asking for feedback after a presentation, conducting online surveys, and holding focus groups. Having a third party conduct the feedback sessions may help enhance the authenticity of the feedback. Using open-ended questions that target the key messages helps ensure the feedback is viable and actionable. TD professionals should adjust the key messages or the communication plan based on the feedback.

3.4.7.7 Ensure Inclusion of All Staff
Make sure that all communication methods, messages, and access are inclusive and tailored to the needs of all staff, including remote or hybrid audiences and employees with accessibility needs.

3.4.8 Skill in Communicating How Talent Development Strategies and Solutions Support the Achievement of Targeted Business and Organizational Results

> **I. Communicating the Value of Talent Development**
>
> TD professionals should understand and communicate the value of their work to their organization. They are thought leaders in the broad world of work who share that knowledge with their organizations. TD professionals are involved in a wide array of business topics and should partner in many ways with different departments to show the viability and value of their work.

3.4.8.1 Partnering With Leadership
Building a partnership with leaders is imperative to success. Leadership endorsement and advocacy are essential to sustaining support for TD initiatives, programs, and activities because the rest of an organization will be watching and will see leaders' involvement as a stamp of approval. TD professionals can build relationships that provide this visibility and support with senior leaders by asking them to:
- Serve as mentors and coaches.
- Introduce new events.
- Speak at and attend learning programs.
- Serve on a governance board.

Giving senior leaders these roles and keeping the communication lines open will help build partnerships. Being involved in high-level organizational discussions and decisions—also known as having a seat at the table—facilitates communication between TD professionals and the leadership team. Once this respect is earned, TD professionals should actively engage in organizational discussions and explain how their efforts can influence the organization and accomplish its objectives. Communicating authentically will build trust and credibility and provide visibility for the TD function's effectiveness and impact. [See 3.2]

3.4.8.2 Building and Sustaining the Partnership Relationship

Building a partnership with leaders is like building any other relationship—getting to know and understand others, keeping commitments, and being accountable all instill trust and credibility. Good partnerships garner support and advocacy for TD initiatives in an organization.

TD professionals can begin to build their relationships with leaders by:
- Getting to know them and their organizations better
- Speaking the language of executives and the industry
- Having a clear understanding of their organization's strategic imperatives and goals and its plans to achieve them
- Understanding and helping solve their problems
- Clearly defining how the TD function supports them
- Demonstrating collaboration and accountability
- Being a systems thinker
- Establishing credibility by delivering programs on time
- Having a positive, can-do attitude

3.4.8.3 Communicate the Value of the TD Function's Contribution to Organizational Outcomes

Articulating the overall value and specific impact of learning and development initiatives is an essential skill for TD professionals. Sharing data and information about the outcome of learning programs and the positive results to the business can help TD functions gain credibility, influence, and the resources they need to increase their impact. TD professionals should collect data about outcome measures, such as efficiency and effectiveness, and analyze it so they can answer key strategic questions facing their organization. For example, a strategic question an organization may have is, "How have the engagement scores of the learners who have gone through the leadership development program changed over time?" Having a plan for collecting data, evaluating results, and communicating them to the necessary audiences will ensure TD professionals have the answers to these kinds of questions. [See 3.4.2.1.4]

Leaders at different levels in an organization will focus on different results and want to hear about the topics that are most pertinent to them. If a TD professional discusses an LMS and its functionality, for example, it may not be as interesting to senior leaders as information on how the learning content offered to employees through the system has positively affected the organization or how having the system helped reduce costs in some way. Most executives want to understand the intent behind and the end result of an initiative or project. [See 1.1.8 and 3.4.3.4]

3.4 Talent Strategy & Management

When communicating contributions to their organization's outcomes, TD professionals should:
- Link results to key performance indicators or strategic objectives when possible.
- Turn TD acronyms and terminology into language that will be understood by leaders and executives.
- Keep the message concise and as simple as possible; use appendices for details.
- Communicate the purpose of the presentation or document up-front so leaders understand what is coming.
- Incorporate executive summaries at the beginning of presentations or documents to provide context and an overview of the content.

3.4.8.4 The Value Proposition of Talent Development

A value proposition is a statement that communicates why a customer should buy from a seller. For TD purposes, the value proposition is the same: Why should customers get their learning and development from TD professionals? In approaching learning like a business, TD professionals should know the products and services they offer, who their clients are, the processes for buying their products and services, and the costs of doing so. Knowing this, they can create a value proposition that draws customers to their offerings.

Many times, internal functions like talent development are viewed as the low-cost, customized provider. In other words, the value proposition is that customers can get their learning and development products specifically customized for their needs better than they would by going outside their organization. Other value propositions depend on the analysis performed on customers, products, offerings, and costs.

Regardless of the specific value proposition, it can be included in advertising and marketing efforts along with measures of success. Helping stakeholders understand the value proposition helps build visibility and support for TD initiatives. [See 1.1.8 and 3.1.3.3]

3.4.9 Skill in Communicating the Value of Learning and Professional Development

I. Communicating the Value of Continuous Learning and Development

TD professionals should be able to demonstrate the value of investing in people through learning and development offerings. Doing so helps shift the perspective of TD activities from an expense to an investment.

3.4.9.1 Develop a Business Case for Lifelong Learning

Lifelong learning is the ongoing, self-motivated quest by an individual for knowledge to develop personally or professionally. Closely related is *continuous learning*, which is the way knowledge and skills are constantly passed throughout an organization. Whether through lifelong learning or continuous learning, TD professionals will need an intentional approach to inspire people to value learning because it will not happen on its own. Creating a learning culture is a never-ending challenge that requires attention, time, clear and aligned communication, and support from everyone in an organization. [See 1.7.1 and 3.1.7]

Three essential characteristics exist in a high-performance organization's learning culture: a sufficient budget to meet learning needs, a dedicated learning function, and senior-level responsibility for organizational learning.

It may take several years to instill the shared values, assumptions, and beliefs of a learning culture that appreciates lifelong learning. They may align with an existing organizational culture or represent a totally new paradigm for an organization.

There are many advantages to having a lifelong learning culture, including improved:
- Employee engagement levels [See 3.3.11]
- Overall organizational performance
- Talent retention
- Ability to meet changing business needs and objectives
- Competitiveness [See 1.7.1]

To develop a business case for lifelong learning, TD professionals should partner with leaders to determine what learning means to their organization. Is it valued? What is the implicit or explicit philosophy regarding learning? What do leaders want the philosophy to be? By answering these questions, TD professionals will have a current-state analysis that determines what changes, if any, are needed. They can incorporate any changes into their strategic TD goals and plans and measure them accordingly.

3.4.9.2 Communicating the Value of Lifelong Learning

A key part of successfully building a learning culture is ensuring leaders and managers know it is their responsibility to develop their employees. The TD professional's role is to serve as the catalyst and support for leaders and managers in this regard and provide learning opportunities for them to sharpen their talent management skills.

Not everyone values lifelong learning. Some employees may be content in jobs that they have mastered. As employees become more accountable for their own development, their interests and desire to learn may increase. TD professionals can use role-based learning journeys to meet employees' learning needs and help them map their careers. [See 1.1.3]

3.4.9.3 The Value of Lifelong Learning

Organizations want a ready pipeline of talent that ensures the best people are in the right jobs at the right time and at the right costs. Having talent ready to assume new or different responsibilities or roles as organizational needs change requires them to be prepared. A learning culture provides the opportunities for employees to do that. Unfortunately, research shows that one of the most significant barriers to creating a culture of lifelong learning is the difficulty demonstrating measurable impact (ATD 2018). [See 2.8]

Employers want their organization's talent to possess more than a degree; they want employees who have the requisite competencies to perform effectively in their current jobs and future roles. Degrees, experience, performance, professional credentials, certifications, certificates, and potential all lead to organizational decisions on promotions and mobility. When organizations provide clear career paths coupled with learning journeys, and employees develop themselves, it creates a clear win-win situation. [See 1.7.1]

Being a lifelong learner has numerous advantages to individuals. It can:
- Offer more opportunities to improve their quality of life.
- Boost their confidence and self-esteem.

- Challenge their beliefs and opinions.
- Increase their ability to adapt to change.
- Enhance their ability to achieve a more satisfying life.
- Improve their personal and professional development.
- Foster their desire to take more risks.
- Lead to them adopting a growth mindset.
- Expand their career advancement opportunities. [See 1.7.1]

3.4.9.4 Modeling the Value of Lifelong Learning

TD professionals need to model lifelong learning by demonstrating a growth mindset, learning ability, emotional intelligence, and personal mastery. They should communicate the value of learning by demonstrating the learning outcomes for all employees.

3.4.10 Skill in Developing Workforce Plans That Articulate Current and Future Talent and Skill Requirements

> **I. Strategic Workforce Planning**
>
> TD professionals should work in collaboration with senior leaders to develop a plan that forecasts future talent needs and skill requirements and compares those needs to current workforce capabilities. The objective is to ensure a steady talent flow.

3.4.10.1 Roles of the TD Professional in Strategic Workforce Planning

TD professionals assume many roles during an SWP process, including:
- **Analyst**—assessing current organizational realities, investigating future needs, and analyzing skills gaps
- **Implementer**—designing learning strategies, applying best practices, and focusing on continuous improvement
- **Evaluator**—measuring the transfer and impact of L&D programs to ensure they are developing talent to assume the needed roles
- **Partner**—helping the organization improve employee engagement, skill and knowledge, and knowledge transfer efforts, as well as reduce turnover and promote creativity and problem solving [See 3.3.12]
- **Change agent**—helping the organization initiate or implement organizational change to increase employee adoption (Burkett 2015) [See 3.6 and 3.2]

3.4.10.2 Strategic Workforce Planning for the Future

Working with senior leadership, TD professionals should help examine the future of their organization. SWP sessions typically examine future scenarios in the environment, the industry, the competition, or technology and how those may affect an organization; after that, the organization creates strategic objectives that include the talent needed to meet them. [See 3.4.2.1]

First, TD professionals need to estimate future talent needs based on the strategic objectives. Questions to ask include:

- How many workers will be needed to meet organizational demand?
- In what roles?
- Which roles are critical to success?
- What are the current in-house capabilities?
- What roles and skills are critical to short-term and long-term organizational goals?
- How large is the talent gap between what is needed and what is available in house?
- If a talent surplus exists, what action will be taken to reduce staffing levels or relocate employees?

The output from the SWP process can show the gaps in existing capabilities and allow TD professionals to begin developing a talent strategy that includes how to address those talent gaps. Workforce plans can include identification of strategic and key roles necessary to achieve organizational goals as well as core and transactional roles that support operations.

Once the types of roles are identified, an organization can conduct job analyses that identify the competencies necessary to perform specific jobs. Competency modeling can be conducted based on the results of a job analysis. [See 3.4.13]

The competencies developed for the roles (along with the KSAs) are then used to hire employees, develop them, manage their performance, and recognize and reward them. These competencies are the same across the talent management process to ensure consistency and fairness.

The organization can use the six Bs to decide whether to buy, build, borrow, bound, bounce, or bind talent for different roles in the workplace. This will determine the scope of the workforce and address questions such as:

- Are contingent workers included in the plan?
- Are gig workers part of the plan?
- Are outsourced organizations used to meet the gaps? [See 3.4.15]

The talent strategy that is derived from the workforce plan informs the development of talent management strategies. If roles are found to be lacking the necessary talent, organizations may decide to *buy* the talent from external sources. If the talent need is ongoing, the organization might decide to *build* internal capabilities through development and internal talent mobility. These strategies are all aligned with the strategic objectives of the organization.

3.4.10.3 Requirements That Inspire an Agile Workforce

To succeed in times of change, organizations need agile workplaces. When organizations can change direction and adjust swiftly to a changing marketplace, environment, or technology, they are more likely to prosper and grow. A workforce must be led by leaders who provide a practical leadership framework that helps individuals adapt to changing environments and effectively respond to recurring problems. This concept is based on the four principles of emotional intelligence, organizational justice, development, and character (Heifetz and Linsky 2017).

Several factors are involved in creating and maintaining an agile workplace:
- **Leadership** must be strongly aligned to strategy, speed of decision making, and speed and clarity of communication.
- **Innovation** is the act of translating a new method, product, or idea into a service or goods that create value. In organizations, product should satisfy customer expectations. An agile workplace must reflect processes that generate and share new ideas using networks.
- **Strategy** (or the intent or direction) is valued more than any particular initiative, and it must include the development of an agile workplace.
- **Culture** represents the collective assessment of an organization based on deeper, relatively enduring, often unconscious values, norms, and assumptions; to maintain an agile workplace, the culture must reflect policies and practices that align with the value of agility.
- **Change capacity** is the degree to which an organization provides employees with the capability to enact changes.
- **Structure** reflects an organization's ease of reallocating resources, existence of broadly shared (versus siloed) measures of success, and clarity of authority.
- **Growth mindset** is a concept developed by Carol Dweck (2006) that argues people believe they are in control of their abilities and can learn, improve, and develop them; a growth mindset is required to ensure an agile workforce.

3.4.11 Knowledge of Succession Planning and Talent Review Processes

> ### I. Succession Planning and Talent Reviews
> TD professionals should understand the role of succession planning and talent reviews in meeting their organization's talent needs. These reviews help ensure talent is available for higher-level positions and provide opportunities for people to move into other roles inside an organization instead of having to pursue growth elsewhere.

3.4.11.1 Succession Planning Defined

Succession planning is the systematic process of identifying, evaluating, and developing personnel who have the potential to assume leadership or mission-critical positions upon the resignation, termination, transfer, promotion, or death of an incumbent. It is a focused process for keeping talent in the pipeline. *Talent pipeline planning* is similar to succession planning; however, pipeline planning is a proactive approach taken to fill current or anticipated staffing shortages in specific job categories or families. A succession planning process can be used with a talent pipeline planning process when specific talent pools are examined, but the two processes can also stand alone.

Who might be considered a candidate for a succession plan depends on numerous factors. Typically, qualified employees are selected based on performance, experience, potential, and competence. They may also be differentiated by readiness—whether they are ready now, ready in one to two years, ready in more than three years, and so forth.

The structure of the succession plan typically begins at the top with the CEO—by identifying and considering each direct report to the CEO for succession. Additionally, each C-suite role is analyzed for successors. How far down the plans go are based on organizational needs and desires.

3.4.11.2 Succession Planning and Talent Reviews

Talent reviews are formal meetings that leaders use to discuss information related to an individual's past performance and future potential. They may be part of a succession planning process, or they could be a standalone activity to ensure a robust talent pipeline for a specific job category. Organizational reviews may also include talent reviews to assess how individuals performed during a defined time period or on a specific assignment.

Succession planning and talent reviews can provide visibility of high-potential talent to senior leaders and help ensure that talent pipelines and succession plans have available talent to meet organizational needs. Both can be integrated with other talent management practice areas, including:
- The SWP process, which can identify critical talent needs and the competencies required of high-potential employees and succession candidates.
- Performance management data, which can help leaders identify and select high-potential employees and succession candidates.
- Special compensation plans and reward structures, which can be used to incentivize or reward high-potential employees and succession candidates.

3.4.11.3 Actions Required for Succession Planning

Guidelines on completing succession plans are typically provided by the CEO or other senior leaders and strategic HR partners. They usually include guidance such as:
- How to identify and analyze critical roles, including growth, decline, and other changes affecting these roles
- How to calculate potential attrition from critical roles
- What tools can be used to identify high performers and high-potential employees, such as scenario planning, assessment instruments, or the nine-box grid model (SHRM 2018)
- How to gauge the readiness of successors
- What the talent mobility strategy is for identified successors

Once a talent review or succession planning meeting has been held and successors identified, managers and TD professionals can implement a talent management strategy. The actions associated with this step include:
- Determining the communication plan for selected and nonselected candidates and their managers
- Deciding on internal versus external acquisition of talent
- Creating development and mobility programs
- Assisting with the creation of individual development plans
- Monitoring attrition and candidate progress
- Discussing talent at all senior-level meetings
- Agreeing on any compensation, incentives, or recognition for selected candidates

3.4.11.4 Alternative Models of Succession Planning and Talent Reviews
Three other succession planning approaches are:
- **The nine-box model** was developed by McKinsey and Company in the 1970s. It's now used to compare individuals in a three-by-three grid that rates employees on two dimensions of performance and potential. Ratings of high, medium, or low are used within the two axes regarding their readiness for promotion.
- **Talent pools** are created if there are two or more potential successors for a specific role. When used properly, they prevent having only one qualified successor for an open position.
- **Individual development plans** use career mapping and follow a process in which employers and employees work together to build plans that support an organization's goals and an individual's career goals.

3.4.12 Knowledge of Approaches for Identifying and Developing High-Potential Talent

> **I. Developing High-Potential Talent**
>
> TD professionals should know how to identify, select, move, and develop employees who have long-term potential to advance in the organization. This keeps talent pipelines full.

3.4.12.1 Defining Criteria for High-Potential Employees
Each organization must determine the criteria for high-potential employees. Generally, this process will begin by understanding what the organization needs in the future. Some organizations establish a percentage of leadership positions that need to remain filled, such as the top 3 percent of senior leadership positions. The list may also include critical positions that are difficult to fill.

High-potential criteria include the characteristics, expertise, experience, and readiness that employees require to be successful in a position. To specifically define high-potential criteria, organizations must determine the long-term strategic needs for each position, the timeline, and the strategy for filling the positions. TD professionals should define readiness and fit, outline performance requirements, and do internal and external research about future readiness requirements and how they align with their organization's current and future needs.

Organizations look for characteristics such as past and current performance, respect of leaders, acceptance of feedback, critical thinking, a drive for results, organizational commitment, and a fit to the culture. Finally, TD professionals need to ensure that the criteria selected are measurable.

3.4.12.2 Process for Identifying High-Potential Employees
A program to identify and develop high-potential employees begins with alignment to organizational goals. TD professionals should know which roles will be key to their organization's success, what capabilities exist currently, what talent gaps exist, and how to close those gaps.

3.4.12.2.1 Identify High-Potential Employees

Successful organizations put effort into developing high-potential employees; therefore, the program or process to identify them must be effective. Having an explicit purpose for the program helps TD professionals confirm expectations, set goals, align with other talent management processes and programs, set selection criteria, and measure effectiveness.

A design may involve many elements that must be customized to an organization and integrated with other talent management practices. TD professionals should work with senior leaders to ensure the program is fair and consistently applied, meets their organization's talent needs, and involves all relevant stakeholders.

High-potential employees can be identified either through a candidate referral process, a self-nomination process, or the nine-box model, which helps TD professionals review employees' performance and future potential to help gauge their likelihood of success. There is no right way to select who will participate, and there are pros and cons to each process. Consider which roles are critical and where the need to keep a talent pipeline full is of paramount importance.

When deciding eligibility for the program, consider the person's:
- Level in the organization
- Time in role
- Performance level
- Supervisory recommendation
- Diversity considerations.

3.4.12.2.2 Selection Process

Whether their organization uses a self-nomination process or a referral process for leaders to nominate candidates, TD professionals should clarify the process, ensure the instructions are clear, and provide sufficient time. Documents for submission may include:
- Application
- Talent profile (including demographic information, employment history, a self-assessment, a supervisory assessment, performance level, potential assessment, and career interests)
- Supervisory endorsement

Using different instruments with candidates may also provide insights into their potential—simulations, games, assessments, panel interviews, or other tools may reveal a more balanced view and make selection easier.

Once assessments and discussions have taken place, TD professionals should score candidates against the established selection criteria and then rate them against one another. Typical selection criteria include:
- Current performance
- Potential as gauged by a nine-box assessment or similar instrument
- Exhibition of role-based leadership competencies
- Formal assessment results

3.4.12.2.3 Inclusivity

TD professionals should define terminology and criteria to prevent any misunderstandings and enforce consistency during candidate recruitment, nomination, evaluation, and selection. These definitions ensure leaders and others involved have a clear course for the process.

In addition, TD professionals should consider involving a diversity, equity, and inclusion (DEI) committee to expand diversity in leadership and other critical roles. This committee could also serve as the selection committee to enable a fair and accurate selection process. Using a panel of leaders from across an organization who know the candidates and can attest to their abilities may generate a robust discussion of capability. The discussions should be focused on objective, job-related selection criteria. [See 1.4]

Once candidates have been selected for a high-potential program, they and their supervisors should be informed. However, some organizations keep that information confidential to avoid implying a future promotion or other employment action. There are organization-specific pros and cons to transparency that TD professionals should consider when making this decision.

3.4.12.2.4 Exceptions

There may be times when selected candidates do not meet expectations. In this case, TD professionals should make plans that address the issues and have a process for releasing these candidates from the program. They should be aware of how candidates are performing and address any early warning signs of derailment.

3.4.12.3 Developing High-Potential Employees

There are many types of internal and external development opportunities, some of which involve a cost that an organization typically pays. TD professionals should target the right development for the individual, considering cost-effective and high-quality development programs. Examples of development programs include:

- External opportunities
    - Academic assignments
    - Advanced degree education
    - Development classes
    - Loaned executive programs
    - Professional associations
    - Executive education programs
- Internal opportunities
    - Committee and task force involvement
    - Immersive management
    - Monthly leadership sessions
    - Self-development opportunities
    - Stretch assignments
    - Rotational assignments
    - Action learning programs
    - Communities of practice

3.4.13 Knowledge of Methods to Identify Critical Requirements of Tasks, Jobs, and Roles

I. Identifying Tasks, Jobs, and Role Requirements

TD professionals should understand how to conduct job analyses that identify tasks and duties performed for specific jobs and roles so they can specify performance gaps and recommend learning and development solutions.

3.4.13.1 Job Analysis Steps to Identify Work Requirements

A job analysis identifies all duties (responsibilities) and respective tasks performed on a daily, weekly, monthly, and yearly basis for a single job or role. The steps for conducting a job analysis include:

- **Identify job results relevant to organizational goals.** Examine the expected outcomes of a job or role and ensure alignment with the organization's goals and objectives.
- **Identify tasks in each job result.** Identify the key tasks that have a substantial influence on the accomplishment of goals.
- **Identify steps within the task.** Break down each task into subtasks.
- **Identify knowledge, skills, and attitudes required to perform each step.** Examine what it takes to accomplish each step or subtask, including the knowledge, skills, abilities, and other competencies.
- **Document task analysis.** Summarize everything needed to perform the job or role successfully.

3.4.13.2 Job Design

Job design is a follow-on activity to job analysis that specifies how a job is done, including the contents, methods, and arrangement of tasks. The design should meet technical and organizational requirements, reduce sources of fatigue and human error, and meet the needs of the job performer. It also addresses the relationship and links between jobs in an organization. [See 3.3.5]

Proper job design is critical for increasing the effectiveness of operations and the employee's efficiency and satisfaction. If designed well, job design components can help enhance employee engagement; the reverse is true if they're poorly designed. These components include:

- **Skill variety**—the extent to which a job requires an employee to use a wide range of skills, abilities, or knowledge
- **Task identity**—the extent to which a job requires a worker to perform all the tasks necessary to complete that job from the beginning to the end of the production process
- **Task significance**—the degree to which a worker believes their job is meaningful because of its influence on people inside the organization (such as co-workers) or people outside the organization (such as customers)
- **Autonomy**—the degree to which a job gives an employee the freedom and discretion needed to schedule different tasks and decide how to carry out those tasks
- **Feedback**—the extent to which performing a job provides workers with clear and direct information about how well they have completed the job

3.4.13.3 Addressing Skills Gaps

Job analysis and job design may identify skills gaps, which are significant gaps between an organization's current capabilities and the skills it needs to achieve its goals and meet customer demand. An organization with significant skills gaps risks not meeting customer demand, because it may not be able to grow, compete, or prepare for the future.

Talent development has assumed an increased role in addressing skills gaps, and there is now more accountability for individual managers. However, success in identifying and closing these gaps depends on the involvement of key stakeholders across an organization.

To address skills gaps, organizations should:
- **Upskill.** Design training to augment existing skills with new or significantly enhanced knowledge to enable individuals to continue to succeed in the same profession or field of work; upskilling does not refer to normal, ongoing development.
- **Reskill.** Design training to help individuals gain new knowledge or skills to enable them to perform new jobs or enter new professions.
- **Multi-skill.** Train employees in new or related work areas to increase their use in different areas of the organization.
- **Right skill.** Train employees to meet the future needs of the organization regardless of their current capabilities (Souza and Fyfe-Mills 2018).

Strategies for addressing skills gaps include:
- Clarifying and understanding an organization's performance metrics
- Identifying key stakeholders to support closing a skills gap
- Outlining competencies and skills that map to strategies and performance metrics
- Assessing the skills gap
- Setting goals and prioritizing the path to filling gaps
- Implementing solutions and monitoring sustainability
- Communicating the impact

Skills gaps continue to affect organizations and pose a risk to organizational success. The shelf life of many skills is shrinking, thanks in part to advances in technology making them outdated as jobs are reshaped, eliminated, or automated. TD professionals should address skills gaps through agile L&D programs that keep talent pipelines filled.

3.4.13.4 Competency Analysis and Competency Modeling

Competencies are the skills, knowledge, and attitudes of employees who are performing their jobs at a high level of proficiency; they are not simply the requirements listed in a job description. Competencies pinpoint the unique characteristics of successful employees, which are commonly captured and organized into a competency model. Knowledge of these success factors allows TD professionals to develop learning and development programs that target the competencies needed by their organization.

Competency modeling supports the integration of talent management practices in an organization to create a sustainable workforce. To conduct a competency analysis, TD professionals should:

- **Define the job and key competency areas for successful performance.** Using expert performers in the roles can help evoke the correct competencies.
- **Define results for each competency.** Know what the competency produces as an outcome.
- **Define the actions for each result.** Link the outcome to the actions taken to produce it.
- **State behavioral indicators for each action.** These are objective descriptions of behavior that demonstrate whether someone has a competency. They may be stated in a positive or negative way: "Asks others for their opinions" versus "Does not seek input from others."
- **Identify KSAs for each behavioral indicator.** Ask, "What are the knowledge, skills, and attitudes that produce this behavior?"

Once they examine the role down to the behavioral-indicator level, TD professionals should condense the statements into a small number of similar skill areas, and then break each grouping into smaller subgroups. This process allows competencies to emerge so TD professionals can categorize them into a model.

3.4.13.5 Competency Model Categories

Most organizational competency models include three areas:
- **Executive**—KSAs and behaviors required to create vision, lead, strategize, influence, plan, negotiate, and recognize talent
- **Managerial or supervisory**—KSAs and behaviors required to supervise, direct, counsel, discipline, coach, organize, and develop people
- **Functional**—KSAs and behaviors required to perform specific tasks, such as operating a machine, creating a website, or writing a technical training manual

Organizations can use competency models in:
- Talent acquisition for hiring
- Talent development for assessment development and creating L&D programs
- Compensation and rewards for inclusion in job descriptions
- Succession planning and talent reviews for assessing candidates
- Performance management for evaluation

Consistency in usage of competencies across all talent management practice areas is one way to integrate these functions.

3.4.13.6 Competency Model Analysis Techniques

Developing a competency model entails understanding the role or roles thoroughly, which can be validated with an in-depth job analysis. TD professionals who are developing a competency model should involve the people performing the role, communicate thoroughly, and use relevant competencies that pertain to all roles covered by the model.

Suggested approaches to competency model development include:
- **Interview.** TD professionals can ask a series of questions to uncover what a person does on the job. These interviews may be done one-on-one with high performers or supervisors. The primary drawback of an interview is that people may have difficulty recalling everything they do; however,

if only a high-level overview of a job is needed, this won't be an issue. An interview is best when predetermined questions are available, and it is especially useful for professional jobs.

- **Survey or questionnaire.** If a general overview of a job is all that's required, surveys or questionnaires may be good options. An open-ended questionnaire should be used when getting input from employees and managers or analyzing a large number of jobs. Off-the-shelf surveys and online tools are available. However, there are limitations to written instruments primarily because they can be cumbersome to fill out in detail.
- **Observation.** This approach means sitting with the job performer and observing or recording all tasks as they are completed. Observation is used to provide a realistic view of daily activities. However, it can be time consuming because people rarely perform every task in their job descriptions in the span of a day—so this method is best for short-cycle jobs in production. Also, the presence of an observer can sometimes skew behavior. The benefit of this method is that the analyst gains first-hand knowledge of the tasks performed and can ask questions along the way. But because the focus of a job analysis is primarily on the *what* of a job, observation is probably best suited for task analysis.
- **Focus group.** This approach involves a group of people in a specific job function coming together to brainstorm all the duties and tasks of their job. Essentially a group interview, a focus group allows participants to use each other as sounding boards to generate a task list. It is efficient because a group can collectively think of all the tasks performed on the job more quickly than an analyst can compile a list by observing tasks over time.
- **Work diary or log.** Although this method can be used for most jobs, a diary or a log often provides too much data and is difficult to interpret.

3.4.13.7 Leadership Competency Development Models

Leadership competency models are widespread and follow the same process of competency identification that's used for other roles. However, leadership competencies may be more generic across organizations, and customizing leadership competencies from the public domain may be sufficient. Consulting firms and TD suppliers may offer a library of leadership competencies from which TD professionals can start.

Leadership competency models should be designed with simplicity to communicate expected behaviors in an easy-to-understand way. Too many competencies or behaviors can create confusion. Scoping the model in a concise, clear, and relevant way helps leaders apply the competencies to their roles and makes it easier for the organization to use the model to assess, hire, develop, and recognize talent. Competency models may use the same competencies for leaders at all levels and simply provide different descriptions for the specific roles.

To ensure buy-in and acceptance of the leadership competency model, TD professionals should work with the appropriate stakeholders to validate or offer modifications.

3.4.14 Knowledge of Talent Acquisition Strategies and Concepts

I. Talent Acquisition Strategy and Concepts

TD professionals should be aware of what constitutes a talent acquisition strategy and what is required to integrate it throughout their organization.

3.4.14.1 Talent Acquisition Strategy

Talent acquisition is a process for filling vacancies in a timely manner. An organization's talent acquisition strategy must flow from its objectives and be customized to address its unique needs. What works in one organization may not work in another. Thorough research and internal measures should guide the talent acquisition strategy. Different strategies for sourcing, recruiting, and hiring can be based on the talent segments identified in the SWP process as well as the organizational objectives. [See 3.4.13 and 3.4.10]

An organization's brand attracts new employees; the employee experience retains them. The *brand* is the comprehensive marketing concept that differentiates one organization from another. The *employee experience*—sometimes called the employee journey—is the employees' perspective of an organization, which is influenced by their workspace, communication, work-life balance, interactions with teams and supervisors, tools and technology, and many other touchpoints. The organization's brand and the employee experience require systems thinking to ensure consistency and applicability across the organization. [See 3.3.13] The brand describes the organization and the benefits of working there, not just the hiring process. Employees won't stay long if they are promised one thing in the talent acquisition process only to find a much different culture when they come aboard. The organization's mission, vision, and values should inform talent acquisition communications.

TD professionals can assist talent acquisition by contributing to activities such as creating assessment instruments to select candidates, providing interview support, and sharing ideas for global recruitment. They should be sure talent acquisition is using validated and reliable instruments and that they use the same competencies for development and compensation decisions. Typically, these competencies are developed as part of the job analysis process. [See 3.4.13 and 2.2.2.3.2]

3.4.14.2 Active Versus Passive Recruiting

Attracting potential candidates who are not actively looking for a job can be an investment whether the organization chooses passive or active recruiting. Passive recruiting is typically done via social networks (virtual or otherwise) by leveraging relationships that may be sources of talent for future opportunities. However, there are some drawbacks to passive recruiting, such as candidates not having up-to-date resumes or the interview process failing to convince the candidate to move. Also, longer searches may be necessary.

Active recruiting occurs when an organization searches for relevant candidates even before a job is available. The jobs may be visible on the organization's website or LinkedIn, or an organization may target a specific demographic. The drawbacks to this type of recruiting are that it can take longer and cost more—by the time the job opens, hiring managers may feel the pain of lost productivity, which may pressure them into hiring the wrong person (Peterson 2018).

3.4.14.3 Planning for Future Demand

Estimating future demand is part of the SWP process and can identify the types of roles where there is a talent gap. [See 3.4.10.2] Once these segments are identified and the decision to acquire them from outside the organization is made, detailed plans can be developed inclusive of the measures of success. These detailed plans can be informed using data about the current state of the role, such as:
- How much turnover is in the role?
- How much of the hiring demand is based on growth?

- In what geographical area is the role located?
- How difficult will this role be to fill?

3.4.14.4 Distinguishing Between Talent Acquisition and Development

TD professionals should help leadership understand the difference between acquisition and development. *Talent acquisition* is a process for filling vacancies in a timely manner. *Talent development* refers to the efforts that foster learning, employee engagement, talent management, and employee development to drive organizational performance, productivity, and other results. To some, talent development is an important tool for unleashing human potential. To others, it is a set of practical capabilities for creating the processes, systems, and frameworks that advance training and development strategies, succession planning, and learning opportunities. Talent acquisition and talent development should work together to identify qualified high-potential employees and succession candidates. Keeping the pipeline full by offering internal employees mobility opportunities can help improve engagement and retention.

TD professionals can support talent acquisition efforts to identify and onboard competent candidates. They can also create learning journeys that map career progression and the associated knowledge with each role to enhance the mobility of internal talent.

3.4.15 Skill in Comparing and Evaluating Advantages and Disadvantages of Talent Development Strategies

> **I. Sources of Talent: Build, Buy, Borrow, Bound, Bounce, or Bind**
>
> TD professionals should be able to articulate the pros and cons of acquiring talent from outside their organization, developing talent from within their organization, or a combination of approaches to ensure that the right talent is available to meet organizational demand.

3.4.15.1 The Six Bs to Meet Talent Demands

The decision to develop internal employees or externally acquire talent is an important choice for any organization. Developing a workforce plan that compares a current workforce's capabilities to the forecasted needs creates talent management strategies and objectives that include decisions to *buy* or *build* talent or some combination of the two. The six Bs of meeting talent demands are:

- **Build.** Develop talent through education, formal job training, informal training, job rotation, special assignments, and action learning.
- **Buy.** Acquire new talent by recruiting individuals from outside or from other departments or divisions within the organization.
- **Borrow.** Partner with consultants, vendors, customers, and suppliers outside the organization in arrangements that temporarily transfer skills and knowledge.
- **Bound.** Move people through the organization and into higher positions.
- **Bounce.** Remove low-performing or under-performing individuals from the job.
- **Bind.** Retain employees with high growth potential and valued talent (The RBL Group 2009).

There are many instances when several of these approaches will be used in one organization, depending on the organizational objectives and workforce plan. The specific approach may be outlined in the talent management objective.

TD professionals can provide insight about the capacity of current talent because of their participation in development programs. Patterns may emerge that indicate the need for a change in recruiting practices or a modification of job descriptions and competencies. For example, during a series of facilitated workshops for a retail organization, a TD professional may observe that many recent hires lack basic customer service skills. Discussing this pattern with their organization's recruiters may lead to a change in the job description and result in better talent acquisition for roles requiring customer contact.

3.4.15.1.1 Build: Develop Internal Employees
TD professionals should consider these factors when developing talent internally:
- Will the position be difficult to fill?
- Is an internal selection strategically important?
- Are there potential internal candidates, including identified high-potential employees or successor candidates?
- Does the position have a steep learning curve?
- Does the position require continuity and institutional knowledge?
- Do internal learning opportunities exist?

3.4.15.1.2 Buy: Hiring External Employees
An organization may want to consider acquiring external talent if any of the following are true:
- A change is desirable.
- The open position signals a new direction for the organization and requires a fresh perspective.
- Limited internal capacity exists.
- The organization is experiencing high growth.
- An external hire could bring key relationships and intellectual capital.

3.4.15.1.3 Borrow: Using a Contingent Workforce
The use of freelancers, consultants, and contract workers (a contingent workforce) is expected to rise as organizations continue seeking ways to lower costs. These workers are not on the organization's payroll and are used on an on-demand basis. There are many benefits to using a contingent workforce:
- Provide more resources to staff.
- Have access to the necessary talent with the right skills when it is needed.
- Lower other related payroll expenses because the workers are not full-time employees.
- Incur fewer labor costs when demand is low. [See 1.6.6]

Using contingent workers requires an organization to decide how those workers should be treated. Are they part of the internal workforce and included in meetings or learning events? Do they have access to the same perks as the internal workforce? How will they be managed compared with the internal workforce? Poorly managed contingent workers can negate many of the benefits associated with using them.

3.4.15.1.4 Bound: Moving Employees

Moving employees through the organization and into higher positions helps retain talent and keeps the talent pipeline filled. When an employee's career aspirations match the move, their engagement and motivation will be high. In other instances, effective rewards—such as flexible hours or work arrangements or job sharing—may help motivate employees in the short term and engage them in the long term.

3.4.15.1.5 Bounce: Removing Underperformers

Removing low performers or underperformers should be done according to organizational policies. Sometimes, development efforts are tried and expectations are explained, but an employee's performance doesn't improve. In these cases, removal from the position is the only option. If possible, employees should be moved to another more suitable position; otherwise, they should be removed from the organization itself.

If a large group of employees is being let go due to a downturn, organizations can help by offering early retirement, severance packages, or outplacement assistance. The TD function may be able to provide additional services for downsized employees like reskilling, resume writing, or interviewing skills programs.

3.4.15.1.6 Bind: Retaining Top Talent

A special focus on retaining identified top performers, high-potential employees, and successor candidates helps an organization maintain a talent pipeline. These talent groups tend to have many opportunities in the job market and will take those opportunities if they are not being actively prepared for new roles within the organization.

3.4.15.2 Comparing the Options for the Organization

There are pros and cons to each of the six Bs. The effects of using these different approaches may result in unintended consequences for an organization or factor into an employee's decision to either remain with the organization or find a new opportunity elsewhere. Also, if employees think nothing is being done to support their careers, engagement levels will be affected. [See 3.3.10]

Developing talent can take time, especially if the needed competencies are not closely related to the individuals' current capabilities. Nevertheless, if time is available, developing talent in such situations may be the best long-term solution. If an organization's strategy is to grow in a certain market or segment, it may be worthwhile to build the talent according to the organization's specific needs. On the other hand, if efforts are made to upskill or reskill some employees, the employees not selected for the development opportunities may think their careers are being stalled.

Acquiring new talent from outside an organization can also take time and may be difficult to source if a job is in demand. Current employees may get upset if they see others with less experience being hired at salaries higher than their own. Salary compression occurs when newer employees earn more than current employees and complicate established compensation and reward plans.

If time is of the essence and an organization does not have the proper skills mix to meet its objectives, it may decide to borrow talent by using a contingent workforce or subcontracting workers. However, current employees may perceive contingent workers as possible replacements and fear losing their jobs. The costs could be much higher than acquiring or building talent, but over time, as internal workers take on the roles of the outsourced workers, the costs may decrease.

Moving employees into higher positions may help retain an experienced workforce, but if policies regarding work hours and workplace are not viewed as fairly administered, an organization may not be able to retain the desired workforce.

Underperformers must be addressed as soon as possible, or employees who are performing may become disgruntled. On the other hand, reassignments or removal must be transparent and clear to avoid creating unintended fear.

Efforts to retain top talent through binding decisions can backfire. Some organizations may offer "stay" bonuses if employees resign, but this practice can prompt numerous resignations as other employees hope for the same bonus. It may be better to focus on developing this talent and moving them while they are still employed. The TD function has a large role in binding employees to the organization.

TD professionals should build a solid business case for using any of these approaches for succession planning. The business case should address the pros and cons as well as any unintended consequences and risks associated with each approach.

3.4.16 Skill in Designing and Implementing a Performance Management Strategy

> **I. Performance Management**
>
> TD professionals should design and implement a performance management process that effectively meets the needs of their organization and its employees and is integrated with other talent management processes and programs. Proper management of individual and team performance leads to better engagement, retention, and organizational success.

3.4.16.1 Designing Performance Management

There are many types of performance management tools, and organizations may have different tools for different roles.

- **Rating scales** indicate an employee's performance level:
  - Critical incidents list specific behaviors that separate effective from ineffective performance.
  - Graphic rating scales list different factors used to rate performance on an incremental scale, such as job knowledge, work quality, and competencies.
  - BARS (behaviorally anchored rating scales) combine critical incident and graphic rating scale approaches.
- **Management by objectives (MBO)** is a flow down of top-level organizational goals that specify the tasks, deadlines, and measures of success. The goals typically include *what* will be accomplished in very specific terms and *how* (what competencies are exhibited).
- **Narratives** assess an employee's strengths, development needs, past performance, potential performance, and recommendations for improvement.
- **Comparisons** look at one employee's performance with that of one or more others.
- **Checklists** can be simple or weighted and use performance elements.

- **360-degree feedback** allows an employee to receive anonymous feedback on performance from peers, direct reports, and supervisors, and compares the feedback to a self-assessment. [See 3.1.4.3 and 3.3.10.3]

TD professionals should be aware of the problems many of today's performance management systems have. Performance management has become an annual check-the-box administrative activity. Performance reviews are also used for multiple purposes—determining compensation actions, providing feedback on performance, and identifying potential succession candidates, among other things—which can lead to confusion and devalue the main objective of managing and enhancing an employee's performance. Lastly, the tools used for performance reviews are not always suited to the role. For example, jobs that are routine in nature may not lend themselves to an MBO (management by objective) approach that sets stretch performance goals. Forcing a tool to a role leads to a lack of effectiveness in the process.

TD professionals should also be aware of new performance management approaches. Many of these approaches start by removing ratings and rankings, which provides a better opportunity for a focused discussion on performance without the concern of making compensation decisions from one data point (such as the rating). In addition, many organizations are shifting from a once-a-year event to more frequent conversations on performance. Employees expect feedback more than once a year, and if they are continuously provided feedback, they can adjust their performance and succeed.

3.4.16.2 Implementing Performance Management

Implementing any performance management process involves significant work to ensure the process is robust and effective. TD professionals should also train managers in the process and hold them accountable for its successful implementation.

All performance management processes have these activities in common:
- At the beginning of the performance period:
  - Clarify responsibilities and expectations of the role.
  - Establish accountability for goals, standards, and expectations.
- During the performance period:
  - Provide learning opportunities and build capabilities.
  - Develop action plans for development and skill enhancement.
  - Review progress.
  - Provide coaching and feedback.
  - Take corrective action when necessary.
- At the end of the performance period:
  - Provide feedback and evaluation on the entire performance period.
  - Identify new learning and development actions.

3.4.16.3 Integration With Other Talent Management Processes

Many organizations integrate performance management with other talent management processes. This is a natural starting point for creating a seamless, talent-focused organization. [See 3.4.1.7]

Here is how performance management can be integrated:
- Strategic workforce planning produces job descriptions and competencies that can be used for managing performance.
- Gaps in competencies and other skills identified in a performance management process can be identified and addressed through TD programs.
- Performance management can be aligned with an employee's career development goals, providing direction to achieving those goals.
- Performance evaluation typically drives compensation, succession, and high-potential employee decisions. Alignment with these processes can be based on the use of the same knowledge, skills, and attitudes used in the performance management process.
- Performance management has a significant impact on employee engagement and retention. If done well, it can enhance employee engagement and retain talent. [See 3.3.10]

REFERENCES

ATD (Association for Talent Development). 2018. *Lifelong Learning: The Path to Personal and Organizational Performance*. Alexandria, VA: ATD Press.

Bennett, N., and G.J. Lemoine. 2014. "What VUCA Really Means for YOU." *Harvard Business Review*, January–February.

Biech, E. 2018. *ATD's Foundations of Talent Development: Launching, Leveraging, and Leading Your Organization's TD Effort*. Alexandria, VA: ATD Press.

Boller, S., and L. Fletcher. 2020. *Design Thinking for Training and Development: Creating Learning Journeys That Get Results*. Alexandria, VA: ATD Press.

Business Dictionary. 2007. "What Is Creative Thinking?" Business Dictionary, January 31. businessdictionary.com/definition/creative-thinking.html.

Burkett, H. 2015. "Talent Managers as Change Agents." Chapter 20 in the *ATD Talent Management Handbook*, edited by T. Bickham. Alexandria, VA: ATD Press.

Burner, T., L. Supinski, S. Zhu, S. Robinson, and C. Supinski. 2019. *The Global Skills Shortage: Bridging the Talent Gap With Education, Training, and Sourcing*. Alexandria, VA: SHRM Research Department. shrm.org/hr-today/trends-and-forecasting/research-and-surveys/documents/shrm%20skills%20gap%202019.pdf.

Center for Talent Reporting. n.d. "Home of Talent Development Reporting Principles (TDRp)." centerfortalentreporting.org.

Dweck, C.S. 2006. *Mindset: The New Psychology of Success*. New York: Random House.

Galagan, P., M. Hirt, and C. Vital. 2020. *Capabilities for Talent Development: Shaping the Future of the Profession*. Alexandria, VA: ATD Press.

Heifetz, R., and M. Linsky. 2017. *Leadership on the Line*. Boston: Harvard Business Review Press.

Loughlin, S. 2022. "8 Talent Ecosystem Building Blocks." *CTDO*, October.

Peterson, T. 2018. "Recruiting Active vs. Passive Candidates." The Predictive Index, March 14. predictiveindex.com/blog/recruiting-active-vs.passive-candidates.

The RBL Group. 2009. "The Six Bs Overview." Tool 5.1 in *HR Transformation: Building Human Resources From the Outside In*. hrtransformationbook.s3.amazonaws.com/Documents/5.1%206Bs.pdf.

SHRM. 2018. "Succession Planning: What Is a 9-Box Grid?" Society for Human Resources Management. shrm.org/resourcesandtools/tools-and-samples/hr-qa/pages/whatsa9boxgridandhowcananhr departmentuseit.aspx.

Souza, A., and K. Fyfe-Mills. 2018. *Bridging the Skills Gap: Workforce Development and the Future of Work*. Alexandria, VA: ATD Press.

Recommended Reading

Bersin, J. 2022. *Irresistible: The Seven Secrets of the World's Most Enduring Employee-Focused Organizations*. Oakton, VA: Ideapress Publishing.

Lawler, E. 2017. *Reinventing Talent Management: Principles and Practices for the New World of Work*. Oakland, CA: Berrett-Koehler Publishers.

Minocha, S., and D. Hristov. 2019. *Global Talent Management: An Integrated Approach*. London: Sage.

Oakes, K., and P. Galagan. 2011. *The Executive's Guide to Integrated Talent Management*. Alexandria, VA: ASTD Press.

Schmidt, L., and T. Hodges DeTuncq. 2013. *Integrated Talent Management Scorecards: Insights From World Class Organization on Demonstrating Value*. Alexandria, VA: ASTD Press.

Yeung, A., and D. Ulrich. 2019. *Reinventing the Organization: How Companies Can Deliver Radically Greater Value in Fast-Changing Markets*. Boston: Harvard Business Review Press.

3.5 PERFORMANCE IMPROVEMENT

Organizational competitiveness is fueled by improvement in human performance. Performance improvement is a holistic and systematic approach to meeting organizational goals by identifying and closing human performance gaps. This is a results-based effort that includes the ability to analyze performance issues, plan for future improvements in human performance, and design and develop solutions to close performance gaps.

3.5.1 Knowledge of Theories, Models, and Principles of Human Performance Improvement

I. Principles of Performance Improvement

Performance improvement is a results-based, systematic process used to identify the model of successful performance, uncover performance problems, analyze influences, select and design actions, manage workplace solutions, measure results, and continually improve performance within an organization. It is based on open systems theory or the view that any organization is a system that absorbs environmental inputs, uses them to transform processes, and expels them as outcomes. [See 3.3.3]

Human performance improvement (HPI) helps businesses target superior solutions. When using HPI models, a TD professional's goal is to enhance organizational and individual performance by targeting efforts to important business goals that will have the greatest benefit to identified performance gaps. Tools to achieve this goal include analysis, partnering skills, straightforward systems and change, and project management.

3.5.1.1 Purpose of Performance Improvement

Most performance problems are not caused by a lack of skills or knowledge, which means that training cannot solve all problems. Instead, they could be caused by performance challenges such as outdated tools, lack of incentives, lack of resources, poor work environment, poor processes, volume of work, or lack of information.

Performance improvement may also be referred to as human performance improvement (HPI), human performance technology (HPT), performance consulting, or the performance approach. The basis for the current focus of performance improvement is work conducted in the late 1960s and early 1970s by individuals such as Thomas Gilbert, Joe Harless, Robert Mager, and Geary Rummler.

3.5 Performance Improvement

The purpose of performance improvement is to boost organizational results by strengthening individual and organizational performance. Using a systematic approach, performance improvement aims to:
- Identify organizational goals incurring performance problems.
- Define the gap between desired performance and actual performance.
- Identify the causes of a performance gap.
- Select appropriate solutions that will address those causes.
- Implement the solutions.
- Evaluate the results.

Performance improvement expands the search for solutions beyond training. *Training* aims to improve individual performance; however, *HPI* improves individuals' performance as well as organizational performance. It has a wider focus, so training is only one possible solution. TD professionals recognize that the performance of an individual or group of individuals may not be the only source of an organization's inability to achieve its performance goals.

3.5.1.2 Human Performance Improvement Definitions
TD professionals should be familiar with several HPI terms:
- **Clients** are the goal owners who sponsor a project or have engaged a TD professional for support, to complete a project, or to improve a performance.
- **Key performers** are individuals in the target job who consistently produce outcomes with above average results.
- **Stakeholders** may be a single person, group, or the organization that has an interest in the project and can influence its success.
- **Standard performers** are individuals in the target job who are meeting most performance standards.
- **Target job** is the specific job the performance improvement project or effort is focused on.

3.5.1.3 Human Performance Models
There are several different HPI models. Each uses unique definitions and labels, but all follow the same principles and have a similar overall process. The models discussed here are the most prevalent and widely used.

3.5.1.3.1 ATD's HPI Model
ATD's HPI Model is a results-based, systematic process for identifying performance problems; analyzing the influences; selecting, designing, and managing performance solutions in the workplace; measuring results; and continually improving performance within an organization (Figure 3.5.1.3.1-1). The ATD HPI Model follows five sequential steps plus two steps that occur throughout the entire cycle:
- **Step 1. Business analysis** is the most important part of the model. TD professionals should examine the factors affecting the organization's strategic imperative, goals, and outcomes related to the performance problem for two reasons: to produce measurable, time-bound, outcome-focused goals that are the prime targets for the organization or business unit and to identify why the goal is a priority and what its relationship is to other organizational goals. This step ensures that necessary resources and stakeholders are identified and potential issues and risks are recorded. Although business analysis is the first step in the HPI process, TD professionals must also remember that they should have an ongoing understanding of their organization's business, including the processes, operations, goals, external influences, products, and services. Having an ongoing insight into their

organization's strategies, goals, and outcomes is essential to maintaining a strategic role with top management. [See 3.1.1 and 3.1.2]

- **Step 2. Performance and key performer analysis** identifies and clarifies the problem or performance gap by focusing on three areas: desired performance state, actual performance state, and the gap between the two in terms of outcomes. The purpose of this analysis is not to identify problems but to identify factors in the environment that both support and hinder performance.
- **Step 3. Influence analysis** identifies the factors contributing to the performance gap. It answers the question, "Why does the performance gap exist?" How TD professionals complete the influence analysis depends on their circumstances and preferences. They must identify all influences that support and prevent or hinder performance at the desired level.
- **Step 4. Solution selection** requires TD professionals to recommend performance improvement solutions to the client, providing information about their features, benefits, and advantages to enable the client to select solutions that have the desired business effect. The ease of selecting a solution depends on how well the analysis was completed.
- **Step 5. Solution planning and implementation** requires TD professionals to consider available resources, sequencing, timing, and other factors to ensure successful implementation of the approved solution.
- **Evaluation and results** provide data for making decisions. Although it appears to be the last step in the process, it begins during business analysis, which is the first step in the process. Both formative and summative evaluations are important. *Formative evaluation* in performance improvement is the assessment that measures the progress throughout the model, such as a client's expectations, whether the key influencer has been identified, or the use of subject matter experts (SMEs). A *summative evaluation* determines how the solution affected the organization.
- **Manage change influences** surrounds the entire model because, starting with the first step, TD professionals and performance improvement initiatives cause change within the organization. To ensure the performance improvement solution is ultimately successful, TD professionals should manage the change.

Figure 3.5.1.3.1-1. ATD's Human Performance Improvement Model

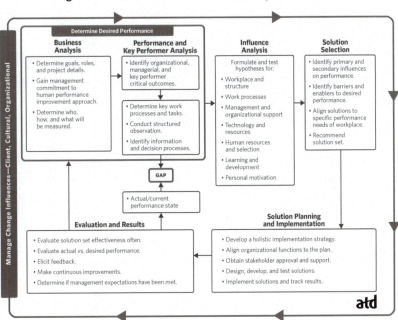

©2015–2024 Association for Talent Development. All rights reserved. For use by permission only.

3.5.1.3.2 Gilbert's Behavior Engineering Model

Gilbert's Behavior Engineering Model identifies six major sets of factors that can either hinder or facilitate workplace performance (Gilbert 2007). Three of these factors—information, resources, and incentives or consequences—are environmental; thus, they are outside the individual performer's control. The three individual factors are knowledge and skills, capacity, and motivation.

3.5.1.3.3 The Sanders and Thiagi Model

Since Gilbert developed his model, many variations have used his approach as a foundation while adding important details. Ethan Sanders and Sivasailam "Thiagi" Thiagarajan, developed their own six-box model that examines the same question as Gilbert: What factors enhance or delay human performance? However, the authors replaced *capacity* in Gilbert's model with *wellness*. In this instance, *wellness* can refer to physical health, mental or cognitive capability, or levels of stress at work.

3.5.1.3.4 The Rummler-Brache Nine-Box Model

Rummler and Brache's model describes the introduction of systems thinking into the organization by defining three performance levels and three performance needs (Figure 3.5.1.3.4-1). A failure at any level will prevent optimal performance.

Figure 3.5.1.3.4-1. The Rummler-Brache Nine-Box Model

The Three Performance Needs

The Three Levels of Performance Needs	Goals	Design	Management
Organizational Level	Organization Goals	Organization Design	Organization Management
Process Level	Process Goals	Process Design	Process Management
Job/Performer Level	Job Goals	Job Design	Job Management

Source: Rummler and Brache (1995).

3.5.1.3.5 Harless's Front-End Analysis Model

Harless's model is a diagnostic model designed to identify the cause of a performance problem. It focuses on three forms of analysis: business, performance, and cause. The steps of front-end analysis are project alignment, analysis of new performance, diagnosis of existing performance, and planning for integrated initiatives.

3.5.1.3.6 International Society for Performance Improvement's HPT Model

The HPT model shares many of the same characteristics as the ATD HPI Model, including operational analysis, performance analysis, cause analysis, solution selection and design, performance solution implementation, and evaluation. One main difference is the elevated importance of change management in the ATD HPI Model, which ISPI's HPT model includes in the solution implementation phase.

3.5.1.3.7 Mager and Pipe's Model of Performance Analysis
Mager and Pipe's model for analyzing performance problems begins with identifying a specific problem and then following a structured flowchart to determine its importance and what would happen if it was solved or ignored. If the problem is important, TD professionals determine whether a skill deficiency is the cause.

3.5.1.3.8 The Holloway-Mankin Performance DNA Model
The Performance DNA Model is the first significant advancement in performance improvement thinking in recent years. While all previous models focused exclusively on finding and correcting performance deficiencies, this model seeks to identify exceptional or key performance and the barriers preventing its attainment. The four analysis phases are business analysis, performance analysis, key performer analysis, and influence analysis.

3.5.1.4 Principles of Performance Improvement
Performance improvement models share three fundamental principles:
1. **Use a results-based, systematic approach.** TD professionals have three options when they respond to a client's request: the wants-based approach, the needs-based approach, and the results-based approach. The results-based approach must be driven by a business need and a performance need and must also be justified by the results of the cause analysis. TD professionals should not assume that the client has correctly identified the problem. Instead, they should identify a measurable performance gap and articulate a relationship between it and an organizational goal.
2. **Focus on outcomes rather than behavior.** *Outcomes* refer to the specific outputs individuals are asked to achieve. *Behavior* refers to the ways that people perform tasks leading to outcomes. Outcomes are easier to detect and measure because many behaviors are not visible (such as planning). Focusing first on the desired end state before looking at the behaviors necessary to reach that performance is logical because "behavior is a necessary and integral part of performance, but we must not confuse the two" (Gilbert 2007).
3. **Organizations are systems.** One of the basic ideas of performance improvement is systems thinking. Geary Rummler, Chris Argyris, and Peter Senge popularized looking holistically and strategically at organizational problems. According to Senge (2006), "The harder you push [on the system], the harder the system pushes back. A name for this phenomenon is "compensating feedback" when well-intentioned interventions (solutions) call forth responses from the system that offset the benefits of the solution." A practitioner can use expertise to fix one component of an organization, but accurately predicting the effect of this change on other parts of the organization is difficult.

3.5.1.5 Organizational Goals and Initiatives
All organizations (for-profit or nonprofit and large or small) have a wide range of goals that exist at various levels in the organization and hold varying degrees of importance, such as strategic initiatives, sales targets, or monthly membership goals. Organizational goals are the drivers; the business analysis determines which performance issues are most important to drive those goals and how to use resources wisely. Performance improvement takes these goals and initiatives into consideration when identifying improvements.

3.5.1.6 The Importance of Change Management Skills

Managing change is necessary during any performance improvement project. Change is one of two steps that occur throughout the entire ATD HPI Model (the other is evaluation). It disrupts the status quo by breaking momentum and continuity in organizations, processes, and performers. Change shocks each of these levels out of a comfortable place and moves them into one of discomfort. This is true even if the change is perceived as positive and useful. Two aspects profoundly influence the course of change in an organization and its effect on people:

- **Change and the forces for change introduce disruptions**, which can significantly diminish both the organization's and the performers' capacities to envision a clear and positive future. The more disruptive a change is to the status quo, the more it diminishes the capacity to envision the future, and the more likely it will have a negative effect on personal and organizational self-confidence, competence, morale, and self-esteem.
- **The path of change is unpredictable.** Leaders may think they know where a change will take them, but disruption of a stable system always produces unintended consequences. Often, organizations get more than expected—and none of what they wanted (Russell and Russell 2003).

TD professionals should start to manage change as soon as the performance improvement project begins. Failure to do so may prevent successful performance improvement results. [See 3.6]

3.5.2 Knowledge of Performance Analysis Methods and Techniques

> **I. Business, Performance, and Gap Analysis**
>
> TD professionals must have knowledge of a variety of analysis methods and techniques to clarify a desired outcome, understand the system, and determine what is preventing an organization from achieving its desired outcome.

3.5.2.1 Business Analysis

A business analysis shows what is important to an organization, and TD professionals should focus on all issues that influence business outcomes. They should identify the important goals, clarify that they are the appropriate goals, determine how specific and measurable the goals are, and ensure there is buy-in and agreement from the client and all stakeholders. Some clients assume that whatever they want is important to the business because they know the business's priorities. However, no matter how insistent clients are, TD professionals should avoid implementing a solution without first conducting an analysis. They need to focus on the business goals and determine how performance is relevant to them.

3.5.2.2 Cultural Analysis

One way to analyze an organization's culture is to complete a culture audit. According to Cynthia Solomon (2004), "The culture audit is the tool to use to get at the substance of an organization's culture so that the organization understands where and how to drive change toward the preferred culture. The preferred culture is one in which the shared ways of thinking and behaving are aligned with other elements of the organization—people, systems, procedures, and structure—to support the strategy of the organization."

3.5.2.3 Performance Analysis

During performance analysis, TD professionals identify the environmental factors that either support or hamper employee performance. They do this by determining the desired performance, the actual performance, and the gap between the two:

- **Defining the desired performance** may involve collecting information from the organization's current and potential customers, suppliers, competitors, stakeholders, and regulatory authorities. TD professionals interview key performers, standard performers, and managers to determine what outcomes are required to achieve the organization's goals. This includes identifying key work processes and tasks. This step answers the question: What outcomes are required to achieve the organization's goals?
- **To measure actual performance,** the TD professional conducts a comprehensive assessment of employees' capabilities and the efficiency of the organizational structure. This may include identifying key work processes and tasks, conducting structured observations, or gathering other information that affects performance. [See 3.5.5.3]
- **The result of the analysis** should reveal the gap between the desired and actual performance levels. Gap analysis describes the difference between desired results and actual (current) results. It combines all the performance issues and forms the basis for the next step in the process—identifying the cause of the gap. [See 3.5.2.7]

An in-depth analysis avoids the risk of optimizing one part of the organization at the expense of others. During the performance analysis, the TD professional gathers data on the causes for both success and failure. This unbiased approach is an important feature of HPI, distinguishing it from other data gathering approaches. It enables TD professionals to identify the model of successful performance while highlighting any significant barriers or gaps to its achievement.

3.5.2.4 Gap Analysis

A gap analysis identifies the performance gap. The process used to gather information includes reviewing documents and other records to learn about current levels of performance and anticipated directions for the organization. TD professionals may use various data-collection instruments and techniques to gather the information, including interviews, surveys, observations, and focus groups. TD professionals should identify both current and desired states of performance. The gap is the discrepancy between current and preferred performance levels. [See 3.5.2.3]

3.5.2.5 Process Analysis

A *process* refers to how people, materials, methods, machines, and the environment combine to add value to a product or service. Everything that happens is a part of the process. Process analysis identifies:

- How the work is completed
- The roles and responsibilities of each individual in the process
- All resources and systems used

A flowchart—a graphic list of sequential steps in a process—is used to help individuals and groups visualize a process by identifying the discrete tasks in the sequence of the activity. Several activities are frequently included under a large task, especially if it's complex, like in the example in Figure 3.5.2.5-1.

3.5 Performance Improvement

Figure 3.5.2.5-1. Flowchart Example

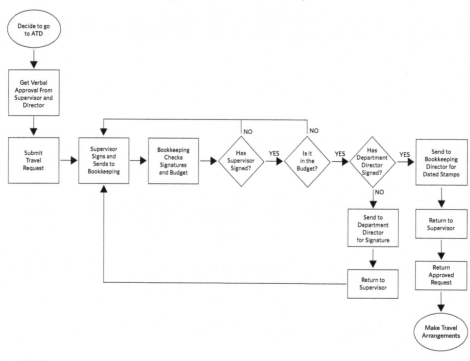

Source: Biech and Danahy (1991).

By defining process boundaries, TD professionals can learn what is included in the process, what is not included, and what the outputs from a particular process are. They can also learn what the inputs are and what departments and individuals are involved in a particular business process. In addition to flowcharts, TD professionals may use other tools and techniques to support analysis, including affinity diagrams, interrelationship digraphs, interviews, focus groups, surveys, and questionnaires.

3.5.2.6 Influence Analysis

TD professionals can conduct an influence analysis if the reason for a gap in performance is not evident.

While TD professionals might think they know why a performance gap exists, they may miss factors that are hindering performance or fail to address all factors, leaving the implemented solution incomplete or unsuccessful. To avoid this, they should focus on employee performance from two perspectives: What do key performers do that makes them successful, and what is preventing all employees from performing at the desired level?

Influence analysis answers the question, why does the performance gap exist? Tools that are most useful include:

- **Cause-and-effect diagrams.** Also called a fishbone diagram or Ishikawa diagram (because it was developed by Kaoru Ishikawa), this is one of the most effective tools for identifying the causes of a performance gap. To use a cause-and-effect diagram, TD professionals should assemble stakeholders (including employees, managers, and executives) in a group setting and document their perspectives within the diagram. [See 2.8.6.4]
- **Five whys.** This tool tells the story of effects starting from the end to the beginning. It provides depth and is useful for complex problems or performance gaps that stem from multiple causes. The steps include asking, "Why?" five times to uncover the root cause of a problem.

- **Pareto analysis.** A Pareto chart is a bar chart that displays the relative importance or frequency of collected data. The Pareto principle, as used in process improvement, states that 80 percent of effects are the result of 20 percent of causes. Joseph Juran (2003), a leading quality expert, called the 20 percent the "vital few" and the rest of the causes the "useful many." Although the percentages are rarely an exact 80/20 proportion, a Pareto chart draws attention to the vital few factors that likely exhibit the greatest payback. Attending to the vital few allows TD professionals to focus their resources on providing solutions that will have the greatest influence on the performance issue. Only after the vital few are addressed should the other 80 percent be tackled.
- **Brainstorming.** This tool requires listing as many ideas as possible and then reducing them down to the most promising. Any number of people can participate, but seven to 10 people in a group is ideal. TD professionals should ensure that participants have enough knowledge about the current problem to provide reasonable input. [See 3.8.3.4]

3.5.2.7 Measurement Criteria and Desired Performance Outcomes

TD professionals should be adept at using measurement. To ensure that desired performance improvement outcomes are achieved, they should use evaluation methods to state whether the objectives were met by measuring the change between baseline performance (presolution) and current performance (postsolution). The ATD HPI Model uses two types of evaluation methods to measure performance outcomes: formative and summative. Formative evaluation in performance improvement is the assessment that measures the progress throughout the model, such as a client's expectations and whether influences have been identified. Summative evaluation of performance improvement is the assessment at the end of the project that determines the effect the solution had on the organization. [See 2.8.1.7 and 3.5.1.2]

According to Robert Brinkerhoff (1998), the purposes of formative evaluation are to:
- Determine if the real cause has been identified.
- Decide if the initiatives are properly designed and selected.
- Ensure that the client's and the stakeholders' expectations are being met.
- Identify lessons learned for the next performance improvement project.

Summative evaluation measures show:
- The initiative's effect on the business goals
- The initiative's effect on the performance goals
- Stakeholders' expectations
- Return on investment (ROI)

3.5.3 Knowledge of How Human Interactions With Work Environments, Tools, Equipment, and Technology Affect Individual and Organizational Performance

I. Influences on Individual and Organizational Performance

TD professionals should understand how employee performance is affected by the environment, the tools and equipment they use, the available technology, and other influences.

3.5.3.1 Identifying Influences

Many things can cause employees to be unable to complete their assigned work. For example, the environment could be filled with conflict, or the work processes could be confusing. The employee could receive conflicting tasks or might not have the equipment and technology required to perform the job. On the other hand, key performers consistently produce outcomes with above average results, so TD professionals should also determine what they are doing to create those results. Seven categories affect an employee's ability to perform as expected:

- Workplace and structure
- Work processes
- Management and organizational support
- Technology and resources
- Human resources and selection
- Learning and development
- Personal motivation [See 3.5.5.2]

3.5.4 Skill in Conducting a Performance Analysis to Identify Goals, Gaps, or Opportunities

> **I. Conducting a Performance Analysis**
>
> TD professionals should be able to conduct a performance analysis, which is the process to measure the gap between the actual and desired performance.

3.5.4.1 Conducting a Performance Analysis

TD professionals begin with a business analysis to define the context in which the performance occurs. This involves collecting information about the organization's current and potential customers, suppliers, competitors, and regulatory authorities to provide a clear picture of the environment in which the work occurs.

The performance analysis follows the business analysis, and TD professionals should identify organizational and key performer outcomes that will be critical to the performance analysis process. To begin, they identify key performers, who are important to performance improvement because they consistently produce outcomes with above average results. Observing and interviewing them will help uncover whether they add, remove, or change steps in a specific work process; use information others don't have; create or use their own job aids; have better tools; or use a different approach.

TD professionals may use other techniques during the performance analysis, such as interviewing SMEs, conducting focus groups, and observing customers, suppliers, and other performers. The goals are to:

- Identify the desired and actual performance levels to calculate the gap.
- Understand the differences between how standard and key performers produce outcomes.
- Uncover potential barriers and enablers of performance.

3.5.5 Skill in Designing and Developing Performance Improvement Solutions to Address Performance Gaps

> **I. Selecting HPI Solutions to Address Gaps**
>
> TD professionals should be able to design and develop solutions that close performance gaps. In addition, they should be able to articulate the features, advantages, and benefits of solutions to stakeholders and decision makers. They should also provide sufficient details about proposed solutions so clients can make informed decisions.

3.5.5.1 Solution Selection Overview

After determining what is influencing the performance problem, TD professionals should select an appropriate performance solution. If the analysis was done correctly, this should be an easy task.

TD professionals should identify primary and secondary influences on performance as well as barriers and enablers to achieving the desired performance. They then review possible solutions and each one's ability to close the gap. However, before recommending a solution, they should confirm that:

- The data suggest clear recommendations to close the gap.
- A full range of possible solutions has been considered.
- The proposed solutions are directly related to the cause of the performance gap.
- They can determine the costs, timelines, and risks associated with each solution.
- They know whether the solution can be implemented internally or if external resources will be required.

3.5.5.2 Barriers and Enabling Forces

TD professionals should recognize that barriers and enabling forces may influence the actual performance, and they should know how to determine these forces. They can use a force field analysis, developed by Kurt Lewin, to identify the forces that maintain the status quo (barriers) and those that support a change (enabling). Lewin called these restraining and driving forces. Once the forces are identified, TD professionals can determine ways to eliminate or weaken the barriers and strengthen or add enabling forces to move from the current state to the desired state. [See 2.8.6.4, 3.3.3.2, and 3.6.3.2]

3.5.5.3 Performance Improvement Solutions

The ATD HPI Model presents seven primary categories that may influence performance. TD professionals should formulate and test hypotheses before selecting an appropriate solution.

3.5.5.3.1 Workplace and Structure

The workplace and structure category addresses influences caused by the workplace and the effectiveness of its structure. It includes tangible resource factors that are extrinsic to the performer and can be changed regardless of who is doing the task. It also considers how conducive the environment is to sustaining high-level performance. Examples of influences in this category include:

- Work area that is favorable to performing the task with limited distractions
- Safe workplace that is free of hazards and risks

- Comfortable and ergonomically appropriate location
- Availability and accessibility of tools and equipment
- How equally the work is distributed
- Collaboration and teamwork

Performance improvement solutions in this category provide smoother and more efficient and effective methods for employees to complete their work. Resources can include tools, equipment, furniture, hardware and software, temperature, and lighting. Examples of solutions include:
- Adjustment of ergonomic and human factors [See 3.5.7.6]
- Review of the adequacy of equipment, tools, and fixtures
- Culture reshaping
- Performance appraisals
- Safety review
- Teambuilding exercises

3.5.5.3.2 Work Processes

The work processes category focuses on the structure and sequence of workflow. For example, an illogical sequencing of tasks or an impractical allocation of work across individuals and work units can affect performance results. This includes how the work gets done, in what order, and who is officially supposed to do it. Examples of influences in this category include:
- Extent to which processes are redundant or complete
- Appropriate sequencing of work processes
- Error-free work compared with rework
- Number of processes that flow through multiple functions
- How often work is completed on time and to standards

Performance improvement solutions in this category provide smoother and more efficient and effective processes for employees to complete their work. Examples of solutions include:
- Process redesign
- Job reviews
- Process improvement
- Lean Six Sigma efforts
- Creating a flowchart of the process

3.5.5.3.3 Management and Organizational Support

The management and organizational support category includes the willingness and ability for management and organizations to support the workforce. Influences include:
- Alignment of workers and managers to the work that needs to be completed
- Competition for resources among managers
- Availability and access to managers and supervisors
- Presence of external opportunities and threats
- Logical reporting structure and relationships
- Accountability for results

Examples of solutions include:
- Negotiating a solution for the employee and organization
- Involving union representatives
- Reviewing structure and cross-department efficiencies
- Commitment of resources
- Meetings and dialogue
- Conflict management
- Reorganization

3.5.5.3.4 Technology and Resources

The technology and resources category focuses on the effective distribution, management, and storage of information. Influences pertain to the effective exchange of data among people or machines and should improve information exchange within the organization. Example influences in this category include:
- Timely receipt, accuracy, and availability of information
- Effective use of technology to manipulate information and data
- Effectiveness of technology and data standards
- Valuing data for its level of volume, velocity, variety, veracity, and value
- Ability to convert data from one system to another

To prevent performance issues, data must be transmitted effectively among two or more people, between a person and a machine, or within an information management system. Examples of solutions include:
- Knowledge management repositories
- Networks for information
- Automation and computerization
- Physical resource management
- Communication vehicles, such as emails or webinars
- Availability of data in the appropriate volume, velocity, variety, veracity, and value [See 3.7.1.1]

3.5.5.3.5 Human Resources and Selection

The human resources and selection category focuses on whether the performer is a good fit for the job and the work to be performed. It also considers whether the performer's physical and mental health influence job performance. Influences in this category include:
- Match of role to the employee's natural strengths
- Level of employee engagement
- Job design and job description clarity
- Hiring evaluation criteria
- Interview process and selection
- Adequacy of onboarding
- Mental and physical health or disabilities
- Substance abuse potential

Examples of solutions include:
- Reviewing the recruitment and hiring process
- Relocating an employee to a job that is a better match
- Work-life balance
- Employee assistance programs
- Counseling
- Violence prevention

3.5.5.3.6 Learning and Development

The learning and development category focuses on the knowledge and skills required for job performance. There is a broad array of solutions to help the performer master a variety of technical and interpersonal skills. Examples of influences include:
- How well employees know how to perform a task
- Availability and access to quality training
- Accessibility of SMEs and job coaches
- Ease of obtaining on-the-job support
- Availability of appropriate task feedback
- How well employees understand the appropriate context

An inadequate number of skills, inappropriate behaviors, inappropriate skills, or underdeveloped skills cause performance barriers. These skills can be technical or interpersonal in nature. Examples of solutions include:
- Coaching or mentoring
- Conference attendance
- Electronic performance support systems or job aids
- On-the-job training or online programs
- Training (for example, case studies, role plays, and experiential activities)
- Self-directed learning such as reading
- Job shadowing

3.5.5.3.7 Personal Motivation

In the personal motivation category, motivational factors are intrinsic to the performer but may be influenced by the work environment. Learning what motivates key performers is critical. On the other hand, a lack of urgency, importance, or value for the desired behaviors can be negative influences. The level of motivation could be caused by experiences the employee has had in the workplace or by a factor outside the workplace, such as the performer's personal values or family obligations. Examples of influences include:
- Meaningfulness of a job
- Level of feedback
- Number of competing or aligned priorities
- Alignment of personal and organizational values
- Appropriate use of rewards and appreciation
- Adequate compensation, benefits, and other monetary rewards

The solutions should identify intrinsic factors, and key performers will be a good resource. Examples of solutions include:
- Rewards and recognition
- Compensation systems
- Motivation systems
- Employee surveys

3.5.5.4 Partner With Stakeholders for Solution Selection
To reach success, TD professionals should work in partnership with learners, clients, stakeholders, and others. They should help clients approach performance problems by coaching them to define the problems and using a systematic process for improving performance. They should involve key stakeholders in every step of the performance improvement process, especially solution selection.

Solution selection may involve working with specialists in their areas of expertise, which requires good listening skills, trust, and respect for their knowledge and expertise. Through this partnering process, TD professionals gain the credibility needed for clients to agree to a solution that will achieve business results.

As TD professionals analyze all improvement solutions, they should involve stakeholders or clients in the discussions, including the cost and expected returns. TD professionals should be able to discuss how these factors fit into the approved budget for the initiative. If a solution costs as much to implement as the anticipated effect on the organization will return, another choice might provide greater gains.

3.5.5.5 Selecting Solutions Using Decision-Making Methods
Several decision-making tools exist to help with the solution selection process:
- **Multivoting or nominal group technique** is a structured method a team can use to brainstorm a wide range of responses to an issue, clarify each response, and rank the responses from most to least important. The outcome of multivoting is a rank-ordered list of causes or solutions—each clearly defined and understood by team members.
- **Affinity diagrams and interrelationship digraphs** are useful in selecting performance improvement solutions because they enable stakeholders to see which influences have the greatest effect on business results.
- **Countermeasure matrix** enables TD professionals and stakeholders to identify appropriate countermeasures for the influences that are causing the issues and rank one to three potential solutions. The actions required to implement each solution are identified as well as the cost and time required for each action. Each solution's rank is based on identified costs, the time required for each action, and the anticipated effectiveness of solutions.

3.5.5.6 Ethics and Integrity
Performance improvement work has ethical implications, so TD professionals will need to make many decisions about ethics:
- How will they treat sensitive information found in their analyses?
- How will management use the information? (For example, is the project being done only to eliminate jobs?)
- Was anything uncovered during the analysis that has internal political implications? Legal implications? Ethical issues?

3.5 Performance Improvement

Because of HPI's influence on individuals and the organization, TD professionals must model ethics and integrity throughout the process. They should use their organization's code of ethics or standards for performance and integrity to guide their decisions when faced with any ethical dilemmas. [See 1.6]

3.5.5.7 Implementing Solutions

TD professionals should develop a holistic implementation strategy by obtaining stakeholder approval and support and aligning organizational functions to their plan. The plan may include designing and testing solutions. The goal of this step is to implement the solution to the target audience.

3.5.5.8 Evaluating Performance Improvement Solutions

Performance improvement can only be accurately gauged using measurement because it results from assessment, evaluation, and reflection. TD professionals should approach performance improvement measurement by determining:
- How to measure
- What to measure
- When to measure (or not measure)
- How much to invest in measurement

To accurately measure the success of a performance improvement solution, TD professionals should possess strong knowledge of:
- Formative and summative evaluation measures
- Measurement processes
- Goal attainment models
- Output models
- Levels of evaluation
- Balanced scorecard approaches

Using this information, they can build an evaluation plan that provides input throughout the process about whether they are moving in the right direction.

3.5.6 Skill in Designing and Implementing Performance Support Systems and Tools

I. Designing and Implementing Performance Support

TD professionals should have the skills to design and implement performance support systems and tools. They should also understand that few employees can learn everything they need to do their work, so providing performance support systems and tools is one way to support them. TD professionals should also be able to discuss the advantages that performance support tools can provide by optimizing employee performance on the job, reducing the costs associated with on-the-job errors, and enabling continuous performance improvement.

3.5.6.1 Performance Support Defined

Performance support provides just enough information to complete a task when and where a performer needs it. It is embedded within the natural workflow and is organized for use within a specific context, such as the location or role that requires completion.

3.5.6.2 Five Moments of Learning Need

There are five fundamental moments of learning that make up the full spectrum of learning and performance support requirements. They provide a framework for helping performers become and remain competent in their roles. Performance support is addressed in each moment:

- **Apply.** Performers need to act upon what they have learned, including remembering what they forgot or adapting to a new situation.
- **Learn new.** Performers are learning how to do something for the first time.
- **Learn more.** Performers are expanding what they've learned.
- **Solve.** Performers address problems when they arise or when things don't work as intended.
- **Change.** Performers need to learn a new way of doing something, requiring them to change skills that are deeply ingrained in their practices.

3.5.6.3 How Performance Support Tools Aid Performance

Providing training and development for everything an employee needs to know about a job isn't possible or preferable. Tapping into the apply moment of learning—when employees need to perform on the job—may require instant access to tools that are tailored to their role and situation that they can apply to complete the job.

Multiple changes in today's work environment often require employees to learn something new in real time on the job. In these moments of performance, they may need to use performance support tools to learn new information or learn more information if they lack the time to step away from their jobs.

In the *solve* moment of performance, a well-designed support tool can be used to diagnose and solve a problem an employee may encounter. In the *change* moment of performance, tools can be designed to help employees understand what has changed and how. When these changes are factored into the performance support tools, employees can continue with their work.

3.5.6.4 Designing Performance Support Tools

To design an effective support tool for learners, TD professionals should think about it from the learner's perspective, consider the physical environment, and make it easy to access. Designing a tool begins at the moment of need in the workflow. The TD professional should conduct a rapid job-task analysis, which is a systematic approach for identifying what employees need to do at the learning moment. This involves SMEs who understand the environment as well as the tools (such as software applications) that are required to complete specific job tasks. Although performance support can be complex, it must be easy for users to access what they need. TD professionals should have a learner test new performance support tools before distributing them to a wider audience.

3.5.6.5 Examples of Performance Support Tools

TD professionals should be aware of and understand how to use tools and support systems to increase employee performance and reduce the amount of time they spend looking for information related to their jobs. Performance support tools such as checklists, job aids, or other electronic support systems should be available to employees when and where they need them.

Examples of electronic performance support systems (EPSS) include:
- E-learning
- Mobile apps
- Learning portals
- Interactive PDFs
- How-to videos
- Searchable knowledge bases

Examples of nonelectronic tools include:
- Quick reference guides
- Infographics
- Job aids
- Process maps
- Frequently asked questions (FAQs)
- Decision trees
- Checklists

3.5.7 Skill in Conducting Analysis of Systems to Improve Human Performance

> **I. Analysis of Systems to Improve Performance**
>
> TD professionals should understand the principles of performance improvement as well as the models and theories that inform the systematic approach to the process. TD professionals must also recognize, respect, and address the internal and external elements that influence the entire system.

3.5.7.1 Systems Thinking for Performance Improvement

Systems thinking is the process of understanding how things influence one another within a whole. In nature, examples include ecosystems in which air, water, movement, plants, and animals work together to survive or perish. In organizations, systems consist of people, structures, and processes that work together to create an effective organization.

Systems thinking plays a significant role in performance improvement because it examines problems holistically to find the most effective place to create an appropriate performance solution. It allows TD professionals to determine what underlying, fundamental relationships are causing the problem rather than being forced to react. Once the underlying barriers and enablers are determined, TD professionals can make changes to improve performance.

Because performance improvement involves introducing changes to an organizational system, systems thinking increases awareness of the effects that those changes will have on the entire system and on desired business results. Consider these systems thinking concerns and their links to performance improvement:

- Many problems are complex, and a simple solution may not actually be so simple. Any actions taken may have other consequences that may make the overall situation worse.
- When dealing with a complex system and its many interdependencies, the main objective is to look for the best places for performance solutions, remembering the interconnectedness of all people, processes, equipment, and materials in a system.
- System boundaries are defined to reduce a problem's scope and maintain an analysis focus. Boundaries that are defined too broadly create a complex analysis. Boundaries that are defined too narrowly lead to a localized analysis, possibly excluding significant variables.
- An open system can be influenced by events outside the system; a closed system is self-contained, and outside events can have little influence on it. In reality, many things are a mixture of open and closed systems.
- In a complex system, the influence may not be found near the symptom.
- Resistance behavior will usually get worse before it gets better.
- Many of the interconnections in a system operate through the flow of information. When improving a process, determine where the information exists.
- The least obvious part of a system, its function or purpose, is often the most crucial determinant of the system's behavior.
- Everything humans think they know about the world is a model, but the models fall short of fully representing the real world (Meadows 2008; Senge 2006).

To take a systems perspective, TD professionals require knowledge of many factors that may affect performance improvement.

3.5.7.2 Cultural and Global Awareness

Changes made within an organizational system will affect organizational culture. In turn, the culture of an organization also affects any implemented solutions. TD professionals should be aware of the influence that culture can have on performance improvement efforts and the achievement of strategic goals.

All organizations—especially global organizations—are part of a larger system: the environment in which they operate. TD professionals should be aware of the effects of the global environment on the organizational system.

Some cultural and global factors that can influence an organizational system include:

- Economic factors, such as pricing and local currencies
- Social interactions, such as the norms of the society within which the organization operates and local practices [See 1.4]
- Traditions, such as local holidays

3.5.7.3 Organizational Transitions

Mergers, acquisitions, downsizing, and other organizational transitions involve changes in organizational structure that must be managed. How they are handled depends on the organization's culture.

The effects of organizational transitions on people are often overlooked. Many organizational transitions fail because management doesn't consider the human factors when merging different cultures. Anger, confusion, sadness, and withdrawal are normal reactions to change, and employers who recognize that these reactions will occur during a restructuring can help employees through them. Such assistance may reduce some of the negative side effects. People going through transitions, such as mergers and acquisitions, experience four reactions: disengagement, disidentification, disorientation, and disenchantment.

3.5.7.4 Industry and Corporate Knowledge
TD professionals should be knowledgeable about their organization and its industry so they can better recognize and address the internal and external elements that affect the system when making performance improvements.

3.5.7.4.1 Industry Knowledge
To enact changes that improve organizational results, TD professionals should have a broad understanding of the industry in which their organization operates. For example, this could involve benchmarking to learn more about the industry.

The business analysis phase of the performance improvement process uses the organizational strategy and business environment to identify:
- The organization's rationale for a goal and why it is a priority
- Other organizational goals, including ones that may be competing or contradictory
- Other strategies that have been identified or tried previously to meet the goal
- The competitive environment and what the organization's competition is doing, as well as new and emerging technologies, innovations, market demands, and so forth
- Compliance issues, such as health, safety, and financial reporting requirements by industry, country, or region [See 1.6]

3.5.7.4.2 Organizational Knowledge
To gain a sense of the organization's entire system, TD professionals should develop broad company knowledge, typically in the business analysis step of the ATD HPI Model. This information identifies important business goals and where the organization is not achieving those goals. In addition, this knowledge provides a broad overview of the organization, which enables TD professionals to identify the areas where the most successful changes can happen. Broad corporate knowledge includes:
- The industry segment
- Organizational structure
- Formal and informal power structures
- Knowledge transfer
- How the organization might affect its own industry
- Potential changes

3.5.7.5 How Organizations Learn
To conduct an analysis of the systems to improve human performance, TD professionals should determine how their organization learns. The goal of organizational learning is for the organization to acquire the ability

to successfully adapt to changing environments, increase efficiency, and be more competitive. Organizations gain knowledge through experience from four sources:

- **Individual learning** occurs when individuals learn skills or ideas and implement or transfer the new knowledge to their work, perhaps increasing their productivity. The individuals may or may not share their knowledge with others. When they leave the group without sharing what they know, the organization ultimately loses the knowledge.
- **Team learning** occurs when individuals within a team acquire and share their experience and knowledge with others. If the group uses this information to modify their future actions, group learning has occurred, which promotes teamwork. Peter Senge (2006) defines three dimensions of team learning as the ability to:
  o Think insightfully about complex issues.
  o Take innovative, coordinated action.
  o Create a network that will allow other teams to take action as well.
- **Organizational learning** is the method an organization uses to create knowledge that relates to its mission and organize it in a way that subunits or functions can use. It may occur in every organizational function and activity, at different speeds, and in different ways.
- **Inter-organizational learning** also adds to the company's knowledge base. It depends on alliances, collaboration, and a willingness to learn from one another, occurring in fixed business models, such as franchising situations. By learning from other organizations, an organization may be able to reduce time or expenses, decrease risks, or learn faster by applying the same ideas or modifying them. This is one way to increase innovation.

3.5.7.6 Human Factors of Learning

Human factors, sometimes referred to as ergonomics, is an established scientific discipline used in various industries, especially where safety is critical, such as healthcare and aviation. Other organizations are also becoming more focused on human factors of learning, for example, consumer product design and web engineering. Human factors are the link between knowledge, the environment in which work is conducted, personal circumstances, and communication between team members.

TD professionals should always examine five factors that affect human performance, which are grouped as intrinsic and extrinsic factors:

- **Intrinsic factors**
  o **Knowledge** relates to the cognitive abilities a performer needs to do the job and involves the development of intellectual skills. The effects of a lack of knowledge on individual performance are the inability to identify essential behaviors necessary for effective job performance; the use of incorrect or inefficient actions on the job; and lack of familiarity with systems, processes, and tools.
  o **Skill,** which is closely related to knowledge, refers to physical movement, coordination, or the use of motor activity to accomplish a task. Lacking skills has a similar effect as a lack of knowledge. Training can improve both knowledge and skills and can thus solve performance issues that are based on the performer's inability to do a job correctly.
  o **Desire** is a factor that training cannot improve. The performer may be perfectly capable of doing the task but simply is not motivated to do so. A lack of desire or motivation does not imply that

the performer is unmotivated—it can be caused by lack of feedback; differing priorities; conflicts between personal values and job requirements; rewards for incorrect behavior; punishments for appropriate behavior; lack of appreciation for accomplishments; or lack of adequate compensation, benefits, and other rewards. Motivation issues can originate at individual, organizational, or process levels.

- **Extrinsic factors**
  - **Environment** refers to a lack of resources, such as tools, equipment, furniture, hardware and software, and inappropriate physical conditions. If the environmental conditions are unsuitable, the effect could be the inability to perform. The environment must be at least manageable to support the desired performance.
  - **Opportunity** relates to whether the performer is actually able or allowed to do the job. Employees who constantly have too many tasks that do not support organizational goals may not have the time to do the work that supports those goals.

TD professionals who are addressing performance improvement should use the study of human factors as a starting point to determine if they might be mitigated or avoided during the solution stage. Human factors can be related to the steps in the job, process interactions, individual characteristics—including mindset, skills gaps, or attitudes—or organizational expectations such as workload or limited resources.

REFERENCES

ATD (Association for Talent Development). n.d. "Human Performance Improvement Certificate Program Reference Manual." Alexandria, VA: ATD Education.

ATD (Association for Talent Development). 2016. *Building a Culture of Learning: The Foundation of a Successful Organization.* Alexandria, VA: ATD Press.

Biech, E. 2017. *The Art and Science of Training.* Alexandria, VA: ATD Press.

Biech, E., and M. Danahy. 1991. "Diagnostic Tools for Total Quality." *Infoline.* Alexandria, VA: ASTD Press.

Brinkerhoff, R. 1998. *Moving From Training to Performance.* Alexandria, VA: ASTD Press.

Brinkerhoff, R., A. Apking, and E.W. Boon. 2019. *Improving Performance Through Learning: A Practical Guide for Designing High Performance Learning Journeys.* Self-published.

Gilbert, T. 2007. *Human Competence: Engineering Worthy Performance.* Hoboken, NJ: John Wiley & Sons.

Juran, J.M. 2003. *Juran on Leadership for Quality: An Executive Handbook.* New York: Free Press.

Kotter, J. 2012. *Leading Change.* Boston: Harvard Business Review Press.

Meadows, D. 2008. *Thinking in Systems: A Primer.* White River Junction, VT: Chelsea Green Publishing Company.

Rummler, G., and A. Brache. 1995. *Improving Performance: How to Manage the White Space on the Organization Chart,* 2nd ed. San Francisco: Jossey-Bass.

Rummler, G., and A. Brache. 2013. *Improving Performance: How to Manage the White Space on the Organization Chart,* 3rd ed. Hoboken, NJ: John Wiley & Sons.

Russell, J., and L. Russell. 2003. *Leading Change.* Alexandria, VA: ASTD Press.

Senge, P.M. 2006. *The Fifth Discipline: The Art and Practice of the Learning Organization,* rev. ed. New York: Currency/Doubleday.

Shorrock, S., and C. Williams. 2016. *Human Factors and Ergonomics in Practice: Improving System Performance and Human Well-Being in the Real World.* Boca Raton, FL: CRC Press.

Solomon, C. 2004. "Culture Audits: Supporting Organizational Success." *Infoline.* Alexandria VA: ASTD Press.

Recommended Reading

Elliott, P., and A. Folsom. 2013. *Exemplary Performance*. San Francisco: Jossey-Bass.

Robinson, D., J. Robinson, J.J. Phillips, P.P. Phillips, and D. Handshaw. 2015. *Performance Consulting: A Strategic Process to Improve, Measure, and Sustain Organizational Results*, 3rd ed. Oakland: Berrett-Koehler.

Rummler, G. 2004. *Serious Performance Consulting According to Geary Rummler*. San Francisco: Pfeiffer.

Sanders, E., and S. Thiagaran. 2005. *Performance Intervention Maps*. Alexandria, VA: ASTD Press.

Wallace, G. 2020. *Conducting Performance-Based Instructional Analysis*. Self-published.

Willmore, J. 2016. *Performance Basics*, 2nd ed. Alexandria, VA: ATD Press.

3.6 CHANGE MANAGEMENT

Talent development professionals are well positioned to facilitate change because they connect people, process, and work. Change management is the capability for enabling change within an organization by using structured approaches to shift individuals, teams, and organizations from a current state to a future state. Once initiated, change follows its own nonlinear path in response to uncertainties, reactions, and guidance from those involved. There are tools, resources, processes, skills, and principles for managing the people side of change that practitioners should understand and implement to achieve preferred outcomes. Research shows that most companies don't manage change well, which makes capability in this area a differentiator for talent development professionals.

3.6.1 Knowledge of Change Management Models, Theories, and Tools

> **I. Change Management Models, Theories, and Tools**
>
> TD professionals should understand change management theories, models, and tools and be prepared to support and facilitate their organization's change efforts. Additionally, every solution they implement is a change—they act as change agents, driving positive outcomes that advance the people and organizations they serve.

3.6.1.1 Introduction to Change Management Models

Change is a constant for organizations that expect to maintain a competitive advantage. TD professionals should understand change theories, models, and tools to help their organizations successfully navigate change.

Whether planned or unplanned or deemed positive or negative, all changes affect an organization and those who lead or facilitate it. The need for change is often driven by external factors occurring within the broader society in which the organization operates. When change is implemented within the organization, the impact ideally affects the intended targets of the change but may also lead to unintended consequences for other stakeholders inside and outside the organization. Change is part of growth and learning, and it will occur regardless of what else happens. It needs to be championed to achieve certain strategic or operational objectives while minimizing the discomfort, disruption, and disequilibrium it can create for employees and customers. The organization's leaders, supported by TD professionals, balance the importance of today with changes in the future.

Change management models can serve as road maps for TD professionals to offer guidance and cautions along the road to change. Models demonstrate action and steps that flow from start to finish. Change management tools offer detailed process guidance and can help assess change efforts.

3.6.1.2 Lewin's Three Stage Model of Change

One of the pioneers of change management, Kurt Lewin first presented his three-step change model in 1947. It details three categories:

- **Unfreeze** is preparing an organization for change by breaking down the status quo before implementing a new way of working. Key steps involved in unfreezing include emphasizing the "why" by determining the business case for change, framing the importance in a compelling message, and communicating the change.
- **Change** is the phase focused on helping people work through the change by communicating, dispelling rumors, addressing resistance, and mitigating risks.
- **Refreeze** occurs once the organization and employees are ready for the change to occur. A new organizational structure, policies, job description, and technology are in place and ready for implementation (Lewin 1958).

The *change* category is sometimes called "transformation and movement." Lewin also contributed tools to the change management field, viewing situations as being affected by "a sea of forces in motion." Some forces are positive and desirable, while others are negative and undesirable. His force field analysis tool demonstrates how these forces push against each other to maintain a status quo. Force field analysis is a useful concept to identify the forces that are producing the status quo and find ways to strengthen the positive forces and weaken or eliminate the restraining forces. [See 3.6.3.2]

3.6.1.3 Kotter's Change Model

John Kotter's eight-step model, first published in the *Harvard Business Review* in 1995, begins with an admonishment to create a sense of urgency. From there, the steps include forming a powerful coalition, creating a vision for change, communicating the vision, removing obstacles, creating short-term wins, building on the change, and anchoring the changes in corporate culture. Kotter is a strong proponent of creating short-term wins along the way, believing that nothing motivates more than success. TD professionals should determine how to establish smaller targets that can be achieved along the way to the final change goal and ensure these short-term wins are communicated and celebrated.

3.6.1.4 The ATD CHANGE Model

Most change models and approaches are rooted in Kurt Lewin's original three-step model, and the ATD CHANGE Model follows a similar approach. As the cyclical model shows, organizations are in a constant evolving state, and each change project informs the next change project (Figure 3.6.1.7-1; Biech 2007, 2016, 2022). The six-step model, conceptualized for the TD profession, is easy to remember—the first letter of each step spells CHANGE.

3.6 Change Management

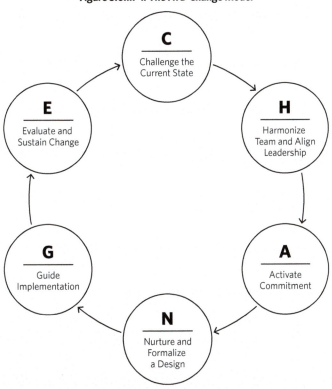

Figure 3.6.1.7-1. The ATD Change Model

The six steps in the ATD CHANGE Model are:
1. **Challenge the current state.** This step recognizes that something can be different—a preferred future that dares the status quo to innovate. It addresses the question, "why?"
2. **Harmonize and align leadership.** This step addresses the need to ensure that leaders are clear about the vision, magnitude, and required actions for leading a change effort. It answers the question "what?"
3. **Activate commitment.** This step is about the employees and processes needed to reach the ultimate goal. There is a need to build commitment, not just compliance, for the effort from everyone. This step answers the question, "How?"
4. **Nurture and formalize a design.** This step encourages change agents or facilitators to use tools to formalize the design, create a communication plan, conduct a risk assessment, select appropriate metrics, and deploy other implementation plans.
5. **Guide implementation.** This step requires that change agents or facilitators keep the implementation moving forward while generating short-term wins and identifying ways to increase resilience.
6. **Evaluate and institutionalize.** This step ensures that the change is embedded into the organizational culture and transforms it to become the new reality.

3.6.1.5 The ProSci ADKAR Model
Introduced in 1999 by the training firm ProSci, the ADKAR model describes five core building blocks necessary for an individual to change the way they work:
- Awareness of why the change is needed
- Desire to change one's behavior to support the change
- Knowledge of how to change by learning the skills to realize the change

- Ability to change focused on time, resources, and support from coaching
- Reinforcement needed to sustain the change by recognizing goal achievement and successes (Hiatt 2006)

Change leaders are advised to manipulate these core building blocks, focusing especially on:
- Project management [See 1.5]
- Communication and training strategies that help employees understand what will change and why, how, and when they will be affected
- Their role in bringing about the change
- Resources available to build skills needed in the changed environment
- Other tools that support the change

3.6.1.6 Bridges Transition Model

Although transition is different from change, it is a concept TD professionals should be aware of. *Transition* is the internal psychological process employees go through when they come to terms with a new situation because of change. William Bridges believed that people need to start with the ending of the former situation prior to addressing the change. The stages in his transition model include *ending*, when people need to deal with their tangible and intangible losses; *the neutral zone*, when repatterning takes place; and *new beginnings*, when people need to develop a new identify and experience new energy. He also believed that leaders will be more successful if they provide the workforce with the four Ps when introducing change:

- Purpose for the change
- Picture of the expected outcome
- Plan for navigating from the current situation to the future
- Part that the employee will play in making the change successful

Bridges encouraged change leaders to establish a transition monitoring team for each change initiative. The team should be made up of a group of employees who don't have formal responsibility for planning the change or authority to make decisions related to it, but who help support two-way communication throughout the change. [See 3.3.3.2]

3.6.1.7 Kubler-Ross Stages of Grief Theory

Although not grounded in scientific research, Elisabeth Kubler-Ross's model recognizes that humans go through five phases following a loss or change. In the 1960's, her work involved the families of dying cancer patients. Her change response cycle phases are denial, anger, bargaining, depression, and acceptance. Kubler-Ross determined that people perceive change as a loss and may move through similar phases.

3.6.1.8 Nudge Theory

Economists Richard Thaler and Cass Sunstein introduced nudge theory in 2008, based on the perspective that people support and embrace change when they maintain their sense of personal control and choice. The theory recommends providing perceptual and motivational nudges, or subtle cues, that guide employees to understand the need for change and to care about changing, to listen to employee feedback about how best to implement the change in their work area, to engineer choices so employees make their own decisions about changing the way they work, and to focus on simple, incremental changes that employees can adopt with minimal effort (Tahir 2020).

3.6.1.9 Six Sigma

Six Sigma is a methodology used for improving customer satisfaction and business processes by reducing process variation. It was developed in the 19th century around the concept of normal distribution, and then Walter Shewhart expanded it in the 1920s. But it wasn't until Motorola brought it into the mainstream in the 1980s that it gained prominence as a methodology to improve business efficiency, improve process quality, and increase bottom-line profits. Six Sigma is a data-driven methodology that provides tools and techniques to define and evaluate each step of a process. The methodology aims to bring operations to a "six sigma" level, which means 3.4 defects out of one million items or events. Tools associated with Six Sigma include the five whys and root-cause analysis. Although not exactly a change management theory or model, it is a methodology that creates positive change in organizational processes.

3.6.1.10 Lean

Lean is a set of management practices used to improve efficiency by eliminating waste based on reducing and eliminating nonvalue-adding activities. It is often associated with Six Sigma and sometimes used in conjunction with it (Lean Six Sigma) because there is overlap between the two disciplines. The key difference between them is that lean management practices focus on reducing waste, while Six Sigma emphasizes reducing variation. In addition, lean practices use fewer technical tools and Six Sigma depends on statistical data analysis and hypothesis testing.

3.6.1.11 Change Management Tools

To help organizations implement change, TD professionals deploy a variety of tools and processes. Most of these processes are designed to help ensure change leaders make more informed decisions about planning and implementing the change, build participation and engagement among individuals affected by the change, foster understanding and support for the change, and ensure employees develop knowledge and skills needed to succeed in their roles in the changed environment. Some of the most used tools include:

- **After action review (AAR)** was first developed by the US Army to encourage individuals to learn for themselves after an activity, project, or task by evaluating and analyzing what happened, why, and how to improve performance. It can be used to assess progress toward a project's goals, identify what's working and what isn't, and agree on lessons learned that can be applied to current or future projects (Zukof 2021).
- **Appreciative inquiry (AI)** is David Cooperrider's approach to large-scale organizational change that involves the analysis of positive and successful (rather than negative or failing) operations. The AI 4-D cycle (discovery, dream, design, and destiny) includes identifying areas for improvement, analyzing previous successes, searching for solutions, and developing an action plan. "AI is about the search for the best in people, their organizations, and the strengths-filled, opportunity-rich world around them" (Stavros, Godwin, and Cooperrider 2015). This positive perspective approach is used throughout a change process to learn (by inquiry) about the strengths and possibilities that can be used in the solution.
- **Commitment charts** are used in change management initiatives to plot key players that will ensure the success of the project. Labels identify how important they are to the effort and may include no commitment needed, let change happen, help change happen, and make change happen. The change agent or facilitator may review the chart to determine where players are and where they need to be

for success. Questions to ponder include "Do they need resources?" "Do they need development?" and "Do they need coaching?"
- **Communication plans** are critical for change efforts to provide details about who will communicate information about the change, specific messages, communication mediums that will be used, and the timing of each message. [See 1.1.5] Deploying strategies for two-way communication should be emphasized (Zukof 2021).
- **A project charter** is a tool used in project or change management that outlines the requirements for the product, service, or process that will be created, and it may include a schedule, key milestones, assigned resources and roles, a budget, a communication plan, or other elements.
- **RACI** is a responsibility assignment matrix that defines the participation level expected of each stakeholder or group for decisions and activities involved with a project or change effort. RACI stands for responsible, accountable, consulted, and informed.
- **Resistance management plans** identify stakeholder groups and individuals who may resist the change, their rationale for not supporting the change, and actions that may be taken to mitigate resistance (Zukof 2021).
- **A risk analysis** identifies and measures risk that accompanies proposed change solutions. It includes compiling a list of all the potential things that could prevent stakeholders from achieving the outcome; rating the probability that each risk event will occur; and identifying causes and possible strategies that could be deployed to mitigate the risk (Zukof 2021). [See 3.6.3.1]
- **A stakeholder analysis** specifies in detail who is affected by the change and how, including the extent to which each group of stakeholders will be affected, their level of influence over successful adoption of the change, concerns, and potential points of resistance (Zukof 2021).
- **SWOT** stands for strengths, weaknesses, opportunities, and threats. It is an analysis tool that identifies an organization's internal strengths and weaknesses, as well as its potential external opportunities and threats. The analytical framework provides input for planning.

3.6.2 Knowledge of How Change Affects People and Organizations

I. The Impact of Change on People and Organizations

During change efforts, TD professionals should recognize the likelihood of a natural tension occurring between an organization and some of its employees.

3.6.2.1 TD Professionals Can Reduce the Negative Impact of Change

An organization's need for change may conflict with its employees' needs to maintain their sense of personal security. Organizations need to keep up with the rapid pace at which their sectors are evolving or risk losing out to their competitors. This means employees need to know what knowledge and skills their organizations will require in the future and what they need to learn to keep pace with the those requirements. When employees learn that organizational change will occur, they may initially experience negative thoughts due to fear of what the future may hold. Whether valid or not, there may be conflicting interests between what the organization requires and what the employee can offer.

Many reasons exist for why individual employees may feel negative about a change, ranging from fearing a loss of status, to feeling a loss of being "in the know," to mourning the loss of friends who voluntarily or involuntarily exit the organization because of the change. At times, employees may be concerned about the additional workload the change may add. Negativity may also arise when employees feel that their sense of competence is threatened if they are unable to meet new expectations.

TD professionals can help prevent as well as decrease the impact of change by partnering with leadership and following these best practices:

- Ensure that senior leadership keeps employees informed about the organization's continuous need to change and the organization's future.
- Make sure employees have opportunities to develop skills the organization will require in the future to address change.
- Coach leaders at all levels to learn the skills required to lead change.
- Understand how talent requirements and resourcing levels may need to be adjusted.
- Build a resilient workforce.
- Confirm that leaders and employees are aware of the needs and expectations of the other, involved in planning for the future, and working toward the same goal.

TD professionals should help employees overcome their resistance by understanding typical human reactions to change, such as Kubler-Ross's stages of grief. They can use the Bridges transition model, which refers to the internal psychological transition process individuals experience as they come to terms with a changing situation. TD professionals can also reduce the negative reaction some employees may feel by encouraging their involvement and engagement in the change process. [See 3.6.1.6 and 3.6.1.7] TD professionals should be prepared to help organizations implement change to reduce any negative impact throughout the change process. [See 3.6.2.4]

3.6.2.2 Forces of Change on Organizations

Most TD professionals have experienced many changes—some may be major organizational shifts while others may be smaller programmatic changes. Change occurs more frequently now than ever, so it's incumbent upon TD professionals to possess the knowledge, skills, and tools to facilitate it. The key is to be aware of the driving forces that are the indicators of change. Factors that cause change may come from outside or inside an organization. Outside factors—such as technological innovation, major societal events, global competition, changes in customer demands, and shifts in the natural environment—motivate leaders to implement changes within their organization as they strive to retain a competitive advantage. Organizations may apply environmental scanning skills and capabilities to try to anticipate external factors, which all have the potential to produce internal change. [See 3.8.2]

3.6.2.2.1 Speed of Change

The growth of content, innovation, and technology is faster now than in any other era in history due to the marked increase in complexity and the rising rate of uncertainty. This growth drives the speed of change in organizations. External change is outpacing organizations' ability to drive internal change, and better ways to adapt are needed (Kotter, Akhtar, and Gupta, 2021). Today's leaders and organizations must keep up with this rapid pace to succeed, establishing the expectation for employees that change will be continuous.

Peter Senge, author of *The Fifth Discipline* (2006), points out that leaders cannot keep up with rapid change through the traditional top-down control mentalities or without a formal structure or process because total chaos would ensue. Today's leaders need to find the right balance between too much and too little organizational structure so that organizations can rapidly adapt their capabilities to survive.

3.6.2.2.2 Technological Innovation

The pace at which organizations adopt new technologies is advancing at a rapid pace, typically driven by the desire to achieve or sustain a competitive advantage. Some of the technology trends predicted for the next few years include:
- Data fabric, which integrates data across systems and users, increasing user access to data while simultaneously reducing the need for human data management
- Advances in the need for and tools used to provide cybersecurity
- Decision intelligence, artificial intelligence, and other resources to support integrated data analytics that are designed to help employees make more informed business decisions (Gartner 2022)

TD professionals also experience rapid technology change in their organizations with the increase in remote and hybrid work, as well as in the TD profession with an increase in immersive, blended, hybrid, and online learning programs of all kinds.

3.6.2.2.3 Global Competition

Globalization in its literal sense is the transformational process of local or regional phenomena into global ones. It can be described as a process of blending or homogenization by which the people of the world are unified into a single society and function. It is a combination of economic, technological, sociocultural, and political forces. Globalization is often used to refer to economic globalization, which is the integration of national economies into the international economy through trade, foreign direct investment, capital flows, migration, and the spread of technology. The changing landscape of competition from other countries often forces organizations to change to keep pace and remain competitive in the global market. Globalization may lead an organization to shift operations to places outside its country of origin, where there are lower costs, more readily available resources, and new markets for goods and services. Changes in the labor pool due to globalization may also lead to changes in the demographic composition of work teams and the creation of more virtual work teams with members physically located in different locations.

3.6.2.2.4 Customer Expectations

The product development cycle has accelerated. New products and services that used to take years to introduce are now hitting the market in a matter of months. Customers expect their needs to be met faster and with more personalized service. This may lead an organization to implement completely new business models to meet customer demands and to modify the systems and processes used to develop, produce, and deliver products and services, driving changes to its structure and the skills it needs to operate (Kulkarni 2018). In addition, Salesforce (2020) reports that customers expect consistent connected interactions across all departments, believe companies should offer new products and delivery services, and expect data collection. Finally, *Forbes* reports that customers have a lower tolerance for delayed product development (Ranjan 2021).

3.6.2.2.5 Government Regulation

As political administrations change, legislative priorities often shift, creating new and modified regulations and requirements. Changes in the economic and geopolitical environment can lead legislative bodies to enact new laws and policies, which create pressure on organizations to modify their own work processes, policies, and procedures. Changes to government regulations may lead organizations to embark on change initiatives they had not planned. As government regulations shift, organizations may find that they need to re-evaluate business priorities and steer resources toward initiatives that ensure compliance.

3.6.2.2.6 Restructured Organizations

For organizations to work, several elements must align, including structure, strategy, work and job designs, systems and processes, people, rewards, and culture. When an organization restructures due to a merger, acquisition, downsizing, redesigned operating model, technological improvements, or outsourcing work, there is a chance that people and processes will no longer align with the organization's business goals and objectives. Recently, many organizations have restructured to address a hybrid workforce.

3.6.2.2.7 Succession Planning

Succession planning is a systematic process for identifying and developing candidates to fill leadership or management positions. As senior and experienced workers leave an organization or move into other roles within the organization, a potential knowledge and skills gap can exist unless the organization is proactively developing its talent to fill these gaps. Even so, different people in different positions typically create opportunities for change. [See 2.5]

3.6.2.2.8 Skills Gaps

The skills gap, or the difference between employees' current abilities and the skills needed for their jobs, continues to grow. *Fortune* magazine reports that 71 percent of CEOs anticipate that a skills and labor shortage is their greatest business disrupter (Conklin 2022). They estimate that 85 million jobs will go unfilled globally by 2030 due to a skills gap. This issue continues to be a huge force of change as organizations make adjustments, but it is an opportunity for TD professionals to help their organizations understand what is needed to position their workforce for the future.

3.6.2.2.9 Employee Expectations, Turnover, and the Balance of Power

Today's workers have extensive skills and knowledge, and knowledge workers are often critical for holding an organization and its processes together. With competitors offering better salaries, career advancement, and job security, today's employees are less likely to build lifelong careers with their employers than previous generations. In addition, they are more likely to move to different organizations during their careers in search of improved job satisfaction. The threat or reality of turnover can drive change in an organization, shifting power away from leaders to employees that the organization wishes to attract and retain. The tide of incoming and outgoing people may also bring different perspectives and work experiences. It may take some employees time to adjust to the organizational culture and processes of a new employer; it may also take time for some employees to adjust to the perspectives and styles of newly hired co-workers. Turnover can create challenges for all employees as they lose or gain co-workers.

3.6.2.2.10 Transferred Knowledge to Emerging Leaders

Leaders who move up the management chain face special challenges as they transition from one level of responsibility to the next. With each step up the corporate ladder, a leader's responsibilities expand, and their decisions affect more people. Although emerging leaders and the transition process are a significant force of change, some organizations lack a development program for the transition into strategic leadership. [See 1.3.7 and 1.3.8]

3.6.2.2.11 Senior Leadership Hired Externally

When organizations hire external candidates for top leadership and management positions, the new leader or manager may bring numerous advantages and serve as a force of change in the organization. Executives from other companies or other industries often bring fresh ideas and processes, particularly in key functional areas such as HR, finance, and supply chain management. They may also be hired explicitly to help an organization shift its work culture to provide more competitive advantages. Whether an external hire succeeds in the new position often depends on the company's TD team, which must understand the organization's business strategy and put systems in place to ensure new executives easily transition to the new culture.

3.6.2.2.12 Increased Diversity in the Workforce

Integrating diversity (genders, ages, races, and cultures) into organizational change efforts can enhance the success of most types of organizational change. In fact, organizational change and diversity efforts are linked because most organizational changes involve components of diversity. To manage how generation gaps and diverse leadership affect today's work environment, TD professionals should understand what motivates each group, ensure equity and inclusivity, and provide learning opportunities that are flexible and accessible enough to meet the needs and interests of each group. They should also help others be aware of how increased diversity requires changes to organizational expectations, such as customs, business norms, dress codes, relationships, and communication. [See 1.4]

3.6.2.3 Impact of Change on Employees

TD professionals acting in a change agent role focus much of their attention on the behavioral effects of change, but psychological and social aspects are important too. Psychological and social influences prompt predictable questions from the people affected by change. TD professionals involved in the change process should anticipate questions and reactions that will arise when the change is implemented. They should demonstrate empathy by placing themselves in the position of those whom the change affects.

TD professionals should understand that when a change is introduced, it often triggers a person's survival instincts. Any change may create doubts and questions in their mind, and some are predictable. Social considerations include changes to an individual's relationships with others in their work group and their relationship with the organization as a whole. In essence, changes may trigger stress responses for some individuals.

A person's sympathetic nervous system responds to stress in two ways: fight or flight. The brain tries to maintain homeostasis to protect the body from threats, and change—whether good or bad—is a disruption of this state. As a result, the body's natural reaction kicks the limbic system into gear, creating the fight or flight response. Knowledge of this genuine physical reaction to change provides insight about how employees deal with change initiatives, and TD professionals need to know how to address employees' responses.

Neuroscience demonstrates that the brain is wired to conserve energy, with uncertainty and ambiguity registering as a threat or error—"something that must be corrected before one can feel comfortable again" (Rock 2008). [See 3.6.4.10] Even a moderate degree of ambiguity can be debilitating and feel stressful because the brain needs to work harder, spending more neural energy to resolve what it perceives as an error condition. However, a mild degree of uncertainty may be perceived by the brain as a challenge and feel energizing instead of depleting because the body releases adrenaline and dopamine. TD professionals should help leaders plan and communicate change in a way that balances creating enough novelty and uncertainty to spark employees' interest, attention, and desire to solve problems, without being debilitating. [See 2.1]

When TD professionals understand human reactions to change, they will be better prepared to support and lead a change effort. Knowing about Kubler-Ross's stages of grief and Everett Rogers's model will help them understand how change affects people. [See 3.6.1.7]

Everett Rogers (2003), a professor of rural sociology, researched human reactions to change and introduced a model that predicts them. This model has become a standard reference when planning and guiding organizational change processes. Understanding how some people will adopt a change early while others lag behind is key to informing a change strategy. However, employees should not be permanently labeled. An employee may be an early adopter for one type of change but a laggard for another. For example, an employee may be an avid supporter and early adopter of a technology change but then cling to an existing HR process they don't want to give up. The model is a bell curve composed of five categories:

- **Innovators** make up 2.5 percent of individuals and are the first to embrace the change; they are proud of being adventurous (Rogers 2003). This category is usually placed at the beginning of a bell curve on the left side.
- **Early adopters** make up 13.5 percent of the population and like to take on new challenges. They are trend setters who stay informed and are generally the influential members of organizations.
- **The early majority** makes up 34 percent of individuals. They are thoughtful about change initially, become positive about the change based on their observations, and then become deliberate acceptors of the change. This category and the late majority form the peak of the bell curve.
- **The late majority** includes 34 percent of the population who are skeptical about change. They may only accept the change because of peer pressure.
- **Laggards** include 16 percent of individuals who hold onto the past and resist change. This outlook becomes problematic if they reject the change completely. This category is reflected in the downslope of the bell curve on the right side. [See 2.1.4.4]

TD professionals may focus much of their attention on the behavioral effects of change, but they must not forget the psychological and social aspects. They should use change management tools and processes to help anticipate questions and reactions that will arise when change is implemented. The key lies in TD professionals placing themselves in the position of people whom the change will affect.

3.6.2.4 Prepare for How Change Affects People and Organizations

Change is constant and the pace will continue to get faster. TD professionals should be prepared with a specific skill set to address the constant churn of change in their organization. Many of these skills are similar to those required of a change agent or facilitator, including:

3.6 Change Management

- Strong communication skills [See 1.1]
- Empathy [See 1.2]
- Knowledge of project management [See 1.5]
- Deploying innovative, targeted learning initiatives [See 2.2 and 2.3]
- Coaching leaders, stakeholders, and others in the change process [See 2.7]

Although TD professionals are uniquely positioned to act as change agents, they should be aware of the many tactics for change because their role and assigned tasks will vary for each initiative:

- Practice resilience or the ability to adapt to difficult events that disrupt others' lives.
- Maintain a positive attitude.
- Demonstrate flexibility and adaptability.
- Learn new skills.
- Practice deploying change management tactics, tools, and processes.
- Schedule time to reflect and think about the exciting future and the positive, available options.
- Learn or relearn time management skills, such as focusing, chunking projects, and trying not to multitask.
- Adopt a growth mindset, help others try new skills and behaviors, assess what's working, and make changes to fix what isn't working.

Recognize individuals who project valued roles such as early adopters, change champions, or change agents who ensure an organization's change management success.

3.6.2.5 Difference Between Planned and Unexpected Change

TD professionals typically know when a planned change will occur because they will inevitably play some role in ensuring it is successful. Often, change is addressed by planning for and maintaining employee involvement; ensuring consistent communication; and helping employees develop the skills they need to be successful in the changed environment.

Although a planned change is more manageable, unexpected changes occur too, sometimes leading to a feeling of chaos or crisis in the work environment. During crisis, TD professionals have less time to react and plan to manage the change effectively. Typically, organizations that use an Agile approach to change fare best during unexpected changes. [See 3.6.4.4]

When addressing an unplanned change, TD professionals need to attend to the same areas they do for a planned change, such as employee involvement, communication, and skill development; however, they will likely take on a more intense focus with an abbreviated timeline. TD professionals can expect some of these adjustments:

- **Engaging** employees may require TD professionals to identify a new method to attain involvement after leaders plan the change, as opposed to ideally before the plan. They may need to identify techniques to gather employee input quickly, such as online polling. They will need to decide what input they are looking for based on the phase of change that is underway. At times, more general involvement may be needed, such as broadly asking employees what they think will and won't work with the change.

- **Communication** should be timely and frequent, even when the message has not been perfected. The critical requirement is to provide information as fast as possible to prevent inaccurate information from spreading. Often, all the answers will not be available, but it is critical to deliver what is known and to be transparent about what is not known. TD professionals may consider creating frequently asked questions or other information sources that can be shared with all managers to ensure that everyone is disseminating the same message. They should also use as many communication methods as possible. It is highly unlikely that employees will be concerned about having too much communication.
- **Development,** or creating the necessary learning and growth opportunities to equip employees for the change, may take on more of an intense approach as TD professionals learn what new skills, processes, or relationships are needed. Assessing, identifying, and documenting these skill or process requirements is an important part of the TD professional's responsibility to ensure a successful change in addition to creating and deploying the learning content itself. Additionally, employees may need more short-term temporary supports, such as help desks or online Q&A sites. TD professionals will want to maintain ongoing communication with supervisors to stay abreast of what employees need.

As any unexpected change occurs, TD professionals will need to be ready with short answers and fast solutions. For example, recognizing that supervisors may be the best solution to fast and accurate communication or that reaching out to employees directly through crowdsourcing may be the best way to get immediate involvement. TD professionals should be prepared for unplanned changes by reviewing their change management processes and asking how they would fare in an unexpected crisis.

3.6.3 Skill in Assessing Risk, Resistance, and Consequences to Define a Change Management Approach

> **I. Assessing Change Risk, Resistance, and Consequences**
> To be successful in planning for and implementing change efforts, TD professionals should be skilled at managing the problems that will arise, including risk, resistance, and unforeseen consequences.

3.6.3.1 Risk
Risk is a measure of the potential inability of an organization to achieve its objectives as planned. It has two components:
- The probability or likelihood of failing to achieve the planned outcome
- The consequences or impact of failing to achieve the planned outcome

Risk management is the process of addressing risks, which may include identifying, analyzing, or developing options; monitoring risks; or mitigating potential risks. A *risk assessment* is a tool that helps identify and measure risks accompanying a change solution. TD professionals may use a specific instrument, electronic tool, or follow these steps:
- **Risk identification** involves compiling a list of all the potential things that can occur to prevent achieving the outcome of the change effort. It can be completed by asking individuals or groups or by reviewing past lessons learned.

3.6 Change Management

- **Risk analysis** begins by examining the risk events and assigning a risk rating based on a definition and numeric scale. This number is usually posted on a risk level chart as shown in Figure 3.6.3.1-1. The assigned rating places "probability of occurring" on one axis against "impact to the effort" on the other.
- **Option development** includes identifying the basic causes and mitigating strategies that will minimize the risks if they happen.
- **Monitor and address risks** requires the TD professional or other responsible individuals to ensure that the identified mitigating strategies (which modify, alleviate, or prevent the risk from occurring) are implemented as needed (Biech 2007).

Figure 3.6.3.1-1. The Risk Level Chart

Impact to the Effort

	1	2	3	4	5	6	7	8	9	10
10			Finance / Testing				Network	New Versions		Data Conversion
9			Budget Execute							
8					Expert Turnover					
7							Business Changes			
6										
5										
4										
3								Regain Momentum		
2			Smaller Network Needs							
1										

Probability of Occurring

Probability		Impact	
1-2	Remote	1-2	Program objectives unchanged
3-4	Not Likely	3-4	Minor impact on people and process
5-6	Possible	5-6	Reduced capability; still mission-capable
7-8	Highly expected	7-8	Significant; affects ability to obligate funds
9-10	Near Certainly	9-10	Quality and quantity reduced; unable to meet organizational requirements

Source: Biech (2007).

3.6.3.2 Resistance

Resistance occurs when employees engage in actions designed to prevent or delay change from progressing. By understanding who the change will affect and how, and by establishing open communication with affected stakeholders, TD professionals can determine the reasons employees might resist change and help change leaders identify actions they can take to prevent resistance from occurring or to minimize its impact. Most change management models include a discussion about resistance to change; some even divide resistance into two categories: resistance as a natural phenomenon or as a more nefarious action intended to block the change.

Ideally, employees who don't support a change will openly share their concerns with TD professionals. These concerns may be valid, especially if the change plan is based in part on mistaken assumptions or includes oversights and errors. In these cases, employees may think that it's their obligation to resist changes they believe won't succeed or will damage the organization in some way.

While there are cases when employees look forward to a change, resistance occurs when they believe the change threatens something tangible or intangible that they value. Employees may resist a change if they fear the change will lead to a loss of status, autonomy, important relationships, or job security or permanently increase their workload (Rock and Page 2009). They may also resist a change if they perceive that it has been forced upon them, as opposed to something they chose.

As organizations embark on successive or simultaneous changes, employees may resist if they feel overwhelmed by the pace of change. Employees may also resist supporting a change if an organization has failed to implement changes successfully in the past.

Sometimes, leaders assume that anyone who isn't supporting a change initiative must be an obstructionist who is attempting to sabotage the effort, establish barriers, or even recruit others to resist the change. That is not necessarily true, and resistance and obstruction must be distinguished from one another. Resistance is something TD professionals should seek to understand and support people through. To successfully change, people need to work their way through the process. They may need time and space for initial failures while learning new skills. They need to understand how the change will be positive. Individuals who obstruct may simply dislike the person leading the change, hold different ideas of success, or be dealing with personal issues. TD professionals must recognize obstruction and conjure up confidence to address it using conflict management skills.

TD professionals need to create opportunities to gather ideas and feedback from employees throughout the change process to ensure legitimate concerns are identified and addressed before problems arise. To be successful, TD professionals acting as change agents or facilitators should never make personal judgments about individuals, introduce resistance as an observation, or allow obstructionists to share their perspectives. TD professionals may also need to clearly express expectations for future behavior, actions, or decisions.

A tool that is effective for addressing resistance (but also for many other needs in change management) is a force field analysis, which is a tool used to assess which forces within an organization will support or prevent the attempt to introduce a change. Often, the tool produces a clear understanding of what needs to be done for organizational success and understanding personal needs.

Force field analysis, created by Kurt Lewin, recognizes two types of forces: driving and restraining (Figure 3.6.3.2-1). Driving forces help implement a change, whereas restraining forces inhibit change. Because they are defined based on their positive or negative effect on the change, forces that may appear to be driving can be restraining. For example, although incentive systems are generally regarded as a positive benefit, if the existing system is not reinforcing the new behaviors, it becomes a restraining force. [See 2.8.6.4 and 3.6.1.2]

Once TD professionals identify driving and restraining forces, they should develop strategies to either take advantage of driving forces or reduce the effects of restraining forces. By increasing driving forces or reducing restraining forces, the status quo can move toward the wanted change. In addition, because systems move toward equilibrium, it is advantageous to reduce restraining forces while increasing driving forces. However, TD professionals should be aware that an increase in driving forces may naturally increase restraining forces.

3.6 Change Management

The plan for reducing resistance should consider the time necessary for the people and the organization to react to the change. It should also account for the fact that although it's necessary to allow time for adjustment, the timeline still needs to be met.

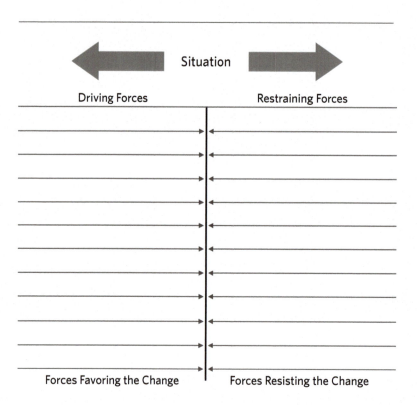

Figure 3.6.3.2-1. Force Field Analysis

Source: Biech (2016).

The best strategy for addressing resistance is to prevent it from occurring in the first place. TD professionals should guide leaders to:

- Implement changes (when possible) in manageable chunks that limit change fatigue and avoid overwhelming employees.
- Create opportunities for employees to make choices regarding how they will incorporate the change and get involved so they have ownership of the change.
- Establish two-way communication channels to ensure leaders can hear and address employees' concerns.
- Use every communication medium available to keep employees informed and reduce uncertainty.

Finally, TD professionals should not be surprised if a leader shows signs of resisting change. Sometimes leaders may be the biggest barrier to change.

3.6.3.3 Consequences
TD professionals should be aware of the consequences that can occur during a change effort. First, change and the forces for change introduce disruptions that can diminish both an organization's and its employees' capacities to envision a clear and positive future. The more disruptive a change is to the status quo, the more it diminishes the capacity to envision the future, and the more likely it will have negative consequences on personal self-confidence, competence, morale, and self-esteem.

Second, the path of change is unpredictable. Change leaders may think they know where a change will take them, but disrupting a stable system often produces unintended consequences. Organizations may get more than expected—and none of what they wanted—so it's important to focus on risks.

3.6.3.4 Overcoming and Preparing for Issues Related to Change
TD professionals should not attempt to manage a change with a one-size-fits-all strategy. Change is personal, and risk, resistance, and the consequences of change are often attempts to maintain the status quo. TD professionals can use change management tools or try these tactics:
- Establish clarity around the purpose, goals, and realities of the change including who will be affected by the change and how.
- Identify specific reasons for the issue and address the root causes.
- Create mechanisms for candid, two-way communication to identify ideas and concerns and reduce uncertainty.
- Deliver training on resiliency and how to manage change.
- Provide training and resources for employees to build the skills that support the change.
- Establish a way to continuously assess progress, identify what's working or what's not, and take action based on lessons learned. [See 3.6.4]
- Provide opportunities to celebrate and reward successes.

3.6.4 Skill in Designing and Implementing an Organizational Change Strategy

> **I. Designing and Implementing an Organizational Change Strategy**
> TD professionals should be able to use multiple skills to design and implement an organizational change strategy.

3.6.4.1 Change Management Basics
TD professionals should know about change management basics, especially when they are called upon to be a change agent or facilitator. They should be familiar with the change categories and their required actions.

3.6.4.1.1 Change Categories

Organizational change initiatives vary in size and scope, but generally fall into three categories:
- **Incremental change** happens when a change is simple and people are able to continue what they are doing just in a different way. This is a small adjustment made toward a targeted result, such as upgrading to a new version of an existing computer system.
- **Transitional change** occurs when a change is more complex, but other organizations have undertaken it and their best practices (or benchmarks) can help guide it. An organization could, for example, offer new services or create new products to achieve a goal such as increasing revenue.
- **Transformational change** is the most difficult type of change. It may disrupt a business' operating model, alter the direction of an industry, or put the business at the forefront of a new paradigm. External forces—such as a significant decrease in revenue or increases in competition—are usually the driving forces for transformational changes. Examples include restructuring an organization's business strategy or an overhaul of products or services.

Within these categories, TD professionals may find themselves focusing on different factors, such as strategy, processes, or people. Each one will have a different influence on the expectations, planning, timeline, and goals. Largescale change initiatives often require attention in each of these areas:
- **Strategy focus**—leadership, structural, re-engineering, divestitures, acquisitions, mergers, consolidation, and systemic organizational initiatives
- **Process-oriented focus**—initiatives involving technology, software development and installation, systems, continuous (process) improvement, total quality management, and business expansion
- **People-centered focus**—culture, customer relationship management, HR services, and other actions that affect the workforce

3.6.4.1.2 Defining the Current State

In most cases, TD professionals acting as a change agent or facilitator will find a pain point that is their organization's motivator for steering away from the status quo. Factors include shrinking market share, increasing customer demands, or continuing inefficient, obsolete processes. The organization may already be experiencing a pain point or may anticipate that it will likely experience the pain point in the future, so the pain or risk of maintaining the status quo is too great. A significant change will be accepted if it is proven to those affected that the present way of doing things is (or will be) more painful than what accompanies the transition. The pain of the present is the prime impetus for movement into the alternate future state.

To define the current state, TD professionals should collect and analyze data, determine their organization's readiness to make a change, and assess the consequences of not changing. They may also build the business case for change, which may include the data that was gathered, the current situation, competitive considerations, business and operational impacts, preliminary risk assessment, cost-benefit analysis, and a timeline. [See 3.1.7.2 and 3.3.1.3]

3.6.4.1.3 Defining Intended Outcomes

In partnership with leaders, TD professionals may be involved in establishing specific, achievable outcomes. This starts with the definition of the business or the organizational need for change. TD professionals may perform an analysis to identify business goals and determine what change is critical to achieving them. Because it is important to start with determining the business goal, it's critical to establish organizational priorities. Ideally, the business goal should be quantitative and time-bound, as well as a legitimate focus of the business.

3.6.4.1.4 Promote the Change

In partnership with leaders, TD professionals should present the need for change to others with a convincing argument based on facts that explains where their organization is, where it needs to go, and why. They may also identify how market forces and customer demands are affecting the organization. Explaining the consequences for the company if nothing changes can be very powerful too.

3.6.4.1.5 Sponsorship

TD professionals help identify and secure organizational sponsorship, which supports the project by committing necessary resources. A lack of commitment to a change management effort can be a serious risk factor.

3.6.4.1.6 Change Management Standards and Resources

The Association of Change Management Professionals (ACMP) is a global community of change management practitioners. The *Standard for Change Management and ACMP Change Management Code of Ethics* provides additional information about designing and implementing change management, processes, professional standards, and other change management basics that can be useful to TD professionals and their organizations as they plan and implement change initiatives.

3.6.4.1.7 Change Management Training and Certification.

If TD professionals find themselves involved with numerous change efforts or if their role is leaning toward managing change in their organizations, they should seek additional change management professional development. A certificate program or certification from ACMP can provide the skill set that is required to be a successful change agent or facilitator.

3.6.4.2 Infrastructure and Roles

Commitment to change means creating an infrastructure to support the change design and implementation and assigning roles to people charged with executing the strategy. Change management roles are unique to every organization. A leader or sponsor champions the effort, giving it credibility; a change leader provides the means to achieve the objectives of the change initiative; and a TD professional coordinates the process and implementation, some organizations may choose to change some of the roles. Although there are many other tasks than those outlined in Table 3.6.4.2-1, it provides several important distinctions.

3.6 Change Management

Table 3.6.4.2-1. Change Management Roles TD Professionals May Hold

Change Leader or Sponsor	Change Agent or Facilitator
• Develops the vision • Provides input to the business case • Establishes a sense of urgency • Assembles a change management team • Shows credible and unwavering commitment • Displays endorsement in actions and words • Removes barriers in the system • Responds to emerging issues • Leads the change implementation team • Communicates the vision constantly • Supports actions addressing reactions • Approves metrics • Holds others accountable to attain metrics • Delivers the implementation plan • Holds others accountable to implementation • Supports practices to institutionalize change • Implements rewards and consequences • Stays the course • Celebrates successes	• Supports the change leader or sponsor • Organizes and drives the effort • Collects and analyzes data • Measures organizational readiness • Assists building a business case • Leads the change management team • Identifies change champions • Coaches leadership and change champions • Recommends implementation team members • Facilitates teams and coaches team leaders • Prepares the implementation plan • Recommends strategies and processes • Coordinates implementation • Ensures milestones are met • Designs the communication plan • Addresses reactions to change • Recommends metrics • Conducts the risk assessment • Identifies and exploits short-term wins • Evaluates change effort • Identifies rewards and consequences • Creates a plan for change-ready organization

Source: Biech (2007).

The planning and design of most change initiatives is the work of the change management team, which is often referred to as a transition or implementation team. This team plays a critical role in implementation and should, therefore, be assembled carefully. TD professionals should begin thinking about potential team members as soon as the change is under consideration by reviewing three issues:

- **Leadership and influence.** Trusted senior managers and others with power and authority will ensure the change keeps moving in the right direction.
- **Business unit representation.** Including representatives of affected departments will ensure smooth implementation within their groups.
- **Knowledge, skills, and attitudes.** Team members who are positive about the change will see themselves as problem solvers and persevere to the end.

3.6.4.3 Process Used to Plan and Implement a Change Strategy

An organizational change strategy is a plan that describes the specific steps that occur to move from the current state to the desired state. TD professionals may use the ATD Change Model to guide them through the process of planning and implementing change. Depending on the size of the organization and the size of the change initiative, others will have roles in planning, organizing, and implementing the effort. Although the final step in the process is evaluate, TD professionals should evaluate progress at every step along the way. [See 3.6.4.4]

The key actions from the ATD CHANGE Model that TD professionals may take to support the change effort are listed here: [See 3.6.1.4]

1. **Challenge the current state** recognizes that something can be different—a preferred future that dares the status quo to innovate. Key actions include:
   o Collect and analyze data.
   o Determine organizational readiness.

- Establish change management roles.
- Assist with building the business case.

2. **Harmonize and align leadership** addresses the need to ensure that leaders are clear about the vision, magnitude, and required actions for leading a change effort. Key actions include:
   - Coach the leader.
   - Prepare the system for change.
   - Help select and build an implementation team.
   - Create a compelling vision.
   - Design a communication plan.

3. **Activate commitment** is about the employees and processes needed to reach the ultimate goal. There is a need to build commitment, not just compliance, for the effort from everyone. Key actions include:
   - Review current information.
   - Create the road map for key steps.
   - Prepare people for the change.
   - Refine the communication plan.

4. **Nurture and formalize a design** encourages change agents or facilitators to use tools to formalize the design. Key actions include:
   - Select appropriate metrics.
   - Formalize the design.
   - Conduct a risk assessment.

5. **Guide implementation** requires that change agents or facilitators keep the implementation moving forward. Key actions include:
   - Encourage involvement.
   - Engage stakeholders.
   - Reach out to naysayers.
   - Build momentum with short-term gains.
   - Identify ways to increase resilience.

6. **Evaluate and institutionalize** is the wrap-up step. Key actions include:
   - Evaluate the impact and the process.
   - Institutionalize the change.
   - Make sure teams have wrapped up.
   - Plan a celebration (Biech 2007, 2016).

3.6.4.4 Agile Change Management

TD professionals should understand Agile change management and how it applies an iterative approach to the change process. When an organization adopts an Agile approach to a change initiative, they plan the change to proceed through a series of short bursts, called sprints, that provide immediately recognizable value to end users. The goal is to create interest in and motivation to change by creating a series of short-term wins. In Agile change management, the focus is on designing the change from the end users' perspectives, using their stories to explain what's changing, establishing priorities from their perspectives, gathering user feedback throughout the change, and adjusting plans based on that feedback and interim results (Bersin 2022).

3.6.4.5 Individual Change Readiness

Employees may experience several readiness stages before they can make a true commitment to change. First, they may not recognize or may even deny that they need to change; next, they may contemplate a change; then, they'll recognize that a problem exists and there are ways to deal with it. Only at this stage are they ready to make a specific, concrete plan. Finally, in the fourth stage, they act on the plan (Prochaska, Norcross, and DiClemente 1994).

TD professionals should recognize that employees will be in different stages of the change process, and some may need help to feel motivated. In general, the percentage of people motivated to change depends on how the change is communicated versus some innate lack of commitment. If a sense of urgency or clear business imperative is created, the benefits of a change are explained, and individuals have an opportunity to influence the change outcomes, the percentage of those committed to change can be considerably higher sooner. [See 3.6.2.3]

3.6.4.6 Pacing and Transition Strategies

Today's organizations may exist in a continuous state of change—one initiative after another is introduced due to market conditions or leadership's desire to respond to trends or requirements (Pasmore 2015). This constant upheaval can create change fatigue among employees. If possible, one way to balance the pace of change is to intersperse major change initiatives with carefully paced small steps that are implemented and evaluated over time.

There are two types of pacing methods:
- Time-based pacing involves setting milestone dates, which can then be adjusted as needed.
- Event-based pacing involves triggering actions when the right event occurs.

Pacing also requires TD professionals to realize that changing marketplace realities will influence how rapidly a change needs to be implemented. In other words, goals and timelines still need to be established, but their pace may need to be stepped up or delayed for reasons out of their control.

Celebrating milestones is another way to provide a pacing break because it provides an opportunity to not only evaluate but also reflect on a change and celebrate the contribution of team members and colleagues. A celebration lifts spirits, reinforces important values, and promotes a sense of accomplishment. A final celebration also establishes closure for a successful project.

Transition Schedule

To ensure full implementation and acceptance of a change, change leaders, sponsors, and TD professionals should create a transition schedule that considers several factors. A transition schedule should:
- Initiate open dialogue with affected employees to listen effectively and respond to their concerns.
- Identify customers' expectations to avoid unexpected backlash.
- Put temporary procedures and processes into place in case a system or process does not work correctly.
- Plan for financial concerns that may emerge if the change goes over budget.
- Prepare the organization's workforce to ensure seamless integration.
- Coordinate the timing of other events in the organization to avoid change fatigue among employees.

3.6.4.7 Communicating Change

TD professionals should use the six Cs of communication to manage change effectively by being clear, correct, complete, concise, coherent, and courteous. [See 1.1.1.3]

Successful organizational change is directly tied to effective communication, both verbal and nonverbal, in person and digitally. TD professionals should create a communication plan at the start of a change effort to guide the change. Knowing who is affected by the change and applying the appropriate communication style is helpful. If the TD professional's verbal and nonverbal communication expresses confidence, then gaining employees' acceptance of the change plan will be easier. Written communication should also be clear and concise, a skill that greatly contributes to credibility and alignment.

The communication process is made up of a two-part (dyadic) system: speaking and listening. When planning a change communication, TD professionals should consider the environment, message, sender, medium, and feedback elements of the communication process. [See 1.1.1.2]

The sponsor of the change initiative, business leaders and department managers should communicate the reason for a change to help employees understand and recognize the need for change—they must first know where the organization is currently and the goals of the change. When they understand the current state of the company and its goals—through a state-of-the-organization address from upper management, for example—employees can better appreciate the value of the impending change. Regular updates should be part of the communication plan.

Strategic communication is critical when implementing major changes and should be part education and part marketing. Change leaders should consider the implementation as they would a new product, focusing on how to convince customers they need it and building trust in the new product. Strategic communication necessitates evaluating what employees need to do and persuading them why it is in their best interest to change behaviors. When communicating about a change initiative, TD professionals should project the desired change in a way that makes it relevant and appealing to those affected while simultaneously being honest about any downsides of the change effort. Employees can easily see through and reject any effort to sell to them. Instead, to build trust, communication must be honest and complete. Additional considerations for effective communication include providing periodic updates on how the change initiative is progressing and establishing appropriate communication channels for employees to provide their input to leaders.

To build engagement and support for a change initiative, TD professionals need to design practical communication plans that provide many opportunities for employees to voice their input, ideas, and concerns throughout the change initiative. TD professionals need to create communication plans that leverage the most effective source for each message, so they should:

- Ensure the change sponsor and business leader convey the overall business purpose of the change, rationale, and intended outcomes.
- Provide supervisors with the information they need to share with their employees.
- Confirm that supervisors have the details about the change before they are shared with employees to prevent putting supervisors in an awkward position.
- Enlist the support of supervisors and department managers to reinforce messages about the change with their teams.

3.6 Change Management

Communicating about changes may occur in formal meetings, informal conversations, emails, newsletters, shared collaboration spaces, websites, social media, or visual reminders (such as posters, videos, and surveys). Often the most compelling messages:

- Use storytelling.
- Convey information to targeted employees that they need to understand.
- Connect with employees on a rational, emotional, and action-based level.

TD professionals need to select the appropriate communication medium for each task, ensuring a mix of information sharing and listening. [See 1.1.5] Actions often convey far more than words, so TD professionals should coach leaders to modify their behavior so that it serves as a model of the behavior expected of employees.

3.6.4.8 Practices to Build Critical Mass

Active support and participation are always required to achieve business or organizational goals. TD professionals' ability to engage others in the identification, assessment, and solution of problems and issues is a critical success factor in change management. They should support this by demonstrating the need, developing employee competencies, and owning the process.

Demonstrate the Need

Before an organization can transform itself, it must recognize the need to do so. Failure to identify the need for change is among the most common barriers to an organization's ability to adapt to new requirements. Attitudes like, "We've always done it this way," "It has always worked before," and "If it ain't broke, don't fix it," are roadblocks on the way to change. Management's commitment is critical to the success of any organizational transformation.

Leaders must have a clear vision of where they want to lead their organizations and a plan for accomplishing it. The first step is to break from old, self-limiting paradigms—preconceived ways of looking at the world are major barriers to change. Lasting change requires adjusting an organization's culture by changing its shared expectations, values, and beliefs. TD professionals can help by partnering with leaders to assess the need by:

- Conducting external and organizational scans
- Collecting data to identify business needs
- Identifying potential change initiatives
- Analyzing the data
- Delivering data analysis feedback [See 2.2.2 and 2.8.3]

Develop Employee Competencies

It is easier to build critical mass when employees throughout organization have the required change management and statistical data competencies. Six Sigma, a data-driven approach to analyzing and solving root causes of business problems, is one way to develop these competencies among employees. [See 3.6.1.9] At the strategic level, Six Sigma delivers improvements and dollars to the bottom line.

At the operational level, Six Sigma ensures customer specifications are met and decreases process variation—the cause of defects that affect customers negatively. It provides specific tools and approaches (process analysis, statistical analysis, lean techniques, and root-cause methods) that organizations can use to reduce defects and improve processes, which increases customer satisfaction and drives down costs. To successfully use Six Sigma in an organization, individuals must develop competencies in statistical data analysis and process redesign and share those approaches with their colleagues.

TD professionals have a huge opportunity to initiate and deploy Six Sigma or other approaches that support data-driven, evidenced-based decision making. It takes intensive training to give employees the appropriate skills, but the payoffs are enormous.

Owning the Process

The details of the change management plan should explain how employees will be personally involved in the change because involvement is a key way to foster commitment to the change. Although the plan identifies where the organization needs to go and what it will do to get there, employees still need to decide how work processes will be redesigned to meet the changing needs. Their involvement allows them to increase their learning and problem-solving skills and gives TD professionals an opportunity to coach them. The effort to redesign work also provides employees with opportunities to work through the feelings and emotions that are part of adapting to change.

3.6.4.9 Motivating Employees During Change Efforts

Change is a business decision that has significant emotional and political effects on people. What motivates employees will vary, but TD professionals can help them understand why motivating factors are critical elements to consider. Motivation helps minimize resistance and avoid failure to institutionalize the change. Failure to maximize retention during a major change can also affect its outcome.

Motivation is classically defined as the desire to work, or the amount of effort put forth on a job. Everyone has a mindset that determines how and why they behave in a certain manner, and these actions are based on motivational factors, such as personal goals, organizational and personal reward systems, and job enrichment.

Motivating employees to achieve their potential is one of the most difficult challenges facing any manager or supervisor. During a change initiative, the need is expanded, and TD professionals can help management understand how to sustain and even build employee motivation during a transition. Employees may be asked to serve double duty by continuing their current jobs and taking on additional responsibilities as part of the change management team. Training managers and supervisors in employee motivation theory allows them to better understand what motivation is and how to elicit it from their employees. For example, the most valuable recognition comes directly from an employee's manager (Clifton and Harter 2019).

To help managers correct course, TD professionals should create a practical list of motivating ideas they can share with managers, including personal discussions about the future, professional growth opportunities, or giving their employees a chance to lead a project. One of the best things TD professionals can do is help management understand how to motivate employees during a change initiative by rewarding those who have embraced change and providing support to those who have not.

According to Daniel Pink's (2009) motivation theory, people have an innate need to direct their own lives, learn and create new things, and contribute to their organization and the world. His theory uses three terms for these needs:

- **Autonomy** gives employees some freedom over some aspects of their work.
- **Mastery** allows employees to master their own learning.
- **Purpose** gives employees a chance to contribute to a cause greater than themselves.

TD professionals should help managers leverage employees' innate motivations by incorporating opportunities for employees to decide how best to implement the change in their own workspace.

In today's workplace, it's also not unusual for employees to recommend and become the driving force behind changes that are adopted. Many workplaces ask employees to suggest ideas for making continuous improvements in the way work is performed in the organization. In these cases, employees may need to motivate their managers to adopt a change! Some organizations have invested in software to support listening to employees with pulse surveys. TD professionals can help their organizations establish and manage processes for employees to recommend needed changes.

3.6.4.10 The SCARF Model

The SCARF model, developed by David Rock (2008), may aid TD professionals as they guide changes. Rock's neuroscience model is based on research that implies that five social domains activate the same threat and reward responses in the brain that are relied on for physical survival. When change is likely, the five domains of human social experience—status, certainty, autonomy, relatedness, and fairness (SCARF)—activate either the primary reward or primary threat circuitry of the brain. The model is based on three central themes:

- The brain treats social rewards and threats with the same intensity as physical rewards and threats (Lieberman and Eisenberger 2009).
- The ability to make decisions, solve problems, or work together is reduced by a perceived threat and increased by a perceived reward (Elliot and Fryer 2008).
- A threat response is more intense (and more common) and needs to be minimized in social situations (Baumeister et al. 2001).

TD professionals who understand that the five domains automatically trigger a human response can prepare the environment when planning for a change effort. The five domains are:

- **Status**—the relative importance of self to others
- **Certainty**—concern about predicting the future
- **Autonomy**—addresses the sense of control over future events
- **Relatedness**—a sense of safety with others
- **Fairness**—a perception of how fair interactions are

The SCARF model reminds TD professionals about the concerns and perceived threats employees experience during a change effort. [See 3.6.2.3]

3.6.4.11 Mindset and Mental Models

Employees bring unique knowledge, skills, and experiences to their workplaces. When working in a change management role, TD professionals should be prepared for all types of employees and their mindsets and be skilled at gathering data, gaining buy-in, addressing reactions, fostering collaboration, and implementing change decisions. TD professionals must bring out the best in employees by understanding their mindsets and mental models and how to best tap into them.

In addition, TD professionals should be knowledgeable about their own mindsets and mental models so that they recognize how their assumptions, behaviors, and communications affect individuals and teams working to manage the change process. During a change process, TD professionals may find their own assumptions challenged, and their success as a change agent or facilitator may depend on their readiness to expand their thinking, accept others' ideas, and use new tools. TD professionals should be knowledgeable about management styles, social styles, and emotional intelligence and the role each plays in managing change. [See 1.2 and 3.3.7.1]

To build change management skills, TD professionals should look at every aspect of their own work as a change effort and apply change management models, tools, and processes to their work. By modeling a willingness to incorporate sound change management theories and practices to their own projects and initiatives, TD professionals build credibility as partners who can help business leaders plan and implement successful business change initiatives.

REFERENCES

ACMP (Association of Change Management Professionals). 2019. *Standard for Change Management and ACMP Change Management Code of Ethics*. Washington, DC: ACMP. cdn.ymaws.com/www.acmpglobal.org/resource/resmgr/files/ACMP_Standard_2019_03_21.pdf.

Baumeister, R., E. Bratslavsky, C. Finkenauer, and K. Vohs. 2001. "Bad Is Stronger Than Good." *Review of General Psychology* 5(4).

Bersin, J. 2022. "Rethinking Change Management From Management to Agility." *Governance Matters*. chandlerinstitute.org/governancematters/rethinking-change-moving-from-management-to-agility.

Biech, E. 2007. *Thriving Through Change: A Leader's Practical Guide to Change Mastery*. Alexandria, VA: ASTD Press.

Biech, E. 2010. *The ASTD Leadership Handbook*. Alexandria, VA: ASTD Press.

Biech, E. 2016. *Change Management Training*. Alexandria, VA: ATD Press.

Biech, E. 2022. *ATD's Handbook for Training and Talent Development*. Alexandria, VA: ATD Press.

Bridges, W. 2003. *Managing Transitions: Making the Most of Change*, 2nd ed. Cambridge, MA: Da Capo Press.

Carr, P. 2006. "Implementing Culture Change." *Infoline*. Alexandria, VA: ASTD Press.

Clifton, J., and J. Harter. 2019. *It's the Manager: Gallup Finds the Quality of Managers and Team Leaders Is the Single Biggest Factor in Your Organization's Long-Term Success*. Washington, DC: Gallup Press.

Conklin, H. 2022. "The Skills Shortage Is 2022's Biggest Threat." *Fortune*, April 8. fortune.com/2022/04/08/online-learning-workforce-training-digital-skills-gap.

Elliot, A.J., and J. Fryer. 2008. "The Goal Construct in Psychology." In *Handbook of Motivation Science*, edited by J.Y. Shah and W.L. Gardner, 235–250. New York: The Guilford Press.

Gartner. 2022. *Top Strategic Technology Trends for 2022: 12 Trends Shaping the Future of Digital Business*. Stamford, CT: Gartner.

Hiatt, J. 2006. *ADKAR: A Model for Change in Business, Government and Our Community*. Loveland, CO: Prosci Learning Center Publications.

Kotter, J.P. 2012. *Leading Change*. Boston: Harvard Business School Press.

Kotter, J.P., V. Akhtar, and G. Gaurav. 2021. *Change: How Organizations Achieve Hard-to-Imagine Results in Uncertain and Volatile Times*. Hoboken, NJ: John Wiley and Sons.

Kulkarni, R. 2018. "The Need for Managing Change." *HumanCapital*, June.

Lewin, K. 1958. "Group Decision and Social Change." In *Readings in Social Psychology*, edited by E.E. Maccoby, T.M. Newcomb, and E.L. Hartley, 197–211. New York: Holt, Rinehart, and Winston.

Lieberman, M., and N. Eisenberger. 2009. "Pains and Pleasures of Social Life." *Science* 323(5916): 890–891.

McArdle, G., and C. Hanson. 2006. "An Eight Step Change Model." *Infoline*. Alexandria, VA: ASTD Press.

Pasmore, B. 2015. *Leading Continuous Change: Navigating Churn in the Real World*. Oakland: Berrett-Koehler.

Pink, D. 2009. *Drive: The Surprising Truth About What Motivates Us*. New York: Riverhead Books.

Prochaska, J.O., J. Norcross, and C. DiClemente. 1994. *Changing for Good*. New York: William Morrow.

Ranjan, N. 2021. "How the Pandemic Has Impacted Customer Expectations." Forbes Council Post, February 4. forbes.com/sites/forbesbusinesscouncil/2021/02/04/how-the-pandemic-has-impacted-customer-expectations/?sh=6b9b14b03185.

Rock, D. 2008. "SCARF: A Brain-Based Model for Collaborating with and Influencing Others." NeuroLeadership Institute, June 15. neuroleadership.com/portfolio-items/scarf-a-brain-based-model-for-collaborating-with-and-influencing-others.

Rock, D., and L. Page. 2009. *Coaching With the Brain in Mind: Foundations for Practice*. Hoboken, NJ: John Wiley and Sons.

Rogers, E.M. 2003. *Diffusion of Innovations*, 5th ed. New York: Free Press.

Salesforce. 2020. "State of the Connected Customer." salesforce.com/resources/articles/customer-expectations.

Senge, P.M. 2006. *The Fifth Discipline: The Art and Practice of the Learning Organization*, rev. ed. New York: Currency/Doubleday.

Stavros, J., L. Godwin, and D. Cooperrider. 2015. "Appreciative Inquiry: Organization Development and the Strengths Revolution." In *Practicing Organization Development: A Guide to Leading Change and Transformation*, 4th ed., edited by W. Rothwell, R. Sullivan, and J. Stavros. Hoboken, NJ: John Wiley and Sons.

Tahir, U. 2020. "What Is Nudge Theory?" Change Management Insight, January 18. changemanagementinsight.com/nudge-theory-in-change-management.

Zukof, K. 2021. *The Hard and Soft Sides of Change Management: Tools for Managing Process and People*. Alexandria, VA: ATD Press.

Recommended Reading

Biech, E. 2007. *Thriving Through Change: A Leader's Practical Guide to Change Mastery*. Alexandria, VA: ASTD Press.

Kotter, J.P. 2012. *Leading Change*. Boston: Harvard Business School Press.

Kotter, J.P., V. Akhtar, and G. Gupta. 2021. *Change: How Organizations Achieve Hard-to-Imagine Results in Uncertain and Volatile Times*. Hoboken, NJ: John Wiley and Sons.

Pasmore, B. 2015. *Leading Continuous Change: Navigating Churn in the Real World*. Oakland: Berrett-Koehler.

Zukof, K. 2021. *The Hard and Soft Sides of Change Management: Tools for Managing Process and People*. Alexandria, VA: ATD Press.

3.7 DATA & ANALYTICS

Data and analytics are key drivers for talent development and therefore overall organization performance. The ability to collect, analyze, and use large data sets in real time can affect learning, performance, and business outcomes. Discerning meaningful insights from data and analytics about talent—including capability, experience, and outcomes—enables the talent development function to leverage itself as a strategic partner in achieving organizational goals.

3.7.1 Knowledge of Principles and Applications of Analytics

> **I. The Importance of People Analytics**
>
> TD professionals should be knowledgeable about analytics and its importance to talent development. Data analytics enables TD professionals to make decisions and recommend actions based on science and evidence rather than preference or previous practices. Data and analytics refer to the process of discovering, interpreting, and reporting patterns in data.

3.7.1.1 Principles and Applications

People analytics, sometimes called human capital analytics, describes using data to align talent development initiatives to organizational needs, assess causes for performance gaps, identify turnover risks and burnout victims, improve performance, or measure the organizational impact of programs and initiatives. The available data varies based on the collection tool and may include typical statistics (such as turnover, cost per hire, and the number of learners attending courses) and organizational impact (such as the correlations between employee engagement, performance improvement, and profit margins). These types of data can be used to predict which leaders will be most successful, what experiences will help employees advance in their careers, or which new hires are most likely to succeed. With analysis, TD professionals can also provide direction to senior leaders about the impact of talent development initiatives and future investment and budgeting requirements related to learning, or to employees about their career development paths.

By analyzing the impact of talent initiatives on an organization, TD professionals can help inform decisions about which efforts are worth pursuing for another fiscal year. Data can be captured through many methods, including employee and manager surveys (both annual and periodic pulse surveys), always-on listening platforms, questionnaires, focus groups, and human resource information systems. It can also be obtained from external sources (such as LinkedIn profiles) or acquired as a by-product of employee activities (such as training and day-to-day work).

3.7 Data & Analytics

To better grasp these processes and applications, TD professionals should understand the following related terminology:

- **Analytics.** TD professionals should be familiar with four types of analytics:
  - **Descriptive analytics**—a summary of historical data that provides the details of what happened.
  - **Diagnostic analytics**—examines data to explain why something happened and may use data mining or data discovery.
  - **Predictive analytics**—any approach to data mining with four attributes:
    - An emphasis on prediction (rather than description, classification, or clustering)
    - Rapid analysis measured in hours or days (not the stereotypical months of traditional data mining)
    - An emphasis on the organizational relevance of the resulting insights
    - An emphasis on ease of use, thus making the tools accessible to all users
  - **Prescriptive analytics**—a form of advanced analytics that examines data or content to answer the questions, "What should be done?" or "What can we do to make X happen?"
- **Big data.** Made up of data sets that are too large to capture and process using common methods for analysis, big data's significance depends on the five Vs (volume, velocity, variety, veracity, and value). [See 2.4.10.6]
- **Business intelligence.** This umbrella term includes applications, infrastructure, tools, and best practices, enabling access and analysis of information to optimize decisions and performance.
- **Data lakes.** A data lake is a centralized repository that stores an organization's structured and unstructured data.
- **Data management.** Data management includes practices, architectural techniques, and tools for achieving consistent access to and delivery of data to meet the data requirements of all business applications.
- **Data mining.** Data mining is a process of discovering meaningful correlations, patterns, and trends by sifting through stored data.
- **Data visualization.** Data visualization means the graphic images or symbols that depict the data.
- **Machine learning.** This involves algorithms that are composed of many technologies (such as deep learning, neural networks, and natural language processing) and guided by lessons from existing information.
- **Metrics.** Metrics are a method of measuring something or the results obtained from measurement.
- **Organizational network analysis.** This is a tool to measure and graph connections and patterns of collaboration between people within and across the organization.
- **Predictive modeling.** This common statistical technique is used to predict future behavior. Predictive modeling solutions are a form of data-mining technology that works by analyzing historical and current data and generating a model to help predict future outcomes. A model is validated (or revised) as additional data becomes available.
- **People analytics.** Also called talent analytics, this is the application of statistics, expertise, and technology to numerous large sets of data that provide a way to combine information and data to make better organizational decisions (Gartner 2019).
- **Sentiment analysis.** This is a process of computationally identifying and categorizing opinions expressed in a piece of text.
- **Text analytics.** This is an automated process of translating large volumes of unstructured text into quantitative data to uncover insights, trends, and patterns.

3.7.1.2 Analytics in the Workplace

TD professionals should be prepared to help their organizations as they increase the use of analytics to predict what will happen in the future along with the impact of what happened in the past. Although these are the most important uses, organizations also use analytics to increase efficiency, improve performance, and make better, more strategic decisions. This trend has been fueled by the availability of more data and technology, which allows organizations to capture and analyze data faster and more economically. The additional dependence on data raises four requirements that TD professionals can support:

- Data is captured, stored, and accessible.
- Employees are skilled and data-fluent.
- The integrity of data used to make decisions is maintained.
- Data is used and applied in an ethical way.

3.7.1.2.1 Increase Data-Fluent Expertise

Although organizations recognize the value of data analytics, many lack skilled employees who know how to identify, collect, analyze, interpret, report, and use data. Gartner's annual chief data officer (CDO) survey cited "talent shortages" as the highest barrier to organizational success (Gartner 2022). This has been exacerbated by the COVID-19 pandemic, which increased reliance on electronic devices capable of collecting and reporting data. Research also shows a 65 percent increase in the expected emphasis on technical skills in the workplace (Agarwal et al. 2018). As organizations become more data driven, they will need employees to become experts in data gathering, artificial intelligence, analytics, and advanced technology.

Intelligent machines are an integral part of the analytics solution because artificial intelligence (AI) can help learners as they struggle with new skills. However, learning opportunites are reduced when on-the-job learning is replaced by "the introduction of sophisticated AI, analytics, and robots" (Beane 2019). TD professionals will need to resolve this.

Another study found that 85 percent of TD leaders want to use big data and analytics to improve learning (Miller 2017). This means that TD professionals must assert their desire for more accountability in this discipline by developing individuals who are proficient in a combination of both business skills and analytics. The fusion of analytical and business skills in one curriculum is one solution to ensure more employees have the required expertise (Chin et al. 2017). TD professionals must lead the effort to build analytical capability.

3.7.1.2.2 Ensure Data Integrity

As more organizations become more dependent on the complex analytics that support their decisions, their data must be accurate and complete. According to Forbes, 84 percent of CEOs are concerned about the quality of the data they use to make decisions (Olenski 2018). In fact, this has become one of the most critical issues in data and analytics (Onay and Öztürk 2018; Spotless Data 2017; Reynolds 2016). TD professionals should ensure that the data they use comes from the correct audience segment, originated from humans, and has been properly curated.

TD professionals should assess their function's analytical capabilities and focus on what is most important to their organizations' success. The TD function should develop its own long-term plan and find ways to automate the delivery of information for itself and the rest of the organization.

3.7.1.3 Data Available in Real Time

TD professionals support their organization to live its mission and achieve its strategic objectives and goals; therefore, they should prioritize data that bolsters stakeholder needs. Dashboards can provide stakeholders with insights about engagement, skills, and learning paths. In the past, collecting and analyzing people analytics data was a labor-intensive process that took a significant amount of time. The advantage of using analytics and AI is that data can be analyzed and delivered to leaders in real time so better decisions can be made faster.

Analytics and AI deliver more powerful searches by eliminating extraneous content. They can also:
- Ensure alignment of the content to what's needed to contribute to the bottom line
- Be used to match mentors and coaches to employees
- Provide real-time data about safety and where an organization might be at risk
- Potentially address how, when, and what people are learning from one another, as well as pinpoint any gaps
- Match employees' skills and capabilities to internal opportunities, such as jobs, roles, gigs, and projects
- Identify high-potential leaders
- Predict turnover or identify how to best incentivize the workforce

3.7.1.3.1 Dashboards

Dashboards distill the most important data so that TD professionals and leadership can view indicators at a glance. They are often used to monitor how an organization is executing on strategy, and they are equally valuable in strategic, tactical, operational, or analytical formats. Dashboards may also provide users the ability to interact with data and study needed information at any time. Real-time access makes it easier for TD professionals to advise and inform leadership. In some cases, access to real-time dashboards can be provided directly to senior leaders so they are able to access the information they need, when they need it.

3.7.1.4 People Analytics Components

Data analytics provides insights into the health and performance of an organization. Having timely access to pertinent information can lead to more improved business decisions that may result in better outcomes related to hiring, staffing and resourcing, product development, customer service, and operational efficiency. Data analytics can also provide insights into reducing costs, cycle times, and waste. The purpose of analytics for the TD function is similar, and its interest in big data includes being able to:
- Evaluate the effectiveness of learning and development initiatives.
- Improve learning delivery methods.
- Evaluate the impact of L&D on organizational results.
- Enhance decision making within talent development departments (ASTD 2014).

TD professionals also use analytics in activities beyond L&D, including:
- **Hiring**
    - Improving hiring decisions
    - Predicting candidates' success
    - Analyzing video interviews
    - Predicting future workforce requirements
    - Matching experience to job success

- **Ongoing feedback**
    - Measuring and monitoring the employee engagement experience
    - Evaluating individual and team performance
    - Determining if departments have the right skill set and talent
    - Demonstrating correlations between coaching and engagement
    - Analyzing employee time management patterns
    - Providing employees and leaders with structured feedback to identify strengths and improvement opportunities
- **Organizational support**
    - Evaluating the effectiveness of employee policies
    - Quantifying safety and accident risks
    - Tying talent development actions to organizational results
    - Identifying overtime and other forms of payroll leakage
    - Determining improved practices in workforce management

These options can contribute to increased employee satisfaction and engagement, which is often attributed to increasing retention and productivity. [See 3.3.10]

3.7.1.5 Talent Development Contributes to the Bottom Line

As TD professionals use data analytics to gain knowledge about what and how learners learn, they can use analytics, dashboards, and AI to help leaders see the influence learning has on their organization. With the right data and analysis, the TD function can prove its contribution to the bottom line. For example, TD professionals can measure data related to employee frustration with a lack of information to do their jobs. Panopto's 2018 *Workplace Knowledge and Productivity* survey showed that the average large US organization loses $47 million in productivity annually due to insufficient knowledge sharing. Using an analytic approach to determine what information is needed, when, and by whom, increases the availability of information and decreases employee frustration. This gives TD professionals a way to contribute to the bottom line.

3.7.2 Skill in Gathering and Organizing Data From Internal or External Sources in Logical and Practical Ways to Support Retrieval and Manipulation

I. Selecting a Project for an Analytics Initiative

TD professionals should be able to gather and organize data to use for an analytics initiative.

3.7.2.1 Selecting Initial Talent Development Analytics Projects

TD professionals require a basic understanding of data analytics and the ability to communicate the results of TD projects to stakeholders. To build data-fluent expertise, TD professionals should select a project that they can learn from and that their organization will benefit from—one that has the potential for increasing their competency while also demonstrating real value to senior leaders. These early projects offer a way to determine how well the organization will adapt to using TD dashboards.

TD professionals should collaborate with senior leaders to identify a business challenge and establish and agree on a clear outcome. To increase the chances of success, TD professionals should ensure that they have access to the required data and identify a project that has a good probability of success, isn't too complicated, and avoids anything that may be politically charged. The project should also be important to the C-suite, such as reducing costs or increasing sales.

An ideal TD project has two important qualities. First, it should be a quick win, such as something that improves an existing process. This means that TD professionals will be able to demonstrate success rather than trying to improve something in the future and waiting for the results. Second, the project should be something that uncovers an insight or has a business impact that will create interest among senior leaders.

3.7.2.2 Steps to Gather and Organize Data

Once a project is selected, TD professionals should begin by using a clear process that includes these steps:

1. **Define the question** that needs to be answered.
2. **Set clear research objectives,** including determining what to measure and how to measure it.
3. **Conduct a data audit** to identify available data, which will inform the data collection strategy.
4. **Design the data collection and data analysis strategies.** The plan needs to be accepted by stakeholders so everyone agrees on the approach. By creating a plan and getting agreement, the data scientist then has a road map that can be replicated in the future and serve as valuable documentation if a stakeholder questions the approach. Planning is key to all good analytics projects.
5. **Collect the data.** TD professionals should consider what information exists in current databases, how the data is stored and filed, and how to collect the data. Cost, bias, and confidentiality will be factors.
6. **Analyze the data.** This might mean manipulating data in several ways, such as creating pivot tables, plotting it, or finding correlations. Several analysis tools and software applications can be used.
7. **Interpret the results.** As TD professionals interpret the results, they should return to the original question to determine if it has been answered. They should organize the data to answer the original question and use visuals to present it to ensure that a productive conclusion has been found.
8. **Report results.** Who expects the data and in what format?
9. **Evaluate the process.** What worked? What didn't? How can the process be improved? What's the return on investment (ROI) of this project?

3.7.2.3 Talent Development Function's Role in Selecting Future Analytics Projects

Ultimately, TD professionals will want to establish a portfolio of analytics projects. They should meet with senior leaders or other stakeholders to show how these projects could deliver short- and long-term value for their organization. TD professionals must be prepared to make recommendations about the projects based on both the level of impact and the ease of implementation. They should follow these best practices:

- **Ensure the talent strategy aligns with organizational success.** Organizations that are most successful have created a talent strategy that enhances their business strategy. Goals, strategy, and outcomes should have a corresponding plan for how employees will help achieve what the organization wants to accomplish. The talent strategy should align with how the organization measures success—it is the direct connection between the TD function and the organization. TD professionals should have a clear understanding of the organization and how it makes money (or if it's a nonprofit, what it is expected to accomplish) to ensure that leadership will be interested in the results of TD initiatives and help demonstrate that the TD function is a valuable resource and critical business function. [See 3.1.2]

- **Engage multiple stakeholders.** Some of the TD professional's key stakeholders include the organization's leaders and the other department leaders they serve. During future projects, additional stakeholders may be added, which is why it is important to identify consistent definitions of the organizational challenge, the measures, and the assumptions.
- **Determine the support needed.** Because every project will likely require support beyond the TD department, TD professionals should determine what support they will need and from whom. To do so, they'll need to obtain buy-in from other departments that may have access to different data or other experts throughout the organization who may need to help gather additional data (extant data or through interviews) and assist with building a measurement plan or analyzing what was learned. Building these relationships will be valuable in the future.
- **Don't over promise.** Not all analytical projects deliver significant measurable findings. Helping others understand this can help TD professionals gain buy-in from senior leaders.

3.7.3 Skill in Identifying Stakeholders' Needs, Goals, Requirements, Questions, and Objectives to Develop a Framework or Plan for Data Analysis

I. Developing a People Analytics Plan

TD professionals should be skilled in identifying stakeholder requirements so they can develop a people analytics plan.

3.7.3.1 The Stakeholder's Desired Purpose

When working with a stakeholder, it is important to understand what the stakeholder wants and needs to know—their goals, motives, and requirements. This forms the framework for a data analysis plan. The TD department owns valuable information for other departments, such as skills needed to improve organizational performance, how to predict turnover, data to measure the impact of leadership development programs, or how to determine the effectiveness of onboarding programs.

3.7.3.2 Conduct Stakeholder Analysis

TD professionals should be adept at conducting a needs assessment because the stakeholder analysis may be broader and deeper than is typical. Identifying stakeholders and determining their power and influence are critical first steps. It is also important to segment the stakeholder group, which can be done in a few ways, including:

- **Hierarchy**—such as team leads, department heads, or directors
- **Function or department**—such as sales, marketing, or operations
- **Decision-making authority**—which differs from hierarchy because in unique situations, a stakeholder group can have responsibility across departments (Anand 2017).

3.7.4 Skill in Analyzing and Interpreting Results of Data Analyses to Identify Patterns, Trends, and Relationships Among Variables

> **I. Analyzing Data and Interpreting Results**
>
> TD professionals should be skilled in analyzing results so they can identify trends and relationships among variables. They can do this by analyzing data and interpreting what it means.

3.7.4.1 Process for Data Analysis

Once questions have been asked and data collected, TD professionals should use a deeper data analysis to identify useful information and initial conclusions. They can begin by plotting the data to find correlations or creating a pivot table that allows data to be sorted and filtered using different variables. They should also calculate the mean, maximum, minimum, and standard deviation of the data.

As they sort and filter it, TD professionals may find that they need to collect more data or ask different questions to obtain the necessary data. In either case, what they learn about correlations, trends, and outliers helps focus the analysis and reach an accurate conclusion.

3.7.4.2 Pitfalls of Initial Data Analysis

Before beginning to interpret results, TD professionals should make sure they haven't fallen into any data analysis traps. Data must be skillfully analyzed, and TD professionals should understand some of the most common consequences of poor data analysis, such as:

- Jumping to conclusions—or worse, starting with a conclusion
- Unconscious bias
- Overusing the mean and avoiding the mode and median
- Incorrectly defining the sample size
- Hypothesis testing without accounting for the Hawthorne effect or placebo effect
- Assuming that correlation implies causation (it is impossible to deduce a relationship between two events solely based on an observed association or correlation) [See 2.8.6.2]

It is important to examine the processes used and the assumptions made before interpreting results.

3.7.4.3 Interpret Results

TD professionals should interpret results by referring to the original plan and purpose of the data analysis initiative and gathering some additional important information:

- Know the number of respondents and the total number of ideal respondents—this provides the sample size.
- If a survey was used, determine the response rate by dividing the number of responses by the number of respondents who were asked to complete the survey.
- Review the aggregated number of responses to each question—this is simply counting the totals.

Next, TD professionals need to make sense of the quantitative and qualitative information:

- **Quantitative data** is a good place to start. Working with the numbers first provides an initial focus or direction for the results. When working with numbers, it can be easier to compare percentages than whole numbers, so TD professionals should convert most of their data into percentages.
- **Qualitative data** should be compiled after the numbers are quantified. It will be used to provide a rationale for the quantitative data message.

TD professionals should provide context and meaning to their analysis. Benchmarks are standards or reference points that data can be compared to. Potential benchmarks include a comparison to a previous survey, another organization's data, or industry best practices. However, when benchmarking, it is critical to compare exact questions to avoid misinterpretation of the data.

It is also possible to make comparisons using cross-tabulation by breaking data into different categories. A cross-tabulation or crosstab table is a multidimensional table that records the frequency of respondents that have specific characteristics defined in each table cell. These tables show valuable data about the relationships of all the variables to one another and help analyze cause-and-effect or complementary relationships. For example, the crosstab table between a question about age and a question about professional development might lead to a conclusion that 20 percent of employees older than 50 want more professional development opportunities. [See 3.7.4.4]

While interpreting the data, TD professionals should use good judgement and question any results that don't seem right. They should also determine *correlation* (when two variables move at the same time) and *causation* (if one variable directly causes a change in another). [See 3.7.7.2]

As TD professionals interpret their analysis, they must remember that it is not possible to prove a hypothesis true. Instead, they can only fail to reject the hypothesis. This means that no matter how much data is collected, chance could always interfere with the results. Asking these questions while interpreting results helps determine the legitimacy and usefulness of the conclusions:
- Are the conclusions likely to be beneficial?
- Do the results answer the original research questions?
- Does the analysis explore all perspectives?
- Does the data address any objections?

TD professionals have likely reached a useful conclusion if these questions can be answered in the affirmative.

Armed with this data analysis and interpretation, TD professionals can determine the best course of action, make recommendations, and report their findings.

3.7.4.4 Using Data Visualization to Tell the Story

Once TD professionals interpret the results and determine they are accurate and serve their intended purpose, they can determine which visualization tools will make the most important point—what the data says.

3.7.4.4.1 Data Visualization

Although the numbers are important, audiences will want to know the story the data tells. TD professionals can use the data to create images that help the audience interpret the data. For example, an image could compare current statistics to a previous year. In other cases, benchmarks could be used for comparison to help interpret results.

Each method of presenting data has a different intended purpose. Charts can show relationships, distribution, comparisons over time or among items, or static composition. [See 3.7.6.2] Crosstab tables show a pictorial comparison of the results of two or more questions relating to factors like demographics (such as respondents' age), organizational position, between departments, or longevity. Two guiding principles for these tools are scaling and integrity—*scaling* shows proportions and relationships, while *integrity* focuses on the presentation's truthfulness and accuracy. [See 3.7.4.3]

TD professionals should create or select graphs that present the results in the most useful format—one that clarifies the intended point (Evergreen 2020). They will deliver their message best if their graphs:
- Induce viewers to think about the message rather than methodology, graphic design, and technology used to create the graphic.
- Avoid distorting what the data says.
- Make large data sets coherent.
- Encourage the eye to compare different pieces of data.
- Reveal the data at several levels of detail, from a broad overview to the fine structure.
- Serve a reasonably clear purpose, including description, explorations, tabulation, or decoration.

3.7.4.4.2 Data Storytelling
Once TD professionals understand the basics of data visualization, they can use imagery to craft a story that turns the data into action, which is called *data storytelling*. It brings together quantitative and cognitive sciences to effectively communicate data. Data storytelling helps audiences interpret complex information to better understand the "why" behind the data and helps them make more informed decisions (Duarte 2019).

Data storytelling requires TD professionals to understand the data they will be presenting, consider the audience, and think about the message they want to deliver. What story do they want to tell? Data storytelling contextualizes and personalizes information so that it is clear and piques listeners' interest. To engage the audience, data storytelling requires three components:
- Collected data
- Data visualization graphics
- Narration of what the data means and why listeners should care (Dykes 2020)

To be effective at data storytelling, TD professionals should incorporate four critical elements in their story:
- **Consider the audience.** What do they want to know and why should they care? Do they prefer a big picture or details? Do they trust the narrator? What action should listeners take?
- **Choose effective data visualization techniques.** What images and graphs will deliver the most information with the least effort? What visuals will be most familiar to the audience? [See 3.7.5.3 and 3.7.6.2]
- **Personalize the story.** What will attract the audience's attention? What can they connect the data to and how will it improve their lives? What quotes might they use to interpret the data?
- **Keep it simple.** How will animation or color affect the audience's ability to listen? How can cognitive load be reduced?

Effective data storytelling should help audiences answer the question, "So what?" Overall simplicity is key for maximum clarity. To evaluate the results, TD professionals should be certain that their audience will take action by answering the question, "Now what?"

3.7.4.5 The Analytic Spectrum

TD professionals typically evaluate TD initiatives using measures, metrics, and targets. "Thanks to plentiful data and smart analytics, companies can gain the insights they need to diagnose problems and make sound decisions" (Dearborn 2015). Using analytics along a progressive spectrum, TD professionals can use four different analyses to measure the value and effectiveness of various training programs and other initiatives (Pease and Brant 2018):

- **Descriptive analytics** are used to explain *what happened*. This is the analysis TD professionals are most familiar with, such as assessment scores, summary activities, opinions, satisfaction, and evaluation surveys.
- **Diagnostic analytics** are used to explain *why something happened* using a variety of techniques, such as data mining and data discovery. They provide correlations for focusing on the reason something did or did not happen as expected. They can save time by identifying where to apply and concentrate next steps.
- **Predictive analytics** use both descriptive and diagnostic data to predict *what will happen in the future*. By having a sense of what the data has uncovered, TD professionals can take this information one step further and build models to predict future outcomes and provide suggestive data for planning efforts.
- **Prescriptive analytics** are used to show *how to make something happen*. They offer the best opportunity to influence a different outcome. This is the least developed analytic because each organization has different requirements. TD professionals can use prescriptive analytics to personalize learning by matching a learner's preferences to make something happen.

3.7.5 Knowledge of Data Visualization, Including Principles, Methods, Types, and Applications

> **I. Data Visualization Principles**
>
> TD professionals should be knowledgeable about the principles and applications of data visualization as it relates to what the data shows. They need to know how to make their point using data visualization to communicate information by displaying data in the best, most accurate way possible.

3.7.5.1 Visualization Principles

Data representation is the form in which data is stored, processed, and transmitted for use, usually in digital format. When TD professionals are asked to display information in a data visualization format, they should follow several basic principles:

- Consider how and where the data visualization will appear to the user. For example, should the design consider mobile-first indexing?

- Balance the design by choosing:
  - Symmetrical visuals—both sides are the same.
  - Asymmetrical visuals—each side is different but has a common visual weight.
  - Circular visuals—use the center as an anchor, placing the components around it.
- Plan for a contrasting background color (white is the easiest); then, use a consistent color palette throughout.
- Optimize images before uploading.
- Use color, form, spatial positions, and other properties to enhance clarity.
- Emphasize key areas.
- Maintain consistency using themes, but also include some variety to keep the audience engaged (Healy 2019).

3.7.5.2 Rationale for Using Visualization

TD professionals use visualization when they create a dashboard for leaders that displays the relationships between multiple data sets. Data visualization is a combination of computer science, mathematics, cognitive science, and engineering. It ensures that an audience can gain insight from and form a mental image of large, complex data sets, which might represent events, processes, concepts, or objects (Telea 2014).

Data visualization helps TD professionals communicate complex information in a way that is easily and quickly comprehended and remembered because the human brain processes information faster when it's presented in a visual format. Visual graphs add credibility to the data and lead to a more persuasive argument. TD professionals should use data visualization:

- As a means for communicating large amounts of data that may be highly complex
- To help audiences glean insights and patterns that they would not otherwise discern from the raw data
- To summarize the data in a way that brings relationships and themes to light

In her book, *Effective Data Visualization*, researcher Stephanie Evergreen (2020) confirms the valuate of visualization: "Research tells us that data are more persuasive when shown in graphs. One factor may be that we are primarily visual beings and that most of us, most of the time, are skimming the narrative for things that pop out at us and catch our attention. Data visualization does just that—it provides the pop."

3.7.5.3 Optimizing the Visualization of Data

TD professionals should ask questions about what they want to show using the data. Once they know the point they are trying to make, they can select the right visualization technique to display it. Options include:

- Distribution of a single continuous variable
- Relationships between two or more variables
- Comparisons
- Distribution of multiple variables
- Connections
- Composition of parts of a whole
- Location

Each option has several types of charts from which to choose. For example, comparisons can be displayed as slope graphs, side-by-side column charts, back-to-back bar charts, or dot plots, among others.

3.7.5.4 Data Visualization Methods

Many decisions are involved when designing a complete visualization system. Example methods TD professionals can use include:

- **Color mapping** is the choice of colors that are linked to specific data. The goal is to easily and accurately recognize the original data set, and could include:
  - Telling the absolute data value at all data points
  - Identifying which of two data points is greater
  - Showing the difference between two data points
  - Telling which points represent selected data values
  - Showing the speed of change or the value of data at specific points (Telea 2014)
- **Texture mapping** is a visualization technique used to define high-frequency details in 2D images that correspond to a 3D model. They can be created using photos painted in a graphics software program or application.
- **Plots** can be shown in two ways: *Line plots* display data points, called markers, which are connected by straight lines. *Scatter plots* allow each data point to have its own x or y axis value, which shows trends or correlations; data points aren't connected by lines.
- **Word clouds** are viewed by data visualization experts as limited at best. However, people often want to use them more seriously than intended, even though they lack insight into the data (except how many words were used how often). Word clouds are best used to show data in a comparative sense.

3.7.6 Skill in Selecting or Using Data Visualization Techniques

> **I. Selecting Data Visualization Techniques**
>
> TD professionals should be able to select data visualization techniques based on what the data needs to show. They should also have the skills to create and use them appropriately.

3.7.6.1 Presenting Data to Stakeholders

TD professionals should have an understanding of how data driven their organization is prior to planning projects and selecting or using data visualization techniques. Five factors define a data-driven organization:

- Strong company culture
- Experimentation mindset and objectively learns from failures
- Digital technology influence
- Focus on the future
- Organizationally agile (Sinar 2018)

These characteristics help TD professionals understand an organization's preparedness level to use data for decision making.

If there isn't a specific request from leadership or another stakeholder, TD professionals should define an outcome they would like to influence. They should consider the main purpose of talent development and identify which TD reports leadership uses to make their decisions. They can also look for organizational metrics that are tied to performance, such as increased sales or reduced turnover. TD professionals can determine the decision they would like to influence, which becomes a likely candidate for gathering and analyzing data for a visualization first step.

Before moving forward, TD professionals should ensure that their selection is not in conflict with what their stakeholder might be doing or planning. This requires them to know the stakeholder's goals and to predict their questions before introducing the idea.

3.7.6.2 What to Display

TD professionals should determine how they want to display data. The visual they choose will depend on the audience and what will be most meaningful to them, as well as which visual will provide the best aesthetic and be the most effective. The following visualization techniques can be used to show different relationships:

- **Distribution of a single variable**—columns, histogram, scatter chart, or bar chart
- **Relationship**—bubble charts or scatter chart
- **Comparison**—bars and columns, timeline, line chart, or scatter plots
- **Distribution of multiple variables**—heat maps or bubble charts
- **Connection**—relationship or connection maps, heat maps, or Venn diagrams
- **Composition of the whole**—pie chart or stacked bar chart
- **Location**—maps, building diagrams, or processes

3.7.7 Knowledge of Statistical Theory and Methods Including the Computation, Interpretation, and Reporting of Statistics

> **I. Principles, Definitions, and Applications of Statistical Theory**
> TD professionals should know fundamental statistical terminology.

3.7.7.1 Fundamental Statistical Concepts and Processes

Talent development and organizations have ample data at their disposal. In fact, there's often too much data for them to be able to make a clear decision. TD professionals should be able to sort through data to draw accurate conclusions using fundamental statistical knowledge, including:

- **Algorithms** are logical sets of rules that create a method to solve a problem. They include calculations, data processing, and reasoning, and depict physical steps or behaviors and the rationale that supports them.
- **Business analytics** are solutions used to build analysis models and simulations to create scenarios, understand realities, and predict future states. Business analytics include data mining, predictive analytics, applied analytics, and statistics, and are delivered as an application suitable for users with prebuilt industry content (Gartner 2019).
- **Causal inference** is the process of drawing a conclusion based on the conditions of the occurrence of an effect.
- **Clustering** is the capability to define resources on one or more interconnected midrange systems available to users and applications from within a specified group of loosely coupled systems in a local- or metropolitan-area network (Gartner 2019).
- **Computations** are mathematical calculations.

- **A data set** is a collection of separate elements or related information that can be manipulated as one group.
- **Mean** is the average of a group of numbers. It is most affected by the presence of rare extreme values (outliers).
- **Normal distribution** is a continuous probability distribution that is symmetrical around its mean with most values near the central peak.
- **A range** is a series of values between two outer values.
- **Standard deviation** is a measure or indicator of the amount of variability of scores from the mean. The standard deviation is a statistic that's often used in formulas for advanced or inferential statistics.

3.7.7.2 Methods to Analyze Data

TD professionals can use several methods to analyze data:

- **Correlation analysis** is a statistical method used to determine whether a relationship exists between two variables and if so, how strong the relationship is. TD professionals should consider all factors to ensure that the statistics represent more than a causal relationship. For example, correlation analysis can show a relationship between courses taken and employee advancement.
- **Multiple regression analysis** quantifies how certain behaviors are tied to outputs. For example, if customer satisfaction surveys indicate that car insurance customers rate their experience as satisfactory (output) when service time on the phone is eight minutes, regression analysis helps define the service behaviors that drive the rating (such as use of the customer's name, times placed on hold, or politeness).
- **Significance testing** verifies correlation and multiple regression analysis. Because statistics can have many sources of errors (such as sampling errors, research bias, and validity), complete certainty that a relationship exists between two variables is difficult to achieve. Statistical significance means that the probability of a relationship existing between two variables is true.
- **Inferential statistics** are statistical techniques for making decisions based on only partial information or a sample of data. The most used statistical analyses are t-tests and analysis of variance—groups are compared to each other and probability is used to discover if differences are statistically significant.
- **Experimental design** is the concept of creating an initiative in a controlled environment with the purpose of establishing a relationship between the independent and dependent variable. For example, if understanding which of two training methods produces the best outcomes, an experimental design would be to randomly select participants in the training program, collecting data prior to the training program and outcomes after the training program.
- **Natural experiment** describes the unique situations that create opportunities to conduct natural experiments. For example, many organizations moved employees to work remotely during the COVID-19 pandemic. Was employee engagement affected by the shift to remote work? Comparing data collected prior to the pandemic to data collected during the pandemic provides a natural experiment to study the impact of remote work on engagement.
- **Text analytics and sentiment analysis** are also important because even though analytics is typically quantitative, the need for and use of qualitative methods such as ethnography, anthropology, and other phenomenological methods are increasingly being used. Understanding a person's lived experience has never been more important in light of the move toward greater inclusion in the workplace.

3.7 Data & Analytics

The findings from these types of analytics can help TD professionals guide organizations in determining what talent initiatives to implement, which types of training yield the best return on investment, and how to prioritize the use of limited resources

3.7.7.3 Ethical Use of Data and Analytics

Data analytics is a relatively new field and people analytics is one of the newest segments of the discipline. As a result, there are few principles to guide its use. The European Union's General Data Protection Regulation (GDPR) enforces regulations for using personally identifiable information (PII). PII is data that could be used to identify an individual, such as a social security number, bank account number, passport number, driver's license number, or even an email address. GDPR requires organizations to request consent from people to use their data and to tell them how it will be used, among other things. When data is being transmitted between an organization and its customers, data processing agreements are the legally binding agreements that outline the terms associated with the data's treatment.

Using people analytics has expanded concerns about privacy, transparency, and how PII can be used in the workplace. As TD professionals begin to use statistical theory and methods in data analytics for talent development programs in their organizations, they should know what protocols their organizations have established regarding processing and security for using personal data. For example, providing predictive analytics around attrition to managers could lead them to reconsider whether they offer learning and development opportunities to some employees versus others. Internally sharing data and analyses could result in unintended consequences, ranging from unfair or unequal treatment to self-fulfilling prophecies, such as employees most at risk of leaving doing so at a greater rate. [See 2.4.1.9 and 2.4.7.2]

Having proper protocols in place becomes more important when data is segmented by gender, race, age, performance, or other sensitive categories. TD professionals need to understand their role in balancing privacy issues with data for decision making. Application of both is a requirement to provide positive results for employees and organizations alike. [See 1.6.3 and 2.8.6.3]

REFERENCES

Agarwal, D., J. Bersin, J. Schwartz, G. Lahiri, and E. Volini. 2018. "AI, Robotics, and Automation Put Humans in the Loop." *2018 Global Human Capital Trends*. London: Deloitte.

Anand, P. 2017. "Executive Dashboards to Win Over the C-Suite." *TD at Work*. Alexandria, VA: ATD Press.

ASTD (American Society for Training and Development). 2014. *Big Data, Better Learning? How Big Data Is Affecting Organizational Learning*. Alexandria, VA: ASTD Press.

ATD (Association for Talent Development). 2018. *2018 State of the Industry*. Alexandria, VA: ATD Press.

Beane, M. 2019. "Learning to Work With Intelligent Machines." *Harvard Business Review*, September–October.

Bersin, J., E. Volini, J. Schwartz, I. Roy, M. Hauptmann, Y. Van Durme, and B. Denny. 2019. *2019 Deloitte Global Human Capital Trends: Leading the Social Enterprise: Reinvent with a Human Focus*. London: Deloitte.

Cappelli, P., and A. Tavis. 2018. "HR Goes Agile." *Harvard Business Review*, March–April.

Charas, S., and S. Lupushor. 2022. *Humanizing Human Capital: Invest in Your People for Optimal Business Returns*. Dallas, TX: Matt Holt.

Chin, J., M. Hagstroem, A. Libarikan, and K. Rifai. 2017. "Advanced Analytics: Nine Insights From the C-Suite." McKinsey and Company, July. mckinsey.com/business-functions/mckinsey-analytics/our-insights/advanced-analytics-nine-insights-from-the-c-suite.

Cross, R.L. 2021. *Beyond Collaboration Overload: How to Work Smarter, Get Ahead, and Restore Your Well-Being*. Boston: Harvard Business Review Press.

Dearborn, J. 2015. *Data Driven: How Performance Analytics Delivers Extraordinary Sales Results*. Hoboken, NJ: John Wiley and Sons.

Duarte, N. 2019. *Data Story: Explain Data and Inspire Action Through Story*. Oakton, VA: Ideapress Publishing.

Dykes, B. 2020. *Effective Data Storytelling: How to Drive Change With Data, Narrative, and Visuals*. Hoboken, NJ: John Wiley and Sons.

Evergreen, S. 2020. *Effective Data Visualization: The Right Chart for the Right Data*, 2nd ed. Thousand Oaks, CA: SAGE Publications.

Ferrar, J., and D. Green. 2021. *Excellence in People Analytics*. London: Kogan Page.

Gartner. 2019. "Gartner Glossary." gartner.com/it-glossary.

Gartner. 2022. "Gartner Survey Finds Successful CDOs Link Data and Analytics to Prioritized and Measured Business Outcomes." Gartner press release, April 20. gartner.com/en/newsroom/press-releases/2022-04-20-gartner-survey-finds-successful-cdos-link-data-and-analytics-to-prioritized-and-measured-business-outcomes.

Harford, T. 2021. *The Data Detective: Ten Easy Rules to Make Sense of Statistics*. New York: Riverhead Books.

Harbert, T. 2020. "People Analytics, Explained." Analytics. MIT Sloan School of Management, May 12. mitsloan.mit.edu/ideas-made-to-matter/people-analytics-explained.

Healy, K. 2019. *Data Visualization: A Practical Introduction*. Princeton, NJ: Princeton University Press.

Miller, B. 2017. "How L&D Leaders Can Demonstrate Value." LEO Learning, July 20. leolearning.com/2017/07/learning-business-impact-towards-maturity.

Olenski, S. 2018. "Three Barriers to Data Quality and How to Solve for Them." *Forbes*, April 23. forbes.com/sites/steveolenski/2018/04/23/3-barriers-to-data-quality-and-how-to-solve-for-them/#6cd2c11b29e7.

Onay, C., and E. Öztürk. 2018. "A Review of Credit Scoring Research in the Age of Big Data." *Journal of Financial Regulation and Compliance* 26(3): 382–405.

Panopto. 2018. "Inefficient Knowledge Sharing Costs Large Businesses $47 Million per Year." Panopto press release, July 17. prnewswire.com/news-releases/inefficient-knowledge-sharing-costs-large-businesses-47-million-per-year-300681971.html.

Pease, G., and C. Brant. 2018. "Fuel Business Strategies With L&D Analytics." *TD at Work*. Alexandria, VA: ATD Press.

Phillips, P.P., and J.J. Phillips. 2014. *Making Human Capital Analytics Work: Measuring the ROI of Human Capital Processes and Outcomes*. New York: McGraw-Hill.

Reynolds, V. 2016. *Big Data for Beginners: Understanding SMART Big Data, Data Mining & Data Analytics For Improved Business Performance, Life Decisions & More!* Self-published.

Russ-Eft, D.F., and H.S. Preskill. 2009. *Evaluation in Organizations: A Systematic Approach to Enhancing Learning, Performance, and Change*. New York: Basic Books.

Schwartz, J., L. Collins, H. Stockton, D. Wagner, and B. Walsh. 2017. *Rewriting the Rules for the Digital Age: 2017 Deloitte Human Capital Trends*. Deloitte. deloitte.com/content/dam/Deloitte/global/Documents/About-Deloitte/central-europe/ce-global-human-capital-trends.pdf.

Sinar, E. 2018. "Leading With Data-Driven Decisions: The Culture and Skills Driving Higher Returns on Data." *DDI Global Leadership Forecast 2018*. ddiworld.com/glf2018/data-driven-decisions.

Soehren, M. 2019. "It's All About the Impact." *TD*, June.

Spotless Data. 2017. "Big Data's Fourth V." October 5. spotlessdata.com/blog/big-datas-fourth-v.

Telea, A. 2014. *Data Visualization: Principles and Practice*, 2nd ed. Boca Raton, FL: CRC Press.

Recommended Reading

Charas, S., and S. Lupushor. 2022. *Humanizing Human Capital: Invest in Your People for Optimal Business Returns*. Dallas, TX: Matt Holt.

Duarte, N. 2019. *Data Story: Explain Data and Inspire Action Through Story*. Oakton, VA: Ideapress Publishing.

Evergreen, S. 2020. *Effective Data Visualization: The Right Chart for the Right Data*, 2nd ed. Thousand Oaks, CA: SAGE Publications.

Newbauer, K. 2023. *Aligning Instructional Design With Business Goals: Making the Case and Delivering Results*. Alexandria, VA: ATD Press.

Reynolds, V. 2016. *Big Data for Beginners: Understanding SMART Big Data, Data Mining & Data Analytics for Improved Business Performance, Life Decisions & More!* Self-published.

3.8 FUTURE READINESS

The pace of change demands continuous upskilling and reskilling of the workforce. Future readiness requires intellectual curiosity and constant scanning of the environment to stay abreast of forces shaping the business world, employees and their expectations, and the talent development profession. Monitoring emerging trends and technologies is essential to prepare for the demands of future learners. A commitment to ongoing professional development is essential to ensure there is capability to handle the changes in how work is done in the years ahead. Fostering environments that promote innovation and creativity will help position organizations to become future focused and future ready.

3.8.1 Knowledge of Internal and External Factors That Influence Talent Development

> **I. Influences on the Workplace of the Future**
>
> In times of continuous disruption, innovation and agility are keys to success for any organization. TD professionals should be constantly scanning the internal and external business environment to anticipate, adapt, and thrive in this disruption by making sense of the inherent complexity in organizational systems.

3.8.1.1 Factors Influencing Talent Development

The factors that influence talent development are changing constantly both within organizations and in the broader environment. Factors that TD professionals should monitor include:

- **External factors that influence organizational strategies and goals.** TD professionals should monitor external factors by routinely conducting a PEST analysis—a tool used for environmental scanning that examines the political, economic, social, and technological events and trends that can affect an organization. A first-time PEST analysis needs to be thorough; updates require less effort (PEST Analysis Tool 2019). The results are reviewed to be better understood within the lens of the industry and on a global scale.
- **Internal factors and organizational decisions.** Factors include organizational strategies and goals, organizational structure, products and services produced, the systems and processes that produce results, the organization's growth rate, mergers and acquisitions, changes in leadership, changes in organizational structure, financial and budgetary issues, natural and man-made disasters, and labor relations. TD professionals should know this information to predict how it might influence talent development initiatives. The information could identify organizational capabilities and the

impact on technology and platforms; organizational design and ways of working; as well as process re-engineering and skills that TD professionals may need to acquire.

- **Talent-specific factors that directly influence talent development.** TD professionals should monitor these factors carefully by remaining in touch with their professional organizations, staying current with reading, and forming groups to explore the future. Factors influencing the TD department include:
  - Employees accepting ownership of their development
  - The expectation that managers should develop their employees
  - Technology that has enabled new distribution channels
  - Emphasis on how the department can partner with the C-suite
  - Opportunities for TD professionals to co-create solutions with others in the organization
  - How diversity, equity, and inclusion (DEI) initiatives are implemented throughout the organization
  - The need for content that is ready when and where learners need it (Biech 2018)

All these factors require targeted development for TD professionals and all TD leaders. TD professionals should be aware of how agile ways of working and new approaches to leading others are shaping the new workforce, which is also being transformed by new talent pools and the independent workforce that is emerging in all markets.

3.8.1.2 Forces Driving Change

Several forces are currently driving change within the workplace. TD professionals should consider the effect they will have on the delivery of their products and services and the learning experience.

3.8.1.2.1 Reimagining Performance Management

TD professionals need to address the expectations for performance management; for example, many organizations are opting for real-time, ongoing feedback. A change for talent development is the decoupling of development planning from the performance review process. Performance management is shifting toward meeting the needs of employees and focusing on supporting future performance. The future-ready organization is also building new systems of feedback for cross-functional teams and agile self-managed teams working on missions as opposed to processes.

3.8.1.2.2 Democratization and Transparency in the Workplace

TD professionals should recognize the influence of democratization (things accessible to all) and transparency (honesty and openness) on their deliverables. They need to address things such as who gets developed, how they are developed, and what capabilities become development targets. In the future, development may encompass a wide array of services and resources that are available for everyone inside and even outside an organization.

Today's environment is becoming more transparent and it's nearly impossible to limit the spread of information. Employees (and nonemployees) have access to substantial amounts of information about many organizations, their performance, the activities of their leaders, and their future plans. Development options that are not available to everyone may be viewed as exclusive and thus decrease engagement. TD professionals need to navigate this new workplace dynamic, which demands a combination of digital literacy, analytics, and a new talent system that's more responsive to the real-time needs of the employee and the organization.

3.8.1.2.3 Workplace Digitization

TD professionals should be part of any decisions about workplace digitization (the advanced use of technologies to connect people and spaces to organizational processes). The goal is to improve productivity, reduce costs, engage the workforce, and encourage innovation. TD professionals can be trusted advisors to the C-suite as they make decisions about the best technology to explore for the workplace and recommend tools that provide the greatest value. The profession is evolving, and the future organization will likely form digital strategy teams to align talent strategies within the digital ecosystem.

3.8.1.3 Anticipate the Workplace of the Future

TD professionals should begin to consider how the workplace will change in the next few years and how work will be conducted. Current changes are likely indications of the workplace of the future, such as rapid technological advancements; new, tougher competition; a demographically changing workforce; increased globalization; higher customer expectations; greater employee expectations; and a constantly increasing rate of change. TD professionals need to attend to an increasingly large number of pressures that are placed on organizations and their employees.

TD professionals should be prepared to help their organizations move into the future by considering recent changes and current dilemmas. They can then select those they think will have the most influence and explore how they can prepare for the future workplace (Biech 2018). Some dilemmas they may encounter include:

- **Leadership gaps.** There is an ongoing need to fill the leadership pipeline with diverse leaders who exhibit new capabilities. Executives are struggling with leadership gaps at all levels. Center for Creative Leadership (2022) research shows that "today's leadership capacity is insufficient to meet future leadership requirements."
- **Leadership skills.** The leadership requirements of tomorrow may be very different and will likely require the skills to form and reform teams to resolve problems. While these leaders will be less constrained, they'll also need entrepreneurial skills (Johansen 2012). They will need to be more focused on self-directed development, change management, and the ability to lead distributed teams. Future leaders must be comfortable sharing power with employees.
- **Connected world.** People, organizations, and countries are all more connected, which offers opportunities for information exchange and employee support. This is good in many ways; however, smaller organizations may not have the necessary systems for fully integrated data to be able to make decisions 24 hours a day. TD professionals should challenge themselves about the best way to leverage this opportunity.
- **Learning where the work is.** Continuous learning is taking over the workplace. TD professionals should determine how they can create an environment that is supportive of and conducive to learning. They need to work with senior leaders to create a learning culture that supports continual learning, as well as fostering mentoring efforts, helping managers be better coaches, introducing performance support tools where needed, and helping employees take ownership of their development.

3.8 Future Readiness

- **Agile teams.** Dynamic and agile team structures are becoming the norm, and contractors and employees are equally in demand as members of these teams. Future organizations will likely get their work done using self-directed teams, and TD professionals can support this direction by providing awareness and development throughout their organizations. TD should consider building a talent architecture inclusive of these new agile teams that reinforces the need for on the job learning and sharing.
- **Ecosystems.** As markets become more connected, small businesses will find increased opportunities in specialized product and service niches that satisfy customized demands. In addition, most organizations will increase partnering options across larger business ecosystems (Johansen 2012). Organizations will also continue to shed assets and pay for the capabilities of other firms, resulting in outsourcing many parts of the business value chain. The TD function should assess its role and value in each of these partnerships.
- **Employees work from everywhere.** Work is becoming a thing you do, rather than a place you go, as more people work remotely from their homes or satellite locations. TD professionals need tools to help employees manage themselves and their work in an increasingly dynamic, virtual workplace. Productivity is one of the basics for an organization's success, so ensuring high levels of productivity and engagement when employees are off-site is required. TD professionals should also consider the personalization of the employee experience.
- **Rapid change of job skills.** Rapid advances in technology are putting pressure on employees to not only build skills for their current job, but also to change jobs and even career paths. To support this phenomenon, TD professionals may consider offering short courses or stackable credentials that work both as certificates and as building blocks toward certification or a degree. Advantages may include cost efficiency, satisfying employees' need to feel valued and developed, and accelerating the obtainment of new knowledge and skills.
- **Employee balance of power.** The balance of power is shifting toward employees. TD professionals need to understand what this means for employees and their organizations and be clear about their own responsibilities to manage expectations. When employees are empowered to influence change in their workplaces, they may feel more valued. Finally, employees want more development, and TD professionals need to be clear about how they can fulfill this desire.
- **Reputation is critical.** An organization's reputation is key. Employees want to work for an organization with a positive reputation, and organizations want to hire candidates with a reputation built on a strong track record. In fact, most job seekers will even accept a lower salary to work for an organization with a good brand. TD professionals can assist their organizations by creating and taking advantage of an excellent reputation.
- **Analytics for increased efficiency.** While 70 percent of company executives cite people analytics as a top priority, most companies still face critical obstacles in the early stages of building their people analytics capabilities, preventing real progress (McKinsey 2020). By taking advantage of this data, TD professionals can partner with their leaders to find practical, meaningful results and apply appropriate interpretations to business decisions. Gartner research has predicted that analytics will be the top focus for many organizations (Bersin 2016). [See 3.8.4 and 3.7]
- **Social issues.** ESG stands for environmental, social, and governance, and it represents an organization's corporate interests that focus on sustainable and ethical impacts.

Investors use these measures to value a company's risk, but they are equally important to employees. When a company uses ESG practices that focus on doing good it motivates employee loyalty, commitment, and engagement. TD professionals are critical to ESG because they are involved with training, retraining, and engaging talent. It's now up to HR leaders and teams to play a greater role in addressing ESG initiatives because they matter to all stakeholders and influence their engagement and productivity. In addition, TD professionals can expect to facilitate ESG teams. More broadly, ESG represents:

- **The environment,** or the organization's impact on the planet
- **Society,** or the impact an organization has on people, including employees, customers, and the community
- **Governance,** or how transparently and ethically an organization is run

According to executives, building the organization of the future is the most important challenge they face (Bersin et al. 2017). This signals a shift in thinking. Most organizations were designed to be efficient and effective with predictable patterns. However, this design is not aptly suited to the unpredictability and disruptions facing organizations today because they need to be designed for speed, agility, and adaptability. This means shifting away from hierarchical teams to a more flexible model of small team networks. TD professionals should help their organizations become more agile and innovative with a dynamic talent strategy that's responsive to internal and external disruptions.

3.8.1.4 The Workforce of the Future

TD professionals should begin to examine the workforce of the future and the skills it will require. There are several current trends that will likely reshape the workforce and the work. These include (Biech 2018):

- **Freelancing as a way of life.** The definition of an employee is on the cusp of a transformation. In the future, employee attitudes and expectations for flexibility will likely influence where, when, and how people work. Today, contractors and consultants make up more than 40 percent of the current workforce; soon they will outnumber full-time employees (Akeroyd 2021). There will also likely be an increase in contingent labor rather than full-time work. One issue facing TD professionals is to decide what is important for contingent labor to learn—if anything. Few organizations have this figured out. TD professionals need to create a process to get contingent employees up to speed quickly.
- **Demographics are changing.** This is not new, but as retirements increase, they cause major shifts in workplace demographics, leadership pipelines, and talent availability. One of the biggest needs TD professionals can support is succession planning. Demographics affect talent development in two ways: An unprepared young workforce requires organizations to plan how to bring them up to speed quickly. Meanwhile, an aging world population will place pressure on organizational and social systems.
- **Finding and retaining talent is critical.** Sixty-five percent of global companies have had problems finding employees with the skills they need (Bersin 2016). Unique talent in specialized occupations is more important for organizational success, yet it's harder to find. TD professionals should understand what it takes to attract people, create involvement, engage employees, and provide an active learning experience. They should recognize that employee satisfaction starts with an effective onboarding program that creates a superior first impression (Bersin 2016). Organizations should leverage technology to identify opportunities to simplify their talent acquisition processes.
- **Job flexibility motivates future employees.** Employees are interested in work that provides maximum flexibility. TD professionals should determine how they can tap into flexibility for more successful

recruiting and retention. They can help their organizations determine how to offer time-shifted hours, frequent sabbaticals, or results-only work environments. Some organizations focus on using asynchronous teams to provide greater flexibility for employees.
- **Robots will have real jobs.** Artificial intelligence (AI) will upset the job market; it has the potential to eliminate up to 50 percent of jobs (Zahidi et al. 2020). This is already happening in law offices, where computerized searches have slashed the number of available jobs. The positive perspective of AI is that it frees up humans for more interesting and creative work. TD professionals will have to take on the task of helping employees work with and perhaps even for robots. This will have a positive impact on productivity and new capabilities that could produce an exponential competitive advantage for companies. TD professionals should get involved with these efforts as soon as they are discussed in their organizations.
- **Innovation will be the norm.** Organizational growth and success will depend on how creative and innovative organizations can be. TD professionals should help their organizations demystify what innovation is by offering a framework and tools they can use to diagnose or implement innovation in their organizations.

3.8.1.5 Prepare for the Future

To prepare for the future, TD professionals should deliberately shift their vision from a single horizon to the periphery. Ideas that will affect organizations can come from many places. TD professionals should track emerging topics to look for patterns and understand how these topics can make a difference in their organizations. For example, they should look for connections between these new ideas or how they connect to current practices. The critical question is, "How could this new idea help people learn more, better, faster, or cheaper than today?"

TD professionals should use a combination of approaches to deliberately focus on the future:
- **Ask questions about the future.** Watch for signs that things are changing. Be alert for those who are trying a new approach or using a new tool or technology.
- **Observe generational differences.** Are newer departments or younger workers doing things differently? Do new processes leverage technology that older ones do not?
- **Heed experts' forecasts.** Who are the experts and what do they say? What does the wisdom of the crowd believe?
- **Watch for indirect effects.** Some changes may not be noticed until they have second- or third-order results and unintended consequences.
- **Challenge the data.** Don't assume the data is accurate. Things may have changed or taken on new meaning or importance.
- **Adopt human-centered design.** Most employees are seeking to be part of the design and development of programs that affect them. Allow for design thinking and inclusive design.
- **Encourage discussions and tracking ideas.** Sometimes patterns only become clear when written or articulated, so it's important to keep a running dialogue.

TD professionals should realize that preparing for the future is not easy. It requires constant attention to keep talent development relevant today while at the same time thinking about the future. To maintain their organization's competitive advantage, TD professionals should track the trends their leaders believe are important to meeting future needs. They must be comfortable synthesizing the data they collect and analyzing it with a focus on the organizational capabilities their businesses need to identify and build to compete in the marketplace. This requires investments in talent analytics tools that are accessible to the HR community as well as business leaders.

3.8.2 Skill in Conducting Environmental Scanning to Identify Current and Emerging Trends in the Economy, Legislation, Competition, and Technology

> **I. Environmental Scanning**
>
> In a time of constant disruption, TD professionals should be constantly searching for information to understand what is changing and how it will influence the products and services they provide.

3.8.2.1 Environmental Scanning Defined

Environmental scanning is the organized and deliberate study and interpretation of the internal and external events and trends that can influence an organization. Scanning can identify threats and opportunities toward the organization's future plans. The primary concerns of environmental scanning are reducing the randomness of information flowing into an organization and providing early warnings of changing conditions (Aguilar 1967).

Scanning also promotes future-oriented thinking and planning. It can help TD professionals anticipate the needs of an organization and develop new plans, policies, and approaches to meet them. They can also use scanning to identify new technologies, new services and products, and different markets. Scanning can help them see emerging competitors, threats, and opportunities, as well as their own strengths and weaknesses.

3.8.2.1.1 Types of Environmental Scanning

Astute TD professionals will likely find themselves scanning regularly and asking what it means for the future of talent development and their organization. Scanning will be more beneficial when TD professionals use formal methodologies to obtain information for specific purposes. Formal environmental scanning can be either centralized or comprehensive:

- **Centralized scanning** looks at specific components of the environment or proposes a hypothesis that is assumed to influence current issues, such as research on the use of virtual reality. For example, it could be used to identify a partnership with an AI-powered company that predicts the tasks being handled by robotics and automation. The results could help TD professionals prepare for reskilling of declining skills in their organizations.
- **Comprehensive scanning** looks at the broader environment without a specific hypothesis. It often leads to a decision to do one or more centralized scans to gain further insight. It might be used, for example, for scanning business intelligence regarding customer behaviors leading to new lines of business. It could also be used to scan the global economy for the migration of skills to different countries. Comprehensive scanning could also be used to scan the talent pools available to build a skill-access plan through partnerships or an independent workforce.

Conducting both centralized and comprehensive scanning at once is referred to as *mixed scanning* and is often the optimal approach.

3.8.2.2 Value of Environmental Scanning

Environmental scanning is an essential element in an organization's strategic planning process and a direct link exists between scanning and organizational performance. It is also essential to plotting the future course for talent development.

Environmental scanning improves TD professionals' ability to implement change, capitalize on opportunities, and better meet their customer's needs. It connects them with their organization and positions them to be business partners. It also highlights threats, the needed decisions, and the capabilities required to move into the future. [See 3.2]

The results of these scans feed directly into the products and services that TD professionals produce. If they understand how environmental factors affect leaders, managers, and employees, they can deal with those issues in programs and initiatives. The information they gather can serve as situational context for tools and development support. TD professionals then can predict the preferences of new generations of learners and implement the technologies and delivery platforms that are most likely to have the greatest impact (Brown and Weiner 1985; Choo 2012; Fahey and Narayanan 1986).

3.8.2.3 Process for Environmental Scanning

TD professionals should follow this process to conduct an environmental scan:

1. **Set direction.** Determine the purpose for scanning and what questions should be answered. Develop a project plan outlining the approach, participants, timeline, resources, and deliverables.
2. **Gain skills.** Determine the skills needed for scanning and how to get them. External expertise may be available. Scanning for the future is a capability TD professionals may want to obtain.
3. **Gather information.** Decide what information sources will likely be most useful and collect a wide range to ensure comprehensive data collection.
4. **Assess the information.** Look for patterns, trends, and other useful information, including answers to the original questions.
5. **Co-create the plan.** Allow for divergent ideas from leaders and employees to ensure diverse and inclusive data interpretation.
6. **Communicate the results.** This may be for internal use by TD professionals or shared with the broader organization. The key is to deliver the results of the scan to the decision makers.
7. **Take action.** Use the results to create a plan that will position talent development for the future.
8. **Monitor or repeat to stay current.** Although continuous scanning is ideal, it requires more effort and resources than many TD professionals have. It may be possible to partner with the planning department or other stakeholders in this effort.

3.8.2.4 Internal Scanning

Conducting environmental scans of an organization is often referred to as internal scanning. TD professionals could do internal scans of their organization, functions, processes, jobs, and technology:

- **Organization scans** provide a high-level overview of an organization and clues to what areas need an in-depth assessment to determine talent development needs. An organization scan reveals information about culture and values, strategy and structure, and strengths and weaknesses. It signals the kinds of development initiatives that will have the greatest impact on the organization.
- **Functional scans** explore a specific function within an organization and its influence on the organization's goals and effectiveness.
- **Process scans** explore a specific process to see how an organization operates and whether anything needs to change. A process scan also reveals best practices and identifies any skills gaps that need to be addressed for best results.
- **Job scans** identify the skill and behavioral dynamics that are required for success in a job. The job's manager and top performers provide input in a job scan.
- **Technology scans** can add value because technology has become such an organizational driver. A technology scan may help TD professionals understand where their organization is leveraging or dependent on technology and how likely that technology is to change.
- **Organizational capability scans** synthesize the findings prior to sharing results with others who may need TD professionals' help to fully understand the opportunities that could increase their effectiveness and competitive advantage.

3.8.2.5 Internal Scanning Techniques and Methods

TD professionals should know about these techniques for scanning:

- **Prior knowledge.** Employees and experts may already know how things are done. While this is a place to start, it is rarely enough.
- **Document analysis.** Looking at reports, budgets, presentations, operations reviews, statistical updates, and a host of other documents can reveal a great deal about how things work.
- **Questionnaires.** When done well, questionnaires can be informative, but the numbers can be hard to interpret. Open-ended questions are rich with data and it takes time to study them. Today, algorithms allow for continuous, real-time data collection.
- **Interviews.** These can be done with individuals or groups. Structured interviews are more manageable, but unstructured interviews can reveal more inside information.
- **Direct observation.** This can be an excellent source of data if done as part of a well-designed approach. At the job level, a common approach is to observe key performers. In this process, at least three key performers are identified, and then each is observed by more than one person.
- **Verification.** This is a lesser used approach and is always done in combination with others. It doesn't work at the organizational level, but it often can at a function, process, or job level. In short, benchmark against other organizations that have already conducted scans. [See 2.8.4 and 3.4.13.6]

When completing internal scanning at any level, TD professionals should include both key performers and average performers to learn what they know. It will be valuable to consider what is likely to change and what will drive that change. Try to uncover the difference between the "as is" and the "should be," and remember that just because something is written, it may not actually occur that way. Scanning is about gaining a broad understanding, not fixing a specific problem.

3.8.3 Knowledge of Techniques to Promote, Support, or Generate Innovation and Creativity

> **I. Fostering Innovation and Creativity**
>
> TD professionals have a responsibility to enable their organizations to reach goals on time, within budget, and with the highest quality possible. They should also help their organizations develop creativity and innovation to accomplish things they have never achieved before.

3.8.3.1 The Difference Between Innovation and Creativity
Creativity is the act of producing original ideas. *Innovation* is the act of translating a new method, product, or idea into a service or good that creates value. In organizations, innovation satisfies customer expectations or meets their needs. It is possible to be creative without innovating simply by not doing anything with a new idea. It is also possible to be innovative without being creative by taking someone else's idea and implementing it. In most organizations, the two are linked (Surbhi 2018).

3.8.3.2 The Value of Innovation and Creativity
Creativity and innovation are important to organizations because they help with:
- Inventing new businesses or lines of business
- Providing the means to do more with less by increasing productivity and reducing cost
- Fueling problem solving and process improvement
- Creating new products and services to meet new customer needs and preferences
- Attracting employees who want to work in innovative environments
- Diverging from industry norms in search of new value drivers
- Identifying new partnerships
- Uncovering organic or inorganic growth options

3.8.3.3 Promoting and Supporting Creativity and Innovation
Talent development is a lever that promotes creativity and innovation, and TD professionals can strengthen their brand by knowing how to support creativity and innovation in their organization by following these practices:
- **Promote and support an innovative culture.** TD professionals can lead the growth of skills in communication, collaboration, teaming, and problem solving, which are at the heart of innovation. TD professionals can help their organization improve how it delivers feedback, celebrates ideas, and values diversity. They can also promote the symbols of creativity and track the benefits of innovation.
- **Help leaders champion creativity and innovation.** TD professionals can help leaders develop the knowledge and skills to model creativity and innovation. They can provide tools and training to recognize and reward creativity, risk taking, and productive failure. Open communication and frequent feedback are hallmarks of an innovative organization.
- **Make creativity and innovation part of the culture.** TD professionals can help their organization be more deliberate by supporting these efforts:
    - Enable design thinking, human-centered design, inclusive design, and other design methods.
    - Sponsor brainstorming sessions, hackathons, and idea competitions.

- o Set aside times dedicated to creative thinking.
- o Introduce innovation as a formal part of every job description.
- o Make collaboration tools universally available.
- o Develop and manage innovation labs.
- o Encourage creativity and innovative social networks.
- o Create virtual and live forums for suggestions.
- **Organize for creativity and innovation.** Creativity and innovation happen most often in teams, so TD professionals can promote, train, and empower teams. They can also help their organization embrace flatter structures, implement flexible work schedules, and spread decision-making authority. Further, TD professionals can develop people to serve as innovation champions—employees who are passionate about and encourage innovation throughout their organization. Organizations should adopt after action reflection as a standard step in any project. TD professionals can also help create physical spaces that encourage creativity, where employees can gather to exchange ideas and collaborate, as well as explore technology and other tools to serve hybrid workplace needs.
- **Benchmark.** TD professionals can study other organizations that are best at creativity and innovation and bring those lessons to the organizations they serve. This ensures that best practices and next practices are shared throughout the organization.
- **Create a common language.** Two popular approaches for promoting innovation are design thinking (which is applied broadly to organizations) and the lean approach (a methodology to eliminate waste and improve quality of processes). Either can provide a discipline to create a common language for innovation. [See 3.8.3.4 and 2.2.13]
- **Drive creativity and innovation skills.** It is not enough to simply encourage people to be more creative or innovative. These skills must be developed, encouraged, and reinforced. TD professionals can introduce these skills into the regular flow of learning within the organization. TD professionals need to go beyond developing skills to be more innovative—talent development needs to be a driver for the organization.

3.8.3.4 Techniques to Generate Creativity

Creativity techniques can be divided into two primary categories: divergence and convergence. Best practices in creativity and innovation promote the use of multiple techniques in both categories.

3.8.3.4.1 Divergence

Divergence means generating a maximum number of ideas from which to choose.
- **Brainstorming** is the most common divergence tool for sparking creativity. There are numerous variations, including reverse brainstorming (what would someone do if they were trying to accomplish the opposite of the current goal) and random adjective brainstorming (applying random adjectives to ideas to spark more ideas).
- **Lateral thinking or perspective shifting** is the practice of considering the problem or opportunity from an unusual point of view; for example, "How would a five-year-old view this?"
- **Analogy thinking** takes concepts from other industries or organizations and applies their best practices in a new context.

- **Benchmarking** against other organizations can be especially useful when adopting new technologies or finding ways to expand markets.
- **Jamming** is a method of driving divergent thinking across an entire organization. Facilitators organize a conversation that may occur in person or using online tools. Jamming differs from brainstorming in that it incorporates other creative thinking tools such as pairing random words. The amount of time for jamming may last for weeks or it may be limited to a period of 24 to 48 hours.

3.8.3.4.2 Convergence

Convergence means starting with many ideas and then analyzing, filtering, and combining them to get more new and better ideas. Convergence techniques are crucial for converting creativity into innovation because they help narrow ideas into something that can produce innovation.

- **Mind mapping** starts by placing the objective into the center of a diagram and then organizing thoughts and ideas into branching subcategories, connections, and trends.
- **The Six Thinking Hats** approach designed by Edward de Bono (1999) is used to generate and analyze ideas from multiple perspectives to get convergence.
- **Idea shopping** uses voting to sort ideas by a group. Each individual gets currency and can spend whatever amount they choose to "buy" the ideas they like best.
- **Feasibility or value graphs** help teams position ideas based on their ease of implementation and value to the company and customers.

Other convergence techniques include clustering ideas to see if they can be combined, using paired comparison to select ideas, and forms of evaluation matrices. [See 1.2.7.2]

3.8.3.5 Design Thinking

Design thinking is a human-centered approach to innovation or problem solving that integrates the needs of people with the needs of the organization. Although design thinking was recently developed, its roots have been planted in global conversations for decades, starting with the melding of aesthetics and engineering principles by John Dewey in 1935. It was also influenced by the work of Horst Rittel and Richard Buchanan and focuses on finding the right solution rather than solving a problem. Design thinking follows five phases:

1. **Empathizing** requires a clear and empathic understanding of a problem.
2. **Defining the problem** requires compiling and synthesizing what was learned in the first phase.
3. **Ideating** begins once there is a clear understanding of the users and their needs, along with a solid background created by compiling the data. Like brainstorming, the idea is to gather as many ideas or solutions as possible at the beginning of the phase. By the end of the ideation phase, TD professionals should be able to investigate and test a couple of ideas to find a good option.
4. **Prototyping** requires the team to produce several scaled down versions of the solution. This is an experimental phase.
5. **Testing** is the final phase to evaluate the final product. However, given the iterative aspect of the process, the results generated are often used to redefine the problem and inform the users (Lewrick, Link, and Leifer 2018; Gibbons 2016). [See 2.2.13]

3.8.3.6 Lean Approach

Lean is a management approach that uses creativity techniques to focus on eliminating waste while improving quality. The goal is to cut costs by making an organization more efficient and responsive to the marketplace. The lean approach began in manufacturing, initiating the Six Sigma movement, and it's now applied to all aspects of business. In 2008, Eric Ries adapted the principles to high-tech startup companies, and it is now viewed as a way for companies to emulate the innovation and nimbleness of startups. There are five steps in the approach:

1. **Define the value.** The definition uses the customer perspective to establish customer-based objectives for every development experience that is delivered and produces only those elements that meet the objectives.
2. **Map the value stream.** Process mapping describes each step of the process and every activity that produces the customer value. This allows non-value-added activities to be identified. Unnecessary activities are eliminated and those that are necessary are streamlined.
3. **Create the flow.** The focus is reducing cycle time and expense and increasing quality and satisfaction. Process users implement the streamlining by employing several tools, including cross-training, workload leveling, changing job responsibilities, and reconfiguring the process.
4. **Establish pull.** Creating a pull-based system is a just-in-time production, which means work is done in time to meet customer needs and no sooner. In talent development, it may mean creating learning experiences in small chunks according to the greatest need, rather than based on a curriculum design.
5. **Pursue perfection.** The last step is challenging and perhaps the most pertinent to innovation. It is working to make continuous improvement a part of the culture. This step demands that the organization constantly learn to be better.

3.8.4 Knowledge of Emerging Learning Technologies and Support Systems

> **I. Evaluating Emerging Learning Technologies**
>
> New technologies emerge regularly, creating two critical obligations for TD professionals: to ensure that their organization and the people in it take full advantage of these breakthroughs and to prevent waste, disruption, or damage from technology that is not viable or appropriate. This means that TD professionals need to take initiative to know what technology and support systems the organization requires.

3.8.4.1 Stay Informed About Future Technologies

TD professionals should stay current regarding emerging technologies. For example, they should consider joining groups that discuss emerging technologies or identifying groups, associations, and nonprofits that take a broader societal view, focusing on technology and its potential impact. TD professionals can also attend conferences and programs offered by associations, governments, and universities. They should identify the technical skills their organization needs. [See 2.4.15]

Other approaches to staying current include networking, reading publications, following blogs, or simply getting to know someone who is deeply involved in new technology, such as an IT manager. TD professionals can track the technology trends of their customers, their consultants, and other organizations with whom they partner by asking about the technology they are using, what they are exploring, and what they plan to adopt. They can also search online for tools or whitepapers written by people analytics and talent intelligence firms. Finally, TD professionals can study those who predict future events such as Josh Bersin or Bob Johanson who are referenced in this chapter.

3.8.4.2 Prepare the Organization for Disruption

Perhaps the first step in preparing an organization for new TD technology and the disruption it can bring is to determine the organization's current readiness. TD professionals should do this by developing insights in four areas:

- **Determine organizational readiness.** Consider the level of technology awareness, sophistication and use in the organization, how much support there will be, and how easy access will be.
- **Decide if there are process issues.** Make sure the new technology doesn't conflict with existing policies or procedures and that it will be supported by existing systems.
- **Prepare the TD staff.** Make sure the team has the expertise to build or buy the program, roll it out, and sustain it.
- **Develop skills.** Ensure that TD staff can facilitate process improvement initiatives and use basic tools such as root-cause analysis, flow charting, cause-and-effect diagrams, histograms, Pareto charts, and others.
- **Obtain necessary support from IT.** Often, new learning technology will require staff's time, server space or cloud connection, and other services from IT. Make sure they're bought into these plans.

TD professionals can also assess what new capabilities and levels of expertise will be required of the target audience to make effective use of the new technology. They can follow several practices to prepare their organization for new learning technology:

- **Foster a digital culture.** A digital transformation will be more likely to succeed if the organization embraces a digital culture. Research shows that 90 percent of organizations that had successful digital transformations focused on culture first (Hemerling et al. 2018).
- **Provide ample information about the technology.** Communicate well in advance about any technology that may be viewed as a significant change. Learn who is using it, where, how, and for what, and then share that information. Although most employees won't need a lot of guidance, it is the TD professional's job to create awareness of the vast array of digital tools at their disposal.
- **Ensure that systems, processes, and rules are supportive.** TD professionals should help organizations identify and address any systemic issues that could prevent an effective adoption of digital learning tools.
- **Provide training on effective and secure use.** Employees need to understand common mistakes and potential misuses for any new technology. This will help them understand what support they can expect from the TD and IT departments, as well as where and how to report issues and get help. TD professionals can support the creation of a workforce that embraces technology.
- **Reward effective use.** TD professionals can promote technology that has proven effective and recognize the pioneers and early adopters of new technology. They can apply metrics to determine the effectiveness of traditional electronic performance support systems (EPSSs) to technology-based learning and be sure to credit the initiators when it originates outside the department. [See 2.4]
- **Maintain a data security focus.** The chance of an organization experiencing a data security breach increases every day. TD professionals can stay involved and informed about how to prevent breaches and help ensure their organization has a cybersecurity information team.

3.8.4.3 Current Technologies in Talent Development

TD professionals should be knowledgeable about technologies that will have a broad impact on talent development. As AI systems, robotics, and cognitive tools improve, almost every job is being reinvented, creating an augmented workforce. This trend is growing rapidly, causing organizations to reconsider job design and how work is organized. TD professionals should stay current with emerging technologies:

- **Artificial intelligence (AI).** AI refers to a set of computer science techniques that enable systems to perform tasks normally requiring human intelligence, such as visual perception, speech recognition, decision making, and language translation. In some organizations AI is already a key part of talent development, enabling personalized learning and development using algorithms to respond to individuals' needs and adapt to their preferences. One example of this personalization is chatbots, which take the place of a human coach or instructor for some parts of the learning experience. Most experts believe that some jobs will be replaced with AI, while others will be dramatically changed. Even though TD professionals may not have ultimate control of AI, they must at least have an opinion, create a plan, and hold their organization accountable for the ethical use of AI in the workplace. The TD function's plan must be part of a larger plan. And if there is no larger plan, TD professionals should take the lead to put one in place for their organization to ensure the integration promotes an approach that is aligned to the organization's values.

- **Analytics and evidence-based talent development.** TD professionals will likely use data to drive decisions, not just show impact. Moving from measurement to analytics will require them to do things differently. Impact management analytics is the practice of setting up an evaluation so it feeds back into the initiative in real time. This means acting on evaluation findings during the initiative rather than just at the end. [See 3.7.1]

- **The internet of things (IoT).** IoT refers to enabling communication between devices and humans across a network, such as the internet or a private intranet. This technology can be used to create more comfortable places to learn. For example, smart speakers allow TD professionals to access information and resources more easily. Devices that can announce when they need attention or repairs create efficiencies and may soon be able to teach people how to best interact with them. For example, interactive whiteboards are currently available for educators to use, and a significant part of IBM's $3 billion investment into IoT will be for education (Thompson and Smith 2019).

- **Wearable technology.** As wearables become common tools for everyday life, TD professionals should stay informed about the technology and its potential to transform learning experiences. Future workers may wear monitoring and computing devices that help them access learning resources in real time or check their performance against company goals and standards.

- **Augmented reality (AR).** AR technology layers information onto the existing world by "seeing" where the user is and matching the information to that context. As TD professionals endeavor to embed microlearning into work processes, they'll find growing applications for AR.

- **Virtual reality (VR).** VR can provide a highly immersive, completely simulated world in which people can learn. In its most sophisticated form, it can create entire learning experiences. As this technology becomes less expensive to create, TD professionals should uncover where it can add value.

- **Virtual collaboration tools.** These tools have become critical with the expansion of remote employees who require ways to ensure clear communication, a mechanism to get immediate feedback on work, and a way to connect with their colleagues. Video conferencing tools are a

3.8 Future Readiness

requirement for conducting virtual meetings. Collaboration tools such as digital whiteboards, polling and surveying software, project management software, and file management tools are also important for supporting synchronous and asynchronous work.

- **Simulations and serious games.** Talent development has seen a recent resurgence in these tools. Gamification is the application of typical elements of game playing (such as point scoring, competition, and rules of play) to development initiatives that are used as either the optimal learning approach or simply as a technique to encourage engagement. Simple, cost-effective, and short simulations offer a way for TD professionals to use that technology (Aldrich 2019).
- **API and xAPI.** It is possible that Tin Can API may soon overtake SCORM as the standard for learning record storage as the TD function seeks to capture a wider range of development experiences. [See 2.4 and 3.7]

3.8.4.4 Considerations for TD Professionals of the Future

TD professionals should be aware of these issues as they relate to emerging learning technologies and support systems:

- **TD professionals should sponsor development options.** They should serve as the sponsor of both quality and utility of technology resources and options for their organization. They can create guides for self-service and portals that prioritize trusted sources and solutions. The goal is to make it easy and natural for employees to use well-vetted methods and sources. [See 2.8.1.5 and 3.8.4.2]
- **TD professionals have a responsibility for guidance.** They should serve as guides and consultants to help their organization and each person in it understand what technology is available, what they need, and how to locate it. As development and career pathing partners, TD professionals can help employees identify the most useful technology. The organization should have an infrastructure that individuals can use to create their own development experience, and TD professionals can help those who need support. These responsibilities require TD professionals to become more involved in the adoption of new technology.
- **TD professionals should adopt and encourage an experimental mindset.** They should embrace experimentation on their own part and on the behalf of learners when it comes to development opportunities. They can act as role models to design training solutions. In the experimental environment, there is rarely control of or even predictability about results. TD professionals should encourage individuals and groups to launch their own development experiments and support their experimentation by helping them find the experiences that are most relevant to their development needs and most valued by the organization. If individuals are increasingly in charge of their own development, development experiments should also be in their hands. TD professionals can influence how much and how well individuals experiment by offering options or tools; recommending websites or actions; inventing challenges through competition or games; delivering reminders of encouragement; and sharing development experiences.
- **TD professionals should do more coaching and consulting.** Coaching is beneficial to organizations because it promotes organizational consistency, furthers leadership development, reduces turnover, and helps ensure solid leadership succession. Likewise, with continual change ahead, TD professionals need to be effective internal consultants for their organizations. Consultants have a unique set of competencies that go beyond the typical TD professional's role. Both coaching and

consulting benefit TD professionals, who become more respected contributors. In addition, when they practice coaching and consulting skills, TD professionals increase their own capacity for leadership and enhance their ability to support their organizations (Biech 2018). [See 2.7 and 3.2]

- **TD professionals should adapt to an increasingly distributed and hybrid workforce.** A hybrid workforce is made up of employees who work remotely and those who work from an office or central location. There is an immediate need to implement new ways of learning and working for employees as well as gig workers who have become an integral part of the workforce. TD professionals need to assist with dividing asynchronous work into components that can be offered as tasks across the organization.

3.8.5 Knowledge of Information-Seeking Strategies and Techniques

I. Identifying Information Sources

TD professionals should know where to locate quality resources and be able to guide others who are seeking them. [See 2.5.9]

3.8.5.1 The Standard Information-Seeking Model

Information seeking is a relatively new topic. Research on how searchers interact with search engines started just before 2000 and is still forming; so far, it has focused on the models used and the kind of searches conducted. When seeking information, TD professionals should know the value of conducting both horizontal and vertical searches:

- **Horizontal searches** are general and typically produce many results over a wide range. Searching for the phrase "coaching for leaders," for example, will get hundreds of thousands of hits that vary and may include anything from how-to videos and books to university programs and executive coaches.
- **Vertical searches** are targeted, usually producing limited results, such as searching for "brainstorming tools."

A standard information-seeking model is used most often and has two variations: the first is presented in stages and the second is a strategic process. The steps in the standard information-seeking model represent the impact of iterative searches:

1. Recognize, accept, and formulate the problem.
2. Express the problem.
3. Identify all possible sources.
4. Select best sources (most reliable information and answers; Hearst 2009).
5. Examine the results.
6. Reformulate the problem (Marchionini and White 2008).

3.8.5.1.1 Information Seeking in Stages

Information seeking in stages is often used in complex searching, beginning with recognition of need. However, this first stage may not be clear because the searcher needs highly complex, sophisticated, or extensive information. Information seeking in stages allows for a more deliberate approach to complex issues.

The six stages are:

1. **Initiation.** Recognize the need for information. (I wasn't trained as a TD professional, and I need those skills.) Early searches will be general, trying to better understand the nature of the problem or opportunity.
2. **Selection.** Select the general area of the search. (I need to understand instructional systems design.)
3. **Exploration.** Determine the best way to get the information on the general topic. (What is available to help me become an ISD expert?) This step includes discovering several possible approaches and resources (such as getting a degree, attending conferences, or watching webinars).
4. **Formulation.** At this point, the search becomes better planned, and some sources and options are eliminated. A sequence or a timeline may be developed.
5. **Collection.** This is the gathering of the specific information over time to meet the need. At this point, the process can become iterative and branch.
6. **Presentation.** The search is complete and a judgement is made as to whether the search has been successful. If the need has been met, the process is complete.

3.8.5.1.2 Information Seeking as a Strategic Process

Information seeking as a strategic process is based on the belief that a search can be more strategic if it is done consciously. This awareness incudes three elements:

- **Be aware of the exact terms of the search.** Searchers track how and when the query changes. Often, when a searcher doesn't obtain the desired results, they'll change a word or phrase and start a new path. Recording these changes maintains what occurred for continued searches. Sometimes the search engine suggests word changes or provides a list of related searches.
- **Record the pathways taken.** Many sources contain hyperlinks to other documents or cited sources. When taking any of these paths, it is easy for the searcher to lose track of how they got there. More significantly, it is possible to assume that they've obtained all the pertinent information before being fully exposed to the sources they originally sought. If the approach changes, it should be done consciously, and the reason should be recorded.
- **Check on progress.** Searchers must ensure that they track any cost or time parameters that are part of the search. Compare progress to the timeline set for the search.

It's also important that the person knows when the search is complete. The most obvious indication is that all the needed information is in hand. But there are other reasons to stop as well:

- It isn't all the available information, but it's enough to do what's required.
- The cost of further searching isn't worth the expected results.
- The search itself proves that having the information is not as valuable as thought.
- New priorities call for a different search.
- The circumstances that prompted the search may have changed (Hearst 2009).

3.8.5.2 Identifying Resources

Steps three and four of the information-seeking model are critical, and TD professionals should not assume everything they need is on the internet. It isn't. TD professionals should consider visiting a library because librarians can be knowledgeable and provide expert tips for locating specific information. Consider looking for scholarly papers and professional articles that will delve into the research to reveal best practices and informative examples to apply.

TD professionals should begin by determining the purpose of the search they are conducting, such as to inform, persuade, or describe a process. They should then identify all possible sources, depending on the kind of information they need to support their process. Examples include:
- **Current statistics or data**—news articles, databases, government reports, journal articles, almanacs, research papers, and surveys
- **Historical facts**—encyclopedias, books, and research paper references
- **Recent information**—online newsletters or magazines, news site indexes, and interviews with experts
- **Opinions**—newspaper op-eds, magazines, and websites

3.8.5.3 Selecting the Best Resources

TD professionals should ensure that the sources of information they use are reliable, credible, and current. To determine this, they should consider where the information originated, whether the author is an expert, whether the organization is viewed as an industry leader, and whether the information was presented as opinion or fact. They should also:
- Note how current the date is.
- Determine the author's credentials.
- Verify the legitimacy of the organization, group, or individual.
- Examine whether the information was cited.
- Track specific data to the originating source or verify it with another source.
- Determine whether quotations are opinions or backed by data and facts.
- Review the content for evidence of bias.
- Cross industry boundaries to check other industries' knowledge.

3.8.6 Skill in Applying Previous Learning to Future Experiences

> **I. Learning Agility**
>
> TD professionals should be lifelong learners who can apply what they have learned to new situations. In this era of perpetual disruption, the products, services, and strategies that work today may not work tomorrow. The best performing organizations require TD professionals and employees who thrive on change.

3.8.6.1 Understanding Learning Agility

Learning agility is the ability and willingness to learn from experience and subsequently apply that knowledge to perform under new or first-time conditions. Learning agility is based on these attributes:
- **Self-awareness**—knowing oneself well, understanding one's capabilities and where there is room to grow, and knowing how one affects those around them.
- **Mental agility**—breaking down complex problems, seeing patterns and connections, and considering multiple possibilities.
- **Change agility**—a hunger for learning, a willingness to take risks and experiment, and the ability to effectively deal with ambiguity and change.
- **People agility**—understanding and relating to others, harnessing diversity, and understanding other viewpoints and motivations.
- **Results agility**—finding a way to meet goals and produce results in new and changing situations (Knight and Wong 2017).

Other attributes commonly associated with learning agility are speed, flexibility, collaboration, feedback seeking, and the ability to be coached. All attributes have a common denominator that's the foundation of new knowledge and the application of experience. Self-acceptance of flaws and past mistakes allows for new thinking to emerge.

3.8.6.2 Learning for Personal or Professional Development

The resources for personal and professional development are virtually unlimited. While every TD professional may not possess every attribute of learning agility, there is at least one requisite: a hunger for learning. TD professionals must avail themselves to multiple resources to enthusiastically pursue lifelong learning. [See 1.7]

3.8.6.3 Benefits and Value of Learning Agility

Learning agility is increasingly critical to individual and organizational success. Learning agility is often a required characteristic for high-potential employees, and its link to organizational success is reflected in the increasing appearance of the concept in corporate annual reports. According to Josh Bersin (2016), "Organizations with a strong learning culture are 92 percent more likely to develop innovative products or processes, 52 percent more productive, and 56 percent more likely to be the first to market with their products and services." A high level of learning agility was found to be a key predictor of executive leadership success in a study that also recommended strategies such as executive coaching to develop this competency (Goebel and Baskerville 2013).

Learning agility is rapidly becoming the key to organizational survival and success. "Learning agility (mediated by job content on-the-job learning) was found to be a better predictor of being identified as a high potential than job performance. Career variety was also found to be positively associated to learning agility" (Dries, Vantilborgh, and Pepermans 2012).

3.8.6.4 Personal Mastery

According to Peter Senge, personal mastery is the "discipline of continually clarifying and deepening our personal vision, of focusing our energies, of developing patience, and of seeing reality objectively. People with a high level of personal mastery are able to consistently realize the results that matter most deeply to them" (Senge et al. 1994).

Senge (2006) introduced the concept with seven pathways to personal mastery:
- **Personal vision** is the ability to clearly picture the best person possible and work toward that vision with focus, determination, and diligence.
- **Personal purpose** is the drive to make a difference.
- **Personal values** means knowing the things that matter most.
- **Personal alignment** means a person's personal vision, purpose, values, and behaviors are congruent with each other.
- **Personal perception** is an awareness of the frames of reference through which people perceive things.
- **Personal awareness** means how much people know (or are willing to know) about themselves.
- **Personal transformation** means a person's capacity to reshape themselves to be more in harmony with their personal vision, values, and purpose.

3.8.6.5 Past Experience

When people look at current situations, they are not merely comparing them to what they have already experienced. The brain tries to apply rules, criteria, and categories to connect the new input. Learning from past experiences rewires the brain so people can categorize the things they experience and respond appropriately—currently and in the future. In the last two decades, the use of functional magnetic resonance imaging (fMRI) has shown that this rewiring is not just functional, but physical (Adlaf et al. 2017).

In the brain, new knowledge changes connections between neurons. Increases in cell-to-cell cooperation produce reliable and sustained learning. Stronger connections between teams of neurons representing separate moments in time let the brain predict what happens next. Neuroplasticity is the term coined to describe the brain's ability to reorganize itself, both physically and functionally, due to the environment, behavior, thinking (learning), and emotions.

When the brain strengthens a new connection, it also weakens other connections that may interfere or conflict with the new information. The more difficult the change, the bigger the required brain change. The more important the change is perceived to be, the bigger the change. Spaced training has shown that if the new information is repeated within five minutes and then again within 30 minutes, it is more likely to be retained. TD professionals should remember that initial changes in the brain are temporary and devise effective means to refresh and repeat new skills to ensure mastery and retention.

Past experiences control the process. When people practice, the brain discards the less perfect, remembers the better attempts, and enables progressive improvement. Mental rehearsals trigger the same kinds of neural changes as real-world practice sessions. But this can only happen when the brain is ready. If a person is alert and prepared to learn, the brain releases the chemicals to enable change. If the person is uninterested or distracted, it doesn't.

Mindfulness and other reflective practices have been introduced to TD professionals to support personal and professional growth. Carol Dwek's ideas about growth mindsets and fixed mindsets, and emerging knowledge about the importance of training brains to learn new pathways through neuroplasticity, have shown great results in creating the conditions in which employees can learn, retain, and practice new knowledge, skills, and attitudes. [See 1.7.1.8]

3.8.6.6 Learning Theories
TD professionals should understand the foundational learning theories:
- **Behaviorism** assumes that all behaviors are a response to certain stimuli in the environment, which are a consequence of a person's history, especially reinforcement and punishment.
- **Cognitivism** focuses on thinking, knowing, memory, and problem solving with the goal of affecting the thought processes in a learner's mind. Learning happens when a new situation disturbs the equilibrium and requires the learners to accommodate the new information into an existing schema.
- **Constructivism** articulates that learning is an active process, directed and managed by a learner. People can add new information, assimilate it into existing understanding and practice, or completely rethink and change what they do. Constructivism fits well with the concepts of individualized, learner-directed development. [See 2.1.1.2]

- **Social learning theory** assumes that the acquisition of knowledge can be directly related to observations from social interactions, media, and experiences; essentially, through interacting with the environment. Learning is optimized when the environment is supportive of learning. [See 2.1.3.10]

Whether improving their own learning agility or developing others based on one of these theories, TD professionals should remember several basic principles that support learning agility:
- **Understand the learners' perspective.** TD professionals should analyze the current state to determine the rewards and punishments in the environment and how they will be perceived by learners. Find out what they already know and why they may want to learn new content.
- **Create tools and resources that adapt to varying levels of readiness.** In a personalized world of learning, learners will start from different places. Adaptive learning means that individuals can move through a totally customized development process.
- **Confirm the information is relevant.** Find ways to understand the learner's goals to help them see learning relevancy and connect it to their current mental models.
- **Structure learning in easily consumable pieces.** The most valuable aspect of microlearning is that it allows learners to add information in easily digestible chunks.
- **Measure progress in real time.** With the right system, TD professionals can get feedback they can use to improve the resources immediately. [See 3.7]

3.8.6.7 Techniques to Apply Knowledge in the Future
TD professionals should leverage what they know to project their work into the future using these ideas:
- **Reflect on what has been learned.** Before it can be applied in a future context, the new information must be fully understood. Part of that reflection can include challenging assumptions or finding others who will. Talking or writing about what has been learned can also be effective.
- **Create a strategy and a plan for the future.** Doing so will predict the actions in practical terms that apply to TD professional's work:
  o Focus on the relevance of the knowledge to the strategy, and plan to anticipate emerging issues that apply to the future.
  o Determine which short- and intermediate-term goals can help pave the way to the future.
- **Understand and manage disruptors.** Events, situations, or politics may force a short-term view. They may be important now, but don't eliminate a long-term focus.
- **Anticipate consequences.** Predict the rewards for individuals and the organization if the knowledge is applied into the future. Predict the consequences if it isn't applied.
- **Practice and reinforce concepts in a future context.** For example, the information could be implemented in a progressive part of the organization or delivered via an external network or association of like-minded thinkers.
- **Track and measure.** Create a plan to apply new skills in the future, use milestones, and measure against them.

3.8.6.8 Commit to Applying Learning for the Future

TD professionals should create a strategy and plan for future learning. It is a big step, but they could consider a "goal a month" or a "goal a quarter" approach. For each month, identify one way to apply what has been learned to the future. Ideally, these goals should be expressed in measurable, behavioral terms.

Several tools can help TD professionals organize how they can apply what they're currently learning for the future:

- **The "Think–Puzzle–Explore" tool** can help organize broad and disconnected thoughts to find patterns in prior learning by simply adding the words "in the future" to the explore column (Ritchhart, Church, and Morrison 2011).
- **The KWL chart** is a simple three-column tool to record what a person knows, what they want to know, and what they've learned. In that same spirit, an LPD chart notes what was learned, what the plan was or is for acting on it, and what has been done.

Finally, TD professionals can join a group such as a community of practice that explores the future and how to apply new knowledge and skills as they emerge. Sharing goals and milestones among group members creates a focus and commitment to meet them. Such groups celebrate success and share advice. Technology is available to support writing plans, tracking progress, keeping journals, and documenting wins.

REFERENCES

Adlaf, E.W., R.J. Vaden, A.J. Niver, A.F. Manuel, V.C. Onyilo, M.T. Araujo, C.V. Dieni, H.T. Vo, G.D. King, J.I. Wasiche, and L. Overstreet-Wadiche. 2017. "Adult-Born Neurons Modify Excitatory Synaptic Transmission to Existing Neurons." *eLife* 6:e19886. elifesciences.org/articles/19886#xa7f04b22.

Aguilar, F.W. 1967. *Scanning the Business Environment*. New York: Macmillan.

Aldrich, C. 2019. "Short Sims: The Pedagogy for the Next Generation." shortsims.com.

Akeroyd, K. 2021. "Five Reasons Why the Rapidly Expanding Contingent Workforce Is a C-Suite Priority," *Forbes*, August 6. forbes.com/sites/forbestechcouncil/2021/08/06/five-reasons-why-the-rapidly-expanding-contingent-workforce-is-a-c-suite-priority/?sh=7d525fb63475.

Bersin, J. 2016. "Becoming Irresistible: A New Model for Employee Engagement." Deloitte University Press, January 26.

Bersin, J., B. Pelster, J. Schwartz, and B. van der Vyver. 2017. *Rewriting the Rules for the Digital Age: 2017 Deloitte Global Human Capital Trends*. Deloitte. deloitte.com/content/dam/Deloitte/us/Documents/human-capital/hc-2017-global-human-capital-trends-us.pdf.

Biech, E. 2018. *ATD's Foundations of Talent Development: Launching, Leveraging, and Leading Your Organization's TD Effort*. Alexandria, VA: ATD Press.

Brown, A., and E. Weiner. 1985. *Supermanaging: How to Harness Change for Personal and Organizational Success*. New York: McGraw-Hill.

Center for Creative Leadership (CCL). 2022. "The Leadership Gap: How to Fix What Your Organization Lacks." CCL Leading Effectively, October 4. ccl.org/articles/leading-effectively-articles/leadership-gap-what-you-still-need.

Choo, C.W. 2012. "Environmental Scanning as Information Seeking and Organizational Learning." University of Toronto. choo.ischool.utoronto.ca/FIS/respub/chooIMreader.pdf.

De Bono, E. 1999. *Six Thinking Hats*. New York: Back Bay Books.

Dries, N., T. Vantilborgh, and R. Pepermans. 2012. "The Role of Learning Agility and Career Variety In the Identification and Development of High Potential Employees." *Personnel Review* 41(3): 340–358.

Fahey, L., and V. Narayanan. 1986. *Macroenvironmental Analysis for Strategic Management*. St. Paul, MN: Cengage.

Gibbons, S. 2016. "Design Thinking 101." Nielsen Norman Group, July 31. nngroup.com/articles/design-thinking.

Goebel, S., and R. Baskerville. 2013. "From Self-Discovery to Learning Agility in Senior Executives." Third Annual International Conference on Engaged Management Scholarship. Atlanta, GA. September 19–22. dx.doi.org/10.2139/ssrn.2327668.

Hearst, M. 2009. *Search User Interfaces*. Cambridge: Cambridge University Press.

Hemerling, J., J. Kilmann, M. Danoesastro, L. Stutts, and C. Ahern. 2018. "It's Not a Digital Transformation Without a Digital Culture." Boston Consulting Group, April 13. bcg.com/en-us/publications/2018/not-digital-transformation-without-digital-culture.aspx.

Johanson, B. 2012. *Leaders Make the Future: Ten New Leadership Skills for an Uncertain World*. San Francisco: Barrett-Koehler.

Knight, M., and N. Wong. 2017. "The Organizational X-Factor: Learning Agility." Korn Ferry, November 22. focus.kornferry.com/leadership-and-talent/the-organisational-x-factor-learning-agility.

Lewrick, M., P. Link, and L. Leifer. 2018. *The Design Thinking Playbook: Mindful Digital Transformation of Teams, Products, Services, Businesses, and Ecosystems*. Hoboken, NJ: John Wiley and Sons.

Marchionini, G., and R.W. White. 2008. "Find What You Need, Understand What You Find." *Journal of Human-Computer Interaction* 23(3): 205–237.

PEST Analysis Tool. "PEST (PESTLE/STEEPLE) Market Analysis Tool." Business Balls. businessballs.com/strategy-innovation/pest-market-analysis-tool.

Ritchhart, R., M. Church, and K. Morrison. 2011. *Making Thinking Visible: How to Promote Engagement, Understanding, and Independence for All Learners*. Hoboken, NJ: John Wiley and Sons.

Senge, P.M. 2006. *The Fifth Discipline: The Art and Practice of the Learning Organization*, rev. ed. New York: Currency/Doubleday.

Senge, P., A. Kleiner, C. Roberts, R. Ross, and B. Smith. 1994. *The Fifth Discipline Fieldbook*. New York: Currency/Doubleday.

Surbhi, S. 2018. "Difference Between Creativity and Innovation." Key Differences, December 4. keydifferences.com/difference-between-creativity-and-innovation.html.

Thompson, N., and B. Smith. 2019. "Virtual Summit: AI and the Future of Work." IBM Watson AI. ibm.com/watson/future-of-work.

Zahidi, S., V. Ratcheva, G. Hingel, and S. Brown. 2020. "The Future of Jobs Report 2020." Geneva, Switzerland: World Economic Forum. weforum.org/docs/WEF_Future_of_Jobs_2020.pdf.

Recommended Reading

Ball, M. 2022. *The Metaverse and How It Will Revolutionize Everything*. New York: Liveright Publishing Corporation.

Canton, J. 2006. *The Extreme Future: The Top Trends That Will Reshape the World for the Next 5, 10, and 20 Years*. New York: Dutton.

Eubanks, B. 2019. "Meeting Tomorrow's Skills Demands Today." *TD at Work*. Alexandria, VA: ATD Press.

Jesuthasan, R., and J. Bourdreau. 2018. *Reinventing Jobs: A 4-Step Approach for Applying Automation to Work*. Boston: Harvard Business Review Press.

Lewrick, M., P. Link, and L. Leifer. 2018. *The Design Thinking Playbook: Mindful Digital Transformation of Teams, Products, Services, Businesses, and Ecosystems*. Hoboken, NJ: John Wiley and Sons.

Weise, M. 2021. *Long Life Learning: Preparing for Jobs That Don't Even Exist Yet*. Hoboken, NJ: John Wiley and Sons.

GLOSSARY

360-degree feedback evaluation is a process created by the Center for Creative Leadership (CCL) that is based on opinions and recommendations from superiors, direct reports, peers, and internal and external customers on how a person performs in any number of behavioral areas.

4-D cycle is the approach used in appreciative inquiry consisting of four phases: discovery, dream, design, and destiny.

4-Ds are the four steps in David Cooperrider's appreciative inquiry model for change: discovery, dream, design, and destiny.

508 compliant is shorthand for an amendment to the United States Workforce Rehabilitation Act of 1973 that requires that all electronic and information technology developed, procured, maintained, or used by the federal government to be accessible to people with disabilities.

70-20-10 is a framework identified by the Center for Creative Leadership (CCL) to demonstrate the ways that people often learn in workplace settings: 70 percent through experience or learning on the job, 20 percent through social development or learning from others, and 10 percent through formal learning such as courses, workshops, or reading. There is no empirical evidence behind this theory, yet it can be used as a guideline for learning design professionals to create a mix of learning resources or in conversations with stakeholders.

A

Academic assignment is a development action that allows individuals to partner with others in an academic environment to extend their learning through activities such as co-authoring articles and leading initiatives.

Accelerated learning (AL) is the practice of using a multimodal, multisensory approach to instruction to make learning more efficient. It's accomplished by honoring the different learning preferences of each participant and using experiential learning exercises (such as role plays, mnemonics, props, and music).

Accessibility most often refers to ensuring that employees with temporary and permanent disabilities have comparable access to information or services as those without disabilities.

Accommodation is part of Piaget's constructivism theory, which describes how learners must reshape or change what they already know. (This is a more substantial change than assimilation.)

Achievement oriented describes leaders who set challenging goals and encourage high performance as a means of showing confidence in a group's ability.

Action learning is a process of organizing small teams of individuals to solve real problems in their work environment while reflecting on their actions and what they are learning throughout the process.

Action planning is a written acknowledgment of the current coaching situation. It expresses specific goals with steps to attain them and lists timelines, expected outcomes, and ideas about the coach's role.

Action research, a term first coined by Kurt Lewin, is also known as participatory research. It is learning by doing that occurs when a group of workers or teams as part of a community of practice identifies a problem, develops a resolution, implements the solution, and then analyzes the final results. Transformative change occurs through the simultaneous process of taking action and doing research, which are linked by critical reflection.

Active listening describes a process in which a listener has a high level of interaction with a speaker, listening for content, meaning, and feelings.

Active training is an approach that ensures participants are involved in the learning process. It is based on cooperative learning, in which participants learn from one another in pairs or small groups, such as in group discussions, games, simulations, and role plays.

Adaptive leadership framework, introduced by Ronald Heifetz and Marty Linsky (2017), is the ability to adapt and thrive in challenging environments. It is based on four principles: emotional intelligence, organizational justice, development, and character.

Adaptive learning is defined as an approach that works to tailor the learning experience to the specific needs of the individual, often using technology that makes it scalable across a larger number of learners.

ADDIE is an instructional systems development model composed of five phases: analysis, design, development, implementation, and evaluation.

Adjourning stage is the last stage of the five-stage Tuckman model, when a team prepares for termination. Once the goal is achieved, the team recognizes its own accomplishments, may be rewarded by others, and disbands.

ADKAR model is an approach for planning and executing change. The model describes five core building blocks necessary for an individual to change: awareness of why change is needed; desire to change one's behavior to support the change; knowledge of how to change; ability, time, and resources to apply the new knowledge; and reinforcement to sustain the change.

Adult learning theory is the collective theories and principles of how adults learn and acquire knowledge. Popularized by Malcolm Knowles, adult learning theory provides the foundation for talent development professionals to meet learning needs in the workplace.

Advanced degree education is participating in higher education programs for exposure to fresh and innovative best practices.

Affective objective is a learning goal that specifies the acquisition of a particular attitude, value, or feeling.

Affinity diagrams are used to organize a large number of ideas (often generated by brainstorming) into logical groups based on the natural relationships among the ideas. Each idea group is defined and labeled. The tool is effective when a group of people need to make a decision. See also *interrelationship digraphs*.

After action review (AAR) was first developed by the US Army to encourage individuals to learn for themselves after an activity, project, or task by evaluating and analyzing what happened, why, and how to improve performance.

Aggregation is the act of curating the most relevant information about a particular topic into a single location.

Agile change management is an iterative approach to planning and executing change, with change planned to occur in short bursts, called sprints, that provide immediately recognizable value to the end user.

Algorithm is a logical set of rules that create a method to solve a problem. It includes calculations, data processing, and reasoning. It depicts physical steps or behaviors and the rationale that supports them.

Americans With Disabilities Act (ADA) is legislation passed by the US Congress in 1990 that prohibits discrimination in employment, public services, transportation, public accommodations, and telecommunications services against persons with disabilities. An individual is considered to have a disability if they have a physical or mental impairment that substantially limits one or more major life activities, has a record of such an impairment, or is regarded as having such an impairment. The ADA prohibits discrimination in all employment practices, including job application procedures, hiring, firing, advancement, compensation, training, and other terms, conditions, and privileges of employment.

Analysis is a systematic examination and evaluation of data or information that uncovers interrelationships by breaking it into its component parts. Standard analyses in talent development include training needs analysis, training design analysis, root cause analysis, job analysis, and SWOT (a matrix analysis of strengths, weaknesses, opportunities, and threats). In addition, as the first phase in the ADDIE model, analysis is the process of gathering data to identify the who, what, where, when, and why of the design process.

Analytics is the discovery and communication of meaningful patterns in data; for example, talent management analytics refers to the use of HR and talent data to improve business performance.

Analyzing is the systematic examination and evaluation of data or information. It uncovers interrelationships in the data by breaking it into its component parts and requires sorting, tabulating, and comparing raw data.

Andragogy (from Greek and meaning adult learning) is the method and practice of teaching adults. It was advanced by Malcolm Knowles, whose theory outlines five fundamental principles of adult learning: self-concept, prior experience, readiness to learn, orientation to learning, and motivation to learn.

API (application programming interface) is a way for computer programs or software to communicate with one another.

Appreciative inquiry (AI) is David Cooperrider's approach to large-scale organizational change that involves the analysis of positive and successful (rather than negative or failing) operations. The AI 4-D cycle (discovery, dream, design, and destiny) includes identifying areas for improvement, analyzing previous successes, searching for solutions, and developing an action plan.

Apprenticeships describe a relationship-driven learning model between an expert and a novice. The expert works closely with the novice to develop skills and knowledge needed to become independent. In some situations, it may refer to a combination of on-the-job training and related classroom instruction. The apprentice learns the theoretical aspects of a highly skilled occupation in the classroom, as well as the practical elements while being supervised by a more experienced professional on the job.

Artificial intelligence (AI) is typically defined as the ability of a machine to simulate human cognitive processes, such as perceiving, reasoning, learning, interacting with the environment, problem solving, and creativity.

As is refers to the current state of performance. Usually, a performance or a knowledge gap is expressed in terms of "as is" versus desired or "to be" or "should be."

Assessment refers to the process of collecting data to understand an issue, situation, opportunity, or problem. It is an ongoing interactive process to monitor progress and areas that need improvement. Both assessment and evaluation use measures, but assessment is formative, and evaluation is summative and applied against standards. See also *evaluation*.

Assessment center is a process that organizations use to determine candidates' suitability for a job or during a performance appraisal. It may include various activities such as simulations, problem analysis, interviews, role plays, written reports, or group exercises.

Assimilation is part of Piaget's constructivism theory and describes how a learner fits an idea into what they already know.

Associate Professional in Talent Development (APTD) is a certification for talent development professionals who are in the early part of their careers or whose professional roles and aspirations are focused on foundational areas of the field. The capabilities included in the APTD are the basics of talent development that professionals can use every day, no matter their level within an organization or company. It may be a destination for some or a pathway to the CPTD for others.

Association for Talent Development (ATD) is a global not-for-profit association for professionals who are involved in learning, development, training, or talent development.

Assumption is something that is accepted as true without proof. The "without proof" part of an assumption is what people often forget when they evaluate a situation.

Asynchronous training or learning is when the trainer and the learner do not participate simultaneously in time or location; for example, a self-paced e-learning module is asynchronous.

ATD Human Performance Improvement (HPI) Model is a results-based, systematic process used to identify performance problems, analyze root causes, select and design solutions, manage solutions in the workplace, measure results, and continually improve performance in an organization.

Attitude is the disposition, belief, feeling, or opinion an individual has about something or someone else.

Attending and focusing skills indicate that TD professionals are giving their physical attention to others. They are nonverbal messages that show the speaker that a listener cares and is listening.

Attentive listening describes a situation in which the listener has no interaction with the speaker, such as listening to the radio or a podcast.

Audience analysis is conducted to gather data about a target population, demographics, and other relevant information prior to job analysis, training, or other solutions.

Augmented reality (AR) overlays digital information onto real-world environments through a mobile or head-mounted device. This information may include navigation directions, location information, or many other location-based details. AR is valuable for talent development as a means of performance support because targeted information can be displayed in context without requiring users to stop their work.

Augmented workforce refers to the use of nonemployees—including consultants, contingent workers, freelancers, and even AI and robots—to support an organization's work.

Authoring tools are software programs that allow a content expert to interact with a computer in everyday language to develop courseware.

B

Balanced scorecard approach is a strategic planning and management system for measuring and tracking an organization's performance through four perspectives: the customer, learning and growth (or innovation), internal business processes, and financial.

Baseline is a measured starting point used for comparison.

Behavioral career counseling is a scientifically precise approach to career decision making that leverages concepts from psychology.

Bench strength is the capability of members of an organization's staff to move into positions of greater responsibility when required.

Behavioral objectives are goals that specify a new observable skill or knowledge that a learner should be able to demonstrate after training or a learning event.

Behavioral leadership theory focuses on the actions of leaders, such as democratic, autocratic, and laissez-faire leaders.

Behaviorism is a learning theory focused on observable and measurable behavior. It is usually associated with psychologist B.F. Skinner, who predicted that animal and human behavior occurs through conditioning, which is the reinforcement of desired responses.

Benchmark is a standard or a reference point against which things may be compared or assessed.

Benchmarking is a measure of quality that compares business process metrics to standard measurements or the best industry measures. The purposes of benchmarking are to compare and analyze similar items to learn how other organizations achieve performance levels and to use this information to make improvements.

Best practices are techniques that are believed to constitute a paradigm of excellence in a particular field.

Bias is prejudice in favor of or against one thing, person, or group compared to another, usually considered unfair.

Big data is a term used to describe multiple lists of data sets that are too large to capture and process using common methods for analysis. Its significance depends on the data's volume, velocity, variety, veracity, and value.

Blended learning is the practice of using several media in one curriculum. It refers to the combination of formal and informal learning events, such as classroom instruction, online resources, and on-the-job coaching.

Block diagram, more often called a flowchart, is a drawing of a system in which the principal parts or functions are represented by geometric shapes (squares or rectangles) connected by lines that show the relationships of the parts to one another. This terminology is most often used in electronic, software, and hardware design.

Bloom's Taxonomy, developed by Benjamin Bloom, is a hierarchical model used to classify learning into three outcomes or domains—cognitive (knowledge), psychomotor (skills), and affective (attitude)—referred to as KSAs. The domain categories use verbs to define behavior in a hierarchical relationship that becomes progressively more complex and difficult to achieve. The taxonomy is useful for writing learning objectives.

Bot, short for robot, is a device or software that can interact with other computer systems to reply to messages or perform tasks automatically. Bots can be chatbots, social bots, web crawlers, or malicious bots that, among other things, may be used to crack passwords.

Boundary spanning is the act of employees who communicate with one another and share information across department lines.

Brainstorming is a group process used to generate multiple ideas through spontaneous and unrestrained participation.

Branding references the comprehensive marketing concept organizations use to differentiate themselves.

Business analysis is the process of identifying and clarifying primary organizational goals, targets, or needs. It is also a step in ATD's HPI model that examines the factors affecting an organization's strategic imperative and outcomes related to performance.

Business acumen is a combination of knowledge and skill informed by experience: knowledge about key business issues, the skill to apply that knowledge, and the confidence to take action. It includes the ability to provide a big picture view of a situation and to influence both strategic decisions and decision makers.

Business analytics are solutions used to build analysis models and simulations to create scenarios, understand realities, and predict future states. Business analytics includes data mining, predictive analytics, applied analytics, and statistics, and is delivered as an application suitable for a business user with prebuilt industry content (Gartner 2019).

Business awareness is the understanding of key factors influencing a business, such as its current situation, influences from its industry or market, and factors affecting growth. Having business awareness is essential to strategic involvement with top management.

Business case is a presentation of the rationale and justification for initiating a project or task.

Business intelligence (BI) is an umbrella term that includes applications, infrastructure, tools, and best practices enabling access and analysis of information to optimize decisions and performance.

Business intelligence tools are systems that retrieve, analyze, and report data to help organizations make more informed strategic decisions or identify inefficient processes. Tools can range from spreadsheets to sophisticated software for querying, data mining, or predictive analysis.

Business process is how people, materials, methods, machines, and the environment combine to add value to inputs to produce a product or service. It is a series of structured tasks that produce a product or service (output) for a customer.

Business process analysis is a structured method of observing and documenting related processes and functions to uncover hidden inefficiencies or highlight strengths that could be leveraged to increase productivity.

Butterfly effect, which is related to chaos theory, describes how a small local change can result in differences in another location.

Buzz group is a small, intense discussion group that usually involves two to three people briefly responding to a specific question during a learning event.

C

Call to action is a written action plan that acknowledges a current situation and expresses specific goals and action steps, timelines, and expected outcomes. It may be used in coaching situations.

Capability is a combination of behaviors, skills, processes, and knowledge that affects an outcome. See also *competency*.

Capital investment refers to a specific amount of money that has been provided to an organization to finance its goals. It can also refer to an organization's acquisition of long-term assets, such as buildings, property, or equipment.

Career advising is professional guidance for making vocational and occupational decisions. It may include outlining required development options.

Career advisor is a professional responsible for helping individuals grow and develop in preparation for new job options. This person is also called a career coach.

Career development is a planned interaction process between an organization and an individual that allows the employee to grow within the organization.

Career models and paths are methods that help employees develop and progress within an organization or through their careers.

Career planning is a process for assessing an employee's interests and capabilities, and then encouraging development that fulfills their aspirations and meets the organization's needs.

Career profile is a summary statement highlighting a person's work history, skills, and competencies.

Case study is a learning method in which an actual or fictitious situation is presented for analysis and problem solving.

Causal inference occurs when a conclusion has been made based on the conditions of the occurrence of an effect. In other words, something made a difference and it would *not* have happened otherwise.

Cause-and-effect analysis is a technique that helps identify all likely causes of a problem. It uses the fishbone or Ishikawa diagram to visualize the data.

Central tendency bias describes the tendency to avoid committing to either end of a scale when completing a survey, and instead selecting a response near the middle.

Centralized scanning is looking at specific components of the environment or proposing a hypothesis that may have an impact on current issues.

Certificate is a document that identifies knowledge or skills acquired using attendance and program completion as the requirements; competencies are not tested.

Certification is a standardized process designed to test the knowledge, skills, and abilities required to perform a particular job, and, upon successfully passing a certification exam, to represent a declaration of a particular individual's professional competence, typically with a designation. In some professions, certification is a requirement for employment or practice.

Certified Professional in Talent Development (CPTD) is a certification for more tenured talent development professionals with a broad range of TD experiences. Focusing on more strategic aspects of talent development, it is designed to assess professional judgement and measure a professional's knowledge and skill application across the breadth of talent development capabilities as defined by the Talent Development Capability Model.

Chain-of-response (COR), popularized by Patricia Cross in 1981, is a model asserting that adult participation in a training program results from a complex series of personal responses to internal and external variables that either encourage or discourage learning.

Change agent is any person or group responsible for initiating or implementing organizational change to increase employee adoption of that change. They also understand organizational and personal change dynamics and seek to affect a different condition in an organization.

Change fatigue may occur when employees feel unmotivated to embrace a change or actively resist it because they feel overwhelmed by the continuous succession of change initiatives occurring in their lives.

Complexity theory is a concept model referenced during change management. It is the study of how complicated systems generate simple behavior.

Change management is the process for enabling change within an organization by using structured approaches to shift individuals, teams, and organizations from a current state to a future state. It is considered an organizational impact capability in ATD's Talent Development Capability Model.

Chaos theory is a concept model referenced during change management. It is the study of how simple systems can generate complicated behavior. It is an interdisciplinary theory that says there are underlying patterns, constant feedback loops, repetition, and self-organization even in the apparent randomness of chaotic, complex systems.

Characteristics of adult learners (CAL) is a framework developed by Patricia Cross to describe why adults learn. Using cross synthesized research about motivations and deterrents to adult learning, it incorporates assumptions about andragogy into the framework as a means for considering the changing adult developmental stages.

Charismatic leaders are generally driven by a commitment to their cause, deriving their influence from their charm and persuasiveness.

Chart of accounts is a list of financial categories that identifies each class of items for which money is allocated in a budget.

Chat room is a synchronous feature used in virtual training events that allows participants and facilitators to interact by sending text or audio messages in real time. They are similar to breakout rooms in face-to-face training sessions.

Chief learning officer (CLO) oversees organizational learning in a corporation. The role came about in the late 1980s to align corporate learning strategy and people development with business goals. Since then, CLOs have helped make organizational learning a key factor in the success of an organization.

Chief talent development officer (CTDO) represents the talent development function at the executive level of an organization. Known in some organizations as the chief learning officer, this role reports directly to the CEO.

Chronology is a form of curation that organizes historical information by date to show an evolving understanding of a particular topic.

Chunk, as a noun, is a discrete portion of content that may consist of several learning objects grouped together to improve learner comprehension and retention; as a verb, it refers to the process instructional designers use to break down and group, or chunk, larger pieces of information into smaller, easier-to-process units.

Classroom learning is characterized by having a facilitator who is physically located in the same room as the participants.

Client is the goal owner who sponsors a project or has engaged a TD professional for support, to complete a project, or to improve a performance.

Climate represents individuals' collective assessment of an organization regarding whether it is a good or bad place to work.

Closed-ended is a form of questioning that limits the information collected to either a yes or no or a specific content response. It's used to check for understanding or test for consensus.

Clustering is used in statistics to organize similar data points.

Coach is a qualified professional who partners with individuals or teams to maximize their potential through a process that involves establishing goals, using strengths, pursuing development, and achieving results; they may work internal or external to an organization.

Coaching, as defined by the International Coaching Federation (ICF), is partnering with clients in a thought-provoking and creative process that inspires them to maximize their personal and professional potential.

Codec (short for coder or decoder) encodes a data stream or signal for transmission, storage, or encryption, or decodes it for playback or editing. Codecs are used in videoconferencing, streaming media, and video editing applications.

Cognition is the mental process of acquiring knowledge and understanding through the five senses, thought, and experience. The word dates to the 15th century and means thinking and awareness.

Cognitive dissonance theory states that when contradicting beliefs occur, the human mind invents new thoughts or beliefs or modifies existing beliefs to seek consistency and minimize the amount of conflict between them.

Cognitive empathy is the ability to understand another's perspective.

Cognitive load refers to the amount of mental effort used to process information by working memory, which has a limited capacity. TD professionals can improve learning results by designing content that does not overload this capacity. The term was invented by John Sweller, who argues that instructional design must reduce irrelevant cognitive load to improve learning results.

Cognitivism is a learning theory that attempts to answer how and why people learn by attributing the process to inner mental activity (thinking, problem solving, language, concept formation, and information processing) and how information is processed, stored, and retrieved.

Cog's ladder is a team development model with five stages: polite, purpose, bid for power, performance progress, and synergy.

Cohort is a group of people with a shared characteristic.

Collaboration is behavior that occurs when two or more individuals, teams, or organizations work together toward a common goal with equal opportunities to participate, communicate, and be actively involved. During conflict, collaboration occurs when both parties work together to develop a win-win solution.

Collaborative learning is an instructional approach that involves two or more learners working together to discover, learn, solve problems, and share information either in person or online. It may be used by facilitators to encourage engagement and involvement.

Collaborative overload describes working situations in which employees spend as much as 80 percent of their time in collaborative activities, such as attending meetings, making phone calls, and responding to emails. As a result, they end up needing to take work home, and their performance suffers because they are overwhelmed with requests for advice, access, input, or meeting attendance.

Collaborative learning software includes platforms for virtual classrooms and meeting spaces, as well as collaborative work.

Comfort zone is a psychological state in which individuals feel safe and at ease and believe they are in control of a situation.

Commitment charts are used in numerous initiatives, such as change management, to plot key players that will ensure the success of a project. Labels identify how important they are to the effort and may include: no commitment needed, let change happen, help change happen, and make change happen. The facilitator or change agent may review the chart to determine where players are and where they need to be for success. Questions to ponder include: Do they need resources? Do they need development? Do they need coaching?

Committee and task force involvement is a developmental option that might broaden perspectives and heighten awareness of issues that may also apply to the organization.

Communication plan is a tool that outlines details about who will communicate information related to an organizational initiative, including specific messages, communication vehicles that will be used, the timing of each message, and who is responsible for executing the plan.

Communication process is the transmission of a message from a sender to a receiver. The sender uses a medium to send the message, which goes through the sender's and the receiver's filters before the receiver decodes the message. The receiver's interpretation of the message becomes part of the feedback to the sender. Elements of communication include:

- **Environment**—the conditions or circumstances within which the communication process operates; it may enhance or block communication
- **Message**—the information that is communicated
- **Sender**—the person communicating a message
- **Filter**—a mindset, bias, or opinion that hinders the flow of information between the sender and receiver, which is usually based on past experiences
- **Medium**—the method used to convey the message, such as voice, report, or email
- **Receiver**—a person or device that receives the message and decodes or processes it
- **Encoding**—the process of translating the message by the sender
- **Decoding**—the process of translating the message to thoughts and understanding
- **Feedback**—communication that gives individuals information about the effect of their communication

Communication's six Cs are the six essential attributes required for sending a message or sharing information:

- **Clear.** Choose audience-appropriate words that are precise and descriptive.

- **Correct.** Select words that ensure accuracy and use correct grammar; avoid misusing words.
- **Complete.** Articulate comprehensive messages that include all the details.
- **Concise.** Use short specific sentences and phrases; avoid rambling.
- **Coherent.** Maintain consistency, select simple sentence structures, and present in an easy-to-follow order.
- **Courteous.** Form respectful and authentic messages with words that are friendly, positive, gender neutral, and sensitive; avoid accusing or blaming.

Community of practice (CoP) is a group of people with a common interest in a competence area who share the experiences of their practice.

Compensating feedback describes a situation in which well-intentioned initiatives or solutions call forth responses from the system that offset the benefits.

Competency is the measure of how a person performs a capability. See also *capability*.

Competency modeling is a process to define the knowledge and skills required to perform a specific job. Corporations may use this process to align the skills and knowledge of various job roles with the organization's strategic goals.

Competency-based learning is an instructional approach focusing on individual skills or outcomes, known as competencies (usually defined in a competency dictionary created from an occupational analysis of the skills required for successful performance). The approach is focused on individual learners who work on one competency at a time, with the ability to skip a learning module if they can demonstrate a mastery of the skills contained within it. It's applied most often to skills-based learning.

Completely randomized design is a model that assumes treatments are randomly allocated to experimental units.

Completely randomized block design occurs when participants are put into experimental groups—known as blocks. Each block has the same number of participants as treatments. Then, each member is randomly assigned a different treatment. Each block sees each treatment exactly once.

Complex systems are structures that feature numerous components with processes that are not linear but self-organizing. Studying the networks within the structure produces patterns that help make sense of the whole system.

Complexity theory defines an organization as a complex, adaptive system that needs to respond to its external and internal environment by remaining on the edge of chaos while at the same time self-organizing and continuously reinventing itself. In complexity theory, the future is unknowable.

Compliance is an action that is mandated by a law, agency, or policy outside an organization's purview. It is generally accompanied by a training program requirement.

Comprehensive scanning looks at the broad environment without a specific hypothesis and often leads to a decision to do one or more centralized scans to gain further insight.

Computation is a mathematical calculation.

Computer-based training (CBT) is any learning course that encompasses the use of computers in both instruction and management of the teaching and learning process. There is no single definition because many other terms are included under the CBT umbrella, including computer-aided instruction, computer-managed instruction, and computer-based instruction.

Concurrent validity is the extent to which an instrument agrees with the results of other instruments administered at approximately the same time to measure the same characteristics.

Confidence interval is the defined range a set of values is expected to be within.

Confirmative evaluation is a process that is applied after the results of summative and formative evaluation have been completed for some time to provide assurance that instruction is still effective in the future.

Conflict management is the ability to limit the negative aspects and increase the positive aspects of disagreements, battles, and differing opinions and desires.

Conflict of interest is a conflict between the private interests and official responsibilities of a person in a position of trust; the person may derive personal benefits from specific actions.

Confounding variable is an unknown or uncontrolled extraneous factor that produces an unexpected effect in an experimental setting. It is an independent factor that the evaluator didn't recognize or control for, which may explain some of the correlation.

Constraints analysis see *resource analysis*.

Construct validity is the degree to which an instrument represents the variable (such as a skill) it is supposed to measure.

Constructivism is a learning theory that states that people construct their own understanding and knowledge of the world through their experiences and by reflecting on them. Swiss developmental psychologist Jean Piaget, who was a key proponent of constructivism, suggested that learners construct knowledge from assimilation and accommodation.

Consultant see *independent consultant*.

Consulting is the short-term, internal or external defined process for solving problems and helping individuals, groups, or organizations move from a current state to a desired state.

Content management system (CMS) is a computer software system that supports the creation, organization, and modification of digital documents and other content by multiple users for an organization's web content or digital assets.

Content validity is the extent to which the instrument represents the program's content.

Contingency theory suggests that there is no one correct or best leadership style and that the optimal style depends upon internal and external options and constraints.

Continuous learning is the way knowledge and skills are constantly passed throughout an organization on an ongoing basis.

Continuous variable is a quantifiable data point or element that can be broken down into smaller and smaller units (for example, time, speed, or distance) and can be seen along a scale.

Control group is a group of participants in an experiment that is equal in all ways to the experimental group except that they have not received the experimental treatment, benefit, or training. This group represents a reference point for comparison (for example, a group that has undergone training versus a group that has not). Types of control groups include:

- **One-way analysis of variance.** This model compares several groups of observations, all of which are independent but possibly with a different mean for each group. A test of great importance is whether all the means are equal. All observations arise from one of several groups (or have been exposed to one of several treatments in an experiment). This method classifies data one way—according to the group or treatment.
- **Two-way analysis of variance.** This model studies the effects of two factors separately (their main effects) and together (their interaction effect).

Glossary

Corporate social responsibility (CSR) is an international self-regulating business model that helps an organization define and integrate social and environmental concerns in its strategy and business operations. CSR means an organization strives to have a positive impact on the world, society, and its community while at the same time enhancing its brand and increasing employee engagement.

Correlation is a measure of the relationship between two or more variables; if one changes, the other is likely to make a corresponding change. If such a change moves the variables in the same direction, it is a positive correlation. If the change moves the variables in opposite directions, it is a negative correlation.

Correlation analysis is a statistical method used to determine whether a relationship exists between two variables and if so, how strong the relationship is.

Correlational research is a type of nonexperimental research that assesses the statistical relationship (correlation) between the measures of two variables.

Cost-benefit analysis is a type of return-on-investment analysis used to prove that an initiative either paid for itself or generated more financial benefit than costs.

Counseling is the professional assistance or guidance provided to individuals to evaluate and resolve personal, social, or psychological difficulties and to learn more productive behavioral patterns.

Covariates are the multiple dependent variables in a study with multiple independent variables.

Creation and capture is a knowledge management element that defines where knowledge is created and how it can be gathered to be shared and reused. Knowledge mapping is a technique for this process.

Creative thinking is a way of looking at problems or situations from a fresh perspective that suggests unorthodox solutions. Creative thinking can be stimulated by an unstructured process such as brainstorming and by a structured process such as lateral thinking.

Creativity is the act of producing original ideas.

Criterion is a measure, gauge, scale, or standard on which a judgement or decision may be based.

Criterion validity is the extent to which an assessment can predict or agree with external constructs and is determined by looking at the correlation between the instrument and the criterion measure.

Criterion-referenced is a kind of test or assessment that measures learners' performance against a specific set of predetermined criteria or standards.

Critical path method (CPM) is a chart that is similar to a program evaluation review technique (PERT) chart. A CPM chart indicates the critical path, which is the path of tasks that together take the longest time to complete.

Critical thinking is a form of analysis that helps evaluate an issue to form a judgment that is logical and well thought out. It does not accept all arguments and conclusions at face value. Instead, it requires viewing the evidence that is involved to support an argument or conclusion. The skills that comprise critical thinking include analytical thinking, open mindedness, problem solving, and decision making.

Cross-functional job rotation is the movement between jobs in different parts of an organization over time to develop relationships and knowledge of operations.

Cross-sectional research uses groups of people who differ in the specified variable but have other common characteristics (such as industry, educational background, or tenure).

Crosstab or crosstabulation is a multidimensional table that records the frequency of respondents that have specific characteristics defined in each cell. These tables record the data about the relationships of all the variables.

Cultural analysis is an organizational assessment used to determine the alignment of shared thinking and behaving (culture) with other elements (people, structure, and procedures) of an organization.

Cultural awareness and inclusion refers to the ability to convey respect for different perspectives, backgrounds, customs, abilities, and behavior norms, as well as ensure all employees are respected and involved by leveraging their capabilities, insights, and ideas.

Cultural competency is the awareness, knowledge, skills, and processes for functioning effectively in diverse situations.

Culture audit is an assessment used to examine current practices, programs, and processes and identify how culturally appropriate they may be for multicultural or global audiences.

Culture represents the collective assessment of an organization based upon deeper, relatively enduring, often unconscious values, norms, and assumptions.

Cumulative frequency is the running total of data points or elements of a class up to a current point and all the data points or elements below it.

Curation is a process for selecting, collecting, organizing, and presenting content, information, or resources.

Curation, enrichment, and sharing is a knowledge management element that defines how the accuracy of the knowledge elements can be confirmed, what additional context is required, and where the knowledge is needed.

Current capability assessment is a measure of an organization's talent and how current skills match the organization's needs now and in the future.

Customer experience management is the action required to manage customer interactions through the touchpoints that lead to customer loyalty. Customer experience is vital to an organization because it directly affects the bottom line.

D

Data is the unstructured facts and numbers that are specific but not organized in any way. Data has no context and is limited by direct experience or interaction.

Data analysis is the process of discovering and interpreting meaningful relationships in data and summarizing empirical results.

Data collection is the act of gathering all facts, figures, statistics, and other information for analyses and assessments; examples of data collection methods or tools include questionnaires, interviews, and observations.

Data isolation is the control determining when and how a change to the data made by one action becomes visible to another. The goal is to allow numerous transactions simultaneously without influencing each other.

Data literacy is the ability to read, understand, create, and communicate data as information. It focuses on the competencies involved in working with data.

Data management includes practices, architectural techniques, and tools for achieving consistent access to and delivery of data to meet the data requirements of all business applications.

Data mart is a specialized version of a data warehouse that provides insight into operational data, such as trends that enable management to make strategic decisions. Data warehouses hold large amounts of detailed information on many subjects; they often hold summarized information on a single subject.

Data mining is a process of discovering meaningful correlations, patterns, and trends by sifting through stored data.

Data storytelling is the concept of crafting a compelling narrative based on complex data and analytics to explain the information presented in a way that influences and informs the audience.

Data visualization is the graphic images or symbols that depict the data.

Database management system (DBMS) is software or a collection of software that enables users to access and manipulate data.

Data set is a group of related sets of information composed of separate elements. Each set can be manipulated as a unit by a computer.

Deep learning is a type of machine learning that can process a wide range of data resources, requires less data preprocessing by humans, and often produces more accurate results than traditional machine-learning approaches.

Define, measure, analyze, improve, and control (DMAIC) methodology is a five-step data-driven improvement process used for reduction of defects, process improvement, and customer satisfaction. It is the core tool used to lead Six Sigma projects.

Delivery is any method of transferring content to learners, including instructor-led training, virtual training, and books.

Dependent variable is what is affected during an experiment because its outcome is the reaction to the independent variable and covariates.

Descriptive analytics summarizes historical data that explains what happened, such as assessment scores, summary activities, opinions, satisfaction, and evaluation surveys.

Descriptive statistics summarizes the data numerically or graphically in four ways: frequency, central tendency, dispersion or variation, and measures of position.

Design is the second phase in ADDIE, in which objectives are determined and planning occurs.

Design thinking is a human-centered process that provides a means for defining problems from multiple perspectives, brainstorming possible solutions, prototyping those solutions, and then testing and iterating to optimize the best approach. It focuses on the spot where business needs, user needs, and technology or environmental constraints meet. It combines user needs with the feasibility and viability of creating the product to specifications.

Desire is a strong wish for something. In talent development, it refers to the inability of training to improve employees' performance if they are not motivated (desire) to improve performance.

Development is the acquisition of knowledge, skills, or attitudes that prepare people for new directions or responsibilities. It may also refer to the third phase in ADDIE, in which training materials and content are selected and developed based on learning objectives.

Developmental feedback is a coaching term that focuses on the future and is designed to improve performance or prepare a person for the next level of effort.

Device compatibility describes the capacity for one program or device to work with another program or device when connected for the same purpose.

Devil's advocate is a term used to describe a role used during decision making or when exploring options. It occurs when an individual says a contentious opinion to provoke debate or test the strength of the current proposition.

Diagnostic analytics means examining data to identify why something happened using a variety of techniques, such as data mining and data discovery. It provides correlations to determine the reason something did or did not happen as expected.

Dichotomous variable is a quantifiable data point or element that falls into one of two possible classifications; for example, test results (pass or fail). An artificially dichotomous variable is imposed for classification purposes; for example, age is classified as retired (>65) or not retired (<65).

Digital divide refers to the gap between people who have affordable, reliable internet service—as well as the skills and devices needed to take advantage of that access—and those who do not. The digital divide may be more pronounced in developing nations. Factors affecting the digital divide include little or no geographical coverage; differences in price and availability of access between rural and urban areas; and demographics such as age groups, educational levels, and, in some nations, gender.

Directive leaders give specific advice and establish ground rules and structure by clarifying expectations and specifying or assigning precise work tasks to follow.

DiSC personality profile is a behavior assessment tool based on William Molton Marston's work that provides a four-dimensional model and four profiles: dominance, influence, steadiness, and conscientiousness.

Discovery learning is a specific learning process in which participants encounter a problem in an activity, respond to the problem, identify useful knowledge or skills gained, debrief what was learned, and plan for transferring what they learned. This process is also known as experiential learning or experiential learning activity. See also *experiential learning activity (ELA)*.

Discrete variable is a measure in which the data points are in whole numbers; for example, the number of children or the number of defects cannot be in fractions.

Disenchantment is a reaction to change distinguished by the feeling of being disappointed with something and no longer believing that it is good or worthwhile. In change management, disenchanted employees may become negative or angry and seek support.

Disidentification is a reaction to change that occurs when employees believe they have lost their identities and become vulnerable.

Disorientation is a reaction to change that occurs when employees are lost and confused or do not know where they fit in or what they think. Because they don't know the priorities or have direction, they spend time determining what should be done instead of how to do it.

Distance learning is an educational delivery in which the instructor and students are separated by time, location, or both. Distance learning can be synchronous or asynchronous.

Distillation is the act of curating information into a more simplistic format that only shares the most important or relevant ideas.

Diversity is the presence of differences that may include, but are not limited to, race, gender identity, sexual orientation, religion, ethnicity, nationality, socioeconomic status, language, physical or mental ability, and age. Diversity may also include differences in personality, political perspective, learning requirements, and communications preferences.

Double-loop learning is changing underlying values and assumptions as decision making progresses. It is also referred to as reframing or changing the context.

E

Ebbinghaus Forgetting Curve was proposed by Hermann Ebbinghaus in the late 1800s to demonstrate the decline of memory retention over time when no attempt is made to retain it.

Economic globalization describes the integration of national economies into the international economy through trade, foreign direct investment, capital flows, migration, and the spread of technology.

Educator (or professor) is responsible for teaching learners through an academic institution or course of study. This role encompasses those who work in primary education, secondary education, higher education, and executive academic education.

Glossary

Effect size is a way of quantifying the difference between two groups using standard deviation. For example, if one group (the treatment group) has had an experimental treatment and the other (the control group) has not, the effect size is a measure of the difference between the two groups.

Elaboration is a deliberate practice technique that involves learners putting content into their own words and connecting it with existing memories, such as skills or knowledge they already have.

E-learning is a structured course or learning experience delivered electronically; it can also include performance support content. There are many different elements that can make up an e-learning program, such as live or prerecorded lecture content, video, quizzes, simulations, games, activities, and other interactive elements.

E-learning professional is an individual who serves in a role that supports the creation of structured courses or learning experiences delivered electronically, including online or computer-based learning, virtual classrooms, performance support materials, and digital collaboration and knowledge sharing.

Electronic bulletin board is the computer equivalent of a public notice board where messages can be posted for viewing and responding by other users. It is also called a threaded discussion.

Electronic performance support system (EPSS) is software that provides just-in-time, on-demand information, guidance, examples, and step-by-step dialog boxes to improve job performance without the need for coaching by others.

Elevation refers to curation with a mission of identifying a larger trend or insight from smaller daily musings posted online.

Emotional empathy is the ability to feel what someone else feels. It is useful when developing and coaching others, interacting with stakeholders, and reading group dynamics.

Emotional intelligence is the ability to accurately identify and understand one's own emotional reactions and those of others. This eighth intelligence, based on Gardner's multiple intelligence theory, was popularized by Daniel Goleman in his book *Emotional Intelligence*.

Empathetic listening is confirming with speakers if an intuition about their feelings is accurate.

Empathic concern is the ability to sense what one person needs from another. It enables a TD professional to sense not just how people feel, but what they need.

Empathy means recognizing the emotional needs of others and effectively supporting them in the way that they require. It is the ability to view and understand others' feelings, needs, and concerns, and it is key to effective interpersonal relationships.

Employee experience, sometimes called the employee journey, is the perspective employees have about an organization that is influenced by their workspace, communication, work-life balance, interactions with their teams and supervisor, the technology and tools they use, and many other touchpoints of their jobs.

Employee resource groups (ERGs) are voluntary employee-led groups that foster a diverse, inclusive workplace aligned with their organization's vision, mission, values, goals, and business practices.

Employee training and development includes any activity that helps employees acquire new, or improve existing, knowledge or skills. *Training* is a formal process that talent development professionals use to help individuals improve performance at work. *Development* is the acquisition of knowledge, skills, or attitudes that prepare people for new directions or responsibilities.

Enabling objectives are goals that define the skills and knowledge learners must achieve during a learning event. They are also called supporting objectives because they support terminal objectives by breaking the terminal objectives into manageable chunks. See also *terminal objectives*.

Encoding, the first step to creating a new memory, begins with converting information to a relatable concept that is stored in the brain for later retrieval.

Engagement is a heightened emotional and intellectual connection that employees have for their jobs, organizations, managers, or co-workers that, in turn, influences whether they apply additional discretionary effort to their work.

Enterprise resource planning (ERP) is business management software. It is typically a suite of integrated applications that an organization uses to collect, store, manage, and interpret data from all business activities and departments.

Environment is the setting or condition in which an activity occurs. It is a factor that affects human performance and can include tools, equipment, furniture, hardware, software, and physical conditions, such as light, temperature, and ventilation.

Environmental analysis is part of the strategic planning process that determines an organization's strengths and weaknesses (internal) and opportunities and threats (external). It's also known as a SWOT analysis.

Environmental, social, and governance (ESG) framework represents an organization's corporate interests that focus on sustainable and ethical impacts. Investors use ESG as part of their analysis to identify an organization's material risks and growth opportunities. A strong ESG position can increase an organization's value. There are three pillars of ESG:
- **Environmental**—an organization's impact on the planet
- **Social**—an organization's impact on people, including its employees, customers, and community
- **Governance**—how transparently an organization is governed

Environmental scan is an inventory of the political, economic, sociological, cultural, global, technological, and employment forces that influence how an organization functions.

Environmental scanning is the organized and deliberate study and interpretation of internal and external events and trends that could influence an organization. Monitoring can provide early warnings of changing conditions that could identify threats and opportunities affecting the organization's future.

Equal Employment Opportunity Commission (EEOC) is the governing body that dispenses regulations to govern the hiring, promotion, and discharge of employees, as well as training guidance.

Equity promotes justice, impartiality, fairness, and equal access to opportunities, advancement, and participation. Equity addresses structural inequalities and barriers through fairness in procedures, processes, practices, and the distribution of resources. It differs from equality in that equality implies treating everyone as if their experiences and backgrounds are the same, whereas equity considers differences in people's experiences and backgrounds when determining what fairness looks like.

Estimation is using data to approximate the data and relate it to the larger population.

Ethical behavior defines individuals' moral judgement about right and wrong and whether they are acting in ways that are consistent with what society, the organization, and the profession believe exhibit good values.

Ethics are the moral principles that govern a person's behavior or how an activity is conducted.

Evaluation is a multilevel, systematic method for gathering data and comparing it to a standard to determine the effectiveness of training programs. Measurement results are used to improve the offering, determine whether the learning objectives have been achieved, and assess the value of the program to the organization. Although assessment is formative feedback, evaluation is summative in that it gauges the quality and value of what is measured.

Evaluative feedback is a coaching term that focuses on the past and is designed to grade performance such as in a formal performance-appraisal process.

Expatriate adjustment training is a delivery of knowledge and skills that employees and their families receive before departing for an assignment in a foreign country. It may include language training.

Experience-centered instruction is a philosophy of adult learning that focuses on the learners' experience during instruction and the production of fresh insights.

Experiential learning is a specific learning process in which learners participate in an activity, review the activity, identify useful knowledge or skills that were gained, debrief what was learned, and transfer what was learned to the workplace. It is also known as discovery learning. See also *experiential learning activity (ELA)*.

Experiential learning activity (ELA) is a specific learning process that emphasizes experience and reflection using an inductive learning process that takes learners through five stages: experiencing, publishing, processing, generalizing, and applying. Learners participate in an activity, review the activity, identify useful knowledge or skills that were gained, debrief what was learned, and transfer what was learned to the workplace. This is sometimes called discovery or experiential learning. See also *experiential learning*.

Experimental design is a method of research that includes a controlled factor or group that is given special treatment for purposes of comparison with a constant or controlled group.

Experimental group is the treatment group; participants receive the remedy or instruction.

Explicit knowledge, sometimes referred to as know-what, is typically captured in information systems. It is found in databases, memos, notes, documents, and so forth, and is easy to identify, store, and retrieve.

Extant data refers to archival or existing records, reports, and data that may be available inside or outside an organization. Examples include job descriptions, competency models, benchmarking reports, annual reports, financial statements, strategic plans, grievances, turnover rates, and accident statistics.

External knowledge (accessed reference) is knowledge stored outside a performer's memory; for example, in a system or other storage option. This is possible in contexts where performance requirements allow more time for knowledge retrieval and access.

Extraneous variable is an undesirable variable or factor that influences the relationship between the variables an evaluator is examining.

F

Face validity is the extent to which a test is subjectively viewed as covering the concept it purports to measure. Does the test appear effective in its stated purpose?

Facilitating usually refers to taking less of a delivery role, being learner-centered, and acting as a catalyst for learning. When a trainer uses facilitative methods, learners assume responsibility for their own learning.

Facilitation refers to the process of guiding discussion and co-learning among participants. It is distinct from the training process, which is more content based and focuses on delivering information and sharing knowledge. A trainer is more directive and makes sure learning happens, whereas a facilitator does more questioning and coaching.

Facilitator is a TD professional who minimizes delivery of information, is learner-centered, and acts as a guide and catalyst for participant learning. Facilitators encourage participants to share and discuss content and take control of their own learning. A facilitator differs from a trainer by emphasizing learner involvement. The term facilitator is also used to describe a consultant who is conducting organizational initiatives, such as strategic planning, team building, or process improvement.

Fact finding is a process used by individuals or a group to discover and establish the truths of an issue.

Fair use is the doctrine (in US copyright law) that allows for brief excerpts of copyrighted material to be quoted verbatim for purposes—such as criticism, news reporting, teaching, and research—without the need for permission from or payment to the copyright holder.

Fairness is a lack of bias, equitable treatment in testing, equality of outcomes of testing, and an equal opportunity to learn.

Feedback is advice or information from one person to another about how useful or successful an event, process, or action is. In coaching and all TD activities, learners receive feedback regarding their progress, which helps with learning retention and behavior change.

Five moments of need is a model for achieving a higher performance and includes five fundamental moments of learning: when you learn something for the first time, when you want to learn more, when you try to apply or remember, when something goes wrong, and when things change.

Five Vs of big data are dependent upon volume, velocity, variety, veracity, and value for accuracy and value.

Flat management model is a model in which authority flows from the top to the lower levels of an organization. Managers on each level have authority over their areas and employees, who, in turn, have authority over others, and so on. Each employee reports to a single immediate supervisor.

Flipped classroom is a "pedagogy-first" approach to teaching in which course materials are introduced outside class, and in-class time is repurposed for inquiry, application, and assessment to better meet the needs of individual learners.

Flowchart, sometimes called a process map, is a visual representation of the process steps in sequence using standard symbols connected by arrows that show the flow of the process.

Following skills is a listening technique that helps individuals stay focused on the speaker.

Force field analysis, developed by Kurt Lewin, is a tool to identify the driving forces and the resisting forces that create an equilibrium that resists change; individuals can influence change by strengthening the driving forces or weakening the resisting forces.

Forced-choice is a type of survey question that does not allow participants to choose a neutral response.

Forecasting is the process used to predict future happenings based on data from the past and present.

Formal learning is a planned learning program that consists of activities within a structured learning setting and includes instructor-led classrooms, instructor-led online training courses, certification programs, workshops, and college courses. There is a curriculum, agenda, and objectives that occur within a pre-established timeframe.

Formative evaluation occurs throughout the design of any talent development solution. Its purpose is to improve the draft initiative and increase the likelihood that it will achieve its objectives. For example, in performance improvement, the assessment measures progress throughout the HPI model, such as a client's expectations and whether the root cause has been identified. TD professionals should conduct a formative evaluation while an initiative is being developed and use this information to immediately revise it to make it more effective. Formative evaluation ensures the effort is understandable, accurate, current, and functional; it could include pilot tests, beta tests, technical reviews with SMEs, production reviews, and stakeholder reviews.

Forming stage is the first stage of the Tuckman model, which is characterized by team members' reliance on past behavior. Members display uncertainty, look to the team leader for guidance, and try to avoid controversy.

Framing is the boundary placed around a problem to define, describe, or present it to listeners.

Frequency describes how often something occurs.

Frequency distribution is a list, table, or graph that shows the frequency of numbers or items in a sample. It can show the actual number of observations falling in each range or summarize them using graphs or summary numerals. In the case of percentage of observations, the distribution is called a relative frequency distribution.

Front-end analysis is a part of the performance improvement process that includes the business analysis, the performance analysis, and the influence and root cause analysis stages.

Functional context describes training related to actual job circumstances and is based on the belief that training is successful only when participants can carry out learned tasks at their workstations. For example, a learner may be able to diagnose a mechanical problem and perform a series of repair steps in a logical, timely way during a training course, but if actual work conditions are noisy and chaotic, those conditions may need to be simulated during training. See also *competency-based learning*.

Functional requirements (or specifications) in a technology system are based on business requirements and focus on what the user expects. Functional requirements define *what* the system must do.

Future readiness refers to intellectual curiosity and constant scanning of the environment to stay abreast of forces shaping the business world, employees and their expectations, and the talent development profession, as well as how to handle the changes in the way work is done in the years ahead.

G

Gagné's Nine Events of Instruction were developed by Robert Gagné, a pioneer in the field of instructional design. The nine events are meant to help ensure that learning occurs—from gaining attention and informing learners of the objective to assessing performance and enhancing retention and transfer.

Gamification is the application of typical elements of game playing (such as point scoring, competition, and rules of play) to the design of development initiatives. It is used as either the optimal learning approach or as a technique to encourage engagement.

Gantt chart, when used in project management, is a bar chart used to provide a graphical representation of a schedule so project tasks and milestones can be planned, coordinated, and tracked.

Gap is the discrepancy between desired and actual knowledge, skills, and performance.

Gap analysis describes the difference between desired results and actual (current) results.

Gardner, Howard, developed the multiple intelligence theory, which suggests there are other domains of intelligence beyond a person's cognitive abilities. Gardner devised a list of intelligences: linguistic-verbal, logical-mathematical, spatial-visual, bodily-kinesthetic, musical, interpersonal, intrapersonal, naturalistic, existential, and emotional. While there is no empirical evidence to support this theory, he suggests our profiles of each intelligence will vary based on genetics and experience.

General Data Protection Regulation (GDRP) is a set of guidelines that defines the legal use for collecting and processing the personal information of those who live in the European Union.

Gig economy is the workforce environment where temporary, independent, and short-term engagements are routinely used to staff an organization's employee needs.

Gilbert's Behavior Engineering Model, created by psychologist Thomas F. Gilbert, identifies six factors that can either hinder or facilitate workplace performance: information, resources, incentives or consequences, knowledge and skills, capacity, and motivation.

Ginzberg's theories reflect a way to view career development as a lifelong process occurring in stages starting when a person is 18 years old. Individuals move from career exploration toward a series of events, including educational specialization, which leads toward a specific career path and a final commitment to a career. Eli Ginzberg was an early theorist in the field of career development.

Globalization is the transformational process of local or regional phenomena into global ones. It can be described as a process of blending or homogenization by which the people of the world are unified into a single society and function. This process combines economic, technological, socio-cultural, and political forces.

Goals are the end states or conditions toward which human effort is directed.

Great man theory assumes leaders are born, not made.

Groupthink is an unhealthy group decision-making behavior that occurs when all group members conform their thinking to the perceived consensus of the group.

Growth mindset, developed by Carol Dweck is a concept in which people believe they are in control of their abilities and can learn, improve, and develop them.

H

Hackathon is an event that started in the technology industry and involves a large group of people with expertise from multiple professions gathering to quickly create new software or hardware. The event has spread to other professions, occurring when large numbers of people gather for a day or more to collaborate in small groups to work on a project or create a new approach or venture.

Hard data is an objective, quantitative measure that is commonly stated in terms of frequency, percentage, proportion, or time.

Harless's Front-End Analysis Model is a diagnostic model designed by Joe Harless to identify the cause of a performance problem. It is based on the belief that the cause should drive the solution.

Hawthorne effect, named for an industrial experiment by Western Electric in the Chicago suburbs, demonstrates that people modify their behavior when they know they are being observed.

Heat map is a visual representation of data, using color to show data locations.

Help desk is a support provider typically run by an IT or customer care department.

Herrmann Brain Dominance Instrument is a method of personality testing developed by W.E. (Ned) Herrmann that classifies learners in terms of preferences for thinking in four modes based on brain function: left brain, cerebral; left brain, limbic; right brain, limbic; right brain, cerebral.

Holland's Occupational Congruency Model, developed by John Holland, seeks to match individuals to their best career choices through interviews that deal with six types of work environments:
- **Realistic**—physical strength, motor coordination, and concrete problem solving
- **Investigative**—ideas and thoughts and intellectual activity
- **Artistic**—less personal interaction and self-expression
- **Social**—interaction with others
- **Enterprising**—use of verbal and social skills
- **Conventional**—rules and regulations

Horizontal information searches are general, use a broad topic, and typically produce a large number of results over a wide range.

HR or OD professional may serve in various roles aimed at optimizing talent and organizational processes or systems to achieve business goals.

Human capital describes the collective knowledge, skills, competencies, and values of the people in an organization.

Human-centered design is a process to incorporate user needs and feedback throughout the development process. It differs from *design thinking*, which combines user needs with the feasibility and viability of creating the product to those specs.

Human performance improvement (HPI) is a results-based, systematic process used to identify performance problems, analyze root causes, select and design actions, manage solutions in the workplace, measure results, and continually improve performance.

Human performance models identify knowledge, skills, desire, environment, and opportunity (with some variation in the precise terminology) as key factors that affect human performance. See also *desire*; *environment*; *knowledge*; *opportunity*; and *skills*.

Human resource audit is one component of a succession planning system, which builds on the identification of successors and addresses employee mobility regarding various positions.

Human resource development (HRD) is the term coined by Leonard Nadler to describe the organized learning experiences of training, education, and development offered by employers to improve employee performance or personal growth. It is also a former name for the field and profession sometimes called training or training and development.

Hybrid learning is a comprehensive approach to combining face-to-face and online learning simultaneously. Learners can participate live, in person, or remotely using tools such as video conferencing hardware and software. All elements of the session need to be tailored to the hybrid learning format.

Hybrid workforce is made up of employees who work remotely and those who work from an office or central location.

Hypothesis testing is used to determine whether the data supports the theory or premise.

I

Icebreakers are activities conducted at the beginning of training programs that introduce participants to one another, may introduce content, and help participants ease into the program.

Idiosyncrasy is a behavior that is viewed as peculiar and specific to a person or group.

Immersive class is a four- to 10-day class focusing on one topic to provide in-depth knowledge.

Impact analysis is a structured process for looking at a proposed change and identifying as many negative effects as possible. It helps evaluate whether to implement a change, as well as how to prepare for issues that may arise if change proceeds.

Implementation is the fourth phase in the ADDIE model, in which a course is delivered in person or virtually.

Inclusion is creating and fostering an environment in which everyone, including members of traditionally underrepresented or marginalized groups, feels respected, welcome, and that they belong.

Inclusive is the complete integration of diverse individuals into a workplace.

Inclusive design describes methods to create products that enable individuals of diverse backgrounds and abilities; it may address accessibility, age, culture, education, gender, geographic location, language, and race.

Incremental change involves making a simple change in which an organization essentially allows people to continue what they are doing but asks them to do it in a new way.

Incurred expenses are those owed by an organization for receiving goods or services.

Independent consultant in the talent development profession helps teams and organizational leaders assess employee learning and performance gaps and recommends or creates solutions to address those gaps.

Independent variable is what influences the dependent element or variable during an experiment; for example, age, seniority, gender, or level of education (independent variable) may influence a person's performance (dependent variable).

Indirect reporting structure occurs when any department does not have a direct reporting relationship to the CEO or more senior leader.

Individual development plan (IDP) is a plan for personal improvement in a current job or for job advancement. Content may be tied to performance data; however, a development discussion is usually held at a different time from a performance appraisal discussion.

Industry awareness is the clear understanding of what is changing or is new in a specific business, commerce, or trade area.

Inferential statistics uses analysis to surmise deductions about a larger data population than was actually sampled and models the relationship within the data.

Influence analysis in performance improvement identifies the root causes for lack of performance results.

Informal learning is what occurs outside a structured program, plan, or class. This type of learning occurs naturally through observations, trial and error, and talking and collaborating with others. It is usually spontaneous and includes coaching, mentoring, stretch assignments, and rotational assignments. It can also include reading books and blog posts, watching online video platforms such as YouTube, listening to podcasts, searching the internet, and retrieving other digital content.

Information is data that is contextualized, categorized, calculated, and condensed. Data with relevance and purpose may uncover trends or indicate a pattern of business in a particular period.

Information architecture is a description or design specification for how information should be labeled and organized so it can be found and used, such as in a knowledge management system.

Information sharing is the process encouraged by organizations through collaboration, mentoring, and socialization to inform people and support informal learning.

Innovation is the act of translating a new method, product, or idea into a service or goods that create value. In organizations, the purpose should satisfy customer expectations.

Innovation champion is an employee who plays an active role in encouraging creativity and innovation in an organization. The role is often not a part of the person's job description.

Input, process, output (IPO) is a graph commonly used in process improvement efforts to describe how the system works. A defined set of data, resources, and materials enter the system as inputs, which are then transformed by the tasks defined as the process, which then produces the products and services that flow out as the output. Everything completed in an organization follows the IPO model.

Inquiry skills follow a process that starts by asking questions prior to reflecting and interpreting the answers.

Instructing others, when used as a development opportunity, means providing knowledge to others to deepen understanding of and appreciation for how they learn.

Instruction is imparted knowledge as well as the practice of instructing—it is used to fill a learning need. In the workplace, instruction covers many types of content and can be delivered in many formal and informal ways.

Instructional design is an essential element of an effective learning effort. The creation of learning experiences and materials is what results in the acquisition and application of knowledge and skills. See also *instructional systems design*.

Instructional designer is an individual who applies systematic methodologies rooted in adult learning principles and instructional theories and models to design and develop content, experiences, and other solutions that support the acquisition of new knowledge or skills. They may also create mechanisms to assess the learning and evaluate its impact on individuals and organizations.

Instructional methods are activities created by instructional designers and implemented by facilitators to deliver content to learners. They are also known as methods, activities, instructional strategies, design strategies, training techniques, and exercises; examples include case studies, ELAs, games, and simulations.

Instructional system is the combination of inputs (such as subject matter and resources) and outputs (such as curriculum and materials) transformed by the process of building a training course.

Instructional systems design or instructional systems development (ISD) is the practice of creating learning experiences. It is a systems approach to analyzing, designing, developing, implementing, and evaluating any instructional experience based on the belief that training is most effective when it gives learners a clear statement of what they must be able to do as a result of training and how their performance will be evaluated.

Integrated talent management (ITM) is a series of HR processes that are integrated for competitive advantage. For example, ITM builds an organization's culture, engagement, capability, and capacity by integrating talent acquisition, employee development, retention, and deployment. ITM ensures that these processes are aligned to organizational goals and strategy. It is sometimes described as putting the right people with the right skills in the right jobs at the right time.

Interim goals are indicators of final goals and progress toward the end result. For example, if the final goal states that 100 percent of the components of a leadership development program are completed, an interim goal could be "80 percent of all leadership development program components are completed by end of year."

Interleaving is a deliberate practice technique that alternates topics within the instruction—so one is started before the other is completed. This technique weaves topics together and repeats them.

Internalized knowledge (learned reference) is the knowledge stored in the performer's memory, which provides immediate access to required information.

International Coaching Federation (ICF) is a not-for-profit, individual membership organization for professionals worldwide who practice business and personal coaching.

International Society for Performance Improvement (ISPI) Human Performance Technology (HPT) Model is a performance improvement model that begins with an operational analysis to identify an organization's vision, mission, values, goals, and strategies. The phases of the HPT model are performance analysis, cause analysis, solution selection and design, solution implementation, and evaluation.

Interrelationship digraph is a follow-on tool to affinity diagrams that chart cause-and-effect relationships among groups of ideas. See also *affinity diagrams*.

Interval variable is a measurement with a difference that is meaningful enough to make it possible to rank measured items and quantify and compare the size of the differences between them.

Interview protocol is a guide used during an interview, which may include an introduction, defined purpose of the interview, a set of interview questions with room for notes, a confidentiality reminder, and other practices an interviewer uses to remember important steps and ensure consistency.

Intranet is a computer network accessible only to authorized users; for example, to employees of an organization.

Intrapreneurial is a situation in which an employee works internally but is expected to act using entrepreneurial attributes.

J

Job aid is a tool that provides guidance about when and how to carry out tasks and steps. Job aids reduce the amount of recall needed and minimize error. They may take the form of checklists, video demonstrations, or audio instruction.

Job analysis identifies all duties and job responsibilities, as well as the respective tasks completed on a daily, weekly, monthly, or yearly basis that make up a single job function or role.

Job description is a document that explains the general duties of a job, but not the specific tasks a person must complete to fulfill the stated duties.

Job functions are the primary responsibilities of programs or departments that have specific outputs and outcomes for internal and external clients.

Job shadowing occurs when an employee works alongside a professional in a certain field or department to observe requirements firsthand.

Just-in-time training is instruction delivered when it's needed, where it's needed, and usually on the job.

K

Kepner-Tregoe is a practical decision-making process that divides criteria into musts and wants. The musts are then divided into either/or categories. The wants are those measures that are important but do not have yes or no answers. Charles Kepner and Ben Tregoe published their Rational Process Technique in 1965.

Key performance indicators are quantifiable measures used to evaluate the success of an organization in meeting its objectives.

Key performers are individuals in the target job of a human performance improvement project who consistently produce outcomes with above average results.

Kirkpatrick, Donald, was a pioneer of training evaluation who first proposed his evaluation model in the 1950s. The model has four levels of evaluation: reaction, learning, behavior, and results. See also *evaluation*.

KM self-help is a knowledge base or FAQ for knowledge management questions and support.

Knowledge implies understanding that is a product of an individual's experience and education. It encompasses the norms by which people evaluate new inputs from their surroundings.

Knowledge audit is a process used to clarify the type of information employees need, and to highlight any barriers to sharing organizational knowledge.

Knowledge base is the data and information captured and stored in a central or distributed electronic environment.

Knowledge dissemination is an embedded knowledge management process and mechanism for spreading information including collaboration, communities of practice, and peer networks.

Knowledge exchange, also known as a knowledge exchange network, enables different groups in an organization to share documents and information, create lists of links in simple web pages, and discuss issues of mutual interest.

Knowledge management (KM) is a systematic approach to achieving organizational goals by creating, capturing, curating, sharing, and managing an organization's knowledge to ensure the right information and knowledge flow to the right people at the right time in the right way for the right reasons.

Knowledge mapping is a process for identifying and connecting the location, ownership, value, and use of knowledge and expertise in an organization. Examples of knowledge maps include network charts, yellow pages of experts, or a matrix relating knowledge to key processes.

Knowledge repository is the storage location of information and data in a knowledge management system.

Knowledge sharing refers to the exchange of employees' knowledge, skills, and experiences.

Knowledge sourcing is the successful retrieval and dissemination of information. Sourcing can be extended through different media such as the internet, intranet, and extranet.

Knowledge survey is a tool used to determine the types of information that employees have as well as the information they need to do their jobs.

Knowles, Malcolm, is considered the father of adult learning theory. He defined six assumptions about adult learning and published *The Adult Learner: A Neglected Species* in 1973.

Krumboltz's model, known as DECIDES, is a decision-making process with seven steps: define the problem; establish an action plan; clarify values; identify alternatives; discover probable outcomes; eliminate alternatives systematically; and start action.

KSA is an abbreviation that stands for two different things, depending on who is using it:
- *Knowledge (cognitive)*, *skills (psychomotor)*, and *attitude (affective)* are the three objective domains of learning as defined by Benjamin Bloom's taxonomy in the 1950s. Bloom's classification of learning objectives is used in education and training to determine the goals of the educational process.
- *Knowledge*, *skills*, and *abilities* are the KSAs used by the US federal government and some private hiring agencies to distinguish qualified candidates.

Kubler-Ross change curve is a model and framework used to clarify personal transition stages during change. The five stages are denial, anger, bargaining, depression, and acceptance.

L

Ladder of inference is a thought process model that describes the stages individuals go through, usually without realizing it, to get from a fact to a decision or action. The thinking stages are like rungs on a ladder; individuals select certain aspects of events that they introduce into their thinking, feelings, and interactions.

Leadership assessments are tools used to identify the developmental needs of current and future leaders at all organizational levels.

Leadership development is any activity that increases an individual's leadership ability or an organization's leadership capability, including activities such as learning events, mentoring, coaching, self-study, job rotation, and special assignments to develop the knowledge and skills required to lead.

Lean approach is a management methodology that focuses on eliminating waste while improving quality, with the goal of cutting costs by making the business more efficient and responsive to the marketplace.

Learning is the process of gaining knowledge, understanding, or skill by study, instruction, or experience.

Learning and development (L&D) is a function within an organization that is responsible for empowering employees' growth and developing their knowledge, skills, and capabilities to drive better business performance. The function may be organized centrally, either independently or within human resources; decentralized throughout different business units; or a hybrid (sometimes referred to as federated) structure.

Learning agility is the ability and willingness to learn from experience, and subsequently apply that knowledge to perform under new or first-time conditions.

Learning content management system (LCMS) is software technology that provides a multi-user environment where developers, authors, instructional designers, and subject matter experts may create, store, reuse, manage, and deliver digital e-learning content from a central object repository. An LCMS focuses on the development, management, and publication of content that is typically delivered via a learning management system (LMS).

Learning experience platform (LXP) goes beyond a traditional LMS to provide personalized social and online learning opportunities.

Learning information systems are complementary networks of hardware and software that are used to create, deliver, and administer learning programs. LMSs and LCMSs are examples of such tools.

Learning management system (LMS) is software technology for delivering online courses or training to learners while performing learning management functions, such as creating course catalogs, keeping track of learners' progress and performance across all types of training, and generating reports. An LMS is not used to create course content; that work is performed using an LCMS.

Learning modality is how information is received through the five senses: hearing, seeing, smelling, tasting, and touching.

Learning objectives are clear, observable, measurable goal statements of behavior that a learner must demonstrate for training to succeed.

Learning objects are self-contained chunks of instructional material used in an LCMS. They typically include three components: a performance goal, the necessary content to reach that goal, and some form of evaluation to measure whether the goal was achieved.

Learning organizations are, according to Peter Senge (2006), places "where people continually expand their capacity to create the results they truly desire, where new and expansive patterns of thinking are nurtured, where collective aspiration is set free, and where people are continually learning how to learn together."

Learning portal is an intranet site that offers a gateway to the organization's resources. It's often used to house prework, course assignments, a discussion board, and downloadable tools for training programs.

Learning record store (LRS) is a system that stores and retrieves xAPI (Experience Application Programming Interface) statements.

Learning science is the interdisciplinary, research-based field that furthers the understanding of learning, learning innovation, and instructional methodologies.

Learning strategy is different for individuals and organizations. For individuals, it is a plan for how they will develop efficiently. For an organization, it is what an organization needs to know and do to achieve its overall business value and reach its goals.

Learning technologist manages and executes the technology infrastructure necessary to enable an organization's talent development strategy.

Learning technologies refers to the tools, platforms, systems, applications, and software used to enable an organization's talent development strategy. This can include resources for administration, content authoring, training delivery, assessment, and talent development.

Learning transfer evaluation measures the learner's ability to use what they've learned on the job.

Lecturettes are short lectures.

Lesson plan is a sequential set of events that leads to a desired learning goal.

Level 1: Reaction is the first level of Kirkpatrick's Four Levels of Evaluation. It measures participants' reaction to and satisfaction with a training program.

Level 2: Learning is the second level of Kirkpatrick's Four Levels of Evaluation. It measures the participant's acquisition of cognitive knowledge or behavioral skills.

Level 3: Behavior is the third level of Kirkpatrick's Four Levels of Evaluation. It measures the degree to which training participants are able to transfer what they've learned to workplace behaviors.

Level 4: Results is the fourth level of Kirkpatrick's Four Levels of Evaluation. It measures the effect of the learning on organizational performance.

Lifelong learning is the ongoing, self-motivated quest by an individual for knowledge to develop personally or professionally.

Likert scale is a linear scale used in data collection to rate statements and attitudes; respondents are given a defined scale, such as 1 to 5 or 1 to 10.

Listening is the receiving end of communication. It requires the person to identify speech sounds and process them into meaningful messages.

Listening for clarification means paraphrasing comments and dialogue into different words to help increase understanding.

Listening for knowledge means listening first for facts and logic and then mentally listing things in a sequence or pattern to form conclusions.

Loaned executive program occurs when someone works in another organization (for example, a nonprofit) while maintaining existing employment to broaden their leadership skills, increase knowledge of community issues, and establish local business contacts.

Longitudinal research is a research method that involves repeated observations of the same variables, such as people over short or long periods of time.

M

Machine learning incorporates algorithms that are composed of many technologies (including deep learning, neural networks, and natural language processing) that operate guided by lessons from existing information.

Mager and Pipe Model for analyzing performance problems was developed by Robert Mager and Peter Pipe. It is a popular troubleshooting model that solves performance problems by identifying their causes and finding realistic, economical solutions. An important step in the process is determining whether a skill deficiency is involved.

Mager, Robert, defined behavioral learning objectives with three elements: what the worker must do (performance), the conditions under which the work must be done, and the standard or criterion that is considered acceptable performance.

Management or transactional theory is a leadership theory that focuses on the role of supervision and group performance.

Management training courses are sessions designed to provide learning that improves supervisory and managerial skills.

Marketing strategy is a set of strategies, tactics, systems, and processes that identify offerings; communicate key messages about them to help potential users select what they need; and enable customers to find and obtain them easily.

Mash-ups are unique, curated juxtapositions that show a new point of view by merging existing content.

Maslow's Hierarchy of Needs is a motivation theory that Abraham Maslow introduced in his 1954 book *Motivation and Personality*. Maslow contended that people have complex needs, which they strive to fulfill and which change and evolve over time. He categorized these needs as physiological, safety and security, social and belongingness, esteem, and self-actualization. He contends that basic needs must be satisfied before a person can focus on growth.

Matrix model is an organizational structure that is not based on a simple chain of command; instead, individuals may report to two or more bosses. It is used in complex organizations to integrate diverse areas of expertise.

Mature learning organizations exist where business executives and employees throughout the organization are aligned around continuous learning, aided by the adoption of strategic tools for talent development and a flexible, agile structure where processes, practices, and programs are fully optimized to support a range of development needs that shift over time. Achieving optimal levels of process maturity is a transformative process characterized by distinct, iterative phases of development.

Mean is the average of a set of numbers.

Measure is a standard used to evaluate the degree or quality of the results of a solution.

Measurement defines or quantifies specific attributes of an observation. In research, it is the process of quantifying assessment data and providing the information required to make sound decisions about an issue or situation.

Measures of central tendency are three statistical averages:
- **Mean**—the average of a group of numbers
- **Median**—the middle of a distribution where half the numbers are above the median and half are below
- **Mode**—the most frequently occurring value in a group of numbers

Measures of dispersion or variation show the number spread by stating them as intervals (range or standard deviation). It is used to show how the spread of the data compares.

Measures of frequency show how often something occurs or a response is given (such as count, percent, or occurrences).

Measures of position describe how numbers relate to one another (such as percentile, quartile ranks, or standard scores). It is used, for example, to compare a number with a predetermined norm.

Measures of variance are either properties of a probability distribution or sample estimates of them.

Median is the middle of a distribution arranged by magnitude; half the numbers are above the median, and half are below it.

Mentoring is a development opportunity that encompasses receiving valuable information, wisdom, guidance, and feedback from an experienced individual to gain an understanding of organizational culture and unwritten norms.

Mergers and acquisition management is a task created for a TD professional when two or more organizations are combined. The TD professional supports the changes that occur in the organizational structure and culture as a result of the merger.

Meta-analytic research is a statistical procedure for combining data from multiple studies. When the effect size is consistent from one study to the next, meta-analysis can be used to identify a common effect.

Metaverse, coined by Neal Stephenson in his 1992 novel, *Snow Crash*, is a vision of what many believe is the next iteration of the internet. It can be described as a single, shared, immersive, 3D virtual space where humans, as avatars, interact with one another to experience life in ways that could not be experienced in the physical world.

Metacognition is the analysis or awareness of a person's own knowledge, or the processes used to assess and monitor their own cognitive processes.

Metric is a number generated by a standardized procedure and method of calculation; a measurement could result from a different calculation or measuring technique each time.

Microlearning enhances learning and performance in the most efficient and effective manner possible through short pieces of content.

Mind-mapping is a creative, converging technique that organizes thoughts and ideas in branching subcategories around one central topic.

Mindset is an established set of attitudes, beliefs, and thoughts that predetermine how individuals interpret and react to situations, events, and comments.

Mission statement defines the purpose of an organization or function, its reason for existing, and its direction. It may also list the products and services delivered, market segments, and the operational area.

Mobile learning is learning that takes place via wireless devices, such as smartphones, tablets, or laptop computers.

Modality decisions occur in the design phase and define how learning will be delivered.

Mode is the most frequently occurring score in a distribution and is also used as a measure of central tendency. Because it is subject to sample fluctuations, it's not recommended as the only measure of central tendency. Some distributions have more than one mode, which is called multimodal.

Model is a representation or example used to describe an idea, object, process, or phenomenon.

Modeling uses mathematical equations to describe the relationships between two or more variables.

Modules, sometimes called lessons, are units of learning that provide content and practice based on predefined learning objectives. Each module contains objectives, information, task content, practice activities, and an assessment mechanism to determine whether the objectives were reached.

Motivation involves the ability to understand emotional tendencies that facilitate reaching goals. A person who is highly motivated demonstrates an internal passion to achieve and pursues goals with energy and commitment.

Motivation theory is based on the idea that when people have the right environment to work in, they will be inspired to grow and connect to that environment. This theory is essential to coaching.

Multi-dimensional databases (MDBs) are often generated from relational databases and are designed to optimize analytical processing.

Multimedia is a computer application that uses combinations of text, graphics, audio, animation, and full-motion video. Interactive multimedia enables users to control various aspects of training, such as content sequence.

Multiple intelligence theory, popularized by Howard Gardner in *Frames of Mind* (1985), describes how intelligences reflect how people may have multiple different intelligence domains. Gardner believed that most people are comfortable in three to four of these intelligences and avoid the others.

Multiple regression analysis is a statistical technique for predicting unknown values of variables based on the known values of two or more variables, which are called predictors.

Multi-rater feedback, also known as 360-degree feedback evaluation, is information gathered from superiors, direct reports, peers, and internal and external customers to assess how a person performs in several behavioral areas.

Multisensory learning engages the learner and increases retention by using different senses. When the brain receives information visually, it stores that content differently than if the information was heard or gained using the other senses. If more senses are involved in learning, more of the brain is involved in storing the information.

Multi-skill means training employees in new or related work areas to increase their use in different areas of the organization.

Myers-Briggs Type Indicator (MBTI) is an instrument that helps determine personality type based on preferences for extraversion or introversion, intuiting or sensing, thinking or feeling, and judging or perceiving. It's often used in career development and team building.

N

Needs analysis is a systemic process of collecting and synthesizing data and information to determine the difference between the current condition and the desired future condition.

Needs assessment is a process for identifying and measuring the discrepancy between current and desired conditions.

Needs-based approach is a performance improvement solution that is implemented for employees who show a documented performance gap.

Neurodiversity is a term originating in the autism community used to explain the normal variations of how individuals' brains learn or think. It describes people who have a broad range of brain functions and behavioral traits such as attention deficit disorder (ADD), dyslexia, autism spectrum disorder, and visual processing disorder.

Neuroplasticity describes the brain's ability to reorganize itself, both physically and functionally, due to environmental, behavioral, learning, and emotional influences.

Nine-box grid is a widely used tool for facilitating conversations about employee development and succession planning. (This should not be confused with the Rummler-Brache Nine Box Model.)

Nine box model is a tool developed by Rummler and Brache. It is used in performance improvement to define three performance levels and three performance needs.

Nominal data is a number or variable used for labeling or to classify a system, such as the digits in a phone number or numbers on a sports jersey.

Nominal group technique is a group process used to identify a problem, generate solutions, and make decisions to solve it.

Normal distribution refers to a specific way in which observations tend to gather around a certain value instead of being spread evenly across a range of values. The normal distribution is generally most applicable to continuous data. Graphically, the normal distribution is best described by a bell-shaped curve.

Norming stage is the second stage of the Tuckman model, when the team begins merging into a cohesive group. More cooperation and understanding occur and the group's goals and objectives are decided and owned by its members.

Nudge theory is an approach introduced by Richard Thaler and Cass Sunstein in 2008 that contends that people respond most positively to change when they receive perceptual and motivational or subtle cues, which help them understand the need for change, and when they are provided with opportunities to exercise choice and personal control over how change is implemented.

O

Objective is a target or purpose that, when combined with other objectives, leads to a goal.

Objective-centered describes a theory of instruction that concentrates on observable and measurable outcomes. It is based on behaviorism, the primary tenet of which is that psychology should concern itself with the observable behavior of people and animals, not the unobservable events that take place in their minds.

Observation occurs when participants are directed to view or witness an event and be prepared to share their reflections, reactions, data, or insights. Observation is also a methodology for data collection.

Observation bias is the tendency for observers to see what they expect to see based on past experiences and knowledge. To prevent it, observations should be conducted in the least obtrusive manner possible, preferably by multiple people. Observers should receive training, as well as a checklist, to aid in their observations. The Hawthorne effect is a well-documented phenomenon that can negatively influence research observations.

Onboarding is process through which organizations equip new employees with the knowledge and skills they need to succeed at their jobs.

One-way analysis of variance allows the comparison of several groups of observations, all of which are independent but may have a different mean. A test of great importance is whether the means are all equal. All observations arise from one of several groups (or have been exposed to one of several treatments in an experiment). This method classifies data one way—according to the group or treatment.

Online is an overarching umbrella term that refers to any type of internet-connected training program, using "live online" when referring to virtual instructor-led training.

Online help is a computer application that provides online assistance.

Online learning describes technology-enabled training via computers, mobile devices, the internet, an intranet, or other technology. It is broader than a virtual classroom because it also includes synchronous and asynchronous training.

Open space technology is an approach for facilitating meetings, conferences, symposia, and so forth that is focused on a specific purpose or task—but starting without any formal agenda beyond the overall purpose or theme. Open space meetings ensure all issues and ideas that people are willing to raise are discussed.

Open systems continuously interact with their environment. In organizations, an open system allows people to learn from and influence one another because of their interconnectedness and interdependence within the system.

Open systems theory, also known as living or general systems theory, is the concept that open systems are strongly affected by and continuously interacting with their environments. Organizations are viewed as open systems.

Open-ended is a type of questioning that stimulates discussion. Open-ended questions have no single correct answer and encourage people to use their own experiences and apply them to the current situation or discussion.

Opening exercises, also called openers, differ from icebreakers in that they always introduce or tie in to the subject matter being taught. Openers set the stage and avoid abrupt starts. They make participants comfortable with the formal program they are about to experience. Openers may also energize a group after coffee breaks and meals, as well as open sessions that occur on the second or third day of a program.

Operating expenses are the costs incurred by an organization as a result of conducting normal business activities.

Operational goals, or programmatic goals, define the objectives that must be met to initiate a TD effort, such as the date by which the program will be deployed.

Opportunity (within performance improvement) refers to whether employees are able or allowed to do a job. Employees mired in insignificant tasks may not have time to do the work that supports organizational goals.

Opportunity centered is a theory of instruction that matches individual needs to appropriate instructional experiences. It is based on developmentalism, an adult learning theory also known as transformative learning, which occurs when individuals critically reflect on their environment. Through intense reflection, they transform their thinking and view of the world. Opportunity-centered instruction is useful for helping employees adapt to changes in their work lives.

Ordinal data is a number or variable that allows ranking order of importance from highest to lowest.

Organization development (OD) is the process of developing an organization so that it's more effective in achieving its business goals. OD uses planned initiatives to develop the systems, structures, and process in the organization to improve effectiveness.

Organizational culture is the unspoken pattern of values, assumptions, and beliefs that guide the behavior, attitudes, and practices of people in an organization.

Organizational learning is the systemic implementation of best practices to create, retain, and disseminate knowledge within an entity or organization to ensure improvement over time.

Outcome goals are based on the needs of an organization and the expectations of senior leaders. They measure an initiative's influence on organizational goals

Outcome measures are the numerical results or impact of a learning program or initiative, such as the results of a training program on revenue or how a leadership development program has influenced succession plans.

Outcomes are measures that examine the impact of an initiative on organizational goals and results.

Outlier is a data point that's an unusually large or unusually small value compared with others in the data set. An outlier might result from an error in measurement, in which case it distorts interpretation of the data and may have an undue influence on summary statistics.

Outsourcing training is when an organization uses external services or products to meet its learning requirements.

Over justification effect is seen when extrinsic motivators are offered for something that is already intrinsically rewarding, which can make the activity less intrinsically motivating.

P

Paired comparison is a decision-making tool that combines each option with all the other options to decide on the preferred choice. It is most useful when there are many competing options involved.

Participative leaders share maximum information and consult with their group to make decisions.

Participative theory proposes that the ideal style includes input from others.

Partnering is proactively establishing a long-term relationship based on mutual trust and each partner's expertise to reach a successful common goal.

Passive listening describes a situation in which the listener has no interaction with the speaker, such as listening to the radio or a podcast.

Pedagogy is the art or practice of teaching that usually refers to children. Pedagogy focuses on the skills teachers use to impart knowledge and emphasizes the teacher's role. It is contrasted with andragogy, the teaching of adults, which focuses on the learner who is assumed to be self-directed and motivated to learn. See also *andragogy*.

Peer coaching is conducted in pairs or small groups to provide personal or professional leadership development by supporting, challenging, and coaching one another. It can be a part of formal training, a follow-up to formal training, a stand-alone program, or a support group for entrepreneurs or consultants, often called mastermind groups.

Peer knowledge management (KM) champion is the person assigned to help provide troubleshooting and support for knowledge management issues.

People analytics, also called talent analytics, is the application of statistics, expertise, and technology to numerous large data sets that provide a way to combine information and data to make better organizational decisions.

Percent is a specified amount that is defined as one part in every 100 parts.

Percentile is a statistical value below which a specific given percent of observations exists; for example, the 80th percentile is the value below which 80 percent of the observations will be located.

Perceptual modality, a theory developed by W.B. James and M.W. Galbraith, states that a learner's primary perceptual modality and the attendant preferred mode of learning may be print, visual, aural, interactive, tactile, kinesthetic, or olfactory.

Performance describes the execution and accomplishment of some activity; it is not an adjective that describes the action itself.

Performance appraisal is an assessment of an employee's job accomplishments. It may also be referred to as a performance review, performance evaluation, or employee appraisal.

Performance analysis is the data gathering phase of performance improvement, which measures the gap between what employees actually accomplish and what the organization desires.

Performance consulting is the process of conducting performance improvement. A performance consultant uses the human performance improvement (HPI) process to close performance gaps and achieve organizational goals.

Performance gap analysis is a process that measures, describes, and compares what employees currently accomplish and what is required in the future.

Performance improvement is a holistic and systematic approach to meeting organizational goals by identifying and closing human performance gaps.

Performance management is the ongoing communication process between supervisors and employees to establish expectations that support accomplishing an organization's strategic objectives, including clarifying expectations, setting objectives, providing feedback and coaching, and reviewing results.

Performance support provides just enough information to complete a task when and where a performer needs it. The support is embedded within the natural workflow and is organized for use within a specific context, such as the location or role that requires completion.

Performing stage is the fourth stage of the Tuckman model in which the team identity is complete, and morale is high. This stage is characterized by a high level of trust. Members organize themselves in highly flexible ways and experiment with solutions.

Personal learning network (PLN) is an informal group of people seeking or sharing knowledge in a subject area. Members, who may be inside or outside a work group or organization, enjoy a mutually beneficial relationship.

Personal mastery is the discipline of continually clarifying and deepening personal vision, focusing energy, developing patience, and seeing reality objectively. People with a high level of personal mastery realize the results that matter most to them.

Personality inventory instrument is a questionnaire or standardized instrument that measures and defines aspects of a person's character or psychological traits.

Personality test is a less formal and less accurate assessment version of a personality inventory, which was not likely validated.

Personally identifiable information (PII) is data that could be used to identify an individual, such as a social security number, bank account number, passport number, driver's license number, or an email address.

PERT (program evaluation review technique) chart is a management planning and control tool that enables project managers to analyze a range of task durations to create a project's timeline by estimating the optimistic, pessimistic, and most likely durations for each task.

PEST analysis is a tool used for environmental scanning to identify, evaluate, and track factors that can influence an organization: political, economic, social, and technical opportunities and threats.

Phillips, Jack, and Phillips, Patricia, developed a model for measuring the return on investment (ROI) of training programs called the ROI Methodology.

Pilot test is a small-scale preliminary assessment conducted to verify a project's feasibility and accuracy and identify flaws and problems prior to implementing a full-scale effort.

Pipeline planning is a proactive approach for filling current or anticipated staffing shortages in specific job categories or families.

Pivot table is a tool that summarizes data in rows and columns from a spreadsheet or database, combining and reorganizing data to show different relationships and perspectives.

Plugin is a software component that adds specific abilities to a larger software application; for example, plugins are commonly used in web browsers to play videos, scan for viruses, and display new file types.

Podcast is a series of digital media files distributed over the internet using syndication feeds for playback on portal media players and computers. The term podcast, like broadcast, can refer either to the series of content or the method by which it is syndicated; the latter is also called *podcasting*. The term derives from the words *iPod* and *broadcast*. The Apple iPod is the brand name of the portable media player for which the first podcasting scripts were developed.

Population analysis is used to analyze the demographics and characteristics of stakeholders; determine who will participate in a performance solution; and identify any education or experience factors, physical needs, and cultural influences to be considered and addressed.

Positive reframing is a technique in which the TD professional emphasizes the successes and strengths related to an issue because it allows the customer to see how positive contributions lead to a positive future.

Predictive analytics uses both descriptive and diagnostic data to predict *what will happen in the future*. By having a sense of what the data has uncovered, TD professionals can take this information one step further and build models to predict future outcomes and provide suggestive data for planning efforts.

Prescriptive analytics is used to show *how to make something happen*. It offers the best opportunity to influence a different outcome. This is the least developed analytic because each organization has different requirements. TD professionals can use prescriptive analytics to personalize learning by matching a learner's preferences to make something happen.

Presentation as a verb is the delivery of content or information. As a noun, it is the format and content that is delivered.

Presenter is a professional whose role is to deliver information and knowledge; the delivery is mostly one way with little interaction, such as a conference speaker. Trainers or facilitators may find themselves in the role of presenter if the information is new or needs to be explicit for safety or legal reasons.

Presenting typically denotes delivering a speech to a group of people with little two-way communication.

Producer is a technical expert who assists a facilitator during a live online session; they may specialize in technology-only assistance or cofacilitate sessions.

Products are the tangible or visible items that are made and placed on the market for consumer acquisition or consumption.

Professional association or organization is a group of individuals from the same vocation who seek to further the interests of the profession and develop its members. Joining and participating in associations to gain knowledge and learn about best practices is a typical developmental opportunity.

Professor. See *educator*.

Program is generally made up of more than one related projects that are grouped together.

Program evaluation is an assessment of the effect of a training program on knowledge acquisition. See also *evaluation*.

Project is a temporary task or assignment with a clearly defined beginning and end, as well as a defined scope and resources. It is not a routine operation but a specific set of operations designed to accomplish a single goal.

Project charter is a tool used in project management or change management that outlines the requirements for the product, service, or process that will be created and may include a schedule, key milestones, assigned resources and roles, a budget, a communication plan, or other elements.

Project life cycle is everything that happens from the beginning of a project to the end.

Project management is the planning, organizing, directing, and controlling of resources for a finite period to complete specific goals and objectives.

Project management team is the group of people who complete the tasks and support the project manager to complete project objectives. It requires collaboration with individuals who may not typically work together.

Project manager is the single person who serves as the project steward and is responsible for planning, organizing, and managing the project.

Project scope is the part of project planning that determines and documents a complete list of specific objectives, goals, deliverables, processes, and tasks that will be achieved for project completion.

Project sponsor is the single person who funds a project and is responsible for ensuring the project meets its goals.

Process is a series of tasks that when done in sequence are intended to produce an accomplishment or outcome.

Provocative proposition is a statement used in the design phase of appreciative inquiry that bridges "what is" with speculation of "what might be." It is provocative in that it stretches the status quo, challenges common assumptions, and suggests desired possibilities for the organization.

Proxemics is a term coined by anthropologist Edward T. Hall defining the study of the cultural, behavioral, and sociological aspects of spatial distances between individuals. Perceptions of appropriate spatial distances vary by country and culture. For example, there are four types of space common to people in the United States: intimate (18 inches), personal (18 inches to 4 feet), social (4 to 12 feet), and public (more than 12 feet).

Psychodynamic theory is a view that explains personality in terms of our unconscious and conscious thoughts shaped by childhood experiences. The knowledge of what motivates individuals and what internal conflicts they face can be used in career development to predict career success and choice.

Psychological safety is the belief that you can share your thoughts, opinions, questions, ideas, and concerns freely without being degraded or shamed. The term was originally coined by Harvard Business School professor Amy Edmondson, with respect to teams at work. In that context, it is a shared belief that team members will not be embarrassed, rejected, or punished by other members of the team for speaking up.

Pull-based system is used in supply-chain management and logistics to represent production occurring after requests so that work is completed just in time to meet customers' requirements.

Q

Qualifications are important because they identify competencies that must be mastered to ensure employees have the skills and knowledge to perform specified tasks. This is particularly important where safety is a priority, such as healthcare, chemical processing, and electrical systems.

Qualitative measures yield soft data, which is more intangible, anecdotal, personal, and subjective, such as opinions, attitudes, assumptions, feelings, values, and desires. Qualitative data may be difficult to express in specific numbers because the analysis is often descriptive.

Qualitative analysis is the examination of nonmeasurable data, such as individuals' opinions, behaviors, and attributes or an organization's image, customer support, or reputation.

Qualitative data is information that characterizes, but does not quantifiably measure, the attributes or properties.

Quantitative methods yield hard data, which is objective and measurable and can be stated in such terms as frequency, percentage, proportion, or time. TD professionals can use quantitative data to measure the problem or opportunity numerically and apply statistical analysis to validate a hypothesis.

Quantitative analysis is the examination of measurable data or the quantities of particular items in a situation or event.

Quartile is one of four equal groups into which a set of numbers can be divided.

Quartile rank is one of four equal groups that a population is divided into; the rank is 1, 2, 3, or 4.

Quasi-experimental research designs occur when a treatment is administered to only one of two groups whose members were randomly assigned.

R

RACI is a responsibility assignment matrix that defines the participation level expected of each stakeholder or group for decisions and activities involved with a project or change effort. RACI stands for responsible, accountable, consulted, and informed.

Random assignment is the use of chance in the process of assigning participants to different groups or treatments in a study, ensuring that every participant has the same assignment opportunity.

Random sampling is a method of selecting options (data points, people, or documents) from a statistical population, ensuring that every choice has a definite probability of being chosen.

Random selection is the process of how study participants are chosen from a population for inclusion in a study.

Randomization is a process that uses chance methods (such as a coin flip or random number tables) to assign subjects to experimental groups. It helps diffuse covariates across experimental and control groups.

Range is the highest and lowest value in a set of numbers.

Rapid analysis means measured in hours or days (not months as typical of traditional data mining).

Rapid instructional design (RID) is a flexible approach to the conventional instructional systems design (ISD) model that uses a collection of strategies to quickly produce instructional packages. RID strategies include incorporating existing material, using templates, and using subject matter experts efficiently.

Rating scales indicate an employee's performance level when used in the performance management process.

Reflecting skills are used during communication in which the listener attempts to understand the message and offers the message back to confirm it has been understood correctly.

Reflection occurs when people slow or pause their thinking process to become more aware of how they form attitudes, opinions, views, and beliefs and how they influence their actions.

Regression line is the best-fitting straight line through all value pairs of correlation coefficients.

Rehearsal is an imagined practice of a complete skill or task from start to finish. Sometimes called visualization, the rehearsal may be done completely in the person's mind instead of actual physical or verbal practice.

Relational database management system (RDBMS) stores data in the form of tables linked by a unique identifier.

Relationship or transformational theory focuses on the connections formed between leaders and followers.

Reliability is the ability of the same measurement to produce consistent results over time.

Replacement planning is a process to ensure the continuity of key leadership positions and the stability of tenure of an organization's personnel. Unlike succession planning, it assumes the organizational chart will remain unchanged and lists individuals as backups for each position.

Request for proposal is a document outlining specific requirements for a product or service. It is sent out to vendors as a request to submit a bid or proposal describing how their product or service can meet the needs of the potential customer sending the request.

Research methods are the techniques or processes used to collect data or evidence for analysis to uncover new information or create a better understanding of a concept. Different types of research methods use different tools for data collection.

Resistance occurs when people engage in actions designed to prevent or delay a change from progressing.

Resistance management plan is a change management tool that identifies which stakeholder groups and individuals may resist the change, their rationale for not supporting the change, and actions that may be taken to mitigate resistance.

Reskilling involves developing individuals to gain new knowledge or skills that enable them to perform new jobs or enter new professions.

Resource analysis, also known as a constraints analysis, is an assessment of talent, systems, facilities, materials, equipment, and other input required for a proposed solution during the performance improvement selection phase.

Result is the measure of objectives or goals established by an organization, department, improvement plan, or employee.

Results-based approach is driven by a business need and ensures that the performance need justifies the business need.

Retention is the ongoing ability of an organization to keep its existing workforce. It is often represented by a single statistic; for example, a retention rate of 75 percent means that the organization was able to retain 75 percent of its employees in a specified period (usually a year).

Retrieval practice is a deliberate technique in which learners build retention by recalling a skill or knowledge directly from memory, rather than reading a text or watching a demonstration.

Retrieval, sometimes called recall, is how the brain accesses information that has been encoded and stored.

Return on investment (ROI) is a ratio of the benefit or profit received from a given investment to the cost of the investment itself; for example, it can be used to compare the monetary benefits of training programs with program costs. ROI is usually displayed as a percentage or cost-benefit ratio.

Right fit describes the compatibility requirements when new technology is inserted into existing technology.

Right skilling involves training employees to meet the future needs of an organization regardless of their current capabilities.

Risk is a measure of the potential inability of an individual, group, or organization to achieve its objectives as planned.

Risk analysis identifies and measures risk that accompanies proposed change solutions. It includes compiling a list of all the potential things that could prevent achieving the outcome; rating the probability each risk event will occur; and identifying causes and possible strategies that could be deployed to mitigate the risk.

Risk assessment is a tool used to help identify and measure the possibility or threat of an error or mishap occurring during a planned solution.

Risk management is the process of addressing a risk, which may include identifying, analyzing, and developing options; monitoring risk; and mitigating potential risk.

Roe's Theory of Occupation divides occupations into eight groups of service and six decision levels. It can be used to determine the best career choice for an individual based on an assessment of their interests.

Role play is an activity in which participants act out positions, attitudes, or behaviors that are not their own to practice skills or apply skills and knowledge. Observers may provide feedback to those in a role play.

Root cause analysis, which may be used interchangeably with influence analysis, examines performance gaps and determines the primary factors responsible for those gaps that are actionable.

ROPES model is an instructional design strategy to increase learning outcomes. The acronym stands for review, overview, presentation, exercises, and summary.

Rummler-Brache Nine Box Model is a matrix approach to performance management based on three levels of performance (organization, process, and performer) and three dimensions of performance (goals, design, and management).

S

Sabbaticals are paid extended time off for individuals to study, write articles, or explore new cultures as a part of their development.

Sales enablement supports a sales team in achieving its goals by providing it with the tools and resources it needs to win. The discipline spans sales strategy, sales training, coaching, content creation, process improvement, sales career development, and sales compensation, among other areas.

Sample is a representative portion of the population from whom to gather data when conducting evaluations, experiments, or analysis.

Sampling is the process used to select the population, the number of observations, and the method to gather data for analysis.

Scaffolding is a technique that breaks learning into chunks, which are accompanied by a tool or structure, to help learners move toward more robust and profound understanding.

SCARF model, developed by David Rock, identifies five domains of human social experience, status, certainty, autonomy, relatedness, and fairness; people may perceive each as being either rewarded or threatened when they face change.

Schein's Career Anchors Theory is a concept developed by Edgar Schein to identify employees' self-concept about their talents and abilities, fundamental values, and motives and needs related to their career.

Scope creep occurs when work or deliverables are added to a project that were neither part of the project requirements nor added through a formal change process.

SCORM (shareable content object reference model) defines a way of constructing learning management systems and courses so they can be shared with other compliant systems.

Selection bias is the error of distorting a statistical analysis because the process to choose the sample (of groups, data, or individuals) was not random; therefore, the sample used is not representative of the population to be analyzed.

Self-directed learning (SDL) is when the learner determines the pace and timing of content delivery. It occurs through a variety of media (print products or electronically).

Semiotics is the study of how meaning is created and communicated to form a culture.

Sender-receiver model defines how communication occurs between individuals. The speaker sends a message, and a listener receives it. The message also travels between each individual's filters.

Glossary

Servant leaders lead from a desire to serve others better and not attain more power; they see themselves as servants of their followers.

Server is a computer or computer program that manages access to a centralized resource or service in a network. They're called servers because they *serve* the requests of other computers for files, mail, print requests, learning modules, and so forth.

Services are the intangible (or invisible) items that are also available for consumer use.

Significance testing is a term used to determine whether differences between assessment results occur based on sampling error or chance. The goal is to determine insignificance and show that they do not.

Significant means probably true (not caused by chance) in statistics.

Siloed approaches reinforce the notion that each function within an organization operates independently.

Silver and Hanson's Inventory was developed by J. Robert Hanson and Harvey F. Silver by adapting the Myers-Briggs Type Indicator to create four distinct learning intake modalities: sensing-thinking (ST), intuitive-thinking (NT), sensing-feeling (SF), and intuitive-feeling (NF).

Simulation is a self-contained immersive environment the learner interacts with to learn or practice skills or knowledge. It can range from simple live exercises to complex computer software. A branching story is a common type.

Single-loop learning refers to a type of knowledge acquisition in which people learn and use new skills for necessary but incremental change.

Situational leaders adopt a different style depending upon the requirements of the circumstances and the development level of each person being addressed.

Situational theory is related to contingency theory, where leaders choose the best action.

Six Cs see *communication's six Cs*.

Six Sigma methodology is a disciplined, data-driven approach for improving business processes; the goal is to improve output quality by identifying and eliminating causes for defects. The name originated from statistical modeling in a manufacturing process where 99.99966 percent of products are free from defects or a maximum of 3.4 defects per million opportunities.

Six Thinking Hats is a creativity converging approach designed by Edward de Bono to analyze ideas from multiple perspectives.

Skewness is asymmetry in the distribution of sample data values. Values on one side of the distribution tend to be farther from the middle than values on the other side.

Skill is a proficiency, facility, or dexterity that is acquired or developed through training or experience.

Snowball sample, also called chain sampling or referral sampling, is a nonprobability sampling technique that involves a study subject referring an acquaintance as another subject and that subject recruiting another subject. It can be a low-cost and effective way to locate a specific population; however, a disadvantage is the lack of random sampling procedures.

Social learning occurs naturally when two or more people interact. Organizations use social media tools to enhance learning and knowledge sharing, resulting in more informed, effective workplace collaborations.

Social network theory represents how people, organizations, or groups interact with others inside their network. Networks comprise actors and the relationships between them, referred to as nodes, which can be individuals, organizations, or companies.

Soft data is a qualitative measure that is intangible, anecdotal, personal, and subjective; for example, opinions, attitudes, assumptions, feelings, values, and desires. Soft data is not always measurable, but it often helps explain the measurable hard data.

Solution is a means of solving a problem using a combination of tools and techniques; they're found in every aspect of talent development.

Solution comparison grid is a way to evaluate the advantages of selecting results to a problem.

Sorting data allows TD professionals to see whether the information has been collected correctly.

Sourcing talent is the acquisition, recruitment, and selection of future employees.

Spaced practice is a deliberate technique that spaces learning over time with intervals scheduled between practices, during which the learner may forget parts. It is related to Ebbinghaus's Forgetting Curve and similar to interleaving.

Split-half reliability is a type of test reliability in which one test is split into two parts and the subject's scores on both halves are compared.

Sponsor usually refers to a single individual in an organization who has the controlling share of a project, often providing the financial resources for it.

Stackable credential is part of a sequence of short courses or credentials that can be accumulated over time to build individuals' qualifications and help them to acquire a degree or certification or to move along a career pathway or up a career ladder to different and potentially higher-paying jobs. They are affordable, satisfy employees' need to feel valued and developed, and can boost employees' resumes quickly.

Stakeholder analysis is the process for specifying in detail who is affected by a change initiative and how, including the extent to which each group of stakeholders will be affected, their level of influence over successful adoption of the change, concerns, and potential points of resistance.

Stakeholders may be a single person, group, or the organization that has an interest in a project and can influence its success.

Standard score is the number that has the same mean and standard deviation for comparing what is normal for a defined population.

Standard deviation is a measure or indicator to quantify the amount of variation or dispersion (how spread out) of a group of data values.

Standard information-seeking model is a widely used six-step process for conducting information searches.

Standard performers in a human performance improvement effort are individuals in the target job who are meeting most performance standards and expectations with average results.

Statement of work (SOW) is a formal document that defines the work activities, deliverables, and timeline a supplier must execute in performance of specified work for a client. It may include detailed requirements and pricing, with standard regulatory and governance terms and conditions.

Stay interviews occur between a manager and an employee to discover what makes the employee want to continue working for the organization.

Stop gap measures are temporary or short-term fixes used until a better solution can be implemented.

Storage is how the brain places new information into memory.

Storage and retrieval is a knowledge management element that defines appropriate mechanisms for storing captured knowledge, including IT systems.

Storming stage is the second stage of the Tuckman model, in which conflict and competition surface. Some people experience hostility or defensiveness. As the team tries to work together, disagreements may arise about the goals and objectives.

Strategic planning is the process an organization uses to identify its direction for the future. No single process exists, but it usually includes envisioning the future, defining goals and objectives, aligning structure and resources, and implementing the plan.

Strategic thinking is a form of analysis that generates business insights and opportunities to help differentiate the organization and make it more competitive. Strategic thinking can be part of an organization's strategic planning process or used by individuals to help achieve a goal.

Strategic workforce planning is the process an organization uses to analyze the current workforce and plan for future staffing needs.

Stratified random sampling is dividing a population into groups based on member attributes or characteristics (such as age) and choosing members randomly from each group. This method provides a more representative sample than a random sample. For example, dividing the population into age groups (10–20, 21–30, 31–40, and so forth) and randomly choosing people from each age group creates a stratified random sample.

Strengths, weaknesses, opportunities, and threats (SWOT) analysis is a process that identifies an organization's internal strengths and weaknesses, as well as its potential external opportunities and threats. The analytical framework provides input for planning.

Stretch assignment is a development opportunity that occurs by conducting a specific task or project to develop expertise beyond a regular routine and to expand experience. The objective is to place learners in an uncomfortable situation to encourage their development in a real-time setting.

Structured mentoring is a time-limited process focused on a protégé's acquisition of a particular skill set based on specific behavioral objectives.

Subject matter expert (SME) is an individual who has extensive knowledge and skills in a particular topic or subject area.

Subject-centered is a pedagogy-based instructional approach focusing on the content that will be taught, as opposed to learner-required knowledge.

Subjective information is based on personal opinions, interpretations, points of view, emotions, and judgment instead of measures and numbers. It is sometimes useful to help explain objective information.

Succession planning is the systematic process of identifying, evaluating, and developing personnel who have the potential to assume leadership or mission-critical positions upon the resignation, termination, transfer, promotion, or death of an incumbent.

Summative evaluation occurs after a TD solution has been delivered. It focuses on the results or impact of the solution to provide evidence about the program's value. It may include measuring participants' reactions, the effect on business goals, the initiative's costs, and stakeholder's expectations. A summative evaluation measures the outcome and could include standardized tests, participant reaction forms, stakeholder satisfaction surveys, and final return on investment.

Super developmental framework is a career development theory developed by D.E. Super that is based on the idea that careers move through five phases from childhood through adulthood.

Supportive leaders promote good relations within a group and show sensitivity to employees' needs.

Survey is a data collection tool that may consist of questions or rating statements and appear in an online or paper format; it may also be called a questionnaire, feedback form, or opinion poll.

Synchronous training occurs when a facilitator and learners participate in a training at the same time. It is most often used when discussing virtual training, which can be synchronous or asynchronous.

System is an arrangement of interrelated parts that denotes interdependency, interconnectedness, and a set of elements that constitute a holistic, identifiable whole.

System development life cycle is an organizational process for planning, creating, testing, maintaining, and deploying an information system or software.

System test is the evaluation of hardware or software to ensure compliance with its specified requirements.

Systems thinking is based on the belief that the component parts of a system can be best understood by examining relationships with one another and with other systems, rather than in isolation. The holistic view is important to change initiatives because small changes to any part of a system affect the whole system based on the level of interconnectedness.

T

Tabulating data is the process of extracting and categorizing data from the instruments used to gather it. This process enables TD professionals to review and understand it. The goal is to reduce data from its raw state into some quantified format without changing the meaning.

Tacit knowledge was originally defined by educator Michael Polanyi and is sometimes referred to as know-how. It is primarily experienced based and intuitive, residing in the memory and mind alone, which makes it hard to define and communicate. It is the most valuable source of knowledge because it is based solely on successful experience and performance, is not broadly disseminated, and usually isn't shared or understood by many. Many knowledge management experts view tacit knowledge as the most likely to lead to organizational breakthroughs. Gamble and Blackwell (2002) link the lack of focus on tacit knowledge directly to the reduced capability for innovation and sustained competitiveness. Knowledge stakeholders (holders of tacit knowledge) know about an organization's cultural beliefs, values, attitudes, mental models, skills, capabilities, and expertise.

Talent acquisition is a process for filling vacancies in a timely manner.

Talent acquisition strategy describes the systems and processes that define how candidates will be sourced and from where, as well as who the target audience is, focusing on filling vacancies in a timely manner.

Talent development (TD) refers to the efforts that foster learning and employee development to drive organizational performance, productivity, and results.

Talent development director or executive is a person who leads and sets the strategy for a talent development unit within an organization. This unit may be comprised of multiple functional areas that have broad responsibility for developing talent in the workplace.

Talent development manager is a person who supervises and oversees the work of a group of people and processes responsible for fostering learning and employee development to drive organizational performance, productivity, and results. This individual may serve as a department of one in small organizations.

Talent development professional is an overarching term that refers to anyone whose role is to foster learning and employee development such as a trainer, facilitator, instructional designer, or others.

Talent management analytics is the term used to describe talent data that is used for improving business performance; for example, predicting turnover, business impact of leadership development programs, or effectiveness of onboarding programs to improve time to performance.

Talent segmentation strategy identifies critical roles in an organization where gaps are present and defines strategic objectives for filling the gaps for those specific roles.

Talent strategy and management are the practices used to build an organization's culture, engagement, capability, and capacity through the implementation and integration of talent acquisition, employee development, retention, and deployment processes, ensuring these processes are aligned to organizational goals.

Target job is the specific job in a human performance improvement project that is the objective of a performance improvement effort.

Task is a single unit of work that can be completed by one person in less than half a day. Projects are made up of tasks.

Task analysis is the process of examining a single task within a job and breaking it down into the actual steps of performance.

Task assessment is defined as the systematic identification of the items necessary to perform any job, such as skills, knowledge, tools, conditions, and requirements. They can vary in complexity and scope. For instance, a person could accurately document a simple set of tasks by interviewing current employees.

Taxonomy is a system of order that serves as the foundation for codifying knowledge. For example, a knowledge management (KM) taxonomy focuses on enabling the efficient retrieval and sharing of knowledge, information, and data across an organization. It is built around work processes and knowledge needs in an intuitive structure.

Teaching is generally associated with a pedagogical process of instructing and giving information and knowledge with limited learner involvement.

TD professional. See *talent development professional*.

Team building is a process for transforming an ineffective or dysfunctional group into an efficient, productive team through various experiential learning activities, including reviewing data, conducting interpersonal activities, exploring problems and challenges, and establishing action plans for change.

Team dynamics are the unconscious, psychological forces that influence the direction of a team's behavior and performance, including creating shared experiences and maintaining excellent communication.

Technical requirements (or specifications) for a technology system are based on how something can be achieved, focusing on the precise technical details for how to build what is described including implementation plans, testing, and benefits. Technical requirements define *how* the system accomplishes what it must.

Technology application refers to a practitioner's ability to identify opportunities to adapt and leverage the right technologies at the right time to meet organizational and people development goals.

Teleconferencing is the instantaneous exchange of audio, video, and text between two or more people or groups at two or more locations.

Terminal objective is the final behavioral outcome of a specific instructional event. It's also called a performance objective because it defines the ultimate, specific, and measurable KSA learners demonstrate as a result of participating in a learning event. The terminal objective may be broken down into enabling objectives.

Test scripts are a line-by-line description that includes the information about the system transactions that must be performed to validate the application or system being considered. Test scripts list each step or entry to be executed and the expected results.

Theory X is a theory of human motivation developed by Douglas McGregor in the 1960s. The theory assumes that employees are inherently lazy, dislike work, and will avoid it if they can. Belief in Theory X leads to a management philosophy of close supervision and tight control of employees.

Theory Y is a theory of human motivation developed by Douglas McGregor. In contrast to Theory X, Theory Y assumes that most employees are self-motivated, enjoy working, and will work to achieve goals to which they are committed. Belief in Theory Y leads to a management philosophy of trust that employees will take responsibility for their work and do not need constant supervision.

Total rewards package is the compensation salary—compensation, benefits, work-life flexibility, performance, and recognition, plus growth and development.

Traditional mentoring is the career development practice of using an experienced person or group to share wisdom and expertise with a protégé over a specific period of time. There are three common types of traditional mentoring: one-on-one, group, and virtual.

Train the trainer is an initiative or development program to teach training and facilitation skills to those who are new to training or subject matter experts (SMEs) who have been asked to train others.

Trainer is a TD professional who delivers and enables learning in a traditional or virtual classroom, one-on-one, or on-the-job in an organization to help individuals improve their performance. See also *facilitator*.

Training and development includes any activity that helps employees acquire new, or improve existing, knowledge or skills. Training is a formal process by which talent development professionals help individuals improve performance at work. Development is the acquisition of knowledge, skills, or attitudes that prepare people for new directions or responsibilities.

Training delivery (and facilitation) is a means by which talent development professionals help individuals improve performance at work by learning new skills and knowledge.

Training manager is a TD professional who is primarily responsible for identifying training needs, developing a strategy to meet target audience needs, and securing resources to fill those needs.

Training needs assessment is a systematic process of collecting and synthesizing data and information to determine the difference between the current performance and the desired future performance and decide if training is the solution.

Training objective is a statement of what a TD professional hopes to accomplish during a training event.

Training or talent development coordinator is a person who plans, administers, and implements learning programs, either developed internally or outsourced, that foster employee performance, development, and growth.

Training transfer evaluation is a process to measure the success of a learner's ability to transfer and implement learning on the job.

Trait theory assumes people are born with inherited traits that are suited to leadership.

Trait-factor counseling is a cognitive career counseling approach based on the theory of individual differences. Known as the talent-matching approach, it assumes that each person has a unique pattern of relatively stable traits, interests, abilities, and characteristics that can be identified as an occupational profile. This approach originated in the early 1900s and is associated strongly with vocational theorists Frank Parsons and E.G. Williamson.

Transactional leaders focus on practically managing work and rewarding performance and are most effective in crisis and emergency situations.

Transformational change is the most difficult type of change and is typically driven by external forces. It may alter the direction of an industry or even put an organization on the forefront of a new paradigm.

Transformational leaders encourage and motivate employees following the four Is: inspirational motivation, idealized influence, individualized consideration, and intellectual stimulation.

Transition monitoring team is a group of employees without formal responsibility for planning a change initiative or authority to make decisions related to it, but who are consulted throughout the change about how to implement the change most effectively in their work area or unit. Transition monitoring team members serve as advocates for the change via formal and informal communication with their peers, and by serving as advocates for their peers' needs and concerns via planned meetings with change leaders.

Transitional change involves complex change in which other organizations have undertaken similar change and their best practices (or benchmarks) can help guide the company.

Treatment (experimental) variable is the term researchers and statisticians use to define the manipulated variable in an experiment; for example, the manipulated variable would be attending a training program, whereas a control group would not attend.

Trigger words are statements that stimulate someone to react instantly in a positive or negative manner.

Triple-loop learning is a model (along with single- and double-loop learning) that helps TD professionals understand the dynamics of learning that are frequently defined as "learning how to learn." Learners reflect beyond what they learned to how they learned, how they think about what they learned, and how others feel about what was learned. This causes them to transform by willingly altering their beliefs and values about themselves and the world.

Tuckman group development model is a model that depicts five stages of team maturation: forming, storming, norming, performing, and adjourning.

U

Unconscious biases are learned stereotypes that unintentionally influence behavior. They are deeply ingrained, which causes them to occur automatically.

Unit test is a process (usually in software) in which the smallest testable part of an application is independently scrutinized to ensure that it is free of errors and defects.

Upskilling is training designed to augment existing skills with new or significantly enhanced knowledge. This enables individuals to continue to succeed in the same profession or field of work. Upskilling does not refer to ongoing development.

V

Validity means the evaluation instrument measures what it is intended to measure.

Value propositions represent a promise of value and results that TD professionals will deliver to leadership, stakeholders, or clients. The value proposition states the results they can expect from a prospective program, TD solution, or even the TD function itself.

Variance is a measure of the spread between numbers in a data set—specifically, how far each number is from the mean.

Vertical information searches are targeted and usually produce fewer results, such as searching for brainstorming tools.

Video is a one-way delivery of live or recorded full-motion pictures.

Virtual classroom is an online learning space where learners and facilitators interact from different locations.

Virtual learning is the synchronous, live online, facilitator-led classroom or learning space where learners and facilitators interact, discuss, dialogue, and collaborate.

Virtual reality (VR) is computer-generated simulation that uses head-mounted displays to give learners the ability to explore a fully rendered digital environment and manipulate objects with handheld controls and voice commands. This powerful tool allows learners to perform skills in a realistic, engaging simulation of a real-life environment. It's especially valuable for training learners in dangerous or hard to replicate situations, such as emergencies or heavy equipment simulations.

Vision is an aspirational description of an organization's, function's, or individual's future goals.

VUCA (volatile, uncertain, complex, and ambiguous) refers to four unique challenges or disruptions that represent the environmental conditions and business climate that influence change readiness.

W

Wants-based approach is a response to clients in a performance improvement setting that is implemented based on the idea that what the client wants, the client gets.

WCAG refers to Web Content Accessibility Guidelines, which are published by the World Wide Web Consortium's web accessibility initiative to provide recommendations for making web content more accessible.

Web portal is a specially designed website that brings information from diverse sources (like emails, online forums, and search engines) together in a uniform way. Each information source receives a dedicated area for displaying information, and users can usually determine which sources to display.

Webinar refers to an online event with live, online participants. Webinars can be used to deliver knowledge-based or low-level objectives to a large group. Depending on the web conferencing tools and facilitator's mastery level, these can be interactive and engaging experiences that avoid a lecture-only format.

Web-based training (WBT), more often called virtual learning, is the delivery of educational content via a web browser over the internet, a private intranet, or an extranet.

Whiteboard is a tool used for collaboration or instruction. It can be a physical white surface used for drawing or writing with markers or an electronic interactive display screen that users can write on with a pen, draw on with their fingers, or enter words on from a keyboard.

WIIFM is an acronym that stands for "what's in it for me." It is used by TD professionals to remember to help learners recognize the value of the training to them personally.

Wiki is a collection of web pages in one location on which anyone with access can contribute or modify the content. It's useful for collaboration, knowledge management, and data compilation.

Word cloud is a data visualization method that counts how often words are used in a statement and then depicts the frequency graphically. Typically, words grow in size proportionally to how frequently they're mentioned.

Work breakdown structure (WBS) is a deliverable-oriented decomposition of a project's or department's tasks. It is used in project management and systems engineering.

Workforce is defined as the entire population of individuals who support an organization including full-time and part-time employees as well as contractors.

Workforce plan is a design that identifies the skill and knowledge gaps between today's talent and the needs of the future, as well as the actions required to meet the needs. The workforce plan emanates from an organization's strategic plan and offers managers a framework for staffing decisions that is based on the mission, strategic plan, budget, and desired competencies.

Workforce planning is the systematic process for identifying the gaps between the talent capability of today and the talent needs in the future. It is often completed in conjunction with a strategic plan—analyzing current talent, identifying skill gaps, developing an action plan, implementing the plan, and monitoring and evaluating progress.

Work-life balance is a concept that includes proper prioritizing between professional (career and ambition) and personal (health, pleasure, leisure, family, and spiritual development) activities.

Workplace is the location where work is completed and is not restricted by the confines of the physical environment; it includes the traditional office space, a shop, or factory, as well as remote locations such as shared workspaces or home offices.

Workplace digitization is the advanced use of technologies to connect people and spaces to business processes to improve productivity, reduce costs, engage the workforce, and encourage innovation.

WYSIWYG (pronounced "wizzy-wig") is an acronym that means "what you see is what you get." In computing, a WYSIWYG editor is a system in which content (text and graphics) displayed on screen during editing appears in a form closely corresponding to its appearance when printed or displayed as a finished product.

X

xAPI is the Experience Application Programming Interface, an e-learning software specification to record learning experiences an individual has on and offline. It's also known as Tin Can API or the experience API.

ACRONYMS

4-Ds	Discovery, dream, design, and destiny
ADA	Americans With Disabilities Act
ADDIE	Analysis, design, development, implementation, and evaluation
AI	Appreciative inquiry
AI	Artificial intelligence
AICC	Aviation Industry Computer-Based Training Committee
APTD	Associate Professional in Talent Development
AR	Augmented reality
ATD	Association for Talent Development
CLO	Chief learning officer
cmi5	Computer managed instruction, fifth attempt
CPTD	Certified Professional in Talent Development
CSR	Corporate social responsibility
CTDO	Chief talent development officer
DEI	Diversity, equity, and inclusion
ELA	Experiential learning activity
EPSS	Electronic performance support system
ERP	Enterprise resource planning
ESG	Environmental, social, and governance
fMRI	Functional magnetic resonance imaging
GDRP	General Data Protection Regulation
HPI	Human performance improvement
HR	Human resources
IDP	Individual development plan
ISO	International Organization for Standardization
IT	Information technology
KM	Knowledge management
KPI	Key performance indicator
KSA	Knowledge, skills, and abilities
KSA	Knowledge, skills, and attitude (Bloom)
LAN	Local area network
LMS	Learning management system
LXP	Learning experience platform

Acronyms

M&A	Mergers and acquisitions
OD	Organization development
PERT	Program evaluation review technique
PEST	Political, economic, social, technological
PII	Personally identifiable information
PMI	Project Management Institute
RACI	Responsible, accountable, consulted, informed
RFI	Request for information
RFP	Request for proposal
ROI	Return on investment
ROPES	Review, overview, presentation, exercises, summary
SCORM	Shareable content object reference model
SLA	Service level agreement
SME	Subject matter expert
SOP	Standard operating procedure
SWOT	Strengths, weaknesses, opportunities, and threats
TA	Talent acquisition
TD	Talent development
TM	Talent management
UI	User interface
UX	User experience
VR	Virtual reality
VUCA	Volatile, uncertain, complex, ambiguous
WAN	Wide area network
WCAG	Web Content Accessibility Guidelines
xAPI	Experience Application Programming Interface